THE DICTIONARY OF PAN-AFRICAN PENTECOSTALISM

Volume I: North America

THE DICTIONARY OF PAN-AFRICAN PENTECOSTALISM

Volume I: North America

Edited by
ESTRELDA Y. ALEXANDER

CASCADE *Books* • Eugene, Oregon

THE DICTIONARY OF PAN-AFRICAN PENTECOSTALISM
Volume I: North America

Copyright © 2018 Wipf and Stock Publishers. All rights reserved. Except for brief quotations in critical publications or reviews, no part of this book may be reproduced in any manner without prior written permission from the publisher. Write: Permissions, Wipf and Stock Publishers, 199 W. 8th Ave., Suite 3, Eugene, OR 97401.

Cascade Books
An Imprint of Wipf and Stock Publishers
199 W. 8th Ave., Suite 3
Eugene, OR 97401

www.wipfandstock.com

PAPERBACK ISBN 13: 978-1-60899-362-8
HARDCOVER ISBN 13: 978-1-4982-8477-6

Cataloguing-in-Publication data:

Names: Alexander, Estrelda Y., editor.

Title: The dictionary of pan-African Pentecostalism : volume I : North America / edited by Estrelda Y. Alexander.

Description: Eugene, OR : Cascade Books, 2018 | Includes bibliographical references.

Identifiers: ISBN 978-1-60899-362-8 (paperback) | ISBN 978-1-4982-8477-6 (hardcover)

Subjects: LCSH: African American Pentecostals—History. | United States—Church history. | Canada—Church History.

Classification: LCC BR1644.3 D3 2018 (print) | LCC BR1644.3 (ebook)

Manufactured in the U.S.A.   06/20/2018

Contributors to the Series

Estrelda Alexander, PhD
William Seymour College
Bowie, Maryland

Lewis Brogdon, PhD
Claflin College
Charleston, South Carolina

Glenda Goodson
Independent Scholar
Lancaster, Texas

Jorge Haustein
University of London
London, UK

Ida Jones, PhD
Moorland Spingarn Collection
Howard University
Washington, DC

Jermaine Marshal
William Seymour College
Bowie, Maryland

Joe Newman
First Assembly Christian School
Memphis, Tennessee

David Roebuck PhD
Hal Bernard Dixon Pentecostal Research Center
Cleveland, Tennessee

Candace Shields, PhD
William Seymour College
Bowie, Maryland

Alexander Stewart, MA
Independent Archivist
Irmo, South Carolina

Matthew K. Thompson, PhD
Southwestern College
Winfield, Kansas

William C. Turner, PhD
Duke University
Durham, North Carolina

Michael Wilkinson
Trinity Western University
Langley, British Columbia, CN

LaTonia Winston, MA
Trinity Evangelical Seminary
Deerfield, Illinois

Contents

Appreciation | ix
Introduction to the Series | xi

DICTIONARY | 1

Index of Denominations | 449
Index of Names | 453
Index of Terms | 459

Appreciation

No work of this magnitude is ever a singular effort. Accordingly, I wish to thank the contributors whose research and scholarship helped make this volume a reality. This work would not have been possible, however, without the dedicated and ongoing assistance of my friend and colleague, Alexander Constantine Stewart, who used the resources of his personal collection to provide information that was unavailable elsewhere. The wealth of knowledge he brings to the subject of black Pentecostalism, in general, and to the Oneness Movement, in particular, is invaluable. And his generous giving of his time and advice is greatly appreciated.

Introduction to the Series

To speak of oneself as black and Pentecostal provides only a partial identification. Black Pentecostalism is not a denominational distinction, but rather it is a multi-faceted tradition made up of very small, moderate sized, and large independent congregations; loosely organized fellowships and denominations with as much variety in structure, polity, doctrine and theology, as one can image. These groups are found on every continent on the globe where African descendants are located. Constituents meet in open tents and fields, in borrowed or rented storefront edifices, in reclaimed sanctuaries of former Christian and Jewish congregations that have outgrown their facilities or migrated from neighborhoods to which they are no longer attached. Yet, as the movement has matured and been relatively assimilated into the broader culture, they also meet on some of the most opulent megachurch campuses with the finest accoutrements and all the latest media and technology resources available.

What these groups share in common is an appreciation for and expectation of a direct personal experience of God through the supernatural baptism (outpouring or indwelling) of the Holy Spirit. Except for the Holiness groups, the majority of these bodies also share a common link to the early nineteenth century Azusa Street Revival and through it, to its leader, William Joseph Seymour.

Some groups within the tradition have existed for more than one hundred years—and among Holiness groups nearly a half a century more. Through processes of planting congregations, breaking away from white parent denominations, growth and repeated schism, realignment and amalgamation, however, new members of the community are constantly coming into existence, while others are going into demise. Some have been, localized and short lived, coming into and exiting the religious arena hardly unnoticed. Others have stood the proverbial test of time, having grown to considerable proportions and made a significant impact on the religious and social context of their respective cultures. Still others, have made contributions beyond their national or cultural contexts to forge religious trends that have been reflected, repeated and imitated in other segments of the Christian church as well as in secular society.

Additionally, for much of its life, the tradition has been one that is largely oral. Except for its most visible members, its history has not been documented in academic volumes or published popular history. Rather it has been recorded through domestic vehicles that have rarely caught broad attention. Sermons, official in-house organs, souvenir journals, obituaries, and legal documents help capture as much of its essence as is possible to convey. More importantly its stories have been told and retold, enacted and re-enacted in sermons, testimonies, and liturgies of multiple generations even as the movement has evolved into different forms that bear little resemblance to a founder's visions or that of the generation that birthed the movement into existence.

Additionally within each context, Pan-African expressions of Pentecostalism are influenced by the culture of the people who are involved. While part of those cultures derives from the racial identity of their constituents, they are also colored by their geographical and linguistic contexts and the well of antecedent spiritualities from which they draw. Accordingly, while Pentecostalism within the African Diaspora is different from the Pentecostalism of the majority world, Pentecostalisms within the Diaspora also show distinctive elements from each other.

This variety makes the work of collecting, interpreting and reporting the essence of so vital a movement challenging. Yet, that essence of contemporary Pan-African Pentecostal spirituality, as a movement within the Christian Church borne out of the loins of a son of Africa, is well worth the effort. The volumes in this collection survey a broad range of black Pentecostal spiritualities. They include the Holiness movement with its language of sanctification and Holy Spirit baptism; classical Pentecostalism that insists on the experience of Holy Spirit baptism that is accompanied by the initial physical evidence of glossolalia, or speaking in tongues; the Charismatic movement that focuses more broadly on the presence of a range charismatic gifts as evidence of Holy Spirit Baptism; and Neo-Pentecostalism, which seeks to incorporate the more visible elements of Pentecostal spirituality without losing its own doctrinal identity. Further, the volumes also includes a number of quasi-Holiness or Pentecostal groups, which Deidre Crumley identifies as "Spirit-privileged" that share certain visible resemblances including a common language and many of the same rituals, yet hold underlying theologies that differs significantly from orthodox positions held by Pentecostals. Personality cults, some syncretistic African Initiated Churches, and groups that have incorporated non-Christian elements into their doctrine and worship are included in these volumes to point out disqualifying distinctions from Pentecostalism.

The task has been to identify major Pan-African organizations, individuals, and points in history that have shaped the fastest growing segment of the contemporary Christian faith. Further, it has been to bring to light their contribution to the broad Pentecostal movement, the broader Christian tradition movement as well as to other segments of society. Hopefully, this effort helps correct the false identification of Pentecostalism as a separatist cult that is unengaged with the world.

The first volume of this broad-ranging project takes its geographical focus within North America. The subsequent volumes consider broader global aspects of the movement outside North America.

Several conventions have been employed within these volumes to make this work more accessible for those who stand outside the movement. Language conventions, including standardizing colloquial jargon to bring it in line with broader religious terminology do not deny the reality of Pentecostal experience for adherents but acknowledge Pentecostals as part of the broader Christian tradition. Special titles are used sparingly, not for lack of respect for individual ecclesial structures and polities, but to make the volumes less encumbered and more readable and to overcome the ever-changing nature of the movement. Finally, the obvious variance in depth of coverage between articles in the dictionary does not reflect a lack of research effort or that shorter entries are, necessarily, less important. Rather, it reflects the significant lack of resources regarding some people and segments of the movement. Every attempt was made to provide full names and birth and death dates, but much of Pentecostal historiography excludes this information, even these efforts were not always fruitful. It is my hope, however, that the work that this collection represents will spur a level of interest that generates more research, so that at some point, fuller stories will be made available.

A

Adams, Joseph H. 1926–2003

The first presiding bishop of the **United Way of the Cross Churches of Christ of the Apostolic Faith**. Adams was born in Cascade, Virginia, where he lived all of his life. Adams earned his theology degrees from the Staunton Bible Institute and the Shiloh School of Theology in Stafford, Virginia. He entered the ministry in 1946, and served as associate minister of Shiloh Way of the Cross Church, later founding Bethel Way of the Cross Church in Danville, Virginia. He was ordained as an elder in the **Way of the Cross Churches** in 1953, and in 1969, he was consecrated a bishop.

In 1996, he joined Harrison Twyman, formerly of **Bible Way World Wide**, and James Pritchard, formerly of the **Apostolic Church of Christ in God**, to found the **United Way of the Cross Churches International** and became chief apostle of that body in 1997.

Unlike many black Pentecostal pastors of his generation, Adams was more than a local church leader; he was also a prominent community leader. After his death, a Virginia State Senate resolution recounted his numerous service awards including an Outstanding Service Award from the Henry County School Board, a Distinguished Community Service Award from the Men's Roundtable Club, and an Outstanding Business Leadership for Minorities Award from Patrick County Community College. From 1970 to 1990, he served on the Henry County School Board, including a term as vice chairperson.

At one point, Adams, a charter member of the Sandy River Medical Center, was vice chairperson of its board. He also founded the Bethel Way Adult Center and the Bethel Way Recreation Center, and was appointed to the Governor's Advisory Board for the Aging by Virginia's first African-American governor, L. Douglas Wilder.

Adams, Leonard P. 1866–1945

An early white Holiness evangelist who associated with **Charles Harrison Mason's** African-American denomination, the **Church of God in Christ**. Adams joined with Mason in moving into the Pentecostal camp and remained with him after other white ministers broke with Mason to form the Assemblies of God. Adams was born near Waverly, Tennessee.

After attending law school, Adams worked as a teacher and lawyer before entering the ministry. His ministerial training was received through the Pentecostal Mission and Literary Institute in Nashville, Tennessee that would later become the Tribecca Nazarene University. He first aligned himself with a Holiness group, the **Cumberland Presbyterian Church**. He started evangelistic work in Tennessee, later moving on to Houston, Texas, and finally to Canada before returning to his home state and settling in Memphis,

Tennessee in 1902 to establish a tent ministry. Around that period, he became acquainted with **Mason,** who at that time was still closely associated with **Charles Price Jones.**

Adams received his Pentecostal Holy Spirit baptism experience under the ministry of **Gaston Bernard (G. B.) Cashwell** who had come to the East directly from the **Azusa Street Revival** to spread the Pentecostal message to Holiness groups that had formed throughout the region. After experiencing the Pentecostal Spirit baptism in 1908, he joined the predominantly white Church of God (Cleveland, Tennessee). That same year, he established the Church of God Bible Institute and Training Home. But in 1910, following a disagreement with General Overseer **A. J. Tomlinson,** Adams left that denomination and defied Jim Crow culture to align his congregation, Grace and Truth Church in Memphis, with COGIC. Between 1910 and 1913, Adams and another white minister, Howard A. Goss, worked under Mason's authority to establish white congregations within COGIC. Though Adams was present among other white ministers who had previously been credentialed by Mason at the 1914 Assemblies of God organizing meeting, he did not join the group in breaking away from Mason's leadership.

From 1914 to 1918, Adams published a periodical that carried the name of his congregation, *Grace and Truth*. In 1917, Mason enlisted Adams as part of his strategy to plant COGIC congregations throughout urban communities. In 1918, he relocated to Birmingham, Alabama where he planted a new congregation, leaving the Memphis congregation to a white pastor named Snavel. That congregation eventually affiliated itself with the Assemblies of God. Over time, many of the white ministers and churches that had been under Adams's supervision separated from COGIC to assimilate into other white Pentecostal organizations. By 1930, he had relocated again, this time to Austin, Texas, where reportedly, Adams's group then included a few Latino members. When Adams later sought to break from COGIC and applied to the Assemblies of God to transfer his credentials, the denomination rejected his application, partly because of accusations that he had misappropriated some church funds while he was a member of the **Church of God in Christ.**

Further Reading:

McBride, Calvin, and Leonard P. Adams. *Walking into a New Spirituality: Chronicling the Life, Ministry, and Contributions of Elder Robert E. Hart, B.D., LL.B., D.D., to the CME Church and COGIC: With Some Additional COGIC History.* New York: iUniverse, 2007.

Newman, Joe. *Race and the Assemblies of God Church: The Journey from Azusa Street to the Miracle of Memphis.* Youngstown, NY: Cambria, 2007.

Aenon Bible College

The official institution of higher education of the **Pentecostal Assemblies of the World**, the largest of the African America, Oneness Pentecostal group in the United States. The school was founded in 1940 in Columbus, Ohio as the Pentecostal Bible Training Center by Bishop **Karl F. Smith** and LaBaugh H. Stansbury. For several years, the college served as the major institution for theological training for PAW leaders.

The school held its first classes in January of 1941 with twelve students. Initially, the course of study involved an eight-week curriculum, but this soon expanded into a two-year program. Eventually, a four-year bachelor degree was offered in theology and religious education, and later a Correspondence Studies program was established becoming the mainstay of the school.

Classes were originally held at Smith's church, the Church of the Apostolic Faith. Property was purchased in 1944 for classrooms and dormitory space. In 1947, however, a fire caused extensive damage to the two-story structure. While repairs were being made, classes were again held at Smith's church. Once the structure was restored, classes resumed. The next year, the school moved to Indianapolis, home of PAW headquarters, and was given the name Aenon, meaning "springs," alluding to the waters of educational and spiritual refreshing that would spring from its midst.

In 1972, Bishop **Frank R. Bowdan** established a west coast campus, **Aenon School of Theology & Bible College**, in Los Angeles. Dr. Howard Swancy, a graduate of the Indianapolis school, served as the first President of that branch. A year later, Dr. Norma Sylvester Jackson became dean and served for thirty-two years in various capacities until her death in 2005.

In 1978, a branch of Aenon opened in Philadelphia. In 1981, the main campus was moved to Indianapolis, Indiana, the new headquarters of the denomination. In 1998, Thomas Griffith was appointed president. The current president is Bishop Michael D. Hannah Sr.

Aenon is accredited by A.C.I. (Accrediting Commission International) and is the official academic, degree-granting Institution of Peace Apostolic Church, Inc. Degrees are transferable to other degree-granting institution, colleges, and universities. Aenon operates through host affiliate institutes throughout the United States as well as the Samuel Grimes Bible Institute in Liberia, West Africa.

Currently, the college primarily offers distance education. Through its affiliates in the United States and two affiliates in Liberia—the Samuel Grimes Bible Institute and the Haywood Mission—Aenon Bible College annually enrolls as many as ten thousand students.

Further Reading:

Golder, Morris. *History of the Pentecostal Assemblies of the World.* Indianapolis, IN: Author, 1973.

Aenon School of Theology

The institution was established in 1972 by **Pentecostal Assemblies of the World's** Bishop **Frank Bowdan** as the West Coast branch of the denomination's **Aenon Bible College** in Columbus, Ohio. Howard Swancy, a graduate of Aenon Bible College, served as the first president of the West Coast branch.

A year after Bowdan officially established the school as an extension of the Ohio institution, Dr. Norma Jackson became dean and served for thirty-two years in various capacities. After her death in 2005, the college underwent a transition. In 2007, after several months of negotiations with the Midwest branch that had moved to Indianapolis, the Indianapolis Aenon School of Theology and Bible College reopened its doors.

Aenon School of Theology & Bible College (AST) is accredited by A.C.I. (Accrediting Commission International). It offers graduate leading to Master's and Doctoral degrees and undergraduate studies leading to an Associate or Bachelor degree in Religious Studies, Christian Education, Christian Ministry, and Theology. Dr. Howard A. Swancy remains as president.

Affirming Pentecostal Church International (APCI)

The multi-racial, Apostolic Pentecostal denomination that is the largest LGBTQ-affirming Pentecostal denomination in the world was founded 2010 in Indianapolis, Indiana. APCI has established congregations in the United States, Albania, Kosovo, Portugal, Mexico, Taiwan, England, Argentina, Peru, Colombia, and Guatemala. It also has a heavy presence in Pan-African communities including Brazil, Montenegro, Ethiopia, Kenya, Madagascar, South Africa, Tanzania, Trinidad, Uganda, and Ghana. APCI also has extensive ministries in Nigeria, through their Chicago church, High Praises International Ministries.

Bishop Erik D. Swope-Wise—the white founding pastor of High Praises International Ministries in Chicago, Illinois—is presiding bishop, and African-American Bishop Donagrant McCluney, leader of an affirming Pentecostal congregation in Greenville, serves as Associate Bishop. Temporal authority, however, is vested in the General Board, led by General Overseer Will Horn.

The doctrinal stance of the organization is similar to that other Apostolic Pentecostal churches: the Oneness of God, water baptism by full immersion in the name of Jesus for forgiveness of sins, the baptism of the Holy Ghost with the initial evidence of speaking in other tongues, and holiness of life and heart. APCI adheres firmly to these teachings, and does not give ministerial credentials to those holding other beliefs.

The major distinction from other Apostolic bodies, however, is APCI's stance on homosexuality, bisexuality, or transgendered lifestyles as being biblically acceptable. They base this view on their understanding of the Hebrew and Greek texts of Scripture, as do other LGBT-affirming Apostolic organizations.

The denomination publishes a monthly, free online newsletter, *The Apostolic Voice*. It also operates a Bible college, Apostolic Institute of Ministry.

African-American Catholic Charismatics

The nearly 2.5 million black Catholics in America represent approximately ten percent of the African-American population, but only three percent of the American Catholic population. Many of these live in seven black dioceses of Louisiana, in the three dioceses around New York, and in those of Chicago, Washington, Miami, Los Angles, Detroit, and Galveston-Houston and Beaumont, Texas. It is in these urban center that black Catholic renewal movements have made their heaviest impact.

Charismatic renewal within the Catholic Church came about because of changes in Catholic liturgy and practice resulting from the deliberations of the Second Vatican Council. The changes allowed African Americans and others within the Church to incorporate culturally sensitive elements into masses within their local congregations.

However, it also allowed Catholics to explore new varieties of spirituality without the direct guidance of Church leaders, opening the possibility for exposure to Charismatic Christianity. For black Catholics particularly, this exposure put them in touch with forms of Christian spirituality that resonated with their roots within African spirituality—such as Pentecostalism.

Black Catholic theologian, Diana Hayes, uses the term "Black Catholic revivalism" to describe this form of spirituality that joins the egalitarian Arminianism of Evangelical Christianity with the institutionalized ritual of Roman Catholicism, though not explicitly tied to an understanding Holy Spirit baptism. But spirited gospel masses replete with choirs singing the latest tunes appear to have become a staple in many urban black congregations such as St. Augustine in Washington DC that employed Howard University-trained Leon Roberts—who had been raised in the **Church of God in Christ**—to direct its gospel choir in the 1980s. Not only did the congregation experience phenomenal growth but it gained fame and national recognition.

Some congregations not only employed gospel choirs, but also incorporated Pentecostal elements as fervent preaching peppered with vocal "amens" and "yes, Lord," lively congregational singing, laying on of hands, slaying in the Spirit, anointing with oil, and praying for divine healing. Statistics on the number of parishes that are involved in Charismatic spirituality are not available and the degree to which they employ charismatic ritual varies greatly.

A few parishes within the movement can be characterized as entirely or predominantly Charismatic. Others set aside one or more of their scheduled masses for Charismatic Worship. In both cases, there is also likely to be a Charismatic prayer group that meets outside the mass. Such venues have led to more room for women's leadership than would be found in the traditional mass. The movement has also led to more involvement of Catholic faithful in ecumenical efforts with other Charismatics through such organizations as Women's Aglow and the Full Gospel Businessmen's Association. Yet, renewal within the Catholic Church has not meant an abandonment of Catholic dogma in favor of classical Pentecostal or evangelical theological forms, since the roots of Catholic renewal lie closer to efforts coming out of the 1960s Charismatic revival within the Episcopal Church.

While most black Catholic charismatics have remained within the Roman Catholic tradition, involving themselves in liturgical innovation made possible by Vatican II, one of the most visible, though controversial, expressions of black Catholic charismatic spirituality is the African-American Catholic Congregation founded in July 1989 by Fr. **George A. Stallings**. Stallings pastored St. Teresa of Avila, a predominantly black, Roman Catholic congregation in one of the poorest sections of inner city, Washington DC for twelve years. His congregation became known for enthusiastic worship featuring a crucifix with a black Christ, a full-immersion baptismal fount, and a gospel choir within what became a three-hour mass. Its highly charismatic ritual drew former Catholics back to the church and enticed Protestants to explore Catholic worship, increasing St. Teresa's membership tenfold—from two hundred to two thousand parishioners before Stallings left to form his own organization, the African-American Catholic Congregation. Since Stallings's departure, no other figure has come forward as the dominant leader.

Further Reading:

Hayes, Diana. "Black Catholic Revivalism: The Emergence of New Forms of Worship." *Journal of the Interdenominational Theological Center* 14.1–2 (Fall 1986–Spring 1987) 87–107.

African-American Catholic Congregation

One of the most visible expressions of African-American Catholic, Charismatic spirituality in the United States is the organization founded in 1989 by Father **George A. Stallings** after leaving the Roman Church to establish the new body with nine congregations. Within a year, thirteen congregations had approximately five thousand members in Washington DC, where the organization was founded—New Orleans, Baltimore, Philadelphia, Norfolk, and Richmond. While the Norfolk congregation had closed by the late 1990s, additional congregation rose up in Los Angeles and Richmond, leading to an estimated 7,500 members nationwide today.

Though Stallings refuses to label the blend of Catholic ritual and African traditional religion as charismatic or Neo-Pentecostal, decidedly Pentecostal elements are discernable in its worship and spirituality. The music, dancing, emotive preaching, baptism by immersion and ritual healing are interspersed with elements of traditional Catholic liturgy in its worship. Yet, the group retains elements that are distinct from Pentecostal understandings including openly supporting inclusion of gay or lesbian leadership and ministry in its congregations and maintaining an openness to intimate collaboration with those who stand outside the Christian tradition.

Seven years after the AACC founding, Father Cyprian Rowe, a Marist priest who had served as executive director of the National Office of Black Catholics, with the National Black Catholic Clergy Caucus, and on the board of the National Catholic Reporter, broke from the Roman Catholic Church to join Stallings. He was subsequently ordained a bishop. Rowe, who died in 2008, was an outspoken critic of the Catholic Church's treatment of African Americans and the lack of black leadership in the church hierarchy. However, before his death, Rowe recanted his decision to rejoin the Marist Brothers.

Stallings made significant changes in structure of Catholic worship within his organization. He dispensed with the traditional one-hour mass to hold services that often ran three hours, blending African music, black literature, and African traditional rites including traditional liturgy and invocation of ancestor spirits. This controversial style drew criticism from Catholic hierarchy and, in part, led to his excommunication from the Church in 1989.

While the organization retains the strong social witness of the Catholic Church, including an emphasis on benevolence and political activism, it eschews more traditional Catholic teachings such as the ban on abortion and birth control, as well as its sanctions on homosexual activity, remarriage after divorce, women priests and bishops, as well as the requirement of celibacy for priests. The social witness goes far beyond traditional Catholic moral stances to embrace the full ministry of women, inter-religious dialog, and collaboration with groups as diverse the Reverend Sun Yun Moon's Unification Church, Louis Farrakhan's Nation of Islam, and the Inner Light Unity Fellowship, a predominantly gay congregation.

In 2002, Stallings's openness to ordaining women clergy led him to elevate Wanda Cecelia Outlaw to the priesthood and appoint her senior associate pastor and administrator of his local congregation, Imani Temple. In 2006, dissident African Archbishop Emmanuel Milingo used Imani Temple as the setting for attacking Roman Catholic Church teaching by consecrating four married men—including Stallings—as bishops, an action for which he was excommunicated. In 2013, the congregation again stirred controversy when Bishop Emeritus Diana Williams, not only a woman but openly lesbian, married Bishop Allyson Nelson Abrams, a Baptist pastor from Detroit, Michigan. Abrams subsequently left her pastorate to establish a non-denomination fellowship in the Maryland suburbs of Washington.

Further Reading:

D'Apolito, Rosemary Ann. "An Analysis of the African American Catholic Congregation as a Social Movement." PhD diss., University of Chicago, 1996.

African Episcopal Methodist Church, Neo-Pentecostalism in

Early black Neo-Pentecostals, as represented in **John Bryant** in the African Methodist Episcopal Church, sought to identify the roots of Pentecostal spirituality in a return to the African roots of black spirituality, and infuse this spirituality with a conscious attempt to engage issues of social justice as well as individual and communal wholeness. In doing so, they were incorporating the very elements of African spirituality that the early independent black church leaders, such as Allen and Payne, attempted to downplay.

In the mid-1960s, as a young seminary graduate serving in the Peace Corp in Africa, John Bryant became intrigued by the possibilities of "spirited" worship as he encountered a "realm of the Spirit" that he sensed "could not be explained away." He saw people healed, going into trances and exercising spiritual power—all "without the [Western] notion of Jehovah God or Jesus Christ." The experience led him to re-examine Christian Scripture to discover what it said about the spiritual dimension largely overlooked within traditional African American Methodism. For Bryant, this search led to the conviction that a more vibrant engagement with the Holy Spirit was warranted.

On returning to the United States and entering the pastorate, Bryant, who is considered the father of African-American Neo-Pentecostalism, sought to incorporate this spiritual realm into his own ministry within the most conspicuously Afro-centric denomination in America, the African Methodist Episcopal Church. Bryant began with Bethel AME Church, a small Fall River, Massachusetts congregation that he saw grow from eight to sixty members in two years. Bryant later moved to the historic St. Paul's AME Church in Cambridge, Massachusetts, where he infused AME teaching and worship with his newfound Pentecostal sensitivity without losing the emphasis on the denomination's historic affinity for involvement in social justice pursuits. He saw Pentecostal spirituality as the mechanism for connecting his congregation to their black cultural roots in

Africa, identifying the Spirit as a liberator who could empower the African-American community.

During Bryant's tenure, St. Paul's young, urban, highly educated, middle-class congregation grew from two hundred to over three thousand members. In 1975, he returned to his native Baltimore and brought elements of Charismatic renewal to the historic 600-member congregation. Within two years, membership grew to over seven thousand, making the largest AME congregation in the nation a catalyst for African-American neo-Pentecostalism and positioning him to be elected a bishop in 1988.

While many AME traditionalists were initially disturbed by the push to import Pentecostal spirituality, the largest and wealthiest AME churches have incorporated neo-Pentecostal elements into their worship. The ten-thousand-member Ebenezer AME congregation, led by Grainger and JoAnn Browning in Fort Washington, Maryland, for example, went from twenty-five members to over one thousand in two years after incorporating the new spirituality. First AME of Los Angeles, Bridge Street in Brooklyn, New York, and Payne AME in Nashville, Tennessee, Allen AME in Jamaica, Queens, New York also saw substantial growth.

Within the AME Church, the neo-Pentecostal movement blends the new charismatic spirituality with the traditional AME progressive involvement in social justice issues and its afro-centric aesthetic sensibilities. A further distinction from classical Pentecostalism is the continued emphasis on an educated clergy and laity within the AME movement. Neo-Pentecostal pastors within the AME, like their other clergy colleagues, are generally college graduates and many, or most, have at least some seminary training.

While initially meeting resistance from some stalwarts, especially within more prestigious historic churches, the new neo-Pentecostal vitality within the more traditional black denominations, such as the African American Episcopal Church, has attracted a younger, more educated and upwardly mobile constituency, including more young black men. It has also sparked an upsurge in the number of people going into the ministry from these congregations.

Further Reading:

Gaines, Adrienne. "Revive Us Again, Precious Lord." *Charisma* (2003) 37–38.
Lawrence, Beverly Hall. *Reviving the Spirit: A Generation of African Americans Goes Home to Church*. New York: Grove, 1997.

African Methodist Episcopal Zion Church, Neo-Pentecostalism in

Unlike the African Methodist Episcopal Church, elements of neo-Pentecostalism are less visible within the AMEZ Church and only a small number of the more than 3,200 AMEZ congregations and 1,440,405 congregants throughout the country would openly characterize themselves as charismatic or Neo-Pentecostal. Yet, the neo-Pentecostal movement has not entirely missed the denomination.

Part of the resistance to the spread of neo-Pentecostal within the AMEZ tradition could be attributed to an experience with one of the movement's earliest and most prominent proponents. Over two decades, **John Cherry**'s suburban Washington DC, Full Gospel AME Zion Church congregation grew from a twenty-person Bible study started in his home in 1981 to reach the present estimated 27,000 members, one hundred full-time employees, and television broadcasts on eleven stations, becoming the largest congregation in Prince George's County, the wealthiest black county in the United States. In 1999, however, after a rancorous court battle, Cherry pulled the congregation out of the denomination, renaming it "From the Heart Ministries."

Greater Centennial AME Zion Church pastored by W. Darin Moore in Mount Vernon, New York is another neo-Pentecostal AMEZ megachurch. Under Moore's leadership, membership of the congregation has grown from eight hundred people to more than five thousand, and with the departure of Cherry's church, making it now the largest of the more than two thousand AME Zion churches in the country. Moore grew up in Greater Centennial, a congregation that had been pastored by his grandfather, William Pratt. After his grandfather's death, in 1995, the congregation retained Moore as pastor.

Baltimore's Pennsylvania Avenue AME Zion Church boasts a membership of several hundred. By 2006, its pastor, Dennis V. Proctor, had served as pastor of the West Baltimore congregation for fourteen years. In that time, its neo-Pentecostal spirituality had not moved the congregation into megachurch status, but Proctor had become an outspoken defender of the new spirituality, while still acknowledging criticism from more traditional pastors who saw the black church's involvement in the civil rights struggle as crucial.

By the end of the twentieth century, the denomination's periodical, *The AME Zion Quarterly*, had published a few articles on the work of the Holy Spirit in the ancient and contemporary church, but gave no coverage to any resurgence of Neo-Pentecostalism within its ranks.

Bishop George E. Battle Jr., who served for some time in the Central North Carolina Conference before moving to the Northeastern Episcopal District, has been a voice for neo-Pentecostal renewal within the denomination. Battle has been an advocate of openness to the "full gospel," and some see him as "a breath of Pentecostal fresh air to the AME Zion Church." He was joined in his assessment by retired AMEZ Bishop Ruben Speaks, an avid supporter of charismatic spirituality within the AME Zion church. Yet Speaks is equally insistent that rigid classical Pentecostal definitions of Holy Spirit baptism as always accompanied by glossolalia are inadequate, and insistence that speaking in tongues is the only valid proof of Holy Spirit baptism belies the truth that not all who receive the baptism of the Holy Spirit speak in tongues. Still, tension caused by varying degrees of openness to Neo-Pentecostalism remains within the AMEZ church.

African Universal Church

One of two quasi-Holiness Pentecostal denominations with black nationalist sentiments that formed from the fragmentation of congregations that occurred after the assassination of **Laura Koffey**, founder of the **African Universal Church and Commercial League**. It traces its founding to the 1927 establishment and the 1928 incorporation of her original organization.

From the 1930s through the 1960s, the body was led by Clarence Addison, and though Koffy's assassination most likely came at the hands of Marcus Garvey enthusiasts,

Addison was heavily influenced by Garveyite Black Nationalist teachings. He was a strong opponent of the American Civil Rights movement and found support from white Southerners. He called integration sinful.

Sometime in 1930, Addison moved the headquarters of the group to East Orange, New Jersey, but by 1936 had reincorporated it in Louisiana. Its African headquarters are in Lagos, Nigeria. In 1934, the organization formed the Commercial League Corporation to assist its members with services such as life insurance and other necessities. The church also encourages the use of African Language by distributing free lessons written in Xhosa-Zulu and encourages total economic self-sufficiency of its members.

While the body holds a Pentecostal soteriology, like Koffey's original group, it teaches that there are four specific experience for the believer: justification, sanctification, baptism of the Holy Spirit, and baptism with fire. Further, though, it observes the usual ordinances of the Pentecostal movement, water is not used for baptism nor wine for communion. The polity of the church is episcopal, and Addison held the position of Archbishop. Its assembly meets every four years.

In the 1930s, missionaries from the denomination traveled to the Gold Coast (now Ghana) and to Nigeria to establish branches of the church. I. T. Wallace, a labor organizer and journalist, for example, established a branch in Nigeria in 1931.

The name and headquarters of the organization appears to have changed several times overs its life. Current headquarters for the group, which has approximately one hundred congregations, is apparently headquartered in Webster, New Jersey. It holds no relation to a parallel group with a similar name that also evolved out of Koffey's efforts.

African Universal Church and Commercial League

The quasi-Pentecostal organization that grew out of the work of **Laura Andorker Koffey** in the mid-1920s. The group incorporated classical Trinitarian Pentecostal doctrine with Black Nationalist elements and Ethiopianism sentiments.

Initially Koffey worked closely with Marcus Garvey, founder of the Universal Negro Improvement Association to recruit members for that movement until she fell into disfavor with Garvey who began to see her as a rival. She originally established her organization as the Universal African Improvement Association and Commercial League with plans to develop business enterprises that would join Africans and African Americans together in economic ventures. Her vision was to prepare African Americans to repatriate to the homeland, and she emphasized the relationship between African people and blacks in the United States.

Once she broke from Garvey's group, using Miami as her center, Koffey began traveling throughout the south holding meetings that were a mixture of Pentecostal revival fervor and Black Nationalist ethos for her new organization. She taught followers Bantu as well as the Bible, within the group that generally held to classical Holiness Pentecostalism, but insisted that there were four specific experience for the believer: justification, sanctification, baptism of the Holy Spirit, and baptism with fire.

Following her assassination, her followers killed a Garveyite in retaliation, but initially did little to sustain the organization. Many of the local centers she had established became autonomous, disconnected churches each carrying on her tradition in their own particular manner, and overall interest in her organization within the United States waned and her work fell into decline for a short time. Eventually however, at least two groups—the **African Universal Church, Inc.** led by **Eli B'usabe Nyombolo,** a South African immigrant, and the African Universal Church with **Clarence Addison** at the head—emerged to carry on her legacy. Further, there were a number of smaller groups that came into and out of existence over the next fifty years including the Missionary African Universal Church, the Tabernacle African Universal Church and the African Unity Church. Historiography regarding these group often involves a confusing intermix of names, places, dates, and statistics.

Further Reading:

Bair, Barbara. "Ethiopia Shall Stretch Forth Her Hands Unto God: Laura Koffey and the Gendered Vision of Redemption in the Garvey Movement." In *"A Mighty Baptism": Race and Gender, in the Creation of American Protestantism,* edited by Susan Juster and Lisa MacFarlane, 38–61. Ithaca, NY: Cornell University Press, 1996.

African Universal Church, Inc.

A quasi-Holiness Pentecostal denomination that was forged as one of the two bodies formed in the period immediately following the death of **Laura Koffey,** founder of the African Universal Church. After her death, her followers had dissipated into several autonomous congregations that were disconnected to Koffey's original movement. **Eli B'usabe Nyombolo,** a South African who had recently migrated to the United State and became attracted to Koffey's teaching, launched a concerted effort to resurrect and promote the movement Koffey had started.

Nyombolo built on Kofi's message of connecting with African cultures and traditions. Church services were held in English and Bantu, a family of languages used by hundreds of ethnic groups in Africa. Church children learned from a Bantu primer. In 1944, he established the intentional community of Adorkaville in Jacksonville, Florida to honor Koffey's memory and keep her teaching alive. The eleven plus "African Community," originally consisted of homes, a church and community center. There were plans to build a school, an office building, as well as a building that could be used as an "African Home" for visiting African natives. The intention was to prepare African Americans to return to Africa and develop relationships between businesspeople in Africa and America. Members were taught African language and customs that were incorporated into their lifestyles. The organization was also involved in the import of crafts, goods, exported tools and equipment to Africa. Nyombolo never made it back to Africa himself. However, there was at least one known attempt of six individuals that were sent as pioneers.

By the early 1950s, the congregation had again began to drift apart. In 1953, however, three of the groups from Miami, Hollywood and Jacksonville reunited and reorganized as the **African Universal** Church, Inc. The group first elected John Dean as chair; he served until 1958, when Clifford Hepburn succeeded him, serving until 1970. Gloria Hepburn served until 1974, the same year that Audley Sears took office.

Fifteen years after its reorganization, the group made a renewed effort to locate Koffey's family in Ghana when Earnest Sears traveled to that country for that purpose. He was successful in not only locating the family but also in bringing one of her family members, a nephew, back to the United States. Prior to his trip, the family had not learned of her assassination.

Presently there are seven affiliated congregations in Florida and Alabama with headquarters in Daphne City, Alabama. The doctrine of this body is similar to that of its sister organization, the **African Universal Church**.

All Nations Pentecostal Church

In 1916, **Lucy Smith** left Stone Church, the predominantly white congregation founded in 1906 by Holiness leader William Piper to form a small home prayer band with two other women. Two years later that group had become the beginnings of All Nations Pentecostal Church. By the 1920s the group of followers that had gathered around Smith was holding tent revival services throughout Chicago's South Side. By 1926, the congregation had settled into its own facility, becoming the first church in Chicago built by a woman pastor, the first new church building constructed in the city by an African-American congregation in over two decades, and the only multi-racial congregation on the South Side of Chicago. By the 1930s the church had grown to a congregation of five thousand, the majority working class and poor blacks, whites, and immigrants from several countries.

From its inception, All Nations Church was led almost exclusively by women in a cultural climate where women's ministry and leadership were largely opposed. Yet, Elder Smith was able to form fellowships with other black churches in South Side Chicago. Further, during the Great Depression, Smith's alliances with prominent businessmen aided her in carrying out a substantial outreach ministry throughout Chicago's South Side so that her church became the first African-American congregation in Chicago to regularly distribute food and clothing without regard to race.

The church was noted for its musical program that eventually included several choirs and a four-piece "orchestra," and its "refilling services," where Smith gave special prayer and attention to those seeking Holy Spirit baptism. All Nations Church became one of the first African-American churches to broadcast services on radio. Worshippers across the country flocked to her live worship services, drawn by Smith's fiery preaching and the musical talent of her granddaughter, **Lucy Smith (Collier)**, known as "Little Lucy."

In the late 1940s, Elder Lucy Smith relinquished control of All Nations to her youngest daughter, Ardella Smith. At the time of Lucy Smith's death in 1952, All Nations Church had become one of the South Side's most influential congregations. Her funeral was one of the largest held in Chicago up to that time, as sixty thousand people viewed her body and fifty thousand lined the streets for the processional.

By 1955, conflicts over church debt and property led to a split and ended its radio broadcast. Those opposed to Ardella's leadership reformed as a separate All Nations Pentecostal Church, devoted to the memory of their founder. Ardella subsequently left the ministry and converted to Catholicism. The former church building was demolished in the late 1950s after the entire east wall mysteriously collapsed.

Further Reading:

Wallace D. Best. *Passionately Divine, No Less Human: Religion and Culture in Black Chicago 1915–1952*. Princeton, NJ: Princeton University Press, 2005.

All Saints Bible College

The only undergraduate level, degree-granting institution serving the more than five-million-member **Church of God in Christ**. The four-year institution was established in 2002 in Memphis, Tennessee as a secular college alternative for COGIC youth.

Beginning in 1973, two years after Bishop **James O. Patterson, Sr.** laid out a vision for the **C. H. Mason System of Bible Colleges**, COGIC schools in the Tennessee Headquarters, the Tennessee 4th, and the Tennessee 5th jurisdictions began discussing a merger. In 1998, the three-jurisdictional Bible Colleges within the state merged with the jurisdictional bishops—**G. E. Patterson, J. O. Patterson Jr.,** and Samuel L. Lowe—as co-presidents of the school. Benjamin L. Smith was appointed the first dean and was later succeeded by Perry C. Little.

In 2000, the then-presiding bishop, **G. E. Patterson**, and the COGIC General Board appointed Dr. Alonzo Johnson to guide the merging of the C. H. Mason Bible College of Memphis with the newly proposed All Saints Bible College. When completed in 2002, Johnson was tapped to serve as its first president. In 2003, Patterson appointed Little as the second president. In 2011, Bishop **Charles Blake**, who had succeeded Patterson as presiding bishop, appointed Dr. Granville Scruggs as the third and current president. The school is located on the grounds of the COGIC World Headquarters. The college houses the forty-thousand-volume Bishop G. E. Patterson Memorial Library, which was dedicated in 2012. While the school does not hold accreditation, it has articulation agreements with several local colleges within the immediate vicinity of the All Saints Bible College campus.

Allen, Oliver Clyde (O.C.) III

Presiding bishop of the **United Progressive Pentecostal Church Fellowship**. In 2003, he established the **Vision Church International** in Atlanta, Georgia as a welcoming and affirming community for the gay and lesbian community. Allen and his followers contradict classical Pentecostal understandings of homosexuality as a sin and insist that it is a biblically acceptable lifestyle. Located in the "Bible Belt," a region known for its conservative sexual ethic, The **Vision Church International** has been cited by the liberal press as an "alternative to sexism, homophobia and identity oppression in the Black Church." His congregation grew rapidly to become one of the fastest growing churches in the southern United States.

Allen has been an op-ed writer for CNN and honored by a host of community and national groups including the Georgia House of Representatives in 2012. He is a regional spokesperson for the National Black Justice Coalition LGBT Economic Empowerment Tour for communities of color and has worked closely with the United States Small

Business Administration to provide support to LGBT and other minority entrepreneurs in the community.

A native of southern California, he completed his undergraduate at Morgan State University in Baltimore, Maryland and at Morehouse College in Atlanta and is currently completing degrees at Harvard University Extension School in Cambridge, Massachusetts. Over the twenty-five years of his ministry, Allen has served as a youth evangelist, and as a lecturer around the United States, Canada, and Bermuda, and as a missionary in Ghana, West Africa.

He is CEO of the Vision Community Foundation that addresses socioeconomic and health gaps in the urban community by providing GED training, food distribution, clothes bank for homeless families, and HIV/AIDS counseling and testing. The Vision Community Foundation hosts a national Community Festival for over thirty thousand people on Labor Day weekend to promote community health and wellness. He has launched The Vision Center for Counseling and Behavioral Health to deliver mental and emotional counseling to the community, as well as ministries addressing women, men, youth, health, and wellness. He has held membership in the Joint College of African American Bishops, People for the American Way, and the Atlanta Council of Churches, just to name a few.

Allen and his partner, Rashad Burgess, to whom he considers himself married, and whom the congregation refers to as "First Gentleman," are parents of two adopted children. In 2013, Allen and his family made history by being the first same-gender couple featured in the black periodical *Ebony* as one of the "Top 10 Coolest Black Families" in America. In 2014, Morehouse College inducted Allen into the prestigious Martin Luther King Jr. International Board of Preachers.

Alliance of Apostolic Churches of Christ Jesus (AACCJ)

A Oneness Pentecostal fellowship of ministers formed in 1977 under the leadership of Albert E. Dixon Sr., a bishop in the **Churches of God and True Holiness**. The organization was birthed out of an earlier conversation between Dixon and Bishop Willie Frazier of **The New Born Lighthouse Church of the Apostolic Faith, Inc.**

These two men shared the vision with other Oneness leaders from several small Oneness bodies and independent Oneness congregations. The group was initially organized as the Apostolic Ministerial Alliance in Cleveland, Ohio where many of its first constituents were located. At the organizing meeting, Dixon was elected as president, Loyce Clark was elected vice president, and Raymond Worrell as secretary. Later, the name was changed to the Alliance of Apostolic Churches of Christ Jesus.

Timothy Herrington, pastor of Abundant Life Assembly of Grenada, Mississippi, is the current presider.

Alpha and Omega Pentecostal Church of God of America, Inc.

The **Alpha and Omega Pentecostal Church of God of America**, Inc., was founded in 1944 when Rev. **Magdalene Mabe Phillips**, a former member of the **United Holy Church of America,** began holding a Bible study in the dining room of her residence, along with an outreach ministry to feed hungry members of her community. She then established the original congregation, the Alpha and Omega Church of God Tabernacle in Baltimore, Maryland. It was incorporated in 1945.

At some point Phillips had left the **United Holy Church**, to join a Baptist congregation in Baltimore, and then joined the **Mt. Sinai Holy Church of America**, the denomination founded by Bishop **Ida Robinson.** She was pastoring in Baltimore when she left that organization to found her own group. The name was later changed to **Alpha and Omega Pentecostal Church of God of America**, Inc. There is no clear indication about what prompted the split, however, it could not have been over the leadership of women, since women had continually been at the head of the Mt. Sinai organization as presiding bishop and occupied many of the top organizational positions. Unlike Robinson, however, Phillips's group never had a large measure of success nor garnered the momentum of the parent organization. In the summer of 1952, however, the denomination, became one of the first Pentecostal churches to have an inner-city summer camp for African-American youth.

It is not known what year Phillips stepped down, but she was succeeded by Charles Waters, who later left the denomination to form True Fellowship Pentecostal Church of America. John Mabe, brother of the founder, succeeded him as overseer. It is uncertain how many congregations pulled out with Waters, but by 1970, there were only four congregations in Mabe's body: the Baltimore congregation, one in St. Augustine Florida, one in Philadelphia, and a mission church in Kingston, Jamaica with approximately four hundred total members. In the 1990s the organization had grown to eight churches.

Amos, Barbara M. 1957–

Prominent preacher, lecturer, teacher, church founder, and former bishop in the **Mt. Sinai Holy Church of America**. As a young woman of sixteen, the multi-talented Amos served for five years as a full-time musician for Grammy-award-winning gospel singer, **Shirley Caesar,** who mentored her in music and public speaking.

She left that circuit to begin her ministry by helping a struggling Norfolk congregation of six people, including the pastor and her husband. She took over that congregation in 1986. Within six months, the church was filled to capacity. In 1999, the year Amos resigned from the pastorate, the congregation had swelled to 2,700 and had established numerous outreach ministries including Faith Academy School of Excellence, established in 1992, to offer a curriculum concentrated in mathematics, science, and technology for students in preschool through the eighth grade.

That year, she became Executive Director of Dorcas, Inc., a nonprofit organization promoting spiritual, educational, and economic wellness in impoverished communities in America and globally. Dr. Amos traveled to Haiti and Africa and provided a myriad of resources to many impoverished communities around the world.

In the early 1990s, Amos was elevated to the office of bishop with the **Mt. Sinai Holy Church**, where she was appointed to oversee the denomination in North Carolina, and was being groomed by then presiding bishop, **Amy Stevens** to succeed her. Amos represented Mt. Sinai at the historic meeting that disbanded the white Pentecostal Fellowship of North America to establish the interracial **Pentecostal and Charismatic Churches of North America**. As a charter member of the Executive Council of PCCNA, which represents over forty million Pentecostals around the world, Amos was the only female member of that group.

Though young Amos had been a member of the **Church of God in Christ**, the outspoken advocate for gender equality within the Pentecostal movement, she transitioned into the **Mt. Sinai Holy Church** because of its more liberal stance on gender equity than is usually found in African-America Pentecostal bodies. After Stevens's death, however, the year after Amos resigned from her congregation, she stepped down from the bishopric of the Mt. Sinai organization after being rejected for the position of presiding bishop, when for the first time in the denomination's seventy-five year history that positon was assumed by a man, Bishop **Joseph Bell**.

Subsequently, Amos founded Kinston Christian Center in Kinston, North Carolina. This ministry provides food, clothing, and a free after-school programing to assist families in the Kinston community and Faith Deliverance Christian Fellowship, a fellowship of Charismatic congregation.

Amos holds a BS degree in Criminal Justice from Hampton University in Hampton, Virginia and has done graduate studies in Social Work at Norfolk State University in Norfolk, Virginia. She received a Master of Divinity degree from Samuel DeWitt Proctor School of Theology at Virginia Union University and her Doctor of Ministry from Eastern Baptist Theological Seminary in Philadelphia, Pennsylvania.

Apostle Church of Christ in God

The Apostle Church of Christ in God is a Oneness Pentecostal denominational that was founded in 1940 by five elders—J. W. Audrey, James. C. Richardson, Jerome Jenkins, W. R. Bryant, and J. M. Williams—who separated from the **Church of God (Apostolic)** largely over concern for the authoritarian manner in which Eli N. Neal, acting presiding bishop, conducted the affairs of the church as well as with some personal problems that Neal was experiencing.

Originally, three churches left with the elders, who established headquarters in Winston-Salem, North Carolina. When Audrey was elected the new presiding bishop in 1952, Richardson was elected as a second bishop.

In 1953, after unsuccessfully seeking to be consecrated a bishop, Robert Doub, the overseer of Pennsylvania, challenged Audrey's position as presiding bishop. When the majority of the denomination backed Audrey, Doub left to found Shiloh Apostolic Temple with his Pennsylvania congregations serving as its headquarters.

Ironically, Audrey resigned in 1956, and Richardson became presiding bishop, serving until his death in 1995. Richardson's tenures spurred growth within the denomination. He began the *Apostolic Gazette* (later the *Apostolic Journal*), which served the church for many years. He also instituted a program to assist ministers in pursuing education.

However, his efforts were frustrated by several schisms that slowed the denomination's growth.

The most prominent schism occurred in 1971 when Audrey, the former presider, left to found an independent congregation. By 1980, membership had grown to 2,150 members in thirteen congregations being served by five bishops and twenty-five ministers. The denomination, headquartered in Winston-Salem, North Carolina, is a member of the Apostolic World Christian Fellowship.

Apostolic Assemblies of Christ, Inc.

A Oneness Pentecostal denomination founded in 1970 by **Bishop George Marshall (G. M.) Boone**, along with several schismatic former members of the Pentecostal Churches of Apostolic Faith. When Bishop Willie Lee—the presiding bishop of the Pentecostal Churches—died, questions regarding Bishop Lee's former administration of the denomination led to a church splinter, and one group formed around Bishop Boone and Virgil Oates, who became the vice bishop of the new group.

The organization's headquarters is located in Detroit, Michigan. The body is episcopal in governance. Boone started with seven congregations: by 1980, there were twenty-five churches and approximately 3,500 members. In 2008, the Assemblies reported seventy-seven member ministers in member churches nationwide. Currently there are 259 congregations worldwide.

The leadership of the AAoC consists of a presiding bishop and a board of bishops. The current presiding bishop is Donald Sorrells of Lockland, Ohio who was elected in 2012, when Boone moved to emeritus status. Within the denomination, women function as licensed and ordained ministers, evangelists, and pastors, as well as in jurisdictional and national offices, but cannot hold the episcopal ranks of elder or bishop.

Apostolic Church of Christ

The **Apostolic Church of Christ** is a Oneness Pentecostal denomination founded in 1969 by Bishop Johnnie Draft and Elder Wallace Snow, both ministers in the **Church of God (Apostolic)**. Draft served for many years an overseer in the parent body and pastor of St. Peter's Church, the denomination's headquarters congregation. The separation was not schismatic; Draft expressed no criticism of the **Church of God (Apostolic)**. Rather, he stated that the Spirit of the Lord brought him to start his own organization. The church maintains doctrine that parallels that of the parent group. It differs from its parent body, however, in its development of a centralized church polity. Authority is vested in the executive board, which owns all the church property. Doctrine follows that of the **Church of God (Apostolic)**. Bishop Draft serves as the church's chief apostle.

In 1992, the Apostolic Church of Christ, which is headquartered in Winston-Salem, North Carolina, had six churches, six hundred members, nine ministers, six elders, and two licensed missionaries.

Apostolic Faith Church of Christ (Pentecostal)

The Oneness Pentecostal body was founded in Winston-Salem, North Carolina in 1969 by Johnny Draft and Wallace Snow, both of whom had been members of the **Church of God (Apostolic)**. Draft was a former overseer and pastor of the headquarter church of the former denomination and pastor of the parent denomination's headquarter congregation, St. Peters Apostolic Church. While there was no schismatic concern, Draft simply felt a desire to establish his own body. The polity of this body is almost identical to that of the parent, except that in the new body individual church property is not owned by the parent board.

ACC Headquarters are in Winston-Salem, North Carolina. In 1992, the Apostolic Faith Church of Christ had six churches, four hundred members, nine ministers, six elders, two licensed missionaries, and one bishop. Draft serves as presiding bishop.

Apostolic Faith Church of God and True Holiness

In 1945, after thirty-five years in leadership of the **Apostolic Faith Church of God**, Bishop **Charles Lowe** separated from the Trinitarian denomination he founded under the auspices of **Azusa Street Revival** leader, **William Joseph Seymour**. Taking only one congregation with him, he established the **Apostolic Faith Church of God and True Holiness** as a Oneness Pentecostal denomination. Lowe presided as bishop until 1952 when he appointed Levi Butts in his place. In 1952, the body split when Bishops Jesse Henshaw and Willie Cross and Elder R. T. Butts left to form the Apostolic Faith Church of God Live On!

Lowe died in 1954. He was succeeded by Bishop Levi Butts, who served until 1980. At his resignation, Vice Bishop Robert Lewis Lyons Sr. became the presiding bishop. In 1990, the church, which is headquartered in Jefferson, Ohio, reported twenty-four congregations.

Further Reading

Montier, Gerald, and Carolyn Montier. *Remembering the Past Apostolic Faith Mission Celebrating the Present Apostolic Faith Church of God*. Bloomington, IN: Xlibris, 2011.

Apostolic Faith Church of God Giving Grace, Inc.

A Trinitarian convention of churches founded in the mid-1960s as the New Jerusalem Apostolic Faith Churches of God by Mother Lillie Perry Williams and Bishop Rufus Easter. The vision was brought into reality in 1975 with the official formation of the organization shortly before her passing, championed by her spiritual sons and daughters.

Williams began her first congregation in 1930 in Ante, Virginia and began to draw a sizeable following within the small community south of Richmond. Easter became one of Williams' earliest converts after first attending one of her services to debate the authority of a woman to preach, then being converted to her doctrine and receiving the Pentecostal experience of Holy Spirit baptism. He later joined her in preaching the Pentecostal message throughout North Carolina, Virginia and other parts of the East Coast. Easter and Williams both had been formerly associated with the **Apostolic Faith Churches of God**.

Williams constructed her first church, New Jerusalem Holiness Church, in Garysburg, North Carolina, which was dedicated in 1952. Over the next twenty years, "Mother" Williams (as she was called) and Easter began churches along the East Coast. Along with preaching and praying for healing and deliverance, Williams and Easter carried out an extensive benevolence ministry, providing food, clothing and housing and even automobiles to families and individuals in need. Her concern for the material needs of her congregations resulted in her purchasing farms, stores, houses, and hotels so members could have employment and become self-sufficient. She built a nursing home to care for elderly members within the setting of a "holy place" for those who needed assisted living.

In 1974, Williams and Easter formed the Apostolic Faith Church of Giving Grace Convention, Inc. with elders from the early churches they had established. A year later, after Williams's death, Easter became the presiding bishop and served until his death in 1986, when Bishop Geanie Perry Sr. became presider. In 1990 there were twelve churches. Today there are over twenty-two churches in North Carolina, Virginia, Maryland, New Jersey, New York, and Ohio. The National Convention is held every year in the last week of July in Garysburg, North Carolina, which serves as the organization's headquarters.

Apostolic Faith Church of God Live On!

A Trinitarian denomination formed in Franklin, Virginia in 1952, when bishops Jesse Hanshaw and Willie Cross of Suffolk, Virginia and Elder R. T. Butts left the **Apostolic Faith Church of God and True Holiness** that had been founded only seven years earlier. No doctrinal issues were at stake so the organization is identical in doctrine with the parent body.

Hanshaw, pastor of House of Prayer Holiness Church in Franklin, became the first presiding bishop. Cross became vice bishop and Butts served as overseer. He was followed by Cross who served until his death in 1972. Following him, Elder W. F. Ridley served as presider until his death in 1974. That year, the current presider, Richard H. Cross, Sr., pastor of the headquarters church, Greater El Bethel Deliverance Center in Suffolk, took office.

Headquarters for the group is in Suffolk, Virginia. In 1990, there were approximately twenty-five congregations with several hundred members scattered throughout Virginia, North Carolina, and New York. The body became a member of the **United Fellowship Convention of the Original Azusa Street Mission**. At some point the name was changed to Live On Ministries.

Apostolic Faith Churches of God

A Trinitarian Pentecostal denomination founded in 1911 in Hansome, Virginia. It began two years after **Charles W. Lowe**, following the teachings of **Azusa Street Revival** leader **William J. Seymour**, started a local congregation in that city. The new church was loosely affiliated with Seymour's original church in Los Angeles, but was chartered in Maryland in 1938 following the dissolution of Seymour's original church.

By 1922, following the death of Seymour, a group under the leadership of Isaac Ryles separated from the parent body to form the Apostolic Faith Church of America. In

1927, a second group left to form the Apostolic Holiness Church of America in Mount Olive, North Carolina. Then, in 1935, John Henry Tucker split to form the Apostolic Faith Churches of God and Christ in Hereford, North Carolina.

In 1941, AFCG purchased the former grounds of the Nansemond Colored Training School in Suffolk, Virginia and relocated its headquarters there. Four years later, in 1945, Lowe separated from the church he had founded to create the **Apostolic Faith Church of God and True Holiness**. By that year, there were approximately forty churches in the denomination. The church reorganized and elected bishop Rosie Cleveland Grant as presider.

In 1952, Bishop **Thomas Cox** was appointed presiding bishop by the chief apostle. At the death of Bishop Lowe in 1954, he was voted to be senior bishop. During his leadership, he established churches in Jefferson, Conneaut, and Ashtabula, Ohio and in Erie, Braddock, and Warren, Pennsylvania. Bishop Cox served faithfully until his death in 1964.

In that year, Robert Clarence Butts was appointed senior bishop. During his tenure, the acreage that now houses the **Apostolic Faith Church of God** headquarters in Franklin, Virginia was purchased in 1971. Butts served as the bishop until his death in 1980. In the mid-1960s, however, another group under the auspices of Bishop Rufus A. Easter and Mother Lillie P. Williams, established the New Jerusalem Apostolic Faith Churches of God (later the Apostolic Faith Church of God Giving Grace). In 1979, seven congregations in South Carolina reorganized as the Apostolic Faith Churches of a Living God. Each of the separated bodies essentially maintained the doctrine of the parent group. Further, by the 1990s, none had grown larger than a couple of dozen congregations.

In 1980, **Oree Keyes** was elected and installed as senior bishop. He served until 2004, when his health, which had been deteriorated from Alzheimer's disease, forced him to step down and serve as Bishop Emeritus until his death at age eighty-four. Although he was physically afflicted from a stroke, in 2004, the **Apostolic Faith Church of God** elected Bishop Robert L. Lyons, Sr. to serve as the senior bishop.

The denomination headquarters are in Franklin, Virginia and there are fifteen congregations in that state, Pennsylvania, Ohio, and Massachusetts.

The AFCG was one of the founding denominations of the **United Fellowship Convention of the Original Azusa Street Mission,** an umbrella organization for denominations that trace their lineage directly back to the **Azusa Street Revival** under Seymour's leadership.

Further Reading

Montier, Gerald, and Carolyn Montier. *Remembering the Past Apostolic Faith Mission Celebrating the Present Apostolic Faith Church of God*. Bloomington, IN: Xlibris, 2011.

Apostolic Faith Churches of God in Christ

A Trinitarian denomination founded in 1935 in Hereford, North Carolina by Bishop John Henry Tucker as a result of a split from the Apostolic Faith (Mission) Church of God. Tucker served as presiding bishop until 1965 and was followed by R. Griswould.

Johnnie L. Anderson, pastor of Little Bethlehem Apostolic Faith **Church of God in Christ**, Brooklyn, New York is the current presider.

Headquarters for the body, which has thirteen congregations is in now in Windsor, North Carolina. The denomination is one of the six organizations that formed the **United Fellowship Convention of the Original Apostolic Faith Mission**

Apostolic Faith Fellowship International

The Oneness Pentecostal denomination was established in late 2012 by Bishop Charles Johnson, pastor of the Morning Star Apostolic Church, a suburban Washington DC congregation within the Pentecostal Assemblies of the World.

Six years earlier in March 2006, Johnson presented a position paper entitled, "Should We Have Unsaved Ministers Preach at our Conventions?" to the PAW Bishop Board Meeting in Detroit, Michigan. In it, he delineated specific grievances regarding what he saw as liberal tendencies evolving within PAW. The paper denounced the practice of inviting people who did not hold to the classical Oneness Pentecostal standard of piety to preach at conventions or other organizationally sponsored events, using versions of the Bible other than the King James Version. Johnson specifically denounced leniency regarding the doctrine of regenerational baptism—the understanding that along with repentance confession of faith in Christ baptism in Jesus' name is a requirement for a person to receive salvation.

Johnson insisted that PAW ministers and congregations should not be in fellowship with those who did not hold to strict Oneness or Apostolic doctrine. When Johnson failed to win the majority of the bishops to his point of view over the next years, he withdrew from PAW to form his new body.

Johnson was later joined by several PAW pastors who shared his concerns. Currently, Johnson remains the presiding bishop for the organization, whose headquarters are in Upper Marlboro, Maryland. There are more than fifty churches throughout the United States.

Apostolic Faith Mission Church of God

A formerly Trinitarian Pentecostal denomination that adopted a Oneness doctrine. The denomination was founded in 1906 by **Frank W. Williams**, a close friend of **William Joseph Seymour** who participated in the **Azusa Street Revival**. That year, he returned to the South, starting his ministry in Mississippi, but ultimately had more success in Alabama where an entire Primitive Baptist Church congregation was converted to Pentecostalism. The members gave him their building as the first meeting house for the Apostolic Faith Mission which was organized as an outreach of Seymour's Los Angeles work within the Trinitarian tradition.

In 1915 William broke with Seymour to adopt the Oneness doctrine and establish his own organization. The body continues to place a strong emphasis upon divine healing, allows the ordination women preachers, and practices foot washing with communion. In keeping with its Oneness identification, it practices baptism in the name of Jesus Christ, and without the use of the name, the baptism is considered void. Intoxicants, especially tobacco, alcohol, and drugs, are forbidden. Members are encouraged to marry only those who are believed to be saved.

Within its governmental structure, the denomination is headed by a senior bishop and cabinet of executive officers composed of the bishops, overseers, and the general secretary.

By 2005, there were 10,730 members in eighteen congregations, most of which were in Alabama. By 2009, those figures had dropped to 6,880 members in sixteen congregations. AFMCG headquarters are in Birmingham, Alabama.

Further Reading:

Tucker, Anjulet. "Apostolic Faith Mission Church of God." In *African American Religious Cultures*, edited by Stephen C. Finley and Torin Alexander, 88–90. Santa Barbara, CA: ABC-CLIO, 2009.

Apostolic Overcoming Holy Church of God, Inc.

In 1916 nine years after the **Azusa Street Revival**, and at a time when the Oneness controversy was at its height on the West Coast, **William Thomas Phillips** founded the Ethiopian Overcoming Holy Church of God as a Trinitarian body. The term "Ethiopian" denoted Phillips's emphasis on a religion that would meet the spiritual needs of African Americans in the segregated Southern Region of the United States. Reportedly, after the group had been established Phillips's interest in the life of holiness spurred him to undertake an independent study of Scripture from which he gained what he saw as a revelation of the Godhead without contact with other existing Oneness groups. Within the next twelve years, the denomination would embrace Oneness Pentecostal doctrine.

The denomination was incorporated in 1920 in Mobile, Alabama. By 1927, Phillips desired that his group be more aligned with what he felt was a more biblical, racially inclusive Church. The term "Apostolic" replaced "Ethiopian" as an identifier of this more inclusive posture as well as clearly signifying new Oneness focus. The name of the denomination was officially changed in 1944; this modification did not result in an influx of other races and it remains a predominantly African-American body.

During its earliest period, worship within the AOHC was among the most emotive of the black Pentecostal bodies, with elements some outsiders described as chaotic and even extreme. Yet, Phillips strongly encouraged his members to express their emotions freely.

In the nearly sixty years that Phillips led the church, he traveled extensively, holding revivals and planting new congregations in cities across the southern United States. By the time of his death, the denomination had grown to three hundred churches in the United States, India, West Africa, and the Caribbean with a constituency of more than one hundred thousand including a small number of white congregants. Within the United States, congregations are concentrated in Alabama, Kentucky, Illinois, Oklahoma, and Texas, but a few are found in other states.

The AOHC maintains an interesting stance to other Christian bodies, separating themselves in spiritual matters; its members do not fellowship with other Pentecostal bodies in worship. Yet, the denomination joins with other Christian groups and secular leaders to promote the practical benefit of the black community. In 1965, Phillips's intense involvement in the Civil Rights Movement led to the bombing of his home.

Upon his death in 1973, Phillips was succeeded by **Jasper Roby**, who moved the denominational headquarters to his home church, AOH Cathedral in Birmingham, Alabama. Roby served from 1973 until his death in 2000. At that time, Bishop George W. Ayers assumed the position of presiding bishop. The current presiding bishop is John H. Matthews Jr. of Dayton, Ohio.

AOHC has an episcopal form of government polity and ordains women. Wine is required in communion. Congregations are concentrated primarily on the East Coast with the largest number in Alabama, yet there are also congregations in the Midwest and on the West Coast. Currently there are approximately 130 churches nationwide.

Further Reading:

Arrington, Juanita Roby. *A Brief History of the Apostolic Overcoming Holy Church of God, Inc., and Its Founder: Including "What We Believe."* Birmingham, AL: Forniss, 1984.

Asberry, Richard 1859–1936
Asberry, Ruth 1858–1934

Richard and Ruth Asberry were the owners of the house at 214 North Bonnie Brae Street in Los Angeles where the 1906 **Azusa Street Revival** had its start. Their home, in a working-class section of the city, providentially became the site of the first series of meetings held by **William Joseph Seymour** after he was barred from teaching his newly formulated Pentecostal doctrine from the pulpit of Pastor **Julia Hutchins**'s Holiness church. It was at this house where the first group of mainly African-American service workers met to pray with **Seymour,** who was to become the pastor of the Azusa Street Mission, and listen to him expound this new doctrine.

Richard and Ruth were reportedly the cousins of **Neely Terry**, also a participant, who was responsible for encouraging Hutchins to Los Angeles to assist with building their fledgling congregation. The Asberrys were part of that group. Seymour's Bible study at the Asberry home was not the first such meeting at that address. During the winter of 1905, the residence served as a temporary home for **Julia Hutchins**'s little Holiness congregation where the Asberrys were members.

Ruth was born in Virginia; Richard, a janitor who had previously been employed by the Pullman Motor Car Company, was born in Louisiana. The couple lived for a time in Texas, where their daughter Willie Ella was born.

Once the revival moved to the Azusa Street location, the Asberrys became members of the Apostolic Faith Mission and Richard served on the Board of trustees throughout Seymour's tenure. After the leader's death, he stayed on to assist Jennie Evans Seymour, until the Mission closed.

Assemblies of God, African Americans in

The largest predominantly white Pentecostal organization emerged in 1914, within an era of rigid segregation in the United States, because of a break from African-American

Pentecostal leader **Charles Harrison Mason's** body, the **Church of God in Christ.** From its inception, however, a black constituency represented an insignificant segment of the fellowship. Yet, from the time of the break until well into the American Civil Rights era, AG history evidences ongoing struggle regarding inclusion of black constituents and ministers in the full life of the organization.

After the break, AG leaders reportedly entered into a "brotherly" agreement with Mason to divide the work of evangelizing along racial lines. Accordingly, the AG would reach out to white communities and constituents and COGIC would do the same for African Americans. Though never corroborated, the "sisterhood myth," as this arrangement came to be known, would persist throughout most of the life of the two denominations, coloring racial politics and evangelistic strategies until well after the Civil Rights era.

In 1915, only a year after its founding, **Ellsworth S. Thomas** became the first credentialed black AG minister, and served until his death in 1936. In 1923, **Martha Neeley**, and her husband, **Isaac**—who was the first black person to appear on the cover of the AG magazine *Pentecostal Evangel*—became the first appointed Black AG missionaries.

The racial makeup of the early AG was influenced by the fact that it was a rural, small town and Midwestern denomination. Though congregations were found in other regions, most were in suburban areas with higher concentrations of whites, versus urban cores with large black concentrations. Secondly, during its earliest years the body had no established racial polity and generally honored the sovereignty of local congregations, giving each freedom in handling handle the race issue. Moreover, AG leadership did not want to alienate white Southern sensitivities by promoting integration.

By the late 1930s, however, a small but growing number of African Americans were affiliating with the AG, and some were seeking credentials. **Bruce Gibson**, pastor of an interracial congregation in Winlock, Washington, was credentialed in 1935. He left the AG when he moved east to pastor a black congregation, but rejoined after returning to the Northwest. Increased interest in credentialing for ministers such as Gibson brought the matter of handling these requests to a head. In 1939, a brother Elison, a Bronx, New York pastor, sought credential but was referred to COGIC, prompting the denomination to recommend that black ministerial applicants only be granted license to preach in their own district or be referred to "colored organizations" for ordination. Still, two years later, Harold Thompson was accepted to Eastern Bible Institute, licensed by the Eastern District in 1941, and then ordained seven years later.

Between World War II and the mid-1960s, a number of proposals were put forth regarding the treatment of blacks within the AG. In 1943, the General Council considered a resolution to promote missionary activity among blacks but after considering the situation in the South, the Council referred it to the Executive Presbytery for further study. In 1945, Gibson petitioned for creation of a colored branch within the AG; in response, a resolution encouraged establishment of black congregations that would display the name, Assembly of God—Colored Branch. Yet a year later, the General Presbytery proposed instead establishment of "a separate colored Pentecostal Church to which the denomination would lend "assistance." No action was taken on that recommendation, but two years later a second proposal for a black branch was put forth; again, it failed to materialize.

Seven years later, in 1956, the General Presbytery authorized a study on segregation and integration. A year later, a committee found that the AG had neglected American blacks while investing heavily in African missions, and suggested offering assistance to blacks, rather than integrating. In 1958 a final committee studied the feasibility of establishing some form of "Colored Fellowship," but it would be thirty years before the National Black Fellowship of the Assemblies of God was established.

During the 1950s and 1960s, AG leaders and publications were generally silent regarding the country's civil rights struggles, except to insinuate that protest might be coming from communist agitation. Two articles related to race were the only attention the Pentecostal Evangel gave the issue during that period. One dealt with witnessing techniques; the other dealt with what it saw as dearth of a true biblical witness among blacks. This silence was broken only by a number of caricatures depicting blacks in less than a flattering manner that appears in the Pentecostal Evangel.

Though not the first African American to seek and be denied credentials because of race, **Robert Harrison** became the most visible symbol of the denomination's racial inequity. As an exceptional student at the AG's Bethany Bible College in Santa Cruz, California where he received his bachelor's degree, he caught the attention of his professors. After his 1960 graduation, several encouraged him to seek AG credentials. His request was rejected by the supervisor of the California-Nevada District, however, ostensibly because of a policy against granting credentials to black people.

The cultural shift in US society away from segregation during the Civil Rights era of the 1960s saw a concurrent shift in AG culture. In 1962 after two years of being denied official recognition as a minister because of his race, **Robert Harrison** (by then a prominent member of the Billy Graham Evangelistic Team) was credentialed and ordained.

His well-publicized ordination marked a change in race relations in the fellowship, helping settle ambiguity over inclusion of African-Americans ministers. Another important catalyst in breaking the AG color barrier was the work of David Wilkerson through Teen Challenge, a ministry focused on recovery from chemical addictions that exposed AG churches and pastors to multi-ethnic ministry for the first time. While responses were mixed, some churches began to embrace the ministry of persons of color. Notably, the prominence of Thurman Faison, a Wilkerson convert and church-planting pioneer in Chicago and Harlem encouraged further breaking through of the color barrier. In 1967 he along with Harrison and other influential black ministers spoke to General Council and major church conclaves regarding the need to minister to African Americans.

During the 1970s other blacks achieved prominence with the AG. George Perry served as the president of the National Evangelical Association. Eddie Washington and his wife, Ruth, were the first blacks to serve a regular appointment under the Division of Foreign Missions. Spencer Jones pastored Tampa Assembly of God, an integrated church in the headquarters city of Springfield, Missouri and Southside Tabernacle in Chicago, Illinois, providing leadership inner-city ministry, and becoming the first ethic Executive Presbyter and first president of the **National Black Fellowship of the Assembly of God** in 1989.

While in 1989, the General Council adopted a resolution condemning racism as sin and called for repentance from those who had participated in any form. In 1997 the Council broadened its institutional structure to make room for non-white members through representatives to the General Presbytery from Minority Fellowships.

Still, the AG remains a predominantly white fellowship, and while integration continues to increase, of the major Pentecostal bodies in the United States the Assemblies of God has remained the most racially segregated. As of 2011 persons of color represented 40.4 percent of United States AG adherents. The proportion of black adherents, however, was only 9.7 percent from all black fellowships including the National Black Fellowship with 231 churches as well as the African AG Fellowship, the Ethiopian Fellowship, the Ghanaian Fellowship, the Haitian American Fellowship, and the Nigerian Fellowship.

Currently the highest-ranking African-American national executive in the AG, Zollie Smith, has served since 2007 as the Executive Director of US Missions. Another high-ranking black leader, Malcolm Burleigh, serves as the National Director of Intercultural Ministries. Both Smith and Burleigh are past presidents of the NBF. Along with other influential black ministers and leaders, they continue to provide strategic vision for and work toward racial diversity and reconciliation within the AG.

Recent efforts between the AG and the United Pentecostal Council of the Assemblies of God exemplify the new attitudes regarding race within the denomination. Discussions, which began in 2010, have resulted in a new partnership between the two organizations that split ninety years earlier over the white body's unwillingness to support black missionaries. Leaders of the two organizations signed an agreement of cooperative affiliation that calls for in 2014.

Further Reading:

Kenyon, Howard, N. "Bishop Mason and the Sisterhood Myth." *Assemblies of God Heritage* (1987) 12.

———. "Black Ministers in the Assemblies of God." *Assemblies of God Heritage* (1987) 10–17.

Newman, Joe. *Race and the Assemblies of God Church the Journey from Azusa Street to the Miracle of Memphis.* Youngstown, NY: Cambria, 2007.

Rodgers, Darrin. "The Assemblies of God and the Long Journey toward Racial Reconciliation." *Assemblies of God Heritage* (2008) 50–61.

Associated Churches of Christ (Holiness)

In 1915 William A. Washington was working with a predominantly white Holiness association under which he founded a congregation in Los Angeles. He continued to work with the white group but established an African-American congregation which he incorporated separately. Two years later, when **Charles Price Jones** came to Los Angeles to preach evangelistic campaigns and establish Christ Temple as a local congregation of the **Church of Christ (Holiness),** the two formed a loose cooperative agreement. The Wesleyan Holiness polity and doctrine of the two groups (which places emphasis on the experience of sanctification rather than on the Pentecostal Holy Spirit experience with speaking in tongues) is essentially identical.

For the next thirty years they worked cooperatively, but in 1946, when, because of what the manual of the Associated Churches of Christ (Holiness) calls the "manipulating of some administrative problems in the upper circles of the Church," several West Coast congregations withdrew from the **Church of Christ (Holiness) USA**. After Jones' death, Williams broke with the parent denomination.

Since the separation, the West Coast churches continued to work with Washington under the original incorporation of his group. After Washington's death in 1949, Bishop Whitfield Massengale became presiding bishop.

Headquarters for the small association, which has approximately two thousand members in less than twenty congregations, remains in Los Angeles. The group is variably referred to as the Assembly of the Associated Churches of Christ (Holiness).

Association of Independent Ministries (A.I.M.)

An organization of independent Pentecostal ministers, prominent African-American ministers, and founders of the New Light Christian Center Church based in Houston, Texas. A.I.M. was founded in 2001 by **Dr. I. V. Hilliard.**

A.I.M. provides autonomous churches an affiliation and fellowship beyond their local congregation. It also provides ordination for those who have no body to whom they can turn. Rather than providing ecclesial, governmental, or administrative control over congregations and ministries, A.I.M. offers counsel and oversight and members see Hilliard as either a spiritual father or mentor. A.I.M. membership is equally open to men and women who have a viable, functional, independent ministry; to date, has more than 1,200 affiliate pastors and ministers.

Audrey, J. W.

One of the founding leaders and the first presiding bishop of the **Apostolic Church of Christ in God**, a Oneness Pentecostal denomination established in 1943 with **James C. Richardson**, Jerome Jenkins, W. R. Bryant, and J. M. Williams, five elders who separated themselves from the separated **Church of God (Apostolic)**. Audrey also served as pastor of St. Paul Apostolic Church in Rudd, North Carolina, near Greensboro.

When Audrey resigned in 1956, Richardson, who had been elected as a second bishop in 1952, became presiding bishop.

Ayers, George Washington 1921–2015

Since 2000 Ayers has served as the third presiding bishop of the **Apostolic Overcoming Holy Church of God, Inc.,** a position he assumed when the denomination's board voted to remove then presiding bishop **Jasper Roby** because of failing health setting off a lawsuit by those who disagreed with this action. Ayers served two years as acting president. When the dissident group did not prevail, he was elected as presiding bishop and continued to serve as acting president for two years until John H. Mathews, pastor of Mt. Zion A.O.H. Church of God in Dayton, Ohio was elected in 2015.

Called into the ministry in 1950, Ayers pastored an AOHC congregation in Tuskegee, Alabama for four years and later the Pratt City (Alabama) AOHC Church for three years. In 1953 he received BA degree in Business from Booker T. Washington Business College in Birmingham, Alabama, then went on to receive a ThB degree from Bethel School of Theology, Detroit, Michigan in 1957. In 1977 he received a ThM degree from Maranatha Bible College, Union South Carolina, and went on to receive a ThD in 1990, and a PhD in theology in 1994. He was also awarded both the DD and LLD from the International Bible Institute and Seminary, Orlando, Florida.

Ayers was consecrated a bishop within the AOHC in 1965. While still pursuing his own education, he founded the Western Regional Bible College and Academic Studies in 1975.

Ayers served on the National Executive Board for over fifty years. He also remained as pastor of Phillips Temple A.O.H. Church of God in Mobile, Alabama and Cathedral of the Cross A.O.H. Church of God in Birmingham, Alabama, and presides over the South Alabama Diocese. In 1956, however, he expanded his activities to the West Coast, founding the first AOHC in California in Marin City. That congregation, Faith Tabernacle AOHC, was later relocated to Richmond, California and Ayers also serves over the Western Diocese of the denomination.

Azusa Interdenominational Fellowship of Christian Churches

A fellowship of primarily non-denominational Charismatic congregations founded in 1990 by **Carlton D. Pearson**, the leader of Higher Dimensions Ministries in Tulsa, Oklahoma to address racial and ethnic divisions that were dividing the Pentecostal/Charismatic movement. In 1988, Pearson—a prominent televangelist and pastor of the five-thousand-member megachurch, Higher Dimensions Family Church—hosted the first annual Azusa Conference involving several days of a multi-cultural, ecumenical charismatic worship, and discussion in an attempt to revive the racial harmony in which the classical Pentecostal movement was birthed. The several-day meeting spotlighted the hottest preachers on the televangelism circuit, provided opportunities for black and white Pentecostal and Charismatic men and women to fellowship within the wider Evangelical arena, and regularly drew crowds of 7,500 to 10,000. Its popularity thrust Pearson into spiritual leadership of non-denominational churches that were looking for a covering organization.

AIFCC was born at the third Azusa Conference in 1990 as a coalition of churches and ministries that would network, be accountable, fellowship, and share resources. In 2002, there were more than five hundred congregations affiliated with the fellowship. That year, when Pearson changed his theology to embrace an inclusive soteriology that dramatically differed from both classical Pentecostal and Charismatic understandings, his following, membership and financial support dropped significantly.

By 2005 the membership of his congregation fell from five thousand to under one thousand. Attendance at the Azusa Conferences quickly drastically and most ministers within the fellowship dropped out. Pearson left the Pentecostal movement and aligned himself with the United Church of Christ.

Azusa Street Revival

The 1906 seminal event led by black Holiness pastor, **William Joseph Seymour,** that represents the starting point of the contemporary Pentecostal movement in the United States. The meeting unfolded over from its beginning until late 1913.

When news of the outbreak of tongues traveled through the Los Angeles Holiness community, it became apparent that residence that hosted the **Bonnie Brae Street Prayer Meeting** was too small. The group that had expanded from a handful of mostly black household servants who had gathered around Seymour moved to a converted livery stable at 312 Azusa Street that had once served as the sanctuary of the Stevens African Methodist Episcopal Church.

The first three-and-a-half years were the most intense. Day and night, seven days a week, worshippers came from all over the country and the world to take part in an unparalleled move of God reminiscent of the Upper Room on the Day of Pentecost. Camp-meeting style worship generally ran from ten in the morning until at least midnight and, sometimes, for several hours past that. These ecstatic services were characterized by impromptu sermons, prophesying, singing in English and in tongues, conversions, divine healing, and exorcisms. No count was taken, but most reports estimate that, at least in the early days of the revival, attendance ran in the hundreds and that the mission was scarcely large enough to contain the anxious seekers. Many stood for several hours around the perimeters of the walls; others stood outside on the porch or listened in through the glassless windows.

Stories in the secular and religious press, word of mouth reports, letters and other correspondences from attendees to loved ones and acquaintances drew a steady crowd almost from the beginning. From time to time, the revival was populated with curiosity-seekers, skeptics, some who came to convince Seymour and his followers to abandon their fanatical antics and heretical beliefs and some just wanted a closer relationship with God. Others wanted to add yet another spiritual experience to their lives.

Within months the mission began publishing its own newspaper, the *Apostolic Faith*, and distribution quickly soared from 5,000 to 50,000 copies. The four-page tabloid of the thirteen issues, published more or less, monthly from September 1906 until its demise in May 1908, was filled with testimonies of Holy Spirit baptism, healing, deliverance, and other miraculous occurrences. It carried "word for word" interpretations of messages given in tongues and stories of those going out from the revival to carry the Pentecostal message across the country and around the world. Sermons and teachings provided instruction in doctrine and correction of heretical teachings beginning to circulate through the movement. It also included stories leaders and common worshippers about other Pentecostal revivals around the country and the world. Many who would later become important to the movement such as Thomas Ball Barratt from Norway, Gaston B. Cashwell, the "Apostle to the East," and **Charles H. Mason** of the **Church of God in Christ** sent items. Missionaries from the revival such as **Lucy Farrow**, **Julia Hutchins**, Florence Crawford and Sam and Ardell Mead, reported back. There were also testimonies from just plain folk who in some way, had been touched by the revival at Azusa Street, or at a camp meeting, or in their local congregation through Holy Spirit baptisms, healings and other miracles that filled its pages.

A prominent feature of the meetings was their radically egalitarian nature. Though many worshipers were working class, there was no stratification by class, race, gender, or age. Men and women, adults and children, black, white, yellow, and red freely worshiped God and admonished each other to holiness of life through speaking in tongues and interpretation, prophesy, testimony, song, prayer, miraculous signs, and preaching. Women and men freely participated as they felt God leading them. Even children had a voice in the worship and received Pentecostal Holy Spirit baptism. Ecclesiastical credentials or education played no part in determining a person's role in the meetings. Seymour and others in "leadership" gave freedom to those who led by the Holy Spirit to testify, sing, exhort, pray or preach to do so. People of different races and cultures worshiped side-by-side without the constraint of segregated seating evident even in mixed race meetings of the period.

There was no distinction of ministerial credentials. Black washerwomen prayed with prominent white pastors. Young girls prophetically confronted seasoned men with messages that brought them to repentance and renewed spiritual vitality. Lay people laid hands on clergypersons of all ranks praying for them to receive healing, sanctification, and Holy Spirit baptism. Ministry was based largely on perception of a call that relied on personal testimony rather than ecclesial endorsement, and endowment with specific spiritual gifts for effective ministry rather than church hierarchy was arbiter of a person's fitness for ministry.

These earliest Pentecostals considered ministerial credentialing unimportant. Some were simply "ordained by the Lord" with no human agency affirming ministerial status, asserting that the fruit of their accomplishments determined whether they were truly called. Some were informally set apart by laying on of hands within a group in a home meeting or other non-traditional setting and sought no formal credentials. Others held credentials from local mission churches. Some who had been licensed or ordained with established denominations were forced to forfeit their credentials once they accepted the Pentecostal experience.

People prayed for the sick and reported reversals in their physical, mental, emotional, or spiritual conditions on a daily basis. Other spiritual gifts were manifested as men and women prophesied, gave words of wisdom or knowledge, exhorted and interpreted messages spoken in tongues. People reported God-given dreams and visions encouraging or directing them or the congregation. Seekers and believers in the congregation were excited to hear their mother tongue spoken, ready to affirm it as an authentic language, and eager to give an "interpretation" of what was being spoken. In some cases, that interpretation was a simple "praise to the Lord." In a few cases, it was a strong rebuke or admonition to a single individual or the entire group. In other cases, it was a call or confirmation to ministry or missions. Some, like **Julia Hutchins** and **Lucy Farrow**, reported using xenolalic languages on the mission field. Hutchins saw her language endowment as confirmation of God's call to Africa several years earlier. Her trip gave no occasion to prove the gift, for English was the official language of the area of Liberia in which she ministered.

The revival's heightened spiritual climate also drew a surplus of interest from spiritualist mediums, hypnotists, and others who dabbled in mystical experiences. Seymour was aware of their presence, but their dark power proved no match for the faith of the saints who contended that those who had experimented with the occult were being set free by God's power.

Though Azusa Street was home to many ordinary people, some attendees had already made names for themselves in Holiness and evangelical circles. For example, Alfred Garrison (A.G.) and Lillian Garr arrived in the spring of 1906, had a Pentecostal experience, and were relieved of their Burning Bush Association pastorate. Garr's move, however, helped turn a revival populated by a few—mostly African-American—house servants into the large multi-racial meeting the revival became. Within weeks, the couple sensed a call to be missionaries to India. **Charles Harrison Mason**, founder of the **Church of God in Christ**, came to Azusa Street on the prodding of his co-laborer **Charles Price Jones** to ascertain the validity of its experiences. Once he accepted the Pentecostal message, he returned to find that Jones rejected the doctrine and experience, and the two eventually severed ties, forming two groups: Mason's **Church of God in Christ**, the largest African American Pentecostal denomination in the world and the **Church of Christ (Holiness) USA**, Jones' smaller group. After coming to Azusa Street, Cashwell, a Holiness evangelist from North Carolina, returned to the East, shared the experience with several Holiness groups in Tennessee, Georgia and North Carolina, drawing several Holiness bodies into the Pentecostal movement.

John G. Lake, who met Seymour through Parham while in Houston and reported receiving the baptism of the Holy Spirit under Parham's ministry, visited the revival prior to taking the Pentecostal message to South Africa in 1908 and revisited at least once to report on the progress of that work. He attempted to carry part of the interracial vision of Azusa Street to that country and was disturbed that he could not conduct interracial meetings. Yet, his ministry would become one of the most prolific Pentecostal works on the continent.

From its earliest days, the revival drew criticism. The earliest written ridicule came from the Los Angeles press who sent reporters within days of the revival's move to Azusa Street. The press used racially-toned stories to titillate its readers, alleging that worshippers used fanatical rites and worked themselves into frenzies, or even insinuating the meetings were like orgies, and rarely did articles give Seymour the respect of referring to him by name.

While many former Holiness believers, excitedly receiving news about the revival, came to Azusa Street and received their Pentecostal experience, many who shared these experience with their pastors and fellow believers were derided or forbidden to speak about or exercise their newfound gift, and some were disfellowshipped by their congregations. Some Holiness ministers who left the revival to preach their newfound reality were forced to leave their existing bodies, while others steered their congregations and denominations toward the Pentecostal movement.

Some Holiness leaders saw the movement as not simply fanatical, but as demonic. Phineas Bresee dropped the word "Pentecostal," adopting the title Church of the Nazarene. A. B. Simpson's Christian and Missionary Alliance took a more balanced stance, seeing tongues as one evidence of Holy Spirit baptism, and while not forbidding the experience did not encourage seeking it. Neither did he renounce ties with Pentecostal colleagues. Charles Jones broke with his colleague Charles Mason after he returned from the revival embracing the experience movement. Jones formulated doctrinal statements that refuted the new understanding of Holy Spirit baptism, insisting that, "every true believer is heir to the Holy Ghost as God's gift that was not for a select few." Radical Holiness leader and noted Greek scholar William Godbey used his knowledge of Greek and Latin to fake a Pentecostal experience of tongues at the Revival convincing enough to be invited to preach by Seymour, who he then denounced as one of "Satan's preachers." Burning Bush Association derided Garr, declaring that he was led away by deception. Holiness critiques, however, were not usually racial, with the exception of Alma White, founder of the Pillar of Fire movement who personally attacked Seymour as leading people into "Satan's slime pits," sealing their doom for damnation.

Some of the strongest criticism came from two opposing factions. Fundamentalist leaders such as G. Campbell Morgan, Harry A. Ironsides, Clarence Larkin, and Rueben Archer (R. A.) Torrey, who shared Pentecostalism's high view of Scripture and disdain for modernist ideas, held a literal biblical hermeneutic and cessationist theology that precluded serious consideration of the movement. More liberal, mainline churches reacted in two ways: they dismissed what they saw as machinations of ignorant, uneducated, and "disinherited" people given to hyper-spiritualism, with no respectable outlet for feeling of desperation, or they ignored the revival entirely.

Another significant source of criticism came from some who had come to Azusa Street or other Pentecostal meetings, embraced and received, but later denounced the Pentecostal experience, such as Former Baptist Joseph Smale, pastor of the New Testament Church, who never fully accepted the Pentecostal experience. This incident generated an outflux of some of Smale's members to join the Azusa Street congregation, at least temporarily.

Perhaps one of the most devastating defections came from one who had been prolific in spreading its message. **G. B. Cashwell** preached throughout the Southeast, and his publishing of the Bridegroom Messenger drew hundreds, including many important future leaders and their congregations into the movement. However, Cashwell quickly became disillusioned at the failure of his expectations for the movement, including the delayed Second Coming and the ineffectiveness of xenolalia within the missionary context, and by 1909, he had left the movement.

The seedy neighborhood surrounding the mission was accustomed to noise and excitement, but soon found the constant coming and going and the high volume of activity too much. Local police were kept busy answering complaints of noise into the early hours of the morning. They responded by posting themselves outside the doors to keep volume to a tolerable level and threatened to issue citations if it did not stop. Attendees were regularly subjected to harassment by police and civic officials and ostracized by friends, family, employers, co-workers, and members and pastors of their home congregations. Some harassment involved simple verbal assault or social isolation. Other times it resulted in physical altercation or violence. Whether the lack of acceptance came from the community, the police, or the home pastor and congregation, it was perceived as harassment by the devil and his workers, and only heightened the faithful's conviction that they were doing God's work, spurring them to even bolder efforts in spreading what they saw was the end-time gospel.

While the revival continued, several who came and received their Pentecostal experience moved on to plant their own congregations within a short distance of the mission and many of their congregations grew and expanded at what appeared to be the Azusa Street mission's expense.

No part of the world was untouched by the revival. Stories poured in from every corner of the globe to the *Apostolic Faith* telling of its impact. Following the revival's three-year heyday, however, spiritual fervor within the meetings ebbed and waned for the next four years. Prominent ministers and everyday people visited, and schism and controversy, fueled as much by personality conflicts and style as by doctrinal differences, plagued the congregation. Each ensuing controversy took its toll until, at the end, the Azusa Street Mission was a small African-American congregation that remained faithful to the Pentecostal message but had lost its influence in the broader Pentecostal movement.

Further Reading:

Alexander, Estrelda. *Black Fire: One Hundred Years of African American Pentecostalism.* Downers Grove, IL: InterVarsity, 2011.

Lewis, Scott. "William J. Seymour: Follower of the 'Evening Light.'" *Wesleyan Theological Journal* 39.2 (2004) 167–83.

Nelson, Douglas J. *For Such a Time as This: The Story of Bishop William J. Seymour and the Azusa Street Revival, a Search for Pentecostal/Charismatic Roots.* PhD diss., University of Birmingham, England, 1981.

Tinney, James. "William J. Seymour: Father of Modern-Day Pentecostalism." In *Black Apostles: Afro-American Clergy Confront the Twentieth Century,* edited by Randall Burkett and Richard Newman, 213–25. Boston: G.K. Hall, 1978.

B

Bailey, Annie Lee Pennington 1894–1975

The **Church of God in Christ** evangelist, women's leader, and educator was born in Temple, Texas. Her mother was a socialite; her father was a laborer and Baptist minister. She came to faith as a young girl and rose from a street corner evangelist to the highest office held by COGIC women leaders—the Supervisor of the International Women's Department.

In 1915, Bailey received the Pentecostal Holy Spirit baptism, and by 1919, was traveling as part of a team led by her pastor, J. E. Bryant, on an evangelistic tour through the Midwest and North East, establishing COGIC congregations in New Jersey, Connecticut, New York City, Boston, and Springfield, Massachusetts. Bailey was one of the featured evangelists in New Jersey's first COGIC Convocation and continued evangelistic ministry until 1925 when James Wells sent her to Newark to help establish what was to become New Jersey's largest COGIC congregation—Wells Cathedral.

In 1927, Bailey was appointed Supervisor of Women for state of Maryland, Delaware and Washington DC were added to her oversight in 1928, and New Jersey in 1941. Bailey was a close confidante to COGIC founder, **Charles Harrison Mason** and his family. When Mason became ill in 1929, Bailey took a year's leave of absence to travel and care for him. In 1930, **Mother Lizzie Robinson**, the first International Women's Department supervisor, appointed her the first Financial Secretary.

In 1934, by then widowed, Annie married Elder **J. S. Bailey**, who later became the first assistant presiding bishop to Bishop **J. O. Patterson, Sr.** For the next thirty years, Bailey served in a variety of secondary leadership positions: Assistant International Supervisor to **Dr. Lillian Brooks Coffey** and Vice-President of the Women's International Convention. She traveled as a companion and secretary to Mason in his declining years.

After Coffey's death in 1964, Bishop **O. T. Jones** appointed her International Supervisor of Women. Besides presiding over eleven Women's Conventions, she added numerous units: Business and Professional Women's Rescue Squad, Sunday School Representatives Unit, United Sisters of Charity, National Secretaries Unit Jr. Missionaries, the women's magazine, *The COGIC Woman,* and appointed the first National President of the Sewing Circle-Artistic Fingers.

Further Reading:

Butler, Anthea D. *Women in the Church of God in Christ: Making a Sanctified World.* Chapel Hill, NC: University of North Carolina Press, 2007.

Goodson, Glenda Williams. *Bishop Mason and Those Sanctified Women.* Lancaster, TX: s.p., 2003.

Bailey, Clarence M. (C. M.) 1941 –

The fourth presiding bishop of the **United House of Prayer for All People**, the quasi-Holiness denomination founded by **Charles Emmanuel "Sweet Daddy" Grace**. Bailey is a native of Newport News, Virginia and was the former pastor of the United House of Prayer in Augusta, Georgia, the parent church for that state. Prior to assuming that pastorate, he served as youth pastor of the United House of Prayer in Richmond, Virginia, and as pastor of East Boundary House of Prayer in Georgia, and North Charlotte #1 in North Carolina.

Bailey was ordained an elder in 1967 by the late Bishop **Walter "Sweet Daddy" McCollough**. McCollough consecrated him as an Apostle of the United House of Prayer in 1984 and appointed him pastor of Mother House of Prayer, South Philadelphia, Pennsylvania in 1986. Afterward, he assumed leadership of the Augusta congregation with supervisory responsibility for the states of Georgia, Florida, and Alabama. In 1989, he was appointed as a Judge of the General Council (highest ecclesiastical body of the United House of Prayer), and in 2000, he was selected to head that body. Four years later, Madison chose Bailey as senior minister of the United House of Prayer (to act with all powers of the Bishop in event of a vacancy in the Office). For two consecutive years, starting in 2006 Madison appointed him Moderator of the General Assembly.

Following Madison's death, the General Assembly elected him as bishop by an unprecedented 91 percent of the votes. Once in office he adopted the authoritarian style of his predecessors and inherited the title "Daddy," as well as the veneration that House of Prayers adherents have historically reserved for them. The extent of Bailey's authority is evident in his serving as sole trustee of the United House of Prayer, the Madison Early Childhood Development Center LLC, and the Madison Saints Paradise South LLC (Senior Living Facilities). Further, he is CEO and Executive Director of the McCollough Scholarship College Fund, and General Builder and Executive Director of the Nationwide Bailey Building Program and the United House of Prayer churches and various properties.

Bailey is largely inaccessible to many members of the denomination who revere him in the same manner they did Grace. He reserves his visits for larger congregations and prominent national events. While only members of the Bailey Club—consisting of regular donors—have special access, still many congregations preserve a golden throne wrapped in plastic, with anticipation of a visit.

Despite such adulation, Bailey's absolute reign has not gone without challenge. In 2013, Ronald Benton, a popular former minister whom he fired from the church and excommunicated, sued Bailey on the grounds that he had been wrongfully fired and that Bailey had alienated him from the affections of his wife. Further, his ministry has come under scrutiny by members of the secular media including local organizations such as Charlotte press and national groups including NBC News.

Further Reading:

Peak, Christopher. "By the Grace of Bailey, There Go I." *Yale Daily News*. April 14, 2013.
Rath, Molly. "A House Divided." *Washington [DC] City Paper*. June 9, 1995.

Bailey, John Seth 1896–1984

The founding bishop of the Southwest Michigan Jurisdiction of the **Church of God in Christ** was born in Daphney, Alabama. He converted to Pentecostalism, married his first wife, Anna Thomas, and was inducted into the US Army, American Expedition Force, in 1918. He was discharged a year later. In 1924, his family moved to Detroit, Michigan, and two years later, he answered the call to ordained ministry, and founded Bailey Temple **Church of God in Christ** on Detroit's west side.

By the time Bailey was appointed a District Superintendent in 1934, Anna had died and Bailey married his second wife, **Annie Lee Pennington Bailey**, who at the time of their marriage was COGIC State Supervisor of Maryland and National Secretary of the Women's Department. She later became the International Supervisor.

Sixteen years later, he was appointed Overseer of the State of Southwestern Michigan and, under his leadership, the number of COGIC congregations in the state grew from thirty-four to one-hundred-and-twenty-five churches and missions. In 1953, Bishop Bailey became the pastor of a second congregation, Livingstone Street **Church of God in Christ**, which he simultaneously pastored with the church he founded earlier. That congregation had been established in 1914 as the first COGIC congregation in Michigan. In 1962, however, the congregation renamed the church Seth Temple in honor of Bishop Bailey.

Bailey was a trusted advisor to COGIC founder, **Charles H. Mason** who appointed him to the general board of Bishops. In 1968, he became the first assistant presiding bishop to then presiding bishop, **James O. Patterson, Sr.**

When his second wife died, Bailey married Iner R. Whittler. Eight years later, he died in Detroit.

Baldwin, James Arthur 1924–1987

One of the most famous American novelists, essayists, playwrights, poets, and social critic of his day. James Baldwin was born in New York City as the oldest of nine children. He grew up in poverty as the son of a divorced mother who married a Holiness-Pentecostal preacher, David Baldwin.

At fourteen, Baldwin became a Pentecostal preacher. He served three years as a junior minister at the Harlem's Fireside Pentecostal Assembly, pastored by **Rosa Artemis**

Horn. At seventeen, however, he walked away from the pulpit, his Pentecostal background, and Christianity.

Baldwin began writing in high school by working on the school newspaper. In 1944, at age twenty, he met Richard Wright, who had achieved some notoriety as an author, and who helped him secure a fellowship that provided him with enough money to devote his time to writing. In 1948, Baldwin left the United States and moved to Paris, a location where he perceived he would experience less prejudice, and he went to live and work in Europe with money from another fellowship.

Themes of religion permeate Baldwin's works and he often used Horn's congregation as a model for some of his writings. His first—and best-known—autobiographical novel, *Go Tell It on the Mountain,* was written in 1953. The work graphically depicts such black Pentecostal phenomena as tarrying, speaking, and praying in tongues. His early play, *The Amen Corner,* was published in 1954, the same year he won a Guggenheim Fellowship. It was first produced at Howard University in 1955, and later on Broadway in the mid-1960s, and looked at the phenomenon of storefront Pentecostal religion. That work featured Pastor Margaret, a main character inspired by Horn. In these works, Baldwin frequently criticized the church, citing its failure to be relevant to black social concerns. Though Baldwin was an avid civil rights advocate, many civil rights leaders rejected him because he openly confessed to being homosexual and because of the sexually explicit nature of some of his work.

Baldwin returned overseas in 1973, remaining there for most of the last fifteen years of his life, yet never relinquishing his American citizenship. The citizens of France came to consider Baldwin one of their own, and, in 1986, he was given one of the country's highest honors when he was named Commander of the Legion of Honor. He died in Saint-Paul-de-Vence in southeastern France of stomach cancer at age sixty-three.

Barr, Edmund S. 1868–1925
Barr, Rebecca 1868–1934

Edmund and Rebecca Barr were key leaders in the Church of God (Cleveland, Tennessee) as the denomination expanded its international ministry and ethnic diversity. As the ministry team that first took the Church of God outside the continental United States, the Barrs established both Church of God and **Church of God in Christ** congregations throughout Florida and in the Bahamas.

Edmund was born on the island of Great Exuma in the British colony of the Bahama Islands. He migrated to Florida in 1893 and the next year married Rebecca Clayton, a native Floridian, at an African Methodist Episcopal Church in Arcadia.

The Barrs, who were already serving in the pastorate, came into the Church of God in 1909 under the ministry of General Overseer **A. J. Tomlinson,** who was preaching at the Pleasant Grove Camp Ground in Durant, Florida. Tomlinson issued an Evangelist License to each of them on May 31, 1909. Returning to the Pleasant Grove camp meeting several months later, the couple sensed a call to take the gospel to the Bahama Islands. Attendees at the camp meeting raised money for their travel, and they arrived in Nassau in November of that where they preached and planted churches.

Returning to Florida in 1911, they established a Church of God among Bahamian immigrants in Miami, which they served until 1916. Tomlinson ordained Edmund as a bishop in 1912, and appointed him as state overseer of Black churches in Florida in 19156. Though he was replaced by a white overseer in 1917, he continued to establish congregations for the Church of God until about 1920.

The couple were likely the first persons of African descent in the Church of God, the first Church of God ministers to take the gospel outside the United States, and are believed to have been the first Pentecostals in the Bahama Islands. Arabella and **W. V. Eneas**, who went on to become leaders of the Church of God in the Bahamas, are particularly notable among their converts.

While her husband was a native Bahamian returning to his homeland with the Pentecostal message, as a full member of their evangelistic team, Rebecca retained the distinction of being the first Church of God missionary. The Evangelist's Certificate, which Rebecca received in 1909, also made her the first black woman minister licensed in the denomination. Under her ministry in the Bahamas, men and women were being saved, sanctified and receiving the experience of Pentecostal Holy Spirit baptism.

Having come from the Bahamian society in which black and white citizens experienced much more affirmative interaction than in the southeastern United States, Edmund's experience helped facilitate the inclusion of black immigrants into what was primarily a white denomination. His ordination as a bishop and appointment as a state overseer authorized him to grant ministerial credentials and to set congregations in order. Under his leadership there was an increase in the Church of God from seven to thirteen black churches and from 111 to 200 black members.

Despite their success, the Barrs along with many other black members of the Church of God transitioned to a primarily black denomination. In 1920, the couple moved their credentials to the **Church of God in Christ**. Once there, they pastored congregations in St. Petersburg and Palatka where he died. Rebecca lived her remaining years in Miami and then St. Petersburg where she died.

Further Reading:

Conn, Charles W. *Like a Mighty Army: A History of the Church of God,* 1886–1996. Tribute Edition. Cleveland, TN: Pathway, 2008.

Michel, David. "The Importance of Florida for the Early Pentecostal Movement." Selected Annual Proceedings of the Florida Conference of Historians 12 (February 2005) 102.

Swann, Michael S. *The Holy Jumpers: A Concise History of the Church of God of Prophecy in the Bahamas,* 1909–1974. Longwood, FL: Xulon, forthcoming.

Bass, Sidney Coy Sr. 1899–1977

Born near Durham, North Carolina to parents who had been former slaves and members of **Elias Smith's** pro-African organization, **Triumph the Church and Kingdom of God.**

By the early 1920s, though still in his twenties, Bass had become a leader in the **Glorious Church of God in Christ.** On the death of the first general overseer, **Albart Smith,** in 1928, Bass become General Overseer, and pastor of the headquarters church of the **Glorious Church God in Christ** in Huntington, West Virginia and continued to serve in leadership with founder **Lulu Phillips** until her death in 1939. In 1940, Bass was ordained.

After the death of his first wife, in 1952, Bass went against denominational polity and his own teaching and married a divorced woman, after which approximately half of the fifty-congregation denomination rejected his leadership and reorganized as the **Original Glorious Church of God in Christ of the Apostolic Faith.**

Bass continued to preside over the parent denomination, which retained the original name. He died in an automobile accident in Roanoke, Virginia.

Bay Ridge Christian College

In 1953, Dr. James Horace Germany, a white Church of God minister without theological training, founded a two-year interracial institution of higher education affiliated with the Church of God (Anderson, Indiana). It was built on 150 of 500 acres of his own land in Union, Mississippi. His intent was to prepare African-American leadership for both urban and rural churches and the communities they serve.

In 1960, only seven years after its founding, a group of whites within the community, including Germany's cousin, demanded that the school be closed. At one point more than one thousand members of the community gathered to protest what they saw as the college founders' stirring up racial trouble for their own gain. After being beaten by members of the white Citizens Council of Senatobia and local Ku Klux Klansmen, and being refused a charter by the state on the basis that it would not be in the "best interest of the state," Germany moved the college, for which he served as president, to its Texas location.

In 2008, the college's Board of Trustees announced that Bay Ridge Christian College would become a two-year residential Christian junior college for African-American males.

Bell, Joseph H. Sr.

In 2001, Bishop Joseph H. Bell Sr. accomplished a milestone that is unique within the Holiness-Pentecostal community when he was elevated to the first male presiding bishop in a denomination that had been headed by women for the preceding seventy-five years. Bell accomplished this by become the presiding bishop of the **Mt. Sinai Holy Church of America,** a denomination that had been founded by Bishop **Ida Robinson** in 1925. Bishop Bell's wife, Elder Minerva R. Bell, serves as the historian for the denomination.

Joseph Bell was born and raised in Philadelphia, PA. He accepted Christ and became a member of Mt. Olive Holy Church of **Mt. Sinai Holy Church of America** in 1944, under the pastorate of his aunt, Bishop Robinson.

The highly educated Bell holds a degree in Biblical Studies from the Hawthorne Bible School in Hawthorne, New Jersey, a Bachelor of Science in Physical Science from Howard University, a Master of Arts in Science Education from Columbia University, and courses leading to Certification in Supervision and Administration from City College, Fordham University and Columbia University. In addition, he studied at Sarah Lawrence College and Yeshiva University in Chemistry, Physics, and Mathematics during the 1960s.

From 1949 to 1987, the younger Bell had assisted his father with Bethel Holy Church in New York City, serving as deacon, Sunday School teacher, church secretary, and assistant to the pastor. He delivered his initial sermon in 1964 and was ordained an Elder in 1970. The denomination consecrated him to the bishopric in 1974. Upon the passing of his father, Bishop James Bell in July 1990, he was appointed pastor of his home congregation.

During that same period, Bell taught and served as an administrator in the New York City Public School system for more than thirty years. He taught science in both junior and senior high schools from 1954 to 1970 and became a junior high school principal in the Bronx, New York in 1971. After assuming the pastorate of Bethel Holy Church, he expanded its ministries to include a soup kitchen, clothing distribution and food pantry program, a program to help parents and children in deal with social, peer and academic issues. In 1995, Bishop Bell initiated the launch of the Bethel Community Bible Institute.

At the denominational level, Bell has been a member of the Board of Directors since 1971. During that period, he also served as General Secretary.

Bennett, Harold V. 1962–

The Winston-Salem, North Carolina native currently serves as the President-Dean of Charles H. Mason Theological Seminary, a division of the Interdenominational Theological Seminary in Atlanta, Georgia, a position to which he was appointed in 2005. Bennett also serves as chair of the Division of Philosophy and Religion at Morehouse College, one of the most prestigious historically black male institutions of higher education in the United States, which is also located in Atlanta.

Bennett received his Bachelor of Science degree from North Carolina Agricultural and Technical State University in Greensboro, North Carolina, his Master of Divinity degree from the Interdenominational Theological Center in Atlanta, Georgia. He also earned a Master of Arts in Religion and a Doctorate of Philosophy in Religion and Ethics from Vanderbilt University in Nashville, Tennessee. His scholarly endeavors include having published books, commentaries, and several articles related to the Old Testament.

Bennet was ordained as minister in the **Church of God in Christ** in 1987. While most of his pastoral work has been as a supply pastor in the United Methodist Church, within his denomination, Bennet has primarily been involved in theological or Christian education having served as Senior Content Editor of the Sunday School Curriculum and as a writer of the Young People's Willing Workers (YPWW) literature, as well as a member of the Standardized Ordination Committee and the Manual Review Committee. Dr. Bennett has been a commentator or guest on National Public Radio, and a commentator on Religion, Pentecostalism, and the Black Community in local newspapers and on radio stations in the Atlanta area.

His involvement in scholarly associations include the Society for Biblical Literature and the Society for Pentecostal Studies, and is a member of the Catholic-Evangelic Dialogue of the United States.

He and his wife, Valerie, who holds a PhD in mechanical engineering, serve as the directors of the parachurch ministry, Pentecost 4 Life, that involves a weekly radio broadcast, outreach to married couples, and mentoring and motivational coaching for health and wellness.

Beth-El Churches of Christ, Inc.

A Oneness Pentecostal organization that was founded in 1989 in Richmond, Virginia, by Bishop **Robert Evans Jr.** who resigned from the bishopric of **Highway Christian Church** a year earlier. Under Evans's leadership, the Beth-El Churches sent ministers to establish congregations throughout the United States.

Evans died in 2000, and initially, **Bernard N. Bragg** was called to serve as interim presiding bishop for this transitional period. In 2001, Bragg, who had served as the General Secretary and a member of the Executive Board and had been consecrated to the office of bishop in 1999, was elected presiding bishop.

Beth-El operates under an episcopal form of government. The organization allows women to serve in all levels of leadership including as pastor, overseer, bishop, and on the executive board.

In 2008, the denomination launched The Beth-El Temple College of Theology (BT-COT) as a satellite extension of the North Carolina College of Theology (NCCT). Along with the mother church and other congregations in Baltimore, there are congregations in Massachusetts, North Carolina, and Pennsylvania.

Bible Way Church of Our Lord Jesus Christ, Inc.

In 1957, several leaders led by **Smallwood E. Williams** broke from the Oneness Pentecostal denomination **Church of Our Lord Jesus Christ of the Apostolic Faith** over the perceived authoritative leadership of COOLJC founder **Robert Clarence Lawson** and his decision to rescind their elevation to the office of bishop and instead designate them as overseers. That year, Williams convened a National Pentecostal Ministerial Conference at which he and Elders John S. Beane, McKinley Williams, **Winfield A. Showell,** and Joseph Moore banded together to form an organization of approximately seventy congregations that continued to hold similar doctrinal distinctives with its parent body. Each of these leaders were consecrated bishops.

Thirty years earlier, in 1927, Lawson had sent Williams to Washington DC to start a congregation. For the next twenty-five years, Williams, who served as COOLJC General

Secretary of denomination and was apparent successor to Lawson, had gained a reputation as a charismatic preacher and social activist. For like Lawson, Williams became one of few Oneness Pentecostal leaders consistently to engage social and political issues on behalf of his congregation as well as other blacks in Washington. Under his leadership, the local Bible Way congregation built a moderate-income apartment complex and opened a neighborhood grocery store when larger chains would not serve the surrounding community. Williams used his political influence to forestall the demolition of a major portion of that for construction of Interstate 95, the major north/west highway in the Eastern United States, through the center of it.

In 1995, the denomination had approximately 300,000 members in 365 congregations in the United States and Great Britain, and mission congregations in Jamaica, Trinidad and Tobago, Liberia, and Nigeria. During his lifetime, no major schism occurred in the Bible Way organization.

Williams's original intention was to have his son, Wallace, be heir to the denomination's leadership. The younger Williams was a graduate of Howard University, whose musical talent was instrumental in forming the Howard University Gospel Choir, and whose dynamic preaching style had been instrumental in drawing and retaining young Pentecostals in the organization. Wallace had served on his father's pastoral staff as a rising star in the organization until an alleged adulterous relationship forced the senior Williams to removed him from his staff and future consideration as successor.

Instead, after Williams's death, organizational leaders signed "The Order of Succession and Constitution," declaring that Bishops **Lawrence Campbell** and **Huie Rogers** would preside for consecutive three-year trial terms prior to a vote for a permanent successor. As a result, Campbell served from 1991 through 1994 and stepped down as agreed. At the end of Roger's term, however, he refused to relinquish his position, asking instead that the vote be delayed for a year. The refusal of the majority of bishops to accept the resolution led to a split, in which both factions continued to represent themselves as the original church.

After the split, most bishops, pastors, and churches stayed with Campbell's group, which is incorporated and headquartered in Danville, Virginia and remains the larger of the two with approximately five hundred churches worldwide. Though the two organizations are similar in structure and doctrine, Campbell, began to make progressive changes, including ordaining women to the office of elder. At Campbell's 2006 retirement, Cornelius Showell, son of a founding bishop of the original body and pastor of four-thousand-member First Apostolic Faith Church in Baltimore, Maryland was elected to preside, and the headquarters were moved to his congregation. Showell broadened Campbell's openness to women's leadership, appointing Bonnie Hunter as the first woman District Elder. When he stepped down in 2014, Floyd E. Nelson, who had served as first vice-presider under Showell, took over. At some point after the fracture, this group began to refer to itself as International Bible Way Church of Jesus Christ, Inc.

Bible Way Churches of Our Lord Jesus Christ World Wide, Inc.

During the lifetime of **Smallwood E. Williams**, founder of the **Bible Way Church of Our Lord Jesus Christ World Wide**, no major schism occurred in the Bible Way organization, which itself had resulted from a schismatic break from the **Church of Our Lord Jesus Christ of the Apostolic Faith.** Several years after his death, in 1995, however, the denomination that had enjoyed relative unity was split completely in two. In that year, organizational leaders signed "The Order of Succession and Constitution," stating that two leading bishops—**Huie Rogers** of Brooklyn, New York and **Lawrence Campbell** of Danville, Virginia—would preside over the body for consecutive three-year trial terms before a vote for Williams's permanent successor was taken six years later. Campbell served first, from 1991 through 1994. At the end of Roger's term from 1994 to 1997, however, he called for a sabbath year to forestall voting. The refusal of the majority of bishops to accept the resolution led to a split, with both factions continuing to represent themselves as the original church. Most of the bishops, pastors, and churches stayed with Campbell, and this branch—**Bible Way Church of our Lord Jesus Christ**, Incorporated—is headquartered in Danville, Virginia.

Rogers's group, which retained the name of the parent body as well as ownership of the mother church, Bible Way Temple, in Washington DC has its headquarters in Columbia, South Carolina, and reportedly has approximately 250 churches throughout the world. Though the two organizations are similar in structure and doctrine, the major difference revolves around Rogers's maintenance of Williams's sanctions against the incorporation of women in ordained ministry.

Blake, Charles Edward Sr. 1940 –

In 2007, when **Gilbert Earl Patterson,** presiding bishop of the six-million-member **Church of God in Christ,** died of cancer, Charles Edward Blake, pastor of the 25,000 member West Angeles Church of God, the denomination's largest congregation, was elected to fill the unexpired term. In November 2008, Blake was elected to serve a full four-year term as the seventh presiding bishop. And, again, in 2012 he was re-elected.

Blake was born in Little Rock, Arkansas. The family relocated to San Diego when Bishop Samuel M. Crouch appointed his father, Junious Augustus "J. A." Blake Sr. pastor of Jackson Memorial **Church of God in Christ**. The younger Blake received his BA from California Western University (now known as United States International University), and his Master of Divinity degree from Interdenominational Theological Center in 1965. Bishop Blake obtained his Doctorate of Divinity degree from the California Graduate School of Theology in 1982, and is an Honorary Doctorate recipient of Oral Roberts University.

The church Blake serves was founded in 1943 in a small storefront building in downtown Los Angeles. A year after founding pastor C. E. Church died in 1968, Blake was appointed as pastor of the fifty-member congregation. Prior to moving into that pastorate, young Blake served as assistant pastor in his father's congregation. As the congregation grew, Blake undertook an extensive construction program adding an Education Building and administrative offices. The church opened a bookstore in 1986, and a Bible College and a full time Counseling Department was established in 1987. By early 1979 a Christian Academy was in place and the church had begun holding four Sunday morning services, plus a Sunday evening service. The new sanctuary held its first service in April 2001. That congregation is now one of the largest congregations of any denomination in the United States. It boasts a five-thousand-seat sanctuary valued at sixty-five million dollars, a one-hundred-voice, Grammy-Award-winning choir, and more than two hundred paid employees. The church counts celebrities such as Denzel Washington, Samuel Jackson, Erving (Magic) Johnson, Angela Bassett, and Stevie Wonder among regular attendees, and operates a Community Development Corporation (CDC) that the University of Southern California "designated the #1 CDC Organization in Los Angeles County."

Blake responded to the HIV/AIDS crisis in Africa by establishing two relief organizations, The Pan African Children's Fund (PACF) assisted grassroots and faith-based projects battling the pandemic in sub-Saharan Africa has reached nearly one hundred thousand AIDS-affected children. Save Africa's Children supports more than two hundred thousand children in 340 orphan care programs throughout more than twenty-three nations of sub-Saharan Africa.

Within his home denomination, Blake continues to serve in a number of leadership roles. He was the founding Chairperson of the Board for the C. H. Mason Theological Seminary and has served as an Executive Committee member on the Board of the Interdenominational Theological Center, its host institution. In 1985, he was appointed jurisdictional bishop of the First Ecclesiastical district of Southern California from 1985 until 2009, overseeing more than 250 churches.

Further, he is involved in the broader Pentecostal community in several substantial positions including having served as Chair of the Executive Committee, member of the Board of Directors of Oral Roberts University, and as a member of the Board of Directors of International Charismatic Bible Ministries. He served on the Advisory Committee of the Pentecostal World Conference, and as the founder and co-chair of the Los Angeles Ecumenical Congress (LAEC), an interdenominational coalition of religious leaders and pastors.

Blakely, Jesse Clarence 1883–1954

Little is known about Blakely's early life, except that he was born in Georgia and by 1940 was living in Waycross. Blakely later moved to Jacksonville, Florida where he pastored a congregation in the early 1950s.

In 1913, Blakely and eight other ministers left the Church of the Living God, Pillar and Ground of the Truth, in part because they objected to what they considered a CLG-PGT liberal stance of allowing women to be preachers, to form the **First Born Church of the Living God**.

Served as presiding bishop of FBCLG from 1924 until 1939 when he left to form The First Born Church of Christ Written In Heaven, which eventually became the Church of Christ Written in Heaven.

Bonner Bible College

A Oneness Pentecostal institution of higher education established in 1995 in Columbia, South Carolina by the **Church of Our Lord Jesus Christ of the Apostolic Faith** to prepare pastors, ministers, and missionaries of the church primarily within its denomination. It was named for COOLJC presiding apostle, **William Lee Bonner**, who was instrumental in founding the institution and served as the first president.

The college offers a Certificate of Christian Ministries, as well as Associate of Religious Studies and Bachelor of Arts in Religious Studies degrees. The institution achieved accreditation with the Association of Biblical Higher Education. Prior to its 2014 temporary and voluntary withdrawal from accredited status and transition to affiliate status, the college was the only Oneness Pentecostal African American institution in the United States accredited by an agency recognized by the Department of Education. Bonner also received accreditation by the International Christian Accrediting Association in 1999. Because this organization is a voluntary accrediting association of Christian schools, it does not enjoy standing with the USDOE.

While the emphasis was on education leaders within the Oneness movement and particularly those within the **Church of Our Lord Jesus Christ of the Apostolic Faith**, Bonner College now enrolls students regardless of their denomination. When Bonner stepped down, Elaine McQueen became interim president.

Bonner, Ethel Mae Smith 1918-1999

A pioneer educator, missionary, women's leader, and social advocate. The native New Yorker became the wife of **William L. Bonner**, third and longest serving presiding bishop of the **Church of Our Lord Jesus Christ of the Apostolic Faith, Inc**.

Ethel Smith was serving as secretary for COOLJC founder, **Robert C. Lawson** when she met her future husband. After marrying in 1944, the couple set out in ministry together. In their early years in Detroit, Michigan, Bonner served as a typical pastor's wife, doing all she could to help her husband's ministry, including operating a restaurant, preparing affordable meals to support the congregation, and serving the community.

At some point, Bonner studied at Union Theological Seminary in New York, but also received her bachelor of arts from Hunter College in the same city, and a master of arts from Wayne State University in Detroit. Bonner also received an honorary doctorate of sacred letters degree through the American Wesleyan College of the Northeastern Educational and Theological Consortium and became an instructor in the denomination's Church of Christ Bible Institute.

While living in Detroit, Bonner taught languages and social sciences for Detroit Public Schools. For over thirty years, she promoted the cause of private education within the Christian community and directed private school programs within COOLJC. In addition, she served as an educational consultant for the Detroit systems and for Wayne

State University. Bonner spent three years in Liberia, West Africa, teaching and organizing a school and dormitories, and initiating projects for teacher training as well as to enable the school to raise crops to help meet student needs.

Within COOLJC, "Lady Bonner" pioneered organization of the Ministers and Deacons Wives' Guild to provide training, inspiration, and fellowship for women as they supported their husbands in the ministry and in the leadership of their congregations, became its first elected president, and published the *Apostolic Women* magazine. In 1984 she became executive director of the 24,000-member International Association of Ministers Wives and Minister's Widows, Inc. She also served as president of the Apostolic Wives Association

In the late 1980s, Bonner and her husband became involved in a breach of relationship that played out within the broader COOLJC community. Ethel accused her husband of heavy-handedness in their relationship. William in turn, accused her of usurping authority over men and attempted to silence all of her influence within the denomination, removing her from important posts and forbidding leaders to allow her to speak at public meetings. Though the couple separated, Ethel decided to remain a part of the denomination, where for some time after her death, she remained an inspiration to many women throughout COOLJC.

Further Reading:

Bonner, Ethel. *This is My Story.* Unpublished manuscript.
Moorer, "Beloved Mother and First Lady Ethel Mae Bonner Laid to Rest." *New York Amsterdam News* 9.2 (2000) 39.
Williams, Pandora. *Outstanding Women and their Contributions to the Church of Our Lord Jesus Christ of the Apostolic Faith, Inc.* S.l.: International Missionary Department, 1994.

Bonner, William Lee 1921–2015

The chief apostle and senior prelate of the major Oneness Pentecostal denomination, the General Assembly of the **Churches of Our Lord Jesus Christ of the Apostolic Faith, Inc.** was born in Bolden County Georgia, and had joined the Oneness movement and be baptized in Jesus' name and received the Pentecostal Spirit baptism before moving to New York. Bonner's ministry began in the 1940s under the tutelage of COOLJC founder, **Robert C. Lawson**, for whom he served as a chauffeur and key aide.

His first pastorate was the Green Avenue Church of Our Lord Jesus Christ in Brooklyn, New York. In 1944, Lawson sent Bonner to Detroit, Michigan to pastor a small storefront congregation, the First Church of Our Lord Jesus Christ. Today, that congregation is the twenty-five hundred seat Solomon's Temple—one of six churches over which Bonner presided until his death.

At Lawson's death in 1961, Bonner was elected to the three-man board of presiding bishops with **Herbert J. Spencer** and Maurice Hutner. Spencer was elected to preside, but that same year, Bonner took over the pastorate of Lawson's three thousand-member mother church congregation, Greater Refuge Temple in Harlem, New York. From there, he launched an evangelistic campaign that eventually saw him serving simultaneously as pastor of five congregations. He first took over the congregation in Detroit. After seventeen years, he took over the mother church in New York City. It would be almost another twenty years before he established a congregation in Washington DC that he founded in 1989 with Jackson, a Columbia, South Carolina congregation established in 1993, and a congregation in Jackson, Mississippi.

In 1973, Bonner was elevated as the presiding bishop of the Church of Our Lord Jesus Christ. Under his administration, the assembly grew from one hundred and fifty-five churches to over five hundred churches and missions throughout the world. In 1995, Bonner established W. L. Bonner College in Columbia and served as its president until shortly before his death. At some point, in Bokaytown, Liberia, West Africa, he built a maternal clinic for women from the "Bush" to have their babies in sanitary conditions.

Bonner received his religious education and the Doctor of Divinity through the denomination's Church of Christ Bible Institute in New York City. Bonner was the author of several published works including *The African Story, The Battle of Armageddon, The Uncontrolled Emotions of Young People, Life in the Holy Spirit*, The Three Women: Sarah, Rebecca and Jezebel, *The Apostolic Dilemma, Part I and II, My Father in the Gospel,* and *Add Thou to It.* In addition, his "Hour of Truth" broadcast aired on nationally syndicated television outlets such as BET and The Word Network—as well as radio stations and via livestream. When Bonner vacated the position of presiding bishop to Gentle Groover in 1995, he was elevated to the office of chief apostle and held that office until his death at age ninety-three.

Further Reading:

W. L. Bonner Literary Committee. *And the High Places I'll Bring Down: Bishop William L. Bonner, the Man and His God.* Detroit, MI: W. L. Bonner Literary Committee, 1999.

Bonnie Brae Street Prayer Meeting

The meeting that served as the catalyst for the historic 1906 **Azusa Street Revival**, the seedbed for the contemporary Pentecostal movement. Several months before the Revival moved into full swing, **William Joseph Seymour**, the lead pastor at the **Azusa Street Mission** came to Los Angeles at the invitation of pastor, **Julia Hutchins,** to assist in building her small Holiness congregation. When Seymour's message of speaking in tongues as biblical evidence of Holy Spirit failed to resonate with Hutchins or most members of her congregation, he was forced to discontinue his ministry there.

Once locked out, Seymour found a place for his fledgling ministry at the home **Ruth and Richard Asberry** and sometime between late February and early April 1906, the family opened their home at 214 Bonnie Brae Street to Seymour and a band of mostly black women household workers to gather to pray for a new experience of the Spirit. Initially, Seymour himself had not yet had the experience, and his teaching was seemingly bearing little fruit, except to intensify the seekers' hunger for the experience.

As the meeting slowly grew, the group faithfully studied and prayed, and within a short period, several attendees received the Pentecostal Holy Spirit baptism experience. As more seekers began to experience speaking in tongues, the group grew to fill the house to overflowing. Soon news of the meeting spread through the community, and attendance spilled out first onto the porch, and then onto the street in front of the house.

Jennie Evans Moore, who would later become Seymour's wife, was among the first to receive the Pentecostal experience at the Bonnie Brae prayer meetings. Among other prominent revival participants, Frank Bartleman, early Pentecostal evangelist and Azusa Street historian visited Bonnie Brae Street, but probably received his experience at Azusa Street. **Frank W. Williams** encountered the revival and had his Pentecostal experience here before participating in the Azusa Street meeting then traveling throughout the South, preaching and planting churches.

As news of the meeting continued to travel throughout the Los Angeles Holiness community, the house became too small. Leaders found facilities at a former African Methodist Episcopal sanctuary that had renovated into a livery stable at 312 Azusa Street. The revival transitioned and the historic events that would be immortalized as the beginning of the contemporary Pentecostal movement unfolded over the next several years.

At the close of the revival, the Azusa Street site that was the long-term home of the Revival fell into financial hard times. It was eventually sold in foreclosure and subsequently demolished. However, the Bonnie Brae Street site (the city of Los Angeles later changed the house number to 216) was turned into a museum, and remains the only physical memorial to the beginning of the contemporary Pentecostal movement. It is visited regularly by pilgrims and scholars.

Boone, George Marshall (G. M.) 1920–

The founder and first presiding bishop of the Oneness Pentecostal denomination, **Apostolic Assemblies of Christ, Inc.** was born in Myrtle, Mississippi to parents who were schoolteachers. He grew up during the Great Depression and segregation. Though Boone came to Christian faith and was baptized at age twelve, while he was serving in the military in New Guinea, he received that experience of Pentecostal Holy Spirit baptism through the witness of a **Church of God in Christ** comrade. The following week, after being baptized in water in the Trinitarian formula, he felt the call to preach. On completing military service in 1946, Boone returned to Mississippi. The same year, he became a member of the **Pentecostal Churches of the Apostolic Faith** where he was re-baptized in water in the Oneness formula by his future father-in-law. Boone subsequently won several family members and friends to the Oneness understanding and eventually, his mother and all but one sibling were baptized in Jesus' name, and experienced Pentecostal Holy Spirit baptism.

In 1947 Boone moved his family to Michigan where he served assistant pastor to his father-in-law. He was ordained in 1961 under the late Bishop **S. N. Hancock,** and in 1964, established New Liberty Apostolic Faith Church in Detroit. He was later appointed District Elder and Chairperson of the Michigan State Council of the Pentecostal Churches of the Apostolic Faith.

In 1965, the Board of Bishops elevated Boone to the office of Bishop over his objections. Five years later, in 1970, however, he left that denomination to establish the Apostolic Assemblies of Christ, Inc. starting with seven churches in Michigan, Ohio, and Tennessee. Within the next forty-two years under Boone's leadership, ACPJ established congregations in fourteen additional states—Alabama, Arkansas, California, Florida, Georgia, Illinois, Indiana, Kentucky, Louisiana, Mississippi, Missouri, North Carolina, South Carolina, and Texas, as well as in Liberia and Haiti. In 2012, Boone stepped down from his position of presiding bishop to become bishop emeritus.

Boone, Wellington 1948–

The conservative, Charismatic speaker, and author was ordained into ministry in 1973. In 1981, Boone started a local congregation in Ettrick, Virginia near Petersburg. The next year, he founded New Generation Campus Ministries (NGM).

He incorporated Living Word Evangelistic Association in approximately 1983, and in 1984 moved the church from Ettrick to Richmond, and founded Manna Christian Fellowship. In 1986, he changed the name to Wellington Boone Ministries which serves as a covering for several outreach ministries. By 1999, this para-church ministry had reached students at over fifty colleges and universities through organizations such as Making of Champions, Global Outreach Campus Ministries, and the Inner City Bible Society.

In 1995, Boone stepped down from his Richmond pastorate and moved to the Atlanta, Georgia area to found and become senior pastor of The Father's House Church in Norcross. That same year, The Fellowship of International Churches and its members conferred on Boone the title of bishop. Some time later, he turned the pastorate of the Atlanta congregation over to Bishop Garland Hunt.

Boone has often been a featured speaker for Evangelical and conservative groups such as Promise Keepers conferences and the nationally syndicated 700 Club television program hosted by conservative religious broadcaster, Marion Gordon "Pat" Robertson. Along with serving on the board of Trustees of Regents at Regent University, the institution Robertson established in Virginia Beach, Virginia, Boone has close relationships with several conservative Evangelical Christian organizations including Focus on the Family and the Family Research Council.

Further, Boone founded the Network of Politically Active Christians (NPAC), Kingmaker Women, and the Fellowship of International Churches. Through Goshen

International, Boone set up learning centers in South Africa for Black African and multiracial children, and in 1999 established Global Outreach Campus Ministries.

Bowdan, Frank Reuben Joseph 1910–1976

The early bishop and leader in the **Pentecostal Assemblies of the World** was born in Los Angeles, California as one of four sons of **Azusa Street Revival** participants, Maggie and William S. Bowdan. At age ten, Bowdan received the Pentecostal Holy Spirit baptism, was called to the ministry a year later, and shortly thereafter conducted his first tent revival in Pasadena, California. That year, he was baptized in the Oneness Pentecostal formula by Frank J. Ewart, an early white Oneness leader.

As a young man, Bowdan was tutored by **Garfield T. Haywood**, until the older man's death in 1931. That year, he was ordained to the ministry within the **Pentecostal Assemblies of the World** and appointed to his first pastorate at Glad Tidings Mission in Chicago where he served for sixteen months.

In 1936 Bowdan accepted the pastorate of Bethlehem Temple in Flint, Michigan, serving there for fifteen years until he was called to pastor the Apostolic Faith Home Assembly in Los Angeles which his family had helped charter. Membership of that congregation swelled in membership under his leadership.

Bowdan's rise through the ranks of the PAW leadership began in 1947 when he became Assistant General Secretary. While still in that position, he was elevated to suffragan bishop in 1959, then to full bishop in 1962. In 1964, he was appointed bishop over the diocese of California and Nevada. In 1968, was elected assistant presiding bishop, serving under presiding bishop Ross Paddock and holding that office until 1974.

Though his formal post-secondary education was probably limited to a short period studying Greek at a junior college, when the West Coast Branch of **Aenon Bible College** expanded in 1972, Bowdan was selected as president. The Columbus, Ohio branch of the college conferred the Honorary Doctor of Divinity on Bowdan. He also received a Doctor of Sacred Letters from Fundamental Bible Seminary in Elk City, Oklahoma. Bowdan died in Los Angeles from heart disease at the age of sixty-six.

Bowe, Justus 1873–1951

An early **Church of God in Christ** bishop who separated from that denomination for a time to found and serve as first presiding minister of the **Church of God in Christ Congregational**. Bowe had been part of the original **Church of God in Christ** under **Charles Price Jones** and **Charles Harrison Mason**, and was among the ministers who sided with Mason in his split with Jones over the issue of speaking in tongues. When Mason left Arkansas for Tennessee, he turned the work in that state over to Bowe who established the first **Church of God in Christ** congregation in Hot Springs, Arkansas and became the first overseer of that state in 1907. After the resignation of D. J. Young as Overseer of Texas, Bowe was also assigned to that state where established the Faith Home and Industrial School at Geridge to educate the affluent black COGIC children.

Born in South Carolina, Bowe was a businessman as well as a minister. Besides owning a 325-acre farm, Bowe owned at least one grocery store and was president of the

Universal Oil and Gas Mining Company in Pine Bluff. During the period while Mason and Jones were in litigation, independent-minded Bowe disobeyed Mason's directive to refrain from formally organizing congregations until the issue had been resolved. His failure to heed the founder's admonition resulted in the loss of several congregations and extensive property for the parent denomination.

Bowe served as editor of *The Whole Truth* until 1920. In 1932, Bowe disassociated himself with COGIC to found the **Church of God in Christ** Congregational in Hot Springs specifically over a difference in understanding of the biblical structure for church leadership which for Bowe was not reflected in COGIC's episcopal polity. He served as senior bishop of the new body.

In 1945 a group of COGIC elders convinced him to return to the parent body and bring his new organization with him. When COGICC elders rejected that proposal, Bowe left the smaller body intact under the leadership of **George Slack** and returned to COGIC alone.

Bragg, Bernard Nathaniel 1948–

The presiding bishop of **Beth-El Churches of Christ** was born in Randallstown, Maryland in suburban Baltimore. He was ordained to the ministry in 1986 and served as the General Secretary and a member of the Executive Board for the Beth-El Churches of Christ from the denomination's inception in 1989. In 1999, he was consecrated as a bishop. In 2001, following the passing of the founder, **Robert Evans, Jr.**, Bragg was elected the presiding bishop.

Along with a Bachelor of Science and Master of Arts degrees in special education from Coppin State College in Baltimore, Maryland, Bragg holds two honorary doctorate degrees. Throughout much of his ministry, he also worked in the Baltimore City Public School System as a teacher and administrator before retiring to fulfill his duties as bishop.

His community involvement includes serving on the boards of directors of the Umoja House—a home for troubled youth—Healing Our Land Ministries, and organization that facilitates the needs of HIV and AIDS victims and their families. His broader spiritual commitments extend to serving as spiritual covering for On Broken Pieces—a ministry to hurting women—and the Apostolic Constituent for the Women Pastors Alliance (WPA) headquartered in West Palm Beach, Florida that addresses the concerns of women pastors. Bragg also serves as the Apostolic Constituent for Convening of the Evangelist—a fellowship that promotes five-fold ministry, with emphasis on the office of evangelist. He is also CEO of the New Life Community Development Corporation and Bernard N. Bragg Ministries.

Bram-Bibby, Emily 1916–2007

The evangelist, musician, and recording artist was the first woman in the **Church of God in Christ** to hold an official pastoral post not tied to the ministry of her husband. Her ground-breaking achievement came in the 1950s when **Frederick. D. Washington,** prominent **Church of God in Christ** pastor and bishop, took the unprecedented step of appointing her as his assistant pastor at Washington Temple **Church of God in Christ** in Brooklyn, New York.

Bram-Bibby was born in Garland, Texas, the seventh of nine children. She received her education in Dallas County, Texas. The family moved to Los Angeles when she was a young child, and she experienced Christian conversion at age of ten in a **Church of God in Christ** congregation. As a young woman, she began singing, playing the piano, and speaking in COGIC congregations as well as other denominations.

From there Bibby, a renowned gospel singer moved back to Dallas, Texas, where she served under Elder S. E. Mitchell. In 1984, she married Lucious F. Bibby, Sr., a COGIC deacon and moved to Marion, Louisiana serving at Litro COGIC. In 2005, she moved on to Kansas City, Missouri and served at Redemption and Shiloh Institutional COGIC.

Bibby, who until the time of her death was the oldest and longest serving evangelist with the denomination, served the church for more than eighty years. Throughout that time, she held several leadership positions including National Evangelist and member of the National Advisory Board of the Women's Department, along with serving on the traveling Evangelistic team with the late **Bishop J. O. Patterson Sr.**

As a gospel singer, she recorded with Savoy Records in the 1950s. Bibby, who was singing at churches and programs as late as several months before her death, died in Kansas City, Missouri.

Branch, General Johnson (G. J.) 1881–1949

One of the early fathers of the **United Holy Church of America**. G. J. Branch was born in Duplin County in eastern North Carolina and educated at Hampton Institute, an historically black college. Branch was not a part of the earliest meetings of the group that founded the UHCA, but joined the denomination 1908 when he was twenty-seven years old. He had come into the UHCA from the Freewill Baptist Church and was a moderately wealthy real estate owner whose exceptional business skills helped set the UHCA on strong administrative footing.

In the 1916 election for presiding bishop, Branch ran in the election in which Henry L. Fisher was voted into office and received the second highest number of ballots. After his defeat, he served alongside President **Fisher** as vice president of the **United Holy Church** from 1916 to 1947.

In 1920, Branch joined with Fisher in meeting with other general officers and the independent groups of Holy Churches in Philadelphia and nearby towns to organize the churches into a Northern District Convocation of the **United Holy Church of America**,

Inc. Branch was chosen as the first president of the district embracing the following states: New York, New Jersey, Pennsylvania, Delaware, Maryland and the District of Columbia. In 1924 Branch was elevated to the office of bishop along with Fisher and Elder J. D. Diggs. In 1924 he and Diggs to organize the Northwestern District. In 1948 Branch organized the Southeastern District, originally known as the Florida-Georgia District.

Throughout his career in the UHCA, Branch pastored congregations in Kinston, Zebulon, and Goldsboro, North Carolina. After Fisher's death in 1945, he served as presiding bishop until his own death two years later.

Further Reading:

Turner, William C. *The United Holy Church: A Study in Black Holiness-Pentecostalism.* Piscataway, NJ: Gorgias, 2006.

Brandhagen, Bishop Gladys A. 1907–1992

The third presiding bishop of the Pentecostal Faith Church, Inc. founded by prominent Harlem pastor **Rosa Artemis Horn**. Brandhagen's father brought her to Evanston, Illinois as a teenager, while Horn was ministering there, and she received a miraculous healing, was converted and experienced Pentecostal Holy Spirit baptism.

Following that encounter, Horn adopted Brandhagen—a young white woman of Scandinavian heritage, born in Jamestown, North Dakota—into her family as a foster daughter, and they worked to evangelize and build Pentecostal Faith Church congregations throughout the East Coast.

Brandhagen, who was affectionately known as "Aunt Glady" or "the white angel," served as the first general secretary of the Pentecostal Faith Church, Inc., conduct corporate business for the Church. She worked with her adopted mother, musical producer, and choir director for the congregation's "You Pray for Me Church of the Air." She was ordained as a minister in about 1939. In 1951, she moved to Baltimore and pastored in the inner city Pentecostal Faith Church until her death.

In 1981 upon the death of the second presiding bishop—Horn's daughter, Jessie—Brandhagen became new presiding bishop of the Golden Council of the Pentecostal Faith Church.

Brazier, Arthur Monroe 1921–2010

A progressive Oneness Pentecostal pastor, community activist, social justice advocate, and bishop within the **Pentecostal Assemblies of the World**. The high school dropout was born on the south side of Chicago, Illinois and was raised by a mother who was a Oneness Pentecostal pastor. He was baptized in Jesus' name under the pastorate of Elder Herbert C. Moore, but later joined the Universal Church of Christ, where his mother, under whose ministry he was converted to Christian faith, served. Brazier answered the call to ministry in 1948 and not long afterward, became assistant pastor of his mother's congregation. Three years after her death in 1949, he assumed her pastorate, enrolling in Moody Bible Institute in 1955 for formal preparation for ministry.

In 1960, he was asked to take over as pastor of the Apostolic Church of God, a small congregation with which his church shared space. Accepting that office, he merged the two congregations under the name of the Apostolic Church of God. Brazier served that congregation for forty-eight years. During that period, the church grew exponentially from fewer than three hundred to over twenty thousand members.

Brazier's many civic involvements included serving for nine years as founding president of The Woodlawn Organization, a community-based group that worked strategically to preserve and improve the community surrounding his congregation. He also served as founder and chair of its Woodlawn Preservation and Investment Co., which acquired vacant city property on which it built low- and mixed-income housing. As chair and vice president of the Center for Community Change, a Washington DC based organization, he provided technical assistance to the Community Development Corporation on large-scale housing and commercial projects throughout the United States; he also served as chair of the Fund for Community Redevelopment and Revitalization.

In the 1960s, Brazier marched alongside Rev. Martin Luther King Jr. to protest racial segregation. In 1966, he invited the famous Civil Rights leader to Chicago, and joined with him to protest against segregation in housing and education in the city.

Despite his limited formal education, Brazier addressed United States presidents, international dignitaries, and national and local politicians. He lectured at such prestigious institutions as University of Chicago and Northwestern University law schools, New York School of Social Work, and at Harold Washington College's Social Work and Gerontology. In addition to advocacy and lecturing, Brazier authored several books including, *Black Self-Determination, Saved by Grace and Grace Alone, From Milk to Meat, and Delivery Systems for Model Cities*, and numerous articles in prominent publications.

In 1976, Brazier was elected diocese bishop of the Sixth Episcopal District of the **Pentecostal Assemblies of the World**, overseeing more than eighty churches in Illinois. While he would serve in that position honoring for more than thirty years, in 2007, after seventy-five years, Brazier pulled his congregation out of the PAW. At issue for him was what he saw as the non-progressive mindset of some PAW executive board members, including imposing limitations on appropriate speakers at PAW's national conference. There was also disagreement over the doctrine of eternal security—the doctrine that once the believer is saved, that person will not lose their salvation—since while the organization does not believe in that doctrine, Brazier did. His departure removed a 20,450-member congregation—the largest membership in a state with only 35,000 total members.

Brazier stepped down as pastor to become emeritus in 2008, turning over the reins to his son, Byron T. Brazier. In that same month, he was named the first senior fellow of the Chicago branch of the Local Initiatives Support Corporation, where he had served as the chair of the Board of the Executive Committee of the New Communities Program. Until his resignation in 2010, Brazier was involved starting the Woodlawn Children's Promise Community, an organization of which he was chairperson of the board until that year he continued in his position as a member of the Board of the Public Building Commission of Chicago to which he was appointed in 1986.

Further Reading:

Alinsky, Saul D. *Rules for Radicals: A Pragmatic Primer for Realistic Radicals.* New York: Random, 1971.
Dortch, Sammie M. *When God Calls: A Biography of Bishop Arthur M. Brazier.* Grand Rapids: Eerdmans, 1996.
Gramsci, Antonio. *Prison Notebooks of Antonio Gramsci.* New York: International, 1994.

Bridges, Peter Jan F. 1890–1962

Early Pentecostal leader who founded Beulah Church of God in Christ Jesus, Inc. and served within both the **Pentecostal Assemblies of the World** and the **Church of Our Lord Jesus Christ of the Apostolic Faith**—the two largest black Oneness Pentecostal bodies in the United States. Bridges was born in Washington, North Carolina. As a child, Bridges attended the Methodist Church with his family, but would steal away to visit a sanctified congregation near his home. Bridges later broke with the Methodist to join the sanctified church and had an experience of Pentecostal Holy Spirit baptism.

While in Columbus, Ohio, **Garfield T. Haywood** baptized Bridges in the name of Jesus Christ. Later, he was part of the historic meeting that involved Haywood in a defense of Oneness doctrine before prominent Assemblies of God leaders. He also met **Robert C. Lawson,** who encouraged him to come to New York.

Early in his youth, Bridges had sensed a call to the ministry, and on arriving in New York City, he initially affiliated with Pastor **Susan Lightford**'s church, where Lawson was also affiliated, joined the **Pentecostal Assemblies of the World**, and began preaching. Bridges went on to be an early leader in that denomination, serving, for example, on committee to consider the amalgamation of PAW and Apostolic Church of Jesus Christ. Once in the city, Bridges—who only completed high school—was forced to work at manual labor, but soon got involved in real estate. By the end of his life, he had accumulated five houses. He encouraged his childhood friend, **Frank Clemmons**, to join him in New York, and Clemmons's positive response to that invitation would be significant to the **Church of God in Christ** for he would go on to establish that denomination's first congregation in that borough.

Around 1920 Bridges left PAW to connect with Lawson and his newly formed Church of our Lord Jesus Christ, Inc. While with that body, he served as national evangelist, traveling to preach throughout the United States, and planting a congregation in the Coney Island area of Brooklyn. In 1938 Bridges left that congregation to establish a second congregation, Beulah Church of God in Christ Jesus in the Bedford-Stuyvesant section of Brooklyn, the congregation he pastored until his death twenty-four years later.

Six years later, Bridges separated from COOLJC and brought his congregation into fellowship with the **Churches of God in Christ Jesus** headed by Bishop **Randolph A. Carr.** Once there, he became diocesan bishop of the Eastern Region of the United States with oversight of New York, Delaware, Maryland, Washington DC, Virginia, North and South Carolina, Georgia, and Florida. He stayed with that church body until his death.

At his death, Elder Edward Payne assumed the pastorate of his Brooklyn congregation.

Bright, Crawford F. (C. F.) 1875–1952

An early leader in the **Church of God (Colored Work),** the Florida native was of Afro-Caribbean descent. He was raised in the Primitive Baptist Church, where he was ordained as a deacon. He was again ordained as a deacon in the Church of God in 1911 and began his preaching ministry in 1913. A year later, Bright left the denomination claiming that "the colored would never be recognized with the whites," and worked with his brother John to establish the **Church of God by Faith** in Jacksonville, Florida. Within two years, however, he had resumed ministry within his former denomination, serving in numerous key positons within the Church of God (Colored Work), and urging several other ministers who had left to return or those considering leaving to remain with the organization.

By 1916 he was ordained as a bishop in the Church of God and was appointed by General Overseer **A. J. Tomlinson** to serve on the Questions and Answers Committee of the General Assembly and, in 1919, as overseer of the churches in Pennsylvania, though at the time there was only one white church in the state. In that same year, he preached in the denomination's General Assembly. He was then appointed as overseer of New Jersey in 1920.

He left the Church of God again in 1920 to join the **Church of God in Christ**. However, he returned to the Church of God in 1924 and became a prominent leader within the black community. In 1927, Bright was appointed pastor of the Church of God congregation in Jacksonville, Florida where the headquarters for the Church of God (Colored Work) was established.

Like so many other early black Pentecostal pastors Bright was bi-vocational. A carpenter by trade, he used his skill to help build twenty-eight churches. His tenure as the pastor of the Jacksonville congregation involved him serving as architect and builder of the congregation's edifice, which would serve as the Church of God Auditorium for the Color Work in Jacksonville, Florida. It was completed in 1936 with a maximum occupancy of nine hundred people. He also took a lead role in planning of the Church of God Industrial School and Orphanage in Eustis, Florida.

His pastoral tenure ended in 1942; little is known about his activities after that period.

Brisbin, Lawrence E. 1915–1994

The last white presiding bishop in the predominantly African-American denomination, the **Pentecostal Assemblies of the World**, ending an era of multi-racial leadership within a denomination that had defied social mores of a segregated American Church for decades. Brisbin, who was born in Grand Rapids, Michigan, received the Pentecostal experience of Holy Spirit baptism after being baptized in water in Jesus' name in 1943. Simultaneously, he received deliverance from alcohol and nicotine addiction and joined the Apostolic Faith Church.

In 1945 Brisbin was drafted into the United States Army where he served with a hospital unit. During his military service he began to preach, and on returning from military duty, continued preaching on the streets of Grand Rapids and at the Apostolic Faith Church. He was ordained in Boston, Massachusetts in 1950, and the next year was elected pastor of a Grand Rapids congregation where he had become a Christian and once been a member. From that point, he was active in the Northern District Council and was made a District Elder over the western portion of the Michigan diocese.

In 1962 Brisbin was consecrated bishop and assigned the diocese of Minnesota, Wisconsin, and the Dakotas. He served there for several years before being assigned the diocese of New York and Ontario.

From 1974 until 1980, Brisbin served as assistant presiding bishop under Francis L. Smith. Then, in 1980, Brisbin was elected presiding bishop, a position he held until 1986. After leaving that office he remained in his pastorate until his wife's death. When his health began to fail, he resigned in 1993.

Broadie, Benjamin H (B. H.) 1906–1965

Famed radio preacher, gospel singer, and faith healer. Broadie, who lived in Manhattan, New York, pastored Gospel Tabernacle Church of America in Newark, New Jersey from which his radio program was broadcast nationally. He began his radio career with a Sunday broadcast that was mainly heard in the Southern states and drew hundreds of letters in reply. He encouraged listeners experiencing any type of illness to receive healing by placing one hand on the radio and the other on the part of their body that was ailing or diseased.

Broadie, who carried the moniker, "The World's Wonder Radio Preacher," was named by *Ebony* magazine as a top radio preacher in July 1949. The former barber was born in Wake County, North Carolina and previously had been affiliated with the **Church of God in Christ.** His local, congregation, however, was non-denominational.

As a gospel singer, Broadie recorded on the World Wide label. His major works included two singles, "On the Jericho Road" and "Come on Home," both of which were recorded in 1960 and incorporated preaching and singing with response from the congregation. The cut received short reviews in *Billboard Magazine* (May 1960) and have become collectible items.

Bronson, Audrey Flora 1929–

Educator, civic leader, pastor, and bishop, Audrey Bronson leads the non-denominational Sanctuary Church of the Open Door in Philadelphia. The Bronson family migrated from Florida to the "city of brotherly love," when she was fourteen years old. That same year, she was called to preach within a local Church of God congregation she was attending. Shortly after that call, her pastor allowed her to preach her first sermon. In 1975 after serving as an ordained evangelist for twenty-five years, she established her congregation and the Sanctuary Christian Academy, a private academic school from pre-school to fifth grade in 1978; later, she served at the Sanctuary Bible Institute and the Sanctuary Counseling and Referral Center. In 1994, she was consecrated as bishop and presides over the International Fellowship of Churches, Inc.

Bronson received a Bachelor of Science degree in elementary education from Cheyney University, a Master's degree in psychology from Howard University where she became a PhD candidate in psychology, but left before finishing. She went on to earn a Doctor of Ministry from New York Theological Seminary and was honored with a Doctor of Divinity degree from Bethune-Cookman College and Doctor of Humane Letters from the National Theological Seminary and College.

Bronson comes from a family of ministers and educators. Her father was a pastor and school principal. Her brother, Dr. Oswald P. Bronson, a United Methodist minister, pastored several churches before serving as president first of the Interdenominational Theological Center in Atlanta, Georgia, then Bethune-Cookman College in Daytona Beach, Florida, and finally of Edward Waters College in Jacksonville, Florida.

Dr. Bronson retired from Cheyney University in 1984 as Associate Professor of Psychology after seventeen years of teaching. She served as Dean of the Philadelphia Urban Education Institute, a subsidiary of the African-American Interdenominational Ministries, Inc. (AAIM, Inc.) of Philadelphia in association with the city's major seminaries.

Bronson is considered a leader in the Philadelphia community and noted as much for her community activism as for her preaching. Beginning in 2009, Bronson served as the first female president of the Black Clergy of Philadelphia and Vicinity two and a half years. Early in the HIV/AIDS crisis, when many churches shunned those afflicted with the disease, Bronson urged other clergy to minister to that community. She served on the board of One Church, One Child, Inc., a statewide organization that encouraging African-American Churches members to adopt black children, for two years on the Executive Committee of the Association of Theological Schools and currently serves on the board of the Philadelphia Industrial Development Corporation.

Brooks, Henry Chauncey 1896–1967

The founding bishop of the **Way of the Cross Church of Christ** was born in Franklinton, North Carolina. After the untimely death of his father in 1912, Brooks moved to Washington DC at the age of sixteen with his sister. In 1917, he entered the military serving in World War I in the United States Navy. In 1925 while affiliated with a Baptist congregation in the city, Brooks attended a Oneness Pentecostal revival intending to disrupt it and persuade the preacher of the error of his ways. By the time the altar call was made, Brooks had a change of mind, and he was converted to the Pentecostal faith and baptized by immersion in Jesus name during the meeting. Meanwhile, he continued attending the Baptist Church until he was excommunicated several months later. Brooks initially affiliated with **Robert Lawson's** organization, the **Church of Our Lord Jesus Christ of**

the Apostolic Faith. Yet, when he initially approached Lawson to obtain ministerial credentials, Lawson refused, suggesting that Brooks work on a ministerial staff of an existing congregation.

In 1926 Brooks started his first independent congregation, Emmanuel Tabernacle, in Washington with five people. Over the next six years, Brooks continued to build the congregation and gained Lawson's confidence to the point that he ordained him to the ministry. Brooks's congregation was the first Pentecostal or Apostolic ministry in Washington that worshipped in an actual church building.

In 1933 Lawson consecrated him as bishop, but requested that he merge his congregation with that of **Smallwood E. Williams** and bring his work under that of Williams, reasoning that one large congregation in Washington DC would be better than two small ones.

However, Brooks scoffed at that idea and broke from Lawson's Church of Our Lord Jesus Christ to form **Way of the Cross Churches of Christ**. In 1924, Brooks started a second congregation in Henderson, North Carolina setting his brother as pastor.

Brooks continued to serve as pastor of the headquarters church in Washington DC and bishop of the denomination until his death.

Brown, Rosie J. Wallace 1935–2014

An evangelist, songwriter, and singer whose music career spanned the 1960s and 1970s. Brown was also founder of the First Church of Love, Faith and Deliverance, in Philadelphia, Pennsylvania. Brown was born in Chicago, but migrated to Philadelphia and organized a congregation in 1962 with eight members. The church became known for its choir and music. Brown also helped introduce gospel music to some of Philadelphia's mental and penal institutions.

Brown was a part of several gospel groups, singing first with the Thelma Davis Specials. She was called to the ministry in 1957 while a member of the Imperial Gospel Singers. At one point she formed her own group, Rosie Wallace Brown and the Savettes. As a songwriter, she wrote many of her songs as well as compose for the Christian Tabernacle Radio Choir.

In 1970 she married singer Eddie Brown, with whom she sometimes joined to perform duet recordings. During her career, Brown recorded seven albums, and guested with other gospel singers such as James Cleveland. While a number of these were recorded on her own, others were recorded with her husband or with the First Church of Love, Faith and Deliverance Choir. Along with a choir, she recorded "God Cares," a big hit for Savoy Records in November 1963. A few weeks later, following the assassination of President John F. Kennedy, she recorded "A Light That Shines" in his memory.

The Pillar of Fire College and Pentecostal Seminary of York, England awarded Brown honorary doctorate degrees in human letters and sacred music. Brown died in Philadelphia at the age of seventy-nine.

Brown, Roy Edmund 1943–

Presiding bishop of **Pilgrim Assemblies International** and a founder of the **Joint College of African American Pentecostal Bishops.** Brown was born in Birmingham, Alabama where he was raised within the Methodist Church, and came to Christ at the age of six. At thirteen, he moved with his family to New York City where he completed his education. There he joined a Baptist Church, acknowledged his call to ministry at seventeen, and later began evangelistic work and was ordained in 1964. That the same year, at age twenty-two, he was appointed to his first pastoral position at First Baptist Church of Deer Park, New York. He served there for one year.

In 1965 he became the pastor of Pilgrim Baptist Church in Brooklyn, New York where, over the next twenty-five years, he led the congregation in establishing radio and television ministry. He began a school, Pilgrim Christian Academy; a bible school, Pilgrim Theological Institute; and planted several congregations by renovating of numerous abandoned buildings throughout the New York area into viable churches. His ministry also extends to revitalizing communities and churches in South Africa, West Africa, Trinidad, and Barbados.

In 1989, he was elected Bishop of the Pilgrim Assemblies International, Inc.—the fellowship of churches he had drawn together. Four years later, he consecrated the first eight bishops to serve with him, and in 1996, would consecrate yet four more men, two of whom would establish the initial international presence of Pilgrim Assemblies International on the continent of Africa. During that same year, Brown was elevated to the office of archbishop. In 2006, his Brooklyn congregation, which serves as the headquarters for his organization was renamed the Pilgrim Cathedral of Harlem. He also pastors Greater Temple of Praise in Baltimore, where he began pastoring last April.

Further Reading:

Shelby, Joyce. "A Master Builder of Churches." *New York Daily News*, February 4, 1996.

Brown, William 1933–2009

The Birmingham, Alabama native who was raised in the Roman Catholic Church was founder and General Overseer of the **Salvation and Deliverance Churches**, a non-denominational **Oneness** organization. Brown entered the ministry from the corporate environment, where he was a marketing executive. He held the Bachelor of Science degree in Business Administration, Master of Arts in Sociology, Doctor of Philosophy in Education, and a Doctor of Theology.

After leaving the Catholic Church, Brown was, for a time, an African Methodist Episcopal Church itinerant preacher. He began evangelizing within that denomination in 1970, and for the next five years travelled throughout the East Coast. By 1975, he had established an independent congregation in Harlem, the Salvation and Deliverance Church, which remained under the AME Church. Brown kept his credentials with that denomination until 1981, when he left to establish the new neo-Pentecostal body.

Brown recorded two preaching albums and wrote several books during his ministerial career. His "Hour of Deliverance" radio broadcast was heard in forty-one states in America and forty-six foreign countries. His teaching thoroughly aligned with the tenets of the Holiness movement with an emphasis on personal piety.

Bryant, John Richard 1946–

Considered the father of Neo-Pentecostal spirituality within the African Methodist Episcopal Church, in the mid 1960s, Bryant was a young seminary graduate who served in the Peace Corp in Liberia, West Africa. There he encountered "spirited" worship including healing, trances, and other expressions of spiritual power that led him to re-examine Scripture concerning the spiritual dimension he considered largely overlooked within African American Methodism. On returning to the United States, Bryant served in pastorates in Fall River, Massachusetts before moving to the St. Paul's AME congregation in Cambridge, Massachusetts where he incorporated his understanding of spiritual empowerment into his own ministry.

He infused the conspicuously Afro-centric AME liturgy, teaching, and social justice with an emphasis in Pentecostal spirituality, which he saw as a means of connecting his congregation to their black cultural roots in Africa.

With Bryant as pastor and with his wife, Rev. Cecilia Bryant, at his side in ministry, St. Paul's membership grew from two hundred to over three thousand members. In 1975, he left that congregation to assume the pastorate of Bethel AME in Baltimore, Maryland where his grandfather and father, an AME bishop, had served. By the time he took over that pulpit, the historic congregation's membership had dwindled to six hundred. Within two years, the congregation was over seven thousand, becoming the largest AME congregation in the nation and a catalyst for African-American neo-Pentecostalism.

Bryant served there until 1988, when he was elected bishop and assigned to the 14th Episcopal District, covering 101 churches in several West African countries. The 10th District, headquartered in Texas and comprised of over 250 churches, was added to Bryant's responsibilities in 1991. From there, he moved to the 5th Episcopal District covering California, the Midwest and the Pacific Northwest. Bryant currently serves as bishop of the 4th Episcopal District covering Canada, Illinois, Indiana, Michigan, Minnesota, North Dakota, South Dakota, Wisconsin, and India.

Bryant was born in Baltimore, MD, and earned his Bachelor of Arts degree from Morgan State College (now University), a Master of Theology from Boston University School of Theology, and a Doctor of Ministry degree from Colgate Rochester Divinity School. Bryant served in the Peace Corps in Liberia, West Africa from 1965 until 1967.

His acknowledged leadership in the broader AME church and the black community sees him serving on boards of numerous civil, educational, and religious groups including the Board of Regents of Morgan State University, the National Committee of Black Churchmen, and the board of the World Methodist Council on Evangelism.

Burruss, King Hezekiah 1881–1963

The first president of the National Convention of the **Churches of God Holiness,** was born in Louisiana. In his early years he had been affiliated with the **Church of God in Christ** when it was a body within the Holiness movement. He left that body (probably during the schism between **Charles Harrison Mason** and **Charles Price Jones** over the issue of tongues as initial evidence) to join the Church of Christ (Holiness) where he first served as a minister under **Charles Price Jones**. He established his first congregation, Bethlehem Church of God, Holiness, in 1912 as a congregation within Jones's organization after Jones sent him to Atlanta to establish a church there. By 1920, he had also established a second congregation in Norfolk, Virginia.

After clashing with Jones over personal rather than doctrinal issues, Burruss founded a new congregation and the Churches of God Holiness. He remained with his Atlanta, Georgia congregation until his death in 1963. He was a separatist who declared that there was only one right church—the Church of God. He had standing offer of $40,000 for anyone that could show that the Bible recognized any other church other than the Church of God. During his lifetime, Burruss was the only bishop in the denomination. At least one prominent Holiness leader, **Ligthtfoot Solomon Michaux,** founder of the Gospel spreading church, was ordained under his ministry

Burruss died in Atlanta. At his death, he was succeeded by his son, **Titus Paul Burruss.**

Burruss, Titus Paul Sr. 1910–1999

Second president and General Overseer and the son of **King Hezekiah Burruss**, the founder of the of **Churches of God Holiness, USA** was born in Louisiana, but moved with his family to Atlanta, Georgia as a young boy and later served in his father's congregation. On his father's death in 1964, the younger Burruss took over the lead post and served until his own death in 1999. Following his father's legacy, the son continued the same rigid leadership style. One of his major contributions to the denomination was the institution of the Uniform Policy Manual (UPM). At his death in Atlanta, he was succeeded by Theodore Roosevelt McBride.

Butler, Keith 1951–

The founder and president of the more than 20,000-member Word of Faith International Christian Center in Southfield, a nondenominational, Charismatic congregation he started in 1978 with sixty people. The Kenneth Hagin protégé and 1978 graduate of Hagin's Rhema Bible Training Center was born was born and raised in Detroit.

Ordained in 1974, Butler is also a graduate of the University of Michigan and holds diplomas from Canada Christian College. He also serves as pastor of Faith Christian Center in Smyrna, Georgia, a 2,000-member church, Faith 4 Life in Dallas, Texas founded in 2011, and Word of Life in Brussels, Belgium.

Butler started a local radio broadcast in 1979, and in that same year organized the Word of Faith Bible Training Center. By 2000, his Word of Faith International Ministers Association had grown to include 600 congregations across the United States and in several foreign countries including Brazil and the United Kingdom.

Butler, who became a Republican in 1982, has been active in presidential campaigns, working to get African Americans to vote for Ronald Reagan and George H.W. Bush. In 1989, he won a seat on the Detroit City Council, becoming the first black Republican to do so since World War II. He ran for United States Senate in 2006 but was defeated in the primary. In 2008, he replaced Chuck Yob as a Republican National Committee member from Michigan.

His activism is not limited to electoral politics. His support for conservative causes includes serving on the Executive Board of John Hagee's Christians United for Israel. Butler chaired an effort by Republicans to support the controversial election of justice, Clarence Thomas, to the Supreme Court. In 1991 he helped launch the Coalition for the Restoration of the Black Family, and partnered with Lou Sheldon, president of the Traditional Values Coalition, to lead a group of African-American pastors in opposing legalization of same-sex marriage.

In 2011, Butler installed his son, Andre to succeed him as senior pastor of his Michigan congregation, but remains presiding bishop over the more than thirty Word of Faith churches while pastoring Faith 4 Life congregations in Round Rock and Dallas, Texas, and Word of Faith Bible Training Center in Round Rock which he started in 2008. Butler has written several books, including best sellers in the conservative Charismatic Christian Community.

Bynum, Juanita 1958–

The televangelist, author, and recording artist has been one of the most visible African-American Pentecostal women preachers in the United States. Bynum, the daughter of a **Church of God in Christ** minister, grew up in Chicago where she and her family were members of a local COGIC congregation and her father served as an elder. She attended high school at the denomination's **Saint's Academy** in Lexington, Kentucky where she was a classmate with several young men who would go on to become significant COGIC leaders. Soon after graduation, she started preaching in nearby churches and at revivals.

By twenty-one, Bynum was in a physically abusive marriage that shortly ended in divorce. That experience left her depressed. She subsequently suffered from an eating disorder and was hospitalized for mental illness. Following that, Bynum left the church for several years. After living on public assistance, she returned to Chicago, worked as a beautician, then as a flight attendant, before moving to New York and returning to the church and the ministry.

In 1996, famed pastor and televangelist, **Thomas Dexter (T. D.) Jakes,** invited Bynum to attend one of his singles' conferences. In 1997, she published her best-selling autobiographical book, *No More Sheets*. A year later, she was invited to be a keynote speaker for the annual event. The success of her autobiography and television exposure with major televangelists such as Jakes and Trinity Broadcasting Network founders, Paul and Jan Crouch, quickly pushed her into the limelight. Within a short while, "Prophetess" Juanita Bynum, as she became known, had become one of the most recognizable fixtures of televangelism among Black Pentecostal women.

In 2001, Bynum married Bishop Thomas W. Weeks III, pastor of the Global Destiny Church in Washington DC, and a year later, the couple staged an elaborate one million dollar televised wedding. By 2008, however, this marriage also ended in divorce after a public, physical altercation in a major Atlanta hotel parking lot. Though the highly publicized dissolution of her marriage left her reputation tainted with some followers, Bynum used the media exposure of the incident and following scandal to turn her ministry into a vehicle to campaign against domestic violence, regaining at least part of her following.

Throughout her ministry career, Bynum, founder and president of Juanita Bynum Ministries in Waycross, Georgia has addressed crowds of 50,000–100,000 as a keynote speaker at international conferences and events, and has preached in many of the largest, well-respected pulpits in America and around the world, as well as been a frequent radio and television guest and host. The author's published works include *My Spiritual Inheritance, Matters of The Heart* (which sold 500,000 copies in less than a year), *No More Sheets*, and several others regularly top bestseller lists. Bynum has been featured in popular black magazines such as *Essence* and *Ebony*, and has appeared on the front covers of the leading Christian magazines, *Charisma, Ministries Today*, and *Spirit Led Woman*. The multi-talented Bynum has also combined her musical and entrepreneurial skills to branch into the field of music recording, establishing Sonflower Records to showcase her music ventures.

Further Reading:

Bynum, Juanita. *No More Sheets: The Truth about Sex*. Lanham, MD: Pneuma Life, 1998.
———. *No More Sheets: Starting Over*. Shippensburg, PA: Destiny Image, 2010.

C

Caesar, Roderick R., Sr. 1900–1999

Founding pastor of Bethel Gospel Tabernacle Church in Jamaica Queens in 1932. Caesar was born in the capital city of Castries in St. Lucia, West Indies. He migrated to New York at age sixteen where he joined the US Army transport Merchant Marines and traveled around the world. Caesar was converted in 1923, and joined the Harlem Pentecostal congregation where the revival had been held. He soon became a Sunday school teacher and deacon, and preached in street evangelistic services before being ordained.

In 1928, he launched a congregation, Bethel Gospel Mission, in Jamaica, Long Island. The work began with cottage prayer meetings from house to house, then moved to a storefront facility, before moving into the facility which came to be known as Bethel Gospel Tabernacle. In 1944, Caesar married his wife, Gertrude Brown, an ordained minister who left the congregation she was pastoring in Ohio to join him in his ministry.

Though the majority of the congregation was African American, it also attracted a significant number of Norwegian Americans and a sizable representation of Jewish-Christian converts. In 1947, Caesar organized Bethel Bible Institute, the first Bible Institute in Jamaica, Queens. A year later, he began the "Full Gospel Hour" radio broadcast which is still an outreach of Bethel. The radio broadcast drew attendance at the church's evangelist meetings that were sometimes so large that it set up a "Big Green Gospel Tent," which became locally famous for healing and prayer services. In 1951, Caesar founded the Bethel G.T. Federal Credit Union, which has indeed been a blessing to many.

In 1962, Caesar was elevated to the office of bishop in the **United Pentecostal Council of the Assemblies of God Inc**. From 1964, he served the Eastern District and later as the second president—or, National Bishop—of the denomination. In 1986, he resigned from that position to serve as Bishop Emeritus of the District and National Councils. In the early 1970s Caesar was one of those who joined with presiding bishop, **James O. Patterson, Sr.** to form the **Black Pentecostal Fellowship of North America**.

At his mother's death in 1978, Caesar's son Roderick Jr., who was serving as pastor of Calvary Full Gospel Church, came to serve as Assistant Pastor at Bethel. Six years later, Bishop Caesar, turned the reins of the local congregation over to his son, Roderick Jr. For the last nine years of his life, Caesar was blind, yet quoted Scripture by heart and carried out an active telephone ministry, praying for and counseling those who called. At his father's death, Roderick Jr. took over as pastor of Bethel Gospel Tabernacle.

Caesar, Shirley Ann 1938–

Gospel music singer, songwriter, recording artist, and pastor, known as "First Lady of Gospel Music." Born in Durham, North Carolina where she has lived most of her life, Evangelist **Shirley Caesar** began singing in her **Mount Calvary Holy Churches of America** congregation at an early age. Her father, Big Jim Caesar, who led the family group, died in 1950 of a fatal seizure, leaving her semi-invalid mother to raise thirteen children. Caesar started touring as a gospel soloist with evangelist Reverend Leroy Johnson. She began recording at the age of thirteen. A year earlier, she felt called to preach. It was not until 1961, however, that Caesar began incorporating the sermonette technique into her musical routine.

Her professional singing career began when she was eighteen with the popular gospel group The Caravans, under leader Albertina Walker. Caesar performed with The Caravans from 1958 until 1966. After eight years with them, Caesar left to organize her own group, The Caesar Singers. Recording executives often approached Caesar to "crossover" into rhythm and blues, but she adamantly refused throughout her career. Though she had started North Carolina Central College as a young woman, Caesar interrupted her studies to join The Caravans. She later returned to college to complete her education, graduating from Shaw University in Raleigh, South Carolina with a Bachelor of Science degree in Business Administration in 1984. She also studied at Duke Divinity School in Durham, North Carolina and received honorary doctorates from Shaw University and Southeastern University in Lakeland, Florida.

Caesar, who has sung for every US president since Jimmy Carter, has released over forty albums, and appeared in three gospel musicals, *Mama I Want to Sing, Sing: Mama 2,* and *Born to Sing: Mama 3.* Her work won her eleven Grammy Awards, thirteen Stellar Awards, eighteen Dove Awards, an Essence Award, McDonald's Golden Circle Lifetime Achievement Award, the National Association for the Advancement of Colored People (NAACP) Achievement Award, the Lifetime Achievement Award from the Society of European Stage Authors and Composers, as well as induction into the Gospel Music Hall of Fame. Caesar was inducted into the North Carolina Music Hall of Fame in 2010.

In 1990, Caesar accepted the co-pastorate of the 1,500-member Mount Calvary Word of Faith Church in nearby Raleigh, North Carolina with her husband, gospel singer and Bishop **Harold I. Williams,** whom she married in 1983. The two served as co-pastors for two decades and also made several gospel recordings together. In 2000, when Williams stepped down, Caesar assumed the role of pastor. From this vantage, she also operates Shirley Caesar Outreach Ministries, concentrating her efforts on housing and other care for the poor and elderly in the Raleigh and Durham communities. She also served a term on the City Council in 1987.

Pastor Shirley, as her parishioners call her, has made televised appearances at some of the most prominent venues in the United States including the Disney World Night of Joy and a White House performance for President George Bush.

Further Reading:

Caesar, Shirley. *The Lady, the Melody, and the Word: The Inspirational Story of the First Lady of Gospel Music.* Nashville, TN: Thomas Nelson, 1998.

Cainhoy Miracle Revival Corporation

A Oneness Pentecostal Denomination founded in 1969 by **Helen Smith,** a former member of the **Church of Lord Jesus Christ of the Apostolic Faith,** that is the only **woman-led organization to come out of that denomination.** In 1968, Smith began with a small home group in Cainhoy, South Carolina. The revival soon outgrew the home where it was meeting and the group relocated to a small shack in the same town. Since COOLJC did not acknowledge the preaching ministry of women to preach, Smith was asked to discontinue the revival services by denominational leaders. When she persisted and asserted that the revival was God's doing and she could not stop it, Smith and eleven others who were working with her, were excommunicated from the denomination.

The group kept meeting, and a year later Smith was ordained as the Apostle of the Cainhoy Miracle Revival Center. Beginning with that single congregation, Smith used an evangelistic team to hold revivals in other cities in the region. Smith led the denomination for thirty years, and by the time of her death, the group established fifteen churches in the United States of America and two churches in Trinidad, West Indies.

Smith died in 1999, and Bishop Larry Brown, the pastor of the Summerville Miracle Revival Center (Path of Life Ministries) in Summerville, South Carolina congregation, stepped up to the helm of the body. Several years before her death, Smith had named Brown as her successor and had consecrated him as a bishop in 1996.

Further Reading:

Smith, Helen. *You're Going to Be Somebody.* Mobile, AL: Gazelle, 1999.

Campbell, Lawrence G. 1931–

In 1950 the founding and first presiding bishop of the **Bible Way Church of Our Lord Jesus Christ**, moved his family from Danville, Virginia to Washington DC, joining the Bible Way Church congregation pastored by **Smallwood E. Williams**. After working in several lay ministries within the congregation and participating in street evangelistic Williams sent Campbell to Danville to start his ministry, beginning with several months of preaching in a tent. From this work, Campbell started his congregation, Bible Way Cathedral, in 1953 in Danville. He rose through the ranks of Williams's organization, finally achieving the position of bishop.

He received his Associate of Arts degree from Virginia Seminary and College, his Bachelor of Arts degree from Averett College in Danville, his Master of Science degree from North Carolina A&T State University, and his Honorary Doctorate of Divinity from Virginia Seminary and College in Lynchburg, Virginia.

Campbell was among the few African-American Pentecostal leaders who actively embraced the American Civil Rights Movement. He marched with Dr. Martin Luther King Jr., and lead marches in Danville. Embracing practical ecumenism in 1961, he fought with other clergy leaders in his city from various denominations for the integration of the Danville Public Library and public accommodations. In 1963 his wife Gloria was beaten for protesting against segregation, and Campbell was arrested several times for civil disobedience. An activist inside the church as well as outside, Campbell began the unprecedented practice of ordaining women to the office of elder within the Bible Way organization.

After the death of Bishop Williams, leaders of Bible Way Church of Our Lord World-Wide signed The Order of Succession and Constitution, stating that both Campbell and **Huie Rogers** would each serve a three-year trial term as presiding bishop before the vote for the Williams's permanent successor, with Campbell holding the office from 1991–1994, then Rogers serving for three years. At the end of Rogers's term, however, he called for a sabbath year of no voting, but when the majority of bishops refused to accept the resolution, the denomination split. Both factions, however, continued to represent themselves as the original church. Campbell served as the chief apostle and presiding bishop of the **Bible Way Church of Our Lord Jesus Christ** from 1998 to 2006, leading over three hundred churches in the United States, England, Africa, and the Caribbean.

When **Cornelius Showell**, son of **Winfield Showell**, a founding bishop of **Bible Way World Wide**, was elected to preside, Campbell retained his position as the presiding bishop of the Virginia State Diocese, a position he has held since 1974.

Cannady, Leroy H. Sr. 1922–

Third presiding bishop emeritus of the **Way of the Cross Church of Christ, International** for twenty years until 2015, becoming the only person outside of the Brooks family to hold the lead position. Within the Oneness Pentecostal denomination founded by **Henry Chauncy Brooks,** Cannady has served as founding pastor of the Refuge Way of the Cross Church of Christ, Inc. in Baltimore, Maryland since 1958.

He was born in Franklinton, North Carolina and by age twelve had been converted to Christian faith, baptized in the Oneness formula of Jesus' Name by Brooks and had received the Pentecostal experience of Holy Spirit baptism. That same year, Cannady was serving as Superintendent of Sunday School and assistant to Brooks.

Ordained a deacon in 1949, Cannady became a licensed minister in 1950, and was ordained an elder two years later, and was consecrated bishop in 1970. Cannady served as diocesan bishop for South Carolina, Georgia and Texas for nine years and was consecrated as vice presiding bishop of the denomination in 1982. He assumed the post of presiding bishop in August 1985, after the death of the founder's brother John Luke Brooks. After his retirement, the founder's son, Alphonso Brooks, took the helm of the organization.

Cannady received two honorary Doctor of Divinity degrees, the first from Grace Apostolic College, Inc., School of Religious Education in Niles, Ohio in 1986, and then from Apostolic Christian College, Washington DC in 1999.

Further Reading:

Cannady, Leroy H. *Give Me This Mountain—A Leap of Faith.* S.l.: s.n., s.d.

Carr, Randolph Adolphus 1895–1970

Founder and first presiding bishop of the **Church of God In Christ Jesus Apostolic**. Carr was born in Nevis, West Indies of East Indian and Afro-Caribbean descent. After the death of Randolph's father, he was reared by his grandfather. He migrated to the United States in 1912 at the age of seventeen, where he worked as a shipping clerk and began his ministry of evangelizing and preaching in 1917. However, he did not become a naturalized citizen until 1948. On coming to the United States, Carr first became affiliated with the Oneness denomination, the **Pentecostal Assemblies of the World,** through the ministry of **Susan Lightford** while living in New York City and working as a shipping clerk. He broke with PAW and first joined the Emmanuel Church in Jesus Christ. At some point, he joined the Trinitarian **Church of God in Christ** under **Charles H. Mason** who, in 1934, and pastored the Bible Way Holiness Church located in Chesapeake, Virginia.

In the mid-1930s a "Mother" Mayfield started a church with five members in her house in Baltimore, Maryland. She called Mason for help and he sent Carr. After helping Mayfield with Church of God #3, Carr started holding tent meetings, then purchased a house, remolded to establish his own congregation, known as Church of God in Christ #6.

Twelve years later, Carr reaffirmed his Oneness beliefs and severed ties with COGIC to establish the body which came to be the **Church of God in Christ Jesus Apostolic** in 1947 in Baltimore, Maryland. He renamed his local congregation, "Rehoboth Church of God in Christ Jesus Apostolic."

In 1965, after several years of living as a divorcee, Carr married a woman who was also divorced. The marriage, which was in direct opposition to church teaching, led to a schism within the denomination. Following it, Bishop **Monroe R. Saunders** led a contingent of fellow bishops, pastors and congregation out of Carr's organization to form the **United Church of God in Christ Jesus Apostolic**.

Carr presided over COGICJA, Inc. until his death. By that time, there were congregations throughout the United States, Canada, Jamaica, Bermuda, and Great Britain.

He died in Baltimore, Maryland. He was succeeded as pastor and presiding bishop by William S. Barnes.

Carter, James H. 1950–

The presiding prelate of United Cornerstone Churches International, an organization of more than fifty churches that he founded with Dr. Tony Horne. The native of Caswell County, North Carolina earned a Bachelor of Arts degree from The Bible Institute in Orlando, Florida, and received a Doctorate of Divinity degree from Shiloh Theological Seminary, Stafford, Virginia.

Carter founded Cornerstone Church of Christ in April 1975, and has served as senior pastor for thirty-nine years. He also founded Faith Deliverance Mission of Lexington, North Carolina in 1978 and the Full Gospel Church of Jesus Christ in Summerton, South Carolina in 1980. He is also the co-founder of the United Cornerstone School of Divinity, and also works with the NC Theological University.

Carter was commissioned to preach in 1969 by Bishop Preston Graves of the Smyrna Church of Christ in Reidsville, North Carolina. Previous to assuming the pastorate, he served that congregation as youth director, superintendent of Sunday School, financial secretary and assistant pastor as he also worked as a driver for a delivery service.

Carter was one of the first ministers to affiliate with the **United Way of the Cross Churches of Christ International** after it split from the Way of the Cross Church of Christ and remained with that denomination for thirty years. During his tenure, he served as assistant general secretary, then as general secretary. He was consecrated as bishop in 1986 as well as diocesan bishop of the North Carolina/South Carolina Diocese and later that year was appointed vice presiding bishop. In 1998 Bishop Carter was appointed as Archbishop and Chairperson of the Board of Bishops.

In June 2003, Carter became the presiding prelate, and chief executive officer of the Board of Apostles, and Board of Directors of the **United Way of the Cross Churches International**. Within two years, however, he left that body to co-found UCCCI and quickly rose to become the chief apostle of a newly formed organization. By 2006 UCCCI has chartered over forty-seven churches in North Carolina, South Carolina, Pennsylvania, Maryland, Washington DC, Virginia, West Indies and Africa.

Along with his ecclesial responsibilities, Carter was involved with the vice president of the Thomasville, North Carolina, National Association for the Advancement of Colored People (NAACP) Treasurer of the Ministers United for Christ, Thomasville Medical Center, Habitat for Humanity, Salvation Army, and the Martin Luther King Gospel Fest. This work led Carter to receive numerous local and national accommodations from civic and religious organizations including the 2005 NAACP President's Award.

Carter, Marshall 1920–2003

Marshall Carter organized and incorporated the United Churches of God in Christ Incorporated of Georgia as an independent fellowship of congregations that would "report to" and remain under the authority of the **Church of God in Christ**, headquartered in Memphis, Tennessee.

He was born in 1920 as Junior Carter in Lilburn, Georgia. As a young man, he had several jobs, including farming, working as a mechanic, and as a laundry hand. It was not until he joined the United States Military that he formally assumed his father's first name: Marshall.

In 1952 Carter came into the **Church of God in Christ**. He accepted his call to ministry in 1956, and first served as an ordained deacon, Sunday School superintendent, and musician before being ordained as an elder in 1959. That same year he established his first congregation, the Lynnwood Park Church of God in Christ in Brookhaven, Georgia.

In 1974 he was appointed superintendent of the Lynnwood Park district. Five years following that appointment, when then presiding bishop **James Oglethorpe Patterson, Sr.** dissolved that jurisdiction, pastors within the district were directed to align themselves with another jurisdiction. Instead, since several independent pastors have aligned themselves with his fellowship, but were not officially aligned with COGIC, Carter broke "ties" with the parent body. That year, the **Church of God in Christ,** Incorporated of Georgia was dissolved and the United Churches of God in Christ, Inc. was formed.

In 1980 Carter was elevated to the bishopric and formally installed as the first chief apostle and presiding bishop of the United Churches of God in Christ, Inc. Carter served in that position until his death.

Charles Harrison Mason System of Bible Colleges

A post-secondary educational program conceived by former **Church of God in Christ** presiding bishop, **James. O. Patterson, Sr.**, in 1971. The system, which is distinct from the C. H. Mason Theological Seminary, comes under the auspices of the national church and provides a comprehensive training effort within the denomination through distinct educational institutions on campuses of various sites across the United States that award certificates and associate level degrees in theology and ministry. Each school is established and is under the control of its jurisdiction.

The aim of the system is to provide colleges a standard, unified curriculum for training of laypersons and credential holders that enhances the offerings available through individual efforts of these schools. Dr. A. J. Hines of Houston, Texas, developed the protocols for the system and organized a pilot school, the Charles Harrison Mason Bible College and Institute in Houston. Shortly, other schools, modeled after the Houston project, were developed in various cities around the nation. By 1973 the denomination began offering courses in Memphis' three jurisdictions—the Tennessee Headquarters jurisdiction, Tennessee 4th jurisdiction, and the Tennessee 5th jurisdiction.

In 1998 the three-jurisdictional Bible Colleges merged to form the C. H. Mason Bible College, the only undergraduate level, degree-granting institution serving the denomination, on the campus of the denominational headquarters in that city, with the three jurisdictional bishops serving as co-presidents of the school. In 2000, efforts began to merge that institution with the newly proposed All Saints Bible College. The merger was completed in 2002. Dr. Johnson served as the first president of All Saints Bible College. Currently, the system includes nearly forty schools across the United States.

Cherry, John A. Sr. 1939–

One of African Methodist Episcopal Zion Church's earliest and most prominent proponents of Charismatic spirituality, John A. Cherry's suburban Washington DC, Full Gospel AMEZ congregation grew out of a twenty-person Bible study started in his home in 1981. Within a year, the congregation was meeting in a storefront facility, having grown to eighty-one members. It tripled again to 243 by 1983, moving into a soon overcrowded "house front" that held three services each Sunday. Two years later, the church had purchased a school building, had 1,500 members, and had established a Christian School. By 1989, eight years after its founding, the church had 6,000 members, ultimately reaching the present estimated 27,000 members and becoming, for some time, the largest congregation in Prince George's County, Maryland, the wealthiest black county in the United States.

Along with Pentecostal style worship, Cherry was known for his controversial polemics against the hierarchy of the episcopal structure of the AMEZ church. As an elder in the denomination, he incurred the ire of denominational leaders for ordaining ministers on his own–a role reserved for bishops. By 1999, however, Cherry's disenfranchisement with denominational leaders grew so large that his then 24,000-member congregation broke from the parent body. He renamed the church, "From the Heart Ministries."

In the battle that followed, the denomination took possession of a majority of nearly forty-nine million dollars in church controlled assets, including cash, a national television ministry, two buildings, a Lear jet, and an estimated 120 acres of land.

Cherry has since developed his ministry into an organization that includes eighteen churches in the United States and over 170 congregations worldwide. Additionally, the local congregation has over one hundred full-time employees, including those affiliated with the school and television broadcasts on eleven stations.

Cherry's contentious existence within and prickly departure from the AMEZ Church hampered the promulgation of the Neo-Pentecostal movement within its ranks and the number of congregations remains relatively small.

Christ Holy Sanctified Church

In 1903 members of a white body, Christ's Sanctified Holy Church, based in Jennings, Louisiana, traveled to West Lake, Louisiana to evangelize black members of the Colored Methodist Episcopal Church, intent on bringing the Holiness message of sanctification to Christians who could not testify to the experience. A year later, the work had been so successful that workers organized a separate Colored Church South, soon changing the name to Christ's Sanctified Holy Church Colored. Over the years, members dropped the word "Colored" and, while the two groups remained separate, reclaimed the name of the parent body whose doctrine was almost identical.

Christ Sanctified Holy Church Colored was chartered in Louisiana in 1904 by Joseph Lynch and others who had been excommunicated from the CME Church on embracing Holiness doctrine. By early 1906—before news of the outpouring of the Holy Spirit at Azusa Street had reached the small community—members reportedly had experienced an equally powerful outpouring with Pentecostal Spirit baptism.

The denomination was incorporated in 1910 in Lake Charles as a Pentecostal body by **Judge and Sarah King**, who had earlier established a congregation in Keachie, Louisiana, near Shreveport. Both were converted in the Baptist church, later joined the Methodist church, and by 1890 were part of the Holiness movement. Once assuming leadership of the newly merged organization, King juxtaposed the terms "Sanctified" and "Holy," changing the name to Christ Holy Sanctified Church to differentiate it from the white body. Besides race, a major issue separating the two groups was the observance of the sacraments. The CSHC holds classical Pentecostal understandings of Holy Spirit baptism. The CHSC holds that Holy Spirit baptism adds to a believer's power, and promotes speaking in tongues as the single *initial* evidence.

While news of the Azusa Street outpouring was late in reaching King's group, news of this "localized outpouring" somehow reached the West Coast group. On his way to Tennessee, **William J. Seymour**, leader of the Los Angeles revival, visited the Louisiana group, many of whom had experienced Pentecostal Spirit baptism, to encourage and teach them. After 1915 King moved into East Texas setting up churches. As early as 1916–17 he had moved to Beaumont and Houston, Texas. In 1918 King went to Los Angeles, and in 1923, he travelled through California setting up churches. During his sojourn, he experienced heavy religious and racial prejudice in the area to the point where the Oroville church building was burned down. King moved on to Fresno, California. Then, in 1925, the Kings moved to Oakland, California after setting up churches in San Francisco.

After the death of King's, his son Ulysses became senior bishop. Guidelines for the church were developed in 1946.

In 1949, a year-long revival occurred in the body that spread throughout the southeast region and added large numbers to the church, especially in Texas and Louisiana. Christ Holy Sanctified Church of America, Inc. has congregations in the United States, Mexico, and West Africa.

Ulysses was succeeded by Elmer McBride who served until 1991. James E. Williams served from 1991 to 1998. Billy R. Brown followed him, serving from 1998 to 2005. In 2006, Georgia E. Jones assumed office and served until her death in 2008.

Statistics of the Christ Holy Sanctified Church are difficult to obtain. By 1957, however, there were 600 members in thirty churches. Current headquarters are in Fort Worth, Texas where the denomination maintains Christ Holy Sanctified School.

Further Reading:

King, Judge, ed. *Discipline of Christ Holy Sanctified Church of America.* Oakland, CA: Christ's Holy Sanctified Church, n.d.

Christ's Sanctified Holy Church

A denomination within the Holiness movement that was established in West Lake, Louisiana as the Christ's Sanctified Holy Church Colored in 1904 by C. E. Rigmaiden, Dempsey Perkins, A. C. Mitchell, Lizzie Pleasant, and James Briller, members of the Colored Methodist Episcopal Church. A year earlier, this group had been pulled out of their Methodist denomination to form the Colored Church South, after a schism arose regarding their embracing of the doctrine of sanctification shared with them by members of a white group of that same name that had spread out from the eastern shore of Virginia. Over the years, the black group dropped the distinction colored from their name and adopted the name of the parent group while remaining separated.

Members of the pacifist group do not practice water baptism, holding that the baptism of the Holy Spirit is sufficient, and over time, adopting the belief that such Spirit baptism is associated with speaking in tongues. It also does not practice communion, believing that no act of ritual is necessary for salvation. The major distinction from the white parent group is that ministers within the black church receive salaries.

Headquarters of the black CSHC group is in Jennings, Louisiana. There are approximately 1,000 members in sixty congregation primarily throughout Louisiana and Texas. The group allows men and women to function equally within the church.

Christian Methodist Episcopal Church, Neo-Pentecostalism in

The rise of the Charismatic Movement within the Christian Methodist Episcopal (CME) Church came into place with the development of the Department of Evangelism. In 1922, the General Conference of the Church enacted recommendation of the College of Bishops to establish the department and authorized the college to appoint a connectional leader. The first person to hold the position was Rev. R. O. Langford, a pastor who had acquired a reputation for charismatic preaching, and had become a noted revivalist within the denomination. During this early period, Langford and his immediate successor, Reverend J. M. Reid, functioned as connectional revivalists, holding mass crusades throughout the connection of the CME Church.

William Yancy Bell, a follower of Marcus Garvey, was a Professor Old Testament at Howard University when he was elected bishop in 1938, becoming one of the most prominent Charismatic leaders in the CME Church. The pastor of the historic Williams Institutional CME Church in Harlem, New York, had earned a PhD from Yale University in 1924, was gifted in linguistics, and spoke several languages. Bell possessed the gifts of *glossalalia*, interpretation of tongues, discernment and prophecy. He was noted for his powerful prayers, as well as sermons that resulted in congregations experiencing a visitation of the Holy Spirit.

Despite these early overtures, it would be sometime before any evidence of wider Charismatic renewal made its presence felt in the CME Church. In 1966, Nathaniel Linsey, a civil rights activist in the Alabama Christian Movement for Human Rights in Birmingham and the Southern Christian Leadership Conference, was elected as General Secretary of Evangelism, and twelve years later was elected bishop. Prior to being elected General Secretary of Evangelism, Linsey had pastored in geographical areas that were conducive to the presence of charismata. He served, for example, in an area of South Carolina that was saturated with the Gullah culture. This openness to Charismatic phenomena was evident in the worship at Charleston's Vanderhorst Memorial CME Church. Linsey's most prominent charismatic influence was Bell, while Linsey served as a pastor in Halifax County, Virginia. Under Bell's influence, Linsey introduced local CME congregations to the notion of the visitation of the Holy Spirit. Some suggest that Linsey's emphasis on the charismatic gifts and success as the General Secretary of Evangelism resulted in his election to the episcopacy in 1978.

The presence of spiritual gifts became widespread through the work of Raymond Williams who was elected General Secretary of Evangelism in 1982. Williams, a pastor in the Florida Conference was introduced to the charismatic work of the Spirit through his service as a musician to several Florida Pentecostal churches He was also influenced, however, by other Charismatic CME persons such as Rev. Mary Green of St. Paul CME Church in Gainesville, Florida. Green testified to having died physically but being brought back to life. She would anoint people with oil and lay hands on then so that they would be slain in the Spirit. Another influence on Williams was Mary Howard, a revivalist from of Thomson, Georgia who became known for eating raw eggs before she preached, possessing the gift of *glossolalia* and sticking her finger in her ear and hollering while she preached and people were being slain in the Spirit.

J. G. Brathwaite and his wife Trudie were from the Dominican Republic. Brathwaite served as the presiding elder of the New York district during the 1950s. His wife was an herbalist who experienced trances during district conferences and anointed people through the laying of hands.

Williams became the organizer of the CME Church's Holy Spirit Conferences begun in 1983. He sent correspondences to seventy charismatic CME pastors. The first such conference was hosted at St. Paul CME Church in Savannah, Georgia by the Henry Delaney. It involved three days of spirited praise, worship services speaking, praying and singing in tongues, holy laughter, holy dancing, people being slain in the Spirit, prophetic proclamations, and workshops with dialogue on the Holy Spirit in the life of the church. The success of these conferences has been pivotal in spreading Charismatic spirituality across the connectional church, and regional Holy Spirit conferences have been formed.

As a result, regional leaders have risen in prominence and are sought out for local revival services that advertise through miracles and the baptism of the Holy Spirit. Raymond Williams emerged in Philadelphia, Pennsylvania; Jerome McNeil of Christian Chapel Temple of Faith came to prominence in Dallas, Texas and built his church to more than 5,400 members during his twenty-one years as senior pastor. Henry Delaney and the St. Paul CME Church in Savannah, Georgia conducted revivals in twenty-six states and three foreign countries, and grew his congregation to more than 5,000 members. After he retired from the pastorate, he founded H. R. Delaney Ministries. Samuel Fitten of St. Matthew CME Church of Milwaukee, Wisconsin also gained prominence.

Further Reading:

Othal, H. Lakey. *The History of the CME Church REVISED*. Memphis, Tennessee: CME, 1998.

Love, Henry Whelchel Jr. "My Chains Fell Off: Heart Religion in the African American Methodist Tradition." In *How Long This Road: Race, Religion and the Legacy of C. Eric Lincoln*, edited by Alton Pollard and Love Henry Whelchel, Jr., 203–31. New York: Palgrave MacMillan, 2003.

Christian, William 1856–1928

The founder of the **Church of the Living God (Christian Workers for Fellowship)** was born in Mississippi several years before Emancipation and reared as a slave during his earliest years. The mark left by the experience of slavery would be incorporated into the tenets on racial equality that were part of the structure of the body he founded. Prior to founding CWFF, Christian had been a Missionary Baptist pastor in Fort Smith, Arkansas and a colleague of **Charles Harrison Mason.**

Christian first preached under the label, "The Do-Right Church." After reportedly having a divine revelation in which God instructed him that Baptist doctrine was erroneous and sectarian, Christian was converted to the Holiness faith. Though he has also been a Freemason, after his conversion he came to hold that membership in secret societies such as the masons is incompatible with Holiness doctrine, and left that organization.

Christian founded the Church of the Living God in 1888 in Caine Creek, Arkansas near Wrightsville. Through his organization, he sought to popularize the restorationist teachings of Alexander Campbell and held that denominational terms such as Baptist and Methodist were unscriptural. He rejected popular conversion practices, such as the mourner's bench. He also taught that many of the biblical figures including Jesus, Abraham, David, Jeremiah, and Job were black. Yet, a central theme of Christian's theology was the rejection of racial prejudice.

At some point Christian was jailed for his pacifist leanings and opposition to the World War I. Christian served as the head of CWFF for almost forty years, until his death in Memphis, Tennessee at age seventy-one. After his death, his wife Ethel, who had served with her husband at the head of the organization, took over leadership.

Church in the Lord Jesus Christ of the Apostolic Faith

A Oneness Pentecostal denomination founded by Lenist Hunter as a breakaway group from **Sherrod Johnson**'s denomination, **Church of the Lord Jesus Christ of the Apostolic Faith.** The first congregation was founded in Hartsville, South Carolina in the fall of 1945.

Like its parent denomination, the group takes a strict stance against divorce as well as against women preachers, not even allowing them into the ranks of lay ministry as evangelists or missionaries as some black Pentecostals do. Dress for women members is tightly regulated as women are forbidden to wear make-up, jewelry or clothes that are revealing in any way. The denomination also holds to the classical Pentecostal understanding that the experience of Holy Spirit baptism with speaking in tongues is necessary for salvation.

After the death of Hunter in 1991, Bishop Joe C. Tisdale became Pastor and General Overseer of the church. There are sixteen congregations spread across South Carolina, Virginia, Washington DC, New York, Florida, North Carolina, Pennsylvania, Ohio, and Alabama. Hunter established a radio broadcast in 1956 that continues until today on several stations through the Faith Radio Network. The body also publishes a periodical, *The Whole Truth Gospel Herald*, and maintains a home for the elderly, The White House for Senior Citizens, near Hartsville.

Church of Christ Holiness unto the Lord, Inc.

A Trinitarian Pentecostal denominational founded by Major Solomon Bennett in 1926 in Savannah, Georgia, where the headquarters remains. In 1927, the denomination held its first assembly and elected Bennett as overseer. He served as presiding bishop until 1952.

After Bennett's death, **Benjamin Fields Colty** became presiding bishop. He served until 1959, when he broke with the organization and accepted the Oneness Pentecostal doctrine regarding the nature of the Godhead and the requirement for Christians to be baptized "in the name of Jesus" in order to be saved. The break was less caustic than many within the movement and Colty, and several others who agreed with him went on to form the **New Church of Christ Holiness unto the Lord of the Apostolic Faith**. With Colty's departure, Bishop James Kelly, who had been elected assistant general overseer in 1952, took office and serve until his death in 1979. In that year, Moses A. Lewis, overseer of the state of Georgia, became presiding overseer. He introduced several major changes into the denominational polity: including a system of tithing in which a local congregation sends funds to the General headquarters to support the work of the bishops and other leaders, removing restrictions of women preaching from the pulpit, and giving women full ministerial status as missionaries.

The COCHUTL has thirty-five congregations in Georgia, Florida, South Carolina, North Carolina, New York, and New Jersey, an accredited Bible School—The M. Solomon Bennett Bible Institute—and is affiliated with the **United Fellowship Convention of the Original Azusa Street Mission**. Adherents believe in the Holy Trinity, the Pentecostal baptism in the Holy Spirit with the evidence of speaking in tongues as the Spirit gives utterance, the gifts of the Holy Spirit, The Lord's Supper, water baptism using the Trinitarian formula, and the ritual of foot washing.

Church of Christ (Holiness) USA

The **Church of Christ (Holiness) USA**, (COCHUSA), arose out of intra-group conflict within the black Christian community rather than as a reaction to white racism. Yet, its founders, prominent Baptist pastors **Charles Price Jones** and **Charles Harrison Mason**, were keenly aware of the racial reality in which their black constituency found themselves, and used knowledge of Scripture and slave spirituality to keep the notion of God's intervention in that reality ever before them.

Both were highly respected in black Baptist circles and protégés of Arkansas Baptist College's founder, Elias Camp Morris, who was by this time president of the Arkansas Baptist Convention and later first president of the National Baptist Convention. Additionally, Jones was also a protégé of Charles Lewis Fisher, president of the college.

Jones had sought to bring the Mt. Helm congregation into the Holiness movement, but some members soundly objected. His attempt to promote the Holiness message within the General Baptist Association of Mississippi also aroused objections and friction within the group.

The two leaders joined **J. A. Jeter**, **D. J. Young**, and **W. S. Pleasant** to conduct revivals in Lexington, Mississippi and throughout the Mississippi Valley in which many experienced divine healing and several people testified to being sanctified. The group established new congregations and drew several existing congregations into a loose knit fellowship. During the Lexington meeting, the formal structure for the **Church of God in Christ** was set in place and throughout the following decade, the four men continued establishing new congregations and persuaded existing congregations to adopt Holiness doctrine of sanctification and join the ecumenical fellowship that included Baptists and a variety of Methodists congregations in the Mississippi Valley.

Jones began publishing the semi-monthly periodical, *Truth*, which promoted his understanding throughout the Mississippi Valley. Through such media and numerous revivals and camp meetings, Holiness ferment continued growing among black Baptist and Methodist congregations in the Valley. In 1897, Jones and Mason convened African Methodist Episcopal (AME), Colored Methodist Episcopal (CME), and Baptist clergy and lay Holiness proponents from nine Eastern states to refute denominational "slavery" and create a "communion of the Holy Spirit" among like-minded believers. Jones also insisted that these churches adopt biblical names rather than geographic or sentimental designations. These teachings were unacceptable to many of his Baptist colleagues who began to close their pulpits to Jones and his sympathizers. After a two-year battle, both Mt. Helm Baptist Church and the Jackson Baptist Association ousted Jones, and he and Mason formed the Christ Association of Mississippi of Baptized Believers.

While Jones was the catalyst in forming the association, Mason envisioned the name **"Church of God in Christ"** through what he contended was a direct revelation from God. Jones was elected overseer of the new organization and Mason was appointed overseer of the Tennessee work. Along with the Wesleyan understanding of sanctification, the two also adopted the radical Holiness stance on divine healing that, at first, precluded the use of medicine and conventional medical care.

Once the **Azusa Street Revival** broke out, Jones and Mason decided that Mason and his colleagues, Jeter, Young, and Pleasant, should go to Los Angeles to investigate whether what was occurring was a move of God or simply fanaticism. Mason returned not only convinced that the Pentecostal experience of Holy Spirit baptism was genuine, but having had the experience himself and insisting that it was normative for Holiness believers. Jones found this assertion untenable and insisted that, though he had never spoken in tongues, he had been baptized in the Holy Ghost in 1894, twelve years before the **Azusa Street Revival** was under way. By this, he simply meant that he had a supernatural infusion of God's power for holy living—not the Pentecostal experience coupled with glossolalia. Rather, he held to the understanding prominent within the Holiness movement that such baptism was an "inner work" that manifested itself in a consistent sanctified lifestyle.

Separation from Mason did not signal Jones's complete rejection of speaking in tongues. In his first tract on the issue, "The Work of the Holy Spirit in the Churches," based on an exposition of 1 Corinthians 12, in 1896, Jones validated the experience as genuine, but rejected insistence that all who received Holy Spirit baptism received tongues as initial evidence of such an infilling. For him, "every true believer is heir to the Holy Ghost...[and]...receiving of the Holy Spirit is an integral part of conversion."

Unable to agree, the two parted ways and a protracted legal battle ensued. Both Jones's and Mason's groups claimed rights to the name "**Church of God in Christ**" until 1915, when Mason, insisting that God had personally revealed the name to him, had it incorporated. Though the congregations that had maintained the Holiness distinctive began to use the name Church of Christ Holiness, a protracted court battle ensued. In 1920, when Jones's group lost the suit, it chartered the name **Church of Christ (Holiness) USA**.

Though Jones was a dynamic speaker and prolific hymn writer, the Church of Christ (Holiness) never showed the dynamic growth of its sister denomination. At its height, membership never totaled more than several hundred thousand, while the membership of the **Church of God in Christ** had grown to several million. In its more than one hundred year history, there have been four presiding bishops of the **Church of Christ (Holiness) USA**. Jones held the position from 1928 until his death in 1949. At that time, Rudd Conic assumed the position and held it until 1992, when, Maurice Bingham of Jackson, Mississippi too the position. In 1996, the leadership split so now a senior bishop and a president lead the denomination.

Another major early split within COCHUSA came in 1920 when Bishop **King Hezekiah Burruss** founded the **Churches of God, Holiness** in Atlanta, Georgia using the congregation he founded in that city in 1914 as headquarters. Within three years, there were twenty-two churches in eleven states, Cuba, the Canal Zone, and the British West Indies. By 1965, the younger body had grown to 25,600 members in thirty-two congregations mostly along the East Coast. The doctrine is identical to that of the parent body. A second group, the **Evangelical Church of Christ (Holiness)** was founded in 1947 by William C. Holman. This break was primarily administrative; the doctrine and practice are the same as that of the parent body. In 1990, membership in this group was approximately 500 members in four churches in Washington DC; Los Angeles, California; Omaha, Nebraska; and Denver, Colorado. There were also two mission churches in Los Angeles.

C

Church of Christ Written in Heaven

In 1913, **Jesse Clarence Blakely** was part of a group of other bishops who left the **Church of the Living God, Pillar and Ground of the Truth**, in part, because they objected to what he considered as CLGPGT liberal stance in allowing women to be preachers. The group formed the **First Born Church of the Living God**.

Blakely served as presiding bishop of that body from 1924 to 1939, when he broke from that denomination to form a new denomination headquartered in Jacksonville, Florida. At one point, the headquarters was moved to Waycross, Georgia. The denomination has more than seventy-five congregations in the Eastern United States, specifically in Florida, Georgia, Pennsylvania, New York, New Jersey, Ohio, and North Carolina.

Despite the founders' early position against women preaching, within the denominations women serves as pastors, holding leaders of half of the congregations, and are ordained as elders. No women, however, hold the rank of bishop.

After Blakely's death, Calvin Poller assumed the position of presider. He was followed by Thomas Brown Sr., who served into his late nineties. The current presiding bishop is Willie J. Jones.

Church of God and Saints of Christ

A Hebrew Israelite Holiness group established in Lawrence, Kansas, by **William Saunders Crowdy** in 1896 when Crowdy established congregations throughout the Midwestern and Eastern United States, and sent evangelist Albert Christian to organize locations in at least six African countries. The congregation later established locations in Cuba and the West Indies.

Three years after its founding, the group established its headquarters in Philadelphia. Four years later, the headquarters were relocated to Washington DC. It remained there for fourteen years. Crowdy died in 1908. Before his death, he named Joseph Wesley Crowdy, **William Henry Plummer** and Calvin Samuel Skinner as leaders of the denomination. As early as 1909, local branches of the organization severed their ties with the congregation, forming their own organizations. Today, among the groups not affiliated with Rabbi Jehu A. Crowdy Jr. are headquartered in Cleveland, Ohio and New Haven, Connecticut.

In 1921, William Henry Plummer moved the organization's headquarters to its permanent location in Suffolk, Virginia, which Crowdy purchased for that purpose in 1903. By 1936, the Church of God and Saints of Christ had more than 200 "tabernacles" and 37,000 members. At Plummer's death in 1931, he was succeeded by Calvin Skinner who served in office only a few months. He was succeeded later that same year by Howard Zebulun Plummer who was consecrated head of the organization and served for over forty years until 1975. At his death, Levi Solomon Plummer became the church's leader. Since 2001, the Church of God and Saints of Christ has been led by Rabbi Jehu A. Crowdy Jr., a great-grandson of William Saunders Crowdy.

Under the leadership of Levi Solomon Plummer, the congregation constructed a temple at its headquarters, Temple Beth El, in two phases, the first in 1980 and the second in 1987. The temple serves as a permanent location for national events, including the annual Passover celebration. Afterwards, the congregation began to rebuild the headquarters land in Virginia originally purchased by William S. Crowdy. As of 2005, it had fifty tabernacles in the United States, dozens in Africa, and one in Kingston, Jamaica. The organization also manages businesses and residential properties at its headquarters in Suffolk, Virginia, including a hotel and two living communities for senior citizens.

The denomination describes itself as "the oldest African-American congregation in the United States that adheres to the tenets of Judaism." While the group teaches that are peoples of African descent are among the descendants of the biblical Israelites, it insists that anyone, regardless of race, nationality or ethnicity, can embrace Judaism and become a member.

Members believe that Jesus was neither God nor the son of God, but rather a strict adherent to Judaism and a prophet sent by God, as they also consider Crowdy to be. The syncretistic group blends rituals from both the Old Testament and New Testament, and the doctrine is a blend of Christianity, Judaism, and Black nationalism. Old Testament observances include circumcision, use of the Hebrew calendar, wearing of yarmulkes, observance of Saturday Sabbath, and celebrating of Passover and other Jewish holy days specified. New Testament observances include baptism by immersion, the consecration of bread and water as Christ's body and blood, and foot washing. The church teaches that blacks are descendants of the ten lost tribes of Israel. The denomination is led by a bishop and prophet held to be divinely called to the office and to be in direct communion with God. When the leader dies, the office remains vacant until a new leader receives such a call.

Each congregation bears the identical name, Church of God and Saints of Christ, and is numbered according to chronological founding. The headquarters congregation is communal; other branches are not required to follow the communal pattern. The only prayer is the Lord's Prayer. The church is also known as the Church of God Temple Beth El.

Further Reading:

Church of God and Saints of Christ. Historical Committee. *History of the Church of God and Saints of Christ,* Suffolk, VA: Church, 1992.
Wynia, Elly M. *The Church of God and Saints of Christ: A History of the Black Jews.* New York: Garland, 1994.
Miller; Terry E., and Sara S. Miller. *The Church of God and Saints of Christ in Africa: The First One Hundred Years (1903–2003).* Kent, OH: n.p., 2008.

Church of God (Apostolic)

The oldest of the black Oneness Pentecostal denominations was initially incorporated in Danville, Kentucky in 1897 by **Thomas Cox**. The organization was established as a Trinitarian Holiness body, the Christian Faith Band. While it is uncertain when the body adopted Oneness doctrine, sometime after 1913, Cox converted to the movement through his association with **Robert C. Lawson** who would later found the **Church of our Lord Jesus Christ of the Apostolic Faith**. In 1915 the name of the Church was changed to what leaders considered the more biblical designation of **Church of God (Apostolic)**.

Cox led the denomination for forty years until poor health forced him to relinquish leadership of the church to **Eli Neal**.

When Cox died in 1943, Neal and Bishop M. Gravely assumed positions as co-presiding bishops since neither was willing to submit to the other's leadership. After two years, Gravely was dismissed because he initiated divorce proceedings against his wife on grounds that the denomination considered did not have biblical support. Though the denomination was prepared to let him remain in his pastorate, a lengthy litigation ensued. When Gravely loss the case, he was removed from his congregation and disfellowshipped from the denomination. That same year, the organization was incorporated and Neal assumed sole leadership. Love Odom, who served from 1964 to 1966, was succeeded by David Smith, who served until 1974, when Ruben K. Hash became presiding bishop. Bishop Cecil O. Reid currently presides.

COGA reached its height numerically in 1938 when it had more than 30,000 members in forty-nine congregations. However, the schismatic tendency of the denomination would repeat itself several times, resulting in a drop in those figures. Within a short time, of his coming into office as presiding bishop, Neal's authoritarian style alienated several ministers within the denomination and caused the first split in the 1940s. Questions regarding Neal's autocratic leadership style and personal morality, five elders—**J. W. Audrey, James C. Richardson**, Jerome Jenkins, W. R. Bryant, and J. M. Williams left to form the **Apostle Church of Christ in God** in Winston-Salem, NC.

In 1963, George Wiley, who had founded a congregation seven years earlier in Yonkers, New York, pulled out to found **Mt. Hebron Apostolic Temple of Our Lord Jesus** Christ after his petition to be consecrated as a bishop was refused. Since his wife had worked with the youth department for many years, the couple had developed a following among this group. As a result, many of the younger members of the denomination left with them into the new organization. In 1969, another break occurred when Johnny Draft and Wallace Snow left to establish the **Apostolic Church of Christ (Pentecostal)**.

These groups have generally remained small with largely regional constituencies, but the continued fissure has led to a steady decline in The **Church of God (Apostolic)** which now has 15,000 members in forty-five congregations primarily along the East Coast. Following the death of Bishop Cox headquarters moved from Danville, Kentucky to Beckly, West Virginia. In 1948, the headquarters moved again to its present location in Winston Salem, North Carolina.

The statement of faith of COGA shows important distinctions from that of many Oneness Pentecostal denominations. COGA believes in "One true God, externally existing in three personalities: Father, Son and Holy Spirit." Though they insist that baptism should be "in the name of Jesus Christ," they differ on the regenerational nature of that baptism, stating that along with repentance and Jesus name baptism, "regeneration by the Holy Spirit is necessary for Salvation."

Church of God by Faith, Inc.

A Oneness Pentecostal body within the Wesleyan tradition that teaching that entire sanctification is an instantaneous work obtained by faith, but must be preceded through the consecration of the individual. The group holds a subordinationist view of the Godhead seeing God (the Father) as preeminent while the Son and the Holy Spirit are lesser persons within the Godhead. They also hold to divine healing, while the use of medicine and doctors is not rejected when necessary. The church's articles of faith do not address the issue of speaking in tongues.

In 1914 John Bright began a prayer meeting with two women, Lucretia Scippio and her mother, Della Scippio, in Jacksonville, Florida. They were soon joined by Bright's brother, Crawford, who had formerly been a pastor in the Church of God (Cleveland, Tennessee), and Aaron Matthews Sr., Hubert Steadman and Nathaniel Scippio. Crawford Bright had formerly been a pastor in the Church of God (Cleveland, Tennessee). By 1917, there were enough congregations to host the first Assembly Meeting in White Springs, Florida. By 1919, Crawford had returned to that body, while other members continued to preach and build congregations throughout the East Coast and the national headquarters had been established in Palatka.

In 1923 the denomination was officially chartered and Aaron Matthews, Sr. was appointed senior bishop. At his death in 1959, his son Willie Matthews became senior bishop and served for twenty-five years before becoming emeritus. In 1984, Elder James E. McKnight, Sr. was elevated to the office of senior bishop. He currently serves as bishop emeritus and his son, James E. McKnight Jr. currently serves in that position.

The Church of God by Faith remains headquartered in Jacksonville, Florida. The denomination has approximately 170 churches, with approximately 35,000 members, primarily along the East Coast, with a substantial number in Florida. There are also congregations in Texas, the Midwest, Washington, Canada, Chile, and Africa.

The church does not recognize ordinances or sacraments such as baptism, communion, or foot washing. The denomination publishes a monthly periodical, *The Spiritual Guide.*

Church of God (Colored Work)

As early as the 1920s, **A. J. Tomlinson**, General Overseer of the Church of God (Cleveland, Tennessee) appointed a small number of black ministers to leadership positions beyond the local congregations and limited fellowship of their own churches. Within the decade, five men—**John H. Curry,** W. V. Eneas and William Franks both from the Bahamas, **David La Fleur,** and Thomas Smith—served terms as overseers of states that were not entirely black. Several blacks also served on subcommittees of the General Assembly. Smith and John Shaw served on the Home Missions committee, Thomas Richardson served on the Education Committee and Crawford Bright served on the Questions and Answers Committee.

Despite Tomlinson's efforts, in 1922, a large number of black ministers exited the denomination. Subsequently, when a black delegation requested that a black person again be appointed to oversee their work, Tomlinson agreed to their request and the Committee on Better Government created an autonomous structure for the black churches, The Church of God (Colored Work), appointing Richardson as its first overseer. Richardson's tenure, however, was short lived. A year later, when Tomlinson was ousted as general overseer, the African-American leader left with him to his newly formed organization, The Church of God of Prophecy.

La Fleur was tapped to oversee the work that, by now, had grown to encompass several northern states. In 1925, La Fleur called the first black National Assembly of the Church of God, inviting constituents from the northern states to attend. After another year, black representatives requested that they not only be allowed to continue holding their own Assembly, but to elect, rather than serve under, an appointed overseer. Both requests were granted by the General Assembly, though blacks could still attend the General Assembly. Further, Flavius. J. Lee, the then General Overseer, assured La Fleur that blacks had the option of passing a resolution to remain with the General Assembly. Yet annual National Assemblies of blacks continued for forty years. Some blacks, however, refused to participate in the racially segregated group and approached the General Overseer separately, requesting exclusion from the black judicatory and retention of voting privileges in the General Assembly. As a result, each black congregation was allowed to determine if they would participate in the white General Assembly, black National Assembly, or both.

The South remained the area with the most black congregations—the largest number in Florida, and despite most black churches' desire to maintain the separate structure, no black leader emerged to strategically direct ministers and congregations into forming a separate denomination, and continuing internal problems among precluded them from making the progress they expected. Within two years, black leaders requested that the General Assembly rescind the power to select their own overseer and asked that the Assembly reclaim appointive responsibility, while allowing blacks ratification authority.

When La Fleur resigned in 1928, he was succeeded by Bahamian, **John Henry Curry,** who held the longest continued tenure in that post, serving from 1928 to 1938. During his tenure, the denomination made a major structural change in the governance of black churches. Prior to then, the unofficial overseer of the black work had been the overseer of large contingent of black churches of Florida. With the change, the Florida overseer officially became overseer of the entire black work, including Northern congregations. Yet blacks could still elect to attend either the General or National Assembly or both.

In spite of little material support from the general church throughout this period, the leaders of the black judicatory was determined to meet the physical needs of its constituency. In 1930, it began to acquire resources to build a national auditorium in Jacksonville, to serve the headquarters for the black work, and facilities for the National Assembly. This project made slow progress since responsibility for raising funds for this facility was left entirely up to the blacks. As such, it became a major project for its women's auxiliary. Though it was partially constructed by 1932, the realization of a completed facility took more than twenty years.

The progress of the Industrial Home and School put forward by the black leaders, at first appeared to fare much better. Work on this facility was begun in 1930 The first stage was completed in 1934. A boys' dormitory was added within a short period. Curry was followed by Norbert S. Marcell who served from 1938 to 1946. At the time he took over leadership, the black work was heavily in debt. Under Marcell's administration, the debt for the Jacksonville auditorium was retired and improvements were made in the facility. Additionally, the boy's dormitory of the orphanage was completed.

In 1944, blacks again sought and received permission to elect their overseer, but little else changed for the next twenty years. The first overseer to be elected under this system was Willie L. Ford who served two terms. During his first term, from 1946 to 1949, the debt for the orphanage was paid off and a national missions program was established. This term was followed by that of George Wallace who served from 1949 to 1954. During his tenure, the Jacksonville auditorium was finally completed.

Ford again served from 1954 to 1958. During this second tenure, blacks made slow, but unsteady progress in expanding their congregations. This pace was not acceptable to the white leadership, however, who wanted to spur more tangible growth among the black constituency. Following Ford's second tenure, the authority to elect the overseer was, again, rescinded. This time, however, the first white overseer of the colored work, J. T. Roberts was appointed. While his appointment was initially controversial among the black constituency, he proved to be sympathetic advocate. During his seven-year tenure, the number of black Church of God congregations grew from 102 in nineteen states to 214 in twenty-four states and the membership more than doubled from little more than 2,900 to more than 7,600. Additionally, Roberts was able to negotiate favorable terms with lending institutions for the black constituency that allowed them to construct or improve several edifices. In 1959 and again in 1960, he enlisted instructors from the denomination's still segregated Lee College to conduct summer Bible institutes for black ministers. The southern institute was held in Jacksonville, Florida and the northern in Philadelphia. At the end of his tenure, Roberts presented a motion to the General Assembly to end segregation of the churches.

The last overseer of the black work was David Lemons, the son of an early Church of God pioneer and a prominent pastor who was state overseer and member of the Council of Twelve. However, Lemons was appointed just as the racial strictures within the church had begun to give way and served for only one year. In 1966, the General Assembly voted to disband the colored work of the Church of God and dissolve the position of overseer. In its place, the General Assembly established the office of Black Liaison at its International Headquarters and tapped **Harcourt G. Poitier**, a black Florida pastor to serve at its head.

Further Reading:

Crews, Mickey. *The Church of God: A Social History*. Knoxville, TN: University of Tennessee Press, 1990.

Michel, David. *Telling the Story: Black Pentecostals in the Church of God (Cleveland, Tennessee)*. Cleveland, TN: Pathway, 2000.

Church of God in Christ

The largest African-American Pentecostal denomination and the one of the most prominent African-American Christian denominations in the world was founded in 1895 as a body within the Holiness movement and incorporated in 1897 as the first legally chartered Holiness denomination in the United States. It was established by two former

Baptist pastors, **Charles Price Jones** and **Charles Harrison Mason**, who by then had embraced the Holiness movement and the experience of sanctification and, subsequently, had been dismissed from their congregations and disfellowshipped from their Baptist convention. Beginning with a revival held in a cotton gin in Lexington, Mississippi in 1896, they worked for the next decade, organizing a Holiness denomination that would grow to encompass congregations throughout the Mississippi River Valley.

Mason received permission to use an abandoned gin house in Lexington, Mississippi, for a new sanctuary and for the next ten years his ministry laid the groundwork for one of the leading congregations among the many that would spring up throughout the valley. It would also draw existing congregations to solidify a Holiness organization under the two men's leadership. Though both preached a message of the necessity for sanctification and the empowerment of the Holy Spirit, events of 1907 brought a rift that split their group into two camps—one Holiness, the other Pentecostals.

Several months after the **Azusa Street Revival** began, the two decided to send a contingent consisting of Mason, **John A. Jeter, W. S. Pleasant,** and **David J. Young**, to ascertain the spiritual authenticity and direction of the new movement. After having his own experience of Pentecostal Spirit baptism, Mason returned fully convinced that the experience was biblical. Though Jones had initially supported tongues speaking as a spiritual gift to sanctified, Spirit-filled believers, he chafed at the idea that it was the only evidence of Holy Spirit baptism. When the two could not agree, matters came to a head. At the group's annual convocation in August and September 1907, the debate over initial evidence waged for three days. In the end, Jones' group prevailed and disfellowshipped Mason. The split was almost evenly divided with Mason and Jones each taking about half of the delegates and fourteen congregations.

Following the split, Mason invited ministers across the South who agreed with his understanding to join in forming a new **Church of God in Christ** as a Pentecostal body. Mason held the first Convocation in November of that same year. Between 1907 and 1926, the two bodies found themselves locked in a legal battle over the right the name, **Church of God in Christ**. With Mason finally prevailing in 1909. After a series of appeals, Mason's group officially changed its name in 1922, though appeals continued until 1926.

From 1907 until 1914, the **Church of God in Christ** was the only body within the new movement registered with the federal government to grant recognized ministerial credentials. Thus Mason provided the critical service of signing credentials for both black and white independent Pentecostal ministers who had been dismissed from their congregations and denominations. During that time, he credentialed nearly 350 white ministers. By the end of that period, however, the arrangement proved untenable for the majority of them. Prior to then, several white leaders approached Mason to suggest he no longer issue individual credentials, but that he sign a number of blank forms and allow them to distribute them and handle all their other affairs. Finally, their discontent culminated in the Hot Springs, Arkansas meeting to which Mason was not invited, that birthed a new, predominantly white fellowship, the **Assemblies of God**.

Though not invited, Mason attended at least one session, preached to the assembled delegates, and gave his blessing to the new organization. Like his close friend, **William J. Seymour,** Mason worked to maintain racial unity within the young movement, and not only did a number of white ministers remain in COGIC, white believers continued to participate in COGIC worship services and several black COGIC congregations continued to have white members. Like Seymour, however, Mason could not sustain the desired racial unity within his denomination. Over time, white participation eroded as new white Pentecostal denominations sprang up and by 1924, the growing pressure for separation between blacks and whites led to establishing a minority conference for white congregations and ministers that remained in existence until the mid 1930s. By the mid-twentieth century, white congregations within COGIC had all but disappeared, though individual white members continued to frequent COGIC worship services.

During its first two and a half decades, COGIC's growth was steady, yet relatively slow. In 1926 Mason authorized organizing a constitution outlining the bylaws, rules, and regulations. By 1934 there were approximately 25,000 members in 345 congregations throughout twenty-one states and the District of Columbia. That year Mason appointed five bishops—**Isaac S. Stafford** of Detroit, **Emmett M. Page** of Dallas, **William M. Roberts** of Chicago, **Ozro T. Jones, Sr.** of Philadelphia, and **Riley F. Williams**, who had served as the overseer of Ohio and Alabama—to help govern the denomination. Though all five men were extraordinarily gifted leaders, all but Jones preceded Mason in death.

Within the next three decades, spurred by the Great Migration of blacks into urban areas in the North, growth increased more than ten-fold, so that by the time of Mason's death in 1961, COGIC membership was nearly 383,000. Twenty years later, by 1981, it had increased ten-fold again to more than 3,700,000.

This phenomenal growth made COGIC, arguably, the largest Pentecostal body and second largest African American denomination in the United States (following the National Baptist Convention, USA), as well as among the fastest-growing Christian denominations in the world. Throughout its history, COGIC has distinguished itself among African American Pentecostal denominations by the degree of institutional structure developed within its ranks. From ten churches in 1907, COGIC has become a global religious organization with it more than six million members spread across fifty-nine countries.

Along the way, however, the denomination experienced the same pattern of schism and amalgamation evident is its sister bodies. First, **Elias Dempsey Smith**, founder of **Triumph the Church and Kingdom of God in Christ** joined forces with Mason shortly after his group was founded in 1904. But while Mason was open to interracial cooperation and fellowship, Smith made a distinction between the "church militant" of whites and the peace loving church of blacks. Further, he did not accept Mason's Pentecostal emphasis on speaking in tongues. This union lasted only until 1912 when Dempsey pulled out of COGIC and resumed leadership of his original body.

In 1915 members of a National Baptist Convention congregation, under the leadership of **J. H. Morris**, formed a separate body that they also called the **Church of God in Christ**. In 1921 this group brought their congregations into fellowship with Mason's group, but four years later, withdrew to form the **Free Church of God in Christ**. By 1935 there were nineteen congregations and 875 members in the denomination; by the late 1940s there was only one additional congregation.

In 1927 **Sumpter. E. Looper** of Ohio pulled out of COGIC to form the **Free Unity Church of God in Christ.** Looper concentrated his efforts within that state, and by 1949 had established branches of the body in Cincinnati, Columbus, Akron, Chillicothe, and Barberton.

In 1932 Bishop **Justus Bowe** broke with Mason to establish the **Church of God in Christ, Congregational** after COGIC rejected a proposal to adopt a congregational polity, voting instead to retain episcopal polity. Bowe, had served as overseer of Arkansas, had been among the first group of ministers who responded to Mason's call to reorganize after his split from Jones. But almost from the beginning, Bowe exhibited a more independent spirit that many COGIC clergy; refusing, for example, to heed the warning of **R. E. Hart** and holding a reorganization convocation in Arkansas before the Mason's suit with Jones was settles. His action caused the denomination to lose all the property it owned in that state. In 1934, another COGIC schismatic, **George Slack**, who had been disfellowshiped because he challenged COGIC's tithing system, joined with Bowe and for the next ten years, the two served at the head of the denomination. In 1945 Bowe returned to COGIC, leaving the smaller body intact under Slack's leadership.

One consistent motivation for the formation of new denominations has been COGIC's stand regarding the ordination of women and their involvement in pastoral leadership. **Mozella Cook,** who pulled out in 1947 to form the **Sought Out Church of God in Christ**, left—at least in part—for that reason. Two years later, the denomination had four congregations and sixty members, and probably grew only slightly larger than that figure. Despite these small numbers, however, Cook is significant because she is the first women to pull out of COGIC specifically to move into a position of full denominational leadership. Later, in 1968, **Ernestine Cleveland Reems**, daughter of COGIC bishop, E. E. Cleveland, left to found her own independent congregation, Center of Hope Community Church in Oakland, CA. In 2000, Reems was consecrated bishop of Monument of Faith, International Assembly.

In 2004 the issue of women's involvement in leadership was arguably part of the catalyst for the formation of a another denomination when David Grayson, former COGIC pastor, bishop, and district superintendent, was consecrated as presiding bishop of the **Church of God in Christ** (New Day). The group included about 2,000 members from forty COGIC congregations, primarily in Tennessee, Alabama, Mississippi, and New York. After a court battle with COGIC, the new group was forced to change its name to **New Day Church International**.

These defections left COGIC largely unscathed, with the vast majority of members remaining loyal to the parent body. Conversely, none of the new organizations had anywhere near the success of the parent body, and most have remained fairly small.

The seven years following Mason's death in 1961 saw the denomination wracked by a much larger and potentially devastating schism. In 1926, thirty-five years before his death, Mason had framed the constitution to stipulate that on his demise, leadership would revert to a Board of Bishops who would supervise the election of two or more bishops who would have oversight of the denomination. During his later years, however, Mason had designated **Ozro T. Jones, Sr.**, the only surviving member of the original five bishops as his successor. After Mason's death, Jones assumed leadership and held the position of senior bishop until 1968.

Nonetheless, in 1965, opposition that had been brewing before Mason's death came to a head when some COGIC leaders began calling for regular elections for the position of presiding bishop. After three years of in-fighting between factions led by Jones and Board Chair, **A. B. McEwen**, in 1968, COGIC leaders also convened a court-ordered constitutional convention with the goal of restructuring the denomination among more democratic lines. That year they held a court-ordered election in which Jones was defeated and a group led by **James Oglethorpe Patterson, Sr.**, Mason's son-in-law, who became the first to hold the elected position of presiding bishop. Jones major contribution to COGIC had been holding the denomination together during the turbulent period of uncertainty following Mason's death. Under his administration, the first official manual of the denomination was published. After being defeated, he remained jurisdictional bishop in Pennsylvania until his death in 1972.

During Patterson's tenure, COGIC saw major growth and emerged from its sectarian posture to align itself with major national Christian organizations, including the National Association of Evangelicals, the Congress of National Black Churches, the Pentecostal World Fellowship, and the North American Congress on the Holy Spirit. Under his leadership, COGIC put the steps in place to set up the Charles Harrison Mason Seminary in Atlanta, Georgia, as the first Pentecostal seminary to receive accreditation from the Association of Theological Schools (ATS). Patterson also worked to establish and the **C. H. Mason System of Bible Colleges**, the **Church Of God In Christ** Bookstore, and took over ownership of the Church Of God In Christ Publishing House. He also served as founding president of Founder and President of the **World Fellowship of Black Pentecostal Churches.**

Eventually many of the schismatics returned to fellowship with the parent body. Not everyone, however, was pleased with the outcome of the convention and this was not the last of the schisms. After Patterson's election, COGIC again found itself in litigation, remaining in court for six years as three groups each claimed to be the rightful heir to the denomination's name and property.

Only a year later, fourteen bishops led by Bishop Illie L. Jefferson and David Charles Williams Sr., of Evanston, dissatisfied with the shift from a presiding bishop to the board, declared themselves the original church and invited others to return to the "only constitutional system of government of our church." A major point of contention was the move from a senior bishop with sole power to elected presiding bishop accountable to a board. The splinter group formed the **Church of God in Christ, International** and elected Williams as senior bishop. In 1982, COGIC International reported 200,000 members, 300 congregations and 1,600 ministers.

In 1990, seventy-six-year-old Bishop **Louis H. Ford**, a prominent pastor and political leader in Chicago, succeeded Patterson as interim, then presiding bishop. Ford had used his pastorate of the burgeoning St. Paul Church of God in Christ in Chicago to not only gain prominence in the denomination but to involve himself in the political life of the city and the denomination. As presiding bishop, Ford exhibited what Ithiel Clemmons referred to as "a restorationist vision" for COGIC, wanting to return it to what he saw as its glory days while improving and expanded existing physical, as well as spiritual structures. He spearheaded refurbishing of Mason Temple, the mother church and the facilities of Saints Junior College. Sociologist **Robert Franklin** contends that Ford's political savvy helped raise the political profile of the **Church of God in Christ**. For example, Ford invited than Arkansas governor and presidential candidate, Bill Clinton, to address the 1991 Holy Convocation. Once Clinton was elected Ford drew on their political friendship to support projects for his constituents.

When Ford died suddenly in March 1995, Chandler Owens pastor of Greater Community COGIC in Atlanta, Georgia and Ford's first assistant bishop, was tapped as interim bishop. Four months later, Owens was elected to the office. His style, however, was considered heavy handed by many COGIC leaders and regular members. He attempted to wrest power out of the hands of the board of bishops and centralize it within his position as presiding bishop, asserting at one point that he had authority to make all decisions within the church without disruption or confirmation.

In 1998 Owens' leadership was challenged, when three members—including later Presiding Bishop **Charles Blake** of the twelve-member Board of Bishops—called for a special election and campaigned to unseat him and replace him with **Ozro T. Jones Jr.** of Philadelphia. Their bid was unsuccessful when assembly delegates voted to postpone the voting until the regular general election the following year.

In that 1999 election, the General Assembly voted not to return Owens to his position. Instead, they elected Mason's Grandson, Gilbert Earl Patterson, pastor the Temple of Deliverance COGIC in Memphis. Patterson was re-elected in 2003. By the beginning of the twenty-first century, under his leadership the denomination reportedly had grown to more than six million members in fifty-eight countries.

At his death, **Charles E. Blake,** pastor of West Angeles Church of God in Christ, a megachurch that is the largest COGIC congregation in the nation, was voted into office. Blake's involvement in a number of religious and civic context has been able to gain a visibility for COGIC that goes beyond any previous administration.

Since shortly after its founding, COGIC leaders, including Mason, have attempted to forge educational institutions that would not only help produce a cadre of practically trained clergy, but would also aid in bringing about racial uplift for its constituents. Within less than two decades of its founding, the first three of such institutions were established, but lack of widespread support within the denominations for such endeavors did not facilitate their success. The **Faith Home and Industrial School of Geridge**, Arkansas was established in 1916, for children from the first through twelfth grade in Lonoke County, Arkansas by **Justus Bowe** and closed during the early 1930s. **Saints Industrial and Literary School** in Lexington, Mississippi in 1918, which was run for fifty years by **Arenia Mallory**, permanently closed its doors in 2007. The **Page Normal Industrial and Bible**

Institute established in Hearn Texas in 1919, by Bishop **E. M. Page** and operated until 1934.

Since that time, individual congregations or jurisdictions have provided varying degrees of formal training for their constituents. In 1971, however, Bishop **J. O. Patterson, Sr.** introduced the vision of establishing the C. H. Mason Theological Seminary and the **Charles Harrison Mason System of Bible Colleges** with the seminary being the responsibility of the national church and the system of Bible colleges being established by individual jurisdictions. The proposed Bible colleges offered jurisdictions a unified curriculum for training laypersons and credential holders. Dr. A. J. Hines of Houston, Texas organized a pilot school in Houston, and eventually developed nearly forty schools based on that model in locations throughout the United States. Beginning in 1973, the first additional schools were in three Tennessee jurisdictions—Headquarters, the 4th Tennessee, and 5th Tennessee Jurisdictions. In 1998, these institutions merged to form the All Saints Bible College with the campus located on the grounds of COGIC Headquarters. As of 2014, the college had gained candidate status with the Association of Biblical Higher Education.

At the outset, Mason drew on his Baptist roots to craft a distinctive structure for women that allows them serve as congregational leaders, while reserving the office of pastor and title of preacher for men. Within it, except for where required for chaplaincy work, women are not ordained as elder or consecrated bishop, but may be licensed as "evangelists" or "missionaries" to primarily teach other women and work to materially support congregation, jurisdictional or national programs. To undergird this structure Mason conceived of a Women's Department as an auxiliary to facilitate the dual leadership in which women could take increasingly important, yet circumscribed, places of service by filling significant roles in the local, regional and national church while being excluded from ordained ministry. Over its history, five women have served at the head: Elizabeth (Lizzie) Robinson, who was appointed the first president of the National Women's Department, Coffey, who instigated the International Women's Convent, **Anne Bailey**, **Mattie McGlothen**, and Willie Mae Rivers.

From the beginning, music has been an integral component of COCIC worship and culture and COGIC leaders at every level have been supportive of quality musical efforts. While the movement was still in its infancy within the Holiness camp, cofounder Charles P. Jones wrote a number of hymns that have become standards among Pentecostal and others. And as early as 1906, he published a hymnal, *His Fullness Song Book*. Seventy-five years later, in 1982 COGIC published its own hymnal, *Yes, Lord!*, which included many arrangements and songs written by COGIC and African-American musicians and songwriters.

Throughout the first half of the twentieth century, COGIC men and women such as **Arizona Dranes**, **Rosetta Thorpe**, **Utah Smith**, and **Ernestine Washington** not only produced quality recordings, but also introduced innovative musical elements that have influence gospel and secular artists up until contemporary times. Some of these have been widely emulated by major secular recording artists.

Several individual traditional and contemporary gospel artists as well as music ensembles of every all sizes have gained prominence for themselves and have given COGIC a reputation for quality music. The formal organization of musical efforts came through Dr. Mattie Moss Clarke who, in 1972, was appointed as the first president of the Music Department and served as director of the renowned Southwest Michigan State Choir, which had a number of hits during the later decades. **Sara Jordan Powell** also founded COGIC's Fine Arts Department taking the emphasis on performance beyond music to incorporate other arenas of artistic expression. Later in the 1970s, Clark's daughters, "The Legendary Clark Sisters," carried the family tradition into the twenty-first century. Yet, that group would only be one among many gifted musicians who would come out of COGIC in the latter half of the century. Other family groups who have been just as successful include Edwin and Walter Hawkins who started a family tradition that would be carried through with their sister Vickie, and Walter's wife, Tremaine. The Winans klan first produced the four-brother contemporary quartet, The Winans, who were later follows by a younger brother and sister duo, BeBe and CeCe Winans. Prolific song writer and musician, Andre Crouch and his sister Sandra did not regularly perform together, but later took over and co-pastored their late father's church. Several COGIC faithfuls had significant cotemporary solo careers including **Sara Jordan Powell,** Donnie McClurkin, Deniece Williams, and John P. Kee.

Along with Southwest Michigan States, a number of choirs—including West Angeles Church of God in Christ Choir, The Hawkins' Love Center Choir, and the Institutional Church of God in Christ Choir—have placed the denomination in the musical spotlight. Along the way, many of these choirs have garnered major music awards including Grammy and Dove awards for all facets of performing, writing, and production. Further, music produced within the COGIC arena not only crossed over into other Christian traditions, but also made deep inroads into the secular arena such as musical scores and cross-over club favorites.

Further Reading:

Clemmons, Ithiel C. *Bishop C. H. Mason and the Roots of the Church of God in Christ.*
    Lanham, MD: Pneuma Life, 1996.
Owens, Robert R. *Never Forget! The Dark Years of COGIC History.* Fairfax, VA: Xulon, 2002.
Bean, Bobby. *This is the Church of God in Christ.* Atlanta, GA: Underground Epics, 2001.
White, Calvin Jr. *The Rise to Respectability: Race, Religion, and the Church of God in Christ.*
    Fayetteville, AR: University of Arkansas Press, 2012.

Church of God in Christ, Congregational

In 1932 Bishop Justus Bowe broke with **Charles Harrison Mason** and the **Church of God in Christ** to establish the Church of God in Christ, Congregational in Hot Springs, Arkansas. He was responding to COGIC's rejection of a proposal to adopt a congregational polity and the vote to instead retain episcopal polity. The organizations share the same understanding as the parent body on all other major issues.

Bowe had been among the first group of ministers who responded to Mason's call to reorganize after his split from **Charles P. Jones** and who served as COGIC's overseer of Arkansas. In 1934 another COGIC schismatic, George Stack, who had been disfellowshipped because he challenged COGIC's tithing system, joined with Bowe and for the next ten years the two served at the head of the denomination, with Bowe serving as presider and Slack as assistant.

In 1945 the elders of COGIC convinced Bowe to return and that body and bring his organization with him. When Bowe presented that proposal to the COGIC elders, however, they rejected it. Bowe left the smaller body intact under George Slack's leadership. Slack served as senior bishop until his death in 1972 and was succeeded by his son, Hosea. The younger Slack was succeeded by Robert Smith, who is the current presiding bishop. The headquarters are located in East Saint Louis, Illinois.

By 1971 COGIC Congregational reportedly had forty-three congregations including six in Mexico and four in England. Except on the issues of tithing and governmental structure, its polity is similar to that of the parent body. It differs from COGIC primarily in relationship to its congregational polity. It also objects to the COGIC practice of naming individual congregations after their leaders.

Church of God in Christ International (Arkansas)

A year after **Church of God in Christ** founder **Charles Harrison Mason's** death in 1961, the denomination appointed **Ozro Thurston Jones Sr.** of Philadelphia, the only surviving bishop of the original five selected by Mason, to the office of senior bishop. For two years, Bishop Jones presided over the church in peace. However, in 1968, dissention erupted within the denomination when some within the denomination forced a legal battle to determine the government structure.

That year, Bishops Carl E. Williams Sr., and his brother, William David Charles Williams Sr., left COGIC to form the **Church Of God In Christ International** as a new organization that would return to original COGIC roots. Later the group split into two bodies each carrying the name **Church of God in Christ International,** with this group using the subscript, "Arkansas," to distinguish itself. In the 1970, denominational headquarters was established at Evanston and WDC Williams was appointed as senior bishop and chief apostle.

Under his leadership eighteen dioceses were added. When he died in 1983, Tony Clemon was elected the senior bishop and chief apostle, serving until his death in 1988. The following year, John H. Davis, who had served as National Chairperson under Bishop Clemon, was elected senior bishop and chief apostle. He resigned in 2013. At some time during this period, the national headquarters was moved to Jonesboro, Arkansas. The denomination operates institutions of higher learning, New Life Theological Seminary and the Williams-Clemon-Davis Bible College, which are located in Orangeburg, South Carolina are accredited by the Accrediting Commission International.

In 2013 Richard G. Gatling Sr. was installed as the sixth senior bishop serving only one year and resigning in 2014. Currently John C. Watford of Powellsville, North Carolina serves in the position. Headquarters is located in Jonesboro, Arkansas. The denomination, which is a member of the World Fellowship of Black Pentecostal Churches, has twenty-five dioceses.

Church of God in Christ Jesus, Apostolic, Inc.

The **Church of God in Christ Jesus, Apostolic**, Inc., is a Oneness Pentecostal denomination founded in 1946 in Baltimore, Maryland, by **Randolph Adolphus Carr**. Carr, a native of Nevis, West Indies, had been a pastor within the Trinitarian, **Church of God in Christ**, before accepting Oneness doctrine and affiliating with the **Pentecostal Assemblies of the World**. The doctrine of the new church followed that of the parent body.

In 1934 Carr established Church of God in Christ #6 as a congregation in Baltimore, Maryland. Thirteen years later, he returned to his Oneness Pentecostal roots, left COGIC and the congregation he was pastoring in that denomination to form Rehoboth Church of God in Christ Jesus (Apostolic). The denomination established or drew congregations along the East Coast of the United States, in Jamaica and in Great Britain.

In 1965 several of the leading bishops of the organization including **Monroe R. Saunders, Sr.**, who had served as assistant presiding bishop, **Sydney A. Dunn** of Birmingham, England, John S. Watson of Jamaica, West Indies and Bishop Raymond Murray of Boston, Massachusetts disagreed with Carr regarding his decision to break with denominational polity concerning divorce and remarriage (which he had originally set) to marry a divorcee. The group established the **United Church of Jesus Christ (Apostolic)**, taking several congregations from the parent body with them.

Carr continued to lead the **Church of God in Christ Jesus Apostolic** until his death in 1970. Bishop William S. Barnes then presided until his death in 1987, and was followed by William J. Faison Sr. The current presiding bishop is Keith Allen.

In the United States, more congregations are located primarily along the East Coast. There are also congregations in Jamaica, Bermuda, Canada, St. Kitts, and the US Virgin Islands.

Church of God in Christ United

The **Church of God in Christ United** was born out of the leadership crisis in the 1960s within the **Church of God in Christ** following the death of founding bishop, **Charles H. Mason**. In 1972 James Feltus Jr., the Bishop of Eastern Louisiana Jurisdiction of the **Church of God in Christ**, began organizing a denomination separate from the Mother Church. He developed five principles on which the **Church Of God In Christ United** would be organized. He took a non-sectarian stance and insisted that the local church be the focal point of all church activities, the organization be a fellowship rather than a political federation, and that local commitments and pledges replace national assessments. In 1973, he was joined by Bishop R. A. Campbell of the **Church of God in Christ International** and Bishop Marshall Hebert of the non-denominational organization, Miracle Oil Revival Center, Inc., to create the new body.

In addition to the jurisdictions across the United States, there are congregations in England, Haiti, Virgin Islands, Trinidad, Bermuda, Barbados, Canada, Jamaica, and Africa. Jamaica contains the largest church group, with an excess of one hundred churches, and South Africa holds the largest congregate with 250,000 members.

Feltus remains the presiding prelate with twenty-five Jurisdictional Bishops, and five Auxiliary Bishops. The COGICU celebrates four international meetings a year: The

Mission & Evangelism Conference, The International Youth Congress, The International Holy Convocation, and the International Women's Convention.

Church of God of Prophecy, Race Relations in

The most racially integrated predominantly white Pentecostal denomination within the United States throughout the twentieth century. The Church of God of Prophecy was founded by former General Overseer, **A. J. Tomlinson**, when he left the Church of God (Cleveland, TN) in 1923, reportedly over a number of issues, including wanting more inclusion of their black constituency. A year after its founding, Tomlinson's new organization, which maintained it headquarters in the same city as the parent body, had black constituents in Florida, North Carolina, Georgia, Alabama, Kentucky, New York, Tennessee and the Bahamas. The next year, its General Assembly passed a resolution against the Ku Klux Klan, becoming one of the few white Pentecostal bodies to do so, and COGOP may have been the first church to defy Jim Crow laws in their worship services.

Tomlinson's racially inclusive posture could be traced, in part, to his Quaker sensitivities, his being raised in an Indiana community with a substantial African-American presence and his exposure to black camp meetings. As a young man, he was introduced to the views of famous revivalist, Charles Finney, who denounced slavery from the pulpit. Tomlinson's openness allowed COGOP to forge a racial praxis significantly different from other classical Pentecostals. Unlike other major bodies, COGOP never separated its black members into a satellite organization or steered them to black groups. When, at the 1926 Assembly, Tomlinson brought up the subject of continuing the practice of separate enclaves as a carry over from the Church of God, the Assembly, instead, voted to disband the "colored work," which it considered an unfortunate carryover because, "[the practice] has a tendency to widen the gap between blacks and white races."

Moreover, while some individual congregations were maintained along racial lines, state, regional, and national assemblies have been fully integrated throughout its history. Further, while other white denominations maintained segregated recreational facilities to ensure no unseemly mixing would occur between young people of different races, COGOP camps were integrated and intended for the use of all constituents. Moreover, the denomination proposed building an orphanage for children of color because the church is "for all races," while other bodies maintained separate facilities for these types of ministries. Yet Tomlinson's efforts, as well as those of his successors, were not unnoticed by the secular society or other white religionists. The denomination suffered persecution for its stand, and its ministers were regularly imprisoned or subjected to violence for participating in mixed-race meetings.

For most of the early history of the modern Pentecostal movement, white adherents generally pointed to Charles Fox Parham, the white evangelist who formalized the doctrine of initial evidence of speaking in tongues, as its founder, giving little attention to the contribution of the **Azusa Street Revival** and its black leadership. Alternatively, they maintained the founding of the movement was solely a work of the Holy Spirit with no specific human foundation. Tomlinson, however, was among the earliest white

Pentecostals to praise Seymour for his contribution and give priority to the **Azusa Street Revival** as a progenitor of the movement.

Though historically there was a section of its General Assembly reserved for blacks, they were not required to sit there. Neither were black ministers and members relegated to one section of the Assembly program, but would often take part singing, preaching, praying, serving on powerful assembly committees and participating in the annual "All Nations Parade" through streets of Cleveland, Tennessee.

Early in its development, COGOP black ministers were promoted to places of prominence rarely seen in any other white organization based in the American South. Thomas Richardson, a close colleague of Tomlinson who had followed him from the Church of God to his new work, was originally the only African-American state overseer appointed to his newly formed Council and served on the Bible Government Committee. Yet, when Tomlinson refused to appoint him as overseer of Florida, and offered him Bermuda instead, Richard left the COGOP for a time. When he returned twelve years later, he never regained his previous prominence.

Ralph Scotton, another early leader, joined COGOP in 1930. Tomlinson ordained him a bishop in 1940, and he served as served as a local pastor and evangelist as well as a denominational representative throughout the United States and the Caribbean. In 1941, Tomlinson appointed Scotton as one of two General Field Secretaries for the Church of God of Prophecy, and he served in that position until 1952.

D. M. and Dorothy Deadricks were introduced to COGOP in the early 1930s and built up its black constituency in East Texas. D. M pastored several local churches, received his ordination as bishop in 1936, became a state leader in Tennessee in 1948, and succeeded Scotton as General Field Secretary No. 2 in 1952. His wife often preached in state conventions and the Annual Assembly and served as director of the state youth camp in East Texas, where she was an outspoken proponent of racial unity. E. L. Jones, who had been a district overseer in Mississippi, succeeded Deadrick.

Stanley Ferguson, another early COGOP bishop affiliated with the young Pentecostal denomination shortly after it was established, and, shortly, was appointed as national overseer of the Bahamas. He became a close ally of Tomlinson and achieved near legendary status in the new organization throughout the 1920s and early 1930s.

Other white COGOP leaders shared Tomlinson's concern about reaching blacks, and, at times, called for racial unity from the assembly podium. At one General Assembly, for example, two white state overseers, W. M. Lowman and L. A. Moxley, urged attendees to make efforts to reach all races. Tomlinson's 1941 General Assembly address again returned to the theme of breaking down the "middle wall of partition," but his interest in racial reconciliation was not only targeted to the blacks, but also included Native Americans. His efforts went beyond impassioned general assembly sermons.

Tomlinson befriended, ordained, and promoted numerous black ministers within COGOP until his death in 1943, when his son and successor, Milton, continued the policy of full integration, ensuring that the organization's leadership continued to include blacks at every level, and making COGOP the largest racially mixed denomination in the South between the 1940s and 1960s. Though not openly involved in the Civil Rights Movement, the denomination was one of few white Pentecostal groups to consistently maintain that "racial distinction [is] against the will of God or the purpose of the Church," and to call other Pentecostal church leaders to account on the issue. In 1948, for example, the COGOP declined to join the segregated Pentecostal Fellowship of North America because of its racially exclusive polity, only joining the umbrella group after it reorganized as the interracial **Pentecostal and Charismatic Churches of North America**.

By 1991 African Americans accounted for 16 percent of the denomination's membership—more than any other predominantly white Pentecostal body. Since then, blacks and other minorities have continued to hold leadership positions throughout the denomination, leaving COGOP with the most racially inclusive leadership of any US Pentecostal denomination. Today Afro-Caribbeans, African Americans, and Latin Americans are charged with the leadership of states whose composition includes European Americans as the majority, which rarely, if ever, happens in other white Pentecostal bodies.

Further Reading:

Hunter, Harold. "A Journey Toward Racial Reconciliation: Race Mixing in the Church of God of Prophecy." In *The Azusa Street Revival and Its Legacy*, edited by Harold Hunter and Cecil M. Robeck, 277–96. Cleveland, TN: Pathway, 2006.

Kinder, Christopher. "'The Great Speckled Bird': Prominent Black Ministers and Interracial Fraternity in the Church of God of Prophecy, 1923–1964." Paper presented to the Southern Studies Conference, Montgomery, AL: Auburn University, February 6–7, 2015.

Church of God (Sanctified Church)

The first congregation of the Church of God (Sanctified Church) was originated in 1900 by former members of Mt. Lebanon Missionary Baptist Church in Columbia, TN, under the leadership of Charles Gray, a member of the **Church of God in Christ** while it was still a Holiness group under **Charles Price Jones** and **Charles Harrison Mason.** Gray continued to work with the two leaders until their 1907 split over the issue of tongues. Though he sided with Jones in not holding speaking in tongues as a necessity for Holy Spirit baptism, he later splintered from the parent body, largely over the issue of church polity.

For the next twenty years, Gray drew a number of congregations, but these associated churches remained unincorporated until 1927, when the Church of God (Sanctified Church) consolidated the work under a board of elders. This incorporation led to further controversy and a schism. The new board approved the ordination of women, which Gray opposed. In that same year, he and a group consisting of nearly one-third of the members broke away to form a new body, **Original Church of God or Sanctified Church.**

On Gray's departure, Rucker became board chairperson, serving until 1946, when he was succeeded by Theopolis Dickerson. Dickerson was succeeded by Jesse Evans. The denomination has approximately 5,000 members in sixty congregations in the United States and twelve in Jamaica.

Its statement of faith is insistent on the necessity on instantaneous sanctification, seeing the baptism of the Holy Spirit as simply the present ministry of the Holy Spirit in indwelling the Christian to a sanctified life. Though the church sees "every true believer as heir to the gift of the Holy Ghost" and it sees the initial receiving of the Holy Ghost occurring at conversion.

Gray's body maintained a congregational structure, with the leader serving as board chairperson rather than bishop and local churches calling pastors, rather than depending on episcopal assignment.

Church of God Which He Purchased With His Own Blood

A Holiness organization founded in 1953 in Oklahoma City, Oklahoma by **William Jordan Fizer**, a former minister. Fizer claimed to have a revelation that led him to believe that the parent church's doctrines that water, not grape juice, be served during the Lord's Supper was in error. From this revelation he established a new organization, The Church of God (Which He Purchased With His Own Blood).

Unlike many Pentecostal bodies, the body celebrates the Lord's Supper weekly with grape juice and unleavened bread. Foot washing is administered at the time of one's baptism. The organization does not practice speaking in tongues, but rather teaches that the Holy Spirit is given to the believers who lead a holy life. There are approximately eight hundred members and eighteen ministers in seven congregations predominantly in the Midwest and Southern parts of the United States, as well as in Nigeria and the Philippines. The headquarters remain in Oklahoma City.

Church of Jesus Christ (Apostolic), Inc.

A Oneness Pentecostal denomination founded in Paterson, New Jersey in 1971 by Bishop **Roy C. Williams**, ten years after he planted his first congregation in that city. In 1962 Williams established as a store front congregation, the Church of Jesus Christ (Apostolic), Inc. in Paterson, and from that point in time, traveled and organized congregations primarily along the East Coast of the United States as well as Canada, England, Africa, India, and many parishes in Jamaica, where churches remain today. By 1973, the organization had begun publishing the Apostolic Monthly Publication, and two years later, had started a bible college. By 1979, they had added the "Apostolic Broadcast."

Williams led the denomination for thirty-nine years. At his death in 2010, he was succeeded by Bishop Walter G. McKoy of Englewood, New Jersey. The denomination follows the more rigid social holiness code of bodies led by Afro-Caribbeans in the United States. Women are expected to "dress modestly" and are required to wear head coverings during all worship services. While women are involved in ordained ministry as pastors, they do not serve as elders or bishops.

Church of Our Lord Jesus Christ of the Apostolic Faith

One of the largest Oneness Pentecostal denominations in the United States was established in 1919 by **Robert Clarence Lawson**, a protégé of **Garfield T. Haywood** and a former pastor and elder in the **Pentecostal Assemblies of the World**. While leading a local Columbus, Ohio congregation, the Church of Christ of the Apostolic Faith, Lawson conducted a series of tent and home prayer meetings in the Harlem section of New York that garnered a large enough following to establish Refuge Church of Christ as a PAW congregation and the launching point of his new organization.

Resigning from PAW in 1918, Lawson continued pastoring his Ohio congregation, leaving his assistant pastor **Karl F. Smith** in place to oversee its ministry. Later, when the two disagreed over polity and doctrine issues, Smith returned to PAW taking the congregation with him and Lawson established a second Columbus congregation, Rehoboth Temple Church of Christ. He would personally establish several additional congregations including Emanuel Temple in Bridgeport, Connecticut, Refuge Temple in Bronx, New York, and Greater Refuge Temple in Charleston, South Carolina, as well as send other ministers to pastor churches and establish congregations throughout the East and Midwest.

These ministers, including **Sherrod C. Johnson** of Philadelphia, Pennsylvania and **Smallwood E. Williams** of Washington DC, all of whom had built substantial works by this time, joined to incorporate the new denomination in 1929. However, in 1931—two years after he founded his Philadelphia congregation—Johnson, the state bishop of North Carolina and Pennsylvania, initiated the first major schism within the organization. Citing what he considered Lawson's liberalism in embracing Pentecostal ecumenism with non-Oneness bodies, allowing what Johnson deemed "inappropriate" dress for women, and showing a willingness for non-ordained women to preach, Johnson left to establish the **Church of The Lord Jesus Christ of the Apostolic Faith**. With this defection, Lawson lost churches in North Carolina and Pennsylvania.

The second major defection occurred in 1957, when Williams, then-executive secretary of COOLJC, broke with Lawson over ecclesiastical polity, challenging what he saw as his leader's authoritarian style. Williams convened the National Pentecostal Ministerial Conference through which was established another new body, **Bible Way Church of Our Lord Jesus Christ World Wide**. With this split, the COOLJC lost seventy additional congregations.

Over the years, several other substantial organizations led by men who had been pivotal in Lawson's organization were born from COOLJC. **Zion Gospel Assembly Churches** was established in 1938 as Zion Assembly Church in the Jamaica area of Queens, New York by Bishop J. P. Shields. **Joseph D. Williams** established the **Progressive Church of Our Lord Jesus Christ Columbia, South Carolina** in 1944. **Way of the Cross International** was founded by **Henry C. Brooks** in Washington in 1957. The **Refuge Temple Assembly of Yahweh** was established 1970 by Bishop John W. Pernell, in Richmond, Virginia. The **Evangelistic Churches of Christ** was founded in Boston by **Lymus Johnson in** 1974. Additionally, a host of small organizations, and independent churches of varying sizes have splintered from the body. Despite these losses, COOLJC has grown to be the third largest Oneness Pentecostal denomination in the United States (following the predominantly white United Pentecostal Church International and the **Pentecostal Assemblies of the World**).

At Lawson's death in 1961, there were 111 ministers serving over 125 churches with 75,000 members. At that time a board of bishops was set in place with **Herbert J. Spencer** of Columbus, Ohio, **William L. Bonner** of Harlem, and Maurice Hutner of

New Rochelle, New York at the helm. Spencer was elected to preside and served until 1972, then was succeeded by **Bonner**, who served in that position for thirteen years until 1995. In the interim, Hutner died a year after the election at fifty years of age. Upon his retirement at age eighty, Bonner assumed the position of presiding apostle, and held that position until his death in 2015.

Bonner was instrumental in proposing changes in the COOLJC governmental structure, calling for replacing a sole governing prelate with an episcopal form, including the chief apostle, the presiding apostle, the board of apostles, the board of bishops, the board of presbyters, the executive secretary, and the general council. The highest governmental board is the board of apostles, with each apostle assigned to oversee a geographical region and led by the presiding apostle.

Within COOLJC women are allowed to preach but they are not ordained to the clergy and do not serve as pastors. Further, they are required to wear some form of head covering in public worship, and to refrain from wearing clothing that is considers "worldly," or provocative such as slacks or short dresses.

The official COOLJC publications include a periodical, *The Contender for the Faith*, and an annual publication called *A Minute Book*, which records activities of international auxiliaries and departments, convention minutes and appointments, financial records and a roster of bishops, ministers, missionaries, deacons, and ministers' and deacons' wives. The organization also publishes *The Discipline Book*, which gives the fundamental creeds of the church with rules, regulations, and responsibilities of governing boards as well as local congregations.

Currently, there are approximately 500 churches located through the United States, England, Africa, and the Caribbean. Churches are also located in Canada, Mexico, and India. It is estimated that there are more than 100,000 adherents. The denomination supports a large missions program as well as two educational institutions—Church of Christ Bible Institute, founded in 1929 in New York City under the leadership of **James I. Clark Sr.** and **W. L. Bonner College**, founded in 1995 in Columbia, South Carolina, which is accredited by the Association of Biblical Higher Education. For years, the R. C. Lawson Institute in Southern Pines, North Carolina, established around 1945, provided private elementary and secondary education to hundreds of inner city children.

With Bonner's elevation, Gentle Groover, a Florida pastor who had served as Bonner's executive assistant, assumed the position of presiding apostle, serving from 1995 until 2001. He was followed by James I. Clark Jr., from 2001 until 2007, Matthew Norwood, from 2007 until 2012, and Robert Sanders, from 2013 until the present. With Bonner's death in 2015, leadership of the church reverted to Sanders in the office of presiding apostle. The denomination is headquartered at Greater Refuge Temple Church in New York City.

Further Reading:

Richardson, James C. Jr. *With Water and Spirit: A History of Black Apostolic Denominations in the U.S.* Washington DC: Spirit, 1980.
Spellman, Robert C., and Mabel Thomas. *The Life, Legend and Legacy of Bishop R.C. Lawson.* Scotch Plains, NJ: Privately Printed, 1983.

C

Church of the Living God (Christian Workers for Fellowship)

In 1888 William Christian found himself out of fellowship with the Baptist Church over embracing the doctrine of sanctification. Christian also objected to what he saw in black mainline churches as commercialization of religion. He chided black pastors for enticing their parishioners to purchase household goods, apparel, and even Bibles from the white Northern manufacturers and unjustly profiting from their position at the expense of their members.

Reportedly, after having a series of divine revelations, in 1889, Christian left the Baptist church to form the "Do Right Church," which evolved into the Church of the Living God (Christian Workers for Friendship), as a branch of black Judaism. Christian's denomination preceded that of **Charles Harrison Mason** and **Charles Price Jones**'s body, the **Church of God in Christ**, becoming the first African American Holiness church within the Mississippi/Arkansas delta region. In 1915 the parenthetical designation was changed to Christian Workers for Fellowship. CWFF congregations are designated as temples, not churches, they originally celebrated Sabbath and worshiped on Saturday rather than Sunday, and used water and unleavened bread in the Lord's Supper which is administered to a believer only once. Within the CWFF, the Lord's Prayer and those prayers found in the Psalms are understood as the only prayers that Christians should pray.

The organization sought to popularize the restorationist teachings of Alexander Campbell and held that denominational terms such as Baptist and Methodist were unscriptural. They also rejected popular conversion practices, such as the mourner's bench. CWFF maintained the Holiness tenets of "believers' baptism by immersion, washing of saints feet." Like many Holiness groups, it does not hold speaking in tongues as an initial sign of Holy Spirit baptism, but rather as one of the several gifts that comes with Holy Spirit baptism. While the group allows operation of this gift within its worship, it only permits speaking in tongues in recognizable languages.

CWFF claims to be the first black church in the United States that was not begun by white missionaries, and maintains that prominent biblical figures (David and Jesus, for example) were black. Its statement of faith was crafted, in part, to address racial disparity Christian had experienced as a child of slavery and asserts, "we believe in the Fatherhood of God and the Brotherhood of man" and ". . . that all men are born free and equal." The statement refutes racist teachings, including the claims of some late nineteenth-century Baptist preachers that "[blacks] were not men, but the outcome of a human father and a female beast." It asserts, instead, that "the saints of the Bible belonged to the black race." In other writings, Christian expanded his theology to insist that since Jesus had no earthly father, he belongs to all people and could be considered "colorless," but because he came from the lineage of Abraham and David, Jesus was black.

Prior to forming the church, Christian had been a Freemason. Presumably, since membership in secret societies such as the masons is incompatible with Holiness doctrine, he withdrew from that organization. Several elements of the church's culture, however, are reminiscent of such fraternal organizations. For example, some doctrinal tenets are only known by members of the church.

Within ten years of its formation, Christian's group claimed a membership of ten thousand and had nearly ninety congregations in eleven states. Christian served as chief bishop of the denomination until his death in 1928. At that time, his wife, Ethel who had served alongside him, took over leadership. After her death, their son John succeeded her. He was followed by F. C. Scott, then W. E. Crumes. Elbert Jones Sr. is the current presiding bishop.

Over the next century, the denomination adopted several organizational changes including changing its Sabbatarian stance. By 2006, the denomination had 214 clergy serving 170 churches with a total membership of 42,000.

In 1902 Charles W. Harris led a schismatic group in forming the Church of the Living God General Assembly. John Christian, William's brother was a charter member of the group and worked alongside his brother for several years before breaking with him to establish the Church of the Living God the Pillar and Ground of the Truth. In 1953, a schism was led by **William J. Fizer** who concluded that grape juice or wine, not water, should be used in the Lord's Supper. Fizer formed the **Church of God Which He Purchased with His Own Blood** (WHPHOB). In 1997, the denomination, whose headquarters are in Oklahoma City, had seven churches, eight hundred members and ten ministers. There are also members in Nigeria and the Philippines.

Church of the Living God International

A denomination that emerged in 1994 out of the **The House of God Which is the Church of the Living God the Pillar and Ground of the Truth without Controversy, Inc.** (the Keith Dominion) under the leadership of Bishop Joseph White. In 1969 White was appointed to a Columbus, Ohio congregation of the parent denomination to serve as assistant pastor to his mother, Elder Beulah White. On her death, the younger White assumed leadership, and shortly renamed the church, "The Pool of Bethesda" Church of the Living God. Within the decade, White began reaching into other cities and neighboring states, new churches were started in Columbus, Warren, Urbana, Cleveland, and Springfield, Ohio, and new congregations were established using ministers under his leadership out of the Pool of Bethesda Church. After White was appointed to State Bishop over what was eventually called the "Great Lakes Diocese," he influenced additional churches to join the organization from as far away as Germany, Holland, United Kingdom, Japan, South Korea, Suriname, South America, and Africa.

In 1994 the CLGI broke from the parent church to become an independent denomination. By 1998 it had established a board of six bishops with White, Mary M. Butler, Martha L. Edwards, William Lee III, T. L. Lucky, and Charles D. Smith, each holding jurisdictional responsibility. For, in keeping with the polity of its parent body, the denomination affords women full participation in leadership, involving them in all levels of ministry.

In 2008, the Jurisdictional Bishops became the Board of Directors, part of an ecclesiastical structure that also includes a General Council (elders and pastors), a General Assembly, Jurisdictional Conferences, and Local Churches. The denomination's ecclesiology promotes development of congregations that hold membership to between seventy-five and five hundred members. When the figure reaches three hundred members, CLGI promotes the establishment of a new cell that is encouraged to become a fully functional church within three years.

Church of the Living God Pillar and Ground of the Truth

The original Pentecostal body founded in 1903 when Mary Magdalena Lewis Tate held a series of revival meetings in Greenville, Alabama in which some one hundred people experienced the phenomenon of Pentecostal Holy Spirit baptism. These meetings would serve as the catalyst for a new congregation and the nucleus for a new denomination. Later that year, Tate was ordained bishop and first chief overseer of the **Church of the Living God Pillar and Ground of the Truth** and within a short period had established congregations along the East Coast promoting her doctrine of "true holiness" among family members and others.

The CLGPGT was incorporated in 1908 and Tate led it until her death in 1930. While evidence exists that Tate might have been an early member of William Christian's Holiness group, the Church of the Living God (Christian Workers for Fellowship), the sect adamantly insists their movement arose without ties to the earlier Holiness movement or knowledge of the Pentecostal revival breaking out around them. Tate saw herself as uniquely called to revive the New Testament church.

Originally the group was founded as the "Do Right Group" as part of the Holiness movement. However, following Tate's miraculous healing from a near fatal illness, which was accompanied by a spontaneous episode of speaking in tongues, she was prompted to add the Pentecostal doctrine of initial evidence to her message of sanctification. That year, she organized holiness bands under her leadership into the first congregations of the Church of the Living God the Pillar and Ground of the Truth. Tate took the title of bishop, becoming the first woman to receive that rank in a nationally recognized religious body and the first woman to hold the rank of presiding bishop of a Protestant Christian denomination.

The schism that had become the hallmark of early Pentecostalism also found its way into the CLGPGT. One of the earliest groups to split from Tate's denomination was the **First Born Church of the Living God** established in 1913 by four men, Bishop **C. H. Bass**, Quincy Crooms, Simon Crooms, and **Clarence Blakely**, in part because they objected to what they considered as CLGPGT liberal stance in allowing women to be preachers. By 1914, a second break occurred in which Bishop **R. A. R. Johnson** left to form the **House of God, Holy Church of God, the Pillar and Ground of the Truth House of Prayer for All People** (Hebrew Pentecostal).

By 1916 Tate's organization had spread to nineteen states, Washington DC, and several foreign countries. In that year, a third schism occurred when Bishop Archibald White led his growing Philadelphia congregation into the House of God, Pillar and Ground of the Truth, Inc. This schism was partly over the issue of women's leadership. White—who like C. H. Mason of the **Church of God in Christ** had been initially ordained in the Baptist Church—held a conservative position regarding women's leadership and did not approve of women as bishops.

While the CLGPGT shares core beliefs with other Pentecostal bodies, Tate's primitive, restorationist exegesis insisted that her organization's name was the uniquely divine revelation of the only God-given name for the present day Church and that other designation were not sanctioned by God. Tate understood herself as exclusively called to "reestablish" the New Testament church, restoring a purity even other Pentecostals missed, and ushering in the beginning of last days of true holiness. The reality that even schismatic followers took that assertion seriously is evidenced in the fact that most who broke from the original body retained some portion of the designation "Church of the Living God" and/or "Pillar and Ground of the Truth," as part of their name.

The practical outworking of this ecclesiology led to unique sacramental understandings. Tate used water, rather than juice or wine, and only unleavened bread for communion which she referred to as Passover and which was always followed by foot washing. While not adopting the literal Saturday Sabbath, the denomination holds a Sabbath understanding of Sunday as a day of rest and abstinence from hard work and total involvement in worship services. Tate's rigid personal piety demanded tithing and proscribed eating pork, swearing or taking oaths, and partaking of any alcohol products, including medicines containing the substance. Church membership was limited to those who evidenced Holy Spirit Baptism with speaking in tongues, and fellowship with other churches was prohibited and access to the pulpit was limited to ministers within the denomination.

During Tate's lifetime, CLGPGT grew to little more than one hundred congregations—most with constituencies of less than one hundred members and the total constituency never grew to more than several thousand persons, most of whom had personally sat under Tate's ministry at one time or another. Before her death in 1930, Tate established procedures for orderly succession within the denomination. They called for an Executive Council of Bishops and Elders to determine who should be installed as chief overseer. Though this procedure was followed, no consensus could be reached on a single successor. Instead, the council initiated a "temporary" arrangement in which three people who had worked closely with Tate were selected to run the organization. The office of chief overseer was divided into leadership of three geographical regions called dominions, each encompassing sixteen of the then forty-eight states.

Once the arrangement was in place, however, repeated attempts to resolve the stalemate proved fruitless and a permanent three-way separation occurred. Each body pays allegiance to the legacy of work and doctrine of Tate. Each retains some part of the original title of the founding body. Each dominion has its own independent governing structure and headquarters. Over the ensuing years, the respective dominions have been involved, from time to time, in litigation among themselves concerning the disposition of assets of the mother church.

Tate's daughter-in-law, **Mary Frances Lewis Keith**, took the Keith Dominion, **The House of God Which is the Church of the Living God the Pillar and Ground of the Truth without Controversy, Inc.** headquartered in Nashville, Tennessee. The McLeod Dominion, **The Church of the Living God, the Pillar and Ground of the Truth, Which He Purchased with His Own Blood,** was headed by Bruce McLeod, who was related to Tate by marriage. This dominion has headquarters in Indianapolis and has come to be known as the Jewell Dominion. The original name, **The Church of the Living God the Pillar and Ground of the Truth,** was maintained as the Lewis Dominion, under the leadership of Tate's son Felix, who served as chief overseer until his death in 1968, when his wife Helen Middleton Lewis took leadership.

Each of these, along with smaller groups that came into being because of the early schisms, pays direct allegiance to Tate's original body. Each retains some part of the original title, crediting Tate as founder and maintaining the distinctive elements she established. A final schism occurred in 1994, when the **Church of the Living God International** emerged out of the Keith Dominion.

Further Reading:

Lewis, Helen M., and Meharry H Lewis. *The Beauty of Holiness: A Small Catechism of the Holiness Faith and Doctrine.* Nashville: New and Living Way, 1990.

Lewis, Meharry. *Mary Lena Lewis Tate: Vision! A Biography of the Founder and History of The Church of the Living God, the Pillar and Ground of the Truth, Inc.* Nashville: New and Living Way, 2005.

Church of the Living God Pillar and Ground of the Truth (General Assembly)

A body within the Holiness movement, which was the first to come out of **William Christian**'s group, **Church of the Living God Pillar and Ground of the Truth (Christian Workers for Fellowship).** It was founded in 1902 in Wrightsville, Arkansas by Charles W. Harris as the Church of the Living God (Apostolic Church). In 1908, Harris reorganized the group as the General Assembly Church of the Living God. In 1924, Harris's group united with another group of the same name.

In 1926, a second group, the House of God which is the **Church of the Living God Pillar and Ground of the Truth** that had been established a year earlier by Arthur Joseph Hawthorne merged with Harris's group. Several years after the merger, Emory J. Cain, who had been affiliated with Hawthorne since before the merger, led several congregations in a schism and joined with the **Church of the Living God Pillar and Ground of the Truth of Muskogee, Oklahoma.**

The doctrine is similar to that of the parent body. Speaking in tongues is permitted (as long as the utterances are in a known language), yet not required. The denomination supports two institutions—the Booker T. Washington Home for the elderly and the Edmonson Institute, a school and orphans' home in Athens, Texas.

The strength of the denomination is in Texas, where most churches are located. Headquarters for the parent group is in Dallas, Texas. C. C. Berry Jr. is the presiding bishop.

Church of the Living God Pillar and Ground of the Truth (Lewis Dominion)

One of the three bodies that came into being after the 1930 death of the Mary Magdalen Lewis Tate, founder of the **Church of the Living God Pillars and Ground of the Truth.** That year, her son, **Felix Early Lewis,** was selected as one of a triumvirate of overseers to administer the affairs of the organization she left intact. When the original shared leadership arrangement failed and the body was partitioned in 1931, Lewis become chief presider of the dominion named after him, a position he held until his death in 1968.

Following his death, his wife, **Helen M. Lewis**, served as chief overseer pro tempore. In 1969, she was seated as chief overseer. She, along with her son, **Meharry H. Lewis**, crafted the church's doctrinal treatise, The Beauty of Holiness: A Small Catechism of the Holiness Faith, in 1988.

Like its sister organizations, the Dominion holds the three distinctives laid down by Tate: 1) its name was divinely inspired and revealed as the only biblical designation for the church; 2) God calls women into all leadership positions in the church; and 3) water (not wine or grape juice) is the true New Testament symbol of Christ's blood. Yet, while the dominion maintains the original name of Tate's organization, it has remained comparably small related to its sister bodies, with only approximately twenty congregations and two thousand members. Lewis Dominion congregations are concentrated in the South—primarily in Florida and Mississippi. Headquarters for this dominion is in Nashville, Tennessee.

The present overseer is Tate's grandson, Meharry Lewis, who took over at his mother's death in 2001. The younger Lewis has reestablished the operation of the **New and Living Way Publishing Company**, using it to produce biographical works on the founder as well as doctrinal and historical material regarding the denomination.

Church of the Living God Pillar and Ground of the Truth of Muskogee, Oklahoma

A group within the Holiness movement founded in a schism between **William Christian**, founder of the **Church of the Living God (Christian Workers for Fellowship)**, and his brother John Christian in 1895. It was incorporated in 1915. One of the major issues driving the separation was William's insistence that the Lord's Prayer was the only acceptable prayer for Christians. The schismatic group originally established its headquarters in Pine Bluff, Arkansas. The organization grew and waned as other schismatic groups from the parent body affiliated and disaffiliated themselves at varying times during the twentieth century. In one such instance, Emory J. Cain who had emerged as a leader within the **Church of the Living God Pillar and Ground of the Truth (General Assembly)** led several congregations from that group into a merger with the denomination.

The denomination is centered in the Midwest. Besides Oklahoma, there are congregations in Texas, Kentucky, Missouri, Illinois, and California. Sometime before 1993, the headquarters moved to Decatur, Illinois. In that year, Herbert Dickerson was the presiding bishop.

Church of the Living God, Pillar and Ground of the Truth, Which He Purchased With His Own Blood, Inc. (McLeod/Jewell Dominion)

One of three Trinitarian Pentecostal denominations that is a direct offshoot of the original **Church of the Living God Pillar and Ground of the Truth**, founded by **Mary Magdalena Lewis Tate**. When the Tate died and an experiment in shared leadership by regional leaders failed, the denomination was partitioned into three cooperative, yet autonomous structures. Bishop **Bruce L. McLeod**, Tate's step son-in-law took sole leadership of the branch that became the Church of the Living God, Pillar and Ground of the Truth, Which He Purchased With His Own Blood, Inc. McLeod served from the time of the partition until his death in 1936. His wife—Tate's stepdaughter—Mattie Lou McLeod became interim presiding bishop and was elected permanent presider in 1939. After remarrying, she changed the designation of the organization to the Jewell Dominion, a name it has held since that time.

In early 1950, she founded a veterans' group as well as Jewell's Academy and Seminary, which operated from 1950–1962 and served kindergarten through high school. In 1964, she purchased property in Indianapolis, Indiana for the denomination's headquarters. Jewell died in 1991.

Jewell's granddaughter, **Naomi Manning**, who had been groomed for the role of General Overseer for most of her life, became the next Overseer. She had worked in the church since her childhood, and had served as Second Assistant Overseer from 1964 until 1986 under Jewell, before becoming Assistant Overseer on the passing of her father L. L. Harrison in 1986. Dr. Manning died in 2003.

The current presiding bishop, Faye Moore, a life-long member of the Church of the Living God, was appointed as senior bishop/chief overseer in 2005. Prior to taking that office, Bishop Moore served as chairperson of the board of directors, and several other leadership positions.

The denomination has headquarters in Indianapolis, Indiana and forty-seven congregations in the United States, the Caribbean, and Africa.

Church of the Lord Jesus Christ of the Apostolic Faith

A major Oneness Pentecostal denomination founded in 1931 by Bishop **Sherrod C. Johnson**, a pastor within **Church of Our Lord Jesus Christ of the Apostolic Faith** who left the parent organization because of what he felt was founder **Robert C. Lawson**'s liberalism. The major issues that concerned Johnson were women's apparel, as well as allowing unordained women to preach.

In 1920 Lawson sent Johnson to pastor a storefront Philadelphia congregation, the Church of Christ. Over the next ten years, Johnson built that church into what would become the second largest Pentecostal congregation in that city. In 1934 he began airing Sunday broadcasts on two separate radio stations: WOOK in Washington DC and WIBC in Philadelphia that expanded the influence of the denomination, drawing significant numbers of people to the churches.

Three years after the split with Lawson, there were churches in eighteen states and several foreign countries. Johnson presided over the denomination for thirty years, until his death in 1961. He was succeeded by thirty-three-year-old S. McDowell Shelton who had been a rising leader in the denomination and whose elevation was initially challenged by several within the group. While continuing the majority of Johnson's sectarian polities, Shelton went on to gain a degree of respectability for the organization through a variety of projects to broaden its presence within the city of Philadelphia as well as the broader African-American Pentecostal community.

In 1971 the church built the Apostolic Square complex that included Apostolic Village, a thirty-two-unit independent living apartment complex for seniors and commercial sites. New churches were built and congregations added so that by 1980, the body had grown to more than one hundred congregations in the United States, England, Africa, Jamaica, and the Bahamas.

The denomination is one of a small number of black Oneness bodies that insists that many of the holidays generally celebrated by the Christian community, such as Christmas, Lent, and Easter are unbiblical "pagan" [sic] festivals. The organization insisted that women refrain from straightening their hair and wear a head covering (usually a plain black tam styled hat) and that they wear long dresses and cotton stockings during all seasons of the year. Within its worship, baptism is specifically in the name of the "Lord Jesus" or "Jesus Christ" to avoid confusion with two other biblical figures, Bar Jesus or Jesus Justus.

Since Shelton had no natural heirs and no enforceable plan of succession was in place, following his death in 1991 at age sixty-two, a legal battle erupted among his adopted sons Elder Nehemiah Shelton, Prince Omega Shelton, and Bishop Anthonee Patterson over succession and control over his assets, with each attempting to carry on their adopted father's legacy. Additionally several smaller bodies, each claiming to be direct heir to Johnson and Shelton emerged including **Holy Temple Church of the Lord Jesus Christ of the Apostolic Faith** under Bishop **Randolph Goodwin**, the Apostolic Ministries of America, and the **First Church of Our Lord Jesus Christ** founded by **Gino Jennings**. All of these bodies are actively evangelizing North America, the Caribbean, Europe, and West Africa.

Further Reading:

Johnson, Sherrod C. *21 Burning Subjects: Who is This that Defies and Challenges the Whole Religious World on these Subjects.* Philadelphia, PA: Church of Our Lord Jesus Christ of the Apostolic Faith, 1962.

Richardson, James C. Jr. *With Water and Spirit: A History of Black Apostolic Denominations in the US.* Martinsville, VA: James C. Richardson, s.d.

Churches of God and True Holiness

The Oneness Pentecostal organization established by the late Bishop **John Wesley Garlington, Sr.** in 1927 in Buffalo, New York. Soon churches were added in New York, Virginia, North Carolina, Ohio, Florida, Delaware and South Carolina. Garlington led this organization until his death in 1943, when Thomas Benton of Norfolk, Virginia became the presiding bishop. After Benton's death in 1958, Bishop Frank Jackson of Winter Haven, Florida assumed the post of presiding Bishop serving until 1961. During his tenure, certain undelineated doctrinal issues arose that caused a fracture within the denomination when Joseph Peeler of Buffalo was appointed presider. After Peeler's death three years later, the office fell to John Kennon; who, in 1968, relinquished his to **John**

W. Garlington, Jr. son of the founder, who stepped down in 1975 to move his family to Portland, Oregon, to assume the pastorate of a multi-cultural non-denominational congregation.

Due to a fire at the headquarters church in Buffalo, the 47th Holy Convocation in 1974 was held at the church in Rochester, New York where the host pastor was Elder Paul Garlington. On his departure, Frank Jackson became the new presiding bishop. The national headquarters was relocated to the church in Cleveland, Ohio. At that time, Elder Albert E. Dixon, Sr. was the pastor of the church in Cleveland and the national evangelist of the Churches of God and True Holiness. After Jackson's death in 1978, Dixon was appointed to preside. In 1996, Dixon and Bishop Raymond Worrell were consecrated as Apostles. Dixon presided bishop for the Churches of God and True Holiness for over thirty years. Following his tenure, James Brant, Jr, assumed office. Today, this organization has churches in six states and two countries

At one point during the 1980s, the denomination was accused of placing members in involuntary solitude and its leaders were under surveillance by the Federal Bureau of Investigation for forcibly coercing members to turn over paychecks, welfare checks and food stamps. Today, the organization, which has strict sanctions against women preaching, has churches in six states and two countries.

Churches of God, Holiness

A predominantly black Holiness church founded in 1920 by Bishop **King Hezekiah Burruss**, formerly with the **Church of Christ (Holiness) USA**. Burruss began a church (Bethlehem Church of Christ Holiness) in Atlanta, GA in 1914 that belonged to COCHUSA. By 1920, the Atlanta congregation was large enough that it hosted the national convention of the Church of Christ (Holiness) U.S.A. Shortly after that Atlanta meeting, Burruss formed his own church, using his Atlanta congregation founded as headquarters. Within three years there were twenty-two churches in eleven states, Cuba, the Canal Zone, and the British West Indies.

In 1947 a group led by William C. Holman broke with Burruss's organization to form the **Evangelical Church of Christ (Holiness).** This break was primarily administrative; the doctrine and practice are the same as that of the parent body.

Burruss led the denomination for fifty years until his death in 1963 and was succeeded by his son, **Titus Paul Burruss.** Three years later, by 1965, the organization had grown to 25,600 members in thirty-two congregations mostly along the East Coast. The doctrine is identical to that of the parent body.

At the younger Burruss death, Elder Theodore Roosevelt McBride assumed the positon of presiding bishop serving for only one year when Bishop James C. Taylor Sr. was elevated to the positon that he currently holds.

Churches of God in Christ International

When **Church of God in Christ** founder, **Charles Harrison Mason**, died in 1961, the denomination waited a year before selecting a successor. In the Holy Convocation of 1962, the only surviving bishop of the original five appointed by Mason, **Ozro Thurston**

Jones, Sr. of Philadelphia, was elected to the office of senior bishop. For two years, Bishop Jones presided over the church in peace.

In 1968 at Evanston, Illinois, Bishops Carl E. Williams and his brother William David Charles Williams, Sr., set up a Committee of Recommendations who advised the group to establish the Churches of God In Christ International as a new organization that would return to original COGIC roots.

In 1970 the headquarters was established at Evanston and DWC Williams was appointed as senior bishop and chief apostle. Around that time, Carl Williams split with his brother to establish the new denomination with the identical name. Later the name was changed to Churches of God in Christ, International. Carl Williams assumed the post of presiding bishop in 1976 and held it until 2001 when he chose Bishop **John C. (J. C.) White**, who had been pastor of Institutional Church of God in Christ, who along with his wife, Gloria, had headed the renowned Institutional Church of God in Christ Radio Choir, to serve in his stead. Williams died in 2007 and White has served as presiding bishop since that time.

The headquarters of the organization is in Bridgeport, Connecticut. Affiliate churches are located in New Haven, Hartford, Bridgeport, and Fairfield.

Clark, James I., Jr. 1936–

Pastor, educator, and former presiding bishop of the Oneness Pentecostal denomination, **Church of Our Lord Jesus Christ of the Apostolic Faith**. Clarke is the oldest son of James I. Clarke, Sr. one of the founding Bishops of **Bible Way Church of Our Lord Jesus Christ World Wide** and Dean of the Christ Bible Institute.

After serving in the United States Air Force, he pursued a career in private industry (which spanned close to thirty years in top-level positions at several corporations). During that time, he served as Director of Minority Affairs at Columbia University's Graduate School of Business, and later of Director of Training and Development at Pfizer, Inc.

Clark holds a Doctor of Education degree from Columbia University, a Masters of Divinity from Union Theological Seminary, an MBA from Columbia University Graduate School of Business, and a Bachelor of Theology degree from American Divinity School.

Within COOLJC, Clark rose through the ranks, serving in increasingly responsible positions. First he took over the pastorate of Christ Temple Church of our Lord Jesus Christ from his father, who moved into the presidency of Church of Christ Bible Institute in 1969. For half that period since then, the younger Clark has also served as assistant pastor of Greater Refuge Temple. Formerly, he served as Bishop of the Westchester Diocese, Bishop of Foreign Missions in the Caribbean, Chair of the Board of Bishops and member of the Corporate Advisory Council for the Children's Aid Society, and finally as presiding apostle for the Church Of Our Lord Jesus Christ of the Apostolic Faith, Inc. from 2001 until 2007. Currently, he remains as pastor of the two congregations.

Clark, James I., Sr. 1891–1972

One of the most educated leaders within the Oneness Pentecostal denomination, **Church of Our Lord Jesus Christ of the Apostolic Faith**, where he spent the early years of his ministry helping **Smallwood E. Williams** establish **Bible Way Church of Our Lord Jesus Christ World Wide.** He spent over a decade here before returning to the parent body.

Born in Trinidad, West Indies, Clark migrated to United States as a teenager. Shortly after World War I, he met **Robert Clarence Lawson** of the Church of Our Lord Jesus of the Apostolic Faith, under who he made a commitment to Christian faith and received the Pentecostal was baptism in the Holy Spirit. While with that body, he was called to the ministry and pastored in Chester, Pennsylvania and Paterson, New Jersey before returning to New York to assume the leadership of Christ Temple Church of our Lord Jesus Christ in Harlem.

Clark attended Shelton Bible College in New Jersey and the Institute of Religious and Social Studies in New York, and received his ThD from American Divinity School. In 1940 he was the natural choice to serve as dean of the newly founded Bible institute that Lawson had envisioned and he served in that post faithfully for seventeen years.

In 1957, however, Clark joined Williams along with John S. Beane, McKinley Williams, **Winfield Showell**, and Joseph Moore in breaking with Lawson and COOLJC to the new organization where they would be allowed to function as bishops and have more authority over their local congregations. While in that organization, Clark established the first Bible Way congregation in the city of New York in 1958, Christ Temple of the Apostolic Faith, Inc., but after approximately twelve years returned to the Church of Our Lord Jesus Christ, Inc.

Clark's congregation was divided on his decision. The majority of the members of the congregation decided to remain with Bible Way, and split with him to form another congregation. On his return, he resumed leadership of the Bible Institute over which he was named president in the fall of 1968. After suffering a mild heart attack in 1969, Clark, turned leadership of his Harlem congregation over to his son, James I. Clark Jr. and devoted full attention to the institute for the remainder of his life.

Clark, Mattie Juliet Moss 1925–1994

The innovative and prolific **Church of God in Christ** musician was born in Selma, Alabama. She began playing piano at age six and by twelve, Clark was the music minister at the Holiness Temple Church of Christ and Prayer, where her mother was pastor. After high school, Clark attended Selma University, receiving training in classical music and choral singing. In 1981 she received a Doctor of Humanity degree from Trinity College in Pennsylvania.

She moved to Detroit in 1947 and experienced Pentecostal baptism in the Holy Spirit. Within a short time, she organized the Southwest Michigan State Choir of the

Church of God in Christ, and served as Minister of Music at Bailey Temple Church of God in Christ, as well as for the Southwest Michigan Jurisdiction both under Bishop **John Seth Bailey.** Soon, she was training choirs throughout COGIC. In 1972 COGIC presiding bishop **James O. Patterson, Sr.** appointed her president of the International Music Department, an office she held for twenty-five years. Within this position, she introduced several new concepts into COGIC such as separating vocal parts into soprano, alto, and tenor and helped to edit the hymnal published by the **Church of God in Christ** entitled, *Yes, Lord.* In 1979, Dr. Clark founded the Clark Conservatory of Music.

Among the several gospel music firsts she accomplished during her career, the Southwest Michigan State choir became among the first choirs to record. Clark also was the first person to present a gospel choir at the Apollo Theater in Harlem, New York.

As president of the National Music Department, Clark conducted statewide music sessions to prepare choirs for service on the National Church level, and organized the National Music Convention, introducing the workshop and seminar concept and a program to introduce new talent to the denomination.

Clark received three gold albums with the Southwest Michigan State Choir, and went on to write and arrange hundreds of songs and. She recorded more than fifty albums with the choir and with numerous other artists. She also mentored several notable gospel artists and groups. She helped such artists as **Walter Hawkins**, Hezekiah Walker, and Richard Smallwood get their careers started. As the first gospel artist to earn a gold album, in 1994, "the Queen of Gospel" was posthumourously inducted in the Gospel Music Hall of Fame. Further, her musical influence reached beyond the church. Among other activities, Clark directed Cadillac Motor Company's Christmas Choir for eleven years and conducted community mass choirs for NAACP Freedom Fund dinners.

Her daughters—Jackie, Denise, Elbernita, Dorinda and Karen—were mentored by their mother, and became the "Legendary Clark Sisters." In 1983 she performed with the group at the Grammy Awards. Despite failing health, Clark continued recording into the last year of her life. She died of complications from diabetes at age sixty-nine in Southfield, Michigan.

Further Reading:

McCoy, Eugene B. *Climbing Up the Mountain: The Musical Life and Times of Dr. Mattie Moss Clark.* Nashville: Sparrow, 1995.

Clark, Otis G. 1903–2013

The evangelist and the oldest survivor of the 1921 Tulsa race riot was born in Meridian, Indian Territory in pre-statehood Oklahoma. Clark was eighteen years old when the riot occured, which claimed the life of his stepfather. He witnessed many people die and his family home was burned to the ground. Shortly after the riot, Clark left Tulsa and= joined his father in Hollywood, California. He found work as an extra in the movie industry where he became friends with black comedy actor, Lincoln Perry (whose stage name was Steppin' Fetchit), and worked as a house servant for stars such as Clark Gable, Charlie Chaplin, Joan Crawford, and others.

At age twenty-five, while serving a term in a Los Angeles jail for selling bootleg whiskey during the Prohibition era, Clark converted to the Christian faith. He became a member of the mission in the Azusa Street Mission after the revival ended and William J. Seymour had died. Near the end of the Mission's existence, he was later given power of attorney, and helped in the failed attempt to keep it open. Eventually, however, the property was foreclosed and, susbequently, torn down.

Clark later became an itinerant evangelist and was ordained as a minister in 1946 in the **Church of God in Christ** by Bishop **Samuel M. Crouch**. He never pastored a church, but shortly, he began traveling the United States as an itinerant evangelist. At one point, he returned to Tulsa, but in later years his principal home was in Seattle, Washington where he became bishop of Life Enrichment Ministries, a non-denominational Pentecostal group he co-founded with his daughter, Gwyneth Williams. Clark spent his last years traveling across the world and preaching on mission trips through Africa—the first when he was 103 years old and the second when he was 104. He traveled to the West Indies at 107. At the time of his death at age 109, Clark was reportedly preparing for a Pentecostal revival in Nigeria in January 2013. He was preceded in death by two wives.

Further Reading:

Clark, Otis G., and Gwyneth Williams. *The Azusa Outpouring: Unleashing the Holy Spirit, Signs, Wonders, & Miracles.* Bloomington, IN: Author House, 2011.

Clemmons, Frank 1894–1990

The founder and pastor of the historic First Church of God in Christ in Brooklyn, New York, was born in Washington, North Carolina. Clemmons was raised in an independent congregation within the Holiness movement, but joined the **Church of God in Christ** in 1914 at age twenty and by 1918, was pastoring a flourishing **Church of God in Christ** congregation in Plymouth, North Carolina.

He was ordained in 1924 and after being discharged from the army. Later that year, at the urging of his close friend, **Peter J. F. Bridges**, he migrated north with his family to Brooklyn, worshiping with Bridges for a short time. Eventually, however, he became dissatisfied with Bridges' emphasis on Oneness Pentecostal doctrine. Two years after arriving in the city, he started a family prayer meeting in his home that evolved into a storefront mission church that became the first COGIC congregation in the borough. In the early years, Clemmons, like many black Pentecostal pastors of his era, worked at odd jobs to help support his congregation. Yet, he still found time to plant a second congregation on Long Island, New York and spread his ministry across the eastern part of the state.

Clemmons was consecrated as a bishop in 1959 and appointed over the state of Vermont. He also served as District Superintendent and worked with the State Advisory Committee. In that post, he interacted with some of the prominent black Brooklyn church leaders of that time, including Sandy Ray of Cornerstone Baptist Church, Gardner Taylor of Concord Baptist Church, and William Augustus Jones of Bethany Baptist Church.

At the time of his death, Clemmons had been in the ministry for sixty-six years and was ninety-six years old. His two sons, **Ithiel Clemmons** and **Joseph Clemons**, would follow him into the ministry and would themselves become prominent figures within COGIC, the broad Pentecostal movement, as well as the social and political arena. For the last twenty-four years of Frank Clemmons' life, Ithiel worked as his assistant pastor and helped solidify the place of that congregation in COGIC history.

Further Reading:

Milner, Marlon. "We've Come this Far by Faith: Pentecostalism and Political and Social Upward Mobility among African-Americans." *Cyberjournal for Pentecostal-Charismatic Research,* February 9, 2001. Online: http://www.pctii.org/cyberj/cyberj9/millner.html.

Clemmons, Ithiel Conrad 1921–1999

Churchman, civil rights advocate, and scholar who chronicled the life of **Church of God in Christ** founder, **Charles Harrison Mason**, and was a leader in the push for racial reconciliation within the Pentecostal movement. Ithiel Clemmons was born in Washington, North Carolina, as the son of COGIC pastor, **Frank Clemmons** who would go on to become a bishop in the organization. By the time he was five, the family had moved to Brooklyn, New York where he father founded First Church of God in Christ. He accepted Christ at an early age and committed himself to the Church and its ministries. By the age of five, Ithiel was being called "the Preacher."

Clemmons was ordained by Bishop **O. M. Kelly** in 1943. In 1952 he received his Master of Arts in Education from the City College of New York. Four years later, he received his Master of Divinity from Union Theological Seminary in the same city. He also held an honorary Doctor of Divinity from the Charles Harrison Mason Seminary of the Interdenominational Theological Center at Atlanta, Georgia.

Beginning in 1955, Clemons pastored Gethsemane Church of God in Christ in Clairton, Pennsylvania for twelve years. In 1966, he joined the staff of his father's congregation, the historic, First Church of God in Christ, Brooklyn to serve as co-pastor, taking on the position of pastor at the senior Clemmon's death. At the same time, from 1975, he co-pastored Church of God in Christ Cathedral in Greensboro North Carolina.

In 1967 he served as Preaching Fellow at the College of Preachers of Washington National Cathedral in Washington DC. From 1968 to 1992 he was the National Prayer Leader for COGIC. Among his other responsibilities, Clemmons served as a member of the General Board of the **Church of God in Christ** from 1977 until his death. He was the denominational historian and jurisdictional bishop of Eastern New York First Jurisdiction, presiding bishop to the military, chair of the Executive Committee of the Pentecostal Charismatic Churches of North American (PCCNA)

As a scholar, Clemmons was Adjunct Professor of African-American Religious Studies at Regent University, Virginia Beach, Virginia, and was a lecturer at the Duke

University Divinity School. The past president of the Society for Pentecostal Studies (SPS), he was a frequent contributor to academic dialog and published one of the most recent full biographers of the COGIC founder. *Bishop C. H. Mason and the Roots of the Church of God in Christ* was released by Pneuma Life Publications in 1996.

Clemmons' ecumenical alliances included serving on the North American Renewal Service Committee (NARSC) and working as a member of the planning committee for Harry Emerson Fosdick Convocation convened at Riverside Church, New York City in 1997. He was a member of the Board of Directors of the LeMan Corporation of Longwood, Florida.

Perhaps his most memorable contribution to the Pentecostal movement was the role he played in bringing about the "Memphis Miracle." Clemmons worked with Pentecostal Holiness Church overseer Bernard E. Underwood to forge an agreement that called for the dismantling of the white umbrella group, Pentecostal Fellowship of North America, and the establishment of the interracial Pentecostal and Charismatic Churches of North America. Clemmons was tapped to serve as the first president of the new organization.

Further Reading:

Banks, Margaret Moffett. "Greensboro Bishop is Remembered as a Gifted Speaker and a National Leader." *Greensboro [North Carolina] News & Record.* January 14, 1999.
Milner, Marlon. "We've Come this Far by Faith: Pentecostalism and Political and Social Upward Mobility among African-Americans." *Cyberjournal for Pentecostal-Charismatic Research,* February 9, 2001. Online: http://www.pctii.org/cyberj/cyberj9/millner.html..

Clemmons, Joseph D., Sr. 1929–

The pastor, educator, and politician was born in Brooklyn, New York, five years after his family relocated from Washington, North Carolina. His father, Bishop **Frank Clemmons**, was founding pastor of the historic **First Church of God in Christ**. His older brother, **Ithiel Clemmons**, was also a leader within COGIC and the broader Pentecostal movement.

Clemmons attended Long Island University in New York and Howard University in Washington DC. He was ordained by **Bishop O. M. Kelly** in 1952. In 1955 he founded Zion Tabernacle in Baltimore, Maryland. In 1963 Kelly appointed him to pastor the Miracle Temple Church of God in Christ of Norwalk, Connecticut, where he remains pastor until this day. After that appointment, Clemmons decided he needed seminary training and entered Yale Divinity school in 1965. He received his Master of Divinity degree in 1969. From there, he entered Colgate Rochester Divinity School where he received his Doctor of Ministry degree. In 1975 as a Martin Luther King Fellow, he traveled to Nigeria and Ghana. For a time, he taught elementary school in Baltimore, Maryland and middle and high school in Bridgeport and Norwalk, Connecticut before retiring from the school system in 1979, to devote full-time to the ministry.

Clemmons was first elected to public office in 1995 to serve on the Norwalk Common Council. Following that, he was elected as a Democratic member to the Connecticut House of Representatives from Norwalk in a special election in February 1997. He then was re-elected in 1998, defeating Republican Jon J. Velez, and again in November 2000.

Clemmons, along with his uncle and mentor, **D. Lawrence Williams,** is only one of two Pentecostals (both of whom were COGIC) to have served as former president of the prestigious Hampton University Ministers' Conference in Hampton, Virginia. He continues to serve on its Executive Board. In 1988 he was inducted into the Morehouse College of Preachers.

In 1999 he followed his elder brother, Ithiel, as the third pastor to serve his father's historic First COGIC in Brooklyn, while retaining the pastorate of his Connecticut congregation, leading both up to this point. In 2004, he was elected to a seven-year term as an Associate Justice of the nine-member Judiciary Board of the **Church of God in Christ**.

Clemmons's civic involvement includes serving as a Norwalk Fire Department chaplain and working on a number of ecumenical projects with mainline leaders in organizations including serving on the board of Norwalk Economic Opportunity Now (NEON), and serving as executive director and board member of Norwalk Area Ministry. He also founded Pivot Ministries, a Christ-centered drug treatment program.

Further Reading:

Milner, Marlon. "We've Come this Far by Faith: Pentecostalism and Political and Social Upward Mobility among African-Americans." *Cyberjournal for Pentecostal-Charismatic Research,* February 9, 2001. Online: http://www.pctii.org/cyberj/cyberj9/millner.html.

Coffey, Lillian Brooks 1896–1964

The second International Supervisor of **Women for the Church of God in Christ** was a social advocate who championed racial uplift and the advancement of women. Though she was founder **Charles H. Mason's** first choice for the position, the young woman was only twenty-one years old and she declined. Considering herself too young for the responsibility, she suggested instead that Mason call on **Elizabeth Isabelle (Lizzie) Robinson,** who took office in 1911, setting the organization on a solid foundation.

Coffey, who grew up in Memphis, Tennessee, became acquainted with the **Church of God in Christ** through attending Sunday school at Mason's local congregation that was near her house, and came to Pentecostal faith under his ministry. After joining COGIC in 1903, the daughter of a Baptist minister left home due to her parents' hostility to her beliefs. When both parents died while she was still a young woman, she eventually moved in with Bishop Mason's family. She married in her twenties and worked as a hotel housekeeper, Her marriage ended, however, again in a dispute over her beliefs.

At Robinson's death in 1943, Coffey assumed full leadership of the Women's Department, serving as its head for twenty-one years until her death in 1964. In the interim, she served as Robinson's Assistant Supervisor and managed the administrative affairs of Mason's local church office. She also occasionally accompanied Mason to revival meetings preaching and teaching as an evangelist.

Though Robinson and Coffey worked closely together for a number of years, the two women differed greatly in styles and focus. Robinson adhered to a strict Holiness code of morality and personal piety and her austere approach centered solidly on developing the spirituality of COGIC women. In sharp contrast, without abandoning Holiness principles, Coffey's more contemporary style involved her in a breadth of issues and causes beyond those specifically beneficial to the mundane needs of the denomination.

While serving under Robinson, Coffey steadily rose through the ranks of the Women's Department. She was appointed Michigan State Supervisor at twenty-nine, and served as head of finances, raising funds for important COGIC projects. The exceptional preacher and prolific church founder aided in expanding COGIC influence in the Midwest by working to help establish congregations in Wisconsin, Ohio, Michigan, and Illinois. In one instance, she organized prayer bands in Chicago leading to the first COGIC there. Eventually, she developed a team of evangelists who traveled around the country promoting prayer bands that led to churches.

Within COGIC Coffey initiated several innovations, including founding the Lillian Brooks Coffey Rest Home in Detroit, and organizing the "Lillian Coffey Train," which not only raised money, but exposed the denomination's black women to the experience of travel. A believer in education, she led the department in creating schools and missions in several parts of the world. Yet, Coffey's single most notable accomplishment was establishment of the National Women's Convention. This event, which regularly draws between 20,000 and 25,000 women, was conceived by Coffey in 1950. The event was a key component of Coffey's strategy to developing the missions department as another notable accomplishment. Coffey appointed a Missions Director and a Board of Stewardesses that directing women throughout the denomination in raising funds for missions as well as collecting food and clothing to send oversees. In 1953, her efforts also involved raising funds to build a residence for the Mason family adjacent to the COGIC headquarters.

Nonetheless, her close association with prominent women, including Mary McLeod Bethune and **Arenia Mallory**, pushed her influence beyond COGIC involving her in the broader struggle for "racial uplift" and women's rights that was waging outside the narrow confines of the church. She was a member of First Lady, Eleanor Roosevelt's, Negro Women's League, advising on issues from the perspective of black women. In the early 1960s, she led a group of women on a tour of the White House where President John F. Kennedy greeted them.

At her death at age sixty-eight, she was succeeded by **Anne Bailey**.

Further Reading:

Butler, Anthea. *Women in the Church of God in Christ: The Making of a Sanctified World.* Chapel Hill, NC: The University of North Carolina Press, 2006.
Cornelius, Lucille. *The Pioneer History of the Church of God in Christ.* Self-published, 1975.

COGIC Scholars Fellowship

COGIC Scholars, as the organization is known, is a network of several hundred predominantly African American scholars who are members of the **Church of God in Christ** as well as other African-American Pentecostal bodies. The organization is also open to white, non-African Americans as well as those outside the movement who are actively involved or interested in studying the movement. It provides a forum for dialogue among those who hold, or are pursuing, graduate-level training in religious or theological studies or other related academic disciplines and sponsors academic forums at regularly scheduled COGIC gathering included the National Convocation and the annual AIM (Auxiliaries in Mission) Convention. It also publishes a semi-monthly newsletter, *The Advocate*, detailing publications of members and other African-American Pentecostal scholars

It was founded in 2002 by Raynard Smith, an elder in the **Church of God in Christ** who at the time was a graduate student at Drew University and is currently serving as associate professor of Pastoral Care at New Brunswick Theological Seminary in New Brunswick, New Jersey.

Collier, Lucy Smith 1925–2010

Gospel vocalist and pianist who rose from her grandmother's South Side Chicago congregation, **All Nation's Pentecostal Church**, to become a nationally known gospel pianist and composer. Lucy Austin was born and raised in Chicago, the daughter of the Rev. James Austin and his wife, Viola Smith, older daughter of Pastor **Lucy Smith**. Her mother died when she was two and she was raised by her father and grandmother.

By age four, the talent of the younger Lucy (who was known as "Little Lucy Smith") was evident when she was picking out the tunes that she had heard in church. At ten, her grandmother sent her to Chicago gospel music pioneer Roberta Martin (later her stepmother) for piano lessons. Within two years, she became the organist at her grandmother's church. Smith also received classical training at the Chicago Musical College that allowed her to play a variety of genres, from Chopin to gospel to jazz. Worshippers across the country came to All Nations Church, to her play the organ and her grandmother preach.

In the mid-1950s she organized the Lucy Smith Singers, whose most famous recording was "Somebody Bigger than You and I." From 1955 to 1956, the group, which featured Smith as the vocalist and organist, recorded for the States Record Label. In the 1960s she was pianist with the Roberta Martin Singers, but when the group disbanded in 1971, Collier became the pianist for the Chicago produced "Jubilee Showcase" TV Show.

Sometime during the 1970s, Collier suffered a stroke, which left her partially paralyzed. While she retained the ability to sing, she was unable to play the piano or organ again. Collier continued to sing and write into her later years, recording in the 1980s and 1990s for Anthony Heilbut's Spirit Feel label.

Colty, Benjamin Franklin 1889–1970

Founder of a Oneness denomination, the **New Church of Christ Holiness unto the Lord of the Apostolic Faith** in 1959. Colty came to Christian faith in the late 1920s during a revival in Beaufort, South Carolina in a congregation of the **Church of Christ Holiness Unto the Lord**, a Trinitarian denomination that had been established twenty-six years earlier by Milton Solomon Bennett. After his conversion, Colty was first ordained a deacon and appointed a Sunday School teacher, before becoming one of four elders elected to serve the congregation. By the 1940s the farmer with only an eighth grade education had established churches throughout Florida and South Carolina within CCHUL. From 1950 to 1952, he served as the second presiding bishop of the denomination. He was appointed assistant General Overseer under Bennett, and at the death of the leader in 1952, the highly respected preacher and administrator was elected as the denomination's head. Sometime after Bennett's death, however, he accepted Oneness Pentecostal doctrine and left in 1959 to form his new denomination.

Further Reading:

Brown, Tomie. *Sharing our History with Others: The Churches of Christ Holiness unto the Lord as We Know It*. Bloomington, IN: Xlibris, 2014

Conry, Inez 1897–1977

The second National Presiding Minister of the **House of the Lord and Church on the Mount** founded by **Alonzo Daughtry**. When the senior minister fell into ill health in 1952, he turned leadership of the denomination into the hands of Conry who originally resisted, feeling she was not equipped. But Daughtry allayed her concerns by reminding her of his vision, and assuring her that one of his sons would eventually assume leadership. She accepted the position and became the church's highest officer.

Conry, a native of Detroit, Michigan, was converted at one of the home Bible studies that Daughtry had conducted upon his arrival in New York. Though not ordained a bishop, a few years before his death, Daughtry had ordained her an elder. Elder Conry served as presiding minister of the House of the Lord for eight years, from 1952–1960, without ever taking the title of bishop. Her major contribution was keeping the organization stable until Daughtry's fourth son, **Herbert Daughtry**, took the reins. Under her pastorate, Daughtry's local congregation strengthened its relationships with other local churches. In addition, it sponsored a mission church in another section of Brooklyn.

In 1958 the younger Daughtry was ordained and installed as pastor of the Brooklyn congregation, with Conry still serving as national minister. Approximately one year later, he became the third national presiding minister, and Mother Conry (as she was called), who had remained unmarried during this time, continued to serve in ministry until her death at age eighty.

Cook, Mozella 1899–1951

A former Baptist who was converted to Christian faith by her mother, a self-proclaimed minister, who was also suspected of suffering from a form of mental illness.

As an adult Cook had been associated with the **Church of God in Christ**, the largest African-American Pentecostal denomination in Pittsburgh, Pennsylvania. Since the denomination does not ordain women to pastoral ministry, Cook pulled out of COGIC in 1947 to form the **Sought Out Church of God in Christ and Spiritual House of Prayer**,

Inc. near Savannah, Georgia. Two years later, the denomination had four congregations and sixty members, though probably grew no larger than that figure. Despite these small numbers, Cook is significant because she was one of the first women to pull out of COGIC specifically to move into a position of full denominational leadership. At one point, Cook was arrested because of complaints from some in her community that she might be insane. After authorities could find no basis for the complaint, she was released. After her death, at least one congregation remains in Sylvania, Georgia that is pastored by Mattie Green.

Cotton, Emma 1877–1952
Cotton, Henry 1879–1959

The Cottons were eyewitnesses to the **Azusa Street Revival**, and Emma was one of the first women to publish an eyewitness account of the revival, as well as one of the earliest COGIC women in pastoral leadership. The Cottons came to Azusa Street in the first year of the revival, perhaps arriving as early as the Bonnie Brae Street prayer meeting. Though they played no major role in the revival, they received their Pentecostal experience, and Emma received healing from several physical illnesses including "weak lungs" and cancer at the meeting.

For thirty years following the revival, Emma and Henry evangelized in Louisiana and California, planting congregations in Fresno, Bakersfield, and Oakland before settling in Los Angeles to pastor Azusa Pentecostal Temple. For much of the twentieth century, this large congregation became an important local COGIC church. Though Emma received credentials with COGIC, was considered the more prominent minister, and did the bulk of the preaching, the denomination's posture regarding women pastors would not allow her to officially that role. Thus, the church remained an independent congregation throughout her lifetime. After her death, Henry aligned it with the denomination.

Emma was born in Louisiana in 1877 and was reportedly of Creole descent. At the time of the revival, Henry, also born in Louisiana, was a railroad cook who served the route between Los Angeles and San Antonio, Texas. Though both were in the ministry, Henry's busy work schedule left Emma with abundant time to travel around Southern California and itinerate as an evangelist.

By the 1930s the Cottons became friends with famed evangelist, Aimee Semple McPherson, founder of the five-thousand-member Angelus Temple and the International Church of the Foursquare Gospel. Emma was also among a small number of women who McPherson allowed to preach at Angelus Temple on several occasions, sharing what had become one of the most visible Pentecostal pulpits with her husband.

In 1936 the Cottons led a delegation of black Azusa participants in hosting what was to be a week-long thirtieth anniversary celebration at Angeles Temple. The meeting turned into a six-month event in which Elder and "Mother" Cotton joined other notable Pentecostal speakers to minister daily.

Emma Cotton holds the distinction of being one of only a small number of Azusa Street participants—few of them women—to write an eyewitness account of the revival. "The Inside Story of the Outpouring of the Holy Spirit: Azusa Street, April 1906" in the only extant volume of Message of the Apostolic Faith, a newsletter she personally published in April 1939. Cotton reportedly intended to publish sequels to the initial installment. They never materialized however.

Henry probably was employed with the railroad when they planted their Los Angeles congregation. Emma, considered the more prominent minister, did the bulk of the preaching. Today, that congregation is known as Crouch Memorial Pentecostal Church of God in honor of late pastor, **Samuel Crouch**, whom the Cottons nurtured in the ministry. In 1945 Emma and Henry hosted the thirty-ninth anniversary of the **Azusa Street Revival** at the church that they pastored, though this was a much smaller celebration than was held nine years earlier.

Besides being a preacher, Emma Cotton was a songwriter. Some historians credit her with penning the popular black spiritual tune "When the Saints Go Marching In." The authorship of this piece, however, cannot be corroborated. However, another gospel favorite among early Pentecostals, "John Saw That Number," was penned by Cotton.

After forty-four years of remission, Emma's cancer recurred in an incurable form. She died of the disease in two years later at the age of seventy-five. Henry continued to pastor of Azusa Temple until his death.

Counts, Beulah 1899–

Founder of **Greater Mt. Zion Pentecostal Church of America**, one of several small Trinitarian bodies founded by women. Counts embraced the doctrine of sanctification around 1928 and joined Mt. Calvary Holy Church a **United Holy Church** Congregation. Counts was born in South Carolina and migrated to New York. She had only an eighth grade education and worked as a house cleaner before entering the ministry.

At some point, she had been pastor of the Brooklyn congregation of Bishop **Ida Robinson's** group, the **Mt. Sinai Holy Church of America**. She left that body to join with the **St. Mark's Holy Church of America** under Bishop **Eva Lambert,** which also came out of Robinson's group, and was a boarder in Lamberts home before affiliating with the Baptist church. At the same time, she was holding Sunday school in her home and undertaking a ministry of feeding those in need.

In 1944 she moved out from the Baptist Church to found and pastor the Greater Mt. Zion Pentecostal Church in Brooklyn, New York. At the height of her movement, there were nine churches which were organized into the **Mt. Zion Pentecostal Church of America**. Counts incorporated many of the restrictions of Mt. Sinai into her new organization, including a strict dress code for women that required head coverings and limited apparel to blue, grey, black, or white.

Courts, James A. 1875–1926

An early **Church of God in Christ** educator who worked with Pinkie Duncan to cofound the **Saints Industrial and Literary School** in Lexington Mississippi in 1918. Courts, who had been born in Holmes, Mississippi, was actively involved in COGIC and also worked with **E. M. Page** to establish **Page Normal Industrial and Bible Institute** in Hearn, Texas, which was being founded around the same period. In 1921, Courts was also appointed to the COGIC Board of the Department of Church Extension.

Initially the Lexington school came about because of some informal teaching that Duncan was providing to neighborhood children who could not avail themselves of public education. Since Duncan had limited education herself, COGIC founder **C. H. Mason** originally sought out Courts to take over leadership of the project and he replaced her as head and became the first principal of the institution, which at that time was an elementary school.

Courts successfully led efforts throughout the South to raise funds to purchase twenty-eight acres to and begin constructing facilities for the institution. Eventually, however, Mason became dissatisfied with him and hoped to replace him with Mallory, who had been serving on the factory as a piano instructor. Yet, before he could make that decisive move, Courts became ill and was unable to continue day-to-day leadership of the school. When he died shortly thereafter, Mallory quickly was tapped to take his place.

Cox, John Thomas 1898–1964

The second presiding bishop of the **Apostolic Faith Church of God** was born in Marion, Alabama. In his early twenties he entered the ministry and attended the African Methodist Episcopal Seminary in Memphis, Tennessee. After graduating, he served as pastor in the AME Church, and established churches in that denomination in Pennsylvania, Ohio, and West Virginia.

Cox joined the Pentecostal movement in 1932, and affiliated with the **Apostolic Faith Church of God** in 1936, where he was ordained as an elder by **Charles W. Lowe**. In 1952, Cox was appointed presiding bishop while Lowe assumed the title chief apostle. At Lowes' death in 1954, Cox was voted senior bishop. During his leadership, he established churches in Ohio and Pennsylvania, and served the AFCOG until his death.

Cox, Thomas J. ?–1943

Founder of the Trinitarian, Holiness group, The Christian Band, in Danville, Kentucky in 1898. Cox remained Trinitarian for twenty years after founding the organization. However, he was converted to a Oneness understanding by Robert C. Lawson sometime before 1919. Cox moved his group into the Apostolic camp and renamed the organization the **Church of God Apostolic.**

Cox led the church until he became too ill to govern effectively turned to the leadership over to Eli N. Neal to act in his stead around 1941. He died in Danville two years later.

Crouch, Andraé Edward 1942–2015

One of the most well known and widely respected contemporary gospel artists in the world during the latter part of the twentieth century. Crouch was an award-winning gospel musician, recording artist, songwriter, arranger, and producer. He was born in Pacoima, California outside of San Francisco, into a prominent **Church of God in Christ** family, whose father was a street preacher and later a COGIC bishop. Crouch began his musical involvement at his father's church, singing, playing piano, and writing his own songs (despite being entirely self-taught) before ten years of age. He later sang with local groups and directed a local Teen Challenge choir before signing his first record contract.

Crouch's first group was the Church of God in Christ Singers (COGICS) in 1960, which included later rock personality Billy Preston. The COGICS were the first group to record the song "The Blood Will Never Lose Its Power," a piece Crouch composed that has become a gospel standard in evangelical congregations around the world.

He attended Valley Junior College in California to become a teacher. After sensing a call to the ministry, he left that pursuit to form another group, The Disciples, in 1965. He signed his first record contract in 1971, and the group issued their first release in 1977, but disbanded in 1979.

Crouch continued his solo career, which quickly began to soar, as he kept issuing albums as well as penning a number of gospel tunes such as "My Tribute (To God Be the Glory)," many of which would not only be commercial successes but would also become gospel standards. Throughout that time, Crouch performed globally while collaborating with secular artist such as Elvis Presley, Michael Jackson, Quincy Jones, Madonna, and Stevie Wonder on projects that included Oscar-nominated film scores. Among his many other honors, Crouch received nine Grammy Awards, six Dove awards, and was inducted into the Gospel Music Hall of Fame in 1998. In 2004, he became the only living contemporary gospel artist—and just the third in history—to have his star enshrined on the prestigious Hollywood Walk of Fame. He was sometimes called "the father of modern gospel music." In 2005, Crouch was the recipient of the National Academy of Recording Arts and Sciences' Inaugural Salute to Gospel Music Lifetime Achievement Award.

After his father's death in 1994, Crouch and his sister, Rev. Sandra Crouch—a gospel artist in her own right—took responsibility of pastoring the church his parents founded, Christ Memorial Church of God in Christ in Pacoima, California.

Throughout his adult life, Crouch was plagued by illness. He suffered two bouts of cancer and suffered from diabetes. In late 2014, he was hospitalized with pneumonia and congestive heart failure. He died early the next year from a heart attack.

Further Reading:

Carpenter, Bil. "Andréa Crouch." In *Uncloudy Days: The Gospel Music Encyclopedia,* edited by Mryna Capp, 107–8. Milwaukee, WI: Hal Leonard Corporation, 2005.

Gersztyn, Bob. "Andréa Crouch." In *Encyclopedia of American Gospel Music,* edited by W. K. McNeil, 92. New York: Routledge, 2013.

Crouch, Emma Frances 1911–1997

Emma Crouch rose from humble beginnings in Homestead, Texas, to become the fifth General Supervisor of the **Church of God in Christ** Department of Women. Crouch was born in Daingerfield, Texas as one of the nine children of Mr. and Mrs. Robert Searcy. While a teenager, she received the Pentecostal baptism in the Holy Spirit and after graduating from high school in 1932, entered **Page Normal Industrial and Bible Institute** in Hearne, Texas where she graduated in 1934. After later attending beauty college, she furthered her education at Bishop College in Marshall, Texas before marrying Elder B. J. Crouch, a church builder, who later became a bishop in the **Church of God in Christ**.

Crouch rose through the ranks of the International Women's Department structure beginning in 1942, serving initially as first Chairlady of the Young People's Willing Workers (the denomination's youth training arm), then being appointed Chair of the Texas Department of Women Finance. In 1945, she oversaw the work of the state's Sunshine Band (the auxiliary responsible for children's training). As COGIC grew within the state, it was divided into four jurisdictions and T. D. Iglehart was appointed Bishop of the Southwest Jurisdiction. In 1956 he chose Crouch as Jurisdictional Supervisor of Women. Crouch served as First Assistant Supervisor for Women in Texas for sixteen years, making rounds as an evangelist within a Jim Crow culture that sometimes forced to those in her party to ride in train cars alongside chickens or cows.

In 1958 she became president of the National Usher Board. She served on the board of National Trustees and chaired the Department of Women's Advisory Board. In 1976, she moved from the state to the national circuit, becoming first assistant to the National Mother, **Mattie McGlothen.** At McGlothen's death in 1994, she was appointed International Supervisor of the Women's Department by then presiding bishop, **Louis Henry Ford**.

Couch's major accomplishments in that role include organizing the Christian Women's Council, re-establishing the National Pastor's Aide, creating the General Board of Bishops Wives' Circle and the Board of Deaconess and appointing a National Women's Department historian. During her tenure, President William Jefferson Clinton became the first sitting president to speak at the Women's International Convention, addressing the group at the New Orleans, Louisiana session in 1996.

Crouch served only three years until her death in 1997. She was succeeded by Mother **Willie Mae Rivers**.

C

Further Reading:

Butler, Anthea D. *Women in the Church of God in Christ: Making a Sanctified World*. Chapel Hill, NC: University of North Carolina Press, 2007.

Goodson, Glenda Williams. *Bishop Mason and Those Sanctified Women*, Lancaster, TX: s.p., 2003.

Crouch, Samuel Martin Sr. 1896-1976

Early prominent bishop in the **Church of God in Christ**. Born in Dallas, Texas and reared by his COGIC missionary grandmother, Crouch began his ministry at the age of twelve, riding his bicycle to Texas towns to preach. As a young man, he conducted tent revivals and led two churches—the first in Dennison, Texas and the other in Fort Worth, Texas before relocating to California. Crouch was one of the earliest African American radio preachers, starting his broadcasting efforts in Texas in 1924.

After coming to California in 1927, Crouch pastored in Oakland, Fresno, San Diego and the Watts area of Los Angeles before COGIC founder, **Charles Harrison Mason,** appointed him pastor of Emanuel Church of God in Christ in Los Angeles in 1931. The same year, Mason also appointed him as overseer of the California jurisdiction, succeeding Bishop **E. R. Driver**. At that time, he was the youngest person within the denomination to hold such a role. During his lifetime, he visited nearly every hospital and penal institution in the Los Angeles area and traveled extensively in the United States and abroad. In California, he supported missionaries by maintaining a home where they could live rent-free.

In 1951 Crouch worked with Mother **Lillian Coffey** in hosting the historic, first International Women's Convention held in Los Angeles, California. In 1962 the California jurisdiction purchased what became known as Crouch Temple in Los Angeles, which had a seating capacity of three thousand. Two years later, Crouch established the Emanuel Ontario Gardens, a 252 low-cost housing unit for families with at least one senior citizen.

While Crouch's ministry in California was growing, however, he was gaining stature throughout the denomination. After Mason appointed him president of the International Home and Foreign Missions, Crouch visited forty-eight countries, building orphanages, schools and churches in Africa, Mexico, South America, the Philippines, Japan, China, Korea, Bermuda and Honduras. In 1965 Crouch was elected as a member of the Executive Board that was put in place to help guide the church after Mason's death.

From 1968 to 1972 Crouch served as COGIC's second assistant presiding bishop, and from 1973 until his death, he was the first assistant presiding bishop. Crouch was a member of the advisory board of the World Pentecostal Congress and Chancellor of the Charles Harrison Mason Bible College in Los Angeles.

Crouch mentored a number of men and women who would go on to make important contributions within COGIC and the broader Pentecostal traditional. His great-nephew **Andraé Crouch** was an award-winning gospel artist was among them. In 1976

C

Bishop Junious Augustus Blake, Sr.—whose son, **Charles E Blake Sr.**, is the current COGIC bishop—followed him as overseer of California.

Crowdy, William Saunders, 1847–1908

The founder and first presiding bishop of the **Church of God and Saints of Christ**, a black Hebrew Pentecostal sect, was born as Wilson Crowdy to slave parents in Charlotte Hall, Maryland. At age sixteen, he escaped, changed his name to William, joined the United States Army and served in the Civil War from 1863 to 1865. Where he became a quartermaster sergeant in the Fifth Cavalry before being discharged in 1872. For twenty-five years after the war, Crowdy made his home in Guthrie, Oklahoma. During that period, he joined the Baptist Church, and was ordained a Deacon.

In 1892 Crowdy reported having a vision of God telling him to redeem Israel out of spiritual and mental bondage. Though he first resisted his felt call to ministry, shortly he began street preaching. By the mid 1890s he had moved to Kansas City, where he married and fathered three children before returning to Guthrie where he ran one of the largest African-American-owned farms in the county.

As a businessman Crowdy owned and operated a restaurant, a furniture store, and a café. By mid-1895 his business endeavors failed miserably, leaving him with severe losses and triggering a second visionary call. Crowdy again began evangelizing in Guthrie and soon expanded his ministry to Texas and other southwestern points. In 1896, he moved his family moved to Lawrence, Kansas, where he began preaching, at first on street corners, then organized the first of his congregations—which he referred to as tabernacles—at Emporia, Lawrence, and Topeka. From there, he traveled throughout the Midwest and Northeast, establishing Tabernacles and ordaining an Elder-in-Charge in each city.

While preaching on the streets of Texas, he was arrested twenty-two times. Undaunted, the membership increased so rapidly that Crowdy gained the attention of the major newspapers, who began referring to him as "the Black Elijah."

In 1899 Crowdy moved to Philadelphia, Pennsylvania to reside for four years, naming it as the organization's headquarters and drawing more than 1300 members to the congregation. That congregation established several businesses including a general store, barber shop, restaurant, and printing plant. While in Philadelphia, Crowdy convened a Passover celebration that thousands of adherents from throughout the country attended.

In 1903 the Crowdy purchased forty acres of land for the religious organization at Belleville, Virginia. Over the next years, he sent missionaries to set up congregations in Malawi, Swaziland, Zimbabwe, South Africa, Cuba, and West Indies.

Before his death, Crowdy married a second wife. Though the couple had four children, a later revelation convinced him that second marriages were unlawful. Crowdy died in Newark, New Jersey and was originally buried in Bergen, New Jersey. After Crowdy's death, his successor relocated the ministry to Bellevue, Virginia near Suffolk where his body was reburied.

Further Reading:

Wynia, Elly M. *The Church of God and Saints of Christ: A History of the Black Jews.* New York: Taylor and Francis, 2014.

Cumberland Presbyterian Church in America

The primarily African-American **Holiness** denomination developed out of the predominantly white Cumberland Presbyterian Church. Historians estimate that there were nearly 20,000 black Cumberland Presbyterians prior to the Civil War. Only several years after it ended in 1869, black delegates of the Cumberland Presbyterian Church's General Assembly asked for assistance in organizing a separate body for African Americans, allowing them to become more independent and self-reliant. They wanted to develop their own clergy and other leaders and maintain their own church buildings, all with financial support from the parent denomination. The new church was organized five years later, in 1874, as the Colored Cumberland Presbyterian Church. It later was known as the Second Cumberland Presbyterian Church before assuming its current name.

Relations between the two groups have for the most part been cordial, and many of the CPCA ministers have trained at Memphis Theological Seminary and institution of the parent body. A reunion attempt on the part of both denominations failed to win approval in the late 1980s, however, the African-American church, feeling that otherwise it would be swallowed up by the larger white church, sought but did not win equal representation on all boards and agencies. While the joint committee drafting the plan agreed to the request and reported its recommendation to the General Assembly, many in the predominantly white, rural, southern-based parent denomination did not support this motion.

In 2012 the general assemblies of both bodies agreed to form a unification task force to pursue organic union. The two denominations continue to share a Confession of Faith and cooperate in many common ministries. This statement of faith identifies the CPCA as a holiness body that emphasizes the process of Sanctification as God's setting apart of believers as servants in the world, and speaks of Christians being progressively conformed to the image of Jesus Christ, thereby growing in faith, hope, love, and other gifts of the Spirit through the ministry of the Holy Spirit. It does not contain a reference to a Pentecostal experience of Holy Spirit baptism.

The denominational is headquartered in Huntsville, Alabama. There are 113 congregations, organized into fifteen presbyteries and four synods, in Alabama, Kentucky, Tennessee and Texas and Illinois. Membership is primarily concentrated in Alabama, Tennessee, and Texas, but the church extends north to Cleveland, Chicago, Oklahoma, Detroit and Marshalltown, Iowa.

Curry, John Henry 1894-1955

The first overseer of all black congregations of the predominantly white, Church of God (Cleveland, TN). The Bahamas native was born in Abaco, converted to Christianity in 1913, and migrated to the United States in 1914. He lived in Miami for a time where he worked in a quarry. During World War I, he was among the Pentecostals who claimed exemption from the draft due to the pacifist commitment of the Church of God (Cleveland, TN).

Called into the ministry in 1917, and licensed in 1920, he served in pastorates in Miami, Deerfield Beach, and Fort Lauderdale. He was ordained a bishop in 1923 and served for a period as Overseer of the East Coast District of Florida—the black churches of the state of Florida, before being tapped by General Overseer, S. W. Lattimore in 1928 to serve as the unofficial overseer of the Church of God (Colored Work). The relatively few black churches throughout the country outside the South were then informally and voluntarily tied to this structure. Under his leadership, black churches built an orphanage and school in Eustis, Florida, and initiated plans to build a national auditorium in Jacksonville.

Active in establishing immigrant congregations, Curry served as pastor of the prominent Fifth Avenue Church of God in Fort Lauderdale, Florida, served on the Church of God Executive Council from 1932 to 1938, and served on the Council of Seventy from 1926 to 1929. In 1928 however, Curry officially became overseer of the entire black work, including Northern congregations. He held the longest continued tenure as overseer of the Church of God (Colored Work), serving until 1938. In 1942 he was appointed the pastorate of the Jacksonville, Florida congregation that served as the headquarters for the colored work.

Curry emphasized the need for an educated clergy in black Church of God congregations and was instrumental in the establishment of several local Bible institutes in Black Church of God congregations in a period during which the denomination's colleges would not matriculate blacks.

Further Reading:

Michel, David. *Telling our Story: Black Pentecostals in the Church of God*. Cleveland, TN: Pathway, 2000.

D

Dabney, Elizabeth Juanita ??–1967

Church of God in Christ prayer warrior, church founder, and writer. Little is known about her early life but she learned the value of prayer from her mother, who always kept a family altar in their home. She was also a graduate of Virginia State College. She and her husband, Elder Benjamin H. Dabney, journeyed from the South, visiting several cities before settling in New Jersey. The couple had one son, John, after they relocated North.

In 1926 Bishop **Charles Harrison Mason** tapped Elder **Ozro T. Jones Sr.** to establish a church in West Philadelphia and he asked them to relocate and work with him. The team immediately set up a tent and through much fasting and prayer many souls were added to the kingdom. Her recounting of their efforts is recorded in her classic book, *What it Means to Pray Through*.

In 1929 the couple was sent to start a church in North Philadelphia, with $28 per month, eighteen broken chairs, and a dilapidated pulpit that had been partially destroyed by fire.

She met **Church of God in Christ** founder Bishop **Charles Harrison Mason** and recorded many of his prayers. She asked God if it were possible for a woman to get before him and the Lord said yes, if she was willing to pay the price. She made a covenant with God that if he would break through in the wicked neighborhood they had been sent, she would meet God in prayer for three years at an appointed time each morning. Because of this covenant she was ridiculed; some thought she was mad and attempted to drag her from the altar. Others threw rotten vegetable through the windows, placed dead cats or rats in front of the building, or nailed threatening notes on the doorway demanding that the couple leave the neighborhood. She writes that near the end of the three years, she heard footsteps when she got off the bus. She never looked around and upon her arrival at the church the footsteps stopped. Soon the mission could not accommodate the people and the couple rented a larger space. At the end of her covenant period, news spread of the burden for prayer of the woman whose signature style was a white top and black skirt. Ministers called from across the country resulting in hundreds being saved at once.

Informed of her life dedicated to fasting and prayer, Bishop **Charles Harrison Mason** sent her out across the country with her prayer ministry. Pilgrims began showing up from Syria, Africa, China, India, Australia, England and other parts of the world.

The couple relocated to Los Angeles and a group of businessmen purchased a building for her and Elder Dabney's Garden of Prayer Church of God in Christ. The name was given to her after a Caucasian woman was saved and said that the atmosphere reminded her of a beautiful garden. The church was in such demand, with some bishops taking their vacation to come to the Garden, that Bishop Dabney held services seven nights per week.

In 1942 Mother Dabney started 4:00 a.m. daily prayer because so many of the saints' children were being called to war. She began each day with the words "Good morning Jesus. It's nice having you here." The prayer times were 4:00 a.m., noon, and 7:00 p.m. Monday through Friday. She trained younger women and men in the discipline of praying and her notoriety grew to legendary status. An eighty-year-old woman, Nettie Dillard, remembered an eyewitness account of individuals being brought in wheelchairs but leaving the church unassisted and walking. Responding to demands from service men and women, missionaries to foreign fields and others the church sent out over seven million blessed handkerchiefs, which had been anointed and prayed over at The Garden of Prayer. Through her ministry many people were saved and healed of bleeding ulcers, cancer, heart trouble, blindness, and tumors.

Further Reading:

Butler, Anthea D. *Women in the Church of God in Christ: Making a Sanctified World,* Chapel Hill, North Carolina: University of North Carolina Press, 2007.
Dabney, Elizabeth J. *What It Means to Pray Through.* .Memphis, TN: COGIC, 1991.
Williams Goodson, Glenda. *Bishop Mason and Those Sanctified Women*, Lancaster, TX: s.p., 2002.

Daniels, Calvin Coolidge 1929–2001?

Early Church of God (Cleveland, TN) Bishop who was among the longest serving ministers of any race within the denomination. After serving in the Korean War, Daniels returned to the last days of segregation within the American South to serve in leadership in the Church of God. In 1957 toward the end of segregation in the South, Daniels was appointed overseer of black churches in Mississippi.

The denomination officially ended segregation in most of its jurisdictions in 1966, and disbanded the **Church of God (Colored Work)**, yet the state of Mississippi remained segregated until 1970. During that period, Daniels remained at the helm as overseer and was instrumental in establishing at least nine congregations. He served as pastor for more than fifty years, and as an overseer for thirteen years. He played a key role in influencing several black congregation to remain within the Church of God during a time when many within the denomination were being gravitating to majority black denominations.

Daughtry, Alonzo A 1896–1952

As a third-generation minister whose grandfather was a slave preacher, Alonzo Daughtry was raised in a prestigious Methodist family. In 1926, however, he came under the influence of **Charles Emmanuel "Sweet Daddy" Grace** at the Savannah **House of Prayer for All People.** Within a short time, he had a Pentecostal Holy Spirit baptism experience, became a member of Grace's church, felt called to the ministry, and was ordained.

In 1927 Daughtry traveled to Augusta, Georgia, to establish a congregation and spread Grace's message. Yet, once Grace took a turn toward demagoguery, Daughtry became disillusioned with his new posture and attempted to temper what he saw as undue praise that some followers were giving to Grace. On one occasion, at a service in 1929, he preached a sermon that compared what Grace's followers were doing to the undue adulation Paul was given by the inhabitants of Malta. That move led to a showdown with Grace, and Daughtry was forced to leave Grace's movement. Some, however, joined him to form a new church, which would become the House of the Lord. Soon Daughtry's small group was joined by other Georgia and South Carolina congregations, and in 1942, branches were founded in Harlem and Brooklyn, New York.

From the beginning, Daughtry pushed a progressive social and economic agenda. His congregations were interracial, even in the heart of the South. Within his congregations, he promoted economic development programs that challenged his constituents to be concerned about more than just the spiritual welfare of themselves and their families, but the social welfare of their communities. He purchased burial plots and opened stores to ensure the solvency of his group.

At his death, leadership of his organization passed shortly to **Inez Conry**, who presided until Daughtry's son, **Herbert Daughtry**, who had reclaimed his Christian faith and answered a call to ministry while in prison, could take the helm.

Daughtry, Herbert 1931–

Pastor, activist, and third presiding minister of the **House of the Lord and Church on the Mount**, that his father, **Alonzo Daughtry** founded. The younger Daughtry was born in Savannah, Georgia, and a year later, his family relocated to Augusta, Georgia. His parents separated shortly after, and his mother returned to Savannah. Daughtry moved back and forth between Savannah and Augusta as a child. His father was heavily involved in the church and Daughtry was raised in a highly religious household. When he was eleven years old, his family moved to Brooklyn, New York, and then to Jersey City, New Jersey. As a black child from the South, Daughtry found it difficult to adjust to his interracial environment and eventually fell into a decade-long struggle with gambling, crime, and drug use. In 1950 he joined the army to escape his environment, but he remained on heroin and was discharged after a year.

In 1953 Daughtry was imprisoned for armed robbery and assault charges. While in prison, he experienced a religious conversion that changed his life. On his release, Daughtry returned to the church, becoming a fourth-generation minister. In 1958 he became the pastor of the House of the Lord Church in Brooklyn. A year later, in fulfillment of his father's prophecy, he was named the church's third national presiding minister.

Throughout his leadership, Daughtry expanded the prominence of the House of the Lord Pentecostal Church by involving his local congregation and the denomination in major local and national social issues. He founded the Coalition of Concerned Leaders and Citizens to Save Our Youth, a body that was integral in developing the coalition that led to the formation of the Black United Front, a political activist organization, during the height of the Civil Rights Movement. Daughtry served as its first chairperson from 1980 to 1985

In 1982 Daughtry founded the African People's Christian Organization, whose aim was to create an African Christian nation by highlighting both African origins and biblical teachings. Two years later, Daughtry became a special assistant to Reverend Jesse Jackson during his presidential campaign and accompanied him to the Vatican to advocate for a firmer stand on human rights. In 1991 he was part of the delegation of New York mayor, David N. Dinkins, to South Africa to meet with Nelson and Winnie Mandela. In 2003 Daughtry led a delegation of multi-faith protesters to Iraq in a last-ditch effort to preserve peace in that nation.

Daughtry has published several books. His 1997 work, *No Monopoly on Suffering: Blacks and Jews in Crown Heights and Elsewhere* dealt with the 1991 crisis in ethnic tensions in that neighborhood. He also published *A Seed Planted in Stone—The Life and Times of Tupac Shakur*, a book that follows his relationship with the slain rapper, who joined Daughtry's congregation when he was eleven years old.

Further Reading:

Daughtry Sr., Herbert. *My Beloved Community: Sermons, Speeches, and Lectures of Rev. Daughtry.* Trenton, NJ: Africa World, 2001.

Daughtry, Leah Denyetta 1951–

Third-generation Pentecostal pastor who is involved in Democratic presidential political and social advocacy. The native of Brooklyn, New York served as the chief executive officer for the 2008 Democratic National Convention Committee and chief of staff to Howard Dean, the chairperson of the Democratic National Committee. She was formerly Acting Assistant Secretary for Administration and Management at the United States Department of Labor.

Daughtry directs the Democratic Party's Faith in Action initiative to reach out to Protestant, Catholic, Jewish, and Muslim voters. At the same time, in the 2008 DNC convention, Daughtry denied non-religious groups participation in the interfaith service.

Daughtry has held a number of senior posts at the United States Department of Labor during the Administration of President Bill Clinton, including senior advisor to the Secretary, chief of staff, and acting assistant secretary for administration and management.

The daughter of prominent pastor **Herbert Daughtry**, presiding minister of the **House of the Lord Church and Church on the Mount**, pastors her own Washington DC congregation, while she runs a consultanting firm that offers managerial support to major advocacy and other nonprofit organizations. With her ordination in 2002, Leah joined the fifth consecutive generation of pastors in the Daughtry family. In 2012 she was ordained an elder and presently serves as jurisdictional elder of the organization's Southeast Region.

Daughtry graduated from Dartmouth College in 1984 and serves on the Board of Visitors of the College's Nelson A. Rockefeller Center for Public Policy and the Social Sciences. In fall 2009 she served as a fellow at the Harvard Institute of Politics. And as the Obama presidency draws to the end of its second term, Daughtry, who is a personal friend of former president Clinton and his wife, Hillary Clinton (the 2016 presidential candidate), now finds herself drawn into the small circle of early supporters on whom the former first lady draws for advice.

Deadrick, Donal M. (D.M.) 1915-1986
Deadrick, Dorothy 1910-1993

Early Church of God of Prophecy ministers who were instrumental in building the constituency of the denomination in East Texas. The Deadricks were introduced to the COGOP in the early 1930s by Bishop J. N. Hurley, the white state overseer of that jurisdiction.

D. M. Deadrick, a graduate of Samuel Houston College, began his ministry as a youth minister at his home church in Palacios, Texas. As a young man, he was active in winning several award banners and notoriety at East Texas state conventions and the Annual Assembly. Deadrick pastored several local churches, received his ordination as bishop in 1936, and accepted a state leadership role in Tennessee in 1948. In 1952 Deadrick achieved prominence when he was appointed as General Field Secretary No. 2, succeeding Bishop Ralph Scotton.

Dorothy Deadrick often preached in state conventions and the Annual Assembly, served as director of the state youth camp in East Texas, and assisted her husband in his ministerial duties. She promoted strong Sunday school programs as a vehicle for bringing the COGOP message to African Americans in East Texas. At the Annual Assembly in 1946, she gave a sermon focused on winning more blacks to the church. Even though she did not address the segregation issue directly, she spoke to those in the audience who were sentimental to the segregationist policies of the South.

DeLee, Victoria Way 1925-2010

Grassroots civil rights activist who helped desegregate schools in South Carolina. DeLee was born in Ridgeville, South Carolina to a deeply religious family of tenant farmers. DeLee, the daughter of sharecroppers, worked in the fields as a child, completed only the seventh grade, and witnessed a lynching when she was twelve. During her early years, she attended the Methodist Church, but as a teen she was involved with the Baptist Church. As a young woman, she was attracted to Pentecostalism and was a founding member of the local **House of God** congregation.

She registered to vote in 1947 and was the first black person in her community who had a voter registration certificate. DeLee fought for school integration, education of black voters, and ran as a candidate for Congress. She participated in civil rights marches, including the 1963 March on Washington, and was friends with Jesse Jackson and Martin Luther King Jr. In 1971 *New Yorker* magazine profiled her in an article written entirely in her spoken dialect.

Over her lifetime, DeLee registered thousands of voters, established a day-care center and a school to teach literacy skills to black and American Indian residents. She began efforts to integrate South Carolina's segregated school system in 1964 by demanding that her own children be allowed to attend white schools. As a result, her family was harassed had to sleep on mattresses on the floor to avoid bullets fired through their windows. In 1965, DeLee spearheaded a voter registration drive in 1965 in Ridgeville, and demanded federal registrars local officials denied blacks the right to register. The family's home was destroyed by fire in 1966.

In 1970 DeLee sought US Justice Department protection after receiving mailed threats warning of "booby traps in your home and car," and signed, "your loving friends, the KKK." A year later, she was a candidate in 1971 for Congress running on the United Citizens' Party that she helped found two years earlier.

DeLee made frequent visits to Washington to see members of congress and federal officials and once staged a sit-in at Senator Strom Thurmond's Capitol Hill office. Once Thurmond's attitude on integration began to change, however, the two worked together on some issues.

During her later years, DeLee served on the South Carolina advisory board of the United States Civil Rights Commission and was a leader in her local branch of the NAACP. By the end of her life, DeLee had made it apparent that lack of education was not an insurmountable handicap for effecting change. For her efforts, she received an honorary doctorate from Amherst College. She died at eighty-five from complications from brain surgery.

Further Reading:

Ross, Rosetta. "The Life and Work of Victoria Way DeLee: A Study of Transformative Ethical Practice." PhD diss., Emory University, 1995.

Trillin, Calvin. "US Journal: Dorchester County, SC: Victoria DeLee in her Own Words." *New Yorker*, March 27, 1971.

Delk, James Logan 1888–1963

An evangelist who was formerly associated with the Baptists and Nazarenes, and was possibly the most visible white minister associated with **Charles Harrison Mason** and the **Church of God in Christ.** Delk was born in Pall Mall, Fentress County, Tennessee. In 1904 Delk met Mason in Conway, Arkansas, when the sixteen-year-old heard Mason preaching to a large crowd. After completing a law degree, Delk opened a practice, but by 1914, Mason had ordained him.

The "Kentucky Cyclone" as he was called, was one of few early white Pentecostals to publically and soundly renounce racial disunity. He became a close confidante of Mason's and led COGIC revivals in Cincinnati, Ohio; Springfield, Missouri; Akron, Ohio; and Pittsburgh, Pennsylvania. But he also counted among his associates Elizabeth "Lizzie" Woods Robinson who, after Delk introduced her to Mason, was to become the first leader of the COGIC Women's Department.

In 1933 after an unsuccessful run for governor of Missouri in 1932, Delk returned to Hopkinsville, Kentucky to become pastor of the First Church of God in Christ in that city. He continued to evangelize, traveling west as far as California in 1936, then east to preach in New England.

Even as the number of white ministers in COGIC continued to decline, Delk maintained his affiliation, becoming Mason's close confidante. That association often proved costly for him within the white community. Because of it, he was beaten twice by local vigilantes who reportedly were members of the Ku Klux Klan.

Yet, the colorful figure—who had some run-ins with the law and served some time in prison—was a strong leader in his own right, running revivals throughout the country and hosting a radio broadcast. His political aspirations led him to run for governor of Missouri in 1932, for governor of Tennessee in 1949, and governor of Kentucky in 1959. At the time of his death, at age seventy-five, he was seeking the Democratic nomination for governor of Kentucky. Though he never succeeded in winning public office, he maintained friendships with local and national political leaders, and these friendship netted benefits for himself and COGIC. In the 1940s, when most available steel was directed to the war effort, Delk drew friendships with Senator Alben Barkley, Happy Chandler, Harry S. Truman, and Tom Stewart to help COGIC secure enough of the metal to complete Mason Temple in Memphis.

Delk divorced from his wife, the former Sarah Tompkins in 1907 and subsequently married Sarah L. Brooks. He stayed with COGIC until his death, two years after that of Mason.

Further Reading:

Maxwell, Joe. "Building the Church of God in Christ." *Christianity Today*, April 8, 1996.

D

Dickerson, Ernestine Cleveland Reems 1932–

Prominent pastor, bishop, and leader among African-American Pentecostal women. Dickerson, daughter of **Church of God in Christ** bishop, Elmer Elijah (E. E.) Cleveland, was born in 1932, in Oklamugee, Oklahoma, near Tulsa and raised within COGIC. At age thirteen, she experienced the first of two bouts of tuberculosis, a disease that kept her in ill health for several years. She attended Patten Bible College in Oakland, California, an institution founded by another Pentecostal woman, Dr. Bebe Patten.

By 1951 Dickerson had fully recovered, and began traveling across the country as an evangelist with her brother, Elmer Cleveland Jr., fully aware of and dissatisfied with the denominational limitations on women. For the next seventeen years, however, she gained somewhat of a following within that sphere and by 1968 she left COGIC to found an independent congregation, Center of Hope Community Church, with four charter members in a seedy Oakland, California neighborhood.

In the forty years since its founding, that congregation has grown to more than 2,000 and has initiated a number of innovative programs, gaining Dickerson respect throughout the African American religious community, as well as the political community. She is perhaps known best for establishing the E. C. Reems Women's International Ministries in 1988 to support women leaders who lack such support from their denominations through national and regional conferences as well as other resources that drew considerable attention from women clergy.

She has also been involved in significant local efforts. In 1990, Dickerson constructed the 56-unit senior housing complex. Two years later, she established a transitional housing program for homeless mothers and their children. The Ernestine C. Reems Academy of Technology and Art Charter School was inaugurated in Oakland in 1999, and she recently opened Hope School of Excellence a charter school for pre-school through eighth grade.

At the end of the twentieth century, Dickerson founded Kingdom Builders Ministerial Alliance to mentor urban ministers and support missionary projects in Haiti and South Africa. The organization was renamed Monument International Church Assemblies, and Dickerson was consecrated bishop in 2007. Dickerson's first husband of forty-one years, Deacon Paul Reems, whom she married in 1959, died in 2000; she married Theotis Dickerson in 2003. While retaining that position, she stepped down from the pastorate in 2004, turning over her pulpit to her eldest son, Brandon and his wife, Maria. Still active in a number of venues, however, Dickerson serves as a trustee of the International Charismatic Bible Ministries and as a member of the board of Trustees of Oral Roberts University. Among the honors has received, Dickerson was Named one of the "Top 15 Black Women Preachers in the United States" by *Ebony* in 1997 and "Woman of the Year" by the National Urban League in 2000.

Further Reading:

Jones, Frank A. "The Season of the Woman: Pastor Ernestine Cleveland Dickerson is Chosen Bishop." *Gibbs Magazine,* January 22–29, 2007.

Diggs, Jefferson Davis (J. D.) 1865–1953

Early **United Holy Church of America** leader and educator. Diggs was born in Anson County, North Carolina to a slave mother—who died when he was three—and her white owner. Having little formal education, his grandmother raised him after his mother's death. She required him to study at night and by eighteen he had educated himself enough to work as a teacher and to preach his first sermon.

In 1889 as a Methodist Episcopal Church itinerant pastor, Diggs was appointed to a congregation in Hickory, North Carolina, serving there for three years. He served in other Methodist congregations before embracing the Holiness movement, leaving his prominent congregation and the M.E.C. to found an independent church, the Union Mission in 1904. Coming into the **United Holy Church**, he brought that congregation with him and remained as pastor.

He graduated from Bennett College in Greensboro, North Carolina in 1899 with a Bachelors of Science. He also held a Masters of Ancient Literature that he obtained in 1905 from the Christian College of Oskaloosa, Iowa. The Theological School of Livingstone College, an African Methodist Episcopal institution in Salisbury North Carolina later conferred a Doctor of Divinity on Diggs.

As an educator, he organized the first public grade school in Hickory, North Carolina in 1891, and in 1897 organized the first public school in Maxton, North Carolina. He moved to Winston-Salem in 1899, where he helped lay out the school district to prevent racial friction. Diggs served in the administration of the Boydton Academic and Bible Institute for Colored People, an institution of the Christian and Missionary Alliance that was endorsed by the UHCA for training its leaders. He was one of the founders of Slater Industrial Academy and State Normal School in Winston-Salem, North Carolina that became Winston-Salem State Teachers College.

In 1916, Diggs was among those who received a nomination for president when Henry Fisher won that office. He was consecrated bishop in 1924 and appointed as the first president of the Northwestern district in 1935 to establish the West Virginia district and serve as its presider. Diggs was revered as a scholar in the **United Holy Church**, serving as the Educational Secretary for twenty years. From 1948 until his retirement, Diggs held the post of president of the UHCA Bible Training School.

Shortly before his death in 1953, the Jefferson Davis Diggs Elementary School in Winston-Salem was dedicated to him. In addition, Diggs Boulevard, near property he owned in the city, was named in his honor. In 1987, the Jefferson Davis Diggs Education Wing of the Albert H. Anderson Center at Winston-Salem State University was also named for him.

Further Reading:

Caldwell, A. B. "Jefferson Davis Diggs." In *History of the American Negro and His Institutions*. Atlanta, GA: A. B. Caldwell, 1917.

Turner, William C. *The United Holy Church: A Study in Black Holiness-Pentecostalism*. Piscatawy, NJ: Georgias, 2006.

D. J. Young Publishing House

In 1907 the year that **Charles Harrison Mason** moved the **Church of God in Christ** away from **Charles Price Jones's** Holiness group of the same name, he felt a need to provide an official publishing organ vehicle to keep his message before constituents. Mason selected **David J. Young** to edit *The Whole Truth* magazine as the denomination's periodical. By 1916, Young had expanded his publishing efforts, moving them to Kansas City, Kansas, opening the publishing house from his private home, and editing and publishing material from the International Church Sunday School Lessons to fit COGIC doctrine of the denomination's Sunday School literature.

Young's wife, Priscilla, worked closely with him during the venture. Initially the couple contracted out printing services. The company also served as the publishing house for many black Kansas City area churches, and sent free materials to missionaries in Thailand, Liberia, England, India, and Jamaica. Young died in 1927, and following his death, Mason appointed his widow as publisher and manager of the Sunday School Literature of the **Church of God in Christ**. She carried on the work of the publishing house and continued publishing COGIC's Sunday School literature. Within twenty years, Priscilla had saved enough to construct a separate building and secure printing equipment.

Around 1958 COGIC Bishop **J. O. Patterson, Sr.** and Bishop **F. D. Washington** began to consider the possibility of taking over all publishing operations, and that year, the denomination informed the owners of the publishing house that it had decided to bring its publishing operations in-house and took over publishing of COGIC periodicals and other publications. In the ensuing years, the Young family attempted to salvage its standing as the official publisher, entering into entered a prolonged battle with the denomination. While these efforts failed, as late as the 1970s, individuals and congregations were still ordering tracts and related religious materials from the company. Yet, the dissolution of the official relationship with the church eventually brought the business to closure. Equipment and stored publications remained on site for more than two decades and descendent of young attempted to enlist the assistance of Kansas city officials to preserve the building and its holdings as a historic site. Their overtures were rejected and the building was demolished by the city in 2009.

Further Reading:

Brown, Ladrian. *Great was the Company of Those that Published*. The D. J. Young Papers. Kansas City, KS: D.J. Young Heritage Foundation, 2010.

Dollar, Creflo Augustus Jr., 1962–

African-American pastor, denominational leader, and prominent televangelist who is one of most visible and highly controversial leaders in the Word of Faith movement. Dollar was ordained a Baptist minister in 1983, and converted to Pentecostalism as a teenager. After his hopes to play professional football ended with an injury, he began witnessing to students on the West Georgia College campus. One student, after accepting Christ, introduced ten others to Dollar. By 1981 Dollar and his roommate were teaching a dorm Bible study that quickly grew to over one hundred people and by his graduation in 1984, had grown to three hundred students.

Dollar held the first services of World Changers International Ministries in 1986 in a school cafeteria with eight people. Within three years, membership had grown to five hundred. Twenty years after its founding, Dollar's congregation had exploded to twenty thousand members who worshipped in the 8,500-seat "World Dome" in the Atlanta suburb of College Park. By that time, Dollar had become internationally known through his "Changing Your World" television broadcast, a publishing group, best-selling books, and a recording label, Arrow Records. Six years earlier, in 2000, he had started a second congregation in Manhattan. The church has more than five thousand members, and Dollar regularly commutes between the two congregations, preaching at Madison Square Garden on Saturday evenings, and using his two private planes to return to his suburban Atlanta pulpit by Sunday morning. Through his International Covenant Ministry, Dollar's church has offices in South Africa, the United Kingdom, Canada, and Australia.

Dollar's ministry has not been without controversy. He has been criticized for living a lavish lifestyle which at one time included two Rolls-Royces, private jets, and real estate such as a million-dollar home in Atlanta, a $2.5 million home in Demarest, New Jersey, and a $2.5 million home in Manhattan, In 2007 the United States Senate Finance Committee began an investigation of several ministries, including Dollar's. In 2012, Dollar was arrested in an alleged attack on his daughter. The charges were dropped in 2013 after he attended anger management classes. Later in late 2014, Dollar drew public scrutiny from within and outside the Christian tradition when he allegedly attempt to raise $65 million through public appeals to members of his congregation, supporters, and media to donate $300 each to help in the purchase of a luxury jet that he maintained was required for him to carry out ministry. After a loud public outcry, with the support of his governing board, Dollar retracted the campaign, but not his plans to purchase the plane.

Further Reading:

Mumford, Debra J. *Above All Prosper: A Critical Analysis of the Preaching of Creflo Dollar Jr.* Berkeley, CA: Graduate Theological Union, 2007.
Walton, Jonathan. *Watch This!: The Ethics and Aesthetics of Black Televangelism.* New York: NYU Press, 2009.

Doub, Robert O. Jr. 1924–1989

The founding bishop of Shiloh Apostolic Temple Church, Inc. was born in Winston-Salem, North Carolina and studied at Temple University, the American Bible College New Era, and St. Elvira's Theological Seminary. At age eighteen, his interest in religion was sparked by a service at Bright Hope Baptist Church in Philadelphia. Doub was baptized in the Oneness formula in 1944. By twenty-four, he had been ordained in the **Apostolic Church of Christ in God**. That year, he organized his first service by preaching on street corners in Philadelphia. That same year, he founded a Oneness congregation, the Shiloh Apostolic Temple, and used that congregation as a center for his evangelistic work that resulted in establishing congregations in nearby communities, and eventually becoming ACCG state supervisor of Pennsylvania.

By 1953 Doub's dissatisfaction with the leadership of presiding bishop **J. W. Aubrey**, and disappointment over the denial of his request to be elevated to the office of bishop over the congregations he had founded led to a split from the parent denomination. Following that split, Doub became popular among other Oneness ministers for his business acumen and entrepreneurial skill, earning him the reputation as "the business preacher." He led his congregation to operate retreat camp sites in the Poconos and North Carolina, employed young members in the church's catering business, purchased and rented buses, sold heating oil to members, and developed the Shiloh Haven House Inn—a multiple use apartments, restaurant, and chapel.

When his congregation became the mother church of local congregation-sponsored churches throughout the country, Doub first attempted to align the congregations under his leadership with **Randolph A. Carr**'s denomination, the **Church of God in Christ Jesus (Apostolic)**. When that merger did not materialize, Doub also started the *Apostolic Wave*, a periodical that circulated in the United States, the West Indies, and England, and used radio and television to spread the gospel also.

Doub, who was a life member of the NAACP and a founder of the Apostolic Ministers Conference of Philadelphia, died in a car accident near Scranton, Pennsylvania at age sixty-five. At the time of his death, plans had been developed to build a small shopping plaza on land near the church.

Further Reading:

Richardson Jr., James C. *With Water and Spirit: A History of Black Apostolic Denominations in the US.* Martinsville, VA: s.p., s.d.

D

Douglas, Floyd Ignatius 1887–1951

A presiding bishop in the **Pentecostal Assemblies of the World** who was born in Nelson County, Kentucky into a Catholic family. Douglas was the only child of Betty and Charles Douglas, but by the age of ten both parents had died and he lived with his grandmother, who also died when he was fourteen. Around 1911, he converted to Pentecostalism, felt called to preach, and joined PAW before it became part of the **Oneness Pentecostal** movement. Later that year, he received the Pentecostal Holy Spirit baptism. His call to the ministry came in 1912, the year he established his first church, with thirty-five members, in Louisville, Kentucky.

In 1918 Douglas was elected as a PAW field superintendent. The next year, he was instrumental in establishing the first District Council of Kentucky. By 1923 the denomination had thirteen churches in that state. In 1920 Douglas became one of the twenty-four general elders of PAW. After serving in his pastorate for twelve years, Douglas left the church he had founded and moved to Los Angeles to take over the pastorate of the Apostolic Faith Home Assembly, where he served for twenty-four years. Douglas inherited approximately thirty members, a large financial debt approximating $15,000, but over his tenure, that congregation grew to be one of the most prominent in the denomination. In 1928 Douglas was consecrated a bishop, and in 1934 became senior bishop of PAW. In 1946 he became ill and died five years later.

Dranes, Arizona Juanita 1884?–1963

The gospel music pioneer was born blind in Sherman, Texas. The actual year of her birth and whether she was fully African American or of mixed parentage is debated. Since both parents were illiterate, the surname was written down as it was pronounced. In 1896 Dranes attended the Texas Institute for Deaf, Dumb, and Blind Colored Youth in Austin. She graduated from that institution in 1910. Her correct last name "Drane," was listed in the school's enrollment record for 1896–1897.

Dranes learned to play piano in her early teens, joined the **Church of God in Christ** church in Wichita Falls, Texas and soon was a favored singer-pianist in COGIC circles, often playing for founder, **Charles Harrison Mason**. Around 1920, Dranes helped Ford Washington McGee, a singing preacher, establish a **Church of God in Christ** in Oklahoma City, Oklahoma. She spent years traveling through Texas and Oklahoma and aiding in the "planting" of new COGIC churches.

In 1926, Dranes recorded for Okeh Records, a subsidiary of Columbia Records. She introduced piano accompaniment to Holiness music, becoming the first person to play the piano on a gospel recording, which had previously been largely a cappella and one of the first professional women gospel singers. She developed the "gospel beat" style combining ragtime and barrelhouse traditions to produce a rolling blues sound, introducing a syncopated, ragtime-influenced accompaniment to gospel music.

First as a soloist and later with choirs and other artists, Dranes sang at COGIC meetings in the Bible Belt, touring Texas, Tennessee, and Oklahoma. During the Great Depression, Dranes continued her performances in church services but did little outside the church.

Although she last recorded in 1928, she continued touring through the 1940s. Through her extensive touring and recordings into that decade, Dranes influenced generations of keyboardists and singers such as Mahalia Jackson, Clara Ward, **Rosetta Tharpe,** and Thomas A. Dorsey. In 1948, she moved to Los Angeles, where she lived until her death.

Further Reading:

Corcoran, Michael. *He Is My Story: The Sanctified Soul of Arizona Dranes.* San Francisco, CA: Tompkins Square, 2012.

Dodge, Timothy. *The School of Arizona Dranes: Gospel Music Pioneer.* Lanham, MD: Lexington, 2013.

Driver, Edward Robert Sr. 1869–?

The organizer of the first **Church of God in Christ** west of the Rocky Mountains and the first overseer of the state of California. Driver was born in Nesbitt, Mississippi of mixed parentage. His father was East Indian, while his mother was black. After graduating from LeMoyne Normal School in Memphis, Tennessee, he returned home to teach. Driver then returned to LeMoyne to study law, and began practicing law in 1892. Two years later, he was called and licensed to preach and accepted a pastorate at Salem Baptist Church in Memphis.

Driver had been part of the early black **Holiness** group organized by **Charles Price Jones** and **Charles Harrison Mason.** After aligning himself with their views on sanctification, he was dismissed by his congregation. He was part of the first meeting called by Mason after his 1907 split from Jones over the issue of speaking in tongues. Driver's legal background was helpful when he was drafted to write and file the first articles of incorporation for the **Church of God in Christ.**

Mason sent Driver to California around 1914. After arriving, Driver found a small group of saints worshipping in a tent. They later moved into a building and the church was named Saints Home Church of God in Christ. Under Driver's leadership, over thirty-five churches were organized around the state, and during the 1916 convocation, Bishop Mason appointed Driver as the first Overseer of California, New Mexico, and Arizona. Initially, Driver's multicultural congregation served as the "melting pot" for all races in the Los Angeles community. Driver's outspokenness regarding racial issues was problematic for the **Church of God in Christ** in California. His bluntness was part of the reasons for the decline of white COGIC followers in the California.

Within the broader COGIC community, Driver served as chairperson of the General Council and as associate editor for the *The Whole Truth* newspaper. He was one of the contributors who drafted the Doctrinal Statement of the Church of God in Christ, Inc. Driver, like Mason, was a pacifist and was instrumental in working with **William Holt**, a white COGIC minister to draft the denomination's position paper opposing World War I.

Within the broader African-American community, Driver participated in Marcus Garvey's Universal Negro Improvement Association. This involvement brought him under scrutiny of the Federal Bureau of Investigation.

DuBois, Joshua 1982–

Former advisor to President Barak Obama on Faith-based and Neighborhood Partnerships. DuBois was born in Bar Harbor, Maine and was raised in Nashville, Tennessee where his stepfather was an African Methodist Episcopal pastor. He then moved to Xenia, Ohio, before moving to Boston to attend school. His early religious foundations were in the African Methodist Episcopal Church, but while in the city, he attended Calvary Praise & Worship Center in Cambridge, a small congregation affiliated with the **United Pentecostal Council of the Assemblies of God**. Although DuBois was just a teenager, he started preaching when the pastor was away and was named an associate pastor while still an undergraduate. He also led a Bible study at a halfway house, and fed homeless people in the streets of the city. By then, he had also become an activist. As a seventeen-year-old freshman, DuBois stood in front of a Martin Luther King Jr. memorial in Boston for forty-one hours with a placard that read, "NO MORE" to draw attention to the forty-one bullets New York City police officers used to kill an unarmed Guinean immigrant named Amadou Diallo.

Despite his active involvement in the church and community, DuBois graduated *cum laude* from Boston University degree in political science. From there, he went on to Princeton University's Woodrow Wilson School of Public and International Affairs. He suspended his pursuit of a JD at the Georgetown University Law Center to join Obama's campaign.

DuBois' initial quest for a role in Obama's Senate campaign proved unsuccessful and he received a form letter rejecting his application. Yet, he continued the pursuit, personally driving to the candidate's office on more than one occasion until he was hired as a Senatorial aide working on faith-based outreach. Subsequently when Obama ran for president, DuBois was picked as the religious outreach director for the campaign. After the election, Obama asked DuBois to lead his White House Office of Faith-based and Neighborhood Partnerships, a position created by executive order by Obama's predecessor, George W. Bush. The young minister stepped in to head the office, focused on bridging the intersection of religion and public policy in 2009 when he was twenty-six, making him one of the youngest people ever to hold such a high-ranking position in a presidential administration.

While in office, DuBois who considers himself a progressive black Evangelical was the only ordained minister in the president's inner circle, although black Baptist minister, Suzann Johnson Cook—former president of the prestigious Hampton Ministers Conference—served as his Ambassador-at-Large for International Religious Freedom. Dubois faced the daily challenges of interpreting the possible use of funding for projects provided to religiously oriented institutions to support community projects. He often found himself at odds with various camps on either side of issues that drew strong views such as healthcare and contraception coverage.

DuBois, however, drew on his faith to establish meaningful spiritual traditions within the White House. He began the tradition of the White House Easter Prayer Breakfasts. Further, he sent devotional messages to Obama every morning to keep him focused spiritually. A collection of the messages was published in the edited volume, *The President's Devotional: The Daily Readings that Inspired President Obama and Stories of Faith in the White House* by HarperOne.

DuBois, who now runs the Values Partnerships consulting firm, stepped down in 2013 to finish the book and teach at New York University.

Further Reading:

DuBois, Joshua, ed. *The President's Devotional: The Daily Readings That Inspired President Obama and Stories of Faith in the White House.* New York: HarperCollins, 2014.

DuPree, Sherrie Sherrod 1946–

Historian, archivist, and author on issues related to gospel music, and Holiness and Pentecostal traditions, as well as the struggle for African-American civil rights within American society. DuPree was born in Raleigh, North Carolina. She earned a Bachelor of Science in Vocational Home Economics and Master of Arts in Educational Media at North Carolina Central University in Durham, North Carolina. Additionally, she graduated twice from the University of Michigan in Ann Arbor with an AMLS in Academic Librarianship and an EdS in Instructional Technology.

Major archival collections throughout the United States hold DuPree's work. She founded the African-American Pentecostal and Holiness Collection at the New York Public Library's Schomburg Center for Research in Black Culture. The "Sherry Sherrod DuPree Collection on the African-American Holiness and Pentecostal Movements, circa 1887–2001" is housed at the Smithsonian Institute in Washington DC.

Dupree served as the project director for the Institute of Black Culture at the University of Florida from 1979 until 1985 and as Professor of Library Science at Santa Fe College in Gainesville from 1983 until 2011. She began the National African-American

Holiness Pentecostal Project during the course of which she received several grants to fund her work. In 1988 DuPree was appointed to the Archival Historical Committee of the **Church of God in Christ,** and in 1995, became the Archivist of the Gospel Music Hall of Fame and Museum in Detroit. Beginning in 2000 she served a one-year term as the first African-American woman and only the second woman president of the Society for Pentecostal Studies, the major academic society devoted to scholars who study the global phenomenon of Pentecostalism.

Dupree's collections include newsletters, correspondence, brochures, fliers, magazines, VHS tapes, articles, newspaper clippings, slides, manuscripts, photographs, books, financial documents, audiocassettes, compact discs, diskettes, as well as her research files. Her seminal work, "African-American Holiness Pentecostal Movement: an Annotated Bibliography," is based on the research in this collection, is also present. Other major works on African-American Pentecostalism include the, *Biographical Dictionary of African American Holiness—Pentecostals: 1880–1990; Exposed! Federal Bureau of Investigation (Federal Bureau of Investigation) Unclassified Reports on Churches and Church Leaders;* and *African-American Goods News (Gospel) Music.*

A large amount of her work focuses on the **Church of God in Christ**, of which DuPree is a member. Still, she has given significant attention to African American Oneness Pentecostal**ism**—a group given little attention among some scholars, who considered the tradition heretical. A notable work is this area is her edited volume, *The Silent Spokesman: Bishop Robert Clarence Lawson, Founder of the Church of Our Lord Jesus Christ of the Apostolic Faith, Inc., New York City,* which she compiled with Alexander Stewart. DuPree was instrumental in Stewart and his wife Shirlene donating part of their materials to the Schomburg Collection.

Besides the Smithsonian, Dupree has received funding for her research from the National Endowment for the Arts, The National Council of Churches and the Gatorade Foundation. Her work related to civil rights includes founding the Rosewood Forum, a series of dialogs regarding the 1923 massacre that desecrated the town of Rosewood in Central Florida. Her work has gained her national attention as a scholar of early African-American history.

E

Eason, Willie Claude 1921–2005

A prominent musician within the **Keith Dominion** of Mary Magdalena Lewis Tate's body, Church of the Living God Pillar and Ground the Truth. Eason introduced the steel guitar genre of gospel music into the church. Eason was born in Schley County, in southwestern Georgia. His family moved to Philadelphia, Pennsylvania before he was a year old. His older brother, Troman, learned to play the instrument first then passed the skill to Willie who, as a teenager, played it in the House of God congregation his family attended in Philadelphia in the late 1930s. In 1939 he quit high school to travel throughout the eastern states with House of God Bishop J. R. Lockley and the Gospel Feast Party Band to play for House of God worship services and revivals and later, on street corners.

Over the length of his music career, he recorded total of eighteen sides in the 1940s and 1950s, seven on popular gospel labels, including two with the Soul Stirrers—arguably the most popular black gospel quartet of their day—singing backup as Eason, who was also a powerful singer, sang and played. In the 1950s and 1960s, he produced gospel music concerts with top acts of the day. Between the 1940s and 1960s, Eason often worked in Florida, but he and his family did not move permanently to St. Petersburg until 1986.

Eason developed a technique of imitating singing voices on the instrument and became known as "Little Willie and his Talking Guitar." He influenced dozens of musicians and inspired many to play the steel guitar for worship services in nearly two hundred House of God churches found in more than two dozen states.

Eckhardt, John 1957–

A leading African American figure in the New Apostolic Movement. Eckhardt was converted to Christian faith in 1979, after listening to a Chicago street preacher.

In 1985, he planted Joliet Faith Center in Joliet, Illinois, but three years after the death of the founder of his home congregation, Eckhardt returned to become pastor of his home church.

In the 1990s Eckhardt began to write about the modern apostolic move of the church, and since that time has authored more than forty books. In 1985 he started radio broadcast in 1985 and a weekly television broadcast, Perfecting the Saints, in 1989.

His Chicago congregation has grown to four thousand in weekly attendance. Eckhardt has ministered throughout the United States and overseas in more than seventy nations.

In 1995 Eckhardt founded the IMPACT Network (International Ministries of Prophetic and Apostolic Churches Together). Through this organization, Eckhardt provides apostolic oversight to a large network of churches around the globe that look to him for authority, having helped to establish more than three hundred churches in Ethiopia alone.

Echols, Joseph Henry 1894–1979

A co-founder and the longest serving presiding bishop of the **First Born Church of the Living God**. Echols served for thirty years—from 1949 until 1979. Echols completely reorganized the church, creating four dioceses—Tri-State, South Florida, Central, and North-Northwestern Dioceses. He also expanded the denomination into the Bahamas, Jamaica, Haiti, and England. Echols established the First Born Seminary and Training School in Waycross. The headquarters of the church is housed at H. J. Echols Memorial Tabernacle in Waycross.

In 1914 Echols was pastoring a thriving congregation within the Church of the Living God, the Pillar and Ground of the Truth and had been elevated to the office of bishop.

Ecumenical Alliance of International Fellowships and Ministries (TEAM)

TEAM is a community of churches and ministries that represent convergence around the Evangelical, Liturgical and Pentecostal streams of the Christian Church. The group was organized in 2008 by Bishops George Ward of Oasis Christian Center in Las Vegas, Nevada, Paul Price of Grace Christian Cathedral in Washington DC, Mary Adams of Mount Zion Cathedral in Washington DC, and Henry Washington and Walter Crowdus of Pure in Heart Ministries in Louisville Kentucky.

The individual expression of the three streams within the convergence is deliberately pronounced and maintained. Pentecostal spirituality is expressed through exuberant praise, signs, wonders, an infilling of the Holy Spirit, and an emphasis on personal spiritual growth, holiness and individual call to ministry. The expression of the liturgical tradition sees baptism, communion, laying on of hands, repentance, marriage, and anointing with oil as sacraments, rather than as ordinances as most other Pentecostals. Further, they encourage use of the historic creeds and of liturgy, which is considered supported by biblical and is an historic expression of Christian faith. From the Evangelical tradition, TEAM stresses salvation by faith in the atoning death of Jesus Christ through personal conversion, the authority and inerrancy of the Bible, the necessity of evangelism the ministry of the believer, and the importance of preaching.

The organization does not consider itself a denomination, but rather, an ecumenical fellowship that promotes unity, offers accountable leadership, and promotes fellowship and the sharing of resources, effective ministry training and community outreach. Its headquarters are in Winston Salem, North Carolina.

Eikerenkoetter, Frederick J. II 1935–2009

The eccentric evangelist, dubbed "Reverend Ike," was born in Ridgeland, South Carolina to parents from the Netherlands Antilles. His father was a Baptist minister of Dutch-Indonesian extraction, and his mother was an elementary school teacher who taught her son in a one-room schoolhouse. The couple divorced when Frederick was five.

Eikerenkoetter began his career as a teenage preacher and at fourteen he became assistant pastor at Bible Way Baptist Church in his community. He attended American Bible College in Chicago, receiving a bachelor's degree in theology in 1956. He also attended a Pentecostal seminary and was an ordained Pentecostal pastor for a short while.

After serving in the Air Force as a non-commissioned Chaplain Service Specialist he founded the United Church of Jesus Christ for All People in Beaufort, South Carolina, the United Christian Evangelistic Association in Boston, Massachusetts, and finally, the Christ Community United Church in New York City.

His preaching, which he labeled "Prosperity Now," "positive self-image psychology," or "Thinkonomics," was a forerunner of contemporary prosperity theology espoused by black charismatic leaders **Creflo Dollar** and **Fred Price**. Eikerenkoetter eventually moved completely away from orthodox Christian theology, crafting a doctrine he named the Science of Living and relocating his understanding of God to the interior of the self, calling it "God in me."

His ministry reached its peak in the mid-1970s, as weekly radio sermons aired on 1,700 stations across the United States, Mexico, Canada and the Caribbean, reaching an estimated at 2.5 million listeners. On the air, he touted his "Blessing Plan," encouraging listeners to send money in return for a prayer cloth and a blessing from him that would make them more prosperous. His media ministry was augmented by other endeavors including publications such as the quarterly *Study Guide for Power or Living* and *Action!* His public appearances at revival style meetings across the country regularly drew thousands of followers. In the 1990s, he became active on the Internet and had a syndicated television program.

The flamboyant preacher reported only a modest regular income of $40,000 annually. Yet the church had an estimated value of nearly $6,000,000. Eikerenkoetter drew on a liberal, unlimited, expense account to purchase expensive clothing and jewelry, lavish housing accommodations and pay for other luxuries.

Eikerenkoetter first located his New York congregation on 125th Street in the center of Harlem. He later bought the Loew's 175th Street Theatre in Manhattan's Washington Heights community, restored it, renamed it the "Palace Cathedral"—colloquially known as "Reverend Ike's Prayer Tower"—and erected a large luminous cross that could be viewed from the George Washington Bridge, a major entry point into the city. He was also the "chancellor" of the United Church Schools, including the Science of Living Institute and Seminary (which awarded him, his wife, and his son Doctor of the Science of Living degrees). After relocating to Los Angeles in 2007, he suffered a stroke from which he never fully recovered. He died there two years later at the age of seventy-four.

Further Reading:

Riley, Clayton. *The Golden Gospel of the Reverend Ike.* New York: s.p., 1975.

Elaw, Zilpha 1790–1846?

Holiness evangelist who was born as a free person outside of Philadelphia to a deeply religious family. After the death of her mother in 1802, when she was only twelve, she went to live with and work for a Quaker family and was exposed to Quaker worship. Elaw, however, was not attracted to the quiet, reserved worship. During that time, she began to have religious visions. She joined the Methodist Episcopal Church in 1808 after seeing visions of Jesus.

In 1817, nearly ten years later, Elaw attended a weeklong camp meeting. During one of the services, she fell into trance. After awakening, she gave her first ever public speech. Elaw began testifying about the experience of sanctification in several revivals. The enthusiastic reponse of a number of women in her audiences, confirmed what she sensed was her calling to preach.

Elaw became ill in 1819, and while remaining sick for two years, experienced an angelic visitation. After the death of her husband Joseph in 1823, Elaw opened a school for African-American children in Burlington, New Jersey. In 1825 increasingly sensing a call to ministry, she went on a preaching mission among slaves in Maryland and Virginia, risking being arrested, kidnapped, or sold into slavery. Between 1827 to 1840, Elaw preached in various setting including mixed congregations of whites as well as free and slave blacks throughout the Northeast and Mid-Atlantic amassing a following among both black and white, Methodist and non-Methodist, in southeastern Pennsylvania and western New Jersey.

In 1840, she traveled to England to evangelize. According to her personal memoirs, *Memoirs of the Life, Religious Experience, and Ministerial Travels and Labours of Mrs. Zilpha Elaw, an American Female of Colour,* she preached over one thousand sermons throughout the central region of the country. Despite this broad reception, she faced criticism from religious figures who opposed the ministry of women. While in England, she remarried. Whether or not she ever returned to the United States remains uncertain. Elaw died in 1846, probably in England.

Further Reading:

Elaw, Zilpha. *Memoirs of the Life, Religious Experience, Ministerial Travels, and Labours of Mrs. Zilpha Elaw, an American Female of Colour.* London: Charter-House Lane, 1846. Reprinted in *Sisters of the Spirits: Three Black Women's Autobiographies of the Nineteenth Century.* Bloomington, IN: Indiana University Press, 1986.

Ellis, Jesse Delano II 1944–

One of the four founders and the first chairperson of the **Joint College of African American Pentecostal Bishops** and Founding General Overseer of the United Pentecostal Churches of Christ. Ellis was born into a Muslim family in Philadelphia, Pennsylvania. He is one of twenty-seven children from a father who beat him severely when he converted to Christian faith. The rift that developed between he and his father caused him to leave home at age fifteen.

Ellis received his Bachelor of Arts degree in Sociology and History from Howard University, and holds a Master of Religious Education degree from the Nazarene Seminary in Institute, West Virginia, an Honorary Doctor of Divinity from Morehouse College in Atlanta, Doctor of Canon Law from Birmingham University, Birmingham England, and Doctor of Philosophy from Stafford University, London, England.

Ellis has been affiliated with the **Church of God in Christ** where he began his ministry, as well as the Church of the Nazarene, and Pentecostal Church of Christ. While serving in COGIC, Ellis worked under Bishop **Gilbert Earl Patterson** to form the office of Adjutant and wrote the initial constitution and liturgical order for the denomination. In 1989 when Patterson failed to elevate Ellis to the office of bishop, he broke rank with the COGIC and took advantage of a call to lead a local congregation in the Pentecostal Church of Christ.

In 1993 Ellis, Bishop **Paul Morton**, Bishop **Roy Brown**, and Bishop **Wilbert McKinley** founded the **Joint College of African American Pentecostal Bishops**. Ellis was selected to serve as chairperson, and in 2006 was elevated to the position of Metropolitan Archbishop with authority to set protocol for the elevation of bishops and preside over their consecration to convey apostolic succession. After Patterson's death in 2007, Bishop **Charles E. Blake Sr.** assumed the leadership of the **Church of God in Christ**, bringing with him a greater appreciation for protocol, and Ellis realigned himself with the **Church of God in Christ**.

In 2004 a debilitating battle with leukemia left him in ill health. He turned leadership of the denomination—which included seventeen bishops, more than three hundred congregations and five hundred thousand people in the United States, India, and Africa—into the hands of Bishop **Larry Trotter** of Chicago. When Trotter subsequently went against the denomination's constitution to change the name of the organization to United Covenant Churches of Christ (UCCC), Ellis, who had regained his health, formed a new denomination, the Pentecostal Church of Christ (PCC), taking with him several bishops and congregations who had served under Trotter.

Ellis began his military career as a Civil Air Patrol cadet after he had some trouble with law enforcement. He later enlisted in the Air Force where he was appointed to the Air Police Division in the Military Air Transport Service.

He served for a time as a chaplain of Shelby County Sheriff's Department during which time he organized the Civil Air Patrol. He currently holds the rank of Colonel.

His career includes service with the United States Air Force Auxiliary Air Patrol, a National Chief Chaplain of the United States Air Force, with the Auxiliary Air Patrol. During his tenure as chaplain for the Auxiliary Air Patrol, he founded the Cushite Composite Wing in the Ohio Wing where he was serving as chaplain.

His written works include *Vocati Ad Ministrandum: A Calling to Servant Ministry, The Bishopric, Constitution and Canon of Bishops: A Handbook on Creating Episcopacy in the African-American Pentecostal Church, Homilies from the Pentecostal Pulpit Volumes I and II, Hallmark Sermons of 1993, Eternal Life* and most recently *From the Ghetto to Glory*.

Among the controversial elements of Ellis's career, contrary to the tenets of Pentecostalism, he is a 33rd degree Mason. Ellis has promoted cooperation with the Roman Catholic Church including visiting Rome to learn about shared Christian roots. After Ellis's first marriage ended in divorce, he married Sabrina Joyce Ellis, who serves as co-pastor of Pentecostal Church of Christ.

Further Reading

Ellis, J. Delano. *From the Ghetto to Glory*. S.l.: Trafford, 2014.

Emmanuel Pentecostal Church of Our Lord, Apostolic Faith

After the death of **Samuel Hancock**, the presiding bishop of the **Pentecostal Church of the Apostolic** Faith, in 1963, Bishop **Willie Lee**—then assistant bishop and pastor of Christ Apostolic Temple in Indianapolis, Indiana—succeeded him as senior bishop. A year later, however, Lee left the PCAF to found his own body, Emmanuel Pentecostal Church of Our Lord, Apostolic Faith in Indianapolis. Lee, like Hancock before him, did not believe that Jesus was God, but only the son of God. Lee, who like Hancock had formerly been a leader within the **Pentecostal Assemblies of the World**, had left the PAW with his colleague over this same issue. When his fledgling parent denomination moved its Christology more in line with more classical Oneness Pentecostal, Lee left to establish the new organization.

Bishop James Stewart of Danville, Illinois became presiding bishop at Lee's death in 1969. The denomination is focused largely along the East Coast and there are congregations in New York, North Carolina, South Carolina, and Pennsylvania.

Emmanuel Tabernacle Baptist Church of the Apostolic Faith

The Oneness Pentecostal body was founded in 1916, and incorporated in 1917 by **Martin Rawleigh Gregory**, a former Baptist pastor in Columbus, Ohio, where its headquarters remains. By 1915 Gregory had embraced Pentecostal Spirit baptism and Oneness

Pentecostal theology under the influence of the preaching of Robert **Clarence Lawson**. He was assisted in founding the church by two women who had been members of his Baptist congregation, Lela Grant and Bessie Dockett.

After Gregory's death, O. J. Gentry served in that position until 1976. He was followed by T. H. Carey who served for a year and a half until his death in 1978. From its inception, and in counter distinction with both Gregory's Baptists roots and the prevailing stance with Oneness Pentecostalism, the denomination has held all ranks of leadership open to women, and the denomination holds the distinction of being the first organization to give women a place equal to men, including access to the episcopacy. Bishop H. C. Clark was first appointed to serve as assistant presider with Bishop T. H. Carey in 2006. At Carey's death in 1978, she became presiding bishop and served in that position for twenty-eight years until her death in 2006. She was followed by F. C. Dampier, who resigned in 2013. The current presiding bishop is Edward M. Mitchell.

The ordinances of the church include baptism by immersion in the name of Jesus, the Lord's Supper, and foot washing. In 1995 there were approximately thirty congregations within the denomination.

Evangelical Churches of Christ (Holiness)

A **Holiness** denomination founded by William C. Holman in 1947. Holman had been a Churches of Christ (Holiness) USA pastor in Los Angeles, California. He has served that denomination for twenty years. The break with the parent organization was administrative not doctrinal and the denomination follows the Methodist Articles of Religion.

Headquarters are in Washington DC, and in 1990, the denomination had approximately five hundred members in four congregations in Washington DC; Los Angeles, California; Denver, Colorado; and Omaha, Nebraska.

Evangelistic Churches of Christ

After the death of his wife in 1974, Lymus Johnson, a minister and evangelist in the **Church of Our Lord Jesus Christ of the Apostolic Faith**, left the Church of Our Lord Jesus Christ to found The Evangelistic Church of Christ in Corona, New York. The congregation grew and was later located in Jackson Heights, New York, which is now the headquarters church for The **Evangelistic Churches of Christ of the Apostolic Faith**.

When Johnson died in 2012, Bishop Willie Thomas took the position as presider.

Further Reading:

Walters. Steve B. *A Shepherd's Journey: The Life Story of Apostle Lymus L. Johnson.* S.l.: Steve Walters Ministries, 2002.

Evans, Robert Jr. 1947–2000

Evans was born in Manning, South Carolina and relocated with his family to Baltimore, Maryland when he was five years old. He was called to the ministry in 1967. In 1971 when the pastor of his church became seriously ill, Evans, who attended the renowned Peabody Conservatory of Music, was appointed as acting pastor. In 1972 when his predecessor died, Evans was ordained an elder and installed as pastor of the **Highway**

Christian Church of Christ where he served until his death. Under his leadership, the church changed its name three times. In 1987, it became Bethel Temple Highway Church of Christ; then in 1988 it became Bethel Temple Church of Christ, Inc. Finally, in 1989, Evans changed the name to "Beth-El" Temple to reflect what he understood to be representing God's name.

At one point, he enrolled in the Baltimore School of the Bible and the Howard University School of Divinity in Washington DC while working first in the Income Tax Division of the State of Maryland, then becoming a public school music teacher in Baltimore.

In 1986 the **Highway Churches of Christ** consecrated Evans to the office of Bishop. Two years later, he resigned from that denomination to organize the **Beth-El Churches of Christ, Inc**. In 1994 he was consecrated an apostle and formed the End-Time World Christian Fellowship Association to provide pastoral leadership for pastors from several denominations. Throughout this period, Evans continued his ministry of music as a recording artist and composer.

Exume, Dorothy Mae Webster 1922–2011

The pioneer **Church of God in Christ** missionary was born in Cleveland, Ohio. As a young child in a Baptist Church, Exume heard a message about African missions and decided that she wanted to go and help. Sometime after that Exume became connected with COGIC.

After praying about serving in foreign missions, the Lord gave her a dream that was interpreted by a church mother as a call to serve in Haiti. Exume served as the first COGIC missionary to the Republic of Haiti. On being assigned there by International Women's Supervisor **Lillian Brooks Coffey**, she arrived in Haiti in 1947 accompanied by Coffey and Bishop **A. B. McEwen**. The year that she arrived, she opened the first COGIC school in Haiti.

Exume's education included dual degrees in French and Sociology from Case Western Reserve University, a Masters of Religious Education from the Interdenominational Theological Center and a Doctorate in Christian Education from Union Graduate School. By vocation, Exume was a high school French teacher.

In the thirty years that she served on the impoverished Caribbean island, she worked as the first supervisor of women, and established approximately twenty churches, as well as schools, missions, a multi-family housing project, feeding programs, new missionary training and micro-financing projects for entrepreneurial single mothers.

While carrying out missions responsibilities, Exume also served as COGIC Christian Education Director; secretary to Mother Coffey; member of the planning Committee of the First International Women's Convention; and founder of Aides to the President, a task force group for the Women's Convention. She was also one of two broadcasters for Women's Convention radio programs. She served as both an instructor and a member of the board of trustees for C. H. Mason Theological Seminary. Exume died in Atlanta at age eighty-eight.

F

Faith Tabernacle Council of Churches International

A Oneness denomination founded as Faith Tabernacle Corporation of Churches in 1962 and incorporated in Portland, Oregon, in 1963, by **Louis W. Osborne Sr.** In 1989 the name was changed to the later designation. Organized as an association of autonomous congregations, the council charters churches and ordains ministers but does not require strict conformity in matters of polity. There are approximately fifty-five autonomous churches in the United States, Zimbabwe, and South Africa. It provides these congregations with "Guidelines for Christian Development."

Within the United States, congregations are principally located in the West and Midwest. There are also congregations in Nigeria, Liberia, Zimbabwe, Haiti, and Jamaica.

After Osborne Sr.'s death, his wife **Grace Osborne**—who was elevated to the pastorate in 1986 and consecrated a bishop in 1989—took the reins of the organization as the second presiding bishop. The Council published a periodical, *The Light of Faith.*

Farrow, Lucy 1851–1911

Lucy Farrow was chief among several women who served with **William Seymour** as leaders of the early stages of the **Azusa Street Revival**. She was born in Norfolk, Virginia, fifteen years before the end of the American Civil War, and allegedly was a mulatto daughter of a white slave owner and a slave woman and the niece of famed abolitionist Frederick Douglass. Farrow was either born a slave or sold into slavery after her father's death.

By 1871 Farrow had moved to Mississippi. By 1890 she was pastoring a Holiness mission church in Houston, Texas. She was widowed at least once and gave birth to seven children, though only two survived. In Houston Farrow met **Charles Fox Parham,** the formulator of the doctrine that the initial evidence of Holy Spirit baptism is speaking in tongues and, subsequently, left her pastorate to work as governess for his family as they traveled throughout Kansas holding revivals. While she was serving them, she received the Pentecostal baptism of the Holy Spirit.

William Joseph Seymour, who would become leader of the **Azusa Street Revival**, attended her Houston church before coming to Los Angeles, serving as interim pastor while she traveled with Parham. She introduced him to the doctrine and phenomenon of Holy Spirit baptism with tongues. Subsequently, she also introduced him to Parham, setting up a chain of events that ultimately led to the beginning of the Azusa Street meeting. Initially, Seymour became his student, but shortly after their meeting, Seymour left for Los Angeles.

Seymour and Farrow re-united in Los Angeles, where she arrived with her associate, Joseph A. Warren, to assist her former member. Known for having the gift of impartation—laying on of hands for others to receive Pentecostal Holy Spirit baptism—Farrow took on an important role in the meetings. During the earliest days, before Seymour received the Pentecostal experience, Farrow's testimonies of her own baptism prodded others to the experience. Many who would later become prominent leaders in the Pentecostal movement received the gift of tongues through her ministry.

In August 1906, Farrow left Azusa Street to embark on an evangelistic campaign, conducting revivals in Texas, Louisiana, North Carolina, Virginia, New York, and England on her way to Liberia. While in Texas, she rejoined Parham as part of the ministry team for one of his revivals. It was here that Howard Goss, an early Pentecostal leader in the Midwest and a founder of the Assemblies of God, encountered Farrow. She stopped in Norfolk and Portsmouth, Virginia, holding revivals in which hundreds came receive the Pentecostal Holy Spirit baptism. By the time she left that state, new congregations had been planted in each of those cities.

Farrow stayed in Johnsonville, Liberia, near the capitol of Monrovia for seven months, working with **Julia Hutchins**, Hutchins's husband, Willis, and niece, Lelia McKinney. Reportedly, during her tenure there, she exercised the xenolalic gift of the Kru language, preaching at least two messages to the Kru people in their own dialect. Also, reportedly, some of the Kru people to whom she ministered received the English language with their Holy Spirit baptism. During the revival in Liberia, it was reported that "twenty souls received their Pentecost [and] numbers were saved, sanctified and healed."

On leaving Liberia, Farrow returned to Los Angeles by way of Virginia, North Carolina, and other areas of the South. Back in the city by May 1908, she established a ministry closely linked to the Azusa Street Mission. For several months, she ministered from a "small faith cottage" in back of the mission where people came to receive prayer, healing, and Pentecostal Holy Spirit baptism. Leaving Azusa Street for the last time, Farrow lived the rest of her life in Houston with her son and his wife. In 1911 only five years after the beginning of the **Azusa Street Revival**, she contracted intestinal tuberculosis and died at the age of sixty.

Further Reading:

Alexander, Estrelda. *The Women of Azusa Street.* Laurel, MD: Seymour Press, 2012.

Father Divine 1876–1965

The quasi-Holiness preacher, civil rights activist, spiritual leader and founder of the **International Peace Mission** movement. Known as Rev. M. J. Divine, his full self-assigned name was Reverend Major Jealous Divine, but his probable given name was George Baker. Divine established the group, formulated its doctrine, and oversaw its growth from a small and predominantly black congregation into a multiracial and international organization.

Little is known about his earliest life, and while some place his birth in rural Georgia, other biographers locate it in a poor neighborhood in Rockville, Maryland. Around the turn of the nineteenth century, he had moved to Baltimore as a young adult where he taught Sunday School, became interested in the ministry, and worked as a gardener. In 1906 he traveled to California, where became acquainted with the positive thinking ideas of Charles Fillmore and the New Thought Movement that would inform his later doctrines, specifically the assertion that negative thoughts led to poverty and unhappiness.

By 1907 he was attending a local Baptist Church, where he frequently was allowed to preach. He encountered Samuel Morris, a traveling preacher from Allegheny County, Pennsylvania, who claimed to be the "Eternal Father." Though his message was roundly denounced by most congregations in the area, Divine became Morris's first convert and adopted a pseudonym, "The Messenger," as the Christ figure to Morris's figure of God the Father. Morris began calling himself "Father Jehovia" and the two men were joined by John Hickerson, who called himself "Reverend Bishop Saint John the Vine."

By 1912 Divine started making his way back east and the three-man team collapsed. By then, Divine was denouncing his former mentor's claim to be God and declaring that he, himself, was the only true expression of God's spirit. In 1914 he was arrested in Valdosta, Georgia, as a public nuisance who was possibly mentally ill.

In 1915 he was in New York City with a handful of disciples he had picked up. Settling in Brooklyn, he moved his all-black congregation to the all-white community of Sayville, New York on Long Island. His neighbors' complaints led to his arrest and a thirty-day incarceration. When the judge who sentenced him died two days after the sentencing, Divine claimed that the death was due to his supernatural intervention.

By 1933 Divine and his followers had moved to the Harlem section of Manhattan, where he opened the first of his residential "heavens" where followers lived communally and practiced his teachings, obtained food and shelter, and found job opportunities, as well as spiritual and physical healing. Additional heavens appeared in Philadelphia, where he moved at the end of the depression and remained until his death. Starting in 1941 with the Brigantine Hotel, the movement owned, managed, and staffed six fully integrated enterprises in New Jersey and Pennsylvania.

The outspoken civil rights activist championed gender and racial equality, rejected racial identity, urged people to think of themselves simply as Americans, and called for an end to segregation, lynching, and capital punishment. Membership in the movement numbered in the tens of thousands at its height, including significant numbers of wealthy whites. That membership declined dramatically, however, in part because of the movement's strict dedication to celibacy.

Though denounced by major African-American Holiness and Pentecostal leaders of his day, Divine incorporated many tenets of these movements into his teaching including abstinence from tobacco, alcohol, narcotics, and vulgar language. Despite these strictures, Divine was accused of breaking up families, swindling money from followers, being sexually promiscuous, though the moral accusations were never proven. Part of the accusations may be attributed to the apparent double standard Divine held for himself and his followers. Though admonishing them to live lives of frugality and turn over their material resources to the movement, he was one of the most flamboyant black leaders of the Depression era, living in abundance, residing in splendor and being chauffeured in a Rolls Royce. Further, while demanding celibacy for followers and dividing his communal residences into separate floors for men and women, he married twice.

His first wife, a disciple named Pinninnah, died in 1946. After her death Divine married a twenty-one-year-old white Canadian follower, Sweet Angel Divine, who was a half century his junior and became known as Mother Divine. After that time, Divine went into semi-retirement and was less active in mission projects. He was eighty-nine when he died. After his death, Mother Divine continued to lead the declining movement.

Further Reading:

Mabee, Carleton. *Promised Land: Father Divine's Interracial Communities in Ulster County, New York.* Fleischmanns, NY: Purple Mountain, 2008.

Jill Watts. *God, Harlem USA: The Father Divine Story.* Oakland, CA University of California Press, 1992.

Federated Pentecostal Church International, Inc.

The organization is the umbrella group for eight independently incorporated African-American Pentecostal bodies who are in full fellowship with each other, yet remain autonomous. It was founded by **Ernest F. Morris** as a loose organization in 1934, but not incorporated until 1986.

Member organizations agree on major areas of doctrine including the Trinitarian Godhead, salvation, sanctification, baptism by immersion (in the Name of the Father, the Son and the Holy Ghost) and necessity of Pentecostal Holy Spirit baptism. They each are adverse to certain practices such as spiritualism. Each body maintains its own governmental structure, officers and polity. Further, each maintains its own headquarters.

The member bodies included some well-established groups within the United States including the **Christ Holy Sanctified Church** under **Ulysses S. King** and the **Mount Calvary Holy Church of America**, under **Brumfield Johnson.** They also included some smaller groups such as the **Full Gospel Pentecostal Association** founded in 1970 by S. D. Leffall in Portland, Oregon; **United Full Gospel Church, USA** under Richard Taylor; the **United Interdenominational Prayer and Fellowship Association**, headquartered in Tacoma, Washington; and the **House of Prayer for All Nations**, an organization of five churches founded in Longview Washington; Saint Timothy Holy Church of Brooklyn, New York. The **Mount Zion Lighthouse Full Gospel Church** headquartered in Nigeria represented the single African denomination, but also has congregations in the United States.

At the time of its founding, there were 400 congregations in the United States and Africa. In Nigeria, where the membership is more than 20,000, the organization's collaborative missions efforts support a school and more than one hundred pastors.

Bishop Leffall served as president from 1986 until his death in 2008. After his death, the organization established the S. D. Leffall scholarship in his honor. G. Jones of **Christ Holy Sanctified Church of America** served from 2006 until his death in 2008. Taylor is the current president and the organization is currently headquartered in Bellevue, Washington.

As of 2015, member organizations include the **Christ Holy Sanctified Church** (twenty-seven congregations), the United Full Gospel Church (nine congregations), the Holy Leadership Association (five congregations), the United Interdenominational Prayer and Fellowship Association (five congregations), the House of Prayer for All Nations (four congregations), and the Full Gospel New Life Association (nineteen congregations).

Feick, August 1879-??

Canadian-born August Feick served as General Superintendent of the white congregations of the **Churches of God in Christ** during the 1920s. He came to the United States in 19v13 and became a close associate of famed evangelist, Maia Woodworth-Etter. During Etter's later years, until her death in 1924, he served as her assistant pastor and business manager, and as ghostwriter for Etter's autobiographical work, *Life and Testimony of Mrs. M.B. Woodworth-Etter, Evangelist,* published in 1925.

Prior to her death, Woodworth-Etter appointed Feick executor of her estate. After her demise, he took over Etter Tabernacle, which affiliated with the Assemblies of God, and remained as lead pastor until 1933. Feick, however, surrendered his Assemblies of God credentials in 1926 to help C. H. Mason with **Church of God in Christ** (White) and worked with **William Holt** to craft The Articles Incorporation in that year. These articles list Feick and Eudorous Bell as General Superintendents. For a time, he used the Indianapolis congregation as headquarters for the white Churches of God in Christ. As late as 1932, Feick was leading white fellowships into the **Church of God in Christ**.

Fellowship of Affirming Ministries

A trans-denominational, predominantly African-American fellowship of more than one hundred primarily African-American Christian leaders and laity representing churches and faith-based organizations from all parts of the United States, Mexico and Africa. The fellowship was founded in 2000 by Bishop **Yvette Flunder**, an openly lesbian woman and former **Church of God in Christ** minister.

In June 2003, Flunder was consecrated presiding bishop of the Fellowship, which characterizes itself as "radically inclusive." Churches within the organization range from ultra-conservative backgrounds to more liberal, independent churches; from startup, developing congregations to large, established churches; and from churches that are economically challenged to the very affluent.

Headquartered in San Francisco, California, the Fellowship seeks to create a safe environment for the community they serve, foster development of an inclusive theology, and foster networks to support member leaders and their congregations financially and socially.

Fellowship of Christian Believers

A predominantly African-American organization of autonomous Oneness congregations that began in 1963 as Faith Tabernacle Corporation of Churches in Portland, Oregon, where the organization is headquartered.

The Fellowship is a member of the Apostolic World Christian Fellowship, a global alliance of apostolic organizations throughout the world. Each FCB church is a self-governing body. The Board of Bishops, which is currently chaired by Bishop **Grace C. Osborne**, serves as a covering to support its individual church bodies and pastors by providing education, fellowship, leadership, and ministerial training, ordination and ministerial licensing.

Within the United States, congregations are principally located in the West and Midwest. There are also congregations in Nigeria, Liberia, Zimbabwe, Haiti, and Jamaica.

Feltus, James Jr. 1921–?

The founding bishop of the **Church of God in Christ United**. In 1946 at age twenty-five, Feltus succeeded his father as pastor of the first **Church of God in Christ** congregation in New Orleans, Louisiana. He served as Assistant Secretary of the State Sunday School Department, a district superintendent and member of the Board of Elders before being consecrated bishop of British Honduras in 1953, where he was instrumental in bringing the island to the **Church of God in Christ**. Feltus also served as a member of the Doctrinal Committee, Dean of The National Sunday School Department, member of the Constitution Committee, and the Board of Bishops.

In 1968 Feltus was consecrated Bishop of Eastern Louisiana Jurisdiction of COGIC by presiding senior bishop, **Ozro T. Jones Sr**. Feltus served in that position from 1968 to 1972, holding annual fellowship Convocations annually and attracting several members to COGIC. After the crisis regarding succession following founder **Charles Harrison Mason**'s death and the dissatisfaction with the resolution of the issue, Feltus' leadership was questioned by those who opposed the ousted Jones.

In 1973 Feltus wrote five principles as foundational for the **Church of God In Christ United**: the defense of biblical doctrine, the centrality of the local church, refusal to form a political federation, replacement of national assessments by local financial contributions, and the biblical constitution of the church. Feltus joined Bishop R. A. Campbell and Bishop Marshall Hebert in establishing the **Church of God in Christ United**. He was selected as chief bishop. Herbert became first assistant Campbell second assistant, and Feltus's wife, Hazel, was appointed general supervisor of women.

Feltus holds six graduate and post-graduate degrees taken from five universities, including Xavier University and Southern University of New Orleans, and New Orleans Baptist Theological Seminary.

Fire Baptized Holiness Church of God of the Americas

The African-American Wesley Holiness Pentecostal denomination that resulted from a break from the earlier interracial Holiness group by that same name. In the late 1800s, B. H. Irwin's **Fire Baptized Holiness Church** held interracial conventions and supported integrated congregations throughout the South that proved exceptional to sanctions on racial mixing in worship.

By 1908 it had existed as an interracial Holiness body for six years, and as a Pentecostal body for two, having moved into that camp through **G. B. Cashwell's** evangelistic efforts. In that year, a group of five hundred blacks, under the leadership of William Edward Fuller Sr., separated from the parent body to form an independent denomination. Since the parent body was a predominantly Southern organization, blacks were largely concerned about the disparity of accommodations at denominational conventions as well as for the criticism the denomination received for hosting integrated worship services and having blacks and whites eat together.

The break from its parent had been largely congenial and by mutual consent. While the black group was associated with the larger organization, the former had accumulated $25,000 in its own property and assets. When they left, the breakaway group was allowed to retain these resources. There was little contact between the two, however, after the division, and later historical scholarship from the white group makes no mention at all of the early black faction or of Fuller's contribution.

The new group held its first General Council in Greer, South Carolina in November of that year and decided that to call itself the Colored **Fire Baptized Holiness Church**. By then, there were twenty-seven churches and 925 members; Fuller was elected general overseer. A year later, the first edition of the denomination's periodical, *True Witness*, was published.

The Fuller Normal and Industrial Institute was organized in 1912 in Atlanta, Georgia, opening with one instructor and two students. In 1913 it moved to an eighteen-acre campus in Toccoa, Georgia and then, in 1923, to its present location in Greenville, South Carolina where it consolidated with the Fuller Normal Junior School. The institution now currently operates as a small private Christian school. Its campus also houses the denominational headquarters.

From 1908 to 1922, the church went by the name, **Fire Baptized Holiness Church** of God. During the 1922 General Council, the group decided to change the name to the Fire Baptized Church of God. This Council also elevated Fuller from the position of general overseer to presiding bishop. In 1926 the name was permanently changed to **Fire Baptized Holiness Church** of the Americas.

Fuller served at the helm of the denomination for fifty years, until his death in 1958. By then, there were more than eight hundred congregations in the United States and the West Indies. On his deathbed, the white segment of the **Fire Baptized Holiness Church** approached Fuller to propose that the two bodies re-unite. When the whites refused to yield the chair of presiding bishop to the larger, black denomination, however, no union occurred.

At his death, the General Council put a structure in place whereby it would be governed by a five-member Board of Bishops representing the five episcopal diocese. The first Council was manned by Charles Calvin Chiles who had previously served as secretary and treasurer, Gustavus Guyhart Gary, Cleve A. Mills, Ezell Z. Bowman, and William E. Fuller Jr. Chiles served as the first chairperson of this board.

In 1994 the denomination had about 220 congregations, mostly on the east coast of the United States, but also including one church each in Canada, England, and the Virgin Islands, and fifteen congregations in Jamaica. By that year, there were approximately 24,000 members served by 2,500 ministers. The organization's headquarters relocated to Greenville, South Carolina in 1996. Fuller died in 2007 and Bishop Patrick Frazier assumed the seat as presiding bishop.

The FBHCA is perhaps one of the last of the classical Pentecostal bodies to hold to a rigid, defined standard of personal piety that governs almost all aspects of its members lives. Adherents continue to refer to the denomination's Book of Discipline, to determine appropriate apparel and adornment for the saints, as well as engagement in social activities and worship. That discipline explicitly details strictures that even many other classical Pentecostal Christians have come to see as a matter of personal conscience, including the apparel women should wear, sanctions on gambling, and social activities. Mothers, deacons, pastors, and elders are to be held responsible for the enforcing the rules. Further, the polity of the discipline takes a clearly Wesleyan stand on the possibility of Christian perfection and soundly rejects other theological understandings regarding the nature of salvation, and of the progressive nature sanctification.

These stands regarding polity and theology have ensured that the denomination has not kept up with the growth exhibited it older classical sister bodies, COGIC and UHC. Instead of major schisms within the denomination, however, the FBHC has generally seen its numbers decline through individual member decision to align with more progressive Pentecostal or Charismatic bodies. One exception was the defection of a group under the leadership of Bishops Nathaniel Simmons and Charles Williams who left the FBHCA taking several key congregations with then to establish Sounds of Praise Pentecostal Fellowship Ministries in 1994.

First Born Church of the Living God

One of the earliest groups to split from **Mary Magdalena Lewis Tate**'s denomination, the **Church of the Living God the Pillar and Ground of the Truth, First Born Church of the Living God** was established in 1913 by Quincy Crooms, Simon Crooms, A. M. McNair, M. M. Hall, L. G. Lockhart, E. Goodson, O. C. Ganger, L. O. Golden, and **Jesse Clarence Blakely**, in part because they objected to the liberal stance of the parent organization in allowing women to preach.

Quincy Crooms headed the denomination, whose headquarters is in Waycross, Georgia, from 1913 to 1923. The constitution and by-laws were drawn up in 1921. During the early 1920s the denomination had been home to George Baker, later known as **Father Divine**, the quasi-Holiness cult leader, who founded the **International Peace Mission** movement.

M. M. Holland presided from 1921 to 1924. During his administration, the first constitution and by-laws were introduced, but his sudden death precluded him from seeing the constitution put into effect. Blakely served as presiding bishop from 1924 to 1939, then left to form **The First Born Church of Christ Written In Heaven** (later the **Church of Christ Written in Heaven**). In the mid-1990s there was a second split when twelve of the congregations under the supervision of Bishop Alfred Howard split from the parent body to form the Worldwide Abundant Life Fellowship. Its headquarters is in Mt. Lebanon, Tennessee.

After Blakely's departure, Clinton Miller served as presiding bishop for ten years. The longest tenure in the denomination was held by **Joseph C. Echols** who presided for thirty years, from 1949 to 1979. During Echols tenure, the church was completely reorganized into four jurisdictions: Tri-State, Florida, Central, and North-Northwestern. During the time, the denomination expanded into the Bahamas, Jamaica, Haiti, and England. Its First Born Seminary and Training School was established in 1954. That institution offers both undergraduate and graduate degrees and continues to train leaders within the denomination.

Echols's extended tenure was followed by two short administrations. Bishop C. L. Smith who oversaw the purchasing of the land for a new International Headquarters served from 1979 until his death in 1980. The shortest tenure was held by Bishop R. B. Thompson, who resigned in after only two months due to illness.

Bishop Albert Hill began his tenure in 1980. Under his administration, the denomination added three jurisdictions, started a benevolence fund to help those in need, and completely renovated the international headquarters. Yet, Hill ran into trouble with the Executive Board, which removed him from office in 1994 over an undisclosed matter. In turn, Hill sued the **First Born Church of the Living God** in prolonged litigation. The denomination prevailed in court and the board excommunicated Hill. Prior to his death in 1999, while the trial was still in process, he attempted to install his son-in-law, Leonard Goode, as assistant senior bishop. The court also overruled that action.

In his stead, the board appointed Bishop W. L. Johnson to serve in an interim positon. He served in that position until 1998 when he became presiding bishop. He continued his tenure until 2000. In that year, Bishop J. C. Howard became presiding bishop.

The denomination is concentrated in the Southern region of the United States but has approximately 15,000 members in congregations throughout the country and the Caribbean.

A further split occurred in the new body in 1939, when Blakely broke to form The First Born Church of Christ Written In Heaven. In the mid-1990s there was a second split and twelve of the congregations under the leadership of Bishop Alfred Howard. They started a new affiliation called Worldwide Abundant Life Fellowship. Its headquarters is in Mt. Lebanon, Tennessee.

First Church of Our Lord Jesus Christ

A Oneness Pentecostal denomination founded by **Gino N. Jennings** in 1983. Variously referred to as the Truth of God Movement, Jennings grew the organization from twelve members who worshiped in the basement of his parents' home to fifteen United States congregations mostly along the East Coast as well as nearly two hundred churches in Africa, Asia, and Europe.

The pacifist denomination follows the most rigid lines within the generally more rigid Oneness Pentecostalism, teaching that those who are not baptized in Jesus' name are not saved. Beyond the normal restrictions of classical Holiness-Pentecostal groups, the body follows the rigid restrictions that were first a part of **Sherrod Johnson**'s denomination, **Church of the Lord Jesus Christ of the Apostolic Faith**. There are specific proscriptions regarding women's and men's apparel even to the point that women are forbidden from cutting, dying, or chemically treating their hair. Men are expected to be clean-shaven at all times and are not to wear shorts or short pants in public. Further, women are not allowed to speak in the church or be in ministry.

Like CLJCAF, the denomination teaches that the celebration of Christian holidays such as Easter and Christmas are unbiblical. Contrary to many African-American Pentecostal groups, the ordinance of communion is administered using wine by the use of a common one cup from which all participants drink.

The headquarters of the organization is in Philadelphia, Pennsylvania. By the end of 1990, the Truth of God Radio Program, which began earlier that year, was being aired on eleven radio stations. By the end of the second year, it reached throughout the United States, the Caribbean, Great Britain, Nigeria West Africa, and even as far away as New Zealand. Jennings's uncompromising preaching draws the loyal support of hardline conservative Oneness adherents while repulsing those within the tradition who tend to be more moderate. Detractors who oppose Jennings regularly accuse him of heresy, misogyny, and cult-like control techniques that have been compared to **Daddy Grace**, **Father Divine,** and even Jim Jones.

Fisher, Henry Lee 1874–1947

The third presiding bishop and one of the most influential leaders of the **United Holy Church of America**. He was born in Salisbury, North Carolina to parents who had not long been freed from slavery, and raised in the African Methodist Episcopal Zion Church. Fisher attended Barber Scotia College in Concord, North Carolina, before moving to Wilmington where he began his ministry.

Fisher's introduction to the Holiness movement came in a meeting at the Sam Jones Tabernacle in Wilmington, where the Elijah Lowney was preaching. In this racially mixed gathering, Fisher was exposed to the doctrine of sanctification as taught by certain Methodists, called to the "deeper life," and introduced to one of the three groups that would merge to form the Holy Church of North Carolina and later the Holy Church of North Carolina and Virginia. That same group would be incorporated as the **United Holy Church of America** over which he would preside.

Fisher was ordained in 1900. In 1907, he reported to the Apostolic Faith newspaper from the Azusa Street Mission that he had received the Pentecostal experience of Spirit baptism, possibly under the ministry of **G. B. Carswell** or one of his disciples. The majority of Fisher's career was spent serving as a pastor in Durham Tabernacle in Durham, North Carolina—his permanent home. He began that pastorate in 1905 and founded a second congregation, New Covenant Temple United Holy Church, for members who migrated to that city.

Fisher's tenure as president of the **United Holy Church** began in 1916 after former presider **William Fulford** was discredited for preaching "heretical" doctrine and failed to win re-election. Throughout Fulford's tenure, however, Fisher emerged as an important, behind-the-scenes, player. He served as editor-in-chief of the *Holiness Union*, the organizations' newspaper, as chair of the Foreign Missions Board, and as Sunday School Superintendent. By 1910, he headed up a team responsible for developing a manual. In it, the name was changed to the **United Holy Church of America**. Fisher used the knowledge he had received in the AMEZ Church to write this first manual of polity for the United Holy Churches. Two years later, and four years before he was elected president, the organization was incorporated under that name.

Under his leadership as presider, a network of seven regional jurisdictions known as convocations was established throughout the United States and in Bermuda. Known for his teaching, powerful preaching, and compassion, Fisher gave structure and mission to the young denomination, guiding it through a period when Holiness and Pentecostal people were often held in great suspicion and considered by some as one of a number of proliferating cults, or as schismatic people of questionable sexual morality. He also guided the denomination through the period of Jim Crow race relations in the United States, and so regarded his part of his mission as helping his people to flourish in the face of economic, political, and social deprivation evidenced in segregation, lynchings, and racial violence.

Fisher's reputation as one of the most significant leaders throughout UHCA history stems, in part, from several important operational changes he introduced including a level of organizational structure that had previously been missing. Throughout that tenure, Fisher was aided by **General Johnson (G. J.) Branch**, his vice president, and president of the Northern District. Branch, who had come into the UHC from the Freewill Baptist Church, was a well-to-do real estate owner whose business skills helped set the UHC on strong administrative footing.

Throughout his life, Fisher maintained strong, cordial ties with other black Holiness and Pentecostal leaders of his day, including **Charles Harrison Mason** of the **Church of God in Christ**, **Charles Price Jones** of the **Church of Christ Holiness**, and **William E. Fuller** of the **Fire Baptized Holiness Church of God of the Americas**. He died in Henderson, North Carolina in 1947. After his death, his local congregation was renamed Fisher Memorial United Holy Church in his honor.

For Further Reading:

Fisher, Henry L. *The History of the United Holy Church of America, Inc.* S.L: s.n., s.l.
Gregory, Chester W. *The History of the United Holy Church of America, Inc., 1886–1986.* Baltimore, MD: Gateway, 1986.
Turner, William C. *The United Holy Church of America: A Study in Black Holiness-Pentecostalism.* Piscataway, NJ: Gorgias, 2006.

Fisher, Violet L. 1939–

Violet Fisher represents a cadre of women who successfully navigated between the black Pentecostal movement and the predominantly white mainline church by returning to her roots in the Methodist Episcopal Church. Though eventually elevated to the office of bishop within the UMC, she maintained elements of Pentecostal spirituality as well as relationships with Pentecostal leaders from her own former denomination and several others. Fisher continued to be called upon to minister within Pentecostal, Neo-Pentecostal, and Charismatic circles.

Fisher was the second of five children into a Methodist family on the Eastern Shore of Maryland. Her father was a deacon and her mother was a preacher. Violet's call to ministry began when she was sixteen. During that time, there was no place in ordained ministry for women, especially in the Delaware Conference of the Central Jurisdiction of the United Methodist Church. Not seeing role models within the denomination, she was drawn to the Pentecostal movement, where she found women such as **Carrie Gurry** willing to mentor her.

Fisher graduated from Bowie State University with a Bachelor of Science in 1962. In 1965, at the age of twenty-five, she was ordained an elder in **King's Apostle Holiness Church of God** a Pentecostal body founded by Gurry. Ten years later, in 1975, Fisher was appointed as a national evangelist of the denomination's Northeastern Region and served as a short-term missionary to East Africa, Haiti, and Jamaica.

Fisher founded the Interdenominational World Wide Women Ministers Alliance in 1978 with chapters in the Eastern part of the United States and Bermuda. After receiving a Masters in Education from George Washington University in that same year, she attained a Doctor of Divinity degree from Baltimore College of Bible in 1984 and a Master of Divinity from Eastern Baptist Theological Seminary in Philadelphia in 1988.

During those years, she also taught junior and senior high in the public school systems of Virginia and Maryland because she was unable to make a living in ministry. While the denomination founded by a woman was open to their leadership, it afforded only a limited opportunity for the kind of ministry that would incorporate her gifts and training, and provide full financial support.

In 1983 she returned to the United Methodist Church. After completing Divinity School in 1988, Fisher was ordained a deacon in the Eastern Pennsylvania Conference and appointed as associate pastor of St. Daniel's United Methodist Church in Chester, Pennsylvania. In 1990, she was ordained Elder in Full Connection in that conference and was appointed senior pastor of Sayer's Memorial United Methodist Church in Philadelphia. In 1994, after only six years in United Methodist Church ministry, she was appointed a District Superintendent of the Mary McLeod Bethune District.

Six years later she was elected bishop, becoming the first African-American woman to do so in the Northeast Jurisdiction and becoming responsible for 800 local churches and 1500 clergy in Western and North Central New York. Fisher served as bishop of the Western and North Central New York Annual Conference from 2000 to 2008. She is one of only three women to have ever attained that rank in the United Methodist Church, along with Loentyne Kelly in 1984 and Beverly Shamana in 2000.

By 2006 Fisher was serving as vice president of the General Board of Global Ministries. She served as Dean of the Cabinet from 1998 to 1999; delegate to General and Jurisdictional Conferences 1996 and 2000; delegate to World Methodist Council in 1996; Dean of the North Eastern Jurisdiction, School of Evangelism from 1998 to 1999; member of the General Board of Church and Society from 1996 to 2000; the General Board of Discipleship; and Older Adult Ministry from 1996 to 2000. In 1997 she was elected to serve on the Board of Directors Eastern Baptist Seminary. She retired as bishop in 2008.

Further Reading:

Craig, Judith. *The Leading Women: Stories of the First Women Bishops of the United Methodist.* Nashville: Abingdon, 2004.

Fizer, William Jordan 1907–2001

The founding bishop of the **Church Of God, Which He Purchased with His Own Blood,** had previously been affiliated with the **Church of the Living God (Christian Workers for Fellowship)**. Fizer was born in Memphis, Tennessee. He earned the Bachelor and Master's degrees from the International Bible Institute of Plymouth, Florida and a Doctor of Divinity degree in the field of Minister of Religion from Anchor College of Truth, Devore, California. He began preaching in 1920 at age thirteen. Fifteen years later, at age twenty-eight, he was appointed to pastor the **Church of the Living God (CWFF)**, in Oklahoma City.

In 1953 Fizer claimed having a revelation regarding error in the parent church's polity. He was excommunicated from that group for promulgating his new understanding, and set out establishing the new church and building a denomination throughout the state and nation—an effort to which he devoted the rest of his life.

Flunder, Yvette Adrienne 1955–

Former Pentecostal minister who became a gay activist and is the founding pastor of City of Refuge church and **The Fellowship of Affirming Ministries**. Raised a devout Pentecostal, the native of San Francisco is a third-generation preacher who was a teenage evangelist with roots in the **Church of God in Christ**. She attended COGIC's **Saints Academy** in Lexington, Mississippi for high school, and returned to San Francisco where she graduated from the College of San Mateo. Flunder is also a graduate of the Ministry Studies and Master of Arts programs at the Pacific School of Religion, Berkeley. She received a Doctor of Ministry degree from San Francisco Theological Seminary in San Anselmo, California.

Flunder began her ministry career in the arena of social justice, which has remained a constant theme in her work. She was licensed in the COGIC and later ordained by the

Bishop **Walter Hawkins** of Love Center Ministries where she served as associate pastor and administrator for the Oakland-based Love Center Church. In 1984 Flunder began performing and recording with Hawkins and the Love Center Choir.

She remained with Love Center until 1991 when, after openly revealing her sexual identity as a lesbian, she divorced her husband and planted a welcoming and affirming congregation that became City of Refuge. In keeping with her emphasis on social justice, an integral part of the congregation's ministry is responding to the AIDS crisis through major outreach efforts to provide housing, direct services, education and training for persons in the Bay Area, throughout the USA, and in three countries in Africa.

After leaving COGIC, Flunder was ordained in the United Church of Christ. In 2003 she was consecrated presiding bishop of The Fellowship of Affirming Ministries, a multi-denominational organization founded by her as an umbrella for more than one hundred primarily African-American Christian leaders and laity representing congregations and faith-based organizations from all parts of the United States Mexico and Africa.

Flunder serves as both a Trustee and an adjunct professor at Pacific School of Religion in Berkeley, California. She has been a lecturer, adjunct professor and speaker at numerous seminaries to include Lancaster, Duke, Drew, Eden, Yale and New York Theological. She is the author of *Where the Edge Gathers: A Theology and Homiletic of Radical Inclusion*.

She has been a board member or consultant for several HIV/AIDS related organizations including the National Sexuality Resource Center, San Francisco Inter-religious Coalition on AIDS, the African-American Interfaith Alliance on AIDS, Alameda County Ryan White Consortium, San Francisco HIV/AIDS Planning and Prevention Council, Congressional Black Caucus Health Brain Trust, and the Ryan White Working Group. She is also chair of the Black Adoption Placement and Research Center, and is co-chair of the Religious Advisory Committee of the National Black Justice Coalition.

Within the UCC, Flunder served as president of the Board of Directors for the Northern California Nevada Conference of the United Church of Christ and serves on the UCC Unified Governance Working Group as representative of the United Church of Christ Seminaries.

Flunder was reconciled with her mother who eventually left the **Church of God in Christ** to join with her at the City of Refuge serving as prayer leader for the congregation. She and her wife, Shirley Miller, also a former lead singer for the Love Center Choir and soloist on the record breaking gospel hit, "O Happy Day" have been together more than twenty years.

Foote, Julia A. J. 1823–1900

The **Holiness** Evangelist who was the irst African-American woman to gain ordination as a deacon in the African Methodist Episcopal Zion Church and the second to be ordained as an elder. Her first ordination came near the end of ministry career in 1894, only six years before her death in 1900. She sought ordination earlier and though she was renowned as an evangelist, it was denied.

The daughter of former slaves was born in Schenectady, New York. She converted to faith at age fifteen, and began evangelistic work as a young woman. Several years later, she married George Foote, a sailor, moved to Boston, and joined the African Methodist Episcopal Zion Church of antislavery advocate, Jehiel C. Beman. Convinced of her call to preach, she sought Beman's permission, but when she began to testify and teach about experiences of conversion and sanctification, her husband, parents, and pastor disapproved. They censured her for engaging in ministry in her home, and when she persisted, she was barred from preaching and excommunicated from the church in 1844.

Undaunted, Foote conducted evangelistic campaigns throughout the Northeast, as far west as Ohio and up into Canada from the 1840s through the 1870s. In 1851 she temporarily ceased evangelistic work due to the loss of her voice and the added responsibility of her invalid mother. In 1869 she experienced healing and began to preach again. On one occasion in 1878, an estimated five thousand people heard her preach at a meeting in Ohio. She published her memoir, *A Brand Plucked from the Fire,* in 1879.

Further Reading:

Foote, Julia. "A Brand Plucked from the Fire." In *Sisters of the Spirit: Three Black Women's Autobiographies of the Nineteenth Century,* edited by William Andrews, 161–234. Bloomington, IN: Indiana University Press, 1986.
Pope-Levison, Priscilla. *Turn the Pulpit Loose: Two Centuries of American Women Evangelists.* New York: Palgrave Macmillan, 2004.

Forbes, James Alexander Jr. 1935–

The educator, pastor, author and outspoken commentator the son of a **United Holy Church** bishop, **James Forbes** Sr. Forbes Jr. was born in Burgaw, North Carolina, son of James Forbes and Mabel Clemmons Forbes. His family moved first to Goldsboro, North Carolina then to Raleigh, where he grew up.

He earned a BS degree in chemistry from Howard University in 1957, a year after he was called to the ministry in 1956. In 1962 Forbes completed a Master of Divinity degree from Union Theological Seminary in New York City. He earned a Doctor of Ministry degree from Colgate Rochester Divinity School in 1975. In addition, he has been awarded thirteen honorary degrees from schools such as Princeton University, DePauw University, Fairleigh Dickenson University, and the University of Richmond.

From 1960 to 1973, he pastored congregations within the **United Holy Church** including St. John's in Richmond Virginia, Holy Trinity Church in Wilmington, North Carolina and Saint Paul's in Roxboro, North Carolina. While in Richmond, he also worked as campus minister for Virginia Union University.

From 1976 to 1989, Forbes taught preaching at Union Theological Seminary, and in 1985 he became the first Joe R. Engle Professor of Preaching. Dr. Forbes also teaches at Auburn Theological Seminary in New York.

In 1989 Forbes was installed as the fifth senior minister of the 2,400 member Riverside Church in Harlem, one of the largest multicultural congregations in the nation, succeeding the Rev. William Sloane Coffin, and becoming the first African American to serve in the position. Though the congregation is affiliated with American Baptist Churches and the United Church of Christ, Forbes has been ordained in the American Baptist Churches, yet never relinquished his **United Holy Church** ordination.

Forbes made several progressive changes within the Riverside Church community. First, he involved the congregation in the redevelopment of Harlem, with the consortium of churches in Harlem Congregations for Community Improvement. His charismatic gift of preaching also attracted new members to the congregation. In 2007, however, after eighteen years of service, Forbes retired from this position to become president of the Healing of the Nations Foundation, a national ministry of healing and spiritual revitalization. Around the same time, he resigned from hosting the radio program "The Time Is Now," which aired weekends on the Air America Radio network. Besides contributing numerous essays and articles to edited volumes, his full-length monographs include, *The Holy Spirit & Preaching*, published in 1989 and *Whose Gospel?: A Concise Guide to Progressive Protestantism (Whose Religion?)* published in 2010.

Forbes, James Alexander, Sr. 1914–1999

One of the most prominent leaders in the Southern District of the **United Holy Church of America** who was instrumental in leading the exodus of ministers from that district to form the **Original United Holy Church of America**.

Forbes was born in Pitt, North Carolina. He was the first **United Holy Church** minister to be seminary trained, having received a BB degree from Shaw University in the early 1940s. As a young man, he pastored churches in his native North Carolina including Providence Holy Church in Raleigh.

Forbes was named a bishop in the organization in 1960. Twelve years later, he was elected first vice president of the UHC. That year, Southern District officers under his leadership balked at national leaders' suggestion that the district be subdivided by state. In response, they took the unauthorized action of dissolving the **United Holy Church of America** and drew up a new charter as the Southern District of the **United Holy Church**. While the majority of churches remained in the denomination throughout those years, during the 1977 General Convocation, Forbes declared that the Southern District should break from the parent body. He led that delegation out to form a new body, the Original United Holy Church of the World, Inc.

He served in numerous leadership positions on the district and national level of the OUHCA before retiring in 1986. In 1989, Forbes moved to the Washington DC where he served as an adviser to local UHC churches. At the time of his death at age eighty-five, the retired bishop was president emeritus of the Original **United Holy Church of America**.

Before the schism he served as President of the Bible Training Institute, dean of United Christian College, and before assuming leadership of the Southern District, he was president of the Western District Served. The split lasted for twenty-three years, and Forbes died a year before it was resolved. During that time, several other smaller bodies split from the parent group. In 2000, the two major factions joined with these smaller factions to reunite.

His first wife, Mabel Clemons Forbes, died in 1969, and his second wife, Lillie Williams Forbes, died in 1982.

Further Reading:

"Bishop James A. Forbes Sr. Passes." *New York Amsterdam News* 90:43, October 21, p. 9.

Ford, Louis Henry 1914–1995

The second elected presiding bishop of the **Church of God in Christ** was born in Clarksdale, Mississippi. Ford encountered **Charles Harrison Mason** on several occasions during his childhood, and the elder leader became one of his biggest inspirations, as well as his personal mentor in the Gospel. He began preaching around Lexington, Mississippi while attending Saints Industrial College in the early 1930s. He moved to Chicago in 1933 and preached on the street until founding St. Paul's Church of God in Christ in 1935.

In 1968 when COGIC moved from a congregational to a more episcopal structure, forming a general board, Ford was one of the first twelve chosen to lead the church. After Bishop **James O. Patterson Sr.** was elected presiding bishop in that same year, Ford became the first assistant presiding bishop. When Patterson was diagnosed with cancer in 1988, he declared Bishop Ford to be his successor. When his health declined and as his pancreatic cancer worsened in 1989, Patterson retired from the office of presiding bishop and appointed Ford acting presiding bishop. After Patterson's death in late 1989, Ford was elected and consecrated presiding bishop, serving until his death.

Prior to assuming that position, Ford was presiding prelate of the historic Illinois First Jurisdiction. Ford, an advocate for social justice, first became nationally recognized in 1955 when he eulogized fourteen-year-old **Emmett Till**. The family returned the murdered teenager's body to Chicago and displayed it at Robert's Temple COGIC after he was beat by a white mob in Mississippi. Following the funeral, Ford was asked to become a member of the national executive committee of the National Association for the

Advancement of Colored People (NAACP). He also became involved with the National Urban League.

In Chicago he organized voter registration initiatives and protested against segregated lodging in Memphis, Tennessee during the holy convocations in the midst of the Civil Rights era. He prided himself in returning COGIC to its emphasis on basic holiness. Known for his community and political involvement in the 1970s, he worked as an advisor to Chicago Mayor Richard J. Daley and maintained a close relationship him and his son, Richard M. Daley. He also served for many years on the Cook County Board of Corrections.

Within COGIC Ford was critical of the introduction of high-church liturgy, vestments, and other encroaching elements modernity that he perceived. He reopened Saints Academy and College and constructed the multi-million dollar Deborah Mason Patterson Hall in Lexington, Mississippi. He is noted for bringing then candidate Bill Clinton to address the COGIC at Mason Temple during the Eighty-Sixth International Holy Convocation on November 13, 1993, making Clinton the only United States President to have done so. Prior to ascending to the presidency, Ford developed a close relationship with Clinton-led delegations of COGIC bishops on trip to the Arkansas governor's mansion.

A year after his death at age eighty-one, Ford became the first African-American to have an Illinois expressway named for him when the state renamed the stretch of I-94 formerly known as the Calumet Expressway as the Bishop Ford Freeway. In 2008 Chicago's DuSable Museum of African-American History held a three-month exhibit in his honor.

Ford, Willie L. 1908–1987

When African American constituents of the Church of God (Cleveland, TN) petitioned to reclaim the right to govern their own affairs and elect their own overseer, denomination leaders consented and Willie L. Ford, subsequently, became the first and last African American to hold that position. He was also the only person to serve two terms as overseer of the **Church of God (Colored Work)**. His initial term ran from 1946 through 1950. Then, after a hiatus in which George A. Wallace held the position, Ford resumed the post from 1954 through 1958.

Ford was the Born in Evergreen, Alabama. He was called to the ministry in 1928 and ordained in 1932. Prior taking over leadership of the Colored Work, he had served as district and state overseer. His major accomplishments during his tenure were eliminating the debt on the **Church of God (Colored Work)** orphanage in 1948 and organizing a national missions program for the black churches in 1954.

Following Ford's second term, the denomination again rescinded the right of its black constituents to select their own leader, and leadership of the Colored Work was put into the hands of J. A. Roberts, a white man.

Further Reading:

Michel, David. *Telling the Story: Black Pentecostals in the Church of God.* Cleveland, TN: Pathway, 2000.

Franklin, Robert Michael, Jr. 1954–

Ethicist, educator, pastor, and college administrator. Franklin, a native of Chicago, was raised within a **Church of God in Christ** congregation. He later served as assistant pastor at St. Paul COGIC in Chicago under the leadership of Bishop **Henry Louis Ford.** He is ordained in both **Church of God in Christ** and the American Baptist Churches USA.

Franklin attended Morehouse College in Atlanta Georgia, graduating Phi Beta Kappa. Prior to receiving a Master of Divinity from Harvard Divinity School where he served as assistant director of Ministry Education, he studied at the University of Durham, in Great Britain, as an English Speaking Union Scholar. Franklin earned a PhD from the University of Chicago Divinity School. He is also the recipient of honorary degrees from Bethune-Cookman University, Bates College, and Swarthmore College.

He has served on the faculties of Harvard Divinity School; as professor, dean and assistant director of black church studies at Colgate-Rochester Divinity School in Rochester, New York; and as Presidential Distinguished Professor of Social Ethics at Emory University's Candler School of Theology where he also held the positions of dean and director of Black Church Studies. In 1997, he assumed the presidency of Interdenominational Theological Center (ITC), the theological seminary consortium of the Atlanta University Center, serving there until 2003, and then moving to his alma mater, Morehouse College (the largest all-male college in the nation) as president from 2007 to 2012.

In 2013 he served as a Visiting Scholar in Residence at Stanford University's Martin Luther King Jr. Research and Education Institute before returning to Emory as the James T. and Berta R. Laney Professor of Moral Leadership, and Director of the Religion Department of the Chautauqua Institution. Hs academic work centers on the ethical concerns of the Black Church and community.

Free Church of God in Christ

Founded by former Baptist ministers **John Henry Morris** and his son, **Ernest F. Morris**, who had an experience of Pentecostal Holy Spirit baptism. In 1915 Ernest accepted the call to preach The Gospel of Jesus Christ in a family prayer meeting.

After that experience sixteen persons, mostly family members who were part of the National Baptist Convention, followed the elder Morris in forming a separate congregation which they called the **Church of God in Christ**, but was not related to the larger group. In 1921, however, this group brought their congregations into fellowship with **Charles H. Mason's** group of the same name. Yet, in 1925 members of the smaller group withdrew from the parent body to form the **Free Church of God in Christ.** By 1935 there were nineteen congregations and 874 members in the pacifist denomination, and by the late 1940s there was only one additional congregation.

The denominations differ strategically for most other African American Pentecostal bodies in that it opposes the practice of tithing (donating ten percent of income) as being unbiblical. Further, its polity is semi-congregational rather than using the episcopal polity of most other groups within the tradition. General leadership of the church is vested in a presbytery of ordained elders. Each elder is allowed to individually establish his right to apostleship by establishing seven churches under his leadership. There is no general overseer, however, since that office is also considered unbiblical. Each apostle serves as a bishop or overseer for the churches he has established.

Originally, the denomination was incorporated in Kansas and most of the congregations were in Kansas, Texas, and Colorado. Subsequently, **E. F. Morris** merged the Free Church of God in Christ with the Full Gospel Pentecostal Missionary Association, and the organization took the name of the latter body and headquarters for the group is in Tacoma, Washington.

Further Reading:

Truesdell, Leon Edgar, and Timothy Francis Murphy, eds. "Free Church of God in Christ." *God's Pentecostal Temple.* Online: http://www.godspentecostaltemple.org/History.htm.

Free Church of God in Christ in Jesus Name, Inc.

Seventh-day Oneness Pentecostal organization founded 1927 in Taylor, Texas by Earl Evans and his wife Elizabeth, and incorporated in 1939. The group, which emerged out of the **Church of God in Christ**, is predominantly located in the Western and Midwestern regions of the United States with congregations in California, Texas, Colorado, and Arizona. It promotes compliance with the Jewish Law as recorded in the Ten Commandments including strict adherence to Sabbath keeping sanctions.

Evans, the first senior bishop, had been called to the ministry only one year prior to founding the denomination. He presided for fifty years. When he died in 1987, he was succeeded by Bishop Robert Bailey Johnson. The current senior bishop is Stephen Fowler, who pastors Noah's Temple Free Church of God in Christ in San Diego, California. The church is clustered primarily in the Midwestern section of the United States. Along with congregations in San Diego and in small towns and major cities in Texas—including Taylor, Dallas, Houston, Corpus Christie and Fort Worth—there are congregations in several western cities including Denver, Colorado; Phoenix, Arizona; and Clovis, New Mexico.

Free Unity Church of God in Christ

A small Trinitarian organization that was founded in 1927, when **Sumpter E. Looper** of Ohio pulled out of the **Church of God in Christ**. Looper concentrated his efforts within that state, and by 1949 had established branches of the body in Cincinnati, Columbus, Akron, Chillicothe, and Barberton. By 2006, however, no information was available regarding these congregations.

Fulford, William H. 1855–1925

The second president of the **United Holy Church of America**. In 1886 Fulford, joined leaders of several black Holiness congregations throughout North Carolina in forming an independent fellowship as simply referred to themselves as the Holy People. He had been ordained in the African Methodist Episcopal Church before joining B. H. Irwin's

Fire Baptized Holiness Church and led a large FBH Church congregation in Goldsboro, North Carolina.

After organizing as the **United Holy Church**, L. M. Mason was elected as the first president, but served only one year. At the next annual meeting, after the group incorporated, Fulford was chosen president with W. C. Carlton as vice president.

Though Fulford presided over these formative years, within public accounts of the denomination's history, his name and any accomplishments during this period are conspicuously absence, perhaps as a seemingly deliberate move to dislodge a potentially embarrassing episode from the denomination's history.

Fulford was born in Beaufort, South Carolina, but we know little of his early life. Beginning in 1905 through 1916, he pastored the Holy Church of the New Covenant in Wilmington founded by C. J. Wilcox nineteen years earlier. The congregation grew quickly to more than fifteen hundred members. During that time, he also served as second president of the Second District of the **United Holy Church**.

By 1912, though, he was still pastoring both the Wilmington congregation and a sizable Goldsboro congregation. A theological controversy compromised Fulford's influence on the **United Holy Church**. Reportedly, Fulford was preaching the doctrine of "everlasting life in the flesh," that proposed the understanding that those who are saved remain or earth eternally, immune to physical death.

While most other denominational leaders considered the teaching a heresy and Fulford to be in error, Fulford remained at the helm of the **United Holy Church** until 1916. His unwillingness to recant the teaching led to an official reprimanded by the UHC Board of Elders and Presbyters, and eventually he left the denomination.

Throughout Fulford's tenure, prominent leader **Henry L. Fisher** was a behind-the-scenes actor in the church, and his respect and popularity increased as Fulford's declined. In 1916 when Fulford was not re-elected, Fisher succeeded him as president, but the latter remained within the fellowship of the **United Holy Church** until 1918—two years later. In that year, he was brought before the board of elders for his doctrinal stance. Described as a powerful preacher whose sermons attracted large numbers of followers and placed him in demand as an evangelist, Fulford drew a number of followers who also adopted the understanding. When the Board of Elders censored and disfellowshipped him from the **United Holy Church**, they also reprimanded those followers

During Fulford's tenure as president, the **United Holy Church** experienced substantial growth so that by the time he left, the denomination had more grown substantially, largely through mergers with several smaller Holiness bodies that Fulford helped orchestrate. Sometime during this period, after two decades as a loosely federated Holiness body, the **United Holy Church** was swept into the new Pentecostal movement with a number of other former Holiness groups.

Seven years after leaving the body, Fulford suffered a sudden cerebral stroke after preaching a sermon in Mount Olive, North Carolina. He died shortly after that at the age of seventy.

Further Reading:

Ball, Dennis. *The Spirituality of the Pioneers of the United Holy Church of America, Inc.: A Study of Bishop Henry Lee Fisher.* PhD diss., Pasadena, CA: Fuller Theological Seminary, School of Theology, 2009.

Fisher, Henry. *The History of the United Holy Church of America, Inc.* S.l.: s.n. 1933?

Gregory, Chester W. *The History of the United Holy Church of America, Inc., 1886–2000.* Baltimore: Gateway, 2000.

Full Gospel Baptist Church Fellowship International

The major neo-Pentecostal movement that is a convergence of Baptist polity, Pentecostal spirituality and the prosperity message of the **Word of Faith** movement within the Black Baptist tradition. When the Full Gospel Baptist Church Fellowship, under the leadership of **Paul S. Morton**, held its first convention in New Orleans, Louisiana in 1994, more than 30,000 Baptists from traditional black Baptist conventions including the National, Progressive and Missionary Baptists were present. In the beginning, some of these congregations maintained dual alliance, and while a few still do, a growing number have come to be fully aligned with the FGBCFI. Yet, the organization's polity and practice has been broad enough to not only attract Baptists, but also formerly Pentecostal, non-denominational or mainline congregations into its ranks.

Twelve prominent pastors, who all assumed the title bishop, joined Morton in forming the new organization. Perhaps, the most prominent among them were **Larry D. Trotter**, of the 5,000 member Sweet Holy Spirit Full Gospel Baptist Church in Chicago and **Kenneth Ulmer**, pastor of the 8,000-member Faithful Central Bible Church in Inglewood, California. But the group also included Odis Floyd, of Flint, Michigan's 2,000 member, New Jerusalem Full Gospel Baptist Church; Carlos L. Malone of Bethel Full Gospel Baptist Church in Miami; J. Douglas Wiley of Life Center FGB Cathedral in New Orleans; K. D. Johnson of Little Rock, Arkansas; Larry Leonard of Morning Star Full Gospel Baptist Church in Houston, Texas; Kenneth Robinson of Antioch FGBC College Station, Arkansas; Fred Caldwell of Greenwood Acres Full Gospel Baptist Church in Shreveport, Louisiana; Robert Blake of Greater Love Missionary Full Gospel Baptist Church Dallas, Texas; Eddie Long of 25,000-member New Birth Cathedral in Atlanta, Georgia; and Alton R. Williams of World Overcomers Outreach Ministries Church in Memphis. Eventually, all except Caldwell and Floyd, who is bishop emeritus, eventually pulled out to form their own Charismatic organizations, though they stayed in fellowship with Morton's group.

The majority of FGBCFI's doctrinal beliefs align with traditional Baptist tenets. Nonetheless, the new group has a distinctively Pentecostal pneumatology, rejecting the Baptist's cessationist stance regarding the operation of the gifts of the Holy Spirit. The ethos of the movement is captured by the slogan "the right to choose," conveying Morton's call for allowing free expression of spiritual gifts including speaking in tongues, praying to cast out demons, and laying on of hands to heal the sick within Baptist worship structures, without abandoning the Baptist Church.

Another important distinction of Morton's group from mainline Baptists, involve its adherence to an espicopal rather than congregation polity. Within its structure, there are bishops, overseers, elders, and adjutants—each with specific responsibilities and corresponding clerical garb. There is also an intricate liturgical structure with robed clergy and choirs, processionals, and high-church ecclesial accoutrements. Yet, elements of Baptist congregational polity are retained since bishops have no governmental authority over local congregations regarding matters of congregational government, polity, operations, and discipline. The office of presiding bishop that Morton held, for example, corresponds to the position of president, general superintendent, or general overseer in other non-episcopal organizations, but FGBCFI deems this language more biblical.

A further distinction from traditional Baptist polity has been the FGBCFI's openness to women's leadership at most levels, including bishops. Though members of the Bishop's Council and College of Bishops are all male, general, state, and district overseers and directors can be men or women. By 2006 at least ten women were serving as district overseers, and several more were serving as senior pastors or staff pastors of FGBCFI congregations. Further, several women within the organization serve as co-pastors—alongside their husbands—of some of the fellowship's most prominent congregations. Indeed, women are among the pastors and co-pastors of some of widely recognized mega-churches such as Betty Peebles who served as pastor of the 10,000-member Jericho city of Praise in suburban Washington DC until her death.

The main distinction between the FGBCFI and classical Pentecostalism is pneumatology. The FGBCFI contends that at salvation, Jesus, as the Baptizer with the Holy Spirit, brings men and women into relationship with himself and the Church. Moreover, they contend that the filling of the Holy Spirit is an ongoing ministry of the Spirit in the life of the believer that enables him or her to live a Spirit-empowered life, not a single experience with a single identifiable evidence. FGBCFI theology appreciates speaking in tongues as one of the gifts of the Spirit; it does not see it as either the initial evidence of Spirit baptism or a necessary element of salvation. It holds, rather, that the dichotomy between being filled with the Holy Spirit and be baptized with the Holy Spirit is false, and that all believers are filled with the indwelling Holy Spirit which validates them as members Christ's body. Additionally they hold that all believers should live a Spirit-controlled life and that being filled with the Spirit is a volitional act that results from the believer being submitted to divine control.

After leading FGBCFI for nineteen year, Morton, who had been raised in the **Church of God in Christ** and whose father was founding bishop of COGIC in Canada, retired in 2014. Though allegations surfaced of alleged sexual abuse of several women, Joseph Warren Walker, III, pastor of Nashville Tennessee's Mt. Zion Baptist Church, was elected as president. Following his election, Bahamian Bishop Neil Ellis, who at the time served as vice president and heir apparent to the lead position, left FGBCFI with all eighteen Bahamian congregations to establish **Global United Fellowship**.

Headquarters of the organization is in Atlanta, Georgia. While no solid statistics are available regarding numbers of congregations or congregants, there are several hundred churches with several hundred thousand congregants.

Further Reading:

Lewter, A. C. *Management Manual for the Full Gospel Baptist Church Fellowship*, DMin diss., United Theological Seminary, 1994.

Ulmer, Kenneth. *A New Thing: A Reflection on the Full Gospel Baptist Movement*. S.l.: FaithWay, 1994.

Full Gospel Pentecostal Association

A Trinitarian umbrella organization founded in 1970 in Portland, Oregon by Adolph Wells of Tabernacle of Evangelism Community Church in Inglewood, California; Edna Travis of New Covenant Pentecostal Tabernacle in Tacoma, Washington; and S. D. Leffall of the **Federated Pentecostal Church International, Inc.** of Seattle, Washington. The organization is a loose association of independent Pentecostal congregations that serves as a clearinghouse for information and resources for member denominations, supports a prison ministry, a national women's organization (Full Gospel Pentecostal Association for Women on the Move) and an international fellowship with similar Pentecostal groups in Africa. It publishes three periodicals: *The Epistle, Full Gospel News,* and *Truth.* It is one of several similar bodies belonging to the ecumenical **Federated Pentecostal Church International,** which Leffall led from 1986 until his death in 2008.

Wells served as the first president and currently, Jesse McClellan is the presider.

Fuller, William Edward 1875–1958

The founder and first presiding bishop of the **Fire Baptized Holiness Church of God of the Americas**. Fuller, a native of Mountville, South Carolina, was a Methodist preacher whose experience of sanctification led him to seek membership in B. H. Irwin's multi-racial, Fire Baptized Holiness Association in 1898. From its inception as a predominantly white Holiness body, black people were admitted to Irwin's group with full equality. However, no other Black person achieved the prominence of Fuller who quickly became a central figure. After Irwin's departure from the church in 1900, Fuller was appointed a bishop under the new General Overseer, J. H. King and by 1905, was serving on the denomination's four-member executive board.

Orphaned by age four and raised by an aunt, Fuller was converted in 1892, at the age of seventeen, and joined New Hope Methodist Church in Mountville. He shortly became a class leader and a steward. A year later, he was called to preach and during the next few years, he immersed himself in personal prayer. He was sanctified two years later, and received the Pentecostal experience of Holy Spirit baptism a short while afterward.

Yet Fuller was not convinced that his experience was biblical foundation and struck out to find scriptural warrant for it. During this period, he relinquished his license with the Holiness group, returned to his Methodist roots and began reading J. M. Pike's *Way of Faith*. In 1898, an advertisement in the periodical called his attention to a Fire Baptized Holiness Association convention scheduled for Anderson, South Carolina.

For some time before he attended a FBH meeting, Fuller had been corresponding with B. H. Irwin and struck up a collegial ministerial respect with him. When Fuller showed up at the Topeka Kansas National Holiness Movement convention, however, Irwin was surprised that his corresponding partner was a black man and was unsure what to do with him. Following that episode, the entirely white body decided to accept him.

Since worship within the **Fire Baptized Holiness Church** had been interracial from its inception, Fuller found not only support wavering Holiness faith, but at least on one level, fellowship between black and white Christians that afforded him an opportunity to minister. Known for his zeal in preaching, he often used street corners and homes as venues, alongside traditional church buildings.

Soon after officially affiliating with the Fire Baptize Holiness Association, Fuller resigned his offices and tendered his credentials with the Methodist church. In 1905 at age thirty, Fuller was appointed to the four members of the Executive Board. As one of the earliest and most prominent black members of the group, Fuller became a prolific church planter, establishing churches throughout South. He stayed with the interracial, FBHC until 1908, serving Assistant General Overseer to J. H. King, Overseer of the black churches and planting many congregations that still exist today. By that time, the organization had transitioned from the Holiness movement into the Pentecostal movement and had accepted the experience of Pentecostal Holy Spirit baptism.

While this arrangement was successful for a while, despite the intentions of FBHC leaders, Southern racial mores made true integration impossible. That year, Fuller led other African American leaders within the denomination in proposing a separation along racial lines. King and other white leaders gave their blessing and the group parted amicably. Once agreement was reached, Fuller took five hundred African-American members and twenty-five thousand dollars in property to establish the Colored **Fire Baptized Holiness Church** of God body that eventually evolved into the largely white, Pentecostal Holiness Church. At the First General Council of the Colored **Fire Baptized Holiness Church** in Greer, South Carolina. Fuller, who pastored a congregation in Atlanta, Georgia, became the General Overseer. A short while later, Fuller launched a denominational periodical *The True Witness*. In 1912 he established the Fuller Normal Industrial Institute, a primary and secondary school, in Greenville, South Carolina.

Fuller served at the helm of the denomination for fifty years. Despite the seeming cordiality of the separation agreement between the two groups, white FBH leaders maintained no further contact with fuller throughout that period. He died in Atlanta the day before his eighty-third birthday. At his death, his son, William Fuller Jr. took leadership of the church.

Further Reading:

Frazier, Patrick L. Jr. *Introducing the Fire Baptized Holiness Church of God of the Americas—A Study Manual.* Online: http://www.fbhchurch.org/pf_manual/pdf.
Synan, Vinson. *The Old-Time Power.* Franklin Springs, GA: Advocate, 1973.

G

Garlington, John Wesley Jr. 1937–1986

Pastor and social justice activist in Oregon during the late 1970s and early 1980s. He was born in Buffalo, New York. His father, John W. Garlington Sr. founded the Oneness Pentecostal denomination, **Church of God and True Holiness**, and served as presiding bishop of that denomination from 1968 until 1975.

Garlington moved his family to Portland in 1976 to be pastor of the interracial Maranatha Church in Northeast Portland. During his tenure, Garlington involved Maranatha in issues as funding of Head Start programs and the establishment of Martin Luther King Jr.'s birthday as a state holiday. The church hosted activists including Jesse Jackson and South African Bishop Desmond Tutu.

During his nine years in Portland, Garlington also became a leader and spokesman for social justice issues such as education, employment, police-community relations and ministries to the poor, hungry, and the homeless.

He was president of the Albina Ministerial Alliance, the original chairperson of the Police Internal Investigations Auditing Committee to monitor the Portland Police Bureau's handling of public complaints, and before his death he was due to be installed as the first African American president of Ecumenical Ministries of Oregon.

Garlington also helped found North Portland Bible College in 1982 and served as the first Chairperson of the Board. Garlington and his wife, Yvonne, were killed in a tragic car accident while traveling in Florida in 1986. The Garlington Center, a mental health clinic and social services center located in Portland was named in 1989 in honor of the Rev. Garlington and Yvonne.

Garlington, John Wesley Sr. 1884–1943

The founding presiding bishop of the **Church of God and True Holiness** was born in Lawrence, South Carolina, in the early 1900s he had migrated to New York City. By the 1920's he had relocated to Buffalo, New York was he established The Churches of God and True Holiness in 1927 in that city. Garlington led this organization until his death in 1943.

Garlington died at fifty-five years old, leaving his twenty-seven-year-old pregnant wife financially destitute, living in an inner city Buffalo, New York ghetto with four small children. Among his seven offspring, the senior Garlington was father of two prominent sons: pastor and social activist **John Wesley Garlington, Jr.** who later served a term as presiding bishop of the organization founded by his father; and megachurch pastor, musician, and noted conference speaker, **Joseph Garlington**.

Garlington, Joseph Lloyd 1939–

Garlington was born Buffalo, New York and was one of three sons of Bishop **John Wesley Garlington**, founder of the Oneness Pentecostal body, the **Churches of God and True Holiness**. After leaving the **Churches of God and True Holiness**, Garlington first aligned himself with the **United Church of Jesus Christ (Apostolic)** under **Monroe R. Saunders**, taking over the pastorate of the Washington DC congregation when Saunders moved the denominational headquarters to Baltimore, Maryland. In 1967 Garlington left Saunders to establish Grace Apostolic Church in Washington DC. The next year, the congregation joined with the **Pentecostal Assemblies of the World**. Shortly after, he and his first wife, Thelma Pratt Garlington, divorced.

By 1971 Garlington had relocated to the Pittsburgh, Pennsylvania are where he and his new wife, Barbara, established Covenant Church of Pittsburgh, a multiracial and cross-cultural community of more than two thousand members. The church, located in suburban Monroeville is heavily involved in outreach efforts, collaborating with other organizations in the surrounding community around them. In one instance, for example, he took over an abandoned school in Wilkinsburg, Pennsylvania and converted it into Hosanna House Community Center, a facility that has delivered health and human services to over 35,000 people. Garlington is also president of Building United of Southwest Pennsylvania, an organization that partners with local and national financial institutions and foundations to give low and middle-income families the opportunity to own homes.

An accomplished musician, recording artist, author, and scholar, Garlington recorded several albums with Maranatha Record Company in the 1990s and has published monographs that focus on two of his main passions: Charismatic worship and racial reconciliation. Since 1979 Garlington has been heavily involved in his work with churches in South Africa, even recording one of his album, "Live from South Africa," in that country.

Garlington is involved in the New Apostolic Reformation (NAR) movement that focuses on restoring the offices of prophet and apostle to the Pentecostal and Charismatic faith community. In 2003 he served on the thirty-two member Apostolic Council of Prophetic Elders along with Bill Hamon, Cindy Jacobs, Gwen Shaw, Dutch Sheets, and Tommy Tenney.

Garlington has addressed thousands at national and international conferences within Pentecostal, Charismatic, and even Evangelical arenas. He often speaks in Promise Keepers, the Evangelical men's organization and is one of the featured teachers for

Cleansing Stream, a discipleship, deliverance, and healing ministry founded by Jack Hayford, former president of the International Church of the Foursquare Gospel.

In 1995 Garlington formed Reconciliation! An International Network of Churches and Ministries Inc., over which he resides as bishop.

Gibson, Bruce K. 1888–1975

An early black minister in the predominantly white Assemblies of God who led an attempt to more fully integrate that denomination. Gibson pastored an interracial congregation in Winlock, Washington (midway between Seattle, Washington and Portland, Oregon) and served in ministry several years before he was credentialed in 1935, then left the Assemblies of God to affiliate with the **Church of God in Christ** and move east to pastor a black congregation, but rejoined after returning to the Northwest in 1939. From the 1930s through the 1950s, he evangelized throughout the Northwest and California, even being invited into some white AG pulpits that were closed to other blacks.

When the General Council met in 1945, Gibson pled for creation of a colored branch within the AG. He established a Bible school to train black ministers that he hoped would affiliate with the Assemblies of God. In response, the denomination put forth a resolution to "encourage establishment of Black congregations that would be authorized to display the name, Assembly of God—Colored Branch." Gibson was tapped to head the project, but a year later, the General Presbytery instead proposed establishment of a "separate colored Pentecostal Church" to which the denomination would lend "assistance, counsel and financial aid," though no action was taken on the recommendation.

By 1952 he had moved back east and was attached to the New York-New Jersey District. He lived out his retirement years in the Bronx, New York where he died.

Glorious Church of God in Christ

A Oneness Pentecostal denomination co-founded by Bishop **Cleveland H. Stokes** and Mother **Lulu Phillips**. In 1919, Phillips and Stokes, along with other members of the **Triumph the Church and Kingdom of God in Christ,** moved to Huntington West Virginia and started evangelizing that city, establishing six Trinitarian congregations under the Triumph Church Kingdom of God in Christ.

In 1921, Richard Phillips, Mother Phillips's husband, called a meeting to implement organization structure into the church. Out of this meeting, Stokes suggested the name that was adopted for the church. Around 1921 Phillips encountered and embraced Oneness Pentecostal doctrine; she and fifty other members were baptized in the name of Jesus.

Phillips was named the presiding pastor of the **Glorious Church of God in Christ**. In 1939 Phillips suffered a heart attack. Following her death, though Stokes was still active in the organization, **Sydney Coy Bass** became pastor of the headquarters church and presiding bishop of the organization. Though he served in that position until his death in 1972, a major schism occurred in the organization when Bass went against church polity and married a divorced woman. His actions lead to twenty-five congregations (approximately fifty percent of the membership) withdrawing from the organization to form a new body, **The Original Glorious Church of God in Christ,** under the leadership of **W.O. Howard.** Those loyal to Bass retained the name of the parent organization.

The current headquarters of the parent church is in Richmond, Virginia. At last report, there were thirty ministers and two thousand members within twenty-five churches. Bass was succeeded by his brother-in-law, Perry Lindsay Sr., pastor of the **Glorious Church of God in Christ** in Brooklyn, New York, who died in 2014.

Further Reading:

Leonard M. Payne Jr. *My People Yesterday, Today and Forever: A History of the Glorious Church of God in Christ.* S.l.: Xlibris, 2008.

Goodwin, Bennie Eugene II 1933–

The Chicago-born, pastor, educator, writer, and civil rights advocate was educated at Moody Bible Institute in Chicago, earning a bachelor's degree from Barrington College, an master's degree from Pittsburg Seminary and a PhD from the University of Pittsburg. His dissertation, which he later published as *Martin Luther King, Jr.: God's Messenger of Love, Justice and Hope*, highlighted the civil rights legacy of Dr. King as well as his concern for the education of the black community. With that education, he went on to serve as associate professor of Christian education at the Interdenominational Theological Center in Atlanta, Georgia. He has also served as a visiting professor at religious institutions and theological seminaries across the United States and Europe.

Goodwin was raised in the **Church of God in Christ** where his father, Bishop Bennie Goodwin served the Fifth Jurisdiction of Illinois. Ordained as an elder in COGIC, the younger Goodwin has served as pastor of three congregations including West End Presbyterian Church in Atlanta. Goodwin's social activist involvement included membership in the National Association for the Advancement of Colored People (NAACP) and the Southern Christian Leadership Committee (SCLC). Goodwin has also been involved in more narrowly Christian endeavors such serving as vice president of the National Black Evangelical Association, and more solidly educational venture including creating the Bennie E. Goodwin Educational Foundation. In 1981 Goodwin and his wife, Melody, launched Goodpatrick Ministries, Inc. to publish and distribute Christian Education and Training materials. The prolific writer has written more than thirty-one books. The main focus of his work has been the development of leadership within the African-American church and on the role of the Holy Spirit in bringing about liberative praxis.

Goodwin, Randolph

Founder and first presiding bishop of the Oneness Pentecostal body, **Holy Temple Church of the Lord Jesus Christ of the Apostolic Faith**. Goodwin was born in Columbia, South Carolina and migrated to Bronx, New York where he worked as a barber for several years before being converted. He was called to preach in 1947 and that same year established a small congregation at the back of his barbershop. For several years, Goodwin worked under Bishop **Sherrod C. Johnson** of the **Church of the Lord Jesus Christ of the Apostolic Faith**.

When Johnson died in 1961, and former vice president, S. McDowell Shelton, took over the organization, Goodwin pulled out of the body and used his Bronx congregation to launch his new organization. Goodwin led that body for nearly forty years, until his death in 2002, building it into a denomination with congregations along the East Coast and in the Caribbean, West Africa, and the Philippines. At his death, Bishop Belton Green became Apostle, Pastor and General Overseer.

The Oneness Pentecostal apologist wrote a number of tracts defending essential doctrines of the tradition. Goodwin also took it upon himself to reproduce several tracts that Sherrod Johnson, his former mentor had originally produced. His writings tend to portray the most fundamentalist strand of Oneness Pentecostal doctrine and leave little room for compromise, as his stance on women demonstrates.

Golder, Morris Ellis 1913-2000

A prominent bishop and unofficial historian in the **Pentecostal Assemblies of the World**. Golder was born in Indianapolis, Indiana, and as a small boy attended Garfield Haywood's Christ Temple Apostolic Faith Church where his parents and been converted to the Oneness Pentecostal movement.

As a young man, Golder fell away from the church, and dreamed of becoming a jazz orchestra leader. In 1930, he also experienced conversion as well as a call to the ministry. He was baptized in the Oneness Pentecostal formula of "the Name of Jesus" and received the four months later, received the Pentecostal Holy Spirit baptism with speaking in tongues.

When he was still a teen, Golder came under the influence of **Robert F. Tobin**, Garfield Haywood's successor who radically influenced the young man. In response to the limited Christ Temple opportunities for young preachers, however, Golder did much of his early preaching in street meetings. In 1935 he moved to Saint Louis, Missouri to pastor a small congregation that had no leader. With this appointment, he led the first racially integrated PAW assembly in that city for more than twelve years.

After Tobin's death in 1947, Golder was called to return to Indianapolis and take over the pastorate of Christ Temple. He was installed in 1948, and the church grew to a weekly attendance of over one thousand. Yet, five years later, in 1953, Golder left Christ Temple and began another Indianapolis congregation, Grace Apostolic Church, with thirty charter members.

Golder served the **Pentecostal Assemblies of the World** in various capacities including treasurer, editor of *The Christian Outlook*, vice-chair of the Board of Directors of **Aenon Bible College,** auxiliary director of the National Sunday School Association, and chair of the Board of Directors of Apostolic Light Press. In 1972 he was elevated to bishop as overseer of the 11th Episcopal District that included Kentucky and Western Tennessee.

Golder received an advanced degree from Butler School of Religion (now Christian Theological Seminary) and an honorary doctorate from Aenon Bible College. He authored eight books, including an unofficial history of the **Pentecostal Assemblies of the World.**

Further Reading:

Gary W. Garrett and Nathaniel A. Urshan. *The Life and Times of Bishop Morris E. Golder.* Eureka, IL: Apostolic Christian, 2000.

Gospel Spreading Church of God

A denomination within the Holiness movement founded in 1919 by **Lightfoot Solomon Michaux** in Hopewell, Virginia. Two years earlier, Michaux's wife persuaded him to construct a simple sanctuary and begin his first congregation—Everybody's Mission. At the time, he was ordained with the **Church of Christ (Holiness) USA** under **Charles Price Jones**, and initially brought his congregation into that organization. Soon after, he launched a series of street revivals in Newport News, Virginia that drew a substantial following.

In 1921 after learning that Jones planned to assign him to another congregation, Michaux seceded from COCHUSA to establish an independent congregation. Soon he established a second congregation in nearby Hampton, Virginia and created the Gospel Spreading Tabernacle Building Association to oversee the group's financial affairs. In 1928, its headquarters were moved to Washington DC and the name changed to the Church of God and Gospel Spreading Association. A year later, his radio ministry started as a local broadcast and by 1934, it was being heard weekly on fifty Columbia Broadcasting System (CBS) stations, carrying his sermons and songs to twenty-five million people across the country.

By 1945 the organization had established seven churches along the eastern seaboard. In 1964 Michaux again reorganized what is sometimes called the Elder Michaux Church of God or the Radio Church of God under the new corporate name, The Gospel Spreading Association.

In the mid-1940s, The Gospel Spreading Church became the first denomination to erect a major housing development for African Americans. The 411-unit Mayfair Mansions apartments complex was built in Washington DC between 1942 and 1946. The project was erected with a $3.5 million loan from the Reconstruction Finance Corporation. At the time, it was the largest loan ever received by the leader of an American of African organization.

The denomination also operated the National Memorial to the Progress of the Colored Race in America. This 1100-acre farm in James City County, Virginia housed an amusement park and beach on the grounds. It was located near the place where the first slaves in this country landed, and was the site of various revivals and other religious activities, including his famous mass-baptismal services in which he immersed hundreds of candidates at one time.

As part of the antecedent Holiness movement, The Gospel Spreading Church distinguishes itself from Pentecostals. At one point, his wife made it clear that she hated what she considered the ravings of lower class "tongue people." Yet Michaux had no problem addressing the needs of the lower classes who frequented his congregation. He ran an employment bureau to help people find work and Happy News Café that served affordable food. Still, the church also drew the support of some of the most powerful people in the country at that time, including President Dwight Eisenhower, who was an honorary deacon, his wife Mamie, and First Lady Eleanor Roosevelt.

Currently, the denomination has approximately 4000 members in twelve congregations, mostly concentrated along the East Coast between Newport News, Virginia and New York City.

After Michaux's death in 1968, the denomination came under the leadership of a board of directors with a president. Currently, Bishop Michael A. Clayton, Sr. serves in that position and as General Overseer.

Further Reading:

Ashcraft Webb, Lillian, and Lightfoot Michaux. *About My Father's Business: The Life of Elder Michaux.* Santa Barbara, CA: Greenwood, 1981.

Grace, Charles Manual "Sweet Daddy" 1881–1960

Founder of the **quasi-Holiness** group, **United House of Prayer for All People**, Grace was born Marcelino Manuel da Graca into a Roman Catholic family in Brava Verde, the Cape Verde Islands (then a Portuguese possession) off the western coast of Africa. His family moved to New Bedford, Massachusetts in the early 1900s, where he took odd jobs between 1909 and 1932 he had two failed marriages.

He reportedly was called to preach as a youth and his public ministry began in Charlotte, North Carolina in the 1920s. By 1921 he had returned to New Bedford to found his first congregation in nearby West Wareham. Soon he was known as "Sweet Daddy." Within a few years, his congregation had grown exponentially. By 1927 the organization was incorporated as the House of Prayer on the Rock of the Apostolic Faith in Washington DC. Throughout the 1920s and 1930s, Grace traveled across the United States establishing the **United House of Prayer for All People**.

The group became essentially a personality cult relying on his fiery sermons and captivating persona to draw followers primarily from impoverished Black ghettoes. Grace's brightly colored suits, manicured five-inch, red, white and blue fingernails, massive diamond ring, and shoulder-length hair made him an outstanding figure in any audience. He lived in one of forty-two large and expensive mansions, filled with expensive furniture, works of art and amenities in various states across the United States, as well as a twenty-five-room mansion and fruit farm in Cuba and a coffee plantation in Brazil. He traveled in chauffeur-driven luxury cars. In the mid-1950s his net worth was estimated at 25 million dollars.

Grace saw himself as an "intermediary" and "the path to salvation" for and to God, and claimed that by the power of the Holy Ghost he could raise the dead. He also taught the controversial doctrine of one man leadership—that God only used one man at a time such as Noah, Moses, and Jesus. He saw himself as that man and held absolute control over the administration and doctrine of his churches.

Grace's adherents' belief system boiled down to worship of their leader. Indeed, at one point Grace reportedly declared, "I never said I was God, but you cannot prove to me I'm not." Later he made a more explicit assertion that "Salvation is by Grace only. . . . Grace has given God a vacation, and since he is on vacation, don't worry him. If you sin against God, Grace can save you, but if you sin against Grace, God cannot save you."

After Grace's death in 1960, the IRS charged his estate with nearly six million in back taxes, a testament to the amount of money his churches earned him during his lifetime.

Further Reading:

Brune, Danielle Elizabeth. "Sweet Daddy Grace: The Life and Times of a Modern Day Prophet." PhD diss., University of Texas at Austin, 2002.
Dallam, Marie W. *Daddy Grace: A Celebrity Preacher and His House of Prayer*. New York: NYU Press, 2007.
Sigler, Danielle Brune. "Beyond the Binary: Revisiting Father Divine, Daddy Grace, and Their Ministries." In *Race, Nation, and Religion in the Americas*, edited by Henry Goldschmidt and Elizabeth McAlister, 209–27. New York: Oxford University Press, 2004
Whiting, Albert N. "The United House of Prayer for All People: A Case Study of a Charismatic Sect." PhD diss., American University, 1952.

Gray, Arthur J., II 1958–

The first African American elected to the International Board of Directors within the predominantly white International Church of the Foursquare Gospel, which was founded by famed twentieth-century evangelist Aimee Semple McPherson. Before moving into fulltime ministry, Gray prosecuted violent felonies as Deputy District Attorney of Los Angeles County from 1988 until 1996. He currently also serves as a private attorney. Prior to moving into leadership at Foursquare Gospel, Gray served as senior pastor of Abundant Joy Christian Fellowship in Inglewood, California from 1994 until 2002.

From 2002 until 2011, Gray served as one of six vice presidents for the denomination and was involved in developing guidelines for a newly established national department, advising other offices on supporting urban and multicultural churches. He also developed a national leadership coaching strategy and developed and coordinated national conferences. Gray provided legal support to pastors and churches in the areas of risk management, leases, and immigration issues.

In 2004 when Foursquare established a Department of Urban and Multicultural Ministries to support leaders of urban minority congregations by focusing on church planting and outreach, Gray was tapped to serve simultaneously with his other responsibilities as executive director.

On leaving his high-ranking Foursquare post in 2011, Gray formed and became chief executive officer of Gray Matters Ministry, an organization that specializes in helping people. Gray has worked as an economist, an attorney, a pastor of two churches, an executive of a religious nonprofit and as an overseer of up to 150 local churches. He also serves in adjunct professor positions at A. W. Tozer Seminary and Vanguard University.

At the same time, Gray is the only African American District Supervisor—out of fourteen—in the denomination. He assumed that position in 2010 and serves the Greater Los Angeles area. He currently also serves as pastor of Connections, a Foursquare church in Long Beach, California.

Gray received his bachelor's degree in economics from Loyola Marymount University in 1980, and holds a Juris Doctors degree from Southwestern University School of Law. He received a Doctor of Ministry in Transformational Leadership of the Global City from Bakke Graduate University in 2009. He is also a certified Life Coach from Leader Breakthru Coaching.

In 2012 he joined the faculty of A.W. Tozer Seminary as an adjunct professor in political science and Vanguard University of Southern California in business law and ethics. He also serves as a member of the Board of Trustees of Foursquare's L.I.F.E. Pacific College in San Dimas, California.

Further Reading:

O'Quinn, Doretha A. *Silent Voices Powerful Messages: The Historical Influence and Contribution of the African-American Experience in the Foursquare Gospel Movement.* Los Angeles: International Church of the Foursquare Gospel, 2002.

Grayson, David W. Sr. 1942–2016

Former bishop in the **Church of God in Christ** and founding presiding bishop and chief apostle of **New Day Church International.** He was born in Brooklyn, New York, and entered the ministry at fifteen. While serving in New York, he first pastored Temple of Blessings, formerly known as Inspirational Baptist Church of God in Christ. Grayson Temple and Temple of Blessings Church of God in Christ (COGIC) was founded in 1969, and through it Grayson established one of the first predominantly African-American private, parochial elementary schools in the city of New York in 1980.

By 1991 Grayson had moved to Memphis where he took over the pastorate of Christian Cathedral COGIC. He founded Christian Cathedral COGIC. After serving thirty-five years as a pastor, Grayson was consecrated a bishop by **J. O. Patterson Sr**. From that year until 2000, he served as the second COGIC prelate to be appointed to the state of Maine, and then was moved to the New York Eastern Fourth Jurisdiction.

In 2003 after his request to presiding bishop G. E. Patterson to be appointed as a jurisdictional bishop within Tennessee was rejected, Grayson led thirty-two COGIC congregations and about 2,000 members from forty congregations—primarily in Tennessee, Alabama, Mississippi and New York—out of the denomination to form the Tennessee Evangel Church Planting Association. Later that year, it was changed to Church of God in Christ (New Day) and Grayson was consecrated as presiding bishop of the organization that would finally take the name **New Day Church International**.

By 2015 Grayson was again listed among the members of the Tennessee Jurisdiction of the **Church of God in Christ** as overseer of the Heart of Tennessee District. From his earliest ministry, he has been an advocate for education as the founder and headmaster of the Kiddie Kollege and David Grayson Christian Academy in Brooklyn, New York. He also recently established Excel Academy in Memphis.

Greater Emmanuel International Fellowship, Inc.

A Oneness Pentecostal body founded by bishop **Quander L. Wilson** as the Greater Emmanuel Apostolic Faith Tabernacles. Wilson, who had been a pastor and former General Secretary in the **Glorious Church of God in Christ** from 1953 to 1956, split from that denomination when its presiding bishop, Sidney Bass, violated denominational polity and married a divorced woman.

The organization began with three congregations in Portsmouth, Ohio in 1960. It became incorporated in the state of Ohio in 1961 and today is affiliated with several churches throughout the United States and Africa but primarily concentrated in Ohio, West Virginia, Maryland.

The careers of many well-known pastors and ministers were birthed from this organization. Perhaps, the best known is famed televangelist, Thomas Dexter (T. D.) Jakes, who was a regional bishop in the organization until 1988, when he left to join **Sherman Watkins's** organization **Higher Ground Always Abounding Assemblies**.

In 1986 Greater Life Evangelistic Temple was established and currently serves as the headquarters, and the title was changed to its present name. In the late 1980s a white pastor, Alan McSavage, joined Bishop Wilson to travel extensively with him and evangelize. However, he later left to begin Greater Emmanuel International in Canada as a separate body. In 1988, there were forty-six congregations.

Wilson died in 2003. His elder son, Quander L. Wilson Jr., assumed the leadership of the denomination. Edward E. Shouse Sr., Wilson's stepson, serves as the current presiding bishop and the organization is a member of the World Fellowship of Pentecostal Churches, the Apostolic World Christian Fellowship, and the National Evangelical Association. Its headquarters remain in Portsmouth, Ohio.

Gregory, Martin Rawleigh 1885–1960

The founder of **Emmanuel Tabernacle Baptist Church Apostolic Faith, Inc.,** a Oneness Pentecostal body. Gregory was called to the ministry at age seventeen. In 1903, at the age of eighteen, he was ordained in the Baptist Church, where he served for nine years. During that period, he attended Colgate University in Rochester, New York, studying law and medicine. In 1910, while still in college and still a member of the Baptist tradition, Gregory received the Pentecostal Holy Spirit baptism.

He arrived in Columbus, Ohio in 1914, intent on establishing a congregation. There, he encountered the Oneness Pentecostal movement under the preaching of **Robert Clarence Lawson** who convinced him of the validity of the doctrine. Once baptized in Jesus' name, Gregory severed formal relationships with the Baptist church. In 1916, however, while sick and immobile, he sensed God urging him to keep the designation "Baptist" and giving him the name Emmanuel Tabernacle Baptist Church Apostolic Faith. The church was incorporated with that name in 1917 and Gregory was appointed as the only bishop in 1921, another break from Baptist tradition where historically that title has not been used.

Besides his Pentecostal experience and acceptance of Oneness understandings of the Godhead, Gregory differed from Baptist congregations of that day, as well as with most Oneness leaders (including Lawson), in that he was the first Apostolic Bishop to give women a place equal to men. This privilege was extended even to the rank of bishop.

Grimes, Samuel Joshua 1884–1967

The second and longest serving presiding bishop in **Pentecostal Assemblies of the World** and longtime editor of *The Christian Outlook*, the official publication of PAW. The noted biblical scholar also served as a missionary to Liberia and the Diocesan Bishop of the Eastern District Council of the PAW.

Grimes was born in Barbados, British West Indies. His earliest Christian experience was in the Wesleyan Methodist Church and by age seven, he had a religious conversion and expressed a desire to preach at a young age. He first visited the United States in 1903 and by 1905, he had settled here. In 1911, while living in Philadelphia, Pennsylvania and attending an African Methodist Episcopal Church, he had a renewed spiritual awakening and sensing a call to the ministry. Shortly after, he left his secular job, enrolled at the National Bible Institute of Philadelphia (now Cairn University), and graduated from the National Bible Institute of New York (later Shelton College) in 1917. He began attending **Henry Prentiss'** storefront Pentecostal congregation where he experienced his Pentecostal Holy Spirit baptism, yet continued to worship in the Methodist church until he moved to New York City, where he again enrolled in the Bible school. During his last year in school, he began an extensive evangelistic tour. During that period, he heard Oneness Pentecostal leader **Garfield T. Haywood** preach, accepted the Oneness doctrine, got re-baptized in Jesus' name, and became affiliated with Haywood's congregation.

In 1927 Grimes was nominated for the bishopric, a position he declined at that time. After Haywood's death, he reconsidered, and agreed to the request made by the Eastern District Council and some of the leaders of the Midwest to accept the nomination of bishop, but was defeated.

In 1931 Grimes attended the meeting to re-organize the PAW where he was elevated to the office of bishop. After a failed attempt to reunite PAW with dissident groups that had earlier splintered from the body, Grimes was unanimously elected as the presiding bishop, the post he held for thirty-five years.

Following one of his missionary trips to Liberia, Grimes and his wife, songwriter **Kathleen Grimes**, brought a teenage **Ellen Moore-Hopkins** to the United States and became the driving force behind her establishing the Samuel Grimes Maternity and Child Welfare Center in Kakata, Liberia. Although he pastored churches in Oregon and in West Virginia, his passion was church building and missions.

His first wife, Kathleen, died in 1960, and he married Miss Carolyn Andrew in September of 1963. Grimes died four years later after a series of strokes.

Further Reading:

Golder, Morris. *A History of the Pentecostal Assemblies of the World.* Indianapolis: s.l., 1973.
Tyson, James L. *The Early Pentecostal Revival.* Hazelwood, MO: Word Aflame, 1992.

Grimes, Sobrina Kathleen McDowell Washington (S. K.) 1881–1960

This Canadian-born missionary, author, composer and musician was also the first wife of **Samuel Grimes,** who became the second presiding bishop of the **Pentecostal Assemblies of the World**. After migrating to the United States, she served alongside her husband as a missionary to Liberia from 1919 to 1923. While there, she contracted chronic malaria, a condition that plagued her the rest of her life. After returning to the United States, she and her husband ministered in evangelistic campaigns across the United States and Canada for several years. Apart from their work together, Kathleen played a key role in organizing PAW's women's auxiliary in the United States. They also adopted a Liberian student, **Ellen Moore (Hopkins),** brought her to the United States, and supported her matriculation for several degrees in the health profession. Their investment paid off when Hopkins returned to Liberian to provide for communities there.

Grimes composed her first known song, "Since the Comforter Came," in 1909. It was included in the *Bridegroom Songs* collection published by PAW. Her most sung hymn is "He's the Great I Am," was copyrighted in 1924. The same year, Grimes published an eight-song collection entitled *Echoes of Zion*. Her hymns centered primarily on Oneness themes and one of her most poignant hymns is aptly entitled "Acts 2:38." It speaks specifically of the Oneness contention that regeneration baptism is necessary for salvation. After her death, Bishop Grimes remarried.

Groover, Gentle L. 1932–

The third presiding bishop of the **Church of Our Lord Jesus Christ of the Apostolic Faith,** serving from 1995 until 2001. He was born in Greenville, Florida and attended Community College in Madison. He went on to receive his Doctorate of Divinity from the University of Alabama, and was awarded an Honorary Doctorate of Divinity from the Saint Thomas Christian University. Before joining COOLJC, Groover had been a steward in the Methodist Church, and had been won to the Pentecostal faith by his sister. He received the Pentecostal experience of Holy Spirit baptism at a prayer meeting at her home.

In 1962 he was called into the ministry and sent to establish a church in Jacksonville, Florida, The Greater Refuge Temple, which he has pastored since its inception. Groover was appointed an elder in 1965, taking the position of District Elder of the Northern District of Florida two years later. He became a junior bishop in 1980, and three years later, was consecrate as a full bishop. When the state was divided into regions, Groover was appointed as Diocesan Bishop for the North Florida/Mississippi Diocese.

In 1984 he was elected as an apostle and a year later was appointed to the Board of Apostles, the governing body of the denomination. When vhief spostle, **William Lee Bonner,** initiated the Presidership Training period for the board members, Groover served with Bishop Wilbur Jones as co-presider of the project from 1994 to 1995. Later that year, he was elected as the new presider and served from 1995 until 2001. During his tenure, he helped build churches and schools in Liberia, Ghana, India and other countries and sponsored missionary trips to supply aid to these fields. After serving two terms, the Bonner chose Groover as his executive assistant, a position he relinquished after the elder leader's death. He currently serves as overseer over three districts in Florida, as well as Europe, Mexico and South America.

Gurry, Carrie V 1865–1942

Founder of the **King's Apostle's Holiness Church.** Raised in the African Methodist Episcopal Church, Gurry was exposed to the Pentecostal experience through the testimony of her daughter-in-law and received the baptism of the Holy Spirit with tongues in 1903, three years before the **Azusa Street Revival**. Between 1911 and 1914, Gurry founded and incorporated the first Holiness Pentecostal congregation in Maryland with a small group meeting in her Baltimore home. While she never attended the west coast meeting, it is likely she had the occasion to meet its founder, **William Seymour,** and his close colleague **Charles Mason** as they conducted a revival tour throughout the Mideast in 1914.

Her denomination grew slowly as Gurry traveled through Maryland and Pennsylvania, preaching and teaching. In her lifetime, her group never reached to more than ten congregations located primarily along the Delmarva Peninsula. It played a significant role, however, in the development of a number of black Pentecostal bodies within both the Trinitarian and Oneness traditions and the leaders (several of them women) who spent their formative years within the King's Apostles Holiness Church. In addition, a number of men went on to later found or pastor prominent congregations. Amy Stevens, who was reared in KAHC, later served as presiding bishop of the **Mt. Sinai Holy Church**, founded by Gurry's personal friend, Bishop **Ida Robinson**. **Violet Fisher**, one of only three black women serving as bishop in the United Methodist Church at the end of the twentieth century, also emerged from the KAHC.

Gurry never took the title of bishop, but referred to herself as "evangelist," appointing a man, Walter E. Campher, as National Overseer of the organization, while reserving for herself the title of General Overseer. In this way, she maintained leadership of the denomination while circumventing some of the criticism of female authority over men. Even this solution, however, was problematic for some of the other male leaders who served with her, and several defected to found their own organizations.

Gurry died at the age of seventy-seven. After her death, the denomination continued a pattern of slow expansion. Today, there are nearly thirty King's Apostles Holiness Church of God congregations. Gurry's influence reached far beyond the early days of the denomination she founded through the men and women she nurtured and mentored to become leaders of larger, more highly regarded congregations and denominations.

H

Hackett, Paul Luther Jr. 1925–1995

A prominent educator, pastor and denominational leader within the predominantly white, **International Church of the Foursquare Gospel,** founded by Aimee Semple McPherson. Hackett was born in Alameda, California, but when he was nine, the family relocated to Los Angeles. In 1951, Hackett made a personal commitment to Christian faith and joined a **Church of God in Christ** congregation pastored by Bishop **Samuel Crouch,** where he experienced Pentecostal Holy Spirit baptism.

After sensing a call to Christian ministry, Hackett entered L.I.F.E. Bible College. In 1965, he earned a bachelor or arts in theology from that institution, where he was student body president. He received a master's degree from Azusa Pacific University in Azusa, California.

In 1967 Hackett joined the faculty as an instructor of Old Testament, making him the first African American appointed to the faculty of a predominantly white Pentecostal academic institution. He served that institution in a full-time capacity until 1974 and as a part-time faculty member until 1980. Throughout much of that period, he was the only African-American faculty member and often had to endure racial discrimination from his colleagues. Further, throughout that period, Hackett served in a number of pastoral roles. Hackett traveled throughout the United States and Canada during that time and recruited a large number of black students.

Hackett's first pastoral role was as assistant pastor at West Adams Foursquare Church in Los Angeles before he resigned to teach full time at the college. In 1974, he became full-time pastor of Colin Avenue Foursquare Church in Lynwood, California. After leaving his position at L.I.F.E., Hackett took on a number of leadership positions within the Foursquare denomination—in many cases making him the first African American to serve in a role there. In 1978 he was the first black to be invited to be a plenary speaker at a Foursquare National Convention. He served as one of the first African-America divisional superintendents, with responsibility for the South Bay District, and was appointed to the first leadership position on the executive council, serving there until 1992. He returned to involvement with his alma mater as the first African-American member of its Board of Regents.

Though Hackett served at almost every level of Foursquare leadership, he was relentless in pushing the denomination toward more inclusiveness. After his death, a Paul Hackett Endowed Scholarship was established for a minority student with an interest in ministering to diverse cultures.

Further Reading:

O'Quinn, Doretha A. "Paul Hackett." In *Silent Voices Powerful Messages: The Historical Influence and Contribution of the African-American Experience in the Foursquare Gospel Movement.* Los Angeles: International Church of the Foursquare Gospel, 2002.

Hamiter, Isaiah Warren (I.W.) Jr. 1919–1985

Second presiding bishop of the Oneness Pentecostal denomination, the **Original Glorious Church of God in Christ**. He was born in Cincinnati, Ohio where his father had been a minister. By the early 1930s the family relocated to Huntington, West Virginia where they may have become involved in the **Glorious Church of God in Christ**.

In 1947 when the Young Peoples Union became an organized auxiliary, Hamiter was selected to head it. From 1947 to 1949, Hamiter pastored the Church in Oberlin, Ohio. That year, he was ordained a bishop and assigned to West Virginia, and by 1952 he was living in Akron, Ohio. Hamiter later moved his family to Columbus and took over a storefront congregation in that city. He slowly built that congregation to the place where they were able to purchase a convention center for the denomination's annual meeting in that city.

When **Sidney Coy Bass** defied charter of the **Glorious Church of God in Christ** in 1952 to marry divorced woman, Hamiter was among a group of leaders who left that organization to form the **Glorious Church of God in Christ**. **W. O. Howard** became bishop at that time and served until 1972. At his retirement, Hamiter became presider. Under his leadership, the church grew to include mission programs in Haiti, Jamaica, and India. He served at the head of the denomination until his death and died in Columbus at age sixty-six.

Hancock, Samuel Nathan 1883–1963

Bishop Samuel Nathan Hancock, a leader in the early Oneness Pentecostal movement and founder of The **Pentecostal Churches of the Apostolic Faith** (PCAF), was born in Adair County, Kentucky, south of Louisville. His family moved to Indianapolis, Indiana in 1888 when he was five. Not long after the move, Hancock's father abandoned the family. At age thirteen, young Hancock dropped out of seventh grade to work on the railroad to help support the family Four years later, he was converted to Christian faith at Penick Chapel, an interdenominational church.

In 1914 Hancock began attending **Garfield T. Haywood's** Christ Temple Apostolic Faith Assembly while it was still a Trinitarian congregation, and received the Pentecostal Spirit baptism. Two years later, when Haywood moved into the Oneness Pentecostal movement, Hancock and 465 members of Christ Temple followed. That same year, he felt called to ministry and began preaching on the Indianapolis streets. By 1917 he was serving as Haywood's assistant pastor.

Hancock moved to Detroit, Michigan in 1921 to pastor Greater Bethlehem Temple Church, a church that grew to more than 3,000 parishioners under his leadership.

Hancock was one of the original men selected as a bishop of the **Pentecostal Assemblies of the World**, following its reorganization in 1925. After Haywood's death in 1931, leaders of the predominantly white, Pentecostal Ministerial Alliance approached PAW about a merger, which transpired quickly with the two organizations combining to form the Pentecostal Assemblies of Jesus Christ. Subsequently, when that merger failed, the PAW restored its charter under the leadership of Samuel Grimes. Hancock remained for a while as a PAJC presbyter. In 1938, however, many of the Blacks returned to PAW after racial tension arose in the new body. Hancock returned as an elder and was elected as a bishop for the second time.

By 1940 at height of his ministry within the PAW, Hancock was accused of teaching the heresy that Jesus Christ was only the son of God, not God Himself. After being exonerated by a council of leaders in 1943, he was appointed to the Board of Directors of the denomination's seminary, Aenon Bible School.

In 1955 he joined other members of the Executive Board in signing an affirmation of the Oneness doctrine. However, Hancock left the PAW in 1957 when he founded the Pentecostal **Churches of the Apostolic Faith**. He served as presiding bishop of PCAF until his death at the age of seventy-nine after a brief illness. Once at the helm of PCAF, he continued the controversial teaching, and though a faction within the denomination objected to this deviation, most tolerated it and remained loyal to him as long as he lived.

Hancock was married five times, outliving all but one of his wives: Bertha Valentine Hancock, the mother of his two children whom he married in 1904; Anna Williams Hancock, whom he married in 1916; Ida Haywood Hancock (the widow of **Garfield T. Haywood**), whom he married in 1939; Anna Bell Douglas Hancock; and Bertha Jackson Hancock.

At his death, Hancock left an organization of nearly six hundred churches. Besides a strong congregation in Detroit, during his short, six-year tenure as bishop, the organization established several ministries. A soup kitchen fed the poor throughout the Great Depression, a boys' workshop taught carpentry and trade skills, a church-owned supermarket provided for the community, and a church farm and girls' home provided other needed services. Additionally the congregation established satellite churches throughout in New Haven, Port Huron, Jackson, Delray, and Detroit, Michigan.

Further Reading:

Golder, Morris. *History of the Pentecostal Assemblies of the World*. Indianapolis: s.n., 1973.
Tyson, James. *Earnest Contenders for the Faith*. Indianapolis: Pentecostal, 1982.

Haney, Oliver J. 1945–

From 1974 through 2004, Haney served as the second dean of the Charles Harrison Mason Seminary of the Interdenominational Theological Seminary in Atlanta, Georgia. The ordained **Church of God in Christ** minister has ministered globally as a revivalist and conference speaker. He has also served as pastor of two Presbyterian congregations: Antioch in Dalton and Ebenezer in Rome, Georgia. He has served in two COGIC congregations: Fairburn Church of God in Christ in Fairburn,

Georgia and New Horizons Church of God in Christ in East Point, Georgia. Prior to assuming a COGIC pastorate, Haney served as an associate minister at Cathedral of Faith COGIC in Atlanta from 1975 to 1977.

In 2009 Haney was consecrated as a COGIC bishop and appointed to the Northern Georgia First Ecclesiastical Jurisdiction. He also is a member of the Advisory Board of COGIC Campus Ministry and the Board of Trustees of the Atlanta Regional Consortium for Higher Education.

Harewood, Gladstone Theophilus 1898–1990

Oneness Pentecostal pastor and songwriter, Gladstone Harewood was born in Barbados, West Indies in 1898. His father was a soldier in the British colonial army, and his mother died when he was an infant. The family immigrated to the United States while Gladstone was a young boy in 1908 and the child was raised by his uncle, Fitzherbert Pilgrim, in Chicago.

His brother Richard was a Methodist circuit-riding preacher while Gladstone became involved with the Pentecostals. Harewood lived in several Midwestern states—Illinois, Indiana, Wisconsin, and Iowa—before finally settling in Los Angeles, pastoring there until at least until 1985, and dying there at the age of ninety-two.

Among his most well known songs are, "I Will Walk with Christ my Savior," and "The Precious Blood of Christ Atones," both published in the 1931 addition of *Full Gospel Songs* edited by **Thoro Harris**.

Harris, James Frank 1943–

A former bishop in the **Highway Christian Church of Christ, Inc.** who is co-founder of the **Redeemed Assembly of Jesus Christ, Apostolic** with Douglas Williams from Washington DC. In 1979 Harris assumed the position of presiding bishop and Williams became assistant presiding bishop.

Harris was born in Prince George County, Virginia and received his Pentecostal Holy Spirit baptism at age twelve. Later, within the same year, he began working in youth ministry and assisting his pastor. In 1967 the pastor sent him to lead a small mission church in a storefront, which outgrew its premises in a year. Following the death of his senior pastor, he returned to his home church to pastor that congregation.

Thirteen years later, he and Williams left the **Highway Christian Church** is a schism over the authoritarian leadership of the presiding bishop, **L.V. Lomax**. They established the Redeemed Assembly of Jesus Christ with six churches. Since that time, Harris has financed, organized, and equipped several churches within the national and international organization.

Harris, Robert Lee 1925–2005

The politician and **Church of God in Christ** pastor was the first African American in the history of the state of Utah to be elected to state office when he was elected to the House of Representatives. Harris, a retired railroad worker and businessman, served as a Democrat in the House of Representatives in 1977 and 1978, when he was elected by a predominantly white district, defeating a white Mormon candidate.

Harris was born in Fort Worth, Texas and later settled in Ogden, Utah. He was retired from the Union Pacific Railroad. Harris pastored a **Church of God in Christ** congregation in Ogden and worked as an entrepreneur who operated a restaurant and several grocery stores in Ogden. He became famous for his Best Soul Barbeque Sauce. He gained notoriety as a political, civil, and human rights activist who was arrested over ninety-seven times for various protests and staged dozens of lone lie-ins for a number of causes. On one occasion, he marched to Washington DC to lie down in the driveway of the White House to protest racial inequality. At another time, he openly opposed the Gay Rights movement before it had gained wide support in the late twentieth century by staging a lie-in on the railroad tracks of a train carrying marchers from the West Coast to Washington DC for the 1979 National March on Washington for Gay and Lesbian Rights.

Harris served only one term in the Utah legislature and was defeated for re-election. After his defeat, he announced that he was changing to the Republican party. He also ran for a seat on the Ogden city council but came third in the five-way primary vote.

Further Reading:

"Political Miracle for a Utah Pastor." *Sepia* 26.46 (1977) 53.
"Protester, Ministers Laying on Tracks Halt Train Carrying Rally Bound Gays." *Lakeland [Florida] Ledger*, October 12, 1979, 5A.

Harris, Thoro 1874–1955

Early Pentecostal hymn writer within both the Trinitarian and Oneness traditions. In addition to composing hymns, Harris compiled a number of hymnals, and was one of the first musicians to produce exclusively Pentecostal hymnals: *The Blessed Hope* (1910), *Jesus Is Coming Soon* (1914), *Songs of His Coming* (1919), and *Songs We Love* (1921). The multi-talented Harris wrote both texts and tunes, and sometimes arranged the tunes of other composers.

Harris was born in Washington DC. He was mullato; his father was black and his mother white, and some accounts claim that he sometimes "passed as white." In 1902 after attending college in Battle Creek, Michigan he lived in Boston and Chicago. He produced his first hymnal, which contained many of his own compositions.

After embracing Oneness Pentecostal doctrine and practice in 1916, Harris wrote "Baptized in Jesus' Name" as a rallying cry for the budding Oneness movement. The song was published by leading Oneness proponent L. V. Roberts in Indianapolis on the front page of the first issue of a 1916 volume of his periodical, *The Present Truth*. After his conversion to the movement, Harris co-wrote several hymns with **Alexander Schooler**, a one-time leader in the **Pentecostal Assemblies of the World.**

In 1920 Harris went to Los Angeles to work with Aimee Semple McPherson to compile the *Pentecostal Revivalist*, a 241-selection hymnal. He then moved to Chicago, Illinois at the invitation of popular singing evangelist and hymnal publisher, Peter Bilhorn. For a time, Harris pastored Lake Street Mission in that city. Though he was never Baptist, in 1925 he edited *The New Hymnal*, the first collection for Swedish-American Baptist hymns published in English (and containing thirty-nine of his songs).

Around 1930 Harris moved to Eureka Springs, Arkansas, where owned a boarding house for a time He moved to work for the publishing arm of the predominantly white Oneness Pentecostal Organization, United Pentecostal Church. While there, he played the organ at several churches. He was also known locally for his penchant for walking around with a canvas bag full of handbooks for sale. Throughout his life, Harris worked with a number of famous preachers including the renowned Billy Sunday, Dwight L. Moody, and George Stebbins.

Perhaps his most gospel song is "Jesus Loves the Little Children, and perhaps the most well-known of his hymns, "All that Thrills the Soul is Jesus" in 1917. The tune is a favorite among Trinitarians as well as Oneness Pentecostals and can be found in many hymnals. Many of his songs found their way into the Holiness and Pentecostal congregations and hymnals. "He's Coming Soon" was adapted to the tune of the famous Hawaiian "Aloha Oe" by Queen Liliuokalani and captured the eschatological hope of the imminent return of Christ that was so central to early Pentecostalism. His work was especially popular among white Pentecostals and included in collections of the Assemblies of God as well as other predominantly white bodies. Yet, they are also features in works of the Holiness and broader Evangelical groups and in those of mainline bodies. Harris died at age eighty-one in Eureka Springs.

Further Reading:

Blumhofer, Edith L. *Pentecost in My Soul: Explorations in the Meaning of Pentecostal Experience in the Early Assemblies of God.* Springfield, MO: Gospel Publishing, 1989.

Wallace, Mary H. *Profiles of Pentecostal Preachers.* Hazelwood, MO: Word Aflame, 1983.

Harrison, Robert Emmanuel ("Bob") 1928–2014

One of the most prominent African-American evangelists of the 1960s, who was known as America's "Black Son of Thunder." Harrison ministered across the United States and around the world through his powerful preaching and accomplished music—both as an associate evangelist with the Billy Graham Evangelistic Association from 1960–67 and through his own organization, Bob Harrison Ministries. For over three decades, Harrison played a significant role in numerous capacities within the Assemblies of God (AG) to facilitate black and urban ministries. His highly visible ordination in 1962, following years of paralysis over the question of the ordination of blacks, served as a watershed within the AG for this issue.

Harrison's grandmother, **Cornelia Jones Robertson**, was a participant in the **Azusa Street Revival**, and a close associate of Maria Woodworth-Etter and Aimee Semple McPherson. She was one of the first blacks ordained in the AG.

At an early age, Harrison displayed musical talent and was encouraged by his prominent jazz associates to pursue his education after leaving the military. Following their advice, Harrison first enrolled at the San Francisco Conservatory of Music and completed his Bachelor of Arts degree in music from San Francisco State College. Though he had grown up in the church, he renewed his commitment to Christ at an evangelistic service while at SFSC. Shortly, he began pursuing his call to ministry by seeking theological training, but he was denied admittance to Bob Jones University because he was black.

Harrison eventually enrolled at Bethany Bible College, an AG institution, as the school's first African-American student. While there, he was well liked and heavily involved in sports, music, and ministry. On preparing for graduation, Harrison sought credentials with the AG's experienced a Northern California-Nevada district. Though this same district had ordained Harrison's grandmother several decades earlier, they denied him credentials based on a rigid interpretation of a 1939 General Presbytery ruling regarding racially based limits on licensing and ordination.

Undaunted, in 1952, Harrison set out into pastoral and evangelistic ministry. In 1957 six years after the committee had denied his credentials, a new district superintendent who felt Harrison had been treated unjustly advocated for him and he received his ministerial license. This, however, was after he joined the Billy Graham Evangelistic Association and saw successful ministry throughout Africa. It seemed that his success "embarrassed" the AG into revising its policy on ordination of blacks, ordaining him in 1962, three years before the body passed a General Council resolution officially condemning racism.

Not long after the movement began to address specific questions of social concern and evangelistic strategy. With Harrison's undeniable gifts and abilities in ministry and leadership, they wanted him on board to help, and his ordination paved the way for him to increase his contribution to the AG exponentially.

Harrison began to receive invitations to address AG leadership on how to best reach blacks in America, including one to speak at the General Council of the Assemblies of God in 1967. Continuing to align his efforts with Foreign Missions, Home Missions, and AG educational endeavors, he was named Consultant on Inner City Evangelism in 1972. He began pastoring a racially mixed AG church in Portland, Oregon in 1973, and continued his work in the United States and overseas. By the time of his 1971 autobiography, *When God Was Black*, was published, Harrison had "sung and preached on every continent."

In 1990 Harrison was appointed as National Representative of Black Ministries and played a significant role in the formation of the AG National Black Caucus in 1993 and National Black Fellowship in 1998. Throughout the eighties and nineties, he continued to use his ministry, writing, and speaking to prod AG leadership on issues of racial justice.

For Further Reading:

Gohr, Glenn. "For Such a Time as This: The Story of Evangelist Bob Harrison." *AG Heritage* (2004) 5–11

Harrison, Bob. *When God Was Black*. Grand Rapids: Zondervan, 1971

Kenyon, Howard N. "Black Ministers in the Assemblies of God." *A/G Heritage* 7.1 (1987) 10–13, 20.

McGee, Gary B. *People of the Spirit*. Springfield, MO: Gospel Publishing, 2004.

Olena, Lois. "I'm Sorry, My Brother: A Reconciliation Journey." In *Forgiveness, Reconciliation, and Restoration: Multidisciplinary Studies from a Pentecostal Perspective*, edited by Martin W. Mittelstadt and Geoffrey W. Sutton, 89–105. Pentecostals, Peacemaking, and Social Justice Series. Eugene, OR: Pickwick, 2010.

Hart, Robert Eber 1863–1921

Early **Church of God in Christ** leader who provided legal assistance to Charles Harrison Mason and represented him before the Tennessee State Supreme Court in his 1907 court battle with **Charles Price Jones** over possession of the property and the denominational name to which both laid claimed.

Hart was born in Georgia and grew up in the city of Macon. In 1901 he graduated from Lane College, a Colored Methodist Episcopal institution in Jackson, Tennessee with a bachelor of law degree. He had no desire however, to practice law, but was interested in teaching at the University of West Tennessee in Jackson. After his religious conversion experience, he was called to the ministry. Sensing the need for theological training, he attended Selma University, where he received his first theological degree and became a prominent figure in the Colored Methodist Episcopal church. Once Hart began promoting the message of sanctification, he slowly became a controversial figure in the CME church. He eventually joined Mason, pastoring a local congregation in Trenton, Tennessee and evangelizing throughout Arkansas, Mississippi, and Tennessee.

Hart was a committed supporter of Mason and became one of the first persons appointed to the pastorate by him. In 1907 when Mason withdrew his fellowship from Jones, followers of both men rallied. Hart was among those who attended the reorganization meeting that established Mason's faction as a Pentecostal body. He not only represented Mason in court but also advised Mason and other early leaders on legal strategies in handling the fallout from the schismatic division, advising state leaders, for example, not to reorganize their jurisdictions until all legal claims were settles. While other leaders followed his advice, Justus Bowe did not. As a result, all the property that Mason's group held in Arkansas was lost to the Jones faction.

Within the new structure, he served as the first overseer of Tennessee, president of the Department of Church Extension and an associate editor of *Whole Truth*, the official periodical of the **Church of God in Christ** under Justus Bowe.

Further Reading:

McBride, Calvin. *Walking Into A New Spirituality: Chronicling the Life, Ministry, and Contributions of Elder Robert E. Hart, B.D., LL.B., D.D., to the CME Church and COGIC: With Some Additional COGIC History*. New York: iUniverse, 2007.

Hawkins, Edwin 1943–

Gospel musician, composer, and arranger. Hawkins is one of the originators of the urban contemporary gospel sound. Hawkins was born in Oakland, California where he began singing in his youth choir at Good Samaritan **Church of God in Christ** while still a toddler. By age five, he was playing piano; two years later, was full-time piano accompanist for the family gospel group. Ten years later, at the age of fifteen, he co-founded of the fifty-member Northern California State Youth Choir of the Church of God in Christ with Betty Watson.

Hawkins is best known for his 1968 arrangement of the traditional hymn, "Oh Happy Day." The song was recorded to be sold locally to raise money for the church, but became one of the biggest gospel hits of all time with sales rocketing to of over a million copies within two months, and a perennial favorite among gospel compositions. The single crossed over to the R&B and pop culture then became an international success, selling more than seven million copies worldwide. Hawkins was awarded his first Grammy for it, and the choir was rechristened the Edwin Hawkins Singers

In 1972 the Edwin Hawkins Singers won a second Grammy for "Every Man Wants to Be Free." Throughout the seventies, Hawkins continued to recording prolifically and in 1980 won a third Grammy for "Wonderful"; in 1983 they won a fourth for "If You Love Me." Hawkins also founded the Edwin Hawkins Music and Arts Seminar, an annual weeklong convention offering workshops exploring all facets of the gospel industry and culminating each year with a live performance by the assembled mass choir.

Since the early 1980s, Edwin Hawkins concentrated his work on songwriting, producing, and promoting of young talent. Although he recorded less frequently in the following years, he continued touring regularly. His Music and Arts Seminar continued to grow as well and expanded to include venues in other US cities, Europe, and Japan.

Hawkins, Walter Lee 1949–2010

Grammy-winning gospel composer and singer. Born in Oakland, California, Hawkins was a self-taught keyboard player. He dropped out of high school, but later earned a GED and attended classes in divinity at the University of California, Berkeley. He started his musical career in his brother **Edwin Hawkins'** Northern California State Youth Choir of the **Church of God in Christ**. Later, he worked with his brother Edwin and Betty Watson to co-found The Edwin Hawkins Singers and to produce the hit song "Oh Happy Day," which became one of the first gospel songs to cross over onto mainstream music charts.

In 1970 Hawkins married Tramaine Davis (the granddaughter of prominent COGIC bishop E. E. Cleveland, who became a prominent recording artist in her own right as Tramaine Hawkins) and left The Edwin Hawkins Singers. After two children were born, however, the marriage ended in divorce. The two remained close and often performed together. In the early 1970s, he founded the Love Center Church in Oakland, California a congregation whose own choir had considerable success with their "Love Alive" series that went on to sell over a million copies from the 1970s through the 1990s.

Hawkins was consecrated to the COGIC bishopric in 1992. Yet, his ministry within the denomination and the Pentecostal movement proved to be controversial as reports claimed that he openly supported homosexuality and gay marriage as biblically supported lifestyles and that he maintained friendships with openly gay pastors who used his ministerial organization to perform gay marriages.

Hawkins died of pancreatic cancer at the age of sixty-one.

Haywood, Garfield Thomas G. T. 1880–1931

One of the most prominent, early Oneness Pentecostal leaders who played a central role in the unfolding of the **Pentecostal Assemblies of the World** as a major denomination with the tradition. The pastor, denominational leader, and apologist was born in rural Greencastle, Indiana. By the time Haywood was three, his family had relocated to the Indianapolis area. During his youth, the family attended the city's St. Paul Baptist Church, but Haywood was active in a local Methodist congregation as well, serving as Sunday school superintendent in both congregations by the time he was a young man. He attended prestigious Short Ridge School, one of the country's oldest free high schools, noted for openness to blacks and academic excellence. After his sophomore year, however, Haywood left school to pursue a career as a cartoonist on two black weekly newspapers, *The Indianapolis Freedmen* and *The Indianapolis Reporter* to help support the large family. Haywood's truncated education did not assuage his love for learning; in its place, he read books, newspapers and periodicals on religion and other subjects voraciously and traveled extensively.

After marrying in 1902, Haywood left the newspapers to work in an iron foundry. For the next several years, he was a member of the Knights of Pythias, and eventually a lodge brother who had converted to Pentecostalism witnessed to him. His testimony deepened Haywood's faith, and he soon sensed a call to preach, but finding little support from his wife, he initially backed away from pursuing ministry.

In 1907 Haywood sustained a serious injury that left him incapacitated. During his recovery, he again sensed a call to ministry. On recuperating, he accompanied his friend to the mission church of **Azusa Street Revival** veteran **Henry Prentiss,** where he and his wife received their Pentecostal Spirit baptism on the first visit and he received a definitive call to preach.

Within the year, Prentiss turned the mission church over to Haywood and returned to New York City to evangelize. Shortly, the racially mixed congregation expanded to more than 400 members and Haywood was ordained in the PAW, one of several newly formed Trinitarian Pentecostal denominations. Haywood's congregation quickly began gaining prominence among Midwestern Pentecostals as the largest, most racially integrated Pentecostal congregation in Indiana during a period when Ku Klux Klan influence was at its highest.

By this time, Several Azusa Street veterans, Frank Ewart and Glenn Cook, began promulgating Oneness doctrine and re-baptizing anyone who accepted their message. When Cook initially approached him, Haywood was skeptical, but he, too, accepted the message and was re-baptized, he subsequently re-baptized most of the members of his sizeable congregation. He became a proponent of the "new issue," as some called it at that time.

Haywood's prominence and influence throughout the Midwest drew large numbers of blacks and whites into the Oneness movement, and he joined PAW founder J. J. Frazee, Howard Goss, D.C.O. Opperman, and Ewart in re-forming PAW as a mostly white, Oneness denomination. In 1913, three white leaders—Frazee, Opperman, and Goss—were elected to head the denomination. Haywood and Ewart were tapped to sign ministerial credentials, and four blacks—Haywood, **Robert C. Lawson**, **Alexander R. Schooler** and **F. I. Douglas**—served with several white field superintendents.

Haywood's newsletter, *The Voice in the Wilderness*, published between 1910 and 1922, served as vigorous advocate, first for Pentecostalism, then for Oneness doctrine. In it, he wrote articles and used his artistic talent to illustrate principle Oneness tenets. When PAW consolidated his periodical with Ewart's *Meat in Due Season* and Opperman's *The Blessed Truth* into *The Christian Outlook,* Haywood was tapped as editor, using the new periodical and numerous tracts and pamphlets to promulgate Oneness theology throughout both the white and the African American communities. The publication also helped formulate foundational theological conceptions that are still held by contemporary Oneness churches. As a prolific hymnist, several of his early twentieth century hymns continue to be sung, not only in Oneness circles, but also throughout the African American Holiness-Pentecostal community. One of the most recognizable, "I See a Crimson Stream of Blood," is regularly sung by Pentecostal and other Evangelical congregations. Others, such as "Jesus, the Son of God," "Do All in Jesus' Name," and "Baptized into the Body" are sung by Oneness Pentecostals throughout the world.

When PAW was formally incorporated in 1919, its headquarter moved from Portland, Oregon to St. Louis, Missouri, then Indianapolis and a board of elders was put in place to assist with the growing denomination. While still nearly three-fourths of its membership was white, Haywood was elected to a one-year appointment as general secretary and for the next several years, held positions of ever-increasing authority and influence. He was elected as secretary in 1920, as executive vice chairperson in 1922.

Haywood's popularity and PAW's racial openness continued to attract blacks in such large numbers it changed the complexion of the organization to one where blacks represented the majority, making some whites uncomfortable and heightening underground currents of racial tension. When the 1924 proposal to separate the denomination into black and white branches failed, several whites broke away to form the Pentecostal Ministerial Alliance, while PAW maintained its commitment to racial equality, reorganizing the loose fellowship with congregational polity into an episcopal structure and electing Haywood as presiding bishop.

He served in that post for only five years, from 1925 until 1931. During that time, the denomination continued to grow through a series of amalgamations and mergers that drew those committed to racial unity. He introduced more structure into the organization, creating, for example, a missions department to organize the disparate missions operations into a cohesive unit. During those years, Haywood traveled extensively throughout the United States, Canada, and the Caribbean encouraging pastors and congregations and continuing to promote the Oneness message.

His leadership was challenged during this period, even with the majority of the PAW constituency being black. In the 1930, General Assembly delegates from the powerful Eastern District questioned the financial structure and sought to impose more accountability by creating an associate board of bishops. **Samuel Grimes**, a fellow African American, was elected editor of *The Christian Outlook,* a move that defused some of the Haywood's power. His detractors considered many of his views liberal. He openly supported the ministry of women, for instance, and allowed women to preach from the pulpit of his congregation and encourage them to plant and pastor churches.

At the same time, Haywood drew on his journalistic training to establish a press and use a newspaper, as well as books, tracts, elaborate charts and numerous hymns to elucidate aggressive defend Oneness doctrine. Several full-length works including, "The Finest of the Wheat," and essays including, "The Birth of the Spirit and the Mystery of the Godhead," "Divine Names and Titles of Jehovah," "Victim of the Flaming Sword" appeared under his name, but without dates. Many of these works were translated into several language versions and distributed to African nations, China, Japan, and Russia. He introduced such innovation into his congregation; for example, he used a movie camera to record his trip to the Holy Land, then used those recordings to educate his congregation.

Haywood was among those early Pentecostals who vehemently believed in divine healing and eschewed use of conventional medicine. Yet, he was heir to a hereditary condition, possibly correctable by medical treatment and worsened by his heavy pace, to which he eventually succumbed. At the time of his death at age fifty-one, plans were underway to for a semi-monthly radio broadcast from the sanctuary of Christ Temple on the Columbia Broadcasting System (CBS). By then, Christ Temple Church was the largest congregation in Indianapolis with 1500 members. The racial balance he had been unable to maintain in the **Pentecostal Assemblies of the World** had held within that local congregation, and nearly half its members were white. The church had become among the most prominent congregations in Indianapolis, and Haywood's stature within the city's religious and secular circles had been established. As a testimony to that influence, in 1980, the city of Indianapolis renamed the segment of Fall Creek Drive where Christ Temple is located the "Bishop Garfield T. Haywood Memorial Way."

Further Reading:

Dugas, Paul P., ed. *The Life and Writings of Elder G. T. Haywood.* Stockton, CA: Apostolic, 1968.

Garrett, Gary W. *A Man Ahead of His Time: The Life & Times of Bishop Garfield Thomas Haywood*. Springfield, MO: Apostolic Christian, 2002.

Golder, Morris E. *The History of the Pentecostal Assemblies of the World*. Indianapolis, IN: s.n., 1973.

———. *The Life and Works of Bishop Garfield Thomas Haywood (1880–1931)*. Indianapolis, IN: s.n., 1977.

Hickson, Peter Callahan 1902–1984

The pioneer historian and youth leader in the **Church of God (Colored Work)** was born in South Carolina. When he was ten, Hickson moved to Florida with his family. That year he was converted to Christian faith in the Baptist Church where belonged until he became an adult. Hickson followed his wife into the Holiness movement and received experience of sanctification, then received the Baptism of the Holy Spirit during a Church of God revival.

Hickson was licensed as an evangelist in 1931 and appointed to his first pastorate in Umatilla, Florida. In his early ministry, he served as state superintendent for the Sunday school department, then president of the Young Peoples Endeavor (YPE) for the state, before becoming national president. In latter two positions, he worked to establish youth ministries in black Church of God congregations, encouraged the Church of God Evangel to publish youth resources. He also organized the first nation YPE convention in 1932, the largest youth event of the entire **Church of God (Colored Work)** up to that time. Building on that success, he set out to establish the national youth work on a sound footing, often purchasing and distributing resources at his own expense.

Hickson also sensed a need to preserve the history of the black churches within the denomination since their activities and issues were often excluded from official denominational resources. In 1936 he published the inaugural issue of the Church of God Gospel Herald. Though the periodical was initially published to facilitate youth ministry, it soon developed into the primary voice for black ministries in the Church of God.

In 1947 Hickson was appointed pastor of Jacksonville (Florida) Church of God, and eleven years later installed as Overseer of the Jacksonville District. He served the Jacksonville congregation until 1960. That year, he was appointed to the Daytona Beach Church of God and Overseer of that district.

From his positon as recording secretary for the national assembly of the Colored Work, Hickson was able to serving as the unofficial historian for the Church of God (Colored Work). In 1954 he included a historical survey of the "Church of God (Colored Work)" in the minutes of the 30th General Assembly of the Colored Work. That single work has been critical in preserving the early accomplishment of African Americans within the denomination.

Further Reading:

Roebuck, David G. "Peter C. Hickson: A Pioneer Youth Leader." *Church of God Evangel* (2008) 17.

Higher Ground Always Abounding Assemblies, Inc.

A Oneness Pentecostal denomination organized in 1988 in Columbus, Ohio, by Sherman S. Watkins, an influential Ohio pastor. In 1970 Watkins founded a storefront congregation, Greater Emmanuel Apostolic Church of God in Columbus with eleven members. The church is as one of the largest congregations in Columbus, Ohio, with over three thousand members.

While famed televangelist, **Thomas Dexter (T. D.) Jakes**, has declined to identify himself openly as a classical Oneness Pentecostal, he serves as vice bishop of the denomination, having been mentored and ordained as a minister in the denomination by Watkins who encouraged him to establish his first church in the Charleston, West Virginia area. Jakes contends that HGAAA differs from other Apostolic or Oneness bodies in that it does not hold a rigid definition of the Godhead and does require baptism in Jesus' name.

The association has over two hundred congregations throughout the United States and Canada, and there are mission congregations in the Philippines. Headquarters remain in Columbus.

Highway Christian Church of Christ

Among one of the most theologically conservative African American Oneness Pentecostal bodies, **Highway Christian Church of Christ** was founded in 1929 in Washington DC as a schismatic group of the **Pentecostal Assemblies of the World** by **James Thomas Morris**. It was charted in 1939, and in 1941, PAW bishop Joseph Turpin consecrated Morris as its bishop. In 1955 Raymond F. Davis, who had served in the **Highway Christian Church of Christ** as National Secretary as well as Overseer of the State of South Carolina, resigned his tenure and the birth of the Highway Church of Christ Association, Incorporated. When Morris died in 1959, his nephew, J. V. Lomax, who had left the **Church of our Lord Jesus Christ of the Apostolic Faith** to join his uncle, became presiding bishop.

Lomax's tenure proved to be schismatic and his perceived authoritarian style was contributive to at least two schisms that occurred in the ranks of HCC during his term. In 1976 James Frank Harris and Douglas Williams separated from HCC to establish Redeemed Assembly of Jesus Christ, Apostolic because of their objection to denominational polity allowing the presiding bishop to serve for life. In 1988 Bishop **Robert Evans**, pastor of the Baltimore Maryland congregation resigned to organize the **Bethel Churches of Christ, Inc.**

When Lomax died in 2001, Samuel Redden of Newport News, Virginia replaced him. Redden died in 2006. Herman Girwright is the current presider.

While **Highway Christian Church** does not ordain women as ministers or appoint them as pastors, the organization does ordain women as deaconesses and will accept a woman as pastor who has previously been ordained by another denomination. Further, it encourages members to limit their apparel to black and white and refrain from wearing what it considers ostentatious colors. In 2002 the **Highway Christian Church** had approximately three thousand members in nineteen congregations.

Hill, Edward Victor II 1967–

For more than fifteen years Hill was one of the most prominent blacks in the International Pentecostal Holiness Church and pastor of Calvary Temple Pentecostal Holiness Church in North Hollywood, California. The son of renowned Missionary Baptist pastor and preacher, **Edward Victor (E. V.) Hill Sr.**, was born in 1967 in Los Angeles, California.

The younger Hill received a Bachelor of Arts degree in Communications from the University of Southern California in 1989. He then attended the Whittier School of Law of West Los Angeles, and completed a first year of law school at Pepperdine University School of Law in Malibu, California. After being called to the ministry in 1990, he received his Masters of Divinity from Talbot School of Theology at Biola University in 1995. Hill has been awarded three Honorary Doctorate degrees—in Religious Studies from Los Angeles University, and one each in Divinity from the Golden West Christian University and the St. Thomas Christian College of Jacksonville, Florida.

Though originally ordained in the Missionary Baptist Church in 1996; a year later he was ordained in the International Pentecostal Holiness Church and called to pastor Calvary Temple Pentecostal Holiness Church in the affluent, West Hollywood section of Los Angeles, California. Under his leadership, Calvary Temple mothered six other churches: Iglesia Peniel-North Hollywood and Los Angeles; The Faith, Hope & Love Church of Glendale; Spirit & Life World Ministries Church in Phoenix, Arizona; Calvary Temple Romanian Church-North Hollywood; and most recently The House of Deliverance PH Church of Lancaster.

In 2004 after his prominent father's death, Hill was elected pastor of the Mount Zion Missionary Baptist Church congregation in the black working class section of Los Angeles where the elder Hill had served for forty-two years. At the same time, he remained pastor of his PHC congregation.

While affiliated with the IPHC, Hill held a series of progressively important positions. He was the first African American to serve on the denomination's Conference Board, serving on the Golden West Conference for twelve years. He served on the Bishop's Council, the General Board of Administrators, and as a member of the Evangelism USA Board.

In 2012 Hill resigned from the IPHC. The next year, he founded Spirit of Zion Fellowship Church, a non-denominational, spirit-filled, multi-cultural congregation in the San Fernando Valley, as a satellite ministry of the Mt. Zion Missionary Baptist Church.

Hilliard, Ira Van 1952–

The Prominent **Word of Faith** pastor and televangelist is a native Houston Texan and founding president of the Association of Independent Ministries (AIM). He sensed a call to the ministry as a child and preached his first sermon at the age of ten. Hilliard received a Bachelor of Arts in Biblical Studies, a Master of Divinity, an Honorary Doctorate in Humane Letters, and Doctor of Philosophy degrees all from Friends International Christian University.

Four years before establishing New Light Christian Center Church in 1984, Hilliard was pastoring New Light Missionary Baptist Church. That year Hilliard founded his congregation with approximately twenty-three members. He changed his ministry style from the typical African-American call-and-response preaching to the teaching style more prominent in predominantly white Charismatic and Word of Faith circles. He also intentionally chose not to align with any existing denomination, but to stay nondenominational. Since then, that congregation has grown to over 28,000, increasing at a rate of 400 to 500 monthly, spans six campuses, and includes a worldwide television broadcast that is aired to millions. His AIM fellowship, which serves as a spiritual covering for independent churches and ministers, mentors pastors and other leaders from one thousand plus churches nationwide.

Hilliard and his wife Bridgett serve as co-pastors of New Light. Their annual salary is based on the weekly offering from the church, which is reportedly in the multimillions. The couple owns a large mansion in Spring, TX, Rolls Royces, Bentleys, private jets, and helicopters. They sport such conspicuous wealth as full-length mink coats and large custom made diamonds rings.

The prolific writer has authored several works, which along with dealing with principles of prosperity, also deal with several areas of leadership. Formerly, Hilliard served on the board of Oral Roberts University, but resigned after the scandal with Roberts's son, Richard, regarding overspending and mismanagement of funds.

Holly, John Silas 1901–1979

An early leader in the **Pentecostal Assemblies of the World**, who, at the age of twenty-one, was the youngest person ordained in the Oneness Pentecostal denomination up to that time. Born in Monroe, Louisiana, by 1910 Holly's family had moved to Arkansas where he came to Christian faith at the age of eighteen under the ministry of **Alexander R. Schooler,** one of the **PAW's** first five bishops. Largely self-taught, Holly's extensive study of the Scripture led to his being considered by many one of the most profound Bible scholars in the PAW history.

The itinerant preacher traveled and evangelized throughout the Midwest until around 1919, when founding bishop **Garfield Haywood** began to mentor Holly until his own death in 1931. Around 1930, when Schooler left the pastorate at Apostolic Faith Church in Chicago, Haywood appointed Holly to fill the vacancy, a position he held for forty-eight years.

In 1931 Holly joined the majority of pastors in PAW in the ill-fated merger with the Apostolic Churches of Jesus Christ that created the **Pentecostal Assemblies of Jesus Christ**. Like most of the black leaders, Holly returned to the PAW by 1938.

Holly was elevated to the office of bishop in 1953 and presided over the Eight Episcopal District of Illinois for twenty-six years. In 1957 Holly was consecrated by the original five bishops, led by **Smallwood E. Williams** of new the **Bibleway Church of Our Lord Jesus Christ** in Washington DC—a group that had broken away from the Church of Our Lord Jesus Christ to the Apostolic Faith.

When Holly died in Chicago at age of seventy-nine, he had been a member of the **Pentecostal Assemblies of the World** almost from its inception, sixty-six years.

Further Reading:

Golder, Morris. *Bishops of the Pentecostal Assemblies of the World*. Indianapolis, IN: s.n., 1980.

Holt, William B. 1880–??

Early white **Church of God in Christ** leader and close colleague of COGIC founder, **Charles Harrison Mason**. Holt was born in Fort Worth, Texas and came to California in 1901 where he enrolled in Baptist College in Redlands. By 1903 he was involved with the Pentecostal Church of the Nazarene, a Holiness group. Holt, who had served as a deputy sheriff during this period, was a lawyer and former minister in the denomination before joining with COGIC. In 1908 he enrolled in the Nazarene Bible College and after graduating, joined the **Church of God in Christ**.

The blond-haired German COGIC pastor served as the National Field Secretary before becoming COGIC's first General Secretary from 1910 through 1920. That position placed him as a trusted confidant of Mason, regularly with the COGIC leader as his aide and secretary. He also served as superintendent of COGIC Spanish missions in California and in 1917, called upon his legal background to draft the denomination's rules for government.

The close friendship between Mason and Holt, described as like blood brothers, drew suspicion of both men from the Federal Bureau of Investigation. That organization monitored them during World War I, believing that Mason might incite blacks to align with Germany and Holt might be a German infiltrator. When federal agents arrested Mason and threw him into a Lexington, Mississippi, jail for violating the Sedition Act, Holt raised his bond. After his release, Mason continued to fellowship with whites, while all the time, condemning segregation. On a second arrest, involving both Mason and Holt, the two were jailed, but initially only Mason was released. Holt was initially held on a charge of "conspiring to commit offenses against the government" on a five thousand dollar bond. However, he subsequently was allowed to plead guilty to a charge of vagrancy, fined one dollar, and released.

In 1916 the few white churches that had joined or remained with COGIC were organized into a white branch with Holt as General Superintendent. Holt publicly went against Southern race protocol by openly embracing black fellow worshippers. Though he had repeatedly demonstrated his loyalty to both Mason and COGIC and his racial openness by eating and lodging with black members of the denomination, by 1933 Holt accused COGIC's majority black leadership of racial discrimination. In return they dismissed him from the fellowship, setting off debate about whether whites and blacks could practically work and worship together. With his departure, the COGIC experiment in interracial unity effectively ended.

Further Reading:

Maxwell, Joe. "Building Up the Church of God in Christ." *Christianity Today* (1996) 28.

Hopkins, Ellen Moore 1921–2000

A repatriated missionary in her homeland of Liberia who had a major impact on Pentecostal missions in that country. Hopkins was born in Talla, Liberia, West Africa, to Congolese parents. As a twelve year old, Moore came to America as the adopted daughter of **Samuel Grimes**, the second presiding bishop of the **Pentecostal Assemblies of the World**, and his wife, **Katherine Grimes** who had served as a missionary team in West Africa. She wrote Bishop Grimes requesting help with her education after finding a copy of *The Christian Outlook* lying along a road in her country. The Grimes helped facilitate her education in the United States by providing the resources for Moore to pursue her education. She graduated, first, from Lincoln School of Nursing as a registered nurse. She continued her education at Maternity Center in New York and became a licensed midwife. She studied obstetric management at Margaret Hauge School of Nursing and Pediatrics in Chicago, Illinois. Upon returning to Virginia she received a Bachelor of Science in Public Health Nursing Education from Medical College of Virginia, a Masters Degree at American University, and a Doctor of Divinity degree from **Aenon Bible College**.

After completing her education, Hopkins, a licensed midwife, returned to Liberia to establish an educational program for students from primary school through junior college. In 1946 she established the Samuel K. Grimes Child Welfare Center in Kakata in a renovated warehouse. That work gradually developed into an organized Christian community of fourteen buildings including schools, a thousand-seat church, a maternity hospital, two medical clinics, three dormitories, and two cafeterias. In thirty-three years of service in Liberia, Hopkins cared for seven hundred orphaned and indigent children, delivered approximately five thousand babies and trained 136 nurses who served all over that country.

Hopkins launched an aggressive health education effort aimed at reducing disease by teaching mothers to care for their children's health needs and youth to care for their own needs. Her extensive work gained recognition in both Liberia and United States. In the United States, both the white and black media took note of her work. She was featured in such diverse publications as the *Saturday Evening Post* and in *Ebony Magazine* and was listed in *Who's Who of American Women*. In her homeland, Hopkins was awarded the Tubman Liberian National Award. Like so many others however, Hopkins was forced to flee during the Liberian civil war. She returned to the United States and continued to minister and publish work that encouraged women's physical and spiritual health. She died in Zanesville, Ohio.

Horn, Rosa Artemis 1880–1976

One of the most controversial black Pentecostal women leaders during the first half of the twentieth century. Born in Sumter, South Carolina to the granddaughter of a slave, Horn was one of ten children. She received a private school education, and after graduating, she worked as a dressmaker in Augusta, Georgia. By the early 1920s, her first husband had died. Horn, who had joined the Methodist Church, moved to Evanston, Illinois where she sat under the ministry of famed evangelist and faith healer, Maria Woodworth Etter, who ordained her into the ministry.

After marrying William Horn, she moved first to Evanston, Indiana, then to Brooklyn, New York, where she was unhappy with the coldness of larger congregations. In 1926 out of empathy with others who had been pulled away from their social and spiritual moorings, she established a storefront congregation, Mt. Calvary Pentecostal Faith Church, that was noted for its extensive prayer ministry. Horn became known within the community as the "pray for me priestess."

By 1933 her congregation and personal popularity had grown so much that Horn was invited to begin a radio broadcast on station WHN, making Mt. Calvary the first church in Upper Manhattan wired for broadcasting. The station launched an aggressive advertising campaign promoting a rivalry between Horn and famed Holiness preacher, **Lightfoot Solomon Micheaux.** The often controversial broadcast remained on the air thirty years, and by 1936 was already reaching numerous cities along the East Coast. After Micheaux's death, Horn became embroiled in a second battle when the station filed a lawsuit against charismatic religious leader, **Father Divine**, for trying to intimidate Horn and run her church and broadcast out of Harlem. The publicity from these squabbles quadrupled the station's audience. Still, Horn's aggressive tactics led her to have open confrontations with owners of cabarets, pool rooms, dance halls, and other such enterprises. At times, she engaged the court system in trying to extricate the "dens of iniquity" out of her Harlem neighborhood.

By 1934 Horn's church had branches in five cities along the East Coast. In 1959 she moved to Baltimore where she remained until her death at age ninety-five. In her years of ministry, the most famous member of Horn's congregation was author, **James Baldwin**, who belonged to the church as a teenager, served as a minister for several years, and used the congregation as a model for some of his writings. His play *The Amen Corner* featured Pastor Margaret, a main character inspired by Horn. His autobiographical novel *Go Tell It on the Mountain* depicts Pentecostal worship that would have been so much a part of Horn's congregation.

House of God International

A Sabbath-keeping Oneness Pentecostal denomination established in 1914 in Beauford, South Carolina by Bishop **Rufus Abraham Reid (R. A. R.) Johnson** as the House of God, the Holy Church of the Living God, the Pillar and the Ground of the Truth, the House of Prayer for All People. Its name was later shortened to the present designation. The body, which holds to the necessity of keeping Old Testament law—observing the Sabbath and Jewish feast days and abstaining from certain foods—was incorporated in 1918 in Washington DC.

At the death of Bishop Johnson in 1940, the church had achieved a creditable level of stability. Bishop Johnson was succeeded by Bishop A. A. Smith, who would eventually be established as the first chief apostle of the House of God. New York City became the church's national headquarters under Bishop Smith's administration. Smith's untimely death resulted in a wave of dissension within the church and ultimately a division of church leadership. In 1950 Bishop **Simon Peter (S. P.) Rawlings** of Lexington, Kentucky became the official chief apostle of the House of God. Bishop M. Baker of Jacksonville, Florida left the denomination. After Rawlings's death, Bishop F. C. Scott of Lockland, Ohio served as chief apostle until his death in 2005. Bishop James Embry currently holds that position.

The church did not identify as Hebrew Pentecostal until 1977 when Rawlings reportedly fathered the term as a religious identification. As a Oneness body, The House of God baptizes "in the Name of Jesus Christ" and teaches that Jesus is God incarnated in flesh and manifested in various forms at various times.

The House of God's national temple is located in Lexington. The body has 118 congregations throughout the United States, three in Canada, twenty-six in Jamaica, and one in Australia, as well as congregations in the countries of Botswana, Ghana, Kenya, Malawi, Mozambique, South Africa, Tanzania, Zambia, and Zimbabwe.

House of God, the Church of the Living God, Pillar and Ground of the Truth, Inc.

One of the several groups to break from **Mary Magdalena Tate**'s original organization, the **Church of the Living God, Pillar and Ground of the Truth.** The denomination was founded by **Bishop Archibald White.**

Tate appointed White to Philadelphia, Pennsylvania where he began to pastor a storefront church of approximately twenty people. In a subsequent General Assembly, he was elected senior bishop of all churches connected with the Pennsylvania Group. In 1916 White led his growing Philadelphia constituency into establishing the new organization. This schism, in particular, was partly over the issue of women's leadership. Archibald White—like **Charles Harrison Mason** of the **Church of God in Christ**, who had been initially ordained in the Baptist Church—held a conservative position regarding women's leadership and did not approve of women as bishops. After setting up several congregations throughout the South for Tate's group, White—who had been consecrated as a bishop—separated himself from that organization.

In 1948 the Church of the Living God purchased a "Headquarter" building and sanctuary in West Philadelphia, better known as the "National Temple." In the early 1960s, the denomination purchased a property in Orlando, Florida that houses a building with a seating capacity of 1500 or more and now serves as the National Tabernacle. Along with Pennsylvania and Florida, there are congregations in New Jersey, Delaware, Ohio, Massachusetts, Rhode Island, Connecticut, Georgia, Mississippi, Illinois, Michigan, New York, the West Indies, and Africa. In addition, the denomination supports the Church of the Living God Publishing House, a Convalescent Home, White's Theological Bible School and Business Institute, and a radio broadcast.

White remained the senior bishop until his demise on January 25, 1981 when Bishop James H. Smith was unanimously elected to be the next senior bishop and president general, serving until 1996. He was succeeded by Jesse J. White Sr., who served until 2008. The current President General is Theodore Brown.

Despite White's early rejection of women's leadership, women currently serve at every level of authority including the bishopric and serve on the executive as well as the general boards of bishops. To date, however, a woman has not been elected to serve as presider of the denomination, which informally designates itself, "The White Dominion."

House of God which is the Church of the Living God Pillar and Ground of the Truth without Controversy, Inc. (Keith Dominion)

The largest of the three divisions that inherited the legacy of the **Church of the Living God, The Pillar and Ground of Truth** following the death of its founder, **Mary Magdalena Lewis Tate** in 1931. **Mary Frankie Lewis Keith**, Tate's widowed daughter-in-law, became one of three members of the Supreme Executive Council designated before the founder's death to succeed her and govern specific regions of the country. When, after a short time, the agreement failed and the denomination split, the parent body was partitioned into three independent, self-governing dominions.

Keith became presiding bishop of The House of God which is the **Church of the Living God Pillar and Ground of the Truth without Controversy, Inc.**, the dominion that later contended that its name was the original name chosen by Tate. It suggested that other factions obliterated any records that bear witness to that fact. By 1937 the body reported 300 churches with 5,000 members and was simply being identified as the House of God Church (Keith Dominion).

Keith led the organization for thirty-one years, until her death in 1962 when the church was still reporting 300 churches with 5,000 members. Under her leadership, the organization established the Saints Home for Girls and the House of God Home for Children in East Chattanooga, Tennessee. Keith Bible Institute near Ooltewah, Tennessee offered both kindergarten through sixth grade classes and provided food, clothing, and housing to children of poor families. Following sixth grade graduation, students were enrolled in religious studies courses for young ministers.

Though there has been decline in the number of congregations, the group still claims more than two hundred congregations throughout the United States and Jamaica, and Missions work in Haiti. More than half of the US congregations are in three states: Florida, Georgia, and South Carolina. The rest are clustered primarily in the South and along the East Coast. Headquarters for the denomination is in Nashville, Tennessee.

There are no mothers in the church as is usually true within most congregations within the African American Pentecostal tradition. That honor is reserved only for Tate. Women, however, serve alongside men at all levels of ministry and Bishop Rebecca W. Fletcher is the current chief overseer.

The Keith Dominion is most noted for introducing and popularizing the "sacred steel guitar" music used within its worship to a broader audience. Though the tradition was introduced within the Jewell Dominion, that body primarily retains its use within worship. Keith Dominion musicians were more open to crossing over into secular venues and gained a significant following within that market.

House of the Lord and Church on the Mount Pentecostal Church

A denomination that sprang from a schism within Bishop **Emmanuel "Sweet Daddy" Grace**'s denomination, the **United House of Prayer for All People,** a quasi-Holiness group contemporary classical Pentecostals would denounce as a heretical cult. Though the group was founded as a body within the Holiness movement, Grace maintained most Holiness piety, and his followers began to exalt him as being equal with Christ.

Among those who pulled away from him and found a home in another sanctified setting was Bishop **Alonzo Austin Daughtry**. In 1927 Daughtry traveled to Augusta, Georgia to establish a congregation and spread Grace's message, but soon became disillusioned with Grace's new posture, and attempted to temper what he saw as undue praise some followers were giving Grace. That move lead to a showdown with Grace and Daughtry, and he was forced to leave Grace's movement. Some, however, joined Daughtry to form a new church, which would become the House of the Lord.

Soon Daughtry's small group was joined by a several churches in Georgia and South Carolina. In 1942 branches were founded in Harlem and Brooklyn, New York, accompanied with the opening of church stores to ensure its profitability, among these a candy store and land-buying initiatives. For the next ten years, the church grew in its new northern urban environment, adding converts and working to ensure the good of its parishioners' lives.

Although not classically Trinitarian, the House of the Lord deviates from strict Oneness Pentecostal teaching in that the denomination allows baptism in either the Oneness or Trinitarian formula according to the dictates of the conscience of the person. Its understanding of the Godhead also differs from that of either classical Trinitarian or

Oneness Pentecostals in that the denomination see Jesus Christ and God the Father as one in divine substance and in attributes—making their names interchangeable. They are one in purpose and goals, but serve as separate beings.

The most distinguishing aspect of the House of the Lord is the level of its social engagement. From the beginning, Daughtry took pains to ensure the economic well-being of his congregants, purchasing burial plots and opening stores to ensure the solvency of his creation. He unsuccessfully stood up to local insurers, who battled him for control over selling burial plots. Although he lost the case, his battle ensured the further popularity of his church. Further, he pushed a progressive social agenda. His congregations were interracial, even in the heart of the South. Within his congregations, he promoted economic development programs that challenged his constituents to be concerned about the social welfare of their communities as well as the spiritual welfare of themselves and their families.

When Daughtry fell into ill health in 1952, he turned the reins of the leadership to **Inez Conry**. A few years before his death, Daughtry ordained her an elder, and Conry served as presiding minister of the House of the Lord for eight years without ever taking the title bishop. Her major contribution was to keep the organization stable until Daughtry's son, Herbert, could take over the reins.

Herbert Daughtry, who had been converted to Pentecostalism while in prison, was ordained and installed as the pastor of the Brooklyn Church. Within a year, he rose to be the church's third national presiding minister, in fulfillment of his father's prophecy. Throughout his leadership, the younger Daughtry has extended the national prominence of the House of the Lord Pentecostal Church by involving his local congregation and the denomination in major local and national social issues.

There are congregations in New York, Washington DC, Ohio, Pennsylvania, New Jersey, and Georgia.

Howard, W. O.

The founding bishop of the Oneness Pentecostal denomination, **Original Glorious Church of God in Christ of the Apostolic Faith**. Prior to 1952, Howard had been a leader in the **Glorious Church of God in Christ** under the leadership of presiding bishop **Sidney Coy Bass**. When Bass defied church doctrine in his decision to marry a divorced woman, Howard—with support from several other GCOGIC bishops including Perry Lindsay, James Smith, David Blount and **I.W. Hamiter**—took possession of the group's charter and led half of the denomination's adherents (twenty-five congregations) into the reorganized body.

During Howard's tenure at its head, fifteen congregations were added to the denomination. Howard led the group until 1972, when he retired because of poor health.

Howell, James Richard 1820–??

The founding bishop of the **Reformed Zion Union Church**. Initially, the former African Methodist Episcopal Church itinerant preacher and abolitionist failed to secure an African Methodist Episcopal Church pastorate because he lacked the requisite education. At the same time, he was dissatisfied with what he felt was the growing "ecclesiasticism" of black churches. In 1864 Howell organized a group of Episcopal, Methodist, and Baptist former slaves into the **Union Zion Apostolic Church** as the first black Holiness body in the United States.

That year, the Philadelphia native was sent by the AMEC to the Tidewater area of Virginia to evangelize newly-freed blacks. Working as a carpenter by day, he preached on Sundays and in the evenings. When his efforts bore little fruit in that area, he relocated 150 miles east to Boydton, Virginia and began traveling throughout the state and neighboring North Carolina, evangelizing and looking for a place to establish his ministry.

Despite his lack of education, his persuasive and charismatic delivery drew lay leaders from several Episcopal, Methodist, and Baptist congregations of former slave owners into what he called Zion societies, relating the term to the biblical portrayal of Zion as "the dwelling place of God among men." He drafted a plan of union in 1866, closely followed the discipline of the AME Church, and by 1869, Howell had organized eight established societies into the Zion Union Apostolic Church. That October Howell was elected to a four-year term as president of the Zion Union Apostolic Church of America.

Howell's heavy-handed leadership—including changing the tenure of his position to a life term—eventually caused the dissolution of the new body and by 1874 he had resigned as its leader. When the church re-organized under the present name in the early 1880s, Howell returned to the organization. While the life term for presiding bishop was rescinded and a four-year term was reinstated, he was again elected to head the denomination. Again, his tenure was short lived. Within a year, Howell stepped down because of friction between him and several factions, severing all communication with the group and leaving virtually no information regarding the rest of his life.

Further Reading:

General Education Board of the Reformed Zion Union Apostolic Churches of America. *History of the Reformed Zion Union Apostolic Churches of America.* Brunswick, VA: Brunswick, 1997.

Hunter Lenist J. 1914–1991

The founding and first presiding bishop of the Oneness Pentecostal denomination, the **Church in the Lord Jesus Christ of the Apostolic Faith**, a breakaway group from Sherrod Johnson's parent body, **The Church of the Lord Jesus Christ of the Apostolic Faith.**

Hunter was born in Darlington, South Carolina and was called to the ministry at age twenty-six. Sometime between the late 1930s and early 1940s, he migrated to Philadelphia, Pennsylvania where he preached his first sermon in 1943 with Johnson's congregation.

After about three years, Johnson requested that Hunter return to South Carolina to establish the founder's denomination there. Once back in the South, Hunter began gathering a small group for a congregation. He preached his first sermon four days later, and within a short period had gathered enough of a following to establish a congregation. He located a building to house that ministry; within a few months, however, the property owner forced the congregation to vacate the building. Hunter continued his ministry under a tent for about a year until another building was secured.

Within a short period, Hunter's ministry spread throughout the South, and more congregations were added. Hunter began a radio broadcast in 1956, and established the Faith Radio Network. He eventually separated his work from that of Johnson, though no reason is given for the break and no major schism appears to have occurred. After the separation, Hunter led his organization until his death at age seventy-seven.

Hutchins, Julia C. 1873-??

Julia Hutchins initially was instrumental in bringing **William Seymour** to Los Angeles—the site of the Azusa Revival—and would later become involved in the revival, taking the Pentecostal message from Los Angeles to West Africa.

Hutchins was born in Georgia in 1873. She and her husband Willis were married in 1892 and lived in the Atlanta area before moving to Los Angeles. Hutchins was saved in July 1901, and almost immediately sensed a missionary call to go to Africa. Two years later, she experienced sanctification and a renewed missionary call. By 1905 she was a respected member of Second Baptist Church, the first African American Baptist church and the second black congregation in Los Angeles. Presumably, the itinerant evangelist upheld a baptistic understanding of salvation and Christian piety. In that year, however, she was converted to the doctrine of sanctification as a second work of grace.

This deviation from traditional Baptist doctrine alienated her and many members of the congregation. When Hutchins would not desist teaching the new understanding, she and eight sympathetic African American families were disfellowshiped. For a time the group associated with William Manley's predominantly white Household of Faith Mission. They then moved first to a tent, then to a private home in downtown Los Angeles, before finally moving to a small building. With Hutchins as pastor, those won to Christ by the group included **Jennie Evans Moore**, who was to later marry **William Joseph Seymour** and play a pivotal role in the Azusa Street Mission's ministry and leadership.

It was Hutchins's congregation that invited Seymour to Los Angeles. However, the invitation was short-lived since Hutchins's early understanding of Holy Spirit baptism differed markedly from Seymour's, especially regarding the necessity for the initial evidence of speaking in tongues. Like many contemporary Holiness proponents, she held that proof of such baptism was an inner witness and a piety of life rather than any outward visible manifestation. Hutchins and other members of her congregation who felt that they had already received the baptism of the Holy Spirit with sanctification rejected Seymour's contention that Holy Spirit baptism should be accompanied by glossolalia. She took a further step, however, to settle the issue by arranging a meeting between Seymour and local Holiness leaders including, T. M. Roberts, president of the Southern California Holiness Association. They were not convinced by Seymour's position and forbade him to teach within the Holiness movement. Between the time Seymour was locked out of Hutchins's church and the full swing of the **Azusa Street Revival**, Hutchins became a wholehearted supporter of Seymour and a convert to his understanding of tongues as initial evidence. Following that change of mind and heart, she was a regular participant in the **Azusa Street Revival**. She sought and received the experience herself, and took the Pentecostal message from Azusa Street to Africa. It is not known how long Hutchins stayed at Azusa Street or what role she played there. Hutchins's husband was considered a backslider, but was probably restored to Christian faith during the revival.

Reportedly, Hutchins received the gift of **xenolalia** with fluency in the Ugandan language during the revival. For her, this endowment confirmed her call to Africa. During the fall of 1906, she and Willis, along with her young niece, Leila McKinney, accompanied **Lucy Farrow** as missionaries to Liberia. On their way, the group stopped and held revival services in several cities including Chattanooga, Tennessee, and New York. Throughout the trip, Hutchins kept a journal in which she wrote her testimony of her salvation, sanctification, and Holy Spirit baptism. She sent it back to the group at Azusa Street, where excerpts from it were published in *The Apostolic Faith* newsletter.

Further Reading:

Alexander, Estrelda. "Juilia Hutchins." In *The Women of Azusa Street*. Laurel, MD: Seymour Press, 2012.

I

Intercollegiate Pentecostal Conference International (IPCI)

The first African American Pentecostal student association on the campus of a private non-religious institution of higher education in the United States. The organization was founded in 1965 by James O. Lewis, Leon Wright, and **Monroe R. Saunders Sr.** as the United Pentecostal Association of Howard University in Washington DC. Its initial purpose was to unite the Pentecostal students on Howard University campus and to promote spiritual awareness among the school's student body. The name was changed in 1974, to not to confuse the group with an exclusively Oneness Pentecostal tradition as reflected in the name United Pentecostal Church International. The organization promoted ecumenism among students by representing the various Pentecostal groups within the Howard University community, and has been open to participation from students representing both Oneness and Trinitarian factions.

In 1969 IPCI became a national campus ministry and in the following year, the group held its first conference on Howard's campus which drew an interracial attendance of 4,000 representing Pentecostal and Charismatic participants from twenty-six states. In 1975 the IPCI was incorporated as a national Pentecostal research center to serve as a training agency for Pentecostal campus ministers. It also promoted unity between Pentecostalism's other groups within the Christian tradition. Headquartered in the William J. Seymour House, a facility the organization acquired in the early 1970s just outside of Howard's campus, the IPCI has been active on more than thirty-five campuses throughout the United States.

One of the early leaders of the organization was Steven Short, a former storefront pastor who initially volunteer to serve as advisor to the group. Following the success of the 1970 conference, however, the university officially appointed Short as chaplain of the group.

Further Reading:

Sanders, Cheryl J. *Saints in Exiled: The Holiness-Pentecostal Experience in African American Religion and Culture.* New York: Oxford University Press, 1996.
Short, Steven. "Pentecostal College Movement at Howard: 1946–1977." *Spirit: The Journal Incident to Black Pentecostalism.*

International Bible Way Church of Jesus Christ, Inc.

During the lifetime of founder **Smallwood E. Williams,** no major schism occurred in the Bible Way. After the death of Williams, organization leaders signed The Order of Succession and Constitution, providing that prominent bishop **Lawrence Campbell** and **Huie Rogers** would each serve a three-year trial term as presiding bishop before the vote for the Williams's permanent successor was taken. Campbell held the office from 1991 to 1994. When Rogers's three-year term ended, he called for a Sabbath year of no voting. When the majority of bishops refused to accept the resolution, the denomination split. Both factions, however, continued to represent themselves as the original church.

Most of the bishops, pastors, and churches stayed with Campbell, and this branch—**Bible Way Church of our Lord Jesus Christ**, Incorporated—remains the largest entity of the two with approximately one thousand churches worldwide as of 2012. While the two organizations are similar in structure and doctrine, Campbell began to make progressive changes to **Bible Way Church of our Lord Jesus Christ**, including ordaining women to the office of elder.

When Campbell retired in 2006, **Cornelius Showell** pastor of the 4,000-member First Apostolic Church in Baltimore, Maryland was elected to preside, and the headquarters were move to his home congregation. That year Showell began the practice of ordaining women to the office of elder and appointed Pastor Bonnie Hunter as the first woman district elder.

He also renamed the denomination from **Bible Way Church of Our Lord Jesus Christ** to International Bible Way Church of Jesus Christ, Inc.

International Fellowship of Black Pentecostal Churches

An organization that is variously called the World Fellowship of Black Pentecostal Churches. It was founded in Memphis, Tennessee in 1984 by Bishop **Amy Stevens** along with Bishop James F. Brown Jr. of the **Mt. Sinai Holy Church of America**, Bishop **James O. Patterson, Sr.** of the **Church of God in Christ**, Bishop **Joseph T. Bowen** (President of the **United Holy Church of America**, Inc.) and **Bishop J. Delano Ellis** of the **Pentecostal Church of Christ**. Ten Pentecostal denominations were represented at the first meeting held in March of that year.

Patterson served as founding president, and Bowen succeeded him in 1990. Ellis served both Patterson and Bowen as executive secretary. The organization, headquartered in Portsmouth, Virginia, was initially called the Conference of Bishops and Leaders of Black Holiness Pentecostal Churches in the United States. Its stated purpose is to preserve the history and structure of Black Holiness-Pentecostal Churches and promote education among its members. It was open to all "well-established" Black Pentecostal denominations with at least ten congregations, without regard to the customary schism between Trinitarian and Oneness traditions that was so prominent within white Pentecostal organizations.

Along with the founding denominations, members include Greater Emmanuel Apostolic Church, **Mt. Calvary Holy Churches of America**, Bibleway Pentecostal Apostolic Church, **Church of God in Christ International**, and Way of the Cross Church of Christ.

In the 1980s, several substantive proposals were proffered, such as establishing a publishing house and creating a satellite network, but these did not come to fruition. After the death of the major founding leaders including Patterson, Bowens, Stevens, and Brown, the group has lost much of its significance and influence.

I

International Church of the Foursquare Gospel, Race Relations

The only majority white, classical Pentecostal denomination in which thoroughly integrated congregations are more than minimal. Yet, possibly because blacks are so well integrated into the denomination's congregations, black Foursquare members may be the least visible community of African American Pentecostal believers. The Los Angeles based denomination was established by renowned evangelist Aimee Semple McPherson, whose flamboyant style openly defied many early Pentecostal and societal mores. Not the least of these was her refusal to uphold racial conventions that had solidly re-emerged within the Pentecostal movement by the time she established her church.

McPherson ignored even legal race restrictions, openly allowing people of all races to attend her meetings across the country, even when preaching in the South. Where law or custom made this impossible, McPherson held separate meetings—one for whites and one for blacks. Several blacks served in leadership roles in these meetings, working in the music ministry, as prayer counselors or altar workers. The worship of Angelus Temple, the megachurch congregation she led from the 1920s, regularly featured singing of Negro spirituals and McPherson encouraged the forming of quartets to perform that music. Moreover, McPherson's regard for prolific African-American hymn writer, **Thoro Harris**, led her to work with him to compose at least two hymnals for the congregation.

Three months after building Angelus Temple, McPherson opened the Lighthouse Institute for Foursquare Evangelism (L.I.F.E.) Bible College. Immediately, blacks were admitted and black Angelus Temple members were encouraged to attend. There were four black students in the first class, with thirty-six blacks graduating from the college in the 1920s and 1930s. Most of these found places to minister at Angelus Temple, while others established congregations outside of the Foursquare movement, because unlike their white classmates, the earliest black graduates of the college did not receive Foursquare pastoral appointments–this did not occur until 1942. It was not for another twenty-five years, in 1967, that the first black man, Old Testament professor **Paul Hackett**, joined the faculty—though even this late date made him the first African American appointed to the faculty of a predominantly white Pentecostal academic institution.

McPherson also associated with Christian leaders of all varieties, including African-Americans pastors, **Emma and Henry Cotton**, whom she highly esteemed and on several occasions allowed them to share one of the most visible pulpits in the Pentecostal movement. In 1936 the Cottons spearheaded a six-month long 30th Azusa Street Anniversary Celebration at Angelus Temple that boosted McPherson's then declining congregation and helped bring it back into prominence. During that time, the Cottons joined other notable Pentecostal speakers to minister daily in multiracial worship services reminiscent of old Azusa Street meetings that drew thousands to experience preaching, prayer, shouting, dancing in the spirit, and divine healing. McPherson credited these meetings with being the launching pad that attracted renewed worldwide attention to the Pentecostal movement.

Despite her seeming progressiveness, McPherson's racial politics were puzzling. While she was open to active participation of blacks in the Foursquare Church, she maintained a long-standing relationship with the white supremacist Ku Klux Klan, accepting their money and preaching in secluded meetings. Reportedly, McPherson's Klan association did not stem from common race notions since on several occasions, she openly challenged their racist beliefs and secretiveness. What she held in common with the Klan was a fundamentalist interpretation of religion and morality that supported prohibition, stood against socialism and communism, and stood for "old-fashioned" ideals.

Following McPherson's death, the racial openness in the Foursquare church somewhat abated and leaders were less receptive to full inclusion of the African American constituency. Blacks felt less welcomed in local congregations as well as regional and national denominational meetings. Though no separate black enclave was formed, a single designation "Zion" was added as a code word to the names of all black churches. Further, district superintendents often showed a degree of racial insensitivity when dealing with black congregations, creating a climate of distrust and aggravation for their pastors.

While Foursquare leaders publicly asserted a desire to increase minority participation in missions, going as far as placing an ad in *The Foursquare Advance* and asking blacks to apply to go to the mission field, they found reasons to restrict blacks from missions appointments. When Marie Johnson applied for a missionary appointment to Brazil in the 1940s, for example, her application was denied due to "concern for the health of an African American to deal with the climate differences of foreign countries." She was later to make the trip on her own.

Still, a small number of black Foursquare congregations began to form, and a small number of black individuals and families joined predominantly white Foursquare congregations. In either case, a critical mass of blacks was never formed, but neither did blacks formally break with the denomination, as they did with the **Fire Baptized Holiness Church**, or set up a separate enclave, as did those in the **Church of God (Cleveland, TN)**. Yet, as hostile treatment from leaders continued, members of black Foursquare congregations simply refused to participate in denominational events, choosing rather to attend meetings with black denominations. When black women, for example, felt ostracized at their own women's conferences, they decided to attend those given by the **Church of God in Christ**.

As of 2002, seventy-two of 1,900 US Foursquare congregations have black pastors. The majority of these, like most Foursquare congregations are located along the West Coast in areas that have historically had smaller concentrations of blacks. In recent years, however, Foursquare leaders have made overtures to increase African American representation at all levels of the church. In 2004 they established a Department of Urban and Multicultural Ministries to "assist and support urban leaders serving serve minority congregations" by focusing on church planting and outreach. **Arthur Gray**, an African American who had been appointed two years earlier to the highly visible position as corporate secretary and was to later serve as vice president, was tapped as executive director.

International Women's Department of the Church of God in Christ

The women's auxiliary within the largest black Pentecostal denomination in the United States that was conceived by founder, **Charles Harrison Mason** as a vehicle for support the dual, gendered leadership structure of the denomination that generally does not license or ordain women to pastoral ministry. In the early years of COGIC, Mason conceived of a loose cluster of local prayer and Bible bands, whose structure would mirror the hierarchical system in place for men and in which women could take increasingly important, yet circumscribed, places of service. Within this system, individual women fill significant roles in the local, regional, and national churches that develop the specific attitudes and skills the denomination values, and women gain an increasing degree of visibility and prominence. The structure affords specially-gifted women opportunities to rise to national prominence and exert a level of authority and influence that, at times, rivals or even surpasses that given to some men.

At the head of this system is the office of the International Supervisor, the denomination's highest ranking position for women. The office holder appoints supervisors in each state and oversees the work of women at every level, ensuring that the denomination has a cadre of women organized into various auxiliaries that support local congregations, regional jurisdictions, and the national church. At each level, women are given a degree of recognition that positions them for more responsibility, providing highly qualified women opportunities to attain levels of leaderships not available if they were competing with male colleagues.

Without having full autonomy, these women operate under men's leadership at three levels. At the congregational level, church mothers direct the women's ministry under the pastor's authority. At the state or jurisdictional level state mothers, operate under the direction of the state or jurisdictional bishop. At the national level, the national mother serves under the presiding bishop.

Women's Department auxiliaries involve women in church life "from cradle to grave." At earliest age, boys and girls are grouped together in the Sunshine band, under the direction of women teachers. Gender stratification begins from adolescence: Purity Class trains adolescent girls and in propriety and etiquette, The Young Women's Council, for those between nineteen and forty gives further instruction and direction and the COGIC Women's Council involves women over forty in the church's life.

Within the Women's Department the hierarchical structure that avails among men in the general church is also present and begins in the local congregation. Women can be licensed as evangelist or missionaries to carry out tasks such as visiting the sick, teaching other women, and raising funds. Women within a congregation are organized under a church mother, who reports to a district supervisor of women who is under the direction of a state or jurisdictional supervisor who reports directly to the International Supervisor. This structure provides for the orderly division of labor for amassing resources to support the denomination and its auxiliaries.

The central focus of the Women's Department, however, is the state, local, and international women's conventions. The International Convention was conceived by Lillian Brooks Coffey in 1950 as a means to more fully incorporate women's leadership skills into the life of the denomination while racing the resources for its programs. Its first session convened in 1951 in Los Angeles. The event serves as a venue for spotlighting promising COGIC women as well as some of the biggest names on the Pentecostal preaching circuit as well as raising a major portion of the department's budget. Next to the Annual Convocation, the International Convention has become the largest event in the COGIC year. The impact that the event, which regularly draws between 20,000 and 25,000 women, has come to exert within COGIC and the influence it has garnered with the broader culture is exemplified in the fact the then president William Jefferson (Bill) Clinton addressed the event in 1996.

Starting with Mason, COGIC leaders have taken great care to select the International Supervisor, who exemplifies both godly piety and the worldly sophistication to extend COGIC's influence. Mason's first choice to head the Department was **Lillian Coffey**, who initially declined due to her youth and inexperience. She suggested that he instead call on **Elizabeth (Lizzie) Robinson**. Under her leadership as head of the newly conceived department, COGIC women established new congregations and Bible studies and prayer groups within existing congregations, and engaged in home and foreign missions work. Her crowning accomplishment was organizing what had been a fledgling amalgamation of scattered and often competing prayer and Bible bands into a national effort to raise funds for building a National headquarters for the denomination.

At Robinson's death in 1943, Coffey assumed full leadership of the Department, serving for twenty-one years until her death in 1964. Coffey differed greatly in styles and focus from Robinson whose strict Holiness, austere approach centered on developing the spirituality of COGIC women. Coffey's more contemporary approach addressed a breadth of causes beyond those specifically beneficial to the denomination. Her close association with prominent women involved her in the struggle for "racial uplift" and women's rights, but she also established congregations throughout the Midwest and founded the Lillian Brooks Coffey Rest Home in Detroit, and conceived of the National Women's Convention.

Annie Bailey served as National Mother from 1964 to 1975, after serving in several positions under Robinson and Coffey. Bailey added several auxiliaries to the Women's Department including the Business and Professional Women's Rescue Squad, the Sunday School Representatives Unit, the United Sisters of Charity, the National Secretaries Unit, and the Jr. Missionaries. She also relaunched the magazine, *The COGIC Woman*, and appointed the first National President of the Sewing Circle, Artistic Fingers.

Mattie McGlothen assumed the position of National Mother after having served as supervisor of California and the Northwest for almost half a century. McGlothen founded several new units including the Education and Scholarship Fund, the Bishop's Wives Scholarship Fund, the Screening Committee for Jurisdictional Supervisors, and the Business and Professional Women's Federation. Under her leadership, the department built a home for Bahamian missionaries, furnished a guest house on Saints Junior College campus, and built senior citizens and unwed mothers compounds in Haiti. She also purchased the property that houses the administrative offices of the International Women's Department.

Emma Crouch, the fifth National Mother served from 1994 to 1997. Crouch, like other prominent women, worked her way through the local, state, jurisdictional, and national ranks of the Department. Crouch turned her attention to developing a Women's Council to train COGIC women who were over forty and engage them more in the life of the church. **Willie Mae Rivers**'s COGIC career includes serving as a District Missionary, Assistant State Supervisor, and State Supervisor, before moving into the top position. She demonstrates the possible path to leadership within the COGIC women's structure.

Further Reading:

Butler, Anthea. *Women in the Church of God in Christ: The Making of a Sanctified World.* Chapel Hill, NC: The University of North Carolina Press, 2006.

Cornelius, Lucille. *The Pioneer History of the Church of God in Christ.* S.l.: s.n., 1975.

J

Jackson, Mary Elizabeth 1881–1983

At the age of eighty-eight **Mary Jackson**, a charter member of **Mt. Sinai Holy Church of America**, succeeded Elmira Jeffries as the third presiding bishop of the denomination, serving in that position until her death at age 102, making her the oldest president in the history of the church.

As a child in Florida, Jackson attended the Methodist Church. Later, she met **Ida Robinson**, and had the experience of sanctification. She was called to the ministry, and ordained in the **United Holy Church** in Philadelphia, Pennsylvania. When Robinson left that denomination over the issues of women's leadership to start a new body, Jackson went with her as a charter member of the **Mt. Sinai Holy Church of America**.

From the earliest days of Mt. Sinai, Jackson had an active role in Robinson's local congregation where she taught the preachers' class and assisted Robinson with finances. Further she took leadership roles at the denominational level, serving as the first National Secretary and the first overseer of the denomination's home for elderly and single members of the congregation. In 1955 she became pastor of Bethel Pentecostal Church in Wilmington, Delaware.

On being elevated to presiding bishop in 1964, at age eighty-eight, she assumed the pastorate of the mother church, Mount Olive Holy Temple, in Philadelphia. Jackson retired from active pastorate service, becoming pastor emeritus in 1980, while remaining as president of Mt. Sinai until her death.

Jakes, Thomas Dexter (T. D.) 1957–

One of the most recognizable names in both popular American, and global Pentecostalism, T. D. Jakes is the founding pastor of the thirty-thousand-member Potter's House, an interracial Dallas, Texas megachurch congregation and T. D. Ministries a multimillion dollar enterprise. Jakes represents a classical Oneness Pentecostal leader who has broadened his message to reach a wider segment of the Evangelical Christian community, a constituency that would not naturally have been attracted to the traditional classical Pentecostal tradition out of which he emerged.

Jakes left high school to care for his ailing parents, but completed a General Education Diploma (GED) and went on to complete both Bachelor of Arts and Master of Arts through correspondence courses at Friends University. He eventually added a Doctor of Ministry degree. As a youngster, the former Baptist encountered movement in a small Oneness Pentecostal church revival in Vidalia, West Virginia where, in his teens, he had a Pentecostal experience of Holy Spirit baptism. As a young man, Jakes had such a pronounced lisp that some attempted to discourage him from pursuing ministry, but by seventeen he was preaching. He was licensed in 1977, and ordained in 1979, assuming the pastorate at a small congregation, Temple of Faith Church, in Montgomery, West Virginia, while working part-time to support his family. A year later, Jakes planted Greater Emanuel Temple of Faith, a racially integrated congregation that grew quickly to eventually reach over 300 members.

After marrying in 1981, he began a radio ministry "The Master's Plan," that ran for three years. In 1987 **Quander L. Wilson**, presiding bishop of **Greater Emmanuel Apostolic Faith Tabernacles Inc.**, consecrated Jakes to the bishopric. In the early 1990s he began a Bible study for forty women, that quickly doubled in size, spawning a ministry that led to the 1993, publication of *Woman, Thou Art Loosed*, with $15,000 of his own money. The work, which addressed the pain of rape, sold over three million copies. In 2006 "Get Ready with T. D. Jakes," started airing on national television networks in major markets.

In the mid-1990s, fifty families from Jakes's local congregation followed him from Charleston, West Virginia (a city of 50,000) to Dallas, Texas, one of the largest metropolitan areas in the nation, to establish the Potter's House. The first Sunday he opened the church for membership, 1,500 people joined. Within a year, the congregation had grown to 10,000 members; within three years, there were 17,000 members. Ten years later, the church had grown to more than 28,000 members, with multiple ministries, spiritual, practical, and entrepreneurial enterprises. In a leadership style that combines entrepreneurial skill, dramatic teaching, and administrative sophistication, Jakes has been able to attract a largely middle class, multi-racial following within both the religious and secular culture that has allowed him and the Potter's House to become celebrities.

This charismatic style has drawn several pastors and their congregations into The Potter's House International Pastoral Alliance, a fellowship of several hundred churches throughout the United States, Great Britain, and Africa. In counter distinction to many such alliances, the fellowship fully supports and encourages women in pastoral leadership, both as senior pastors and as members of co-pastoral teams. Further, Jakes has been able to cross the racial divide to attract pastors of white and Latino congregations.

Jakes has never repudiated his Oneness Pentecostal roots, but avoids the Oneness-Trinitarian schism that has splintered other Pentecostals by nuancing his theology, asserting that there is "one God, Creator of all things, infinitely perfect, and eternally existing in three manifestations: Father, Son, and Holy Spirit." He has also downplayed other elements of his theology that are divisive within the Pentecostal tradition by displaying a broader understanding of the Church as, "composed of all . . . who through saving faith in Jesus Christ, have been regenerated by the Holy Spirit." Further, the insistence on the necessity for the experience of Holy Spirit baptism as outlined in classical Pentecostalism is absent.

This nuancing has allowed him to venture into markets that have historically been closed to other Oneness Pentecostals and has garnered him much personal and professional fruit, making him one of the most highly visible Pentecostal leaders in the world. A *Time Magazine* headline asked, "Is This Man the Next Billy Graham?" One article dubbed him, "America's Best Preacher." *Christianity Today* labeled his multi-racial Potter's House congregation one of America's fastest growing mega-churches, contending that it dominated church growth records since its 1996 inception. Moreover, his rallies have increasingly drawn record crowds, at one point even going beyond those of Graham. Comparing him to the multi-millionaire secular talk show host whose name is a household word, one journalist referred to Jakes as "the Oprah Winfrey of popular preachers."

His separate conferences for women, men, youth, and pastors are generally sellouts as are his appearances in other venues across the country. The annual "Megafast," a four-day festival held in Atlanta, Georgia, which he bills as a Family Vacation Event, features some of the biggest gospel artists and secular performers of every ilk. It regularly draws more than 100,000 people of all ages from across the nation and other countries.

Jakes's work has been recognized in almost every segment of American culture. He received a Grammy award for his "Woman Thou Art Loosed"; his release, "Sacred Love Songs" was named one of Billboard Magazine's 1999 top gospel albums; and his books regularly make the top seller lists of major periodicals.

Further Reading:

Lee, Shayne. *T. D. Jakes: America's New Preacher.* New York: New York University Press, 2007.

Wellman, Sam. *T. D. Jakes.* Bel Air, CA: Chelsea House, 2000.

Jefferson, Illie Louis 1896–1983

Co-founder and first presiding bishop of the **Church of God in Christ International** in Kansas City, Missouri in 1969. Jefferson was born in Buenavista, Georgia and was converted to Christian faith in 1916 at the age of twenty. He was called to the ministry in 1918. By 1930 he had migrated north to New England, going first to Springfield, Massachusetts before settling in Connecticut and beginning work as a laborer. By 1945 he was pastoring a rescue mission in Hartford Connecticut. By 1955 he was pastoring Hartford's Holy Trinity Church of God in Christ and Holy Temple Church of God, No. 2 in Springfield, Massachusetts. Within COGIC, Jefferson served as a district elder, and by 1952 had been appointed overseer of Rhode Island before being consecrated as a bishop in 1960. By then he was pastoring Little Zion Church of God in Christ in Stamford, Connecticut.

Nine years later, Jefferson, along with fourteen other bishops objected to a reorganization of the **Church of God in Christ** that shifted government from a senior bishop acting alone, to a twelve-man board. As a protest, they pulled away from the parent group to form the new body, and Jefferson was chosen as presiding bishop. He retired in 1980 and died three years later in Bloomfield, Connecticut.

Jeffries, Elmira 1882–1964

A charter member of **Mt. Sinai Holy Church of America** who followed **Ida Robinson** from the **United Holy Church**. Jeffries started her ministry leading Tuesday tarry service at Robinson's Mount Olive congregation and subsequently pastored several congregations, including Bethel Pentecostal Church in Bridgeton, New Jersey; Mount Nebo in Baltimore, Maryland; Zion Gospel Mission in Newark, New Jersey; and St Paul's Holy Church and Mount Olive Holy Temple in Philadelphia, Pennsylvania.

Jeffries was a charter member of the denomination and became its first vice-president under Robinson. She was elected as the second presiding bishop directly after Robinson's death, serving in that position from 1946 until her death in 1964. Prior to assuming the presidential position, Jeffers held increasingly important positions, and became the corporation's first vice-president.

Born in a Christian home in Littleton, North Carolina, Jeffries became a Christian at age twelve. By age twenty, she had experienced sanctification and the Pentecostal Holy Spirit baptism. Shortly afterwards, she was called to the ministry, but began searching for a church that preached and practiced the Word of God in its fullness. This search lasted fifteen years, but in 1922, brought her to Mount Olive Holy Church a **United Holy Church of America** congregation in Philadelphia, after which she relocated from East Orange to join the congregation.

After the death of Robinson, Jeffries was consecrated to the bishopric by Bishop **William E. Fuller**, President of the **Fire Baptized Holy Church**. She also became president of Mount Sinai Holy Church of America, Inc., and the pastor the Mount Olive congregation.

Jeffries's home in North Philadelphia would later become the office of Mount Sinai's headquarters. She also purchased the Physicians' and Surgeons' Hospital located next door to accommodate the elderly and single saints. Today, it is a brand new, 189-bed, skilled nursing care facility that has been named the Elmira Jeffries Memorial Home in her honor.

Following her death, a third woman, **Mary Jackson** assumed the leadership of the Mount Sinai organization.

Jennings, Gino N. 1963–

Controversial Oneness Pentecostal founder and presiding bishop of the **First Church of Our Lord Jesus Christ of the Apostles' Faith Inc**. His father, Ernest Jennings, was a bishop. Jennings came to faith as a child while the family was worshipping in a congregation pastored by his great uncle, also Bishop Ernest Jennings. The young boy began preaching at the age of thirteen, entered the ministry while a young man, and was appointed to the pastoral staff as the Bible reader and traveling companion for his pastor.

While still a teenager, Jennings reported having a vision in which God showed him that most of the Christian Church was in error and he was called to correct it. After recounting his vision to church leadership, he was silenced from preaching for a year. Later, he was again given the opportunity to speak, but admonished to preach only what was in the doctrine of the church. When his preaching did change, he was silenced again for another year.

In 1984 at the age of twenty-one, he left that congregation to establish the first **Church of the Lord Jesus Christ of the Apostolic Faith**. By 1988 he was ministering in thirteen areas, was holding monthly services in Maryland, Virginia, Illinois, Michigan, Tennessee, and Pennsylvania, and had baptized more than 350 people in the Name of the Lord Jesus.

In 1990 he established a radio broadcast that by the end of the next year had gone global. Over the airwaves, Jennings promulgated his rigid Oneness theology that reinforced his accusation that other Pentecostals along with the majority of the rest of the Christian Church was teaching false doctrine.

Within his own denomination, he wields almost dictatorial power, enforces rigid rules of social and personal piety, and has been seen by some as having cultist influence over his followers. His charismatic misogynist message draws a disproportionate following of males to his ministry which has been compared to that of Nation of Islam leader Louis Farrakhan in its structure.

Jeter, John A. (J. A.) 1855–1945

The former Little Rock, Arkansas Baptist minister was a pastor, missionary and close colleague of **Charles Price Jones** and an associate of **Charles Harrison Mason.** He was born in Henrico County, Virginia, near Richmond and in 1880, **J. A. Jeter** settled in Somerville, Tennessee, where he worked as a drug store porter. By 1885 he had moved to Little Rock, Arkansas, where he served as a deacon in Jones's prominent Baptist Church.

In 1896 Jeter joined Jones, Mason, and **W. S. Pleasant** of Mississippi in conducting revivals to spread the message of the Holiness movement throughout the Tennessee Valley. He presented at the 1897 Holiness organizing convention called by Jones in Jackson, Mississippi for the **Church of God in Christ**, the body that served as the foundation for **Church of Christ Holiness (USA).**

Jeter became a leader of the Council of Holiness Meetings of Jackson. In 1903 he went to Liberia to determine the prospects for a missionary effort in that country. After news of the **Azusa Street Revival** reached the East in late 1906, Jeter was part of an excursion team—which also included Mason, **D. J. Young,** and **W. S. Pleasant**—who were sent by Jones's group to investigate the authenticity of the phenomenon being experienced there.

On returning to the east, Jeter—who had reportedly evidenced the Pentecostal Holy Spirit baptism experience by speaking in tongues—reputed it as invalid, and finally sided with Jones in his assessment that discredited the phenomenon. After Mason and Young were disfellowshipped, Jeter remained a colleague of Jones.

Before the Mason-Jones schism, Jeter held a number of significant positions in Jones's organization, and he continued to do so after the division. He pastored Sweet Rest Church of Christ (Holiness) in Pearl, Mississippi, which he took over from Jones, serving there from 1914 to 1916, then moved to Norfolk, Virginia to pastor the First Church of Christ (Holiness) U.S.A. in that city. He served as Overseer of Arkansas and eventually became a bishop, serving as chair of the first foreign missions board of the COCHUSA.

Jewell, Mattie Lou Tate McLeod 1897–1991

The second presiding bishop of the **Church of the Living God, the Pillar and Ground of the Truth which He Purchased with His Own Blood, Inc.** (The McLeod Dominion) was born in Fort Davis, Alabama, near Tuskegee. The gifted singer and preacher came to faith in the Baptist church. When her father, Robert Tate, married the Mary Magdalena Lewis Street, founder of the **Church of the Living God, Pillar and Ground of the Truth**, around 1914, Mattie became her stepdaughter and the family became a member of Tate's Pentecostal denomination. She received the Pentecostal Holy Spirit baptism in 1912 at the age of seventeen, and received a called to the ministry at age twenty-one in 1916.

In 1919 she married Bishop **Bruce L. McLeod** one of Mother Tate's chief assistants. The couple worked in Philadelphia, Pennsylvania; Jacksonville, Florida; Mt. Vernon, Illinois; and Nashville, Tennessee establishing churches. In 1924 her husband and bishop appointed her to assist him in setting up churches in Paducah, Owensboro, Beaver Dam, and Morgantown Kentucky and throughout Mississippi and Michigan.

After 1931, when Tate's organization splintered into three separate bodies, her husband was given leadership of what would shortly be the McLeod Dominion. Sometime before he died in 1937, she was ordained to the bishopric. After his death, she became head of the body. She later married a CLGPGT deacon, William Jewell, a successful businessperson who served as treasurer of the Pilot Mutual Life Insurance Company of Cleveland, Ohio and was a stockholder in the Southern Potato Chip Company. After the marriage, Mattie appointed William comptroller and senior bishop of the denomination and re-designated it the Jewell Dominion. The couple resided in Cleveland, Ohio, where she pastored a congregation from 1939 to 1947. Jewell was elected presiding bishop in 1939 by the General Assembly in Nashville, Tennessee. Her domain covered Florida, Mississippi, Georgia, Alabama, Louisiana, and Texas. From 1946 she conducted an extensive campaign in Florida, building churches throughout the state, and then in 1947 she established a congregation in the Philippines.

Returning to Nashville, Tennessee in 1948, Jewell founded Jewell Academy and Seminary to serve kindergarten through high school. The school operated from 1950 to

1962. In 1964 she relocated a last time, moving the headquarters to Indianapolis, Indiana where she died twenty-seven years later. At her death, her great granddaughter, Naomi Manning, was elected presiding bishop.

Johnson, Brumfield 1901–1972

The founder of the **Mount Calvary Holy Churches of America** (MCHCA) was born in Charlotte, North Carolina. His early life was spent between various communities in North Carolina including Henderson and Durham with devoted Baptist parents. When Johnson was nine years old and in the eighth grade, his father, a dedicated deacon, died and Johnson left school to help support his mother and siblings.

The family moved to Durham, North Carolina where Johnson encountered the **United Holy Church** when his mother started attending revivals at a local UHC congregation. Soon both Johnson and his mother joined the congregation, and by the age of sixteen Johnson was preaching and conducting revivals for the denomination. After his 1919 marriage, Johnson and his bride moved to East Orange, New Jersey, and then to Summit, New York to pastor United Holy Churches. While in New York, Johnson had an opportunity to minister in Boston Massachusetts and planted a congregation there.

By the mid-1920s Johnson popularity as an evangelist attracted more opportunities for preaching engagements. Yet, he was a UHC prominent minister, and he began to be troubled by some of the denomination's polity and some UHC leadership attempted to curtail his rising popularity.

As a result, in 1929, Johnson left to establish the MCHCA, which he incorporated in Winston-Salem, North Carolina, taking 200 members of his UHC congregation into the new body. Johnson evangelized up and down the East Coast throughout the Great Depression, leaving churches in many cities that he reached. By the time of his death, Johnson had built the MCHCA to eighty congregations in thirteen states. Prior to his death he appointed Bishop **Harold I. Williams** as his successor.

Johnson, Celeste Ashe 1946–

As an educator, Johnson is the first black and first female to serve as an Administrator of the College of New Rochelle, School of New Resources in the Bronx, New York. Before migrating to the North, Johnson had served as the first African-American to hold an office on the Sussex County Virginia Education Association Board after schools were integrated in the 1970s. She is founding president of Educational Consultants, Inc., and currently serves as Chairpersonof the Board of Trustees at the **W. L. Bonner Bible College**, the institution of higher education for the **Church of Our Lord Jesus Christ of the Apostolic Faith** (COOLJC).

Within the religious sector, from 1994 until 2002, Johnson served as the first Pentecostal elected as president in the sixty-three-year history of the International Association of Ministers' Wives and Ministers' Widows, Inc. (IAMWMW), an ecumenical organization with a membership of more than 43,000 within 138 denominations throughout the United States and eighteen other nations.

Johnson holds a Bachelor of Science in Education from Elizabeth City State University in Elizabeth City, North Carolina. She earned her Master of Science in Education from the City College of New York, and studied for the Doctor of Education Degree at the University of Massachusetts, earning the Doctorate in Religious Education from Christ Theological Seminary. She also has honorary doctorates from Virginia Commonwealth University and Richmond Virginia College and Seminary, as well as certification in the Management of Life Long Learning from Harvard University.

Dr. Johnson has produced several publications on education, sexuality, marriage and women's leadership within the church. Further, she has traveled throughout the country making presentations on these topics. As a professional, she has served as a teacher, program executive and educational trainer and administrator at the secondary and post-secondary level.

In 1998 her work was pivotal in the passing of Congressional legislation for the production of 500,000 coins by the US Mint commemorating Crispus Attucks, an African-American man who was the first person to die during the American Revolution. Additionally she has chaired or served on several boards related to community issues such as senior housing and other urban issues. Her involvement in family related matter extends to contract by the federal government as well as faith-based group. In 2006 for example, she worked with the Alliance for Marriage Foundation to draft the Marriage Protection Amendment to the US Constitution.

Within the **Church of Our Lord Jesus Christ of the Apostolic Faith**, besides being an active member of her local congregation, Urban Hope Refuge COOLJC where her late husband pastored until his death in 2013, Johnson served for thirteen years as Dean of Education of the Women's Council's Academy, and founded and directed its Auxiliary of Apostolic Teens. She has also served as President of the Missionary Department of the Diocese of Connecticut, designed the denomination's Chastity Program and trained staff in its use. She is manager of the International Church Convention Planning Committee and a member of the Presiding Apostle's Cabinet.

Johnson has received numerous honors including the Black Revolutionary War Patriots Foundation Award, The IAMWMW Minister's Wife of the Year in 1984, and recognition from the Phoenix Life Insurance Company for her community contributions in the field of education. Dr. Johnson has been featured in Christian and women's publications including *FORUM, the Religious Christian Manager's Association Magazine*, the *Pittsburgh Post Gazette Sunday Magazine* and the *Richmond Free Press*.

Johnson, Charles Edward 1948–

Oneness Pentecostal leader who is the founding presider of the **Apostolic Faith Fellowship International**. Johnson was born in Chester, Pennsylvania. The family later moved to Paterson, New Jersey where he received his education. After graduation, Charles enlisted in the United States Air Force and served his tour of duty in Vietnam and Taiwan before being discharged in 1972. Four years later, he had settled in the Washington DC area where an old friend witnessed to Johnson and invited him to a New Year's Eve night service where he was converted and baptized in the name of the Lord Jesus Christ. Shortly afterward, he experienced the Pentecostal Holy Spirit baptism. By the end of the next year, Johnson was called into the ministry.

Ten years later, Johnson was called to pastor Greater Morning Star Pentecostal Church, a PAW congregation with in Washington DC with approximately 600 members, Under his leadership, six new churches were establish throughout the Mid-Atlantic and Southern sections of the East Coast and Johnson began moving into PAW leadership positions. He served as lay director, a member of the International Foreign Missions Board, on the Board of Directors for **Aenon Bible College**, and Chairperson of the District of Columbia, Delaware and Maryland District Council. In 1996 Johnson was consecrated to the Board of Bishops serving the Diocese of Togo, West Africa. He was later moved to the Eighth Episcopal District in Iowa, Nebraska and Wyoming, before returning to his home district of Washington DC, Delaware, and Maryland as diocesan in 2002.

In the meantime, Johnson's local congregation had grown in membership and in its ministry offerings including regular radio and television broadcast and Bible Institute. Under his leadership, by 2007, the church grew to over 1,200 and relocated to Largo, MD in a new 1,500-seat sanctuary.

In 2012 a growing dissatisfaction with Oneness doctrine and piety led Johnson and some other ministers within PAW to leave that body to establish the **Apostolic Faith Fellowship International**. He was immediately elected as presiding bishop.

Johnson, Lymus Leewood 1922–2012

A Oneness Pentecostal leader who was the founding presider of the **Evangelistic Churches of Christ of the Apostolic Faith**. Johnson was born and educated in Lusby, Maryland. He relocated to Asbury Park, New Jersey at a young age, and after marrying, he and his wife settled in Trenton, New Jersey. He was converted as a young child, began preaching around the age of seven, and experienced Pentecostal Holy Spirit baptism at age of nine while attending a revival. Shortly after that, he preached his trial sermon at his home church St. John Methodist Church. As a youngster, he was deeply influenced by the radio ministry of Bishop **Sherrod C. Johnson**.

After moving to New Jersey, he began attending the church pastored by Johnson and was baptized in Jesus' name. While attending services there he met and married Ruth Robinson, and through her family, he met Bishop R. C. Lawson who would later become his pastor and spiritual mentor. In the 1930s and 1940, Johnson gained a reputation as a revivalist who regularly drew crowds. At one time, while Lawson was on a missionary trip to Africa, he called upon Johnson to run a revival at his church. That revival lasted almost a month, one hundred souls were baptized in Jesus' name, and seventy-five were filled with the Holy Ghost. Following that revival, in 1956,

Lawson promoted Elder Johnson to the office of National Evangelist and Chair of the National Evangelistic Board.

After the death of his wife, Johnson left the Church of Our Lord Jesus Christ in 1974 to found The Evangelistic Church of Christ in Corona, New York. The congregation grew and was later located in Jackson Heights, New York. which is now the headquarters church for the **Evangelistic Churches of Christ of the Apostolic Faith**. He went on to take his gospel to the world by radio broadcast. Johnson died at age ninety.

Further Reading:

Walters, Steve B. *A Shepherd's Journey: The Life Story of Apostle Lymus L. Johnson.* S.l.: Crowned Warrior, 2012.

Johnson, Rufus Abraham Reid (R. A. R.) 1863–1940

The founder of the **House of God, The Holy Church of the Living God, the Pillar and Ground of the Truth, The House of Prayer for All People, Inc.** was born in Crawfordsville, Georgia as the son of slaves. Johnson first served in ministry as an itinerant preacher in his Macon Georgia Methodist Church. He left that body in 1903 to join with Mary Magdalena Lewis Tate who had established **The Church of The Living God, Pillar and Ground of The Truth.** He worked closely with Tate, probably evangelizing and planting church until around 1913. By then, he had become convinced concerning issues on biblical sanctions for keeping the Sabbath.

He left Tate's group to begin an independent group as the Commandment Keepers Church. Johnson incorporated his new organization in Washington DC in 1918; presumably, it was by that time that he also accepted Oneness Pentecostal doctrine, was re-baptized in Jesus' name, and moved his organization into that movement.

In 1922 Johnson met Lena Brown, a member of the **Pentecostal Assemblies of the World.** They married in 1924 and Lena Brown Johnson was ordained and made an assistant overseer by her husband. Sometime after that the national headquarters were moved from Washington DC to New York City where he presided until his death. Johnson was succeeded by Bishop A. A. Smith.

Johnson, Sherrod Charlotte (S. C.) 1897–1961

One of the staunchest defenders of Oneness Pentecostal doctrine in the early twentieth century and founder of the **Church of The Lord Jesus Christ of the Apostolic Faith.** Johnson was born in Pine Tree Quarters, Edgecomb County, North Carolina. His early years were spent in poverty; he began working in the cotton fields at the age of nine—chopping cotton for twenty-five cents per day. When he was twelve, Johnson went to work at a box mill. Yet, he later became one of the wealthiest Oneness Pentecostal leaders of his time. His radio ministry,

"The Whole Truth," which was launched during the Great Depression, was heard in ninety cities around the globe.

Johnson first heard the holiness message in a congregation in Halifax, North Carolina. He later received the Pentecostal experience of Holy Spirit baptism one night while in bed. Soon, he received a call to the ministry and eventually, moved to Philadelphia, Pennsylvania, where he was exposed to the Oneness movement, shortly accepted that doctrine, and was re-baptized in Jesus' name.

In 1919 Johnson joined the **Church of Our Lord Jesus Christ of the Apostolic Faith** under bishop **Robert C. Lawson**. Lawson ordained Johnson an elder in 1920 and assigned him to a storefront Philadelphia congregation, the Church of Christ of the Apostolic Faith. Eventually, Johnson's congregation became the second largest church in Lawson's association. In 1930 Lawson elevated Johnson to the bishopric and assigned him as overseer North Carolina and Pennsylvania. When Lawson incorporated his group as the Church of Our Lord Jesus Christ of the Apostolic Faith (COOLJC) in 1933, Johnson would be one of its incorporators.

Within a short period, however, Johnson would instigate the first organizational split in the COOLJC and secede from that body. For while Johnson accepted the main points of Lawson's theology, the two men differed over what Johnson saw as Lawson's liberalism on matters such as appropriate women's attire, their role in ministry and other issues. In 1932 he started his own organization, taking churches in the states of North Carolina and Pennsylvania with him.

Johnson's ultra-conservative views on sanctification and exclusiveness promoted rigidly modest apparel for women including a prohibition on use of hair straightening products, and sanctions against wearing jewelry or cosmetics. Further, while Lawson allowed women to preach, but denied them ordination, Johnson objected to even this concession.

He insisted that men within his denomination wear dark-colored suits and be clean-shaven. Johnson himself, however, lived lavishly, dressed in expensive suits and drove in expensive cars and limousines.

He condemned the use of traditional medicine, and promoted the usual social sanctions of early Pentecostals against the use of tobacco and alcoholic beverages, listening to radio broadcasts, and viewing television programs and movies. He also stood against education beyond that required by the government, and considered traditional Christian holidays including Christmas and Easter as pagan.

Once convinced of the rightness of his newly adopted doctrine, Johnson published a series of tracts on issues that he considered important and distributed them to whoever would read them. He was willing to debate with anyone who wished to challenge what he preached. At one later point, he offered a $500,000 reward to anyone who could prove him wrong. This contentious attitude even extended to other Oneness leaders who considered him extreme such as **Smallwood E. Williams** of **Bible Way Church of the Lord Jesus Christ World Wide, Inc.** and **Monroe Saunders** who was then with the **Church of God in Christ Jesus, Apostolic.**

At the same time, Johnson was socially and economically progressive. He established restaurants and stores, operated a saw mill, and maintained a farm in Cherry Hill, New Jersey that was operated by members of his church. With his numerous enterprises, he became wealthy and influential in a number of arenas. The July 1949 issue of *Ebony* magazine listed Johnson among the most widely listened to African-American preachers in America.

While on an evangelistic tour in Jamaica, British West Indies, Johnson died at age sixty-three, and was succeeded by Bishop **S. McDowell Shelton.** After his death, many of his members, reportedly, expected that he would soon be resurrected.

Further Reading:

Church of the Lord Jesus Christ. *Condensed Manual of the Doctrines, Rules and By-Laws of the Church of the Lord Jesus Christ of the Apostolic Faith.* Philadelphia, PA: Church of the Lord Jesus Christ, 1944.

McEady, Vivian. "History of the Founder: Biography of Bishop Sherrod C. Johnson, 1919–1950." The Church of the Lord Jesus Christ of the Apostolic Faith. Online: http://www.apostolic-ministries.net/late_bishop_johnson.htm.

Johnson W. J. ("Blind" Willie) 1897–1945

A gospel blues singer, guitarist, and songwriter. Johnson was born near Brenham, Texas. Johnson was not born blind. While it is not certain how he lost his sight as a young child, one report is that when he was seven, his stepmother, fighting with his father, threw lye in Johnson's face, permanently blinding him. After losing his sight, his father would often leave him on street corners to sing for money.

Johnson made twenty-nine commercial studio records for Columbia Records from 1927 to 1930. Though he refused to sing secular blues and sang only religious songs, he is considered one of the most influential guitarists in music history. One song, "Dark Was the Night (Cold Was the Ground)" was chosen for an album placed aboard Voyager 1 spacecraft in 1977.

Johnson remained poor until the end of his life, preaching and singing on the streets of several Texas cities. In 1945 Johnson operated the House of Prayer in Beaumont, Texas. That year, his home burned to the ground. Johnson lived in the burned shell for a month, contracted malaria, and died after the hospital to which he was transported refused to treat him.

Further Reading:

Blakey, D. N. *Revelation Blind Willie Johnson The Biography.* Great Britain: Lulu Enterprises, 2007.

J

Johnson, William Monroe 1913–1975

Founder and first presiding bishop of the **True Vine Pentecostal Holiness Church**. Born, in Darlington, South Carolina, in 1929, Johnson migrated to North Carolina to work for the R. J. Reynolds Tobacco Company. He converted to Christian faith the following year and joined Kimberly Park Holiness Church. In 1931 he began preaching and received his ministerial licensed the same year. He attended Hood Theological Seminary, at Livingstone College in Salisbury, North Carolina, to further his ministerial training.

In 1932 Johnson founded a small mission in Winston-Salem, North Carolina. This congregation became the Macedonia Holy Church. From 1932 to 1946, Johnson built and pastored several churches throughout the Carolinas. Later he co-founded the True Vine Pentecostal Holiness Church with Robert L. Hairston and was consecrated as presiding bishop. Johnson's home church was designated as headquarters for the denomination. In the 1960s, Johnson and Hairston parted ways after the latter accepted the Oneness Pentecostal doctrine and split to form a **True Vine Pentecostal Churches of Jesus Christ (Apostolic Faith)** as a Oneness body.

Johnson headed the True Vine organization until his death, when his son Sylvester assumed leadership. By the time of his death, True Vine churches were located in North Carolina, South Carolina, and Virginia.

Joint College of African American Pentecostal Bishops

An interdenominational ecumenical organization that trains bishops, overseers, senior shepherds, and high-level church staffer primarily within the Pentecostal tradition regarding governmental and liturgical protocol. The organization was founded in 1993 by Bishops **Roy E. Brown** of **Pilgrim Assemblies International**, **Wilbert McKinley** of Elim Fellowship International, **Paul Morton**, of the **Full Gospel Baptist Church Fellowship International** and **J. Delano Ellis II,** presiding prelate of the **United Pentecostal Churches of Christ.** The group was concerned about the lack of training for newly elected Pentecostal bishops. Through consensus among the four bishops, Ellis became the first chairperson, and then in 2006, was elevated to the positon of Archbishop Metropolitan giving him the authority to set protocol for the episcopal elevation of bishops, and to participate in the "laying on of hands" during the elevation, thus providing apostolic succession. Ellis is assisted in governing the organization by a fifteen-member Advisory Board that is populated by male and female bishops from Trinitarian and Oneness Pentecostal traditions as well as neo-Pentecostal and Charismatic groups.

Since its inception, the organization has advocated several changes in Pentecostal ecclesial polity. The office of adjutant, for example has been revived due to the classes offered at the JCAAPB. Classes for this office have been formed into the Adjutant Academy, overseen by a bishop who specifically trains this group.

The college attempts to bring uniformity to a movement that, over its one-hundred-year history, has fragmented into numerous small and larger bodies that traditionally have been able to find little common ground (outside of openness to the experience of Pentecostal Spirit baptism) on which to agree. A special language has developed within the college that allows for conversation over divisive issues. Rather than denominations, branches of the Pentecostal community are referred to as reformations, and leaders of various bodies, regardless of their official title (bishop, president, etc.) are referred to as presiding prelate. They body has adopted designations not previously used among Pentecostals such as archbishop or apostle, applying biblical, as well as historical justification for use of terms commonly found in other Christian traditions. Moreover, it supports events that aim at reconnecting the African American Pentecostal bishops with the broader church. Further, the traditional Trinitarian-Oneness schism that is still fairly rigid among white Pentecostal bodies is absent from its membership. The theological ecumenism it displays regarding this issue has led to some bodies adopting a more nuanced conception of the Godhead.

Moreover, JCAAPB undertook major efforts such as a trip to Rome in 2000 by a delegation of more than two hundred bishops and other members of the college to build closer ecumenical relations with the Roman Catholic Church. The group visited the Vatican, gained an audience with the pontiff, Pope John Paul, and attended a three-day seminar at the Pontifical North American College, an elite seminary for Catholics, and participated in a Roman Catholic mass.

The influence of the college within the Pentecostal movement has been variable. Its annual conference draws more than four hundred bishops from substantial Pentecostal bodies. The Joint College has been enlisted to respond to contemporary issues on which the Pentecostal church has often been relatively mute, such as addressing the issue of homosexuality among its ranks and crafting a response to Bishop **Carlton Pearson**'s newly formulated doctrine of inclusion—in which everyone would eventually go to heavan—and urged its members to refuse Pearson access to their pulpits.

Currently, membership of the Joint College includes seven hundred affiliated ministers and represents more than one hundred Pentecostal denominations and independent black churches, as well as members of neo-Pentecostal Baptist and Methodist communions. Further, while the Joint College originally did not include prominent representation from the **Church of God in Christ**—the largest black Pentecostal denomination—**Charles E. Blake**, presiding bishop of COGIC, now sits on its board.

Further Reading:

Ellis, J. Delano II. *The Bishopric*. Bloomington, IN: Trafford, 2006.
Banks, Adelle M. "Pentecostals Dress like Catholic Bishops." *National Catholic Reporter*, February 24, 1995.

Jonas, Mack E. 1885-1973

The early **Azusa Street Revival** convert and later **Church of God in Christ** leader was born in Edwardville, Alabama and migrated to California as a young man where he attended the early days of the revival. Reportedly, he was the first African American to be converted during the revival. After having the Pentecostal experience of Holy Spirit baptism with speaking in tongues, Jonas quickly became a member of the **Azusa Street Mission** ministry team, and was assigned the responsibility of meeting incoming trains and greeting those who had come to Los Angeles to attend the meeting. On one trip he escorted three visitors from the East Coast who were to become important Pentecostal leaders—**David J. Young, John Jeter,** and **Charles Harrison Mason**, a later founder of the **Church of God in Christ**. Jonas was also responsible for **"tarrying"**—or praying—with those seeking their Pentecostal experience. Among those with whom he tarried was **Charles Harrison Mason**, though he was not present when Bishop Mason received his Pentecostal experience.

In 1907 Jonas was among the first to take the Pentecostal message to Georgia, establishing a congregation there. In 1909 he attended the **Church of God in Christ** convocation, was ordained as an elder by Mason, and brought his congregation into COGIC. In that same year, Mason appointed him overseer of Georgia and Alabama.

In 1917 Jonas pioneered the first African-American Pentecostal congregation in Cleveland, Ohio, which was also the first **Church of God in Christ** within that state. He was appointed the first COGIC overseer of Ohio and stayed in that position fourteen years, until 1931. Five years after taking the Ohio position, he was also appointed one of the first state overseers of Michigan, but only held that position from 1923 until 1924.

Jonas remained a pastor in Ohio until the 1960s. He was ordained a bishop in 1962, and appointed Bishop of Northwestern Jurisdiction of Ohio, which he served faithfully until his passing.

Further Reading:

Patterson, James Oglethorpe. *History and Formative Years of the Church of God in Christ.* Memphis, TN: Church of God in Christ, 1969.

Jones, Charles Price 1865–1949

The founder of the **Church of Christ (Holiness) USA** and prominent early twentieth-century African American Holiness movement leader was born near Rome, Georgia, where he spent his young life. He was steered toward Christian faith at an early age by his mother, a deeply religious Baptist former slave.

She died in 1883—when he was seventeen—and Jones left Georgia to work at odd jobs throughout the South, eventually landing in Memphis where he stayed for four years. In 1887, he moved to Cat Island, Arkansas, where he was converted and joined Locust Grove Baptist Church, pastored by Elias Camp Morris, a renowned Baptist preacher who subsequently was president of the National Baptist Convention. A year later, Jones was preaching in local congregations and three years later, was licensed to the ministry, becoming pastor of Pope Creek Baptist Church in Groat County, Arkansas.

Jones matriculated at Arkansas Baptist College, graduating in 1891. He was called to Bethlehem Baptist Church in Searcy, Arkansas. While there, he became editor of the *Baptist Vanguard Newsletter*. Within four years, was at the head of a successful Baptist congregation, Tabernacle Baptist Church and the College Church of Selma University in Selma, Alabama and was a prominent member of the state Baptist convention, where in 1892, was elected corresponding secretary and appointed as a trustee of his former alma mater. Jones was considered a great revivalist, and he conducted meetings throughout the Mississippi Valley. In 1895 he took over the pastorate of Mount Helm Baptist Church, the oldest black congregation in Jackson, Mississippi.

Two years later, Jones became dissatisfied with his religious state and sought a deeper experience of God. This search led him to embrace the holiness doctrine and experience of sanctification. He was introduced to the doctrine of sanctification through the writing and preaching of white Baptist evangelist, Joanna Patterson Moore, who worked among the freedmen, attempting to help improve their social conditions. The two became friends and the relationship, as well as Moore's writings, profoundly influenced Jones.

He began teaching the doctrine of sanctification, attacking Baptist and Methodist practices he considered worldly, including involvement with fraternal orders, fashionable standards of consumption, and allegiance to secret societies. Jones called on his followers to mark their spiritual birth as sanctified Christians by "pitching their secret order pins . . . out the church windows." This move led to him being expelled from the local Baptist convention and removed from his pastorate. For a short time, Jones worked closely with colleague, **Charles Harrison Mason**, evangelizing throughout the Tennessee Valley and organizing congregations into a loose Holiness fellowship that would eventually become a denomination, the **Church of God in Christ**.

A fissure developed between the two, however, after Mason accepted the Pentecostal doctrine of Holy Spirit baptism being accompanied with the evidence of speaking in tongues. Jones, on the contrary, maintained that Holy Spirit baptism was an inner work of the heart that required no outward sign to accept a life lived in holiness and obedience the Lord. After the split, and an unsuccessful lawsuit, Mason's group retained the original name, and Jones group took the name **Church of Christ Holiness (USA)**.

Jones was one of the most prolific writers within the black Holiness movement; he developed several manuscripts on doctrine. His literary works include, *An Appeal to the Sons of Africa*, a collection of poems, readings, orations and lectures to inspire black youth; and *The Gift of the Holy Spirit in the Book of Acts*, written to refute the claim that speaking in tongues was the initial evidence of Holy Spirit baptism.

Jones penned more than one thousand hymns, publishing his first hymnal *Jesus Only, No. 1* in 1891. He published his second song book *Jesus Only, No. 2* in 1901. Many of his hymns became mainstays of the Holiness and Pentecostal movement. Among his most noted works are "Deeper, Deeper," "I'm Happy with Jesus Alone," and "All I Need."

Jones made his first trip to Los Angeles in 1915 to conduct a revival and help organize and incorporate a congregation there. In 1916 Bishop Jones's first wife, Fannie Brown, died in Little Rock, Arkansas. He moved to Los Angeles in 1917, organized Christ Temple Church of Christ (Holiness) USA, and married Pearl E. Reed in 1918.

He continued to lead the COCHUSA until he became ill in 1943. A year later, he attended his last convention in 1944 in Chicago, Illinois where he was elected senior bishop and president emeritus of the National Convention for life. He died five years later in Los Angeles.

Further Reading:

Castilla. Willenham. *Moving Forward on God's Highway: A Textbook History of the Church of Christ (Holiness)*. s.l.: Author House, 2007

Cobbins, Otto. *History of Church of Christ (Holiness) USA, 1895–1965*. Chicago, IL: National Pub. Board Church of Christ (Holiness) USA, 1966.

Jefferson, Anita Bingham. *Charles Price Jones: First Black Holiness Reformer*. Jackson, MS: s.n., 2011.

Jones, Curtis P. ?–1976

The founding bishop of the **Bibleway Pentecostal Apostolic Church** Jones had served in the Apostolic Church of God where he pastored St. Paul Apostolic Church in Acton, Virginia. In 1933 he was sent to Roanoke, Virginia to establish a congregation. In 1938 he left the COGA, rejecting the leadership of the newly appointed presiding bishop, **Thomas Cox**, to align himself with the **Church of Our Lord Jesus Christ of the Apostolic Faith**, becoming pastor of St. Paul Apostolic Church in Henry County, Virginia.

In 1957 Jones split from Lawson, primarily citing the same rigid authoritative stance as **Smallwood Williams**. The group split to form the Bible Way Churches of Christ World Wide. He also objected to the fact that Lawson did not go far enough in repudiating the ministry of women. He did not, however, align himself with Williams' faction. Three years later, Jones established his own group with two other congregations in Virginia. He served as presiding bishop of Bibleway Pentecostal Apostolic Church until his death.

J

Jones, Ozro Thurston (O.T.), Jr. 1922–2008

Well-known **Church of God in Christ** bishop, educator, and civil rights leader. Jones was born in Fort Smith, Arkansas as the eldest son of former COGIC presiding bishop, **Orzo Thurston Jones Sr.** When Jones was still a boy, the family moved to Philadelphia where his father pastored. He earned a bachelor's degree in education and a master's degree in sociology as well a bachelor's degree in sacred theology from Temple University. Jones became the first COGIC minister with a terminal degree when he earned his doctorate in sacred theology from that same institution.

Jones preached his first sermon at fourteen and was ordained as a minister by his father at sixteen. In 1949 Jones served a four-year tour as a missionary associate minister in Liberia, West Africa. After returning to the United States, he was ordained an elder in 1954, and appointed to Memorial Church of God in Christ, a local congregation in Haverford, Pennsylvania, leading that church until 1964. Once his father assumed his position as senior bishop, the younger Jones became the active pastor of Holy Temple Church in Philadelphia so that his father could devote his full attention to his responsibilities. That year, he also became president of COGIC's International Youth Congress.

Jones progressive ecclesiology kept him a step ahead of many classical Pentecostal on social justice issues. In 1965 Jones hosted Dr. Martin Luther King at the COGIC international Youth Convention in Chicago. In 1985 Jones went against denominational polity to ordain nineteen COGIC women to the ministry. His ecumenical sensitivities won him a seat as a member of board of the American Bible Society as well as on the Board of Regents or Oral Roberts University, a Charismatic institution that did not fit squarely in the classical Pentecostal camp.

Yet, like his father, he was fiercely loyal to COGIC. Like him, he was consecrated bishop in 1973, and in 1980 he was elected to the COGIC General Board. Jones contributed to the body in a number of areas. Like his father, he was a gifted speaker and called on often to speak to COGIC and other congregations across the country. The two worked together to produce Bible study materials for the national *Young People's Willing Workers (YPWW) Quarterly Topics*.

Further Reading:

DuPree, Sherry Sherrod. *Biographical Dictionary of African-American Holiness-Pentecostals 1880–1990*. Washington: Mid-Atlanta Regional, 1989.

Ligons-Berry, Delrio A. "'The Few that Got Through': The Nineteen Women Ordained by Bishop Ozro Thurston Jones Jr. STD (1982–1990)." Paper presented to the Society of Pentecostal Studies. Memphis, TN, 2011.

Jones, Ozro Thurston (O.T.), Sr. 1891–1972

The prominent **Church of God in Christ** bishop who succeeded founder, **Charles Harrison Mason** as presiding Bishop of the denomination. Jones was born into a Baptist family in Fort Smith, Arkansas. By 1912 he had affiliated with COGIC, experienced and confessed salvation and Pentecostal Spirit baptism, and answered a call to the ministry under the guidance of Elder **Justus Bowe**, a COGIC pioneer. Soon afterwards, Jones, his older sister, and a brother developed an evangelistic team in North Arkansas and the surrounding states. Over the next few years, they established eighteen congregations.

In 1914 Jones organized COGIC's Youth Department and served as its first president. Two years later, he founded and edited the *Young People's Willing Worker (YPWW) Quarterly Topics*, a Christian education-oriented journal that has been a staple of the COGIC education department since that time.

In 1920 he was appointed assistant to the state overseer in Oklahoma. In 1925 Jones became pastor of a small congregation in Philadelphia which grew to become the historic Holy Temple Church of God in Christ. A year later, he became state overseer for Pennsylvania, and in 1928, founded the International Youth Congress of the Church of God in Christ.

In 1933 Mason consecrated Jones as one of the five "founding" bishops and later selected him to serve on the executive commission, then headed by Bishop **A. B. McEwen**, to assist the founder in administering. At Mason's death in 1961, the board of bishops nominated Jones as senior bishop and the church's general assembly approved the nomination. While serving in that position, he continued to author the *YPWW Topics* and remained Jurisdictional Bishop of Pennsylvania. His son, **Ozro Thurston Jones Jr.**, became the active pastor of Holy Temple Church in Philadelphia in order that his father could devote full time to his position of senior bishop.

In 1965 opposition that had been brewing before Mason's death came to a head when some within COGIC called for regular elections for the office of a presiding bishop. After the demands ended in a 1968, court-ordered re-election, Jones was defeated, but remained Jurisdictional Bishop in Pennsylvania until his death in 1972, and **James Oglethorpe Patterson, Sr.** won the office of presiding bishop.

Jones, Spencer A. 1946–

One of the most highly visible black pastors and leaders within the predominantly white Assemblies of God (AG) at the end of the twenty-first century. Jones, a native of Pine Bluff, Missouri, received his Pentecostal baptism experience in 1967 while serving in the Vietnam War. In 1972, after becoming one of the first black students to attend and graduate from the AG's Central Bible College in Springfield, Missouri, Jones entered Assemblies of God ministry. While there, he went on a summer missions trip to Chicago, a city he feared, to help plant a church. Jones, who was ordained in 1974, pioneered churches in Indianapolis, Minneapolis, Tampa, Orlando, Fort Lauderdale, Houston, Dallas, Gary, and Charlotte before serving as pastor of Southside Worship Center Assembly of God in Chicago, Illinois since 1972.

Jones has held several prominent positions within the AG. Serving as a featured speaker at the denomination's 1993 General Council put him the limelight. Since then, he has been a nationally appointed home missionary to the inner city since 1996 and is executive director and president of National Inner City Workers conference. Jones serves on the Royal Rangers Committee (the AG equivalent to the Boy Scouts), and was first vice president and later president of the **National Black Fellowship of the Assemblies of God**. In 1999 when the Executive Presbytery voted to expand by one position to include ethnic representation, Jones was elected to represent the ethnic fellowships.

Within his inner city congregation, Jones takes a hands-on approach to urban ministry. He serves as a police liaison, facilitating meetings between the police and his majority African American community. He visits schools on a weekly basis to encourage both teachers and students. In addition, in 2005, he became founder and president of the nonprofit People United to Save Urban America, which focuses on training urban workers, planting churches, and conducting outreach crusades throughout urban centers of the United States.

K

Keith, Mary Frankie Giles Lewis (M. F. L.) 1888–1962

The first presiding bishop of the **House of God which is the Church of the Living God Pillar and Ground of the Truth without Controversy** (the Keith Dominion). Keith was born of mixed race parentage in Lumpkin, Georgia. Her father was white, and her mother was native American from the Cherokee tribe.

She was raised in the Missionary Baptist Church, before the family joined the **Church of the Living God Pillar and Ground of the Truth** during its foundational years. By the time that Keith was twelve years old, both her mother and stepfather had died.

Keith met **Walter Curtis Lewis**, eldest son of **Mary Magdalena Lewis Tate** founder of the parent organization, **Church of the Living God, Pillar and Ground of the Truth** in 1914. After their marriage, she taught school part time and worked alongside him to establish congregations throughout the South. During this time, her mother-in-law developed a close relationship with her and began grooming her daughter-in-law to take over after her death.

After her husband's death in 1921, Tate appointed the young widow to the bishopric to continue serving over the congregations that her late husband had previously overseen. Under her oversight, the territory was expanded into Connecticut, Delaware, Maryland, Indiana, Kentucky, Michigan, New York, New Jersey, North Carolina, South Carolina, Pennsylvania, Virginia, Alaska, and Jamaica.

In 1927 she married Lonnie Keith. They were married for only two or three years before he died. She did not marry again. Despite her remarriage—which brought on the resentment of **Felix Tate**, her brother-in-law—Keith and Mary Magdalena Lewis Tate remained close. Tate provided generously for her daughter-in-law and saw to it that Frankie was designated bishop. During the latter years of Tate's life, Keith served as chief overseer and General Secretary of the parent organization.

When Tate died, Keith became overseer of the entire denomination for a short while. However, her leadership was not without contention. After a year, she became one of the three-member Supreme Executive Council that also included her brother-in-law, and her husband's nephew by marriage, **Bruce McLeod**. When the denomination split, she became presiding bishop of The House of God which is the **Church of the Living**

God Pillar and Ground of the Truth without Controversy, Inc., which later became identified as the House of God Church.

Perhaps the most highly educated leader with in the Church of the Living God tradition, Keith received her Bachelor of Theology and Doctor of Divinity degrees from Moody Bible Institute, worked on a master's degree at Tennessee Agricultural and Industrial State College (now Tennessee State College), and was awarded a Doctor of Letters degree.

Her appreciation for education led her to establish the Keith Bible Institute near Ooltawah, Tennessee in 1943. The institution served kindergarten through sixth grade, made food, clothing, and dormitory housing available to students from poor families. She also founded a school and religious studies courses for young ministers within her denomination, collaborating with Moody Bible Institute to allow many of those completing the ministry training courses to pursue degrees in theology through the Chicago institution. She also assisted many members to attend Tennessee State College, a historically black institution whose campus abutted the denomination's headquarters.

Her other accomplishments include publishing a composition of the elder leader's musical compositions in *Spiritual Songs and Hymns*, a hymnal published in Chattanooga around 1944, and establishing the House of God Home for Children.

Further Reading:

Lewis, Arthur L. *The Morning Breaks: Mary Frankie Lewis-Keith Collected Work, Letters and Manuscripts*. S.l.: s.n., 2014.

Kelly, Otha Miema (O.M.) 1897–1982

An advisor to **Church of God in Christ** leaders **Charles Harrison Mason** and **J. O. Patterson, Sr.** Kelly was born in Hattiesburg, Mississippi, to a Baptist father and Methodist mother who experienced Pentecostal Holy Spirit baptism in 1912. The next year the fifteen-year-old converted to Christian faith and came under the influence of **Mason**. Kelly left Mississippi in 1917 to travel to Chicago, Illinois. There he met Bishop **William Roberts** and Mother **Lillian Brooks Coffey** and became a member of the **Church of God in Christ**. Within a short time, he had the experience of Pentecostal Holy Spirit baptism and threw himself into the work of the COGIC.

In 1924 he was appointed vice-president of the COGIC Youth Department of Illinois and Indiana. A year later, he became president, serving in that position until 1930. At same time, Kelly founded churches in Lexington, Mississippi, the birthplace of the **Church of God in Christ** as well as in New York City and on Long Island, New York.

Early in 1931 he was appointed to a mission congregation in Rockaway Beach, New York that he pastored until 1935, when he moved to the Mother Church of God in Christ. In 1934 Mason appointed Kelly as Overseer of Eastern New York. Beginning with sixteeen mission congregations, he brought Eastern New York Jurisdiction to a strength of 170 churches and missions, hundreds of preachers and missionaries, and thousands of members organized into twenty-two districts.

In 1951 eighty-five-year-old Mason selected Kelly, along with Bishops **J. S. Bailey** and **A. B. McEwen,** as an Executive Commission to assist him in overseeing the administration of the work of the denomination. After the 1968 election of **James O. Patterson, Sr.** as presiding bishop, Kelly became one of his advisors. In 1976, on Patterson's recommendation, the Executive Counsel elected Kelly as First Assistant Presiding Bishop. Kelly became seriously ill in 1981 and died in New York City a year later.

Keyes, Oree Sr. 1923–2008

The fourth presiding bishop of the **Apostolic Faith Church of God**. Keyes was born in Laurel, Mississippi and lived most of his life around Ashtabula, Ohio. He previously served as overseer of the Northern District of the denomination. He served in the United States Army during World War II and worked professionally as a carpenter. Keyes was the founder of an **Apostolic Faith Church of God** congregation in Jefferson, Ohio, using his carpentry skills to build the sanctuary and parsonage, and to help with the construction of other churches within the AFCOG. He also spearheaded construction of the new general headquarters of the Apostolic Faith Church in Franklin, Virginia.

He took the lead in establishing the **United Fellowship Convention of the Original Azusa Mission**, which encompassed the fellowship of six separate bodies that originated from the churches established after the **Azusa Street Revival** (the **Church of God Holiness Unto the Lord, The Apostolic Faith Churches of God,** Scott's Revival Center, Tabernacle of God Holiness Church, and the **Apostolic Faith Church of God Live On**).

In 1980 Keyes was officially elected and installed as senior bishop of the **Apostolic Faith Church of God**. He served as presiding bishop from 1980 until Alzheimer's disease deteriorated his health to the point that he was forced to step down in 2004. He served as Bishop Emeritus until his death at age eighty-four.

Killingsworth, Frank Russell 1873–1976

The educator, minister and founder of the Holiness denomination, **Kodesh Church of Immanuel.** Killingsworth was born near Winnsboro, South Carolina. His father was an African Methodist Episcopal Church minister and presiding elder; yet in his early life, Killingsworth was a socialist and a Mason. He received an associates degree from Livingstone College in Salisbury, North Carolina in 1899 and a Doctor of Divinity degree from South Carolina State College in 1907.

Killingsworth served as a principle of two high schools—one in South Carolina and the other in North Carolina, and of Jefferson grade school in Yorkville, South Carolina before moving to the Washington DC area and serving as the administrator of the Manassas Industrial Institute in Manassas, Virginia from 1911–1915. He was licensed to preach in 1911 and ordained in 1917. His first pastorate was Hosea AMEZ Church in Bowie, Maryland, outside of Washington DC.

He pastored Lomax AMEZ Church in Arlington, Virginia from 1918 to 1926 and Varick Memorial AME Church from 1927 to 1929. By then he had become dissatisfied with the episcopal structure of the AMEZ church and the power invested in its bishops. That year Killingsworth and 120 lay people from the AMEZ founded the Kodesh Church of Immanuel in Philadelphia.

During the early years of the denomination, Killingsworth formulated much of its doctrinal stance. In 1933 Killingsworth wrote the *Junior Catechism of the Kodesh Church of Immanuel*. In 1940 Killingsworth published the *Doctrines and Discipline of the Kodesh Church of Immanuel*. He died at the age of 103.

Further Reading:

Caldwell, A. B. "F. R. Killingsworth." In *History of the American Negro, Washington D. C. Edition, Volume IV,* 230–33. Atlanta: A.B. Caldwell, 1922.
Killingsworth, Frank R. *The Doctrines and Discipline of the Kodesh Church of Immanuel.* Philadelphia, PA: Westminster, 1940.

Kinchlow, Harvey Benjamin "Ben" 1936–

An ordained African Methodist Episcopal Church minister and evangelist, broadcaster, author, and businessman best known for being co-host of The 700 Club from 1975 to 1988 and again from 1992 to 1996 with "Pat" Roberson. Kinchlow also hosted other shows on the Christian Broadcasting Network such as Straight Talk and a radio talk show, "Taking it to the Streets."

Kinchlow was born and raised in Uvalde, Texas. After a period as a Black nationalist, influenced by Malcolm X and the Black Muslims, the son of a Methodist minister became a born-again Christian. He was ordained an African Methodist Episcopal Church minister in 1971. Soon thereafter, he became the executive director of a Christian drug and rehabilitation center and appeared as a guest on The 700 Club, speaking his ministry there. He initially was asked to guest host the show while Robertson was on a trip to Israel. In 1975 he became Director of Counseling with oversight of counseling centers in major American cities He was eventually tapped to co-host the talk show with Christian Broadcasting Network founder Pat Robinson. In 1982 he was promoted to vice-president for domestic ministries for CBN, then in 1985 to executive vice-president.

Kinchlow left the show and the network in 1996 to pursue an independent ministry. Since his departure, the conservative Republican and pro-Israel advocate has served as founder of Americans for Israel, an organization that promotes understanding between Christians and Jews and attempts to foster ties between the Jewish and African-American communities. He co-hosts the "Front Page Jerusalem" radio show, a news and commentary program on American-Israeli relations, contributes to WorldNetDaily a conservative internet newspaper, and serves on the Board of the National Council on Bible Curriculum in Public Schools, to promote returning Bible reading to schools.

As a motivational speaker, Kinchlow travels around the United States conducting men and couples seminars. He is author of several books including his autobiography, *Plain Bread,* and a political history of African-Americans, *Black Yellow Dogs.*

King, Judge 1872–1945

The founder of the **Christ Holy Sanctified Church** was born in Louisiana. As a young convert into sanctification and holiness, King was a rising leader in the Christ's Sanctified Holy Church, a predominantly white body, before breaking away, reportedly over the issue of the nature of New Testament sacraments. King and his wife, **Sarah King**, moved to Los Angeles, California, around 1918 to escape Southern racism. In the early 1920s, the family relocated north to Oroville, California where they opened a small mission church. Yet, even in that area, the Kings encountered strong racial and religious prejudice. Their detractors were not only disturbed by their doctrinal teachings, but also the idea of whites and blacks worshiping together was unconscionable. The church in which they worshipped was burned down, King and other church members were beaten and thrown in jail, and Sarah was shot by a crazed assailant during a worship service.

After moving to Central California, the family fared better and King began to spread his message of holiness and sanctification throughout the state. By 1925 Judge and Sarah had relocated again, this time to the Bay Area, where they settled in San Francisco and established a mission church in the culturally diverse area of West Oakland. From here, they launched an aggressive evangelistic campaign in their home and on the streets of an area known for seedy nightclubs, prostitution, derelicts, alcoholics, and open street violence.

The Kings became colleagues with major Pentecostal leaders throughout California including **William J. Seymour, Henry and Emma Cotton,** as well as **Church of God in Christ** leader, **Charles Harrison Mason.** Judge King served as senior bishop and president of Christ Holy Sanctified Church for over thirty-five years, until his death in 1945. When he died, his son and assistant bishop, **Ulysses S. King Sr.** took the lead of the denomination.

King, Sarah Ann 1878–1971

Little is known of the early life of the co-founder of the **Christ Holy Sanctified Church** except that she was born in Calcasieu Parish, Louisiana. She and her husband, **Judge King**, were converted to Christian faith in the Baptist Church, left to join the Methodist Church, and subsequently moved into the Holiness movement after accepting the doctrine of sanctification. Their first association with that movement was through the predominantly white Christ Sanctified Holy Church. They were dropped from the membership roll of that organization, however, because of disagreement regarding the nature of New Testament ordinances such as foot washing, communion, and water baptism.

King was one of the first of the Holiness group to speak in tongues while worshipping in the Methodist Church. For the experience, she was branded as deluded and demon possessed. Her husband, Judge, who had not yet embraced the Pentecostal Holy Spirit baptism, initially threatened to dissolve the marriage and leave home.

Sarah's mother's home was the site for the historic meeting when William J. Seymour, founder of the Azusa Street Mission, stopped in Louisiana on his way to Tennessee. He spent an unknown amount of time with the small group teaching the Pentecostal doctrine and encouraging them in their evangelistic work.

A preacher in her own right, once Judge King was converted to Pentecostal spirituality, Sarah worked faithfully by her husband's side and suffered many of the same persecutions to the point of endangering her life. One night while she was preaching, a man burst into the worship service and shot her. Often in sharing her testimony, she would declare, "When I get to Heaven, I'm going to present the bullets in my body to Jesus and I'm going to say to Him that I took these bullets for the Gospel of Jesus Christ." Then she would look around and simply ask, "What are you going to present to Jesus when you stand before Him?"

King set up a Home Missionary Department among the small group of women she had gotten together from the surrounding farmlands. Despite having only a ninth grade education, while living in Louisiana, she set up a school to educate poor black children.

A year after Judge King's death, Sarah remained active in the leadership of the denomination. When a division broke out within the denomination, Mother King, as she was known, worked along with her son **Ulysses S. King Sr.**, who had assumed the position of presiding bishop, and a small group of followers to write guidelines for the church.

She died in Berkeley, California at age ninety-five.

King, Saunders Samuel 1909–2000

The noted blues musician was the son of **Sarah and Judge King,** founders of the **Christ Holy Sanctified Church.** As a child, King sang in the choir of his parents' local congregation. Still a child, he learned piano, banjo and ukulele, and took up the electric guitar in 1938 after hearing soloist guitarist, Charlie Christian, in the Benny Goodman band. He first performed at the end of the 1930s as a tenor vocalist with the Southern Harmony Four, a gospel quartet that broadcast over NBC radio in San Francisco, California.

King left the denomination to become a blues musician. He formed his own band and had his first major hit, "S. K. Blues" in 1942. Subsequently, he recorded for Aladdin Records, Modern Records, and Rhythm Records before he suffered a series of misfortunes, including his wife's suicide in 1943, being shot by a disgruntled landlord in 1945, succumbing to heroin addiction, and being sentenced to San Quentin prison for drug possession. He retired from active performance in 1961 and returned to the church where he worked until suffering a stroke in 1999. In 1979 he briefly came out of retirement to play on his son-in-law Carlos Santana's album "Oneness." He died at age ninety-one.

King, Ulysses Stephen, Sr. 1906–1985

The author, orator, historian, musician, and second presiding bishop of **Christ Holy Sanctified Church**, was born in Mansfield, DeSoto Parish, Louisiana. When his father, Bishop **Judge King,** died in 1945, he assumed the position of presiding bishop. At the time, the younger King was serving as assistant bishop. He left seminary for a time to take over helm of the denomination. He pastored the Christ Holy Sanctified Church in Oakland, California where he served until his death.

He was educated at the Center for Urban Black Studies in Berkeley, California, and received an Honorary Doctor of Divinity degree from the same institution, where many of his writings and his memoirs can be found. He was also a member of the Interdenominational Ministerial Alliance, and other community organizations. His vision was to see the local church become a center of influence within the heart of the community.

King's ministry was ecumenical. He traveled across the United States preaching in Baptist, Methodist, other mainline churches, as wells as non-denominational churches at a time when many Pentecostals refused to do so. In 1969 King was elected second president of the **Federated Pentecostal Church International, Inc.,** an umbrella organization for eight independently-incorporated, autonomous Pentecostal bodies who are in full fellowship with each other.

Along with his wife Tryphosa, King was responsible for bringing in over one hundred churches from Nigeria, West Africa into Christ Holy Sanctified Church. The couple began their ministry in 1972 in Uyo, where a congregation was established in 1976.

King's Apostle Holy Church World Ministries

The Pentecostal denomination was established by "Mother" **Carrie V. Gurry**, incorporated as the King's Apostle Holy Temple Church of God in 1911 in Baltimore, Maryland. The group often met in her home. Gurry traveled through Maryland and Pennsylvania, preaching, teaching, and establishing congregations. The first two churches she established were King's Apostle Holiness Church of God, Inc. (KAHC) in Annapolis, Maryland in 1922 and the KAHC in Denton, Maryland in 1924.

In 1925 the name of the movement was changed to "the Holiness Church of God," followed by the change to its present name, King's Apostle Holiness Church of God, Inc., in 1958 under the leadership of Bishop Walter E. Campher of Hagerstown, Maryland, who died in 1971.

Bishop E. Eugene Baltimore, pastor of the Baltimore Temple Church in Ranson, West Virginia, succeeded Bishop Campher, serving for eighteen years until his death in 1999. The senior Baltimore was succeeded by his son, Wilbert Lewis Baltimore, who had previously served as Minister of Music, Moderator of the Youth Conference, National Field Supervisor, and vice bishop. He was elevated to the office of senior bishop and General President. In 1967 Baltimore established Holy Temple Church of God in Jessup, Maryland with five original members. In the intervening years, that congregation became Holy Temple Cathedral, and relocated to 7.2 acres of property in Annapolis.

In 2001 the organization ratified a name change to the King's Apostle Church of God, Inc. to reflect the organization's move into the twenty-first century. It was changed again to King's Apostle Church World Ministries. Currently, there are seventeen congregations throughout New York, New Jersey, Pennsylvania, and Maryland.

Kodesh Church of Immanuel

A predominantly black Holiness church founded as the Kodesh Holy Church of Philadelphia in 1929 by **Frank Russell Killingsworth**, a former African Methodist Episcopal Zion Church pastor. Killingsworth's departure, along with 120 laymen, from the AMEZ Church was due, at least in part, to dissatisfaction with its episcopal structure. In 1934 the group merged with a Pittsburgh organization the Christian Tabernacle Union that held similar beliefs. The denomination differs from other Holiness bodies in that it practices three modes of baptism—sprinkling, pouring, and immersion—leaving the choice to the individual. Further, the denomination does not hold the doctrine of speaking in tongues as initial evidence of Holy Spirit baptism. It views, instead, glossolalia as spiritual gift not all believers possess.

The denomination also includes elements of Killingsworth's former Methodist tradition, including Wesleyan emphasis on entire sanctification as a second work of grace, and organization of churches into Annual Assemblies based on jurisdictions. It diverges from Methodism, however, in that there are no bishops and its leadership is shared by supervising elders.

By 1936 Kodesh Church of Immanuel had nine congregations with nearly six hundred members, and at one time, the membership reached 2000. By 1990, however, the denomination had declined to five congregations located in Philadelphia and Pittsburgh, Pennsylvania and Washington DC with twenty-nine clergy and a little more than three hundred members. There is also a mission church in Liberia, West Africa that has a church, school, medical clinic, and missionary dormitory facilities.

Further Reading:

Killingsworth, Frank R. The *Doctrines and Discipline of the Kodesh Church of Immanuel*.
    Philadelphia, PA: Westminster, 1940.

Koffey, Laura Adorkor 1893–1928

Preacher, organizer, and leader who founded the **African Universal Church**, a **quasi-Pentecostal** group that flourished in the mid-1920s. Koffey was a native of Asofa, Gold Coast (now Ghana) in West Africa and, reportedly, the daughter of an African tribal king, village pastor, and missionary. She carried the title "princess," and was addressed as "Mother Kofi" by her followers.

In 1924 she reportedly began hearing voices and visions from God calling her to help Africans in America. Originally, she refused the call and began traveling to other parts of Africa, even after suffering two near fatal illnesses. After the third near-death illness, however, she relented. Koffey reached the country through Europe, then Canada. She arrived in New York City intent on urging blacks to return to their mother continent. Reportedly, Koffey entered this country with her husband, but the two were separated by the massive crowd of immigrants disembarking in New York and she never saw him again.

She first visited and spoke in churches in major northern cities such as Chicago, , Detroit, and New York City, attracting large audiences. By spring 1927, however, she was traveling and speaking primarily on street corners, and in halls and churches in the South. By then, she also had established churches in Florida cities as well as in Mobile, Alabama. These congregations came under the umbrella of her **African Universal Church and Commercial League.**

After joining with Marcus Garvey's Universal Negro Improvement Association (UNIA), Koffey concentrated her works in Mississippi, Alabama, Louisiana, and Florida serving as a major UNIA recruiter. Her revival style meetings regularly resulted in hundreds of new members for his movement. Yet, her involvement with UNIA eventually ended, and her relationship with some sympathetic black leaders became contentious after she was perceived as a rival to Garvey. Detractors began accusing her of fraud, including some who insisted that she was actually born in Georgia and had American siblings. On more than one occasion, she was arrested, yet never faced formal charges.

Still, her increased personal popularity remained problematic to Garvey's leadership. Within a short time, Koffey began to distance herself from Garvey and the UNIA. Koffey began to criticize the group for practices she considered in conflict with Christian faith, such as holding fund-raising dances and holding drills on Sunday. In return, Garvey publicly repudiated her and she was excommunicated from the UNIA.

In 1928 while she was delivering a message from her Miami pulpit, thirty-five-year old Koffey was shot point blank by an assassin. At the time of her death, she had tens of thousands of followers, with a large portion located in Florida. While she died in March, Koffey's burial did not take place until August since the funeral home waited for burial instruction from her family in Ghana. During the interim, her body remained on display and the funeral home charged twenty-five cents for each person who desired to view it. The funeral service had nearly 10,000 attendants who paid their respects, with almost 7,000 following her funeral procession.

After her death, her organization faltered for a while, and followers scattered into various groups. After several years remnant members reorganized into two separate bodies, the **African Universal Church, Inc.** and the **Missionary African Universal Church**.

Further Reading:

Bair, Barbara. "Ethiopia Shall Stretch Forth Her Hands Unto God: Laura Koffey and the Gendered Vision of Redemption in the Garvey Movement." In *A Mighty Baptism: Race, Gender, and the Creation of American Protestantism,* edited by Susan Juster and Lisa MacFarlane. Ithaca, NY: Cornell University Press, 1996.

L

La Fleur, David 1885-??

One of the first black ministers within the **Church of God (Cleveland, TN)** and a leader within the **Church of God (Colored Work)**. La Fleur was born in Nassau, the Bahamas and first came to the United States around 1913, the year he was ordained a deacon. By 1920 he was serving as pastor of a Church of God congregation in West Palm Beach, Florida. In 1923 when **Thomas Richardson** left with **A. J. Tomlinson** to move to the Church of God of Prophecy, La Fleur was tapped to oversee the Church of God (Colored Work). In 1926 La Fleur was a member of the committee of Black ministers that included Crawford Bright and who requested that a separate general assembly be established for blacks. During his administration, the first three Assemblies of the black church were called. In 1925 LaFleur convened the first Black Assembly of the Church of God. He resigned in 1928 and was appointed to the Council of Seventy.

Lambert, Eva Gertrude Bell 1899-1949

Early faith healer and pastor, "Mother" Lambert, as she was known, was born in Houston, Texas and migrated to Philadelphia, Pennsylvania where she met Bishop **Ida Robinson**, founder and presiding bishop of **Mt. Sinai Holy Church of America, Inc**. Lambert became a member of both the denomination and Robinson's congregation and began working very closely with Bishop Robinson.

With Robinson's blessing, Lambert subsequently left Philadelphia for New York City where she held a series of tent ministries that drew a following large enough so that the group began to seek a permanent facility. By 1926 Lambert had established the congregation that would b the beginning of **St. Mark Holy Church** in the Bedford-Stuyvesant section of Brooklyn, New York. In the 1920s that congregation was one of only a few congregation in New York city that were pastored by a woman. During the 1930s Lambert was one of several progressive Pentecostal ministers to enlarge her ministry through radio broadcasts.

At the end of that decade, in 1939, Lambert was consecrated to the bishopric, and shortly after held the first Convocation of the **St. Mark Holy Gospel Church of America Inc**. At the time of her death, Lambert's body had congregations in nine states with membership running into the thousands. Though her followers lauded her ability to heal the sick, Lambert died in Philadelphia while on route to a tent revival in Berkeley, Virginia, following a prolonged illness.

Latter House of the Lord for All People and the Church of the Mountain, Apostolic Faith

A predominantly African-American Pentecostal church founded in 1936 in Cincinnati by Bishop L. W. Williams, a former Baptist preacher who formed the body in part because of an experience of enlightenment during prayer. Williams was appointed chief overseer for life, and his successors serve the same term.

The body has a strong pacifist stance and members are conscientious objectors. In worship, it uses water instead of wine or grape juice for communion The church combines Calvinist and Pentecostal doctrine.

In 1936, the group, headquartered in Georgia, reported six churches and by 1947, they reported six thousand members.

Lawrence, Mary D. ??-??

Lawrence was born in Eden, North Carolina. She was educated at Rockingham Community College where she received certification in nursing assistance, printing, and business administration. The Christian involvement of the musically gifted Lawrence began at an early age when she trained and directed a 150-voice children's choir in her mother's church. Later she ventured into the professional arena with her husband, Charles J. "Charlie Brown" Lawrence, and sons as the recording group, the True Saints.

In 1990 Lawrence was called to ministry. Subsequently, she founded the Open Door Outreach Center in suburban College Park, Georgia; and became founder of Women Against Violence Evolve (W.A.V.E.), a multi-cultural, interreligious coalition established to deal with widespread violence in society. From the vantage point of her local congregation, Lawrence also attacked the problem of drug abuse with anti-drug and rehabilitation programs. Her outreach to women includes publication of "The Woman/The Compass," a volume which provides perspective on women's "divine" purpose.

In May 2001 Apostle Lawrence was consecrated a bishop within the **United Holy Church of America**, Inc. by Bishop Odell McCollum, making her, at that time, only the second woman to be consecrated in the 112-year history of one of the oldest African-American holiness church in the United States. She was first appointed as the bishop over the denomination's music department, then over the South Central district of the denomination.

Subsequently, Lawrence left the **United Holy Church** to establish Victory International Prophetic Ministries, Inc., an organization she began in 1993, which now has fourteen affiliate ministries. As presiding bishop of that organization, Lawrence's involvement with the Atlanta and Fulton County communities has garnered numerous honors and awards from civic organizations as well as local, state, and federal government agencies, including recognition as one of the Most Outstanding Pastors in Atlanta, and among the Top Ten Women Ministers in Georgia.

Lawson, Robert Clarence 1883-1961

One of the most prominent Oneness Pentecostal religious leaders, civil rights activist of the early twentieth century, and founder of the **Church of Our Lord Jesus Christ of the Apostolic Faith** (the second largest black Oneness body in the United States). Lawson was born in New Iberia, Louisiana, (birthplace of **Azusa Street Revival** leader, **William Joseph Seymour**). His parents died when he was a child and he was raised by an aunt.

Reportedly, as a boy, Lawson planned to become a lawyer and businessperson. After leaving Louisiana as a young man, however, he became a nightclub and tavern singer who traveled and performed throughout the Midwest. While touring in Columbus, Ohio he contracted tuberculosis and was hospitalized. During his hospital stay, he encountered a member of **Garfield Thomas Haywood's** congregation who shared the Christian Gospel with him. He was converted to Christian faith and received the Pentecostal experience of Holy Spirit baptism in 1913 under the ministry of the then-Trinitarian leader of the **Pentecostal Assemblies of the World**.

Once called to the ministry, Haywood sent Lawson to plant churches in the Southwest. Then in 1914, Haywood assigned him as pastor of Apostolic Faith Assembly in Columbus, Ohio. Within the PAW, Lawson rose to the rank of general elder. In 1915 when Haywood adopted the Oneness understanding, Lawson followed suit and was baptized in Jesus' name.

In 1919 Lawson incorporated this church as the Church of Christ of the Apostolic Faith. Using this congregation as his base, Lawson continued to evangelize throughout the Midwest and through his efforts established the Lincoln Park Church of Christ in San Antonio, Texas and the Temple Church of Christ in St. Louis, Missouri. Lawson's departure from PAW was a solitary act; he did not encourage other pastors or congregations to leave with him. His decision, at least in part, was based on doctrinal disagreements with PAW leadership. First, he what he considered their lenient stance on the issue of divorce and remarriage was problematic to him. He also did not accept Haywood's decision to license women as evangelists and pastors. Further, he required women to cover their heads whenever they entered the church building.

During 1919 Lawson traveled to Harlem, New York City and, beginning with a series of prayer meetings and street preaching services, founded Refuge Church of Christ while continuing to pastor his Ohio congregation. He organized the Church of Christ of the Apostolic Faith, named after that Ohio congregation. The rapid growth of the New York work led him to move his headquarters there. In 1920 he incorporated his Harlem church as the Refuge Church of Christ of the Apostolic Faith. From this central point, over the next eleven years, Lawson sent ministers across the country to establish new works.

As a fierce defender of Oneness Pentecostal doctrine, Lawson attended the **Church of God in Christ** national convocation in 1919. Lawson debated his friend and COGIC founder **Charles Harrison Mason** over understandings of Christology. He also contributed numerous hymns portraying the Oneness message. Lawson influenced several others regarding Oneness doctrine. Including Holiness minister **Thomas Cox,** whose Christian Faith Band founded in 1897, the **Church of God (Apostolic)** was incorporated as Oneness organization in 1919. **Martin Rawleigh Gregory**, a Baptist minister, founded the **Emanuel Tabernacle Church** in 1916 and through Lawson's influence accepted the Oneness message. **Karl F. Smith**, later founder of Aenon Bible College, served as a pastor of Haywood's home church before returning to PAW. **Smallwood William**s, who had worked closely with him, would later break with him to establish the **Bible Way Church of Our Lord Jesus Christ World Wide** organization.

In 1925 Smith led a schism in the Columbus congregation Lawson had established, and returned the congregation to PAW. Immediately, Lawson established a second congregation in that city and placed Elder **Hubert Spencer** as pastor. Since the New York congregation was thriving, he moved the headquarters of the Church of Our Lord Jesus Christ of the Apostolic Faith there.

An entrepreneur as well as a pastor, Lawson established numerous businesses including a bookstore, printing company, grocery stores, and funeral parlors to help raise the economic status of the community surrounding the church. His business acumen aligned with his social activism in the establishment of an African American Pentecostal community known as Lawsonville in predominantly white, Shrub Oak, New York in 1927. There, he established a twenty-room summer inn, a cattle barn, a grocery store, a gas station. He also established Emanuel Cemetery with Attorney Sumner H. Lark. In 1932 Lawson initiated the radio broadcast over the stations WGBS. He also broadcasted successfully over WHOM and WINS.

As an educator, he took over a boarding school in Southern Pines, North Carolina that became known as the R. C. Lawson Institute and founded an orphanage there. In 1926 he founded the Church of Christ Bible Institute as the theological training center for his denomination.

Through his civil activities, he worked with political leaders such as Senator Adam Clayton Powell, Jr., the first African American member of congress since reconstruction. This interest also involved him to push for voter registration among his congregates and was participation in the first March on Washington in 1957 to encourage the federal government to grant African Americans voting rights.

Lawson drew on his earlier musical experience to contribute a number of Oneness hymns to the African American Pentecostal repertoire including some that have become mainstays in the Oneness tradition such as "God is Great in My Soul" and "His Name Should be Praised." A prolific writer, in 1925 Lawson wrote the groundbreaking, *The Anthropology of Jesus Christ our Kinsman*, an Afrocentric theological critique of western culture and of race relations within the Christianity tradition.

Socially progressive Lawson served as president of the Ethiopian World Federal, visiting that country in 1950, entertaining Haile Selassie at his home when the emperor visited New York, and receiving the *Star of Ethiopia* from Selassie in 1954. He also sponsored scholarships for two Ethiopians students and adopted an Ethiopian child.

Over the forty-two years of his ministry within the Church of Our Lord Jesus Christ of the Apostolic Faith, Lawson built a community that influenced African American Oneness Pentecostalism more than any figure other than Garfield Haywood. Several Oneness bodies trace their lineage back to his movement and many more indirectly flow from it. By the time of his death, Lawson left the membership at his headquarters Greater Refuge Temple at three thousand members before the megachurch phenomenon had exploded on the scene and without the benefit of the technological revolution. He also left a movement with 155 churches and a combined membership of 45,000. After his death, that movement would swell to over several hundred thousand.

Further Reading:

Anderson, Arthur M., ed. *For the Defense of the Gospel: Writings of Bishop R.C. Lawson.* New York: Church of Our Lord Jesus Christ, 1972.

Spellman, Robert C, and Mabel L. Thomas. *The Life, Legend and Legacy of Bishop R. C. Lawson.* Scotch Plains, NJ: s.n., 1983.

Stewart, Alexander C., and Sherry Sherrod DuPree. *The Silent Spokesman: Bishop Robert Clarence Lawson.* Gainesville, FL: Displays for Schools, 1994.

Layne, Austin Augustus 1891–1967

Bishop Austin A. Layne was born in 1891, in Barbados, West Indies and was converted at the age of ten. Austin came to the United States at the age of twenty-two, settling in New York City. While living in New York, Layne met PAW Bishop **Robert C. Lawson**, who encouraged Layne to contact a group in St. Louis who was looking for a pastor. In the fall of 1918, he made his way to St. Louis.

Layne took a graduate course in theology from Columbia University in New York City. He received two certificates from Moody Bible Institute, and was a member of the Society of Psychology. Raised an Episcopalian, Layne was introduced to the Apostolic Faith through the ministry of Mother **Susan G. Lightford** at Kings Chapel Assembly of the Apostolic Faith in New York (NY).

He began preaching in young people's street meetings as a young man, and accompanied his father on preaching tours. The call of God was ever on his heart.

In the summer of 1915, he was filled with the Pentecostal Holy Spirit baptism. Later, he was enlightened to baptism in the name of Jesus, which he also accepted. The late Bishop G. T. Haywood ordained and appointed him as district elder, and he was called in 1918 to pastor the Temple Church of Christ in St. Louis Missouri, which he did for forty-eight years. Though Layne's church started as a storefront congregations, it grew to be one of St. Louis largest, most progressive Pentecostal congregations, and by 1948, 500-seat sanctuary had been completed.

On more than one occasion, Layne's ministry resulted in a violent confrontation. Once, the husband of a member of his congregation confronted Layne with a knife and threatened his life. At another time, Layne received two bullet wounds (one in his right lung, the other in his right thigh) for preaching the gospel.

In 1951 Austin Layne, Sr. became Bishop of the Midwestern District. Layne was the diocesan of the 12th Episcopal District of the **Pentecostal Assemblies of the World**. He served in that capacity until his passing at seventy-six years of age.

Lee, Willie 1901–1969

The second presiding bishop of the **Pentecostal Churches of the Apostolic Faith** was born, in Starksville, Mississippi. He moved north as part of the great migration settling at some point in Indianapolis, Indiana.

Lee was baptized in Jesus' name at Christ Temple of the Apostolic Faith under the ministry of early **Pentecostal Assemblies of the World** leader, **Garfield T. Haywood,** and received the Pentecostal experience of Holy Spirit baptism in 1925. After moving to Detroit, Michigan, Lee was appointed assistant pastor of Greater Bethlehem Temple under **Bishop Samuel N. Hancock** and became pastor of Christ Temple Church in Muskegon Heights, Michigan.

In 1954 Lee returned to Indianapolis to become the fourth pastor Christ Temple, the mother church of the **Pentecostal Assemblies of the World**, which has once been pastored by Haywood. He served the congregation for fifteen years, until his death in 1969. While there, he was also responsible for the creation of the publication department. Among the publications produced by the department, the hymnal, *The Best of All*, published in the 1940s, features hymns composed by and sung throughout the Oneness Pentecostal community. After the resignation of Bishop **Charles Poole**, Lee also served as diocesan bishop of the Illinois State Council.

In 1957 Lee left with Hancock, Bishop Heardie Leaston, and Elder David Collins to form the **Pentecostal Churches of the Apostolic Faith, Inc.** He took his congregation into that denomination and was elected the assistant presiding bishop.

After Hancock's death in 1963, Lee succeeded him as senior bishop and persisted in teaching the heretical doctrine (which had be tolerated with Hancock but had been repudiated after the founder's death) that Jesus was only a son of God and not God himself. When a majority of the congregations objected, opting to return to the "orthodox" Oneness doctrines, Lee was disfellowshipped. At the end of a year, he founded a new body, Emmanuel Pentecostal Church of Our Lord, Apostolic Faith, in Indianapolis. Lee died in Indianapolis, five years after establishing his new organization.

Lewis, Felix Early 1892–1968

The co-founder, with his mother **Mary Magdalena Tate** and brother, **Walter Curtis Lewis,** of **The Church of the Living God, the Pillar and Ground of the Truth, Inc**. Lewis later became presiding bishop of the Lewis Dominion, which, though it retained the name of the earlier body, is one of the three factions that emerged out of Tate's original body. Felix, the younger of Tate's two sons claimed that God had revealed this name to him in 1903 and that it was later confirmed by his mother.

In 1914 Lewis was ordained to the bishopric at age twenty-two and served as one of the first four State Bishops of the church. The year he was ordained, his mother appointed the younger Lewis over the State of Florida. Moreover, he helped organize congregations throughout the country also in sending missionaries to foreign countries for the church. In 1923 he worked with his mother to establish the church general headquarters in Nashville, Tennessee and established the **New and Living Way Publishing Company** from which he composed and/or edited the literature, including the Constitution, Government and General Decree Book, written for the church by his mother.

At her Tate's death in 1931, Lewis was selected as one of a team of three overseers to administer the affairs of the organization and remained in that post until the three groups split into separate organizations, and he remained in leadership of his new, independent body until his demise.

Bishop Lewis was married three times during his life. His first marriage was to the former Estella Bonapart; the second was to the former Beatrice Giles; and his final marriage was to the former **Helen Middleton Matchett** who succeeded him as overseer. He died in West Palm Beach, Florida.

Lewis, Helen Middleton Matchett 1905–2001

The third chief overseer of the **Church of the Living God, Pillar and Ground of the Truth** (the Lewis Dominion) was the daughter-in-law of founder, **Mary Magdalena Lewis Tate**. She was born in Crystal River, Florida. She received the Pentecostal Spirit baptism at the age of fourteen and was originally a member of the **First Born Church of the Living God**

After her first husband Benjamin Matchett died, she married Tate's younger son, **Felix E. Lewis**. Called to the ministry in 1928, she was ordained and appointed assistant pastor of the congregation at Crystal River, and went on to serve as pastor in Daytona Beach, and West Palm Beach, Florida; and Nashville, Tennessee. She also held the office of presiding elder of the west and east coasts of Florida. Lewis was elevated to the bishopric in 1932. Later, she was appointed district bishop of Kentucky and Indiana, and in 1937, as assistant chief overseer, general secretary, and treasurer.

The family moved to Nashville, Tennessee around 1931 and when the Church of the Living God, Pillar and Ground of the Truth split, Felix became overseer of the Lewis Dominion, which retained the name of the parent body. In 1951 the family moved to West Palm Beach, Florida where she was active in local and community affairs. Following the death of Felix in 1968, she served as chief overseer pro tempore. In April 1969 she was officially selected and seated as chief overseer by the Supreme Executive Council of the **Church of the Living God, Pillar and Ground of the Truth, Inc.** Since that time, she worked with her son, Meharry Lewis, to reestablish the **New and Living Way Publishing**

House and co-authored the church's doctrinal treatise, *The Beauty of Holiness: A Small Catechism of the Holiness Faith* in 1988. She died at the age of ninety-six.

Lewis, Walter Curtis 1890–1921

The older of two sons of David and **Mary Magdalena Tate** was born in Vanleer, Tennessee. In 1903 he worked along with his mother and brother, **Felix Early Lewis**, to establish the Church of the Living God, Pillar and Ground of the Truth. Tate appointed him one of the first four state bishops.

Tate first sent Lewis along with several other church leaders to establish the church in the Northeast. Between 1913 and 1921, Lewis traveled with his wife, **Mary Francis Lewis** to plant or nurture congregations in Dickson and Chattanooga, Tennessee, Philadelphia, Pennsylvania, and Quitman, Georgia.

Lewis died from pneumonia in Churchville, Tennessee at age thirty, six months before the birth of his last child and ten years before the death of his mother.

Lightford, Susan Gertrude ??–1949

An early Oneness Pentecostal evangelist, church planter, and pastor who was instrumental in the ministries of some of the most prominent leaders within the Oneness movement. Lightford was born in Washington DC and raised Baptist. After migrating to Harlem in New York city, she first affiliated with the **Pentecostal Assemblies of the World**, and later joined the prominent Abyssinian Baptist Church pastored by Adam Clayton Powell, Sr., father of the first African American US Senator since Reconstruction.

In 1909 after receiving the Pentecostal Holy Spirit baptism, Lightford began preaching on the streets of Harlem before founding King's Assembly in 1910, the first Pentecostal church in that community, as a Trinitarian congregation. With this, she also became the first black woman to successfully pastor a church in New York City.

Lightford first heard the Oneness message in 1917 through Henry Prentiss, the pastor under whose ministry **Garfield T. Haywood** received the Pentecostal Holy Spirit baptism. Lightford later became a colleague of Haywood, and a pastor within his **Pentecostal Assemblies of the World**, traveling with him and his party on mission trips throughout the Caribbean.

Members of her flourishing congregation included the family of Thomas Wright (Fats) Waller, famous jazz musician, and **Robert C. Lawson**, later founder of the **Church of Our Lord Jesus Christ of the Apostolic Faith**. Lawson ran revivals for her and left with some converts to the Refuge Church of Chris. The Waller family was part of a contingent who left with Lawson.

Other prominent ministers who received the baptism of the Holy Ghost under Lightford's ministry were **Randolph A. Carr**, founder of the **Church of God in Jesus Christ (Apostolic), Peter J. F. Bridges**, who joined Haywood in the Assemblies of God Oneness showdown, then joined PAW, and **Austin A. Layne Sr.**, a prominent PAW leader.

Living Witness of the Apostolic Faith, Inc.

A Oneness Pentecostal denomination that was established in 1963 by **Mattie B. Poole and Charles E. Poole** in Chicago, Illinois, out of Bethlehem Healing Temple, a congregation established in 1932, as a local church within the **Pentecostal Assemblies of the World**. That congregation was primarily noted for the healing ministry of "Mother Poole" and attracted a large following almost since its founding.

In 1957 the couple left PAW to join with **Samuel N. Hancock** and the **Pentecostal Church of the Apostolic Faith**. After Hancock's 1963 death, Mattie Poole led the congregation separating from that body to establish Living Witnesses of the Apostolic Faith, Inc., and, for the next five years, served at its head. Neither of them, however, carried the designation of bishop.

Through extensive travel, preaching, and conducting of healing services, the Pooles added congregations in Brooklyn, New York; Boston, Massachusetts; Atlanta, Georgia; Gary, Indiana; Lockport, Illinois and Chicago's Southside as well as in Ghana, Liberia, and Nigeria, West Africa. Other congregations were added as ministers from Bethlehem Healing Tabernacle, which the church had come to be called. It branched out and established churches throughout the city and other sections of the country. The Pooles also started Living Witness Academy and Theological Seminary in Chicago, and other Bible schools in Brooklyn, New York; Atlanta, Georgia; and Boston Massachusetts.

When Mattie died in 1968, her husband became "Bishop" Charles E. Poole with PAW, serving in that post until his passing in 1984. After his death, the congregation elected Bishop Arcenia C. Richards as pastor of Bethlehem Healing Temple and presider, serving until his death in 2001. After his death, a dispute erupted within the congregation regarding succession. The resulting case went as far as the Illinois Supreme Courts. In 2006 Chester Hudson was elected pastor of Greater Bethlehem Healing Temple, and currently serves in that position.

Looper, Sumpter Eziel (S. E.) 1886–1972

Founder and first presiding bishop of the **Free Unity Church of God in Christ**. Looper was born in Marietta, South Carolina. He completed only an eighth grade education. In 1920 Looper migrated to Cincinnati, Ohio where he was pastoring as a member of Charles Harrison's group, the **Church of God in Christ**. In 1927 he left that body to establish the Free Unity Church of God in Christ.

In 1935 he was living in Cleveland where his congregation, the Free Unity Church of God in Christ, had been established. He was concentrating his efforts within the state of Ohio. By 1949 Looper had established congregations in Cincinnati, Columbus, Akron, Chillicothe, Barberton, and Cleveland, where he eventually died in 1972.

Lovett, Leonard 1939–

First Executive Director of Ecumenical Relations and Urban Affairs for the **Church of God in Christ,** and Dean Emeritus of the first fully accredited Pentecostal seminary in North America, C. H. Mason Theological Seminary, an affiliate of the Interdenominational Theological Center in Atlanta, Georgia. Lovett has served more than twenty years in pastoral ministry. As a theologian and commentator on political, social, ethical, and theological issues, he has written innumerable articles and authored three widely acclaimed books—*Crackpot Preaching, Close Your Back Door, and Kingdom Beyond Color*.

Lovett, a native of Pompano Beach, Florida, is a graduate of Morehouse College, in Atlanta, Georgia, Crozer Theological Seminary, and Emory University. He has taught at Fuller Theological Seminary, Graduate Theological Union, American Baptist Seminary of the West, Ecumenical Center for Black Studies, and Oral Roberts Graduate School of Theology.

His ecumenical career began in 1974 with involvement in the Catholic-Pentecostal Dialogue. He has served as a member of Faith and Order Commission of the National Council of Churches. Since 1994, he has been a columnist for *Ministries Today* magazine. From 2004 until the present he has been CEO of Seminex Ministries, an organization that provides church and leadership development with urban congregations. As a scholar, he contributed heavily to the academic dialogue with numerous monographs, articles and presentations on issues related to race relations, ecumenism, and social justice.

Lowe, Charles Wesley 1876–1954

The founding bishop of the **Apostolic Faith Church of God** was converted to the Pentecostal faith at the **Azusa Street Revival** and kept in contact with revival leader, **William Joseph Seymour** after leaving Los Angeles. By 1909 Lowe was in Hansome, Virginia where he established a Pentecostal congregation.

Two years later, Seymour visited Handsome where he organized the already existing group of congregations as the Apostolic Faith Missions, loosely affiliated this group with his California organization and consecrated Lowe as senior bishop and chief apostle. Under Lowe, the organization grew to include churches North Carolina, Maryland, Ohio, Pennsylvania, New York, and New Jersey, with one foreign mission in Liberia, West Africa.

In 1945 four years after headquarters for the denomination was moved to Suffolk, Virginia, Lowe separated from the organization he had founded and presided over as bishop of for thirty-five years. Taking only his own congregation with him, he founded the **Apostolic Faith Church of God and True Holiness**, as a Oneness body. During that period, he helped form the United Fellowship Convention of the Original Azusa Street Mission. In 1952 he appointed **John Thomas Cox** as presiding bishop. Bishop Lowe died in 1954.

M

Madison, Samuel Christee (S. C.) 1922–2008

The third presiding bishop of the **United House of Prayer for All People.** Madison was born in Greenville, South Carolina, where he joined the House of Prayer. In his youth, he was a boy scout, musician, and deacon in the congregation, as well as a cook for **Charles Emmanuel "Sweet Daddy" Grace.** Later, he worked as a chauffeur for **Walter "Sweet Daddy" McCollough**, and then as presiding bishop. Having receiving the Holy Ghost at age seventeen, he answered the call to be a minister. As a young man, he was sent by Grace to pastor in Salisbury, North Carolina from 1941 to 1942, and he returned there from 1949 to 1964. He also pastored in Hopewell, Virginia from 1943 to 1944; South Mills, North Carolina 1944 to 1949; and in Philadelphia, Pennsylvania from 1964 to 1969.

In 1968 McCollough sent him to pastor God's White House, the denomination's national headquarters in Washington DC, where he served until 1991, while at the same time, serving as chairperson for the DC region and overseer of the state of Maryland. A year after being appointed to that congregation, he joined the church's highest ecclesiastical body, the General Council, where he eventually served as clerk, chairperson of the Constitutional Revision Committee, and judge of that body.

In 1986 McCollough appointed him senior minister, the denomination's second-highest post. In 1991 Madison succeeded his mentor after winning a close election against McCollough's son. During his tenure at the head of the House of Prayer, he erected more than one hundred sanctuaries throughout the country, as well as multi-family housing, retail establishments, and assisted living facilities.

Beyond his ministry within the House of Prayer, Madison was a political activist who firmly opposed gentrification, urban renewal, and encroachment into his working and middle class congregation's inner-city neighborhood. His stance ensured that redevelopment of downtown Washington DC did not exclude single and multi-family housing, retail properties, and assisted-living facilities for moderate income families, or senior citizens and persons with disabilities. His advocacy for education led to oversight of the denominations scholarship funds, enhancement of an education program for ministers, and support for the McCollough Theological Seminary located in Richmond, Virginia.

These efforts earned him several awards from organizations outside the church. In 1995 he received the African American male IMAGE Award from the Phi Beta Sigma Fraternity. He traveled to the Holy Land as a guest of the Israeli government, where he was awarded a distinguished certificate as a Jerusalem Pilgrim. He was also recognized by Bowie State University in Maryland which awarded him the honorary Doctorate of Human Letters degree in 1999.

Madison displayed the same lavish lifestyle as his predecessors, Grace and McCollough, and received a significant amount of adulation as they did. Further, in counter distinction to classical Pentecostal piety regarding participation in secret organizations of any order, Madison was a Mason. He died at eighty-six.

Mallory, Arenia 1904–1977

Church of God in Christ educator, civil rights advocate and community activist. Mallory was born in Jacksonville, Illinois. In her late teens, Mallory was converted to Pentecostalism and received the Pentecostal Spirit baptism during a COGIC tent revival. Following that event, Mallory chose to travel with mission workers and her new religious affiliation placed her at odds with her family while birthing a zeal for evangelistic work in the young woman.

Mallory, whose mother was the first African-American woman to master the Italian harp, trained to be a professional concert pianist. She earned a bachelor's degree from Simmons College of Kentucky in 1927, a master's degree from Jackson State University, and a master's degree from the University of Illinois in 1950. Mallory was also awarded an honorary Doctor of Law degree from Bethune-Cookman College.

In the early 1920s, she accepted a position as a piano instructor at **Saints Industrial and Literary School** and moved south to Mississippi. A year after Mallory's arrival, the school principal, **James Court**, died. With COGIC founder **Charles H. Mason's** approval, the young teacher was appointed his replacement. She took over leadership of Saints in 1926 and served as its president until 1975. Under her leadership, the first black high school in Holmes County, Mississippi, became a junior college by 1945 and a four year institution by 1974. In her fifty years at its helm, the institution trained many men and women whom she personally mentored or inspired to become prominent denominational leaders. Before she retired in 1976, more than 25,000 students from various denominations had graduated from the school.

Intimately involved in the life of the college, Mallory's intellect and wealth of interest took her beyond the realm of most Pentecostal women of her day. She frequently traveled with the Jubilee Harmonizers, a women's choir, raising money and collecting books and clothing for students and county residents. Early in the 1930s, she worked to bring health and welfare services to Holmes County sharecroppers by convincing former Mississippi resident, Ida Jackson, president of the Alpha Kappa Alpha sorority, to set up a Summer school for Rural Teachers. In 1935 the sorority changed its summer educational program into a summer public health program—the Alpha Kappa Alpha Mississippi Health Project—that also operated out of the Saints school.

Mallory, an active COGIC member, participated in the Women's Department and was the leader in the national church. In 1952, she was selected to represent COGIC at the World Pentecostal Convention in London, England in 1955, and also served on the National Education board and the Charles Harrison Mason Foundation.

Outside of COGIC, the long-time member of the National and International Councils of Negro Women, Mallory served as vice president of the umbrella organization of black women's groups from 1953 to 1957. She was also a member of the Regional Council of Negro Leadership, an organization founded in 1951 to promote a civil rights, self-help, and business ownership in Mississippi—serving on its board from 1952 to 1955. In that year, she was a delegate to the tenth anniversary celebration of the United Nations in San Francisco, California. Mallory served as a consultant for the United States Department of Labor in 1963. Further, in 1968, despite the fact that Holmes County was predominantly black, Mallory became the first woman and African American to serve on the County's Board of Education.

Appreciation of Mallory's achievements went far beyond COGIC. As early as 1936, she was featured in issue of Crisis Magazine. In 1956 the Utility Club of New named her Woman of the Year, while a parallel honor was given to prominent African American civil rights leader, Senator Adam Clayton Powell Jr. To commemorate her legacy community facilities in two states were named in her honor: the Arenia C. Mallory Community Health Center in Lexington, Mississippi and the Arenia Mallory School of Religion located in Miami, Florida.

Further Reading:

Dovie Marie Simmons, and Olivia L. Martin. *Down Behind the Sun: The Story of Arenia Cornelia Mallory*. Lexington, MS : D.M. Simmons, 1983.

Tucker, Anjulet. "'Get the Learnin' but don't lose the Burnin': The Socio-Cultural and Religious Politics of Education in a Black Pentecostal College." PhD diss., Emory University, 2009.

Martin, Sallie 1895–1988

Nicknamed "the mother of gospel music," Martin was raised a Baptist in Pittfield, Georgia. In 1916 she moved into the Pentecostal movement joining the **Fire Baptized Holiness Church.** After moving to Chicago during the 1920s, she began her career singing in Holiness churches after coming to Chicago in 1927.

Thomas Dorsey looked down on Martin's rough singing style and Holiness religiosity, but she persuaded him to hire her for a trio he had formed to introduce his songs to churches. She proved to be an able organizer with a shrewd financial sense; she marketed Dorsey's songs, organized his finances, developed new avenues for business and helped launch the National Convention of Gospel Choirs and Choruses, Inc. (NCGCC), serving as its first vice president until her death.

In 1933 Martin traveled to Cleveland to organize a chorus to sing Dorsey's songs; in the following years, she helped set up similar groups throughout the South and Midwest. In 1940 relations between Martin and Dorsey soured to the point that she went solo, teaming with a young pianist named Ruth Jones—later to rocket to fame under the name Dinah Washington—and began touring the country, traveling a gospel circuit. That same year, Martin, gospel composer Kenneth Morris, and financial backer, Clarence Cobb founded Martin & Morris, Inc., a publishing company. In a few years it became the largest sheet music company in the United States.

Martin retired from the Sallie Martin Singers in the mid-1950s. She remained an active force in the NCGCC even after she went out on her own and was a vocal supporter of Dr. Martin Luther King Jr. and of health programs in Nigeria. Until her death, she remained a vigorous proponent of gospel music and defender of her role in bringing it to the churches.

Mason, Charles Harrison 1866–1961

The founder, first senior bishop, and longest serving leader of the **Church of God in Christ**. Mason was born to former slaves in Shelby, Tennessee. When he was twelve, his family moved to Arkansas where they attended a Missionary Baptist Church. He converted as a young boy. Mason grew up intending to be a minister, but as a young man gave up that goal. After contracting tuberculosis from which he was miraculously healed, he renewed pursuit of his call, and was licensed to preach by his local congregation, the Mount Gale Missionary Baptist Church in Preston, Arkansas.

In 1890 he met and married Alice Saxton. Bitterly opposed to his ministerial plans, she divorced him after two years of marriage. Yet, holding the Holiness understanding of having only one living wife, Mason did not marry again until a year after her death in 1904. Lelia Washington became his second wife and the couple had seven children. She died in 1936. In 1943 when he was seventy-seven years old, he married his third wife, thirty-five-year-old **Elsie Louise Washington** who became editor-in-chief of the church's journal, *The Whole Truth*.

After initially attending Arkansas Baptist College for a short while, Mason entered the school's ministerial institute to obtain a certificate. He received his preaching license from the Baptist Church in 1893. Two years later, he met and joined with popular Baptist preacher **Charles Price Jones**, who shared his enthusiasm for holiness teachings to which he was introduced on the writing of African Methodist Episcopal Zion evangelist, **Amanda Berry Smith**.

In 1897 the Mississippi Baptist Association expelled him from his pulpit for preaching the holiness doctrine of sanctification. He and Jones, who was also disfellowshipped by the Baptists, forged an alliance of AME, CME, and Baptist clergy and lay Holiness proponents throughout the Mississippi Valley as the Christ Association of Mississippi of Baptized Believers. Jones was elected the new organization's overseer and Mason was appointed overseer of the Tennessee work.

After soon receiving permission to use an abandoned gin house, the two began traveling and holding revivalistic meetings. Together, they formed the **Church of God in Christ** as a denomination within the Holiness movement. For ten years, they planted churches and recruit other holiness sympathizers throughout the Valley.

Once the **Azusa Street Revival** broke out, Mason led a contingent including **J. A. Jeter, D. J. Young,** and **W. S. Pleasant** to Los Angeles to investigate whether what was occurring was a move of God or simply fanaticism. Mason returned from Azusa Street not only convinced that the Pentecostal experience of Holy Spirit baptism was genuine, but having had the experience himself and insisting that such an experience was normative for Holiness believers.

Reportedly, this was not Mason's first acquaintance with Seymour, whom he had met when the Pentecostal leader visited Arkansas near the turn of the century. Neither was this his first encounter with speaking in tongues, for several years before going to Azusa Street, Mason had experiences of God speaking to him in an unknown tongue and had wrestled with what these visitations might mean. Once he determined that the experience was authentic, however, both Mason and Young received their Pentecostal experience at Azusa Street. After this encounter, at least with Mason, the issue was settled. On route back to Tennessee, he stopped in Portsmouth, Virginia to conduct revival meetings. During this time, more than six thousand conversions were reported. On his return to the East to share his assessment with his colleague, his report was soundly rejected and their collaboration ended. He and Jones found themselves locked in a legal battle over the name of their organization since both laid claim to the name, "Church of God in Christ." Mason's claim that he had originally conceived of the title ultimately prevailed in court and Jones Holiness group went on to become the **Church of Christ (Holiness) USA.**

In September of the year, Mason called a meeting with his colleagues, **David J. Young, Robert E. Hart, Edward R. Driver,** and other leaders who believed in speaking in tongues met in Memphis and re-organized the **Church of God in Christ** as a Pentecostal denomination. During that first General Assembly meeting, Mason was elected chief apostle/general overseer. Many of those in attendance would go on to become important figures in COGIC's history.

Mason quickly became the only leader legally able to ordain those within the nascent Pentecostal movement whose clergy status was recognized by civil authorities. From 1909 to 1914, roughly equal numbers of African Americans and whites came to him for ordination. Mason's interracial and pacifism stances brought him to the attention of the Bureau of Investigation, the forerunner of the Federal Bureau of Investigation (FBI) and the organization that kept a file on him during World War I. In 1918 he was arrested and jailed on suspicion of un-American activity.

Mason was among those who considered Seymour a father in the faith, frequently inviting him to speak at the Annual Convocation for the **Church of God in Christ**. Like Seymour, Mason worked hard to maintain racial unity within the young movement. He maintained close alliances with sympathetic white leaders such **A. J. Tomlinson**, of the

Church of God (Cleveland, TN) and J. H. King of the Pentecostal Holiness Church among his friends. When the majority of white ministers left in 1914 to form the Assemblies of God, a number remained with Mason. Among them was the "Kentucky Cyclone Evangelist" **James Logan Delk.** Mason also maintained relationship with Oneness Pentecostals, such as **Robert Clarence Lawson**, whom he considered a good friend, and on at least one occasion, invited to address the COGIC convocation.

Drawing on his Baptist roots, Mason held that women should play a vital, yet distinctive role from men in the life of the church, and structured a dual system within COGIC that allowed women to serve as congregational leaders, while reserving ordained leadership for men. He allowed women to be licensed as "evangelists" or "missionaries" primarily to teach other women and raise financial support for local, regional and national efforts. Like many other Pentecostal groups, he allowed women to "dig out" congregations in untested fields and nurture them to viability until a male pastor could take over leadership. To ensure that women had a role to play within his denomination, Mason created the International Women's Department, placing former Baptist headmaster Elizabeth (Lizzie Robinson) at its heads.

Mason was a keen tactician in building COGIC as a denomination. During the Jim Crow era and the Depression, he sent strategic ministers to follow the migration patterns of blacks to the urban North, and to establish houses of worship where they could find the kind of spiritual environment they had been accustomed to in the South.

At the time of Bishop Mason's death in 1961, he had served as senior bishop for fifty-four years. Before his death, he earned a doctorate of divinity from Trinity Hall College in 1957. COGIC had spread to every state in the United Stares as well as many foreign countries on five continents, and the denomination had a membership of more than 400,000 in more than four thousand churches.

Further Reading:

Clemmons, Ithiel. *Charles Harrison Mason and the Roots of the Church of God in Christ.* Lanham, MD: Pneuma Life, 1997.
Maxwell, Joe. "Building the Church (of God in Christ)." *Christianity Today*, April 8, 1996.
McBride, Calvin. *Frank Avant vs. C.H. Mason: Mason and the Holy Ghost on Trial.* New York: iUniverse, 2009.

Mason, Elsie Louise Washington 1907–2006

Evangelist, teacher, civil rights advocate and third wife of **Church of God in Christ** founder **Charles Harrison Mason.** Elsie Washington was born in Memphis, Tennessee and raised in the denomination her husband founded. At one time, she worked for the Saints Industrial and Lit4erary Academy in Lexington, Mississippi.

During her younger years, Mason edited COGIC's newspaper, *The Whole Truth,* and worked as a secretary in the denomination's missions department. For three years, the licensed evangelist served as a missionary in Haiti where she founded an orphanage, the Charles Harrison Mason School.

In 1943 seven years after Mason's second wife died, thirty-five-year-old Washington married the presiding bishop who was nearly forty years her senior. Yet, the two would have a relatively lengthy marriage of eighteen years. At the time of the marriage, she was a teacher in the Memphis School System and had previously taught in New York. Though she outlived him by forty-five years, she never remarried. Nearly two decades after her husband's death, she penned a biography, *The Man, Charles Harrison Mason: 1866–1961* that was published by the Church of God in Christ Publishing House in 1979.

The apartment complex adjacent to Mason Temple for physically impaired elderly members of the denomination was designated the Elsie W. Mason Saints Haven in her honor. Ironically, Mason, who fell victim to such an impairment during her older age, became the first permanent resident of the facility. She died at the age of ninety-eight.

Further Reading:

Mason Elsie W. *The Man, Charles Harrison Mason: 1866–1961*. Pioneer Series 1. Memphis, TN: Church of God in Christ, 1979.

Massey, James Earl 1930–

The son and grandson of ministers, Massey is a **Holiness** pastor, educator, writer, and accomplished musician. The man referred to as a "Prince of Preachers" has preached and lectured at more than one hundred colleges, universities, and seminaries in the United States and on four continents.

Massey graduated from Detroit Bible College (later William Tyndale College) in 1961, and Oberlin Graduate School of Theology in 1964. He received his doctorate from Asbury Theological Seminary in 1972. He was later elected to membership on the trustee board there. At the close of his term in 1991, Massey he was named a "Life Trustee."

Beginning in 1954, he served for twenty-two years as senior pastor of the Metropolitan Church of God, a multi-cultural, inter-racial congregation in Detroit, Michigan. Taking a leave of absence from the pastorate in 1963, he became Principal of the Jamaica School of Theology in Kingston, Jamaica, for three years. In 1969, he began serving concurrently as campus minister and professor of New Testament and Preaching at Anderson University, an institution of the Church of God (Anderson, IN). Massey left the university in 1977 to serve as the weekly speaker on "The Christian Brotherhood Hour," the international radio broadcast of the Church of God heard throughout the English-speaking world from 1977–1982. Two years later, he was appointed Dean of the University Chapel and Professor of Religion and Society at Tuskegee University in Alabama and served there until 1989. He later returned to Anderson University to assume the post of Dean of the School of Theology where he currently serves as Dean Emeritus and Distinguished Professor-at-Large of the Anderson School of Theology.

Further Reading:

Massey, James Earl. *Aspects of my Pilgrimage: An Autobiography.* Anderson, IN: Anderson University Press, 2002.

McCollough, Walter M. ("Sweet Daddy") 1915–1991

The second presiding bishop of the quasi-Holiness denomination the **United House of Prayer for All People.** Bishop **McCollough** joined that organization in Charlotte, North Carolina at age of fourteen, and quickly rose through the ranks of leadership. After the native of Great Falls, South Carolina came to Washington in the 1930s, he served as a junior trustee for the young people, senior trustee, choir member, usher, grace soldier, junior elder, and later, as chauffeur for founding bishop **Charles M. Grace.** He went on to become senior elder board chair, pastor, senior minister, and then presiding bishop.

In 1941 he was named pastor of the Anacostia Mission in the inner city Southeast section of the city. In 1956 he was named pastor of God's White House—the Washington DC headquarters of the church. After Bishop Grace died in 1960, McCollough, whom Grace had personally favored, succeeded him, adopting his nickname, "Sweet Daddy." However, in response to some church members' allegation of irregularities in voting process and the handling of church finances, the court ordered McCollough to step down and a court ordered re-election was held with McCollough ultimately prevailing and retaining his position. Once in office, he expanded the denomination's political influence and increased worldwide membership significantly.

McCollough was noted for his long hair and fingernails, abundance of gold jewelry and brightly colored cutaways. Yet, he was also noted for his economic development of the neighborhoods surrounding his churches. Under McCollough's leadership, the church purchased and built hundreds of units of affordable housing for moderate-income families and senior citizens in the predominantly black neighborhoods surrounding their congregations in Washington DC, North Carolina, and Connecticut. He was also considered a power broker within Washington municipal politics.

After his death, House of Prayer leaders interred him in a $500,000 mausoleum at the denominational burial site. When they later informed his widow, Clara McCollough, that she and the rest of her family would not be buried with him, she had the body exhumed and reburied in a family plot. A court battle ensued over the right of the denomination to use him name on the mausoleum they maintained. The court sided with the denomination, which claims that though his body is no longer on their site, his spirit rests there and hundreds still regularly visit that site. At her death fifteen years later, Clara was buried with her husband.

M

McCullough, Jacqueline E. (Jackie) 1950–

The evangelist, pastor, bishop, women's leader, and daughter of two Jamaican preachers, was born in Kingston and relocated to New York City. McCullough came to faith at a young age and became active in the church—teaching Sunday school, speaking to young people, or ministering from a text. At sixteen, she sensed a call to preach. After high school, however, McCullough planned to enter the medical field and preach on her off time. She trained as a nurse, and for the next seven years, worked in that field and as a nurse practitioner, continuing her plans to attend medical school. When she, again, sensed a call to full-time ministry, she resigned her job within the year to pursue that course. Earlier that year, she lost her baby after only two hours of life and her physically abusive marriage ended in divorce.

Soon McCullough began regularly preaching, teaching, and visiting prisons and hospitals. She also undertook graduate study at the Jewish Theological Seminary of America and earned her master's degree from New York University in Philosophy, and a doctorate degree in Ministry by Drew University in Madison, New Jersey.

Seeking a home church for herself and those she had disciple, she joined Elim International Fellowship, under **Wilbert S. McKinley,** and became the minister of evangelism. Since the pay was fairly low, eventually McCullough returned to nursing for one year, before permanently leaving the profession to itinerate full-time. With that move, McCullough's ministry escalated to the place that she preaches approximately 120 dates a year in revivals and conferences and has shared the platform with some of today's most well-known Pentecostal and Charismatic figures.

McCullough is founding pastor of the International Gathering at Beth Rapha, a congregation located in Pomona, New York, and is founding president of Beth Rapha Christian College and Theological Seminary in Tampa, Florida, and is Executive Director of Daughters of Rizpah, a nonprofit evangelic ministry based in Brooklyn, New York. Since 1997 McCullough has spearheaded the "Word Alive Crusade Tour," a humanitarian effort that raises funds for medicine and hospital equipment for hospitals in Jamaica.

McCullough has authored several titles including a devotional entitled, *Daily Moments with God: In Quietness and Confidence,* as well as *Satisfaction of the Soul, 105 Days of Prayer* and *The Other Side of This*. She released her first CD, *This Is For You Lord*, in 1998 on which she produced all of the cuts.

In 1996 *Gospel Today Magazine* called her one of "The Most influential African-American Ministers in the Nation," and in 1997 *Ebony Magazine* identified her as one of "The Fifteen Most Influential African-American Female Ministers in the Nation."

In the early part of the twenty-first century, McCullough continued her full speaking and writing schedule, appeared at some of the most important Pentecostal conferences both within the United States and overseas and continued at the head of her organizations. In 2015 McCullough became one of the most highly respected women on the Pentecostal preaching circuit; she was consecrated a bishop in the Global United Ministries, a fellowship of churches and ministries founder in 2014 by Neil Ellis.

McEwen, A. B. Sr. 1874–1969

An early **Church of God in Christ** leader and confidante to founding bishop, **Charles Harrison Mason**. Born in Mississippi, McEwen spent much of his early life in Washington, DC, before returning to the South. Ordained to the ministry in 1920 by **Charles Harrison Mason**, he was appointed Overseer Tennessee and served from 1922 until 1954. By the end of his term, he had helped establish more than forty congregations across the state. He was also instrumental in establishing the Church of God in Christ Publishing House, and pastored congregations in Covington, Lane City and Memphis, Tennessee. After 1954, the state was divided into two jurisdictions. From that time until 1969, McEwen presided over the Western Jurisdiction and **J. O. Patterson, Sr.** presided over Eastern Jurisdiction.

Among the important posts McEwen held within COGIC were chair of the Home and Foreign Missions Board, member of the five man commission with **I. S. Stafford**, **O. T. Jones**, **Samuel Crouch**, and **James O. Patterson, Sr.** that Mason established to help him with the administrative responsibility of the organization, and head of the COGIC Youth Work. He was the first bishop to travel abroad on behalf of the church when he visited countries including Haiti, Bahamas, Jamaica, and Bermuda as well as nations of Africa and the Middle East.

In 1951 Mason set up a "special commission" to help him with the administration of the church and selected McEwen with Bishops **J. S. Bailey**, and **O. M. Kelly** as his assistants.

Following Mason's death in November 1961, McEwen was elected chairperson of the twelve-man commission (later the Executive Board), put in place to oversee the administration of COGIC. McEwen served in that position for one year and at one time was considered as successor to Mason.

In 1962 however, the board of bishops nominated and the General Assembly elected **Ozro Thurston Jones, Sr.** as senior bishop. Two years later, disagreement between the authority of the Senior Bishop and the Executive Board headed by McEwen led to the development of factions within the organization as executive and administrative decisions were being made by both thesenior bishop and McEwen. The two leaders ended up in court, with McEwen and his followers insisting that the executive board had the right to govern the organization and Jones claiming the opposite.

After the counter demands ended in a 1968, court-ordered re-election, Jones was defeated, but remained Jurisdictional Bishop in Pennsylvania until his death in 1972. **James Oglethorpe Patterson, Sr.** won the office of presiding bishop, but his supporter, McEwen, never got to savor that victory since he died the same year.

McGlothen, Mattie Mae Carter 1897–1994

The Fourth General Supervisor of the International Women's Department **Church of God in Christ.** McGlothen served as a Supervisor in California for sixty-one years beginning in 1933, and as General Supervisor for the International Women's Department and Third President of the Women's International Convention of the Church of God in Christ for eighteen years beginning in 1976.

McGlothen was born in Tehuacana, Texas. She attended Quindaro College in Kansas City, Kansas. In 1921 she was converted to Pentecostal faith; she experienced the Pentecostal Holy Spirit baptism and was healed of tuberculosis in the same night. After marrying Bishop George Wenzell McGlothen in 1923, and acknowledging her call to ministry in 1924, the couple founded and pastored churches in Hugo, Idabelle and Tulsa, Des Moines, Fresno, Los Angeles, Richmond, and Pittsburgh.

In 1933 she was appointed Northern California State Supervisor, and six years later, **Lizzie Roberson** appointed her to the State Supervisor role. McGlothen also served the International Women's Department as President of Hospitality for over twenty-eight years and served as Assistant General Supervisor to Mother Annie Bailey. At the death of Bailey, Bishop J. O Patterson, Sr. appointed her General Supervisor of the International Department of Women and Third President of the Women's International Convention. The appointment marked the beginning of a tenure that would in span work with five Jurisdictional Prelates.

Under her supervision, the Women's International Convention gained the distinction of being the second largest convention held in the **Church of God in Christ**, second only to the National Convocation. Through her initiative, the Women's Department built four missionaries in the Bahama Islands in 1938, furnished the guesthouse on the Saints Academy Campus in Lexington, Mississippi in 1984, and built a pavilion in Port-au-Prince, Haiti for senior citizens and unwed mothers. Further, from 1985 to 1991, three homes were purchased in Memphis, Tennessee that today stand as the McGlothen Complex and accommodate the administrative offices of the International Women's Department. Finally, she gave a visible presence to **Church of God in Christ** women in ministry by introducing the ministry "habit" in which many contemporary COGIC women adorn themselves when ministering or serving in official capacities.

The Dr. Mattie McGlothen Library and Museum, Richmond, California, founded in 1989 by Emma J. Clark houses historic artifacts chronicling McGlothen's life and teachings as well as those of other leaders within the COGIC. The Mother Mattie McGlothen Home of Love and Hope Emergency Shelter in Memphis, Tennessee and Dr. Mattie McGlothen Senior Housing complex in Oakland, California also bear witness to her years of ministry within the denomination and the broader community.

McGoings, Robert J. Jr. 1917–2012

A prominent African-American Oneness Pentecostal layperson who was an expert on the African-American Pentecostal Movement. McGoings, who studied at Morgan State College, worked most of his life as a dining car waiter—first beginning in 1937 for the B&O Railroad, then for Amtrak after B&O passenger operations became part of that company in 1972. He retired in 1979.

As a youngster, he joined the First Apostolic Faith Church in Baltimore; after 1968, he affiliated with the **First United Church of Jesus Christ Apostolic**, where Bishop **Monroe Saunders** was presiding. He also regularly visited **Robert Clarence Lawson's** Refuge Temple **Church of Our Lord Jesus Christ of the Apostolic Faith** (New York, NY) and **O. T. Jones Jr.**'s congregation, **Holy Temple Church of God in Christ** in Philadelphia, becoming close friends with the two pastors.

Throughout his life, McGoings assembled a large library of religious artifacts on the movement. McGoings was a student of Reformed theology and maintained theological dialogue with numerous African-American church leaders. In 2000, the Society for Pentecostal Studies dedicated its 29th annual meeting papers to McGoings.

At his death, McGoings' son, Michael, donated the collection, which includes publications, sermon notes, church programs, audio recordings, and other materials primarily from 1930–2002, to the Flower Pentecostal History Collection of the Assemblies of God. These material are primarily related the **Church of God in Christ**, the **Church of Our Lord Jesus Christ of the Apostolic Faith**, the **Pentecostal Assemblies of the World**, and other Oneness Pentecostal congregations. In tandem with that donation, McGoings' son donated publications that he, himself, assembled related to several large Charismatic African Methodist Episcopal (AME) congregations in the Washington DC area.

Further Reading:

"Robert James McGoings Jr. Collection." *Assemblies of God Heritage* (2012) 74.

McKinley, Wilbert Sterling 1938–2008

Co-founder of the **Joint College of African American Pentecostal Bishops** and presiding founder of the Elim International Fellowship, a neo-Pentecostal reformed Episcopal denomination, in Brooklyn, New York.

McKinley was raised in Panama, and at the age of thirteen, answered the call to ministry. He studied at Zion Bible Institute in Providence, Rhode Island; the University of Pittsburgh, where he received a degree in history; the Reformed Presbyterian Seminary, and the Reformed Episcopal Seminary in Philadelphia, Pennsylvania, where he received a master of divinity degree.

In 1964 McKinley planted his local congregation as a storefront ministry with four members. Since then, it has grown into the interracial, non-denominational congregation that the Hartford Institute for Religious Research now lists as a megachurch. The congregation, which purchased and refurbished the former Catholic edifice that was the Church of the Nativity of Our Blessed Lord, came to be known as the Protestant Cathedral in Brooklyn. With McKinley at the helm, the congregation took over the vacated edifice and was directly involved in efforts to revitalize the surrounding community including a school, three residences, and three other buildings.

McKinley came to be called "Prince Cush" for his sense that he was chosen to carry the message of empowerment to the Cushite race—and specifically to black men. In 1993, he joined Bishops **J. Delano Ellis** of the **Pentecostal Church of Christ**, Roy E. Brown of **Pilgrim Assemblies International** and Paul S. Morton of the Full Gospel Baptist Church Fellowship International in forming the organization to offer education, training, and accountability. He has also served as a mentor to some of the more prominent leaders within the contemporary Pentecostal movement including Brown and Bishop **Jackie McCullough.**

McLeod Bruce Lee 1880–1936

First presiding bishop of the **Church of the Living God Pillar and Ground of the Truth which He Purchased with His Own Blood (McLeod Dominion).** McLeod was born in Macon, Georgia. He joined the **Church of the Living God Pillar and Ground of the Truth** around 1912, and married founder **Mary Magdalena Tate**'s stepdaughter, Mattie Lou Tate in 1919 and soon became a trusted aide and leader in the organization. McLeod was one of the first state bishops appointed by Tate. The couple worked in Philadelphia, Pennsylvania, Jacksonville, Mt. Vernon, and Nashville, and he assisted Tate's son, Felix Early Lewis, in locating and purchasing the site for the Church of Living Way headquarters in Nashville, Tennessee.

In 1924 McLeod appointed his wife to assist him in setting up churches in Kentucky and congregations were established in Paducah, Owensboro, Beaver Dam, and Morgantown. They also established congregations throughout Mississippi and Michigan.

After Tate's death, McLeod became a member of the triumvirate of leader who oversaw three separate divisions of her church. When that arrangement failed and the organization was partitioned into three autonomous, yet cooperative entities, McLeod assumed leadership over one of the three dominions.

Sometime before his death in 1937, McLeod ordained his wife to the bishopric, and following his demise at age fifty-six, she took leadership of the McLeod Dominion, On her remarriage to William Jewell, a deacon, the body was designated as the Jewell Dominion.

McKinney, George Dallas 1932–

Influential **Church of God in Christ** pastor, bishop, author and social activist who has been at the forefront of the push toward racial justice within the Pentecostal movement and American society for several decades. McKinney was born in Jonesboro, Arkansas as the son of a sharecropper in a strictly segregated society. He answered the call to preach age fifteen.

McKinney is a magna cum laude graduate of Arkansas State College where he received a Bachelor of Arts degree. He received his Master of Arts degree from Oberlin College School of Theology in Glendale, California, and partly because of that institution's long history in civil rights, McKinney was drawn into social advocacy. He went on to study at the University of Michigan, School of Social Work before receiving a PhD in Ecclesiology from California Graduate School of Theology, being honored with a Doctor of Divinity from Geneva College in Beaver Falls, Pennsylvania.

McKinney served as a volunteer pastor in Toledo for a short time, and interned for three years with Bishop **Junious Augustus Blake Jr.** In 1962 he founded St. Stephen's Church of God in Christ in San Diego, California, a congregation that houses St. Stephen's Nursery School, Southeast Counseling and Consulting Services, American Urban University and the St. Stephens Retirement Center, which are all located in San Diego.

Since 1970 the former probation officer has also served as a licensed marriage, family, and child counselor. He also served on the board of C. H. Mason Seminary in Atlanta. In 1985, he was consecrated as the Jurisdictional Prelate of COGIC's Second Ecclesiastical Jurisdiction of California. In November 2001, he was elevated to the General Board (the presidium) of the Church, and re-elected in 2004 and 2008.

McKinney is an internationally known speaker and the author of numerous books. His literary contributions include the best-selling book, *Cross the Line: Reclaiming the Inner City for God*, which he co-authored with William Kritlow in 1998. He served as the senior editor for the *African American Devotional Bible*, published by Zondervan in 1977. Currently, he serves as a publisher for the San Diego Monitor Newspaper.

McKinney has received numerous awards for his work in community activism and social advocacy including being named Mr. San Diego, by the San Diego Rotary Club in 1995, and the Racial Reconciliation Man of the Year by the National Association of Evangelicals in 2001. Two years later, that same organization nominated him for US Senate Chaplain, for which he also received an endorsement from Rev. Billy Graham.

McKinney is one of a small number of **Church of God in Christ** bishops who have taken it upon themselves to actively go against what he considered to be unjust policy related to women in ministry.

Meares, John Levin 1920–2011

Faith healer and founder of Evangel Cathedral, one of the largest and most powerful black congregations in the nation to have predominantly white leadership, and bishop of an multinational Charismatic association, the International Evangelical Church and Missionary Association. Meares was born in Largo, Florida and was a member of the predominantly white **Church of God (Cleveland, TN)** and was the nephew of the General Overseer, Zeno Tharp. At eighteen, he enrolled at the Church of God Bible School in Sevierville, Tennessee and received a bachelor's degree from the University of Tennessee four years later. He also received an honorary doctor of divinity degree from Oral Roberts University in Tulsa, Oklahoma.

Meares was ordained in the Church of God in 1943, and had established Church of God congregations in Athens and Memphis, Tennessee. He was expelled from that body in 1957, however, for what leaders characterized as insubordination and Meares maintained was his daring to regularly preach to black people. Two years earlier, he was invited to preach a revival in Washington by famed healing evangelist, Jack Coe in 1955. The meeting drew thousands of black believers. Meares decided to stay in the city, and establish The Washington Revival Center. The congregation grew as Meares started a radio broadcast, "Miracle Time," and the church gained a reputation as a center for "miraculous" spiritual phenomena. From those early roots, his ever-expanding congregation migrated to a converted horse stable, and then to a renovated movie theater, before moving into a newly constructed three-million-dollar building in 1975.

Between the late 1960s and the early 1970s, Meares joined with John McTernan of an Italian Pentecostal body, the International Evangelical Church and Missionary Society, and became vice president of the organization. When McTernan died, Meares became president, inheriting congregations in Italy, Brazil, and Africa. In 1982 Meares worked with other leaders to form the International Communion of Charismatic Churches, an organization that incorporated the IEC with other groups such as Earl Paulk's Gospel Harvesters Association in Atlanta, Georgia. Later that year the other Leaders of the Communion (including **Benson Idahosa** of Nigeria) consecrated him bishop. In 1984 he initiated the Inner City Pastor's conference, which drew mostly African Americans.

Meares's ministry within his congregation was repeatedly plagued by allegations that he and his sons funded its multimillion-dollar expansion on the backs of low-income urban black congregants. In its latest move in 2001, Meares's congregation migrated from the inner city where most of its congregants were working class to a twenty-two-million-dollar sanctuary on a one-hundred acre campus within Prince Georges County, the most affluent African-American county in the United States. The relocation was followed by charges from former congregations that the Meares family used strong-armed tactics to get them to pay for the project, and then abandoned numerous members who were unable to travel easily to the new site. While the earlier locations were called Evangel Temple, with the move, the name was changed to Evangel Cathedral.

Before his death, the congregation had grown to more than 4,200 members; it had become known for putting on lavish Broadway-style musical productions and drawing high-profile evangelists—including **T. D. Jakes**, Oral Roberts, and **Church of God in Christ** bishop **Charles E. Blake**—to its pulpit.

The church dwindled in the aftermath of the 1968 riots following Martin Luther King Jr.'s assassination, but rebounded in the early 1970s as Meares changed the emphasis of his ministry from miracles to teaching and created a Christian Training Institute that offered self-help courses, counseling, Bible studies, and academic classes.

In the 1970s and 1980s, Meares served on an international committee that sought to build bridges between Pentecostal and Roman Catholic leaders. He traveled widely, expanding his church's missionary programs with the help of the IEC. He also continued to be an outspoken leader in the dialog regarding the white churches' role and responsibility in the African-American community.

After his 1982 consecration as bishop, Meares installed his son Donald as senior pastor of the congregation, and continued to be in dialog with and serve as a mentor to other Pentecostal and Charismatic leaders. He died of congestive heart failure.

Further Reading:

Meares, John. *Bind Us Together*. Old Tappan, NJ: Chosen, 1987.

Memphis Miracle

The popular name of the 1994 Pentecostal convocation that was the backdrop for the dissolution of the exclusively white umbrella organization, Pentecostal Fellowship of North America and the establishment of the interracial body as the **Pentecostal and Charismatic Churches of North America** in its place after nearly fifty years of racial separation.

The meeting, held in October in Memphis, Tennessee, was characterized by frank discussion, prayers of repentance, and a dramatic final session that resulted in the end of forty-five years of institutionalized segregation between the major bodies within each camp. The convocation took place after two years of dialog initiated by overtures from Bishop Bernard E. Underwood, presiding bishop of the Pentecostal Holiness Church, who took office of PFNA chair in 1992.

The climactic moment, however, came in the scholar's session on October 18, when after COGIC bishop, **Charles Blake** tearfully addressed the delegates, a young black man uttered a message in tongues and Jack Hayford, president of the predominantly white **International Church of the Foursquare Gospel**, offered the interpretation. Almost immediately, a white pastor name Donald Evans of Tampa, Florida appeared with a towel and basin of water, tearfully knelt before COGIC bishop, Ithiel Clemmons and washed his feet while begging forgiveness for the sins whites against blacks. Blake then washed the feet of Thomas Trask, General Superintendent of the Assemblies of God. In an emotional speech the next day, Dr. Paul Walker of the Church of God (Cleveland, TN) called this event, the Miracle in Memphis, a name that struck and made headlines around the world. When members of the PFNA gathered later that afternoon, the motion to dissolve the organization in favor of a new entity passed. When the new constitution was read to the delegates on October 19, a new name was proposed—Pentecostal and Charismatic

Churches of North America (PCCNA). Before the constitution came before the assembly for a vote, Pastor Billy Joe Daugherty of Tulsa, Oklahoma proposed inclusion of the word Charismatic in the new name to begin healing the rift between Pentecostals and Charismatics as well.

The group also unanimously adoption a "Racial Reconciliation Manifesto" that was drafted in which the new organization pledged to oppose racism prophetically in all its various manifestations and to be vigilant in the struggle. They further agreed to confess that racism is a sin while seeking avenues for partnerships.

Clemmons was chosen as Chairperson and Underwood as Vice-Chairperson. Also elected to the Board was Bishop **Barbara Amos**, whose election demonstrated the resolve of the new organization to bridge the gender gap as well.

The event, in which more than one thousand leaders participated, was widely covered by the secular as well as Christian media. Major national newspapers, including the *Boston Globe* and the *Los Angeles Times*, gave considerable space to the occasion, considering what it might mean for the future of Pentecostalism.

Further Reading:

"The 'Memphis Miracle.'" *Ministries Today* (1995) 36–38
Synan, Vinson. "Memphis 1994: Miracle and Mandate." *Reconciliation* 1 (1998).

Meredith, Don 1964–

The fourth person of African descent, and the first Jamaican to serve in Canadian Senate. Meredith, a Pentecostal pastor, was ordained in 2006 and is the senior pastor at the Pentecostal Praise Centre in Maple, Ontario. He is also founder and executive director of the Greater Toronto Faith Alliance Centre that focuses on youth gangs and gun violence. Born and raised in Jamaica, Meredith immigrated to Canada, and became a Canadian citizen in the early 1980s. He attended Ryerson Polytechnical Institute, and is a graduate of Rhema Studies of Theology Association.

In 2007 he was nominated by the Conservative Party Toronto Centre federal by-election held in 2008. He lost that race, placing fourth, but was appointed to the Canadian Senate in 2010, serving one term. Meredith is a member of the Chief's Advisory Council for the Toronto Police Services and has been a member of the York Region Community Police Liaison since 2004, as well as a member of the Royal Canadian Mounted Police Consultative Committee since 2005. He is the former co-chair of the Black Community Police Consultative Committee. Though he has stayed active in politics, Meredith was expelled from the Conservative caucus in 2015, following allegations of sexual misconduct.

Michaux, Lightfoot Solomon 1885–1968

An evangelist, pastor, denominational leader, early radio and television pioneer, and businessman. Michaux was born in Newport News, Virginia. His father was a local grocer, and Michaux dropped out of public elementary school to help with his father's business. He eventually opened his own combination grocery store and dance studio. During World War I, Michaux obtained contracts to supply food to the defense department.

Initially a member of the **Church of Christ (Holiness)** under **Charles P. Jones, Michaux** served as treasurer for that body. In 1917 he moved his family to Hopewell, Virginia where he was ordained in that denomination a year later. However, finding no church home, in 1919 Michaux launched a tent revival in Newport News to recruit 150 congregants to a new **Church of Christ (Holiness) USA** congregation. However, he served in that body for only two years longer.

In 1921 Michaux formed an independent Holiness congregation. Soon he established a second congregation in nearby Hampton, Virginia and created the Gospel Spreading Tabernacle Association to oversee the group's financial affairs. Michaux moved his home base to Washington DC in 1928. A year later, his radio ministry started as a local broadcast on an Alexandria, Virginia station. By 1934 he was being heard on fifty CBS radio stations on a weekly broadcast carried his sermons and songs to twenty-five million people across the country.

Despite the inferior wattage of **Charles Emmanuel "Sweet Daddy" Grace,** the two used their radio broadcast to hurl epithets at each throughout the 1930s. By 1933 **Rosa Artemis Horn** had also launched an aggressive radio rivalry with the man the *Washington Post* called "the best known colored man in the United States." Michaux, who was daubed "The 'Happy Am I' preacher" by the popular press, took pains to maintain the distinction between Pentecostals and the Holiness movement of which his body was a part. His wife, Mary, hated what she considered the ravings of lower class "tongue people," vowing never to allow them into her husband's church. Yet many of his Holiness adherents would later go on to embrace Pentecostal Holy Spirit baptism with speaking in tongues.

A social reformer and entrepreneur as well as preacher, during the Depression, he crafted the "common plan" and ran an employment bureau and a Happy News Café that fed many hungry persons throughout the Great Depression. In 1942 he collaborated with Jack Goldberg to produce a commercial film entitled, "We've Come a Long, Long Way." The short black and white documentary film, released in 1943, featured commentary by Mary McLeod Bethune and Major R.R. Wright, and footage of George Washington Carver, Joe Louis, Paul Roberson, Lena Horne, and Bill Robinson. That same year, he collaborated with Howard University professor Albert Cassell to build Mayfair Mansions, an affordable, five-hundred-unit apartment complex for Washington's black residents, who were often excluded from other areas by racially restrictive housing covenants. The project was one of the earliest and largest complexes conceived and designed for working- and middle-class blacks.

The denomination also operated the 1100-acre National Memorial to the Progress of the Colored Race in America in James City County, Virginia, near the place where the first slaves in this country landed. Michaux was the first person to fly over the Arctic Circle and air drop copies of the Russian language Bible over the Soviet Union.

President Dwight Eisenhower was an honorary deacon of Michaux's Washington congregation; other supporters included Eisenhower's wife, Mamie and Eleanor Roosevelt. CBS vice president Harry Butcher, and President Roosevelt's personal secretary, Steve Early, became honorary deacons of his congregation. On his death, FBI director J. Edgar Hoover, notorious for his treatment of some black leaders, lauded Michaux as one whose "contribution to human understanding was unforgettable." In 1992 a memorial marker honoring the life's work of the Virginia native was unveiled in Williamsburg.

Further Reading:

Webb, Lillian Ashcraft, and Lightfoot Michaux. *About My Father's Business: The Life of Elder Michaux*. Santa Barbara, CA: Greenwood, 1981.

Mix, Sarah Ann Freeman 1832–1884

Sarah Mix has been Proclaimed as the first healing evangelist to be both African American and female. Her prolific ministry began shortly after the Emancipation of slavery crossed the color barrier. Though she mainly traveled throughout New England, preaching at healing conferences, her healing miracles were documented in the local newspapers as well as Christian periodicals across the country.

Mix was one eleven siblings born to free parents in Torrington, Connecticut. Her mother was Baptist, but her father had fallen from faith. During her childhood, her father contacted tuberculosis and when she was twenty, he died of the disease, leaving Sarah's mother without means to sustain herself. After her father's death, Sarah and her mother moved to New Haven, Connecticut, where Sarah found a boarding home for her and proceeded to work as a maid to sustain them. During this time they were destitute and struggled to survive, but in this time of struggle she came to God. She felt the calling to ministry early in her life yet delayed her response for several years.

Three years after moving to New Haven, her mother also died of tuberculosis, and Sarah briefly returned to Torrington before moving to New York to begin to work again. Within a short time she, too, also contracted tuberculosis, but was able to regain her health.

Sarah married Edward Mix. All of the couple's seven children died at a young age and Sarah again contracted tuberculosis. Sarah and her husband rededicated themselves to the Lord joined with the Seventh Day Adventist Church. Shortly afterward she felt a renewed call to ministry, and though she was still in poor health, began preaching.

In 1877 when she was forty-five, the tuberculosis returned and Mix sought the healing ministry of Ethan O. Allen and received what appeared be a miraculous healing. Allen encouraged Mix to use the gift of healing, which he discerned she possessed, and allowed her to join his ministry. Soon, she began holding her own faith healing and prayer meetings in her home and at private residences and churches. Mix worked primarily among whites and among the many who were healed by her prayers was Carrie Judd, a young, bed-ridden, white woman at the point of death. Judd would subsequently become a prominent faith healer and her story would be published in the widely read book, *The Prayer of Faith*.

Mix's ministry was so powerful that medical doctors recommended patients to her, and even detractors of faith healing acknowledged the impact of her short-lived ministry. During her ministry, she published a monthly journal entitled *Victory Through Faith*. In 1880 she wrote *The Life of Mrs. Edward Mix, Written By Herself*, and in 1882 she published *Faith Cures, and Answers to Prayer*.

In 1884 seven years after embarking on her evangelistic career, Mix, again, was diagnosed with tuberculosis and within several months, died from complications of the disease. Her autobiography was published shortly after her death.

Further Reading:

Mix, Sarah Ann Freeman. *Faith Cures, and Answer to Prayer: The Life and Work of the First African American Healing Evangelist*. Edited by Rosemary D. Gooden. Syracuse, NY: Syracuse University Press, 2001.

Moales, Kenneth H., Sr. 1945–2010

The noted gospel artist, preacher and church and community leader was a native of Bridgeport, Connecticut. He attended Norwalk Community College, Nyack College, and the University of Bridgeport. He received honorary Doctor of Divinity Degree (DD) from Saint Thomas Christian College of Jacksonville, Florida.

Moales was founding pastor of the Cathedral of the Holy Spirit formerly the Prayer Tabernacle Church of Love, which he founded in 1969, when he was only twenty-one years old. He served that congregation for forty-two years and by the time of his death, the congregation had more than one thousand members.

In 1993 the gifted musician, who began singing at age seven, succeeded the Thomas A. Dorsey, as president of the National Convention of Gospel Choirs and Choruses, Inc. He was a member of the New York Chapter of the National Academy of Recording Arts & Sciences, Inc. and was inducted into the International Gospel Music Hall of Fame & Museum. Moales made several guest television appearances on the Trinity Broadcasting Network.

In 1995 Moales turned his attention to the church when he brought together a group of congregations as the **Pentecostal Churches of Jesus Christ** and was installed as presiding bishop of the organization. He was an Executive Board Member of and the **Joint**

College of African American Pentecostal Bishops, for which he served as chaplain. As a community leader, he served on the Regional Advisory Council for Housatonic Community College, served six terms as a fire commissioner for the city of Bridgeport and was appointed by the mayor as a member of the Charter Revision Committee.

Moore, Benjamin Thomas 1927-1988

Prominent leader in the **Pentecostal Assemblies of the World**. Moore was born in Toledo, Ohio. After graduating from Wiley High School in Terre Haute, Indiana in 1944, he attended Highland Park Junior College and the Wayne State University both in Detroit, Michigan with the goal of becoming a doctor. However, his education was interrupted by a stint in the United States Armed Forces, and during his time of service, he acknowledged a call to the ministry. He later attended Butler University in Indianapolis, Indiana, where he graduated with a Bachelor of Arts degree in religion and sociology.

In 1950 Elder Moore was ordained in the **Pentecostal Assemblies of the World**. After several years serving as National Evangelist, he accepted a position with Aenon Bible College in Indianapolis, where he served as instructor and later as Dean. In 1954 Moore moved to Seattle, Washington to establish a congregation. A year later, he worked with Bishop A. William Lewis organized the Pacific Northwest District Council of the PAW. Moore quickly rose through the ranks of the PAW, moving from elder, to district elder, to become the youngest Suffragan Bishop ever appointed in the denomination.

In 1961 he was elevated to full bishop, and sixteen years later, in 1977, was called to Indianapolis, Indiana to assume the pastorate of Christ Temple—the congregation that had once been pastored founding bishop, **Garfield T. Haywood.** He served there until his death. While serving in that post, Moore established the Christ Temple Christian Academy.

One of his many accomplishments was to get Fall Creek Parkway, which runs directly in front of Christ Temple, renamed to G. T. Haywood Memorial Way, in honor of the PAW founder.

Moore, Faye 1928-

The fourth and current presiding bishop and the third successive woman to serve at the head of the **Church of the Living God, Pillar and Ground of the Truth, Which He Purchased With His Own Blood, Inc. (Jewell Dominion),** following the original Overseer, Bruce McLeod. Moore, who was born in Tupelo Mississippi, was appointed as senior bishop and chief overseer of the Church of the Living God-Jewell Dominion in 2005, two years after the death of former overseer Acquilla Manning.

Prior to assuming the leadership of the denomination, Moore pastored in Mt. Clemens, Michigan. She served as chair the Board of Directors of the Dominion, taught Sunday Bible School, established the first Sunday School Books for the denomination workshops and spearheaded the annual

Youth Church Bible Quiz events. She was also very active as Chaplain of the Camp Jewell ministry (a church-owned summer camp for all young people), and was heavily involved in prison ministry. As an advocate for young people, Moore also established the first black-owned foster care service in the Macomb County, Michigan.

Moore has been a life-long member of the Church of the Living God, who was raised by parents who were involved in church leadership. She is, however, the first overseer not to come directly out of the line of the Tate dynasty.

Morris, Ernest Fredrick (E. F.) 1890–1968

Co-founder and first bishop of the **Free Church of God in Christ** and founding president of the **International Federation of Pentecostal Churches.** Morris was born in Memphis, Tennessee. His father, a Baptist minister, was the father of twelve children—six boys and six girls, eight of whom became ministers, and two of whom became bishops. The family moved to Enid, Oklahoma, where Ernest spent his childhood. In 1915 while the family was gathered for in prayer for a brother who had became gravely ill, all twelve family members had an experience of Pentecostal Holy Spirit baptism. That event left a lasting impression on the young man who, subsequently, accepted the call to the preaching ministry.

In 1919 Morris moved to Colorado where he met his wife, Olive, who served in ministry with him as co-pastor. The couple first moved to Tacoma, Washington in 1925 where he first established church. They then settled in Seattle in 1928 where he was the founding pastor of God's Pentecostal Temple, the first congregation of the **Free Church of God in Christ.**

Bishop E. F. Morris incorporated the **Free Church of God in Christ** with the Full Gospel Pentecostal Missionary Association. Morris also consolidated the Central District and the Western District of the FGPMA and established the Full Gospel Pentecostal Missionary Association.

Reportedly, Morris experienced the Holy Spirit outpouring of Azusa firsthand and was closely associated with Bishop **Judge King** of Christ **Holy Sanctified Church**, Aimee Semple McPherson of Angelus Temple Church, and **Emma and Henry Cotton**, Azusa Temple.

Morris, James Thomas 1892–1959

Founder and first presiding bishop of the Oneness Pentecostal denomination, **Highway Christian Church of Christ** in Washington DC and a leader in spreading the early Oneness movement in the area.

Morris was raised Methodist and was called into the ministry in 1918, at age sixteen. He received the Pentecostal experience of Holy Spirit baptism within the **Church of God in Christ.** Later he accepted Oneness doctrine, was rebaptized in Jesus' name and aligned himself with the **Pentecostal Assemblies of the World.**

Morris founded his local PAW congregation in 1929, beginning with a tent ministry and then moving into a storefront building before occupying a more substantial edifice. He also served as a vice chairperson of the Washington DC, Maryland, and Delaware

District of the **Pentecostal Assemblies of the World**. By 1941, however, Morris had formed his own organization. The split with PAW was not schismatic in nature and Morris maintained cordial relationships with many of his PAW colleagues. PAW Bishop **Joseph Turpin** consecrated Morris as bishop. As the denomination grew, Morris relocated to New York City, where he died. At his death, his nephew J. V. Lomax assumed leadership for the denomination.

Morris, John Henry 1858–??

Co-founder of the **Free Church of God in Christ** in Enid, Oklahoma. Morris was born in Tennessee. In 1915 after receiving the Pentecostal experience of Holy Spirit baptism, Morris led others of the National Baptist Convention (who were primarily members of his family) to form a separate Pentecostal body, which they named the **Church of God in Christ**, though it had not connect to **Charles Harrison Mason's** group of the same name. The majority of the members of his original congregations were member of his family.

Morris believed strongly in divine healing and one incident that played a dramatic role in the development of the body occurred when, in 1915, the family gathered for prayer for one of Morris' eleven children—a gravely ill son—when all sixteen people who were gathered experienced Pentecostal Holy Spirit baptism. Morris took as a sign of God's favor.

After forging a relationship with Mason, however, Morris brought his congregation into fellowship with Mason's group. After establishing the church on solid footing, Morris turned the denomination over to his son, **Ernest Morris**. By 1920 he had died and in 1925, a disagreement developed between the two leaders and Morris led his smaller group into withdrawing from the parent body to form the **Free Church of God in Christ**. The younger Morris later merged it with another independent group to form the **Full Gospel Pentecostal Missionary Association.**

Further Reading:

Truesdell, Leon Edgar, and Timothy Francis Murphy, eds. "Free Church of God in Christ." Online: http://www.godspentecostaltemple.org/History.htm.

Morton, Clarence Leslie (C. L.), Sr. 1897–1962

Internationally renowned preacher and pioneer founder of the Canadian and International congregations in the Windsor/Detroit region. Morton, a Canadian citizen, was born near Chatham, Ontario. As a young child, he was sickly and doctors predicted he would not live past fifteen years of age. He was also, however, a bright child and though his sickness kept him from attending school, he learned to read and write.

After fully gaining his health as a young man, he became well enough to do military service, during World War I. However, in keeping with COGIC's pacifist stance,

Morton refused to bear arms and was sentenced to prison. He was freed after the passing of the Conscientious Objector Law.

Morton was ordained with the **Church of God in Christ** in the early 1900s. Coming to the United States, his first pastorate was in West Virginia. He shortly returned to Canada and began his ministry there by preaching on the streets of Windsor, Ontario, establishing first church, Mt Zion Full Gospel Church, in 1926. That same year, he established another congregation in Harrow. All totaled, Morton was instrumental in the establishment of five churches—the later three in Chatham, Buxton, and Amherstburg.

Morton was involved in broadcasting for forty-two years. He used an international radio broadcast begun on CFCO in Chatham in 1935, and later was the first Black minister to broadcast a radio program on Windsor's CKLW. After thirty years, the popular program moved to WGPR in Detroit. He also held an annual River Baptismal Service that brought thousands to the riverfront during the 1940s and 1950s. The event regularly drew thousands of worshippers to Windsor.

In 1935 Morton incorporated the body of churches he had established above the northern border under the name of Canadian Church of God in Christ. In 1951 focused his attention again on the United States. He established a congregation in Detroit—Mount Zion Tabernacle Church of God in Christ—and from that point until his death, pastored both congregations. However, membership in the Ontario Mt. Zion congregation declined after Morton founded the Detroit location.

During his ministry, Morton established eleven churches. Along with those in Ontario, he established six congregations in the United States. After his death, his oldest son, Clarence Leslie Jr. succeeded him as bishop. Another son, **Paul S. Morton** is founding bishop of the **Full Gospel Fellowship of Churches International**.

Morton, Paul Sylvester 1950-

Mega-church pastor, recording artist, and founding presiding bishop of the neo-Pentecostal, **Full Gospel Baptist Church Fellowship International**. Morton was born in Windsor, Ontario. His father, **Clarence Leslie Morton, Sr.,** was a pioneering **Church of God in Christ** bishop who established that denomination in Canada, but died when the younger Morton was twelve. Morton began preaching in 1967, when he was seventeen.

Five years later, in his early twenties, Morton moved to New Orleans, Louisiana to serve as associate pastor at Greater St. Stephen Missionary Baptist Church. In 1974 when the pastor of the church, Percy Simpson Jr. was killed in a car accident, Morton was installed as pastor of the 650-member congregation in January 1975, with his wife, Debra, as co-pastor.

Fifteen years later, Morton founded the FGBCFI, in the wake of a scandal within the 8.5 million-member National Baptist Convention USA, Inc. when its president, Henry Lyons, was charged with stealing millions of dollars from the organization. Though Morton initially backed Lyons, who denied the allegation, Lyons was not accepting of

Morton's belief in speaking in tongues and divine healing, and the two parted ways. Morton's intention was to establish the Neo-Pentecostal FGBCFI to give Baptist congregations and leaders a place to appropriate Pentecostal/Charismatic spirituality within the context of their existing congregations.

In 1992 Morton joined twelve prominent Baptist bishops with Charismatic leanings—Odis Floyd, **Larry D. Trotter**, Carlos L. Malone, I. Douglas Wiley, K. D. Johnson, Larry Leonard, Kenneth Robinson, **Kenneth Ulmer**, Fred Caldwell, Robert Blake, Eddie Long, and Alton R. Williams—to form his new fellowship. All except Caldwell and Floyd, who became bishop emeritus, eventually pulled out to form their own organizations, though they stayed in fellowship with Morton's group. That year Greater St. Stephen Missionary Baptist Church changed its name in 1992 to Greater St. Stephen Full Gospel Baptist Church. In 1993 Morton was consecrated International Presiding Bishop of the Full Gospel Baptist Church Fellowship. That office corresponds to the position of president, general superintendent or general overseer in other Evangelical organizations, but it is deemed by FGBCFI to be language that is more biblical.

In 1997 Morton initiated an investment plan for his congregation as well as other pastors to bring modern banking actions such as online banking to the fellowship. After the group whom he signed to oversee the absconded with more than $200,000, Morton suffered a breakdown from which he eventually recovered.

Morton, an accomplished musician and singer, released his solo album entitled "Crescent City Fire" in 1999. Since then he has produced five albums with the Greater St. Stephen Mass Choir and two recordings with the Full Gospel Baptist Church Fellowship Mass Choir. He was also featured on the all-star recording of the hit song, "Something inside So Strong" a tribute to Rosa Parks. His current project in hot release is entitled "Let It Rain." He founded Tehillah Music Group as a division of the Full Gospel Baptist Church Fellowship.

Though Morton's education ends with attending J. C. Patterson Collegiate Institute, a public secondary school located Windsor, he is a strong advocate of education. In 2004, Greater St. Stephen Christian Academy opened its doors. He is also the president of the Paul S. Morton Scholarship Foundation and president of the PSM Bible College and School of Ministry. Morton's published works include, *Why Kingdoms Fall, It's Time for the Outpouring,* and *What is the Full Gospel Baptist Church*?

In the devastation of Hurricane Katrina in 2005, the once burgeoning New Orleans congregation of more than 20,000 lost its edifice and the majority of its member to the dislocation caused by the storm. The church has re-emerged as a smaller congregation of approximately 5,000 in that city. By 2009, however, Morton moved the base of his operations to Atlanta, where he had planted a new congregation, Greater St. Stephen Full Gospel Church/Atlanta. The church was renamed as Changing a Generation Church, and Morton turned over the pastorate of the New Orleans congregation to his wife, Debra. In keeping with his new focus, "Changing a Generation" daily radio and weekly television broadcasts airs both locally and nationally.

Further Reading:

Morton, Paul S. *Why Kingdoms Fall: The Journey from Breakdown to Restoration.* New York: Albury, 1999.

Mount Calvary Holy Church of America

In 1928 **Brumfield Johnson**, a young minister associated with the **United Holy Church of America** and pastoring a congregation in Summit, New Jersey, traveled to Winston-Salem, North Carolina to conduct a revival. By the end of that meeting, nearly 250 persons were converted to the Pentecostal faith, and many of them wanted a church home shepherded by Johnson.

For some time Johnson had been growing increasingly dissatisfied with the UHCA organization, and he and seven others—Lee R. Ligons, Van L. Pope, William Bryant, Augustus A. Granville, Josephine M. Spencer, Bessie L. Lipscomb, and Nancy Hall—established the structure for Mount Calvary Holy Church of America in Winston-Salem in 1929. In the next year, twenty other ministers joined the group in a conference in Summit to formalize the new organization.

Johnson's main method for building Mt. Calvary was personal evangelistic efforts. From the time he left the UHCA until his death in 1972, Johnson traveled with evangelistic teams of three to five young people who served as advance support teams for his revivals, ensuring that logistical needs were met and forming the core of new congregations established in the wake of these meetings. They first traveled to Huntington, Long Island, New York to hold a revival and establish a congregation there. From there the group traveled to Boston, Massachusetts where they adopted the principles of the MCHCA and chartered the organization. By the early 1930s, the teams had planted churches in cities across the country, including Staten Island, New York, Durham, North Carolina, and Columbus, Ohio.

In 1940 MCHCA opened a Bible School in Lillington, North Carolina to train ministers and Christian workers, but it was short lived. The first headquarters was established in Baltimore, Maryland and relocated to Buffalo, New York in 1942. After the Buffalo facility was destroyed by fire in 1960, the headquarters was moved to Boston where the National Convocations were held until the International Headquarters was established in Washington DC in 1991.

In 1972 two women, **Ardell Tucker** and Dorothy Austin left to form the **National Tabernacles of Deliverance**. That year, Johnson died after having appointed **Harold Ivory Williams** to serve as his successor. Williams led the church for over thirty-seven years. Under his leadership, Mount Calvary grew to include churches in over fifteen states and several countries throughout Europe, Africa, Asia, and the Caribbean.

Johnson's departure from the UHCA was, in part, due to the parent denominations' more open stance on women in ministry. Yet Mount Calvary permitted women to serve as pastors from its inception. It was not until 1994, under the administration of Williams, that MCHCA took the historic step of ordaining two women to the office of bishop, **Gertrude L. Pitts** of Milwaukee and **Nellie Yarborough** of Boston.

In 2008 Bishop Williams chose to take emeritus status, elevating **Alfred A. Owens, Jr.,** to the office of presiding bishop and Bishop Hansel H. Henry to the office of executive vice-bishop.

Further Reading:

Reynolds, Barbara. *Doing Good in the Hood: The Life, Leadership, & Legacy of Bishop Alfred A. Owens.* S.l.: BookBaby, 2007.

Mount Hebron Apostolic Temple of Our Lord Jesus Christ

In 1956 George Wiley, established a local congregation in Yonkers, New York as part of the Oneness Pentecostal body, the **Church of God (Apostolic).** In 1963 after his petition to be consecrated as a bishop was refused, Wiley left that organization. Since his wife had worked with the CGA youth department for many years, the couple had developed a following among this group and established their new work out of the local Mt. Hebron congregation they had established seven years earlier. Within this organization, local congregations are referred to as temples and numbered chronically as they are formed or join the body. The mother church, for example, is Temple No. 1. A second congregation, Temple No. 2, was organized in Manhattan, New York later in 1963. By 1978 however, there were only three congregations after a third temple was established in Wallace, North Carolina.

In 2005 Bishop Jeremiah Ravenell, who had been an earlier associate of Wiley, reconnected with him and the Mt. Hebron organization and two years Wiley appointed him Presiding Apostle. After Wiley's death in 2008, the two New York congregations merged. While the headquarters of Mt. Hebron remains in Yonkers, New York, there are also congregations in North Carolina, South Carolina, and Georgia.

Mount Sinai Holy Church of America

In 1924 **Ida Bell Robinson**, pastor of a Philadelphia **United Holy Church** congregation had gained considerable exposure within the UHC and throughout the community of black Pentecostal congregations along the East Coast for her dynamic preaching and singing. As she regularly travelled with UHC leaders, Bishop **Henry Fisher** and Bishop **General Branch,** to minister in revival meetings throughout the East coast, her ministry piqued the interest of other women, spurring many to seek ordination and more public ministry. However, though UHC was initially open to the ministry of women, the surge in interest in pastoral ministry that Robinson's ministry spawned led to a decision to no longer "publically ordain women," and to restrict credentialed women to lower levels of ministry.

This moved spurred Robinson and several supporters—including many of the women rejected for ordination, as well as male and female pastors sympathetic to her stand to leave the UHC—to establish a body that would be open to women's leadership at all levels. At the denomination's first convocation in 1924, one year after its founding, the seventeen congregations in attendance included several from the **United Holy Church.**

At least two schisms occurred during Mt. Sinai's early years. A dissenting group, dissatisfied with Robinson's the decision to relax the ban on men wearing neckties, left to form Glorious Mt. Sinai Holy Church. By 1926 **Eva Lambert** had withdrawn to establish **St. Mark's Holy Church of America Inc.** Generally, however, though individual congregations left from time to time, additional congregations slowly joined the denomination. In the twenty-two years that Robinson was at its helm, the denomination grew to eighty-four churches, stretching from New England to Florida

By the time Robinson died in 1946, a pattern of women's leadership had been established that would stand for half a century. The next four presiding bishops were women Robinson had personally prepared to move into the highest level of leadership. **Elmira Jeffries**, a charter member of Mt. Sinai from the UHC who started her ministry leading Tuesday noonday tarry service at Robinson's Mt Olive congregation, was elected as presiding bishop directly after Robinson's death and served until her death in 1964. Eighty-eight-year-old **Mary Jackson**, another charter member who had taught the preacher's class at Mt. Sinai and assisted Robinson with finances, succeeded Jeffries, serving until her death at age 102. **Amy Stevens**, who like the others had previously served in a number of capacities including usher and Sunday school teacher, was elected presiding bishop at age seventy-one, serving until her death in 2000 at age eighty-eight. In 2000 **Ruth Satchell** became the fifth presiding bishop, but served only one year before becoming emeritus. In 2001 the current presiding bishop, Joseph Bell, became the first male to hold that position.

Gradually, a pattern of preference for male leadership at the higher levels of authority has developed within Mt. Sinai. As early as 1980, considerably less than one-half of Mt. Sinai's bishops were women and by 2000, only one-third of Mt. Sinai bishops were women. However, the actual rate of participation of women in top leadership positions has continued to decline from the time of Robinson's death until the present. Though there are still large numbers of women in ministry, the proportion of women pastors and the proportion of women with governing and oversight responsibilities continue to slowly, but steadily, fall. Of the 160 ordained ministers who were part of the organization in 1996, 125 (more than three-fourths) were women; eight of the nineteen bishops were women.

The majority of the current women bishops are older women who came into the church and rose through the ranks during or shortly after Robinson's lifetime. These women are highly revered by the membership for the contributions they made during their lifetimes, but most can no longer make viable contributions to Mt. Sinai's governance. The younger, more recently elected, male bishops are the decision makers and the real leadership of the Mt. Sinai organization.

Along with the decline of women in top positions, there has been corresponding decline in women in pastoral leadership. Within the first twenty-six years (nearly one generation), there was only a nine percent fall. However, with the succeeding twenty-four years the rate of decline almost doubled to sixteen percent. By 1996, only forty-five of the 102 pastors were women.

Mt. Sinai Holy Church remains a relatively small denomination, largely unknown outside of the African American Pentecostal community. At its height, in 1988, the denomination grew to 154 congregations, primarily along the East Coast. By 1996 that number down to 102 with approximately ten thousand members, including one congregation in Cuba, seven house churches in India, and two congregations in Guyana, South America.

Further Reading:

Alexander, Estrelda. *Limited Liberty The Legacy of Four Pentecostal Women Pioneers.* Cleveland, OH: Pilgrim, 2008.

N

National Apostolic Fellowship Association, Inc.

An organization within the Oneness Pentecostal tradition established in 1987 by **Robert O. Doub**, bishop of **Shiloh Apostolic Temple Church, Inc.**, in Philadelphia after Doub sensed a need for a unified base of Apostolic (Oneness) ministers and churches. The NAF sought to bring together Oneness ministers from wide organizational backgrounds to address the challenge of empowerment, self-reliance, and independence on the part of the tradition as a whole. At that time, the executive officers were Doub, as President; Bishop Ralph E. Green as Vice-President; Dr. Dennis M. Golphin, Executive Secretary; Overseer William Thomas, Treasurer; and Bishop J. H. Bower, Chaplin. The organization was incorporated in Maryland in 1992 with Bishops Ralph Green, Alphonzo Brooks, Major Foster, R. H. Prince, and Joseph Weathers as the incorporators.

While the major objective of NAF was to bring Apostolic ministers from various organizations together, it also sought to serve as a fellowship for alienated Apostolic churches, to be platform for socio-economic enhancement and stability within these churches, to establish a unified public standard of teaching, and to collectively represent Oneness churches with the region covered by the organization. The NAF planned to establish an Apostolic Theological Seminary, as well as to develop a construction company to facilitate building churches, schools and other facilities, give financial and management support to newly forming congregations, and establish job creation programs.

Doub served as president until his sudden death in 1989—two years after the organization's founding. Foster, pastor of Philadelphia Pentecostal Holiness Church, has served as president since then. By 2012 the organization, whose headquarters were in Accokeek, Maryland, was still in existence though little is known regarding the progress toward its goals.

National Association of the Churches of God (Anderson, Indiana)

A Holiness association primarily constituted of the African American congregations affiliated with the Church of God (Anderson, Indiana), a fellowship of congregations, pastors, ministers and support agencies joined together by covenant to advance practical and spiritual needs. Its headquarters is on the NACOG campground in West Middlesex, Pennsylvania, affectionately known as Zion's Hill.

NACOG was founded independently of the Church of God around 1906 as the "Brothers and Sisters of Love." In 1916 the group organizedin Pennsylvania under the name of The Western Pennsylvania Industrial Camp Ground. Without knowing that a doctrinally similar interracial group had been established in western Michigan, the independent autonomous organization envisioned uniting African-Americans who were migrating from the South and Mid-Atlantic areas.

A year later, the group changed its name to the National Association of the Church of God. Some within the Southern constituency who had joined the group informed the leaders about the Reformation Movement of the Church of God headquartered in Anderson, Indiana. Within a short time, the National Association of the Church of God began affiliating with the COGA as a partner that avails itself of the educational and other resources of the larger body, but remains an independent body.

Today, the association has over 420 churches. The current presiding elder is Miki Merritt of St. Louis, Missouri. Bishop Robert S. Davis, Sr. of Columbia, Maryland is presiding elder emeritus.

National Black Fellowship of the Assemblies of God

One of twenty voluntary ethnic/language fellowship groups within the Assemblies of God. From its inception, NBF has been somewhat controversial in that some both blacks and whites within the denomination believe the title connotes a separatist image. The mission of NBF, however, is focused on urban America, where the majority of black AG churches are located. In keeping with its mandate membership in the NBF is reserved for pastors of churches are at least 50 percent black. Accordingly, half a dozen white pastors, such as Gary Grogan, lead pastor of Stone Creek Church in Urbana, Illinois, belong to the fellowship because of the ethnic composition in their congregations.

The fellowship emerged out of the Inner-City Workers Conference, which began in the late 1970s under the leadership of led **Spencer Jones** of Chicago. It was formed in 1989, and approved in early spring of the next year when the denomination's executive Presbytery recognized the ICWC as the National Black Fellowship. In 1998 the NBF, which represents more than two hundred congregations, became a representative voice for blacks within the AG when its General Council empowered the NBF with seats on the General Presbytery.

Jones, leader of the ICWC, pastored Tampa Assembly of God, an integrated church in Springfield, Missouri and Southside Tabernacle in Chicago, Illinois, before becoming the first ethic Executive Presbyter and first president of the National Black Fellowship (NBF). Other presidents have included **Zollie Smith**, the highly visible AG pastor of Eternal Life Christian Center in Somerset, New Jersey, who had previously been assistant superintendent and later, executive secretary of the New Jersey District. Malcolm Burleigh served as the president from 2008 to 2012 and went on to serve as the first nonwhite director of the Commission on Ethnicity. The current president is Michael Nelson of Jacksonville, Florida.

By 2006, the NBF was called on to help formulate new strategies for including minorities more fully into the life of the AG, and to aid the denomination in increasing the number of blacks attending AG churches. The fellowship continues to sponsor the biennial Inner City Workers Conference as a resource for evangelizing the black community and providing spiritual and practical support to existing black pastors and congregations.

Further Reading:

"National Black Fellowship Formed." *The Pentecostal Evangel* (1991) 29.

Kennedy, John. "National Black Fellowship Seeks Relationship and Revitalization." *Pentecostal Evangel,* November 13, 2014. Online: http://rss.ag.org/articles/detail.cfm?RSS_RSSContentID=28796.

National Church of God, Inc.

A Pentecostal organization of about twenty churches that came into existence in the mid-1960s out of the predominantly white, Church of God (Cleveland, TN) when the parent denomination's bi-annual General Assembly voted to integrate its long-standing Church of God (Colored Work) under the General offices of the denomination. Immediately after the ruling, all offices of the Colored Work were abandoned and the department dissolved. The Annual Assembly of the Colored Work was discontinued as well. These actions met with disfavor from several black pastors who feared they would be subjected to racial inequality in dealing with the larger denomination.

The leader of this group included Rev. Harcourt. L. Cartwright pastor of Washington Park Temple in Fort Lauderdale, Rev. Leonard Josey Sr. of Delray Beach, Rev. J. H. Woodside Port Salerno Church of God, and Rev. J. B. Ferguson who pastored the Church of God in West Palm Beach, Florida. Congregations are located throughout Florida, Georgia, New York, the Bahamas, and Jamaica. The General Overseer is Bishop Otis Williams of Pompano Beach. The new organization set up headquarters in Fort Lauderdale, Florida where the Church of God (Colored Work) had been centered and enlisted several additional pastors to their cause who were prepared to pull their congregations out of the parent body. Several of these backed away from pulling out when the Church of God took the position that all facilities that congregations held belonged to the parent body and would stay with denomination should a congregation withdraw.

Beginning in 1966 a four-year court battle ensued between the Church of God (Cleveland and the National Church of God over the ownership of several black congregations. When it was over, the Church of God had prevailed and some pastors who could not take their church with them stayed or returned to that body. Those who left after three years of litigation were ordered to return their property immediately. One of the main properties in dispute was the Fort Lauderdale facility that had once served as headquarters of black constituents. It, too, reverted to Church of God (Cleveland, TN) ownership.

The organization, which was incorporated in 1968, is the most notable defection of black churches and pastors in the history of the Church of God during a time of heightened racial unrest in the American society. This group has remained separated from the parent body until this day.

National Fellowship Churches of God, Inc.

An interdenominational body that serves as a covering for independent Pentecostal, Neo-Pentecostal and Charismatic churches. The organization, which refers to itself as the "Nation of National Fellowship Churches of God," was established in 1996 by Ivan L.

Grant, Sr. pastor of the former Trinity Apostolic Faith Holiness Church, Inc. in Baltimore, Maryland.

The organization traces its lineage directly back to the **Azusa Street Revival** in 1906 through the **Apostolic Faith Church of God, Inc.** that was founded in 1938 by Bishop **Charles W. Lowe**. Many of the first members of the fellowship were former AFCG congregations who sensed that their parent body was experiencing decline and who sought viable organization with which to affiliate.

Grant, a former overseer in the AFCOG, left that organization in 1994. Two years later, he established the new organization and, in 1997, was elected as presiding bishop and chief apostle. In 1998 Grant, consecrated NFCOG's Ronald E. Riley, Sr. of Bridgeport, Connecticut as First Vice-Bishop and he served at that post until 2006. Grant served at head of the body without assistance from that time until 2012, when Forrest R. Nance, Jr., pastor of Saints in Christ Church in King George, Virginia was consecrated at the second First Vice-Bishop.

Member congregations are in that state and in Maryland and Georgia. There are also covenant (affiliate) churches in other parts of the United States. The organization operates the NFCOG Bible Institute, a non-degree granting school approved to offer Evangelical Training Association (ETA) Church Ministries Courses. New Beginning Apostolic Faith Church of God, Inc., in Jacksonville, Florida, serves as the General Assembly headquarters.

National Tabernacles of Deliverance

In 1970 two women—Ardell E. Tucker and Dorothy Austin—left **Mt. Calvary Holy Churches of America** to form the Mt. Calvary Churches of Deliverance in New Haven, Connecticut. The work grew out of a congregation that the women had established in that city in 1964. By 1966 the two had established additional congregations in Bridgeport and Danbury, Connecticut. Tucker and Austin changed to National Tabernacles of Deliverance when it was incorporated in 1972. Tucker had formerly been a member of the Oneness **Apostolic Faith Church of God**, but had accepted the Trinitarian understanding of the Godhead and had left that body to join Mt. Calvary.

Tucker and Austin served at the helm of the organization until 1986, the year of Austin's death. Tucker continued at the head until 2006, when Austin's grandson, Robert L. Ford, IV took leadership. At that time, the organization had fourteen churches. Reportedly the denomination has grown to fifty congregations throughout the United States.

Neal, Elijah Nathan (Eli N.) 1900–1964

Second presiding bishop of the **Church of God Apostolic** (COGA) after founder, **Thomas Cox**, became too ill to govern effectively. Born in Casville, North Carolina, Neal served as pastor of Saint Peters Apostolic Church of God and state overseer of Virginia.

Cox first selected Neal to preside in his stead for an interim period. At Cox's death, however, the leadership of the denomination was vested in the hands of two men, Neal and Bishop M. Gravely. After only one year, Gravely was disfellowshipped from the

COGA when he divorced his wife and married another woman, and Neal assumed the position of presiding bishop. He served as presiding bishop until 1964.

Neal's perceived authoritarian leadership style led to a schism in the organization with several leading several pastors left to form a new body, the **Apostolic Church of Christ in God**.

Neal continued as bishop until his death in 1964 in Forsythe, North Carolina, and was followed by Love Odum. At the time of his death, he was also serving as pastor of the Holiness Church in Rockingham, North Carolina.

Neeley Isaac S, 1865-1923

Neeley, Martha A. (Mattie) 1866-??

Early black missionaries ordained in 1913, by L. C. Hall with the **Church of God in Christ**. Isaac Neeley was born in North Carolina and Mattie Neeley was born in Princeton, Indiana. The couple was among the few blacks at the originating of the Assemblies of God Hot Springs meeting and left COGIC to align themselves with the AG. The pair, who were supported for a time by a black Pentecostal congregation in Chicago, were missionaries to Cape Palmas (Liberia), West Africa. While there, they received support from congregations that had joined the Assemblies of God. The Latter Rain Evangel, a periodical published by the Stone Church (an Assemblies of God congregation in Chicago), published many of their missionary letters.

The Neeleys returned to the United States on furlough in 1919 and attended the General Council that year at the Stone Church. They received credentials as evangelists with the Illinois District Council of the Assemblies of God in 1920. As the first African-Americans to serve as Assemblies of God missionaries, they were officially appointed as missionaries to Liberia in 1920.

They served as pastors and evangelists in the United States until 1923, while they raised funds to return to Liberia as Assemblies of God missionaries. Before they could get the necessary financial support for their trip, however, Isaac was appointed associate pastor at historic Stone Church in Chicago in 1923. He died suddenly from a stroke that same year, just before their departure. They were associated with the colored mission on Langley Avenue, Chicago at the time of his death.

The next year, Martha travelled to Liberia as a single missionary and took charge of Bethel Home in Cape Palmas, Liberia, serving there until 1930. After her return to the United States, no further record can be in her AG ministerial file inferring that she was no longer held credentialed with the denomination. In 1940, the widow was living back in Chicago, Illinois.

Nelson, Douglas Johnson 1931-

The white social scientist who completed his doctoral dissertation, *For Such a Time as This: The Story of Bishop* **William J. Seymour** *and the Azusa Street Revival, A Search for Pentecostal/Charismatic Roots,* at the University of Birmingham in England in 1981. Nelson's dissertation was the first definitive work on either Seymour or the revival. In undertaking research for the dissertation, Nelson traveled over 14,000 miles and gathered materials including interviews, newspaper accounts, and early scholarly treatments.

Nelson was not Pentecostal and at least one scholar identifies Nelson as a Methodist clergyman, while another as Lutheran. He studied with prominent sociologist and Pentecostal scholar Walter Hollenweger under whom he completed his dissertation.

Born in San Antonio Texas, the ex-Green Beret, who was a military chaplain during the Vietnam War, has spent the latter years of his life in Arlington, Virginia. A second work on the subject of Afro-Pentecostalism, *The Black Face of Church Renewal: A Brief Essay Examining the Meaning of the Pentecostal-Charismatic Church Renewal Movement, 1901–1985*, was also published in 1981.

New and Living Way Publishing Company

One of the earliest Pentecostal publishing companies in the United States was established at Nashville, Tennessee in 1923 by the **Church of the Living God, the Pillar and Ground of the Truth.** The company published church literature including three periodicals (*The Present Truth Gospel Preacher, Another Comforter,* and *The Official Organ*), *The Church General Decree Book*, song ballads, and missives from the founder, **Mary Magdalena Tate** and her son **Felix Lewis**. That year, Tate commissioned Lewis and **Bruce McLeod** to locate suitable properties in Nashville, Tennessee upon which to construct and operate church physical facilities.

The denomination operated the New and Living Way Publishing Company through the early 1940s. After shutting down for a short period, in 1943, **Helen Middleton Lewis**, Tate's daughter-in-law and successor to her husband as presiding bishop, was responsible for attempting to reestablish the company. However, due to financial exigencies and property litigation, formal operations were suspended around 1944.

During the period its demise, the company continued to serve as the archival repository for historical document of the denomination and in 1983, the M. L. Tate, W.C. and F. E. Lewis Foundation entered into an agreement with the Moorland-Spingarn Research Center at Howard University, Washington DC. The library established the Mary Magdalena Tate Collection as the major repository for the personal papers of Tate and other leaders, historical documents, and artifacts of the publishing house, the founders, and the church.

Around the turn of the twentieth century, the operation was reestablished. It is now located in Tuskegee, Alabama under the direction of Meharry H. Lewis, grandson of the founder and fourth General Overseer of the denomination.

New Born Lighthouse Church of the Apostolic Faith, Incorporated

A Oneness Pentecostal body that was established in 1988 by two organizations—New Born Church of God and True Holiness, under the leadership of Bishop Woodrow Roach of Washington DC; and Lighthouse Church of the Apostolic Faith, under the leadership Bishop John W. Lee of Columbus, OH. The groups had been holding joint convocation meetings for several years officially when the merger occurred.

There are six districts with thirty-eight congregations in North Central (Canada, Kentucky, Ohio), North Eastern (Connecticut, New York), South Central (Arkansas, Missouri, Mississippi, Tennessee), East Central (Maryland, North Carolina), South Eastern (Florida, Georgia, South Carolina), and Jamaica. The headquarters for the organization is in Capitol Heights, Maryland, a suburb of Washington DC. The body is led by a three-person executive board whose current members are General Overseer Winfer Turner of Bruce, Mississippi, Vice General Overseer Allen Roach of Capital Heights; and Executive Secretary David Gillispie of Maryland.

Within the denomination, there is an all-male clergy. Further, there are sanctions on women's dress including the requirement that women wear head coverings in worship.

New Century Fellowship of Churches and Ministries–International

A Pentecostal body founded by Bishop **Larry Trotter** in Chicago, Illinois in 2012 after a schismatic break with **J. Delano Ellis** of the Pentecostal Churches of Christ.

Ellis founded the parent organization and led it for several years before ill health forced him to step down from leadership. He tapped Trotter to lead the body and installed him in 2004. While maintaining the doctrine and polity established by the former leader, within five tears Trotter would make several significant changes in the structure of the organization that did not have Ellis' approval or support. These included changing its name to **United Covenant Churches of Christ** and moving its headquarters to Evergreen Park, Illinois. Subsequently Ellis returned to the organization and asked Trotter to step down.

In 2012 Trotter established a new organization and within a month, fifty churches from the United States and two churches from the United Kingdom had joined the New Century Fellowship of Churches and Ministries International. Trotter serves as presiding bishop. Jacquelyn D. Gordon, founder and senior pastor of Shiloh Christian Center in Melbourne, Florida, was elected as second presiding bishop, and there are now approximately seventy churches in the fellowship.

New Church of Christ Holiness unto the Lord of the Apostolic Faith

A Oneness Pentecostal body that formed under Bishop **Benjamin Franklin Colty** in a 1959 split with the Trinitarian denomination, **Church of Christ Holiness unto the Lord of the Apostolic Faith** in which Colty had been presiding bishop.

At the time of the split, the parent denomination had two main jurisdictions—the South Carolina District (which included congregation in the Northeastern United States), over which Colty had been overseer, and the Georgia District. The actual dissolution was peaceful and the two groups continued to fellowship with each other.

A year later, the headquarters of the twenty-one congregation denomination was in Burton, South Carolina. Churches are located throughout that state in small towns such as Long Reach, Hardeeville, Freedman Grove, Ellabell, and in Georgia with at least one congregation in Savannah. There are also congregations as far north as Brooklyn and Albany, New York and Boston, Massachusetts. The denomination was incorporated in

Georgia in 1975, sixteen years after its founding and dissolved as a corporate entity in 1998.

Further Reading:

Brown, Tomie L. *Sharing our History with Others: The Churches of Christ Holiness unto the Lord as we Know It*, S.l.: Xlibis, 2014.

New Day Church International

One of the latest denominations to form as a splinter group from the **Church of God in Christ** ostensibly because of the parent organization's longstanding position against the ordination of women. Yet, the departure also may have been related to then presiding bishop **G. E. Patterson's** refusal to support Bishop **David W. Grayson, Sr.** in his bid to be appointed as a jurisdictional prelate within the state of Tennessee.

In 2003 Grayson, a former COGIC pastor, bishop, and district superintendent, led thirty-two COGIC congregations and about two thousand members from forty congregations, primarily in Tennessee, Alabama, Mississippi and New York out of the denomination. The new denomination is almost identical to the parent body in structure and belief, except that it welcomes the ordination of women as both elders and bishops.

In 2004 the group formed the Tennessee Evangel Church Planting Association and later that year, Grayson was consecrated as presiding bishop of the Church of God in Christ (New Day). Almost immediately, COGIC sued Grayson and his organization for infringement on the parent body's name. After a court battle, the new group was forced to change its name to **New Day Church International**.

From the outset, Grayson extended membership to non-COGIC churches who embraced the full-gospel teachings COGIC and his position on the ministry of women. Within the denomination, whose headquarters is in Memphis, women serve at all ranks of ministry. During its inaugural year, Dr. Bettye J. Alston, founder and pastor of New Beginning Ministries Church of Our Lord and Savior Jesus Christ, was consecrated the first female bishop and appointed Suffragan Bishop of Health Education and Welfare.

Further Reading:

Barker, John. "Alston Named New Day Bishop" *The Commercial Appeal*, May 5, 2007.
Davis, Janel. "A New Day? COGIC Split Puts Church at Odds." *Memphis Flyer* 1.779 (2004).
Wiley, Henry. "COGIC Church Did Not Split: Grayson Says is a New Day." *Tri-State Defender*, January 8, 2004, 1A.

Nyombolo, Eli B'usabe 1904–1970

A later follower of **Laura Adorka Koffey** who attempted to restore Koffey's quasi-Pentecostal, **African Universal Church,** after her 1928 assassination. Nyombolo was not associated with Koffey during her lifetime. During the 1930s, however, he became attracted to Koffey's teachings and joined a remnant group of her followers. Within a short time, he moved into leadership and reorganized the group as the Missionary African Universal Church in Jacksonville, Florida. In 1953, after further reorganization, this group became the **African Universal Church, Inc.**

Born in Pondoland, South Africa, Nyombolo came to the United States to obtain a post-graduate degree from Wilberforce University in Ohio and to teach. By the time he encountered Koffey's teachings, Nyombolo, one of the leading officers in the Native African Union of America (NAUA), had become a nationally known religious writer, speaker, churchman and president of the American branch of that organization.

In 1944, "Lil Brother," as he came to be called by some, moved to Jacksonville where he purchased an eleven-acre site and created the Adorkaville community and Ile Ife Institution to honor Koffey's vision and memory, spread her spiritual teachings, and build on her message of connecting with African cultures and traditions. Within his group, services were held in English and Bantu, the language used by ethnic groups in Africa; children within the community studied from a Bantu primer. Nyombolo also edited the periodical, *African Messenger,* and published some of Koffey's writings including, the *African Universal Hymnal, Mothers Closet Prayer Book, Mothers Sacred Teachings, and Mothers Sayings.*

Though in the twenty years since beginning his efforts, Nyombolo did not return to Africa himself, he worked to prepare returning African Americans as well as to develop relationships between businesspeople in Africa and America. Through his efforts, there was at least one known attempt by six individuals to go as pioneers to locate Koffey's home on the Continent, and they returned to the United States, presumably having met with some of her kin and authenticated her story.

Shortly after Nyombolo's death, several factions split from his group. Presently there are less than ten congregations remaining.

O

Original Church of God or Sanctified Church

An association of predominantly African-American churches within the Holiness movement headquartered in Nashville, Tennessee. The parent body of the organization originated in 1900, around the same period that **Charles Price Jones** was organizing the **Church of God in Christ**. During this time an elder of Jones' church, Charles W. Gray, formed a number of congregations in and around Nashville. At the time of the split between Jones and **Charles Harrison Mason** over the issue of speaking in tongues, a second schism occurs when the churches organized under Gray also from Jones. Though non-Pentecostal and doctrinally identical to Jones' faction, the new body was independent of Jones' body and congregational in polity. Gray's churches were known by the name, **Church of God (Sanctified Church)**. When the organization was incorporated in 1927, the new board approved the ordination of women, which Gray opposed. When the board would not move from its support of women, Gray led a group of members who were supportive of his stand in breaking away to form a new body, the "Original Church of God or Sanctified Church."

Gray remained the leader of the church until his death in 1945. He selected Elder William Crosby of Chicago, Illinois to be presiding chairperson of the annual National Conventions. At his death, Crosby moved into the presiding position, serving there until his death 1952. During his tenure, he is credited with writing a *Handbook of The Church of God*, as well as manuals detailing, *The Duties of the State Overseers*, and, *The Duty of the National Trustees*. He was followed by T. R. Jeffries who had served as Assistant to Crosby. The current leader is George W. Price, Jr., pastor of the Bethesda Original Church of God in Nashville, the site of the denomination's headquarters.

The body includes about sixty-three churches in Tennessee, Kentucky, Indiana, Illinois, Michigan, Ohio, and Pennsylvania. As of the 1970s it had about five thousand members.

Original Glorious Church Of God in Christ (OGCGIC)

The **Original Glorious Church of God in Christ** was founded in 1921 by Lulu Phillips and **Cleveland H. Stokes** as part of a larger Trinitarian organization, the **Glorious Church of God in Christ**. At Phillips's death in 1939, **Sidney Coy Bass** moved into the office of General Overseer of the former organization and pastor of the headquarters church. Sometime between its founding and that date, the denomination adopted a Oneness stance. It also held a rigid holiness piety forbidding remarriage of divorced persons among other moral sanctions.

In 1952, however, after the death of his first wife, Bass defied denominational polity and married a divorced woman. Approximately half of the fifty-congregation denomination rejected Bass and reorganized under the leadership of W. O. Howard. The group lead by Bass kept the original name of the denomination. Howard's group took the name **Original Glorious Church of God in Christ Apostolic Faith**, signifying its claim to its history and retained the founding charter. Further, since the split was not related to doctrinal, the schismatic group retained the doctrine of the parent denomination.

During Howard's tenure, the denomination added fifteen congregations. In 1972, however, he retired because of poor health. He was succeeded by Bishop **Isaiah Hamiter,** the founding pastor of the Original Glorious Church, in Columbus, Ohio. Under his leadership the church has grew to include mission programs in Haiti, Jamaica, and India. Hamiter has also led in the purchase of a convention center for the church's annual meeting in Columbus, Ohio. At his death, his wife became presiding bishop.

By 1979 the denomination had approximately 165 congregations, 300 ministers and 30,000 members. Only sixty-five of these congregations were in the United States, and one hundred of them were in other countries including Haiti, Jamaica, and India.

Though the church has the distinction of being among a small number of Pentecostal bodies founded by a woman, it would be more than ninety years before the first two female bishops were consecrecated. In 1913, Dr. Julia M. Shaffer, pastor of God's House of Prayer and Deliverance Holiness Church of Cleveland, Ohio and Rocine Jackson, pastor of The Original Glorious COGIC of Whitman, West Virginia were elevated to that office.

Original United Holy Church of America

In 1972 a schism began to unfold that caused a rift within the **United Holy Church of America** that would take several years to heal. Since the mother denomination originated in the South, from the beginning, the strength of the denomination lay in the South and the Southern District had been its strongest district. Not only had it been the first district formed and house the largest number of congregations and adherents, but the denomination's international headquarters was located was located in Greensboro, North Carolina. The district held numerous strong churches and many prominent, charismatic UHCA leaders came from its congregations. Bishop **James A. Forbes, Sr.** was one of these leaders.

In an attempt to diffuse some of that influence, UHCA leaders suggested subdividing the district into smaller jurisdictions by state. In response, in 1972, Forbes lead officers of the District in taking the unauthorized action of dissolving the **United Holy Church of America** and drawing up a new charter as the Southern District of the **United Holy Church**.

Relationships between the District and the **United Holy Church** leadership continued to deteriorate until 1977 when most district ministers representing one hundred congregations walked out of the General Convocation and formed a new body, the Original United Holy Church of the World, Inc. That name was later shortened to Original United Holy Church International.

Though the parent body made overtures to allow any Southern District congregations to remain with the body, only seven congregations agreed to do so, continuing to represent themselves as the Southern District of the **United Holy Church**.

The schism resulted in a lengthy trial which over ownership of the properties of individual congregations. Early in that period, Forbes approached the leadership of the International Pentecostal Holiness Church about possible affiliation (not an official amalgamation) and the IPHC General Conference drew up and approved such an agreement.

The split lasted for twenty-three years. During that time, several smaller bodies that had split from the parent group joined the Forbes faction or formed other organizations. In 2000 a year after Forbes died, the two major factions joined with these smaller factions to reunite. By that time, most of the leaders who had been involved in the original schism were out of leadership, and many of the local congregations and individual pastors within these bodies had continued to fellowship with each other.

O'Quinn Doretha Ann 1952–

Since 2014 O'Quinn has served as provost and vice president of Academic Affairs at Vanguard University of the Assemblies of God. O'Quinn is an ordained minister in the International Church of the Foursquare Gospel. She previously served as the vice provost of Multi-Ethnic and Cross Cultural Engagement at Biola University, as associate dean for the School of Education at Point Loma Nazarene University and program director for Graduate Studies in Education at the Inglewood satellite campus for Biola University, and has held faculty positions in Graduate Education at both Biola University and Point Loma Nazarene University.

O'Quinn's education includes a PhD in Intercultural Education, a Master of Arts in Christian School Administration from Biola, and graduate studies at University of California, Los Angeles, and California State University, State Dominguez Hills. She received her Bachelor of Arts in Theology from the Foursquare Church's Life Pacific College in San Dimas, California.

She is author of the book *Silent Voices, Powerful Messages: The Historical Influence and Contribution of African-Americans to the Foursquare Gospel Movement*, and a contributing author of the book *Our Voices: Issues Facing Black Women in America* as well as *Alone in Marriage*. She is also a contributing editor to *Women in Ministry Leadership* published by Foursquare International.

O'Quinn has received several honors including being Distinguished Educator of the Year in 2002, Lifetime Achievement Award for Service to the Foursquare Church, Outstanding African American Educator of the Year from of Phi Delta Kappa National Sorority, and the Los Angeles Community Service Award.

Osborne, Grace C. 1927–

Grace Catherine Schultz Osborne, the second presiding bishop of the **Original Glorious Church of God in Christ**, was born in Kansas City, Missouri. Her father was a senior bishop in the **Pentecostal Assemblies of the World**, diocesan of the 11th Episcopal District over the states of Texas, Arkansas and Oklahoma.

The highly educated leader received her early education in Louisville, Kentucky. She completed her higher education at Franklin University, Capital University, Aenon Bible College, Warner Pacific College, and Portland State University. She received her Bachelor and Master Degrees from International Institute and Seminary and holds an honorary doctorate from Grace Apostolic Bible College in Indianapolis, IN. Throughout much of her ministerial career, she has also served within the public school system. In 1964, she became the first African-American teacher employed with the Head Start Program in the city of Portland, Oregon. She also held the position of principal at Louis I Elementary Christian School and is currently on staff at North Portland Bible College.

Grace was married to the pastor of a congregation in Portland, Oregon who died in the late 1950s. In 1960 the young widow opened her congregation to **Louis W. Osborne** for a series of evangelistic services that would expand the ministries of her **Original Glorious Church of God in Christ** congregation. After being ordained to the ministry in that same year, she served as the Assistant Pastor and Minister of Education for the congregation. In 1962 she and Louis were married, continuing their ministry together until his death in 2009.

Osborne was elevated to the pastorate in 1986 and consecrated a bishop in 1989. With that act, she became the first female to be elevated to that position in her organization. Osborne was elected president of the Oregon Association of Ministers Wives and Ministers Widows and served as a regional vice president, president, board chair in the International Association in which she now serves as treasurer. She has served her community through her involvement as a as a member of officer organization as varied in mission as the Black United Front (founded by Pentecostal bishop **Herbert Daughtry**), and the Apostolic World Christian Fellowship.

Presently, Bishop Osborne pastors Grace Covenant Fellowship Church and is president of Grace Cathedral Ministries, a service organization addressing issues of drug use and abuse, homelessness, and AIDS. She is also chief executive officer of Fellowship of Christian Believers Inc., which her late husband founded in 1963 concomitant with FTCCI.

Osborne, Louis W. Sr., 1922–2009

The founder of the **Faith Tabernacle Council of Churches** was born in Eufaula, Oklahoma. His father pastored a Baptist Church in the city and he and his siblings grew up singing together. During World War II, young Osborne moved to Richmond, California to work in the ship building industry. In 1947, he answered a call to ministry, furthered his education at Oakland, California's Bay City Bible Institute, and joined North Richmond Baptist Church where he directed the Young Peoples' Choir and sang tenor with a quartet named The Golden West Singers.

He then moved on to The New Bethel Church of God in Christ. Shortly thereafter, he accepted the Oneness doctrine. He served as youth pastor as an ordained elder. In 1953 he joined with Pastor Sallie Tolbert in Berkeley, California as a youth pastor.

By 1956 Osborne had relocated to the San Francisco Bay Area, and was evangelizing and setting up congregations that he named Faith Tabernacle. He often told the story of "seeing a great crowd of people who were groping in the darkness, not able to find their way until God gave me a hot ball of something that grew into a burning bright light that began to show the way for the people." It was to be called, "the Light of Faith." That Light of Faith became his hallmark for the rest of his life.

In 1960 he relocated to Portland, Oregon to run a series of revivals and begin another Faith Tabernacle. There he joined with Grace Catherine Schultz Kennedy, a recently widowed evangelist who provided a place for Osborne's fledgling congregation. The couple married in 1962 and continued ministry together evangelizing new congregations as well as affiliating existing congregations. Subsequently, Osborne was elevated to the office of bishop over the Faith Tabernacle Fellowship. After his death, his wife, **Grace Osborne** succeeded him as presiding bishop.

Owens, Alfred A. Jr. 1946–

The third presiding bishop of the **Mt. Calvary Holy Churches of America, Inc.** A native of Washington DC, Owens attended Miner's Teachers College, graduating with a Bachelor of Arts degree in English. He began working as a high school English instructor while he pastored his storefront congregation. In 1985 he received a Master of Arts degree in English from Howard University, and later a Master of Divinity degree and Doctor of Ministry Degree from that institution's School of Divinity.

In 1966 Owens founded Christ is the Answer Chapel. Ten years later the small inner-city congregation merged with another small congregation, Mt. Calvary Holy Church forming what is now Greater Mt. Calvary Holy Church. Since the merger, his original congregation grew from seven members in 1966 to an adult membership of nearly seven thousand. Many upwardly mobile African-American Pentecostals eventually migrated to suburban enclaves, and most of the other Pentecostal congregations joined them. However, Owens kept his congregation within the city limits. As the congregation continued to grow, it became the largest Pentecostal congregation within the nation's capital.

Under his pastorate, the church has established an alcohol and drug abuse treatment program, a food and clothing bank, Calvary Christian Academy for children from infants to the eighth grade, an HIV/AIDS ministry, an employment service, a prison ministry, and several other social outreach services and ministries. It also operates a state-of-the-art Family Life Community Center and a Calvary Bible Institute over which Owens presides as chancellor.

As the congregation grew, so did Owens's presence within the **Mt. Calvary Holy Churches of America**. He was consecrated a bishop in 1988, and Bishop **Harold Ivory Williams** appointed him vice bishop in 2001, and elevated him to senior bishop in 2008, while he took for himself the position of bishop emeritus.

Outside MCHCA, Owens plays a significant role in the broader African-American Pentecostal movement. In 2000 he was appointed as Dean of the **Joint College of African American Pentecostal Bishops**. He serves as adjunct professor at Howard University School of Divinity, where he teaches Homiletics, and Church Leadership, and Administration.

In the spring of 2013, after preaching the early morning message, Owens suffered a mild heart attack while preparing for the second service. In an urban culture and church, he ministers to people from every stratum of society. While his messages have been considered by some Pentecostals as not going far enough to denounce the lifestyles Pentecostals traditionally consider sinful and taboo, others have accused him of going too far. Owens, however, has publically tackled such hard issues as homosexuality, the HIV/AIDS epidemic, and family dysfunction within the African-American community that other Pentecostal pastors have stayed away from.

His wife, Susie Carol Thomas Owens, who is a Doctor of Ministry graduate of Fuller Theological Seminary, serves as co-pastor of the congregation. Along with their two biological children, the couple has been responsible for the care for sixteen foster children.

Owens, Chandler David, Sr. 1931–2011

The fifth presiding bishop of the **Church of God in Christ** was born in Birmingham, Alabama. His father, William, pastored a COGIC congregation, and Chandler, who started preaching as a young man, served as his junior pastor and as an adjutant to COGIC founder, **Charles Harrison Mason.** After completing high school, Owens moved to Detroit, Michigan where he served as a minister under Bishop **John Seth Bailey** who later appointed him to his first pastorate at Wells Cathedral Church of God in Christ in Newark, New Jersey, a congregation he served for thirty-three years. During his tenure there, he was consecrated bishop of New Jersey's Third Ecclesiastical Jurisdiction.

At various times during this same period, Owens also served the denomination as international president of the youth congress, chairperson of the Constitution Committee, second assistant presiding bishop and first assistant presiding bishop and was instrumental in establish several churches, schools and transportation for ministries in the Philippines, India, Malawi and Central Africa. In 1976, at the age of forty-five, he became the youngest bishop elected to the COGIC General Board of the, a seat he held until his death.

In 1991 Owens moved to Atlanta to serve as pastor of the Greater Community Church of God in Christ in suburban Marietta. Subsequently, as appointed the presiding bishop of Central Georgia Ecclesiastical Jurisdiction when then bishop and general board member John D. Husband was stripped of his office and excommunicated after admitting to embezzling half a million dollars of church money and to the sexual abuse of young men under his charge. Owens worked hard to rebuild the jurisdiction, even using his own money to buy several churches in Metro Atlanta for COGIC congregations. His missions interest led him to establish churches, schools, and transportation for ministries in the Philippines, India, Malawi, and Central Africa.

After the 1995 death of Bishop **Louis Henry Ford,** Owens first served as interim presiding bishop. He subsequently won the election for the post against **Gilbert Earl Patterson,** by a single vote. During that tenure, Owens' interest in training leaders within the denomination led him to organize the first annual Auxiliary in Ministry (AIM) conference and established The C. H. Mason Bible Institute throughout the Church of God in Christ. He also developed the *Whole Truth Newsletter* into the *Whole Truth Magazine.*

Despite these accomplishments, Owens' often heavy-handed style rankled many COGIC leaders and laity. They saw him as attempting to wrest power from the board of bishops and centralize it within his position. In 1998, two years after his election, three members of the twelve-member Board of Bishops—including later-presiding bishop **Charles Blake**—called for a special election to unseat him and replace him with **Ozro T. Jones Jr.** Their bid failed.

In the next year's regular general election, Patterson defeated him. Prior to that vote, Owens reportedly had claimed that his spiritual authority was analogous to the pope's. Owens' defeat marked the first time that the **Church of God in Christ** had voted out its presiding bishop.

During his tenure, Owens served on several committees for the administration of President William Jefferson (Bill) Clinton for whom he served as a spiritual advisor and personal friend. He hosted the nation's leader at the COGIC National Annual Holy Convocation in 1993, the Bishop's Conference in 2000, and at the International Women's Convention in New Orleans in 1996.

After leaving the bishopric, Owens returned to his Atlanta congregation. He died there at age seventy-nine.

P

Paddock, Ross Perry 1907–1990

The third presiding bishop of the **Pentecostal Assemblies of the World** was born in Van Buren County, Michigan as the second of three children. Later, Paddock's family moved to Kalamazoo County where he lived for the remainder of his life.

After having attended a small country church in Kalamazoo, Michigan for most of his young life, as a young man, he moved away from the church for a while. At age twenty-one, he converted to Pentecostal faith and was baptized in Jesus' name. Shortly afterwards, he received the Pentecostal Spirit baptism. Within a short period, his entire family—wife, mother, father, sister, and brother—were among his first converts.

Paddock began studying the Bible feverishly. Five months later he conducted his first service. Soon afterward, his pastor was killed in an accident and Paddock was drafted by the congregation to serve as their pastor. Though at the time he refused to take the post because he felt he lacked adequate preparation, five years later, when the then-selected pastor experienced moral failure, Paddock was elected pastor of the small congregation, Blessed Promise Assembly, purchased a new facility and rename the church Christ Temple Church. The new church was dedicated in 1950 and Paddock served as pastor for thirty-seven years.

Initially, as a white man, Paddock affiliated the congregation with the predominantly white Pentecostal Assemblies of Jesus Christ. When Paddock discovered, however, that racial disparity was in the failed merger of that body and the predominantly African American **Pentecostal Assemblies of the World, Inc.,** he resigned from the former organization and in September of 1938, applied for credentials with the PAW.

In 1947 Paddock was elected to the office of Treasurer and as a member of the PAW Board of Directors. In 1952 he was consecrated a bishop, and was assigned the following year to the Mountain State Council. A year later, Paddock was elected assistant presiding bishop of PAW, a position he held for fourteen years. He was appointed Diocesan Bishop over the State of Michigan in 1962. In 1967, following the passing of Bishop **Samuel Grimes**, Paddock was elected presiding bishop to fill the unexpired term. He was elected to two full terms—in 1968, and again in 1971—and served until 1974. He continued his responsibilities as diocesan bishop over Michigan until 1988. He died two years later.

During his lifetime, Paddock contributed to the development and clarification of Oneness doctrine by authoring of several publications centered on confessional theology and PAW history.

Further Reading:

Paddock, Ross P., and Ira Combs. *The Era of Apostolic Excellence: A Chronology of the Teachings of Bishop Ross P. Paddock.* Jackson, MI: Greater Bible Way Temple, 2005.

Page, Emmett Morey (E. M.) 1871–1944

Early **Church of God in Christ** bishop who served as the first overseer of Texas and on the five-man board bishop Mason appointed to help with the administration of the denomination. When **D. J. Young** failed to establish a presence for COGIC in Dallas, Texas, **Charles Harrison Mason** sent Page to the state. More diplomatic than his predecessor, Page gained the respect of the surrounding community and was able to grow the membership of the congregation to more than one hundred members. In 1914, Mason appointed Page overseer of Texas.

Born in rural Yazoo County, Mississippi, Page heard Mason preach in 1902 and was converted at that time. He was among the small group of Holiness leaders who stood with Mason in his split with **Charles Price Jones** over the issue of speaking in tongues, and was at the meeting Mason called to reorganize the **Church of God in Christ** as a Pentecostal body. Afterward, he was among those at the new organization's first general assembly who elected Mason presiding bishop.

Page countered claims of Pentecostal "otherworldliness" by embracing the Progressive era, particularly its emphasis on social uplift of African Americans through civic involvement and education. Deprived of the opportunity for formal instruction, Page was determined to educate himself. In 1926 his ongoing interest in education led him to spearhead the establishment of Page Normal and Industrial Institute in Hearn, Texas.

In 1935 Mason consecrated Page, along with **Ozro Thurston. (O. T.) Jones, Sr.** of Philadelphia, **Edward Robert (E. R.) Driver** of California, **William Roberts** of Chicago and **Isaac Sanford (I. S.) Stafford** of Detroit, as one of the five original bishops of the **Church of God in Christ** and set him over the states of Arkansas, Oklahoma, New Mexico, Texas, California, Tennessee, Mississippi, and Wisconsin.

Page died in Dallas, TX at the age of seventy-three.

Page Normal Industrial and Bible Institute

One of three **Church of God in Christ** schools established in the American South to provide education for African-American students during the period of Jim Crow segregation when they were forbidden to attend white institutions. The trade school was established in Hearn, Texas in 1919 by Bishop **Emmett M. Page,** overseer of Texas, and **James Courts**, an educator who would also serve as president of **Saints Industrial and Literary School** in Lexington, Mississippi. They were assisted by Jerome Robert Delley, a well-known civic leader, organizer, and community developer who was pastor of the Hearne Church of God in Christ and had received his degree in General Agriculture under the instructions of George Washington Carver at Tuskegee Institute in Tuskegee, Alabama.

The school was named after the founder, who served that state from 1914 until his death in 1944, and who used his own resources and his influence as the first COGIC overseer of Texas. Deprived of his own formal instruction, Page was determined that younger black people within COGIC would not suffer the same deprivation. In 1918, at his urging, the Texas COGIC Educational Board purchased 268 acres in Hearne where the administration building and the girls dormitory were the first two edifices constructed. In 1926, Bishop **Ozro T. Jones Sr.,** who by then was overseer for Pennsylvania, donated $50 of the total $394 pledged for educational work. COGIC founder, Bishop **Charles H. Mason,** matched Jones' donation.

The trades offered to boys included carpentry, painting, agricultural vocations, floriculture, and landscape gardening. Girls were offered sewing and dressmaking, domestic science, home crafts, and laundering. Both also received strong religious (i.e., Pentecostal) training, civic and moral lessons, and classes in reading, composition, and mathematics.

In what appears a show of his support, Mason sent his two sons to study at Page. And, during its years of operation, the school trained several persons who would go out to make a solid impact within the denomination. After graduating from high school in 1932, for example, **Emma Crouch** who would go on to become International Supervisor of COGIC's International Women's Department, attended the school, where she graduated in 1934.

The school had strong leadership; besides Page, Courts, and Delley, Emma F. Bradley Barron, who was the daughter of a professor and who had herself been educated at Prairie View A&M University, served as principal. Ultimately, however, Page did not survive more than eight years because funds were allocated to the more prominent schools–Saints and Geridge Academy in Arkansas. After fire devastated the complex in 1932, Page was never fully rebuilt. It closed in 1934.

Further Reading:

Kossie-Chernyshev, Karen. "Constructing Good Success: The Church of God in Christ and Social Uplift in East Texas, 1910–1935." *East Texas Historical Journal* 44.1 (2006).

Patterson, Gilbert Earl 1939–2007

Church of God in Christ leader who was a presiding bishop, pastor, recording artist, televangelist, and social justice advocate. Patterson, the grandson of founder, **Charles H. Mason**, first ran for the post of presider in 1996, losing to Atlanta pastor **Chandler D. Owens** by one vote. In 2000, he ran again and was elected, becoming the fifth presiding bishop and the first to unseat a sitting incumbent in the denomination's history. Four years, later he was re-elected by acclamation in 2004.

Born in Humboldt, Gibson County, Tennessee, Patterson grew up in Memphis, where his father, W. A. Patterson Sr., was a pastor and bishop, and four of his siblings became preachers or church officials. Patterson's uncle was **J. O. Patterson Sr.** the presiding bishop of COGIC from 1968 until his death. His cousin was Bishop **J. O. Patterson Jr.** who was a state politician and chair of the COGIC General Assembly.

As a youth, Patterson moved with his family to Detroit, where his father pastored New Jerusalem COGIC. He studied at the Detroit Bible Institute (later known as William Tyndale College), and LeMoyne-Owen College in Memphis, and later received an honorary Doctorate from Oral Roberts University.

Patterson came to Christian faith in 1951 at age twelve. He received his Pentecostal Holy Spirit baptism, and began his ministry at seventeen, and was ordained an elder at nineteen. In 1961 at twenty-two, he returned to Memphis to become co-pastor with his father at Holy Temple COGIC a congregation of less than one hundred members. In 1964 he led the congregation in three days of fasting and prayer, then launched a thirty-day tent revival that generated fifty-five new members, and began a long growth curve that would continue upwards for the rest of his career.

In 1975 Patterson temporarily left the **Church of God in Christ** to found Temple of Deliverance, the Cathedral of the Bountiful Blessings in Memphis. Four hundred and thirty-six members joined at the church's inception and the congregation grew to 2,000 members in three years before erecting a 5,000-seat worship center. He returned to the denomination in 1986, bringing the congregation with him. Twenty years later, his congregation had grown to more than 13,000 members.

As pastor of one of the largest, most influential congregations in the denomination, in 1990, Patterson became one of the first COGIC pastors to have an international television broadcast by taking advantage of satellite television offered through the Trinity Broadcasting Network (TBN) and Black Entertainment Television (BET). He reached out to constituents who tuned in through his *Bountiful Blessings Magazine*. Nearly ten years after his death, those broadcasts are still being aired. In 1991 Patterson became president and general manager of WBBP, a 5,000-watt gospel radio station

From 1988 until 1992, when he became a General Board member, Patterson served as a jurisdictional bishop of Memphis serving until his election in 2000. During his tenure as presider, he launched a new COGIC charity arm, planned the construction of a substance-abuse center on church-owned land in Mississippi, and worked to expand the church's educational institutions, serving from 1999 onward as president of the Charles H. Mason Bible College. Under him, the church-owned Podium record label began to make inroads into the gospel market.

Patterson's interest in social justice was evident and went far beyond the confines of the **Church of God in Christ**. Within COGIC, during his seven-year tenure, he repeatedly raised the issue of women's leadership. He brought it to a new level of public attention by appointing a woman, DeOla Wells-Johnson, as an associate pastor of his congregation, seating her prominently on the podium with male pastors during worship services that were televised around the world. In the broader Pentecostal realm, he was one of the movers behind an unprecedented effort to foster a new level interaction between black and white Pentecostal bodies. In 1994 his congregation served as the host for the "**Memphis Miracle**" convocation that culminated in replacing the white Pentecostal

Fellowship North America with the interracial **Pentecostal and Charismatic Churches of North America**.

Yet, Patterson's interest went beyond even these bounds. In 1968, he was a part of the nine-person strategy team that invited Martin Luther King Jr. to Memphis for the Sanitation Worker's strike in which he also participated. It was while he was in the city for this event that the civil rights leader was assassinated. President George W. Bush invited him to offer prayer during his 2005 inaugural prayer service at Washington Cathedral. That year, he announced that he was battling prostate cancer.

In 2006 Patterson was nominated for a Grammy Award and a Soul Train Music Award for his gospel album, *Singing the Old Time Way*. A year later, he received a Stellar Award for Traditional Male Vocalist of the Year, for his project, *Bishop G. E. Patterson & Congregation–Singing the Old Time Way–Volume 2*. The next year, the United States Senate passed a resolution, sponsored by Senators Barack Obama, Carl Levin, John Kerry, Lamar Alexander and Bob Corker, celebrating Patterson's life. Patterson died that year of heart failure. The first assistant presiding bishop, **Charles E. Blake Sr.** succeeded him as presiding bishop.

Patterson, James Oglethorpe, Jr. 1935–2011

A politician and statesman who was the son of **James Oglethorpe Patterson Sr.**, the first elected presiding bishop of the **Church of God in Christ**, grandson of COGIC founder **Charles Harrison Mason**, and cousin of COGIC presiding bishop, **Gilbert E. Patterson**. He was born in Memphis, received a Bachelor of Arts degree in Business Administration from Fisk University in Nashville, Tennessee, a Master of Religion degree in from Memphis Theological Seminary, and a Doctor of Jurisprudence degree from DePaul University, Chicago, Illinois.

Patterson began practicing law in Memphis before becoming active in local and state Tennessee politics. He started as a State Representative for one term, a State Senator for two terms, a Memphis City Councilman for five terms. He served as interim mayor of Memphis for twenty days in 1982 and served as a delegate to the Tennessee Constitutional Convention and the Democratic National Convention in 1972, 1976, and 1980.

Patterson's father consecrated him to the bishopric in 1985, appointing him to the First Ecclesiastical Headquarters Jurisdiction of Tennessee. At the time his father's death in 1989, he assumed the pastorate of the Pentecostal Temple Church of God in Christ in Memphis, Tennessee. By then the congregation had 2,500 members, and the younger Patterson continued many of his father's efforts including the J. O. Patterson Crusade, a broadcast, and media ministries and while also assuming the presidency of J. O. Patterson Mortuary, Inc., the business established by his father in 1939.

Patterson was elected vice-chairperson of the General Assembly in 1998, and elevated to chair in 2000, after the demise of Chairperson Frank Ellis. In that position, Patterson supervised sessions of the body that held supreme legislative and judicial authority of COGIC, and is responsible for expressing the doctrines and creeds of the church. As such, Patterson was a contributing writer for the Official COGIC Manual. He also served as a member of the COGIC Legal Counsel, the Board of Directors of the C. H. Mason

Foundation, the Saints Center Board of Directors, C. H. Mason Foundation Board of Directors, and advisor to Women's International Convention.

Patterson died of kidney failure at the age of seventy-six.

Patterson, James Oglethorpe, Sr. 1912–1989

The first elected presiding bishop of the **Church of God in Christ** who served for over two decades from 1968 until his death. Patterson was born in Derma, Mississippi and his family joined the **Church of God in Christ** when he was a young teen. Patterson acknowledged his call to preach in 1932 and was ordained an elder in the COGIC by Bishop **A. B. McEwen, Sr.** in 1935, the same year he married Deborah Indiana Mason, daughter of **Charles Harrison Mason**. He served congregations in Gates, Brownsville, and Memphis, Tennessee, and in East Orange, New Jersey before becoming pastor of Woodlawn Church of God in Christ (now Pentecostal Temple Institutional Church of God in Christ), in Memphis, in 1941. During his forty-eight-year term, that church grew in membership from less than twenty to nearly three thousand. In 1939 Patterson opened J. O. Patterson Funeral Home, a business that would be carried on by his family through several generations.

Patterson was ordained a bishop in the COGIC in 1955, and appointed to the Second Ecclesiastical Jurisdiction of Tennessee. When Mason created the Executive Committee to help carry out his administrative and executive duties, Patterson was appointed to serve on the committee's secretariat. He also served as the COGIC General Secretary and oversaw the operations of the COGIC Publishing House.

At Mason's death in 1961, Bishop **O. T. Jones Sr.**, succeeded him as senior bishop, organized an executive "General Board," and appointed Patterson as the assistant chair of the Board. In 1968 after seven years at the head, Jones leadership was challenged in as controversy over tenure. That year, by court order the General Board organized a General Assembly that voted to create the office of thepresiding pishop and voted Patterson into the position. He also presided over the Headquarters Jurisdiction in Memphis, Tennessee, from 1969 to 1981.

As denominational presider, Patterson consolidated COGIC publishing efforts into a single COGIC Publishing House owned and operated by the denomination. Along with it, he established the COGIC Bookstore, as a natural outgrowth. Further, he poured considerable effort into developing the foundation for the **C. H. Mason System of Bible Colleges** and the Charles H. Mason Theological Seminary, which opened in 1970 at the Interdenominational Theological Center in Atlanta, Georgia.

Patterson worked with leader from other major black Pentecostal bodies including, **Amy Stevens and** James F. Brown Jr. of the **Mt. Sinai Holy Church of America**, **Joseph T. Bowen of** the **United Holy Church of America**, Inc. and **J. Delano Ellis** of the **Pentecostal Church of Christ** to established the **World Fellowship of Black Pentecostal Churches**. Further, he involved the denomination in the Black Church Summit of the World Council of Churches and in the Congress of National Black Churches.

During his tenure as presiding bishop, Patterson built and organized COGIC churches in over forty-four foreign countries and organized many jurisdictions in those foreign countries. Under his leadership, he appointed over one hundred. He also founded the COGIC International C. H. Mason Memorial Choir, to serve as the official mass choir of the denomination, appointing **Mattie Moss Clark** as head and as director of the church's music department. In the 1970s and 1980s he appointed Bishops O. M. Kelly, **Frederick D. Washington, Louis H. Ford** and **Chandler D. Owens** as his assistant presiding bishops (Ford and Owens later became presiding bishops in succession).

In 1988 Patterson was diagnosed with pancreatic cancer, but refused to be treated with chemotherapy, and trusted in divine healing through prayer. As his condition worsened, Patterson retired from the office of presiding bishop and Bishop **L. H. Ford** became the acting presiding bishop until Patterson's death, when he moved into the position.

Further Reading:

Bennett, Harold. "The Legacy of Bishop James O. Patterson, Sr." *Assemblies of God Heritage* (2011) 74–75.

Peace Mission Movement

The quasi-Holiness, social activist organization founded by Rev. **M. J. (Father) Divine** in Harlem, New York. It remained relatively unknown until the start of the Great Depression in 1929. By the end of the 1930s, the mission had extended itself from New York City and the Northeastern cities to Chicago, Los Angeles and Seattle, and then spread internationally with followers in France, England, Switzerland, Germany, Australia, Panama, and Canada. Approximately 85 percent of Peace Mission disciples were black, and at least 75 percent were female.

The organization adopted many of the tenets of the black Holiness movement, including imposing a strict moral code with proscriptions against use of alcohol and tobacco, eating certain foods, and cohabitation. In reality, the moniker, "Divine" was not coincidental. Many members of the movement held their leader, whose given name was George Baker, to be deity.

Besides claiming his divinity, the movement departed from Christian doctrine in a number of ways, rejecting the doctrine an afterlife in Christian eschatology, advocating for creating an egalitarian heaven on Earth, referring to the United States as the "Kingdom of God," and regarding the Declaration of Independence, the Bill of Rights, and the Constitution as divinely inspired. Yet, the group rejected Ethiopianism, which was popular among some urban blacks at that time, downplaying Africa and the black heritage.

In 1939 as the Depression was ending and World War II was beginning, the American economy began to grow and jobs became available, the Peace Mission's communal style lost much of its attraction, and the popularity and influence of the organization began to diminish. In the late 1940s, however, the movement regained some of its influence by mounting a campaign against lynching in which it collected more than 250,000 signatures on a petition to Congress. They also flooded the office of Mississippi senator, Theodore Bilbo with letters attacking the injustice. Gradually, however, Divine retired in quiet wealth at his Woodmont Estate outside of Philadelphia until his death in 1965.

In 1971 the infamous People's Temple cult leader, Jim Jones, who modeled some of his activities after the Peace Mission, arrived at the estate, claiming to be the incarnation of Divine and attempted to take over leadership of the movement, but his attempt was solidly rejected by the founder's widow, Mother Divine.

While, in 1992, the movement's newspaper, *The New Day*, ceased publication, as late as 2003, the International Peace Mission still maintained its estate outside Philadelphia, church offices in downtown Philadelphia, and a budget hotel, the Divine Tracy, near the University of Pennsylvania campus. In 2012 it sold two major hotels that it operated and began construction of a building that would hold archives of the movement.

Presently, only a few hundred members remain within the movement. Fewer than two dozen live with Mother Divine at Woodmont. Despite her advanced age, no successor has been identified to take over leadership at eventual her death.

Pearson, Carlton D. 1953–

Throughout much of the last quarter of the twentieth, Tulsa, Oklahoma pastor, Carlton Pearson was one of the most visible Pentecostal televangelist in the African-American Christian community. At one time, he along with Word of Faith preacher, **Fred Price** was one of only two African-American Pentecostals with a national television presence. A strong proponent of racial and denominational unity among Pentecostals and Charismatics, and a supporter of the ministry and leadership of women, Pearson used his television prominence to build his local ministry into one of the largest black congregations in the country as well help up-and-coming preachers such as **T. D. Jakes** rise through the ranks to national prominence.

Pearson, a fourth-generation Pentecostal minister from a prominent **Church of God in Christ** family, began preaching and was ordained in that denomination at an early age. He attended Oral Roberts University, where his musical ability landed him a slot as a member of the World Action Singers and brought him to the attention of the university's founder and namesake, who took Pearson under his wings and mentored him. In 1975 Roberts commissioned Pearson to begin a two-year stint as an associate evangelist for the ORU association. Pearson traveled with Roberts' son Richard, serving as an opening act for Richard's concert performances. However, his work with the association kept him so busy that he did not complete his degree.

By 1977 Pearson left Roberts' ministry to found Higher Dimensions Ministries as a traveling evangelistic team that grew through the 1980s into a significant, multifaceted ministry. Four years later, he established Higher Dimensions Family Church in Tulsa with a white fellow minister, Gary McIntosh. Within a year, the small congregation of mostly ORU students had grown to nearly 1,000, and eventually the church became one of the largest in a Tulsa—a city saturated with megachurches. At its height, the congregation had more than 5,000 members, and provided a variety of community services from a meals-on-wheels program to an adoption agency, to a multiethnic and multiracial constituency.

From its prominent locale within the Bible Belt, Pearson became one of the first African American televangelists with classical Pentecostal roots to have a major slot on national television and a multi-racial following. His Azusa Conference, first held in 1988, attempted to revive the racial harmony that gave birth to classical Pentecostal movement. It spotlighted the hottest Charismatic and Pentecostal preachers on the televangelism circuit, provided opportunities for black and white Pentecostal and Charismatic men and women within the wider Evangelical arena, and regularly drew crowds of 7,500 to 10,000 people. Its popularity allowed Pearson to parlay his influence into becoming spiritual overseer for another six hundred churches that he formed into the **Azusa Interdenominational Fellowship of Christian Churches,** an affiliation of primarily non-denominational Charismatic congregations. Along with his own broadcast, during this period, he regularly appeared on the broadcasts of other Pentecostal and Charismatic televangelists. He also recorded music albums, wrote books and made guest appearances at some of the biggest congregations and conferences in the country.

Pearson's ministry took a dramatic turn, and his meteoric rise ended abruptly when, following the death of his father who was not a Christian, he enunciated a theology that veered sharply from classical Pentecostal, Charismatic, and neo-Pentecostal understandings of soteriology that everyone, whether they have come to faith in Christ or not, will eventually be saved. Within a few months of his proclamation, the majority of Pearson's 5,000 congregation deserted him and by 2005 membership fell to under 1,000. The ministry also suffered a deep financial loss; attendance at the Azusa Conferences quickly dropped, he lost his viewing public, and many of the ministers who were part of his non-denominational fellowship dropped out. Further, prominent Pentecostal and Charismatic leaders refuted his theology. Some completely distanced themselves from him when he refused to retract the teaching. His renowned mentee, **T. D. Jakes** remained a friend, but publically insisted that Pearson's teaching was erroneous and heretical.

The continued decline of his congregation led to the eventual loss of his 71,000-square-foot worship facility to foreclosure. Oral Roberts University removed him from its board of directors, and he was shunned by the majority of the Charismatic community. Bishop Clifford L. Frazier spoke for the four hundred strong, **Joint College of African American Pentecostal Bishops**, insisting that the organization would no longer fellowship with Pearson and would urge individual members to follow suit and refuse Pearson access to their pulpits.

Undaunted, he established a new congregation, New Dimensions Worship Center, and ultimately affiliated the congregation—which met in a borrowed Episcopal sanctuary—with the United Church of Christ. The new fellowship attracts people who formerly would have been uncomfortable in Pentecostal and Charismatic circles. Subsequently, Pearson has taken other controversial stances at odds with Pentecostal understandings including supporting homosexuality and aligning himself first with Johnnie Coleman's

Christ Universal Temple and then with the more liberal United Church of Christ in which he was ordained in 2006.

Further Reading:

Pearson, Carlton. *The Gospel of Inclusion: Reaching beyond Religious Fundamentalism to the True Love of God and Self.* New York: Atria, 2008.

Pentecostal and Charismatic Churches of North America

The interracial interdenominational partnership of denominations within the American renewal community that was established in 1994 after the dissolution of the exclusively white **Pentecostal Fellowship of North America** (PFNA). In 1948 when leaders from the major white Pentecostal bodies in the United States met in Des Moines, Iowa to establish the PFNA, no black churches were invited to attend the organizing meeting or join the Fellowship.

For the next forty-six years, the body grew from the eight initial member denominations to include other white denominations. Yet, as race relations within the Pentecostal movement suffered essentially the same fate as those among other segments of society, the body remained essentially white, accept for limited participation from African-American members of predominantly white bodies. While several members of the Board of Administration of PFNA deplored this situation over the decades, no move was made to change the structure up until way after the end of the American civil rights era, as the Pentecostal movement, along with most other segment of the church remained among the most segregated arenas of society. However, with the change in racial sensitivities brought about by advances achieved during the American Civil Rights movement and subsequent increased exposure between black and whites at a number of Christian gatherings (especially within the renewal traditions), attitudes about the acceptability of an exclusively white Pentecostal body began shift.

In 1991 Bernard E. Underwood, then presiding bishop of the Pentecostal Holiness Church became Chairperson of PFNA and determined to use his term to end the racial divide between the Pentecostal churches. At a 1992 meeting, its board voted unanimously to pursue the possibility of reconciliation with African/American organizations. The next year it invited Bishop **Gilbert Patterson** of the predominantly black **Church of God in Christ** to address the organization, and a serious dialog began between the two groups.

Subsequently, three meetings were held throughout 1994: a Reconciliation Dialogue in January, a planning meeting involving twenty representatives from the each side, and the final Reconciliation Dialogue/Convocation on October 17–19, in Memphis. It was at this meeting—dubbed the "**Memphis Miracle**" involving three days of discussion, presentation and prayer—that the PFNA officially dissolved itself and in its place, constituted the interracial PCCNA. The group chose an African-American pastor and scholar, COGIC Bishop **Ithiel Clemmons** as the first chair and underwood as vice-chair of a twelve-member executive committee of six blacks and six whites. Bishop **Barbara Amos**, of the **Mt. Sinai Holy Church** who had been the only woman on the organizing committee was, subsequently, chosen as the first woman on the board of the newly formed bi-racial umbrella organization.

While PCCNA also broadened its scope beyond classical Pentecostal groups to include Charismatic denominations and fellowships, it is solidly Trinitarian by refusing to include Apostolics (Oneness Pentecostals) in its ranks. Its statement of faith specifically affirms that, "there is one God, eternally existing in three persons: Father, Son, and Holy Ghost." This succinct statement precludes involvement of Oneness denominations. Also missing from the initial structure was any representation from Hispanic Pentecostal Charismatics. That omission had sense been addressed and currently both Dr. Samuel Rodriguez of the National Hispanic Christian Leadership Conference and Rev. Fermin Garcia of Grupo Unidad serve as members-at-large. In 2015, of the eleven members, seven are white and represent the largest Pentecostal bodies, two are African American, and two are Hispanic. There is currently no female representation and smaller groups have no presence.

Further Reading:

Underwood, B. E. "The Memphis Miracle." *Pentecostal Charismatic Theological Inquiry.* Online: http://www.pctii.org/arc/underwoo.html.

Synan, Vinson. "Memphis 1994: Miracle and Mandate." *Reconcialation Journal* 1.1 (1998) 14–18.

Pentecostal Assemblies of the World

The oldest and largest Oneness Pentecostal organization in American and parent body of most African American and many white Oneness Pentecostal bodies around the globe. The organization was founded in 1906 in Portland, Oregon as a predominantly white Trinitarian body by a group of individuals that included William Pendleton and J. J. Frazee. In 1907 Pendleton—a Los Angeles pastor, who was ousted from his Holiness congregation after his Pentecostal Holy Spirit baptism at the **Azusa Street Revival**—served as chair.

At its first meeting in Los Angeles, the loose fellowship of Pentecostal congregations was neither black nor Oneness. The next year, Frazee, a colleague of Azusa Street associate, Florence Crawford, was elected secretary. After PAW merged with the General Assemblies of the Apostolic Assemblies, Frazee was elected general secretary of the new body; after a year, E. W. Doak replaced him.

When the group was formally organized in 1912, Doak served as the first general superintendent until 1917. When the 1913 "new issue" controversy arose regarding the doctrine of water baptism in "the Name of Jesus Christ" rather than using the Trinitarian formula, it became a pivotal turning point for the young body. The majority of the PAW community accepted both the liturgical change and a "Jesus Only" or Oneness approach to understanding of the Godhead, moving the organization into that camp.

Five years earlier, while the organization was still Trinitarian, **Garfield Thomas** Haywood, a recent African American Pentecostal convert obtained PAW credentials and joined **Henry Prentiss'** PAW congregation. By the time the "new issue" arose, his Indianapolis congregation was gaining prominence as the most racially integrated

Pentecostal congregation in Indiana. When early Oneness proponent, Glenn A. Cook, first approached him, however, Haywood had been skeptical about the new understanding. When he eventually became a major proponent, his influence as pastor of the largest Pentecostal congregation in the Midwest drew large numbers of northern blacks into the movement. In 1915 he joined Frazee and others in re-forming PAW as a Oneness denomination.

Since initially, nearly three-fourths of PAW's membership was white, all the earliest leaders, except Haywood, were also white. At its first general meeting, Frazee was elected General Superintendent and Chairperson, D. C. O. Opperman was chosen as secretary and Howard Goss as treasurer. Haywood and Frank Ewart, two other early white Oneness proponents, were tapped to sign ministerial credentials and four blacks—Haywood, **Robert Lawson, Alexander R. Schooler,** and **F. I. Douglas**—were elected as field superintendents.

The 1918 PAW merger with the General Assembly of Apostolic Assemblies (GAAA) created the only formally organized Oneness Pentecostal denomination in existence until late 1924. That year, a separation occurred mainly along racial lines when several whites split off to form the Pentecostal Church, Inc. In 1919, PAW put a board of elders in place to assist the general secretary, permanently moved its headquarters to Indianapolis and formally incorporated in Indiana. The single action changed its racial complexion from predominantly white to one where blacks represented the majority of its membership; from that point, many of the denomination's officers and a majority of its committee members were black.

With the growing black constituency, the apparent racial harmony of the PAW began to fracture. By the early 1920s, white members began to insist that venues for meetings formerly be held in the North to accommodate the black constituency. In 1922, the Southern Bible Conference was convened to quiet some Southern whites complaints about the economic burden of all meetings being held in the North. The racially mixed climate of the organization hampered growth among other Southern whites. Moreover, they voiced concern that having credentials signed by a black person was problematic for their Southern white colleagues. By way of response, in 1923, the assembly adopted "Resolution No. 4," calling for white credentials to be sign by white presbyters and black credentials to be sign by black and Haywood appointed Howard Goss and T. C. Howard to sign the credentials for the respective groups. The next year, several whites suggested establishing co-existing race-based "Eastern" and "Western" administrative structures with separate places of worship, boards, ministers and printed materials. The blacks rejected this suggestion.

That year the Texas whites took the name Pentecostal Assemblies of Jesus Christ, establishing two parallel administrative structures. When blacks again rejected this move, the majority of remaining whites aligned themselves with the new organization. Yet, a number of white remained within PAW, leaving it still the most interracial Pentecostal denomination in the country. The newly formed splinter body, however, eventually became the largest Oneness denomination in the United States—the United Pentecostal Church International.

A year after the split, remaining PAW ministers, adopted an episcopal governmental structure and elected Haywood presiding bishop, along with an interracial board of two white men—G. B. Rowe and A. F. Varnell, and three black men, Haywood, **Alexander Schooler** and **J. M. Turpin**. By 1931, however, another contingent of white ministers left to join the Pentecostal Ministerial Alliance, a body that had formed in Tennessee in 1925. The relatively few whites who remained with the PAW found themselves in a minority position and ridiculed by white colleagues for their loyalty.

When Haywood died suddenly in 1931, no plan of succession was in place and remaining white PAW bishops attempted to orchestrate a merger with the Ministerial Alliance to reconstitute an interracial PAW. However, when they suggested that any reconstitution be under two race-based administrations, black leaders bulked, and no merger occurred. Several blacks, offended by the attempted move, left PAW to join the Apostolic Churches of Jesus Christ. The remaining black members called a reorganization meeting and **Samuel Grimes**, an early black missionary to Liberia, followed Haywood as presider, remaining in office for thirty-five years, until his death in 1967.

In 1957 Bishop **Samuel Hancock**, one of the original seven presiding bishops who had supported the PMA merger, and who was disappointed that was not elected presiding bishop, left PAW to help form the Pentecostal Assemblies of Jesus Christ. After a short while, however, he returned to the organization and was re-elected to the bishopric. Still he felt he was the legitimate heir as presiding bishop and, again, challenged Grimes. When a forced run-off vote failed to unseat Grimes, Hancock, who had married Haywood's widow, left PAW to found the **Pentecostal Churches of the Apostolic Faith.**

The schism with Hancock was not the first break of an African-American contingent from PAW. In 1919 **Robert C. Lawson,** who had been converted under Haywood's ministry, incorporated his Columbus, Ohio congregation as the Church of Christ of the Apostolic Faith. Lawson's departure from PAW was a solitary act; he did not encourage other pastors or congregations to leave with him. His decision, at least in part, was based on polity disagreements with PAW leadership. First, what he considered their lenient stance on the issue of divorce and remarriage was problematic to him. He also did not accept Haywood's decision to license women as evangelists and pastors. Further, he required women to cover their heads whenever they entered the church building, which Haywood did not. He later renamed his organization the **Church of Our Lord Jesus Christ of the Apostolic Faith,** and it would go on to become one of the most influential black Oneness bodies in the nation.

Though whites comprised a continually decreasing proportion of PAW membership throughout the American Civil Rights era, the denomination maintained its commitment to interracial inclusiveness, deliberately structuring bi-racial partnerships at its head. Grimes was assisted by **Ross Paddock**, a white pastor from Michigan. When Paddock assumed the lead position in 1967, **Frank Bowdan,** a black pastor also from Michigan served as his assistant. That team was followed, in 1974, by **Francis Smith** and **Lawrence Brisbin,** a black presiding bishop and a white assistant. When Brisbin took over as presiding bishop in 1980, he was assisted by James Archie Johnson (black, 1986–1992), Paul A. Bowers (black, 1992–1998), **Norman L. Wagner** (black, 1998–2004). In 2004, **Horace**

E. Smith and his assistant formed a black team. The current presiding bishop is **Charles H. Ellis III**, elected in 2012, is assisted by two African Americans, Richard E. Young and Theodore L. Brooks.

At the end of the twentieth century, the **Pentecostal Assemblies of the World** had succumbed to the dominant American racial patterns and become a predominantly African-American body. However, it remained the most racially integrated of all Oneness or other Pentecostal bodies.

In 1997 PAW reported one million members in 4,200 worldwide, with 1,800 of those congregations in the United States. Between 1919 and 1960, at least twelve separate major Oneness bodies were founded (directly or indirectly) out of PAW. Importantly, almost every existing Oneness body—whether black or white—can somehow trace its heritage back to PAW. Today, the denomination has over 1.5 million members in more than one thousand congregations around the globe.

Hancock's defection would not be the last. In 2007 **Arthur Brazier**, prominent Chicago pastor and civic leader, pulled his several thousand member **Apostolic Faith Church of God** congregation out of what he saw as rigid, dogmatic doctrinal stances. Conversely, in late 2012, **Charles Johnson**, pastor of the Morning Star Apostolic Church, a suburban Washington DC would leave the denomination to form the **Apostolic Faith Fellowship International** in Upper Marlboro, Maryland, over what he saw as increasing liberalism within the parent body.

Along the way, the denomination has managed to established two institutions of higher education to serve its needs in training men and women for ministry. Aenon Bible College was founded in 1940 in Columbus, Ohio, as the Pentecostal Bible Training Center by Karl F. Smith and LaBaugh Stansbury was relocated to Indianapolis, Indiana. In 1972 Bishop **Frank R. Bowden** established the second institution, Aenon School of School of Theology and Bible College in Los Angeles. The denomination also established a publishing facility on the campus of its denominational headquarters.

Women in the denomination are ordained to ministry and appointed as pastors. However, they do not serve as presiding elders or bishops.

Further Reading:

Golder, Morris E. *The History of the Pentecostal Assemblies of the World.* Indianapolis: s.n., 1973.

Tyson, J. Laverne. *A Definitive History of the Pentecostal Assemblies of the World: A Narrative & Pictorial Study in 7 Volumes: Volume 1, 1914–1930*, S.l.: Tyson, 1998.

———. *The Early Pentecostal Revival.* Hazelwood. MO: Word Aflame, 1992.

Pentecostal Church of God (Detroit)

A predominantly black Oneness Pentecostal body headquartered in Detroit, Michigan founded by Willie James Peterson Jr. in the late 1950s. This body is not to be confused with the predominantly white denomination, **Pentecostal Church of God of America**, which has its headquarters in Joplin, Missouri. Peterson, who was born in 1921 and had been raised Baptist, began preaching the Oneness doctrine in 1955 in Meridian, Mississippi and raised up congregations across the South. At the time of his death in 1969 at age forty-eight, Peterson was succeeded by the four bishops of the church, William Duren, J. J. Sears, C. L. Rawls, and E. Rice.

The church holds several unique doctrines that are attributed to God's revelation to Peterson. It teaches one God (in spirit), one mediator (in flesh body) between God and men—Jesus Christ—and one Holy Spirit in the Church. It differs from most Oneness groups in teaching that God is his office, but Jesus is his name. It identifies the Roman Catholic Church with Babylon, the Mother of Harlots, and rejects the doctrine of the Trinity as unbiblical. It also does not observe holidays such as Christmas, Easter, and New Year's Day or participate in human government (which includes practicing pacifism, not saluting the flag, and not voting). Leadership in the church is reserved to men, but women may preach, prophesy, and minister healing.

The majority of the approximately sixty churches within the denomination are spread throughout four districts in the Southeastern United States. It has no relationship to the Trinitarian body of the same name that is headquartered in Joplin, Missouri.

Pentecostal Churches of Christ (PCC)

An organization of churches that characterizes itself as combining Pentecostal Holiness teaching and practice with an ecclesiology and theology that is evangelical, pentecostal, sacramental, ceremonial and celebratory. In 1992 Bishop **J. Delano Ellis**, pastor of the Pentecostal Church of Christ in Cleveland, Ohio, convened several congregations to found an association of churches as United Pentecostal Churches of Christ. Later that year, the group recognized Ellis as their general overseer and president. He served for twelve years, until resigning in 2004 due to ill health.

In his place, he nominated **Larry Trotter**, pastor of 5,000-member Sweet Holy Spirit Church in Chicago, Illinois, to assume the leadership. After his installation, Trotter led the organization until 2009, moving the headquarters office to Evergreen Park, Illinois and changing the name to **United Covenant Churches of Christ International**. The move drew the ire of Ellis who again took over interim leadership of the group and adopted the name Pentecostal Churches of Christ.

The body combines Pentecostal Holiness teaching and practice with openness to larger Christian community, including teachings and practices from the period of the ancient church until contemporary times. It blends Pentecostal tradition and worship with Apostolic teaching and practice and Anglican/Apostolic government while congregations enjoy autonomy and self-determination. The organization does not identify itself as either Trinitarian or Oneness, but rather makes room for both camps. The statement of belief of the parent church lays out an understanding that there is "only one ever-living, eternal God . . . possessing absolute indivisible . . . deity, who manifested himself in the flesh as His Son (Jesus), and as the Holy Spirit, working in the lives of the believers." In 2000, there were 483 clergy serving sixty-two churches with a total membership of more than 7,000. Currently the denomination has approximately 12,000 members.

Pentecostal Churches of the Apostolic Faith

A Oneness Pentecostal denomination founded by Bishop **Samuel N. Hancock** in 1957 with Bishops **Willie Lee** and Heardie Leaston, and Elder David Collins as one of twelve major organizations to be birthed out of the **Pentecostal Assemblies of the World** between 1919 and 1960.

When the 1931 attempt to reunite PAW with white former PAW minsters who had formed the Pentecostal Ministerial Alliance failed, the PAW restored its charter under the leadership of **Samuel Grimes**. A new interracial body, the Pentecostal Assemblies of Jesus Christ, emerged and Hancock remained with that group as a presbyter. In 1938, however, after racial tension arose in the new body, Hancock was one of many blacks who returned to PAW. He first assumed the position of elder, but was re-elected as a bishop

Soon after his return, however, Hancock, began teaching a doctrine that suggested that Jesus was only the Son of God, not actually God himself. While the PAW leaders issued a clarifying statement and tolerated Hancock's teachings, in 1957 they subsequently declined to elect him presiding bishop. Disappointed over that development, Hancock left with three other bishops to form the new denomination.

Once Hancock founded PCAF he resumed teaching his controversial doctrine. Though he met objection from some within the denomination, they tolerated that teaching and remained loyal to him. At the time of Hancock's death in 1963, PCAF claimed nearly 600 congregations.

Hancock's colleague Willie Lee, pastor of Haywood's former congregation Christ Temple Church, succeeded Hancock. Yet, when Lee persisted in teaching Hancock's doctrine, a majority of the congregations objected, opting to return to the "orthodox" Oneness doctrines, and Lee was disfellowshipped. In his place, **Elzie Young** was appointed as presiding bishop, and the denomination returned to traditional Apostolic teachings. Young was the only presider to serve a life term as presiding bishop of the PCAF, remaining in office for twenty-five years until his death at the age of seventy-six. At time he stepped into the position of presiding over the organization, there was $5.00 in the treasury and by the end of his tenure, the organization was worth over $1,000,000.

Dennis Rayford Bell followed Young and served from 1990 until 2000. He was succeeded by Alfred Singleton from 2000 until 2008. Bishop J. E. Moore is the current presiding bishop; Moore was elected in 2008.

By 1980 however, the denomination had declined to approximately 115 churches in the United States, Haiti and Liberia, but membership had grown to 25,000 members with 380 ministers. Today, it has nearly 300 churches across the United States and in several foreign countries. The PCAF headquarters is located in Louisville, Kentucky. *The Voice in the Wilderness* is the organization's official publication.

Pentecostal Faith Church for all Nations

The denomination founded and incorporated by **Rosa Artemis Horn** in 1929 in Brooklyn, New York is one of few Pentecostal denominations whose leadership has remained in the hands of a woman since its inception.

In 1926 Horn founded the Mt. Calvary Assembly Hall of the Pentecostal Faith Church for all Nations as a local congregation. Four years later, she launched a revival crusade in the 3,000-seat Olympia Club. At its close, Horn opened a second church on the second floor of a two-story loft building in Harlem that became her headquarters.

In 1933 radio pioneer Major Edward Bowes, began negotiating with Mother Horn to broadcast her services. In 1934 she launched her first broadcast, "You Pray for Me Church of the Air," and by that year, the organization had spread to five cities along the Eastern seaboard.

During the depression, her local congregation fed thousands of hungry unemployed men and housed women and children. In 1962 the organization established a forty-acre retreat center, Bethel Sunshine Camp in the Catskill Mountains for under-privileged children. Many young people who attended the camp in the sixties and seventies later entered the Christian work ministry. One of the most famous members of her church was novelist and playwright James Baldwin who at the time was a teenage minister. Baldwin would later incorporate themes and reminiscences from his time at church in his work.

After Horn's death in 1976, her daughter, Jessie A. Horn, presided as bishop, serving for only five years. She died in 1981 and was succeeded by **Gladys A. Brandhagen**, Horn's white "adopted" daughter, who served until her death in 1992.

The current presiding bishop is Dr. Betty M. Middleton and there are twenty-eight congregations in Maryland, New Jersey, New York, North Carolina, South Carolina, Virginia, and the Bahamas.

Pentecostal Holiness Church, Race Relations in

Since its founding in the late nineteenth century as one of the four largest white Pentecostal bodies in the United States, the Pentecostal Holiness Church has been primarily a Southern, rural denomination, with an insignificant black presence. During its earliest years, as a member of the racially inclusive Holiness movement, the denomination attempted to maintain an open posture toward admitting blacks and went as far as regularly holding racially mixed conventions and camp meeting. One of the most prominent black to be associated with the group was **William E. Fuller** who became a trusted colleague of the founder and overseer of several, mostly black, congregations.

In 1896, however, the majority of African Americans pulled out to follow William Fuller into a predominantly black organization with the same name. Still, a number of African Americans remained with the parent group until 1913 when they too separated to found the Black Pentecostal Holiness Church. The parent body contends that the decision of Fuller's group to separate was mutual and that the impetus came from the black contingent. Some scholars, however, contend that the black congregations were dismissed by the parent organization.

In 1911 three years after Fuller's group pulled out, the white **Fire Baptized Holiness Church** joined with the predominantly white Pentecostal Holiness Church taking the designation of the latter group as its new name. A separate "colored convention" that was formed within the FBHC sometime before the merger was adopted into the new church and by 1913, there were a number of African Americans in the new denomination.

In that year, the Assembly set aside one of the eight existing regional conventions as a "Colored Convention," again maintaining that that the idea of separating blacks within the parent body was by mutual consent, with the initiative came from blacks. In reality, both groups were cognizant of the criticism interracial meetings engendered from outside whites. Further, the treatment blacks received from PHC leaders often seem patronizing. Eventually rather than suffer the indignity of being partitioned, the black convention withdrew. Instead of joining the existing black **Fire Baptized Holiness Church**, however, they formed the autonomous Black Pentecostal Holiness Church, and within two years, though they shared the name, the two Pentecostal Holiness Church bodies had no official contact with each other.

In response, the General Conference voted to drop the Colored Conference from its rolls and expel the remaining black congregations, leaving almost no evidence of earlier black involvement in the Pentecostal Holiness Church among either official records or popular accounts of denominational history for several years following the last split.

Throughout the intervening years, individual blacks were still attracted to individual white PHC congregations, yet, for a number of reasons, black participation in the Pentecostal Holiness Church remained low. In 1922, for example, while the General Board agreed that persons of all races should be accepted into the denomination, restrictions were immediately put in place including confining black to northern conferences, forbidding them from hold office in an Annual Conference, as well as from being a delegate to a General Conference.

In the years immediately following World War II, the denomination determined that the most practical way of reaching Southern blacks was to "work through established black churches rather than promote integration of blacks into its structure. Yet, as the Civil Rights Movement moved into full swing at the end of the 1950s, such entrenched attitudes began giving way to social pragmatism, and the General Executive Board appointed a committee to investigate avenues of communication between the Pentecostal Holiness Church and black Pentecostals.

By 1965 the Executive Board was instructed to begin communications with the possibility of forming "Negro [sic] Associate Conferences." The 1969 General Conference adapted a resolution affirming the church's commitment not to "not discriminate against any person due to race, color, or economic status." Eight years later, in 1977, PHC leaders appointed Thadeus White as liaison to black congregations within and outside the denomination. During a period of schism within the predominantly black **United Holy Church**, **James A. Forbes, Sr.,** leader of the schismatic faction, approached PHC leadership about a possible affiliation with that group and an agreement was drawn up and approved by General Conference that year.

By 1980 the PHC was taking a more progressive stance establishing and strengthening relations with predominantly black denominations, making specific advances to the **Fire Baptized Holiness Church**, which it had ignored for decades. Three years earlier, the **Soul Saving Station for Every Nation**, an association of autonomous churches who share the same beliefs, began negotiations to enter a loose affiliation. None of the arrangements went beyond that.

In 1991 an entirely different attitude began evolving among PHC leadership. The most tangible evidence of this was seen in the actions of presiding Bishop Bernard E. Underwood. Representing PHC as the president of the white umbrella organization, Pentecostal Fellowship of North America, Underwood initiated steps that would lead to one of the defining moments in late-twentieth-century American Pentecostalism, leading that body to dismantle itself. In its place a new multi-racial umbrella group, the **Pentecostal and Charismatic Churches of North America,** was formed. During the strategic convocation between black and white leaders dubbed "**The Memphis Miracle**," Underwood led pastors in a time of repentance and reconciliation that, presumably, would open a door for change throughout the movement. Two years later, in 1996, Underwood again led the denomination in convening a solemn assembly in which racism was among seven sins for which it repented and issued a missive in regard to the "sin of racism." In 1998 for example, when the FBHC celebrated its centennial, PHC leaders were on hand for the first time with PHC presiding bishop, James Leggett joining Bishop W. E. Fuller Jr., son of FBHCA founder.

In January 2004 Macon Wilson became first Director of African-American Ministries in an attempt to link African-American PHC congregations with training and resources in church planting, church growth and pastoral ministry. In 2005, the denominations held its first National African-American Conference in Houston, TX. In that same year, there were only twenty-seven African-American congregations in the PHC in comparison to 381 Latino congregations. Another one hundred congregations were characterized as multi-cultural. Presumably, these majority white or mixed congregations have some black membership.

By the middle of the first decade of the twenty-first century, one of the most visible blacks in the PHC was **E. V. Hill II,** son of renowned Missionary Baptist pastor and preacher, E. V. Hill, Sr. After being ordained in the PHC, he was called to pastor Calvary Temple PHC in North Hollywood, California. While affiliated with the PHC, Hill held a series of progressively important positions. He was the first African American to serve on the denomination's Conference Board, serving on the Golden West Conference for twelve years. He served on the Bishop's Council, the General Board of Administrators and as a member of the Evangelism USA Board. In 2005 however, he left the PHC to return to pastor his late father's congregation.

While the denomination remains a predominantly white Southern group, it has come in line with current social ethos regarding progressive race relation within American society. PHC set up an African-American Ministries outreach as part of its Evangelism USA campaign. AAM focuses on having African-American representation throughout the PHC and determining the most effective method for addressing the needs of African-American communities The quadrennial goal it had was to reach African-American churches that have an African-American pastor and a majority of African-American congregants throughout the PHC. Stacy Hilliard serves as Director of African-American Ministries.

Phillips, Lulu 1875–1939

One of the founding leaders of two schismatic organizations that trace their historic roots back to her initial evangelistic work was Born in Birmingham, Alabama, and migrated to Indianapolis, Indiana. Before her move, Phillips had been a member or the **Triumph the Church and Kingdom of God in Christ**. By 1919 she had settled in Huntington, West Virginia and embarked on an evangelistic campaign, often preaching under a tree and establishing eight **Triumph Church Kingdom of God in Christ** congregations within two years.

In 1921 Phillips's husband, Richard, also a minister, began implementing organizational structure into the congregations his wife had established that resulted in the forming of the **Glorious Church of God in Christ**. Shortly following that move, Phillips was converted to the Oneness Pentecostal movement accepting the teaching of baptism in Jesus' name and leading fifty followers to be re-baptized in that formula, so that by the following year, the denomination had become a Oneness Pentecostal body.

Phillips led the denomination until her death in Caball, West Virginia. After her death a schism broke out within the group that resulted in an almost even split among the members. On half of the existing congregations left to form the **Original Glorious Church of God in Christ.** Both bodies adhere to Oneness doctrine. Both bodies credit her role in their founding.

Phillips, Magdalene Mabe 1902–1990

The founder of the **Alpha and Omega Pentecostal Church of God of America**. In 1919, at the age of seventeen, Magdalene moved from her home in Pulaski, Virginia, where she was a member within a **United Holy Church** congregation, to Baltimore, Maryland. Once in that city she remained active in the UHC, eventually becoming a minister within that body.

In 1938 she started a home Bible study and became involved in feeding those in need. This group that made up the Bible study became the nucleus for establishing a congregation, the Alpha and Omega Church of God Tabernacle in Baltimore, Maryland in 1945. Later the name was changed to **Alpha and Omega Pentecostal Church of God of America**, Inc. and several small Pentecostal congregations within the Baltimore area joined under her leadership.

There is no clear indication why Phillips left the **United Holy Church** since the doctrine of the two bodies is close. Phillips died in Baltimore at age eighty-eight.

Phillips, William Thomas 1893–1973

The founder and first presiding bishop of the **Apostolic Overcoming Holy Church of God, Inc.,** was the son of a Methodist Episcopal Church minister from Mobile, Alabama. In 1913 he was called to the ministry at the age of twenty.

Phillips left the Methodist Church, where he had served as a minister, after becoming interested in the doctrine of holiness and the process of sanctification. He was converted to the Pentecostal doctrine at age nineteen in a tent revival conducted by **Azusa Street Revival** veteran **Frank Williams**, a close friend of **William Seymour** and founder of the **Apostolic Faith Mission Church of God.** Phillips originally joined the AFMC and began evangelizing 1916 in Mobile, where he established a congregation, the Greater Adams Holiness Church. That congregation was incorporated in 1920 and became the founding congregation of the Ethiopian Overcoming Holy Church of God. By 1927 Phillips's desire for a more biblical, inclusive church led him to replaced the word "Ethiopian" with "Apostolic." Though the denomination he established began as a Trinitarian body by the late 1920s Phillips had embraced Oneness Pentecostal doctrine and had transitioned the denomination into that camp.

Phillips led the AHOC for fifty-seven years. Throughout that period, he traveled extensively holding revivals and planting new congregations in cities across the southern United States. By the time of his death, the denomination had grown to three hundred churches in the United States, India, West Africa and the Caribbean. He was actively involved in the Civil Rights movement and in 1965, this involvement led to the bombing of his home.

Further Reading:

Phillips, W. T. *Excerpt from the Life of Rev. W.T. Phillips and the Fundamentals of the Apostolic Overcoming Holy Church of God, Inc.* s.l.: s.n., s.d.

Pilgrim Assemblies International

A neo-Pentecostal Baptist denomination founded by Bishop **Roy Brown**, pastor of Pilgrim Cathedral in Brooklyn, New York. Brown officially introduced the organization, which characterizes itself as a reformed church with a Pentecostal experience, during his consecration to the Bishopric and Annual Prayer Day in 1990. As such, the denomination does not insist that speaking in tongues is initial evident of Holy Spirit baptism. Rather, it sees such baptism as the normal Christian experience of the filling of the Spirit following conversion and represents the Spirit's endowment of power for life and service, and the spiritual gifts for ministry.

In 1965 Brown became the pastor of Pilgrim Baptist Church and built the denomination through efforts to plant new congregations and draw existing congregations into fellowship. In 1994 he consecrated the first eight Bishops to serve with him, and then in 1996 he consecrate and additional team of four more men, two of whom helped establish the international presence of Pilgrim Assemblies International on the continent of Africa. In addition to congregations in both in South Africa and West Africa, there are churches in Trinidad, and Barbados, as well as in the United Stated with a total of approximately 17,000 members.

Pitts, Gertrude Louise Norris 1914–2005

One of the pioneers who helped to carve out the **Mt. Calvary Holy Churches of America**, Inc. The late founder, **Brumfield Johnson**, appointed her National President of the Youth Church at its inception in 1941, and she served for more than forty-two years in that office. She also is currently the National Missionary President of **Mt. Calvary Holy Churches of America**, Inc. and State Mother of the Wisconsin-Ohio-Michigan-Illinois District.

The Buffalo, New York native attended the Buffalo Bible Institute and the American Bible Institute where she received her Bachelor of Theology degree. She earned her Doctor of Divinity degree from A. E. W. Institute of the Cathedral of the Living Word in Baltimore, Maryland in 1986.

Pitts arrived in Milwaukee, Wisconsin in 1955, to serve as associate pastor under O. E. Evans. After Evans' death in 1957, he took leadership of the congregation. In 1966, when it was forced to vacate its edifice to make room for a new expressway, Pitts led them in building a new structure that was dedicated in 1968.

Though founding bishop, Johnson opposed to elevation of women to the position of bishop, in an historic turn for the denomination, in 1994, Pitts became one of the first two women consecrated as Bishops in the MCHCA. Two years later, she was appointed bishop over the denomination's National Archives. In 2002, Pitts stepped down from the pastorate to serve in emeritus status.

Pleas, Charles 1879–1967

Church of God in Christ bishop, missionary and historian, who personally worked with founder, **Charles Harrison Mason** during the formative years of the denomination. Pleas was born in Holmes County, Mississippi and, as a young boy, was abandoned by both parents and adopted and raised by his grandmother and uncle Charles Pleas. Sr. after whom he was named. Pleas was converted in 1896, at age sixteen as the first convert in a revival preached by **Charles Harrison Mason** and **Charles Price Jones** in the renovated, and became a member of the first **COGIC** congregation pastored by Mason while the elder man was still part of the Holiness movement. When Mason accepted Pentecostal doctrine and the experience of speaking in tongues, Pleas was among those who sided with him in his split with Jones over these issues.

By 1910, Pleas was an elder in the **Church of God in Christ**, and in 1915, Mason appointed him to a pastorate in West Pointe, Mississippi. In 1919, he moved to Kansas where he served as assistant overseer under the leadership of Bishop **D. J. Young**. After Young's death in 1926, Pleas was appointed as overseer and elevated to the office of bishop. During his tenure in that state, Pleas was the first African American to be appointed to prison chaplaincy by the state of Kansas.

In 1945 Pleas accepted the appointment as bishop of Liberia, arriving in the country in 1948, as the first male COGIC missionary to travel to there. A bricklayer by trade, he built the first permanent sanctuary and convened the first COGIC convocation in the West African nation. On returning to the United States, Pleas lobbied denominational leaders to expand its missions efforts on the continent of Africa.

Though Pleas was an adult before he learned to read and write, in 1957, as COGIC celebrated its 50th anniversary of reorganization as a Pentecostal body, the seventy-eight-year-old Pleas authored one of few historical accounts of the denomination, *Fifty Years Achievement (History): Church of God in Christ (Memphis, Tenn)*, which was published by the Church of God in Christ Publishing House.

Pleasant, William S. (W. S.) 1854–1935

Early leader within the Holiness movement and an early associate of **Charles Price Jones** of the **Church of Christ (Holiness) USA** and **Charles Harrison Mason** of the **Church of God in Christ**. The former Baptist pastor was born in Hazelhurst, Mississippi. In 1872, when he was eighteen years old, Pleasant became pastor of the Colored Damascus Baptist Church He became a colleague of Jones and others within the Baptist community who had embraced Holiness doctrine in the late 1800s.

Pleasant was among the ministry associates who worked with Jones to form the Christ's Association of Mississippi of Baptist Believers in Christ in 1900, and was subsequently elected president. In 1896, Pleasant and his congregation joined with Jones, **Church of Christ (Holiness) U.S.A.**, and Damascus Church became one of the first churches to join the Holiness movement, becoming known as Damascus Church of Christ (Holiness) U.S.A. He continued to serve that congregation from 1896 to 1918, an additional twenty-two years, finally resigning to do evangelistic work.

In 1895 Pleasant met **Charles Harrison Mason**. The following year, they conducted a revival in Jackson, Mississippi, and the two, subsequently became closes companions in the ministry. After the outbreak of the 1906 **Azusa Street Revival**, Pleasant was part the four-person team that also included Mason, **D. J. Young**, and **J. A. Jeter**, who travelled to Los Angeles to ascertain the spiritual validity of the phenomenon occurring in the meeting. On returning from the revival, Pleasant sided with Jeter and Jones in refuting the validity of the Pentecostal experience of Holy Spirit baptism with speaking in tongues.

After Jones and Mason separated, Pleasant remained a member of Jones' group which ultimately changed its name to the **Church of Christ (Holiness) USA**. In 1908, Pleasant was a board member of the Christ Missionary and Industrial School and was responsible for conceiving the name of the institution. Over time, the congregation he headed for forty-seven years grew to be one of the most prominent churches in the Church of Christ (Holiness).

Plummer, William Henry 1868–1931

The second presiding bishop of the **Church of God and Saints of Christ**. Plummer was born in Montgomery County, Maryland and orphaned at an early age. His father left home before his birth to fight Indians in the Oklahoma Territory to become one of the famous Black Buffalo Soldiers and never returned. By age five, he had also lost his mother.

Plummer did not begin formal education until he was nine years old and from the age of twelve to seventeen, he served an apprenticeship. He joined the Church of God and Saints of Christ in 1900, in Philadelphia, and was ordained a minister by founder, **William S. Crowdy** who sent him to Jersey City, New Jersey as overseer. Three years later, Crowdy appointed Plummer District Evangelist, and the next year Plummer was elevated to the honorable office of Grand Father Abraham, and appointed General Superintendent over the business of the Church of God and Saints of Christ.

In 1906 Crowdy appointed three successors: Plummer, the founder's brother, Joseph, and Elder Calvin S. Skinner. In 1909 one year after the founder's death, Joseph Crowdy and Plummer were consecrated to the office of Bishop. In 1914 during World War I, Plummer sent a letter to President Woodrow Wilson explaining our beliefs on the issue of war. President Wilson answered by all the men within the denomination Conscientious Objectors status. In 1917 after Joseph's death, the Presbytery Board affirmed Plummer, as Executive Leader of the Church of God and Saints of Christ and affirmed him as General Superintendent and Overseer.

A decade and a half earlier, Crowdy had purchased farmland in Belleville, Virginia as a home for the saints. When the Church suffered financial difficulties in 1909, the land was sold at auction in 1909. Once he became leader, Plummer made it to redeem the land and by 1919, he successfully repurchased and enlisted skilled crafts men from within the denomination to refurbish and expand the property make Belleville a self-supporting community. In 1922 saints from around the country attended the first Assembly held in Belleville. Along with reclaiming the original farm, Plummer purchased additional acreage and established the Belleville Industrial School and Widows and Orphans Home.

Near the end of his life, Plummer took on the pastorate of the church in Boston. As the pastor of the Boston Congregation, he launched several business enterprises. During his tenure there, he became ill and died in Belleville, Virginia.

Further Reading:

Wynia, Elly M. *The Church of God and Saints of Christ: The Rise of Black Jews.* New York: Rutledge, 1994.

Poole, Charles Edward 1899–1984
Poole, Mattie Belle Robinson 1903–1968

The founders of the Bethlehem Temple in Chicago, Illinois a congregation established in 1932 that was famous for its healing ministry, and the **Living Witness of the Apostolic Faith, Inc.** a denomination headquartered in the same city. In 1954, after several changes in location occasioned by growth, the congregation was renamed Bethlehem Healing Temple.

Pastor and faith healer, Mattie Poole was born in Memphis, Tennessee, one of eight children of an alcoholic father and an abusive mother. At thirteen, she was left to care for herself, and then came to Chicago to live with her father. By age sixteen, she had attempted suicide, but a year later, she was attending the Apostolic Faith Church under the leadership of Elder **Alexander Schooler** and Bishop **John S. Holly.** There she had a conversion experience and received the Pentecostal Holy Spirit baptism under the ministry of Garfield Haywood. By age eighteen, Poole began preaching in street services.

Shortly after her conversion, her future husband, whom she had already befriended, was converted. Charles was born in Georgia and was a machinist who had migrated to Chicago. By 1921, the year they were married, he was serving as an associate minister at Apostolic Faith Church. Shortly afterward, the two struck out to plant a storefront congregation that grew to become Bethlehem Healing Temple, a congregation of several hundred, housing numerous ministries in a multi-auditorium facility. In earlier years of their ministry, Mattie, an accomplished pianist and music teacher, who attended Chicago Musical College and the Chicago Conservatory of Music and was tutored by prominent instructor, Lawyer Glassman, played for the churches as well as preached.

She authored several books, numerous pamphlets and edited two periodicals, *The Voice of Living Witnesses* and *God Met Us in the Healing Campaigns*. While she worked as assistant pastor alongside her husband, Charles, she carried on a radio program that, at its height, was broadcasted on twenty-four stations including major markets throughout the country. Yet, it was her healing ministry that began simply in the late 1930s but grew to include major healing campaigns throughout the country, for which she was most renowned. Hundreds of people crowded churches and halls to hear her preach and have her pray for their healing. Following upon the success and notoriety of these campaigns, the Pooles established Bethlehem Healing Temple congregations in Atlanta, Brooklyn, and Boston.

Due to continued growth, the Pooles's congregation relocated several times. While Mattie had worked alongside Charles from the beginning, it was not until 1938 that she became Assistant Pastor, and shortly after that, her healing ministry began to flourish. In 1944 the congregation began to experience Miracles through her gift of healing and the word spread throughout the Chicago and the nation. In 1954 the Pooles established the radio broadcast that drew an international audience, as well as a communications ministry to distributed literature, record albums, and tapes.

With Mattie as the more visible member of the team, the Pooles traveled extensively in healing campaigns across the country; thousands were won to the Oneness movement, received healing and experienced Pentecostal Holy Spirit baptism at her hands. This work led to establishment of Bethlehem Healing Temples and Bible schools in Brooklyn, Boston, Atlanta, Gary, Indiana; Lockport, Illinois; the island of Jamaica; Ghana, Liberia, and Nigeria and other parts of West Africa. Revival Tabernacle, on Chicago's south side also became part of the organization.

In 1957 the couple broke their longtime association with the **Pentecostal Assemblies of the World** and joined the newly formed **Pentecostal Churches of the Apostolic Faith** (PCAF) under **Samuel N. Hancock**. When Hancock died in 1963, "Mother" Poole founded Living Witnesses of the Apostolic Faith, Inc., taking many of the congregations they founded with then. Initially she served at its head though never carried the title bishop. Following her death in 1968, her husband became "Bishop" Charles E. Poole, serving in that post until his passing in 1984.

Portier, Harcourt Garfield (H. G.) 1904–1990

A leader within the **Church of God (Colored Work)** then in the broader Church fof God (Cleveland, TN) who, during sixty-two years of ministry, served as a missionary, pastor, radio minister, and state overseer for Florida, Alabama, Mississippi and Georgia. He also served as secretary-treasurer of the Church of God (Colored Work) from 1949 until 1964. After that rigidly segregated structure was dismantled, Portier was appointed as national representative of Black Affairs at the Church of God`s executive office in Cleveland, TN, and established the church's ministerial and lay enrichment programs in Florida.

He was born in Arthur Town on Cat Island in the Bahamas. He was raised in the Episcopal Church and as a young boy served as acolyte. He converted to the Pentecostal faith at the age of eighteen, presumably in the Church of God, and migrated to Florida with his family in 1920. In 1922 at the age of eighteen, Poitier preached his first sermon at the Deerfield Beach Church of God where he was a charter member. He was licensed five years later, and the next year was back in the Bahamas as a missionary.

Portier moved to Jacksonville from Deerfield Beach in 1924. Portier was one of the charter members of the Deerfield Beach Church of God, and was ordained a pastor in that city in 1945. During his ministerial career, he helped organize twelve churches including congregations in Delray Beach, Yamato, Cocoa, Sharpes, Liberty City, Dania and Liberia, West Palm Beach, Jacksonville Florida and Seaford, Delaware. He also did evangelistic preaching in England, France, Canada and the Bahamas. Portier pastored the Jacksonville congregation that served as the headquarters of the Colored Work from 1974 until 1978. After retiring from the Deerfield Beach church where he had started his career, he continued to have an active ministry to sick and shut-in persons.

Throughout his ministry he served in several civic capacities including as president of the West Palm Beach Ministerial Alliance, the board of directors of the West Palm Beach Welfare Association. As a civil rights leader, Portier worked with the Voter`s League in Palm Beach County, Florida and the Equal Opportunity Commission of Cleveland, Tennessee. Poitier was the uncle of actor-director Sidney Poitier.

His wife, Celestine, with whom he had seventeen children, was the first black women appointed to the national Women's Ministry Board within the Church of God.

Powell, Sarah Jorda 1938–

Well-known soprano who has sung gospel music at the White House before Presidents Jimmy Carter, Bill Clinton, and Ronald Reagan, who appointed her to serve on the Year of the Bible committee. Powell, a fourth generation **Church of God in Christ** member, whose father was a COGIC minister, was born in Houston, Texas, where he pastored Turner Memorial COGIC. She attended Texas Southern University where she majored in English and minored in history and drama. She also attended Southwest Theological Seminary and earned a masters degree from the University of St Thomas. She sang for a while with the Sallie Martin Singers, and after leaving that group joined the Chicago-based Voices of Melody led by Charles Clency.

After her father's death, Powell and her husband returned to Houston to handle the church's affairs. While serving there as a public teacher, she became a highly sought after local artist. An, at first, reluctant Powell began recording in the 1970s at the urging of famed gospel artist, James Cleveland who facilitated her signing with Savoy Records, with whom she released five albums. In 1975 Powell was nominated for the Gospel Music Award of Ebony Magazine, a leading African American periodical. Her biggest hit, "When Jesus Comes," was recorded in 1977. Cleveland, founder of the Gospel Music Workshop of America, appointed Powell as the first Youth Director of that organization and she served in this position for five years. After leaving Savoy for Power House Records, rhythm and blues superstar, Ray Charles produced her next album, "Affectionately Sara," in 1982.

She also founded Fine Arts Department for the **Church of God In Christ** and spent ten years as its executive director, and as well is a member of the **Charles Harrison Mason** Foundation Board of Directors. In 2003 she was inducted into the Oklahoma Jazz Hall of Fame joining such stars as Taj Mahal, Patti Page, and Dave Brubeck.

Prentiss, Henry S. 1873–??

An early Pentecostal leader, who attended the 1906 **Azusa Street Revival** where he received the Pentecostal Holy Spirit baptism experience, then became an early convert and leader in the Oneness Pentecostal movement. Prentiss was born in Staunton, Virginia and migrated to California around the turn of the nineteenth century, possibly settling in San Francisco. He left that city to move to Los Angeles five days after the famous earthquake and became an active member in the revival. In a short time, Prentiss was travelling as part of one of several evangelistic teams to take the message of the revival to Northern California and the Northwest, stopping in Whittier and San Jose, California and Portland, Oregon. At least once, he was a member of a team lead by Florence Crawford, a close colleague revival leader, **William J. Seymour**. As he travelled, *The Apostolic Faith* newspaper published his itinerary.

Prentiss' controversial ministry style often landed him in trouble with the surrounding community and the authorities. In mid-1906 he was nearly lynched for "disturbing the peace" at a tent meeting in progress less than two miles from Azusa, when he pointed his finger at a white Church of God minister's daughter and declared her a sinner. During his evangelistic campaigns, he was arrested several times for disturbing the peace and served thirty days on a chain gang.

In 1907 Prentiss moved to Indianapolis and concentrated his evangelistic ministry within that city's African-American community, taking over as pastor as a group that had been holding house meetings. In 1908 that Trinitarian group became the Apostolic Faith Assembly with Prentiss as their pastor. In the same year, he was back on the front page of the Indianapolis Star, with the press coverage of another Prentiss arrest and trial.

One of his most important converts would become one of the most important early African-American Oneness Pentecostal leaders. For it was at this congregation that, in 1909, Prentiss preached to **Garfield T. Haywood** who was converted and launched into his own ministry. Later that year, he turned the Indianapolis work over to Haywood and was back on the evangelistic circuit. We know little of his ministry after or life after 1914. His marriage ended in divorce in 1915 and by 1917 he was in Chicago, evidently not in ministry.

Further Reading:

French, Talmadge. "Henry Prentiss and the Downtown Indianapolis Mission." In *Early Interracial Oneness Pentecostalism: G. T. Haywood and the Pentecostal Assemblies of the World (1901–1931)*, 78–80. Eugene, OR: Pickwick, 2014.

Price, Frederick K. C. 1932–

One of the earliest and most visible African-American televangelist in the **Word of Faith** movement as well as to inner city black communities through his television broadcast and the Fellowship of Inner City Word of Faith Ministries (FICWFM). Though his parents were nominal Jehovah's Witnesses, as a young man, Price was uninterested in religion. He began attending church to attract the attention of his future wife, Betty, and the approval of her devout Baptist parents. Once married, his spiritual interest quickly waned, but shortly into the marriage, Price was converted in a Baptist revival and called to the ministry. He served as assistant pastor of a Baptist church from 1955 until 1957, and then served as an AME minister until 1959, before landing in a Presbyterian congregation. In 1962 while he was serving that congregation, his eight-year-old son, Frederick III, was struck and killed by a car, throwing him into a crisis of faith.

Price moved into the pastorate of West Washington Community Church in 1965, a Los Angeles congregation of the Christian and Missionary Alliance, but was dissatisfied with what he perceived as the ineffectiveness of his ministry and lack of spiritual vitality in the churches he encountered. During this time, he read a book by healing evangelist Kathryn Kuhlmann and it whetted his appetite for a more vital ministry that would include the operation of spiritual and charismatic gifts.

By the time he received the Pentecostal baptism of the Holy Spirit in 1970, Price had been pastoring for fifteen years. The next year, he founded Crenshaw Christian Center with nine members, five of them from his own family. Several months later, he began reading the teachings of Word of Faith movement founder, Kenneth E. Hagin, and incorporating elements of his teaching into his ministry. Within a short time, his congregation began growing so rapidly that they were forced to secure new facilities.

In 1973 Price moved his three hundred parishioners to the Crenshaw Christian Center on the site of the then defunct Pepperdine University in the working class Los

Angeles community of Inglewood. By 1982 the 1,400-seat sanctuary was not large enough to contain the three worship services that Price was conducting each Sunday. He oversaw the building of the 10,000 seat Faith Dome, at that time the largest dome church in the United States.

Over the next forty years, Price's ministry grew to become Ever Increasing Faith Ministries. The organization includes radio and television broadcasts, heard and viewed by millions around the globe, tape and book ministries, and the Fellowship of Inner City Word of Faith Ministries (FICWFM), established in 1990 to provide support to approximately five hundred Word of Faith pastors in thirty-eight states and nineteen foreign countries. By then, the ministry housed a Christian school, school of ministry, bookstore, cafeteria, day-care center, alcohol and drug-abuse program, and 24-hour prayer service, which is maintained by several hundred full- and part-time employees and a bevy of volunteers, and a second a Latino congregation. The Crenshaw Christian Center-East was established this same year, 2,800 miles away in Manhattan. Though Price would ultimately not serve as its senior pastor, only making irregular personal appearances, the congregation grew to more than 1,100 members within a few years.

Throughout most of his time at the helm, Price's teaching centered on personal and spiritual empowerment, drawing a multi-racial congregation of middle class, and aspiring middle class followers. By late 1990s that focus expanded to include social issues within the black community. At one point in 1997, for example, he took on Kenneth Hagin, Jr., son of his mentor, for disparaging remarks concerning interracial dating and marriage, becoming an outspoken critic of racism, particularly within Evangelical Christianity. His hard line in his nationally televised teaching on the subject elicited strong reactions from both blacks and whites. Several television and radio stations cancelled his broadcast. Almost half of the twenty-four black clergy on the FICWFM executive board resigned, but several supported Price. Still, several prominent leaders who felt his frank criticism was on target applauded him. He was given the Horatio Alger Award, for "exemplify inspirational success, triumph over adversity, and . . . commitment to helping others," and the SCLC's Kelly Miller Smith Interfaith Award for outstanding clergy.

Price completed two years of education at Los Angeles City College, and received an honorary diploma from Hagin's Rhema Bible Training Center in 1976, and an honorary Doctor of Divinity degree from Oral Roberts University in 1982. Yet, the prolific writer has published numerous books on a variety of issues including and going beyond prosperity.

Though later assisted by a cadre of paid staffers and host of volunteers, responsibility for ministry leadership has been held in the hands of family members from the beginning with his wife, son, three daughters and their spouses all playing major roles. By the time he reached his late seventies, Price was ready to relinquish leadership of this congregation to his son Frederick Kenneth Price Jr., who, after being called to ministry at seventeen, had worked alongside his father. After serving as a member of the pastoral staff and as an irregular speaker on the television and radio broadcast, the younger Price was ordained and installed as pastor of the 22,000 member Crenshaw Christian Center at its thirty-fifth anniversary celebration and on his thirtieth birthday in 2009.

Progressive Church of Our Lord Jesus Christ, Inc.

The organization is a Oneness Pentecostal body founded in 1944 by **Joseph D. Williams** Sr., pastor of the Pilgrim Church of Christ in Cleveland, Ohio. This congregation had been established under the leadership of **Robert C. Lawson,** founder of the **Church of Our Lord Jesus Christ of the Apostolic Faith, Inc.** Williams resigned from his pastorate with the blessings of Bishop Lawson, and moved to Columbia, where the denomination's headquarters are located.

The first congregation of the Progressive Church of Our Lord Jesus Christ, Inc. was founded in Columbia, South Carolina in 1944 by Bishop Joseph D. Williams Sr. following the miraculous healing of Helen L. Washington, one of his charter members. Having no baptismal pool, and failing to convince local pastors to allow him access to theirs, his first convert was baptized in a bathtub, at her mother's house. In the 1940s and 1950s he personally traveled throughout South Carolina to preach and establish churches and because of his effort, congregations were established in Killian, Mullins, Denmark, Lugoff, Bishopville, and Florence. In 1963 a major split occurred in the organization. Several of the leading ministers, deacons and members who had worked with Williams for many years left the denomination.

Williams led the denomination for twenty-two years as pastor and presiding bishop. Prior to his death in 1966, he appointed a Board of Elders to provide leadership for the Progressive Church after his demise: Elders Joel G. Washington, Edward Smith, Herman Jackson, Henry J. Breakfield and Ernest Finkley, and left the later decision of who would succeed to his position. After his death, this board collectively governed the church from 1966 to 1973, with Washington serving as Chairperson. While Jackson resigned during this time, each elder was assigned to oversee a district of churches to maintain the unity of the organization.

In 1973 members of the Board of Elders were consecrated to the office of Bishop, and subsequently governed as the Board of Bishops. Washington, Sr. was elected to serve as presiding bishop by members of the board. Finkley resigned from the organization in August of 1976. During the 1970 and 1980, churches were established in North Carolina, Georgia, and Florida. In 1983 the national church ratified a new Church Constitution and appointed Edward Smith as assistant presiding bishop.

When Washington died in 1987, Smith became presiding bishop and remains in that position until this time. He established a National Unity Conference for the National Church that has been held in different cities throughout the southeast. In addition, the Church convenes its Annual Holy Convocation during the first week of July. The Annual Holy Convocation generally convenes in Columbia, South Carolina.

Though there is no official statement in public church records regarding the matter, within the church ordained ministry is reserved for males. The same is true of the majority of all leadership positions outside of the women's department.

Currently, the Progressive Church consists of approximately twenty-five churches and missions in the United States including California, Florida, Georgia, New York, North and South Carolina and on the continent of Africa. In 1999 the denomination dedicated a $2.5 million dollar, 31,000-square-foot Headquarters Church Complex with a 1,000-seat sanctuary, a family life center, a gymnasium, office space, and classrooms. This complex abuts an education and office building, senior citizens apartments, and the old sanctuary built under the leadership of the late Bishop J. D. Williams.

Pure Holiness Church of God

One of several Holiness Pentecostal denominations founded by a woman, The Oneness Pentecostal body was birthed by Mary Rowe in 1927 with the assistance of Isaac Woodley, Lee Blackwell, Elder Bryen, and "Mother Lilla Pittman" in Anniston, Alabama. Though Rowe assisted in founding several of the churches, she never took the position or title of presider. In 1935 Rowe founded a congregation in Clem, Georgia now known as St. John Pure Holiness Churches. A year later, she went to Hiram, Georiga where she started the Pure Holiness Church of God in Hiram, now known as Smith Temple PHC. "Mother" Rowe then traveled to Coosa, Hulett and Senoia, Georgia to extend the PHC brand. In 1952 the Pure Holiness Church of God now known as Timothy PHC was established in Atlanta, Georgia. Later that year, she planted a congregation in Zebulon, Georgia that is now Joyful Tabernacle PHC. She then set her sights on Lineville, Alabama and created a church there.

The denomination holds to some elements of Oneness Pentecostalism insisting in their doctrinal statement that, "God is absolutely and indivisibly one" and in "Jesus dwells all the fullness of the Godhead bodily. . . . He is the self-revelation of the one God, the incarnation of the full, undivided Godhead." Yet the group does not include a requisite for baptism in Jesus' name in its statement.

Though the denomination acknowledges Rowe as its founder, she apparently never assumed the title presiding bishop, and office presumably reserved for male. Once a congregate was established, Rowe turned over leadership to a selected pastor. Woodley served as the first pastor of the Anniston congregation and first presiding bishop of the organization until 1932. John Grayhouse followed Woodley and served until 1939 when he left the organization and return to the **Church of God in Christ**. He was followed by George White, who died in 1947. E. L. Blackwell served until 1958 and was followed by Charles Frederick Fears. During his tenure, two important actions occurred. In 1964 the denomination established the Pure Holiness School of Theology, selecting Judson Ringer as president. After the requirement that the presiding bishop remain unmarried was lifted in 1956, Ringer became presiding bishop, serving until 1965. He was followed by Luther Rex Smith, who served less than a year to be succeeded by Bennie G. Isom, Sr. from 1965 until 1989. Steven E. Ackey served from 1989 until 2013. The current presiding bishop is Carl Montfort. The denomination has more than 3,000 members that are currently served by sixteen congregations spread throughout Alabama, Georgia, South Carolina, and Tennessee.

R

Rawlings, Simon Peter (S.P.) 1914–1991

The second presiding bishop of the **House of God International** was born in Georgetown, Kentucky. He became ill at around the age of six with diabetes and temporarily lost his sight. After six months, his sight returned, but he lived with diabetes for the rest of his life.

Rawlings joined the House of God in Georgetown, Kentucky, at the age of sixteen. In 1933 he was ordained an elder, and later that year was sent to South Carolina to serve as assistant pastor to father of rhythm and blues singer-superstar, Marvin Gaye. A year later, Rawlings returned to Lexington, Kentucky, where he received his Pentecostal Holy Spirit baptism.

In 1935 he returned to Lexington to become pastor of Lexington Temple for fifty-six years building it from a small congregation to and edifice that would become National Headquarters of the House of God. It was from that congregation that Rawlings officiated at the funeral service of famed blues singer Marvin Gaye, whose father was once Rawlings' pastor.

In 1942 Rawlings was appointed to the Committee on Education and was ordained a bishop in 1947, becoming the second chief apostle of the House of God in 1950, a position he held for forty years—the remainder of his life. During the next thirty years, Rawlings traveled many miles to set up and form new temples throughout many parts of the United States.

He received his Bachelors of Theology and Masters of Divinity from Cooper College Institute in Jacksonville, Florida. He received his Doctor of Divinity from the Kentucky College of Contemporary Religion, an institution Rawlings assisted in establishing, and where he later served as president.

Redeemed Assembly of Jesus Christ, Apostolic

A Oneness Pentecostal body formed by James Frank Harris of Richmond, Virginia and Douglas Williams of Washington DC in a 1979 schismatic break from the **Highway Christian Church of Christ**. The organization began with six congregations, three of which had been part of the **Highway Christian Church** and three of which had been independent.

At the death of Highway founder **James Morris**, his nephew L. V. Lomax assumed leadership. His perceived authoritarian style in which he bypassed he control of the ruling elders to seek support for his decision from loyal laity. The new body, which does not have doctrinal differences with the parent organization, has a looser structure as does not have a presiding bishop with a lifetime tenure. Harris served as presiding bishop and

Williams as vice bishop. The organization is governed by an executive council involving all the bishops and an executive board consisting of all bishops and pastors.

The headquarters for the body is in Washington DC.

Reeder, Hilda 1888–??

Raised as a Presbyterian, Reeder once served as president of the Ladies Missionary Society of her local Presbyterian congregation. Reeder received her Pentecostal Spirit baptism in 1912 and shortly after joined the Oneness Pentecostal congregation of **Garfield T. Haywood** in Indianapolis, Indiana. Within a short time, Haywood tapped the public school teacher to assist him and his wife with the administration of his congregation's missions work.

Haywood first appointed her to handle the missionary department of his local congregation, and then as the first National Secretary for Missions of the **Pentecostal Assemblies of the World**. Reeder also had the distinction of serving as the secretary treasurer of the Board of Bishops, a role usually reserved for a man, and was considered the only woman member of the executive board. Reeder continued to serve in that capacity under presiding bishop **Samuel J. Grimes**.

In 1919 Reeder assisted Haywood and Andrew Urshan in organizing the PAW Missions Department after several men had failed to make a go of it. She was appointed secretary treasurer of that department and served in that position until her retirement in 1951. A year earlier she wrote the first history of the Missions Department, *A Brief History of the Foreign Missionary Department of the Pentecostal Assemblies of the World*.

Reformed Churches of God in Christ International

In 2006 Bishop J. H. Davis Sr., along with the executive board of the **Church of God in Christ International**, formed and commissioned the West North Carolina Diocese after seeing a need for growth in the western region of the state. On the recommendation of the Bishop James C. Watford, who serves as overseer of the state of North Carolina, Bishop **Kendrick. J. Rogers** was selected to oversee the new diocese.

In 2010 the West North Carolina Diocese withdrew from the **Church of God in Christ**, with the blessings from the senior bishop, to form the Reformed Churches of God in Christ International. The body sees itself as being a direct descendant of the offspring of Bishop **Charles H. Mason** but trace their Christian heritage back to the original Apostles and embrace what they see as the Apostolic Traditions of the first century church.

Their worship expression incorporates Pentecostal elements such as laying on of hands, speaking in other tongues and dancing in the spirit. But it also embraces traditions of the first-century church. Headquarters of the denomination is in Winston-Salem, North Carolina and there are congregations in North Carolina, New York, and Oklahoma.

Reformed Zion Union Apostolic Church

Unlike numerous other Holiness groups formed at the end of the nineteenth century, the earliest black Holiness denomination did not result from schism in an existing group, but came when **James R. Howell** failed to secure an African Methodist Episcopal Church pastorate because he lacked the requisite education. He was dissatisfied with what he felt was "ecclesiasticism" of black churches. In 1864 after the native Philadelphia abolitionist was sent to evangelize newly freed blacks in Virginia, he moved to the Tidewater area of that state, working as a carpenter by day and as a preacher on Sundays and in the evening. When his efforts bore little fruit, he relocated to Boydton, Virginia some 150 miles east and began traveling throughout the state and neighboring North Carolina, evangelizing and looking for a place to establish his ministry.

Despite his lack of education, his persuasive and charismatic delivery drew lay leaders from several Episcopal, Methodist, and Baptist congregations of former slave owners into what he called Zion societies, which he designation because he related the term to the biblical portrayal of Zion as "the dwelling place of God among men." He drafted a plan of union in 1866 closely followed the discipline of the AME Church, and by 1869, had organized eight established societies into the Zion Union Apostolic Church, and at least six more being organized. That October, Howell was elected to a four-year term as President of the "Zion Union Apostolic Church of America."

Almost from the beginning, the denomination had three major factions: the liberals, who had withdrawn from the Episcopalian communion, the conservatives, who had been in the white Methodist church, and the fundamentalists, who had come from the Baptist churches or were new converts to Christianity made almost unceasing war on each other.

Howell used his powers of appointment to silence or expel ministers with whom he disagreed and eventually his heavy-handed leadership led to the dissolution of the new body. Not only had he imposed the organization's name on the rest of the body, he insisted that the polity change from congregational to episcopal and had himself elected as bishop for life. By 1874 the internal friction completely disrupted the body and Howell resigned as its leader. Several within the body specifically wanted less emotive worship and a more structured organization. In 1877 they forced a vote during which the **Union Zion Apostolic Church** elected to merge with the Episcopal Church. But the minutes from that meeting mysteriously disappeared and no such merger ever occurred.

Bishop William Howell—a more acceptable leader to conservatives as well as liberals and the fundamentalist—was ineffective, however, in resolving the issues between the three groups. In 1880 his attempt to bring about a merger of the Episcopal government led to the adoption of the Common Book of Prayer, but left the Zion Union Apostolic Church organized into thirty-eight Episcopalian churches and missions.

When the church re-organized between 1881 and 1882 as the Reformed **Union Zion Apostolic Church**, after Reverend John N. Bishop gathered several of the dissenters, the life term for presiding bishop was rescinded and the four-year term was reinstated. Howell, who had returned to the organization again took that office and the friction between him and several factions within the body resumed. As a result, several congregations returned to their former Methodist or Baptist roots. Others remained independent. Several leaders who disagreed with Howell or were felt to be undermining his authority were stripped of their pastorates and disfellowshipped from the denomination. Eventually, in 1882, Howell stepped down and left the denomination, severing all communication with the group and leaving virtually no information. While by 1923, RZUAC congregations could be found only in Virginia and North Carolina, by 1965, the denomination had 16,000 members in fifty churches stretching as far north as Philadelphia, Hackensack, New Jersey, and Detroit. After numerous schisms, the denomination is now primarily a Southern church.

Further Reading:

General Education Board of the Reformed Zion Union Apostolic Churches of America. *History of the Reformed Zion Union Apostolic Churches of America.* Brunswick, GA: Brunswick Publishing, 1997.

Refuge Temple Assembly of Yahweh

A quasi-**Hebrew Pentecostal** denomination founded in 1970 by Bishop John W. Pernell, a former leader within the **Church of Our Lord Jesus Christ of the Apostolic Faith**. From 1943 to 1969, Pernell pastored Mother Refuge Church as a COOLJC congregation in Richmond, Virginia. Pernell, who had been mentored by **Robert C. Lawson** was on the five member apostolic board for the COOLJC organization. After Lawson's death in 1961, a three-member board was established with **William Bonner**, Herbert Spencer and Maurice Hutner. When the board was expanded two years later, Pernell was added along as a member. He also served for a time as the editor of the denomination's official periodical, *The Contender for the Faith.*

In 1969 Pernell resigned from the COOLJC when he reported that he had a vision of the importance of the "divine name" and rejected traditional references to Christ by his anglicized name "Jesus." His refusal to back away from this position brought about his total exclusion from the Churches of Our Lord Jesus and he resigned from his pastorate to establish a new congregation in the same city, **Refuge Temple Assembly of Yahweh** and preceded to build in to a body of congregations.

After ordaining twenty-one elders, putting the structure in place for his new body, however, and completing all the required legal work, Pernell lived to presided over one National Convocation. After his death, in 1971, the organization set up a board of bishops. Elder Elmo W. Woodbury of Norfolk, Virginia assumed leadership as presider, a position he held until the present.

While not much information is available on the group, it appears to distinguish itself from other Hebrew Pentecostal bodies in that its emphasis is squarely of the use of the proper Hebrew name for God rather than on keeping Sabbath or other Jewish customs. No statistics are available regarding the size of the body. However, most congregations appear to be in Virginia.

Richardson, James C. Sr. 1910–1995

The second presiding bishop of the **Apostolic Church of Christ in God** was born in Newberry County, South Carolina. The Richardson family was Baptist, and his father served as music director for twenty years. Richardson received a Bachelor of Arts, a Master of Divinity, both from Richmond Virginia Seminary; an Honorary Doctor of Divinity from Virginia Seminary & College and an Honorary Doctor of Laws from Richmond Virginia Seminary.

Richardson left home at an early age traveling first to Georgia, then Florida, and finally to North Carolina where he settled in Winston-Salem to work for the R. J. Reynolds Tobacco Company. While there, he was converted to the Oneness Pentecostal movement by the preaching of **Eli Neal**, was baptized in Jesus' name, and received the Pentecostal experience baptism of the Holy Spirit. Within a year, Richardson accepted the call to the ministry and eventually became the assistant pastor of the Neal's congregation.

In 1935 Richard moved to Martinsville, Virginia where he established the Mount Sinai Church as a mission of the **Church of God Apostolic**. For seven years, he made the weekly two-hour commute between the two cities before relocating.

In 1943 Richardson broke with the COGA with several other ministers to cofound the Apostolic Church of God (now the **Apostle Church of Christ in God**). He served on the board of elders from 1941 to 1952, the Board of Bishops from 1952 to 1956, and then as presiding bishop for thirty-nine years, from 1956 to 1995. During that period, he helped found congregations from Florida to New York, initiated publication of a National Journal and a National Scholar Program; National Youth Jubilee; worked to organized the church through a number of departments including the Junior missionary departments; the National Young People's Apostolic Association; National Deacon/Brothers Association; National Music Department with a Minister of Music; Development of the National Finance Committee.

Further Reading:

Richardson, James C. Jr. *With Water and Spirit: A History of Black Apostolic Denominations in the U.S.* Martinsville, VA: s.n., s.d.

Richardson, Thomas

An early black leader in the Church of God (Cleveland, TN) and later, the Church of God of Prophecy–two predominantly white Pentecostal bodies. As early as the 1920s, when Church of God (Cleveland, TN) General Overseer, **A. J. Tomlinson**, appointed a small number of black ministers to leadership positions beyond the limited fellowship of the African American churches, Richardson was appointed to the Education Committee. Richardson was also among three blacks who served on the Council of Seventy, along with **W. V. Eneas** and William Franks.

During the 1922 exodus of black Church of God ministers, Tomlinson attempted to quiet dissention by appointing to the Committee on Better Government and created an autonomous structure for the black churches, appointing Richardson as overseer. In that post, Richardson held the same authority as that of a state overseer, and could establish or disband churches, grant ministerial credentials and appoint pastors. While Richardson focused his efforts on converting black Americans, winning to the denomination and increasing the black membership in the Church of God, the highly visible figure, who had been appointed to the denomination's council of seventy elders served only one year at that post.

Richardson participated in the 1923 called council within the COG in which Tomlinson responded to charges against him. He may have been the only black present during meeting at which Tomlinson was voted out of the organization, Richardson sided with him. Newly elected overseer, Flavius. J. Lee revoked Richardson's license, appointing **David LaFleur** over black churches. When Tomlinson, left the denomination, Richardson followed him to the newly formed Church of God of Prophecy.

Within Tomlinson's new organization, Richardson was the only African American state overseer appointed he appointed, and served on his newly formed Council and on the Bible Government Committee. Yet, in 1926, when Tomlinson refused to appoint him as overseer of Florida, because he was disbanding separate racial enclaves, and offered him Bermuda instead, Richard left the COGOP. He returned to the denomination in 1927, but never regained the prominence he had previously enjoyed.

Rivers, Eugene F. III 1950–

Social activist and pastor of the Azusa Christian Community, a church he founded in 1974 in Boston's inner city Dorchester neighborhood, co-founder of the Boston Ten Point Coalition, and co-chair of the National Ten Point Leadership Foundation.

Rivers was born in Boston, but spent his early years in Chicago where his parents were members of the Nation of Islam. As a young man he moved to Philadelphia where he was mentored by **Benjamin Smith** of Deliverance Evangelistic Temple and studied painting at the Pennsylvania Academy of Fine Arts, while becoming active in community organizing and black church politics and working with other activists on issues ranging from economic development to gang violence.

In 1970 Rivers was a part of the Black Economic Development Conference working with Muhammad Kenyatta. He later joined Lucius Walker and James Forman in the Reparations Movement. He attended Yale as an unregistered activist from 1973 to 1976. Further, he was officially admitted to Harvard University later that year, but did not receive a degree. While there, he was instrumental in founding the Seymour Society. Though a social activist with progressive views, Rivers, who also attended Eastern Baptist Theological Seminary, is theologically conservative.

Rivers served as president of the Ella J. Baker House, the nonprofit originally created by the Azusa Christian Community. His is president of the Ten Point Leadership Foundation, a local Boston organization he founded in 1994 as the Ten Point Coalition that has expanded to the national level. Through it, he worked to build grassroots leadership in inner city neighborhoods across the United States. Further, he serves as Special Advisor to **Church of God in Christ** presiding bishop, **Charles E. Blake**, for the Save Africa's Children program. Rivers advised both Bush Administrations and the Clinton Administration on their faith-based initiatives and in the foreign policy arena regarding the AIDS crisis in Africa.

Rivers has appeared on major network syndicated programs including CNN's *Hardball*, NBC's *Meet the Press*, PBS' *Charlie Rose*, BET's *Lead Story*, and on National Public Radio. He also has been featured or provided commentary for periodicals such as Newsweek, which once referred to him as, "the savior of the streets," *The New Yorker, The New York Times, The Washington Post, The Los Angeles Times, The Boston Herald*, and *The Boston Globe*. He has also been featured in periodicals such as the *Boston Review, Sojourners, Christianity Today,* and *Books and Culture*. He has authored or co-authored numerous essays, including, "On the Responsibility of Intellectuals in an Age of Crack"; "Beyond the Nationalism of Fools: A Manifesto for a New Black Movement"; "Black Churches and the Challenge of U.S. Foreign and Development Policy"; "An Open Letter to the U.S. Black Religious, Intellectual, and Political Leadership Regarding AIDS and the Sexual Holocaust in Africa"; and "A Pastoral Letter to President George W. Bush on Bridging our Racial Divide." He has lectured at universities around the nation including Harvard, Yale, Princeton, and Calvin College.

Rivers, Willie Mae 1926–

Unlike the women who preceded her as the sixth International Supervisor of the Church of God in Christ International Women's Department, as a child, Rivers was not a member of that denomination. She was raised in the African Methodist Episcopal Church. Rivers was also without the advantage of marrying a prominent husband within the denomination to pave a path to her appointment, and rather rose through the ranks of COGIC's dual leadership system to her position.

Willie Mae Small was born during a period of rigid segregation in the predominantly black town of Goose Creek, South Carolina near Charleston, and came to faith in Christ as a small child in the Mt. Zion AME Church. When she was eight years old, her father died suddenly and she went to work in the tobacco fields with her mother. As a young woman, her religious fervor gained the attention of leaders of her congregation and she was asked to represent the congregation as a delegate at local and jurisdictional AME conventions.

In 1941 fifteen-year-old Willie Mae married David Rivers. The couple raised ten daughters and two sons. In 1946 while attending a revival at a local COGIC congregation, Rivers received the Pentecostal Holy Spirit baptism. Shortly after that, she joined Calvary Church of God in Christ and began working with her pastor in evangelistic and fundraising efforts.

In 1947 at the age of twenty-one, Rivers was appointed church mother of the local congregation (a position she continues to hold). Two years later, she was appointed District Missionary of the Orangeburg, South Carolina District, and in 1968, as Supervisor of the South Carolina State Women's Department, where she still serves.

Among the others positions of local and national prominence Rivers has held within COGIC are International Marshal of the Women's Convention, Chairperson of the Board of Supervisors for the International Women's Department, member of the COGIC Executive Board, as well as rising successively from Third Assistant General Supervisor to Second Assistant General Supervisor to First Assistant General Supervisor.

By the time her husband died in 1997, Rivers's ministry included a radio broadcast "The Evangelist Speaks," which has aired on five stations in the southeastern United States. That year, following the death of Mother **Emma Crouch**, Bishop **Chandler D. Owens** appointed Rivers to the International position. Since her tenure began, she founded the "forty-nine and under" club to encourage younger women, and the Mother Willie Mae Rivers Foundation to provide financial assistance for COGIC students attending vocational and trade schools. She also founded the Community Christian Women & Men Fellowship, an organization that provides spiritual enrichment to people in all walks of life, but is particularly aimed at providing for those less fortunate and bereaved.

In the early years of the twenty-first century, Rivers entered a new venture, recording several albums of traditional gospel music. *Business for the King* was released in 2003 on the Rivers of Melody label, and *Lord, I'm In Your Care*, featuring Mother Willie Mae Rivers & the Family, was recorded in 2011 on the same label.

Further Reading:

Butler, Anthea D. *Women in the Church of God in Christ: Making a Sanctified World.* Chapel Hill, NC: University of North Carolina Press, 2007.

Clemmons, Ithiel. *Bishop C. H. Mason and the Roots of the Church of God in Christ.* Bakersfield, CA: Pneuma Life, 1996.

Goodson, Glenda Williams. *Bishop Mason and those Sanctified Women.* Houston, TX: s.n., 2003

Roberts, William Matthew 1876–1954

An early leader in **Church of God in Christ** who established the denomination in the state of Illinois and was one of the original members of its first Board of Bishops appointed by founder, **Charles H. Mason**. Roberts was born in Okalona, Mississippi and in 1904 he and his wife, Mamie moved to Memphis, Tennessee where they opened a dry goods store and became involved in COGIC after hearing Mason preaching on a street corner. Roberts served as a deacon and later as assistant pastor of Mason's congregation.

At some point, Robert visited the **Azusa Street Revival** where pastor **William J. Seymour** was in leadership, and after Mason returned from that event, he was one of the first to hear his testimony. Convinced that speaking in tongues was a valid sign of Holy Spirit baptism, Roberts was among the thirteen ministers who responded to Mason's initial call to separate from his former colleague and Holiness movement leader, **Charles Price Jones** and his followers, to establish a new Pentecostal group. Over the years, Roberts remained a close colleague of Mason. While he was a young struggling minister, Roberts and his wife provided him clothing from their store. At one time, he used his family's savings of $100 to bail Bishop Mason out of jail.

Roberts left Memphis in 1917, when he was invited by a group of women including **Lillian Brooks Coffey** (later national president of the COGIC International Women's Department) to come to Chicago to establish a congregation. Prior to his taking on the task, several pastors had abandoned the mission, seeing Chicago as too difficult a field to attempt to establish a new COGC work. On arrival, he initially, took a job in the stockyards to augment the meager support the congregation could afford for him. Over the years, however, Roberts built that congregation into one of the largest COGIC church in the United States, and was the first COGIC minister to have a radio broadcast.

He eventually came to serve as the first superintendent of Illinois, Indiana, Kentucky, Iowa, Arkansas, Minnesota, Wisconsin and Nebraska. In 1933, he was consecrated as one of the first five overseers to be consecrated as bishops of the denomination. Several leaders who later gained prominence within COGIC were mentored or tutored by Roberts including Bishop **O. M. Kelly**, who became the first person to be named assistant presiding bishop.

Outside of COGIC, Roberts served as treasurer of the Board of Education of the National Fraternal Council of Negro Churches. In 1941 before the Civil Rights Movement was in full swing, Roberts was a member of the delegation from the organization that went to Washington to demand economic justice in the form of jobs and reparations for African Americans.

Roberts died suddenly of a heart attack during an Annual Women's Convention. After his death, his oldest son, Bishop Isaiah Roberts, took over his congregation, and later became presiding bishop of Prelate of the Northern Illinois Jurisdiction.

Further Reading:

Marovich, Robert M. "William Matthew Roberts." In *A City Called Heaven: Chicago and the Birth of Gospel Music*, 29–31. Urbana, IL: University of Illinois Press, 2015.

Robertson, Cornelia Jones 1881–1967

One of the earliest African-American ministers credentialed by the predominantly white Assemblies of God. The minister and pastor, who received a district preaching license and was ordained in 1922, was the first African-American woman to receive credentials from that organization and, perhaps, its first black woman pastor.

The **Azusa Street Revival** participant was born in Kadiz, Kentucky. She was ordained an evangelist in 1909 and in her early ministry was a colleague of two prominent early white women Pentecostal leaders, Aimee Semple McPherson, founder of the International Church of the Foursquare Gospel, and famed healing evangelist Maria Woodworth-Etter. Later, she became a mentor to **Robert (Bob) Harrison** who received international fame as an evangelist and associate of Billy Graham. Harrison was a close family friend who, though not related to Jones by blood, considered her his grandmother.

In 1922 she founded Emmanuel Pentecostal Church and House of Prayer in downtown San Francisco. She was reportedly a widow at the time she received ministerial credentials from the Northern California-Nevada district of the Assemblies of God in 1923. She preached an average of three hundred sermons per year with her evangelistic work spreading to cities throughout California and the American Northwest.

During the Depression years, her mission handed out food and clothing to many and continued that operation throughout the remainder of her ministry. She is credited with helping more than 100,000 men and boys through the cooperation of merchants and various churches in the San Francisco area.

Jones resigned from the Assemblies of God in 1935 to join the predominantly black **United Holy Church of America** and brought her congregation into the body where she served as president of the Missionary Department in the Western and Pacific Coast District. She led an effective ministry in the black community for the next three decades. Her involvement in a variety of associations ran from serving as secretary of the Interdenominational Ministerial Alliance of San Francisco and an officer of the Women's Christian Temperance Union. Though one of few African Americans listed in the official predecessor to the San Francisco Social Register, she founded and ran the Barbary Coast Mission in San Francisco for fourteen years. After a long illness, Jones died at age eighty-six.

Further Reading:

Gohr, Glenn. "Cornelia Jones Robertson—A Friend of the Needy" *Charisma* (July 2004) 33.
Carter, Jessica Faye. "Known and Yet Unknown: Women of Color and the Assemblies of God." *Assemblies of God Heritage*, 2008.

Robinson, Elizabeth Isabelle Smith Woods (Lizzie) 1860–1943

The first International Supervisor of the Overseer of the Women's Department for the newly formed **Church of God In Christ.** Robinson was born in Phillips Arkansas to slave parents who both had died by the time she was fifteen, leaving her to care for her four siblings. In 1880, she married her first husband, William Holt, with whom she had one daughter, Ida. Holt died a short time afterward, and Lizzie remarried, this time to William Woods. During this marriage, she joined the Baptist church at Pine Bluff, Arkansas, in 1892.

As a young woman, Robinson began reading American Baptist magazine, which she credited with introducing her to the experience of sanctification. After becoming sanctified, she began corresponding with Holiness teacher Joanna Moore who prevailed on the missionary society of the American Baptists to send Robinson to the Baptist Training Academy in Dermott, Arkansas for two years. After matriculating there, she was appointed matron. Robinson remained Baptist until introduced to the **Church of God in Christ** through the preaching of **D. W. Delk**, and received the Pentecostal baptism of the Holy Spirit in 1911, in a revival preached by COGIC founder, **Charles H. Mason.**

The two met while Robinson was serving as matron, and though he was impressed with her leadership ability, Robinson was not Mason's first choice to head the International Women's Department. Rather, when **Lillian Coffey**, a young woman Mason and his wife had personally mentored, sensed she might be too young for the responsibility, she suggested Robinson instead.

Under her leadership, COGIC women established new congregations, Bible studies, and prayer groups within existing congregations, and engaged in home and foreign missions work. Her crowning accomplishment was organizing what had been a fledgling amalgamation of two often competing camps–the prayer bands and the Bible bands scattered throughout the denomination—into a national effort forming the Prayer and Bible Band. She also organized the sewing circle and encouraged the women to support mission work through the Home and Foreign Mission bands. As the church continued to grow, Robinson, a staunch advocate for holiness who taught strict guidelines for the women regarding dress and worldliness, began state organizations and appointed the first state mothers.

In the second decade of the 1900s, after the death of her second husband, Lizzie married Edward Robinson, a COGIC elder. As an evangelist, along with her responsibilities for the International Women's Department, she worked with her husband to dig out and establishing churches. After moving to Omaha, Nebraska, they established the first **Church of God in Christ** in the state in 1916, and persevered in building a COGIC presence in the state by helping establish other congregations. Yet, though an evangelist who traveled across the nation speaking, Robinson did not believe women should preach. Instead, she held that the Bible permitted them to speak or teach. Under her leadership, COGIC women traveled nationwide under this understanding, starting Bible Bands that often became churches.

One of her major contributions to COGIC was raising the funds to build the National Headquarters, and she kept her national drives functioning so she could live long enough to see its dedication. She died shortly after that occasion.

Further Reading:

Butler, Anthea. *Women in the Church of God in Christ: The Making of a Sanctified World.* Chapel Hill, NC: University of North Carolina Press, 2006.

Hill, Elijah L. *Women Come Alive: Biography on the life of Mother Lizzie Robinson.* Arlington, TX: Perfecting the Kingdom International, 2005.

Robinson, Ida Bell 1888–1946

Ida Robinson founded the **Mt. Sinai Holy Church of America**—the largest African-American Pentecostal denomination established by a woman, continually headed by women, and promoting the equality and leadership of women in ministry. A product of the early years of the Great Migration, Robinson was born in Virginia and migrated to Philadelphia in the early 1920s, first working as a laundress and serving as a minister with the Church of God, then the **United Holy Church** (UHC), where she was ordained and appointed pastor of a small congregation. At that time, however, UHC women outnumbered men two to one, and there were few women preachers.

By 1924 Robinson's reputation as a revivalist had spread among African American Pentecostal congregations within and outside of the UHC, and she was ministering along much of the East coast. People regularly filled her church to hear her sing and preach. Many stayed to become members, fueling the congregation's rapid expansion, causing it to move three times to larger locations.

Despite little formal education, Robinson's sharp intellect, excellent leadership skills, giftedness as a preacher and singer, and biblical knowledge did not escape the attention of **United Holy Church** leadership who frequently called on her for ministry. Her success and prominence prodded other **United Holy Church** women to vigorously demand a more public presence. The male leadership responded by finally announcing that they would no longer "publicly" ordain women and would restrict those already ordained to lower levels of ordained ministry. Though her position was secure, Robinson started a new denomination in which women could freely participate in all levels of ministry. When church leaders attempted to change her mind, she responded that God had instructed her to, "Come out on Mt. Sinai and loose the women." Perceiving this summons as a direct command, she asked, "if Mary the mother of Jesus could carry the word of God in her womb, why can't women carry the word of God in their mouth?" Robinson's first steps as denominational head reflected this commitment. Yet, rather than being exclusivist, she employed men and women in the organization's ministry and leadership. From 1924 to 1936, Robinson was involved in setting up almost every new local congregation within the organization. She traveled throughout the East Coast to small towns and larger cities conducting revival services, making new converts and establishing local congregations over which she would place a minister as pastor. Many of these placements were women.

After leading Mt. Sinai for twenty-two years, Robinson died in 1946, at the age of fifty-four. In that time, she had built a denomination of eighty-four churches, stretching from New England to Florida. Since her death, the growth that Mt. Sinai experienced under Robinson was never again realized.

Further Reading:

Alexander, Estrelda. "Ida Robinson." In *Limited Liberty: The Legacy of Four Pentecostal Women Pioneers,* 120. Cleveland, OH: Pilgrim, 2008.

Fauset, Arthur H. *Black Gods of the Metropolis.* Philadelphia: University of Pennsylvania Press, 1944.

Roby, Jasper C. 1912–2006

The second presiding bishop of the **Apostolic Overcoming Holy Church of God, Inc.** was born in Brookfield, Mississippi and raised in Demoplis. Ordained into the ministry in 1942, Roby was founder and pastor of Greater Seventeenth Street Apostolic Overcoming Holy Church of God in Birmingham, Alabama. He was consecrated bishop in the AOHC in 1956, the same year he received the BTh degree from American Divinity School. In 1964 he earned a DD from Universal Bible Institute.

At the death of **William T. Phillips**, he assumed the highest leadership in the denomination, serving in the post for twenty-seven years. On assuming the post, he moved AOHC headquarters to Birmingham. Among his several accomplishments within the AOHC, in 1979, Roby founded the AOHC Theological Seminary and School of Academic Studies. His sermons aired on several Birmingham radio stations for more than forty years and he hosted the television program "The Bishop's Gospel Hour" for more than eight years. A lifetime member of the NAACP, Roby followed the tradition of Phillips in his active engagement as a Civil Rights leader.

In 2000 due to ninety-three-year-old Roby's failing health, the AOHC board voted to remove him from office and install Bishop **George Washington Ayers** as acting president. A faction within the AOHC disagreed with the decision, however, and filed a lawsuit to keep him in office. The Alabama Supreme Court upheld a ruling that ousted Roby, as head of the 30,000-member denomination, and in 2002, four years before Roby's death at ninety-five, Ayers was re-elected to a full-term.

Rogers, Huie 1934–

Long-time leader and presiding bishop of the **Bible Way Church of Our Lord Jesus Christ World Wide**. Rogers was born in Vidalia, Georgia and migrated with his family to Brooklyn, New York where he graduated from Boys High School. He was called to the ministry at fourteen. He graduated from the Church of Christ Bible Institute and the Nyack Missionary College and obtained his honorary Doctor of Divinity Degree from New Haven Theological Seminary in Connecticut.

After its founding, Roger was one of the first twelve elders to be ordained in the Bible Way. He was mentored by **Joseph Moore**, founder of the Bible Way Church of Christ, now Greater Bible Way Temple in Brooklyn, New York. After Moore's death in 1966, Rogers became pastor of that congregation. He founded the Tidewater Bible Way Church in Portsmouth, Virginia where his son, Michael Rogers, now serves as pastor.

In 1991 Rogers was affirmed as an Apostle by Bible Way founding bishop **Smallwood E. Williams,** and after Williams' death, leaders of Bible Way Church of Our Lord signed *The Order of Succession and Constitution*, calling for **Lawrence Campbell** and Rogers to each serve a three year trial term as presiding bishop before any vote for the William's permanent successor was taken. Campbell held office from 1991 until 1994, when Rogers took over. After serving his three-year term, however, Rogers called for withholding the vote for one year. When the majority of bishops denied his request, the denomination split. Both factions, however, continued to represent themselves as the original church.

Rogers's faction is smaller; however, it retained the name of the parent body as well as ownership of the mother church, Bible Way Temple, in Washington DC, though its headquarters are in Columbia, South Carolina.

Rogers is the author of four books: *Power To Turn The World Upside Down*; *No Questions Just Trusting*; *Can I Get A Witness*; and *Tender Loving Care*. He is also founder of the Total Truth Bible School.

Rogers, Kendrick J. 1965?

Chief apostle of the **Reformed Churches of God in Christ International.** The Winston-Salem, North Carolina native was called to preach at age of eight and received his license at age ten. He was ordained an elder in the **True Vine Pentecostal Church of Jesus** in 1989, and consecrated a bishop in the Pentecostal Holiness Church of God in Christ, Incorporated.

Rogers matriculated at Augustine De Leon Bible Institute Seminary—earning a diploma of Biblical Studies—and was awarded an Honorary Doctorate of Divinity. He also studied with New Life Theological Seminary Orangeburg, South Carolina, earning a Bachelor of Theology, a Master of Theology, and Doctorate of Philosophy in Religious Education. He is currently pursuing a Doctorate of Philosophy in Episcopal studies at Faith Christian University.

Rogers has served in ministry within the Missionary Baptist Church, Apostolic, **Church of God in Christ**, Metaphysical Churches of Faith, and Methodist denominations. He established the Unity Cathedral Churches—one church in three states. He is the chief executive officer of the K. J. Rogers Community Development Corporation, and is also the author of books on history within the Pentecostal movement and a member of several community and religious organizations.

R

He is an administer for the Augustine Deleon Bible Institute & Seminary. He also served on the executive board of the Fellowship of Independent and Global Churches. Before affiliating with that group, he served as General Secretary, Dean of the Bishops College, as a member of the Board of Bishops of **Church of God in Christ International**, and bishop of the West North Carolina diocese of the **Church of God in Christ International**, as well as President of the 5th Sunday Union of Churches.

S

Sacred Steel Guitar Tradition

A musical style within the African-American gospel tradition that developed within two derivative organizations from **The Church of the Living God, the Pillar and Ground of the Truth),** headquartered in Nashville and the **Jewell Dominion (Church of the Living God, Pillar and Ground of the Truth, Which He Purchased With His Own Blood, Inc.),** headquartered in Indianapolis. Troman Eason and his brother, **Willie Eason** of the Jewell Dominion, introduced lap steel guitar to worship services in place of the traditional organ. This new instrument was met with great enthusiasm and taken up by others including Bishop J. R. Lockley. The three toured together and later Willie recorded a total of eighteen sides in the 1940s and 1950s.

The instrument, invented in Hawaii in the late nineteenth and early twentieth centuries, is a cross between guitar and a xylophone. It is usually positioned horizontally; strings are plucked with one hand, while the other hand changes the pitch of one or more strings with the use of a bar or slide called a steel. It is often identified with country and western music and virtually unheard of within other African-American churches. Since its introduction by the Church of the Living God, the sacred steel guitar style has grown and flourished within both groups. The most famous and commercially successful practitioner is Keith Dominion guitarist, Robert Randolph, of the Robert Randolph and the Family Band. The son of a deacon and minister, took up pedal steel guitar at seventeen, and within seven years, had become one of the most admired practitioners of the form within and outside the church.

The Easons' nephew Aubrey Ghent has also become celebrated within the secular music realm, presenting the music to a wide audience. Ghent's father, Henry Nelson, who was also schooled by Willie Eason and played sacred steel for over fifty years, sharing the stage with gospel artists such as Sister **Rosetta Tharpe,** The Soul Stirrers, the Blind Boys of Alabama and Mahalia Jackson, becoming the most prominent steel guitarist in the Keith Dominion. Unlike Randolph and the Family Band, Ghent has stayed closer to his gospel roots, like many Jewell Dominion steel guitarists.

The Campbell Brothers, a group composed of three brothers and one son, began as the house band for a Keith Dominion congregation. They released several albums on blues label, Arhoolie Records in the late 1990s and early 2000s before signing with Ropeadope Records, releasing "Can You Feel It?" in 2005, an album that reached the twenty-sixth position on the Billboard Top Gospel Albums chart.

While the Keith and Jewell Dominion worship music is based around the instrument, their sister dominion, the **Lewis Dominion (Church of the Living God Pillar and**

Ground of the Truth) has given little prominence to steel guitar and the majority of its congregations choose to use the traditional piano or organ.

Further Reading:

Stone, Robert L. *Sacred Steel: Inside an African American Steel Guitar Tradition*. Urbana, IL: University of Illinois Press, 2010.

Saint Mark's Holy Churches of America, Inc.

An ecumenical fellowship of interdependent ministries founded in 1939 by **Bishop Eva Lambert,** a former elder in the **Mt. Sinai Holy Church of America** under Bishop **Ida Robinson.** The first congregation of the organization, founded in Brooklyn, New York in 1926, was one of a small number of congregations pastored by women in New York City by that time. In the 1930s, the radio broadcast from that church was among the first to introduce the new genre of gospel music over the airways.

For the next thirteen years, several churches came under Lambert's leadership as she remained in fellowship with Robinson's group. In 1939 she was consecrated as a bishop with Robinson's blessing. That year, St. Mark's Holy Church of America held its first convocation.

After Lambert's death in 1949, Bishop Nathaniel Townsley Sr., who pastored a congregation in Philadelphia and who had been ordained and consecrated to the Bishopric by Lambert, took the helm of the St. Mark Holy Church of America, Inc. Townsley led the church for thirty-five years until his death in 1984. At that time, his eldest son, Nathaniel Townsley Jr. an accomplished musician who, like his father, had previously sung in the group known as the Selah Jubilee Six, used that ability to draw the masses into St. Mark.

Thirteen of those congregations are located in New York, Connecticut, California, Georgia, North Carolina, Hawaii, and Virginia. There are also churches, orphanages, and schools in India, Uganda, Ghana, and the Caribbean.

Saints Industrial and Literary School

The major educational institution serving constituents within the early years of the Church of God in Christ, the largest and most influential African American Pentecostal denomination was established in 1918 through the efforts of Pinkie Duncan and incorporated in 1921 in Lexington, Mississippi. That year, **James Courts** was appointed as president and led fund raising efforts throughout the South that allowed the denomination to purchase twenty-eight acre and begin constructing facilities for the institution. Courts died in 1923, and **Arenia Mallory**, who had been serving on the factory as a piano instructor, was tapped by C. H. Mason to take the job as president.

Mallory served in this post until 1983. Mallory threw her efforts into a massive fundraising campaign. Saints' Jubilee Harmonizers crisscrossed the country on numerous fundraising campaigns. While Mallory's efforts at the helm were laudable, the school experienced varying degrees of success. While she often struggled to raise funds, she enjoyed the support of the International Women's Department and its leaders. By 1936, the high school of Saints Industrial and Literary School had the distinction of being one of the first schools for Mississippi blacks to be fully accredited by the State's Education Department. In 1950, a devastating fire destroyed the boys' living quarters.

From 1951 to 1961, the COGIC Board of Education took over the governance of Saints. In 1954 Saints added a junior college, changing he name to Saints Junior College and expanding its course offerings. With that expansion, some who would become COGIC's most influential leaders enrolled. In 1976 however, COGIC closed the junior college division and the school was converted into a private school for students grades one through twelve. By that year, when Mallory retired, more than 25,000 students from various denominations had graduated from Saints College.

While serving as pastor a COGIC pastor, **Donald Wheelock** accepted a position as the school's academic dean, then president. In 1981 under his leadership, Saints Academy obtained the second-highest accreditation rating (next to SACS) in Mississippi. After the cafeteria suffered a devastating fire in 1983, COGIC leaders closed the school for a year and presiding Bishop **James O. Patterson, Sr.,** effectively dismantled Saints by steering the denomination's attention toward his vision for the C. H. Mason System of Colleges.

When Mississippi native **Louis Henry Ford** assumed the office of presiding bishop, he set out to revitalize his alma mater. In 1990, Ford announced his intentions to refurbish the school and a year later, he led a COGIC delegation on a tour of the site. Within months, he broke ground for the Deborah Mason Patterson building, a structure that included a massive sanctuary, state-of-the-art kitchens, and hotel rooms. Ford selected Goldie Wells, a North Carolina native and third-generation COGIC woman, to lead the school. When Ford died in 1995, the life of the institution was again in danger. Wells lost support of the new administration, and between 1996 and 2007, leadership of the school changed hands several times. At some point, the school was renamed Saints Academy, but it permanently shut its doors in 2007.

Besides Ford, well-known graduates of the school include prominent televangelist, **Juanita Bynum**, pastor and gay activist **Yvette Flunder**, and the inaugural dean of C. H. Mason Seminary, **Leonard Lovett**.

Further Reading:

Tucker, Anjulet. "'Get the Learnin' but don't lose the Burnin': The Socio-Cultural and Religious Politics of Education in a Black Pentecostal College." PhD diss., Emory University, 2009.

Salvation and Deliverance Churches Worldwide

An interracial-intercultural, non-denominational, **Oneness** body that was established in 1981 in Harlem, New York, by **William Brown**. In 1975 Brown established a single African Methodist Episcopal Church congregation and then set out for five years, traveling throughout the East Coast with Prophetess Jane Kelly holding "Holy Ghost Deliverance Revivals" in drug rehabilitation centers, public parks, street corners, and churches of various denominations.

Brown left the AME Church in 1980 to establish the new body. Five years later, in 1985, over one hundred churches had been added in the United States and around the world. The body, headquartered in the Harlem section of New York City, currently has

140 affiliated congregations throughout the United States, and missions in forty-six countries including several within Africa, and in India, Haiti, Jamaica, Argentina, Guatemala, El Salvador, and Panama. Its substantial outreach efforts emphasize feeding the poor, building schools and orphanages, digging pure water wells, and operating medical clinics. It also operates an extensive youth ministry through the International Youth Movement for Christ, Miracle Mountain in Freehold, New York, in the Catskills Mountains, one of the largest Christian resorts on the east coast; and runs an award winning drug abuse rehabilitation program in Harlem.

Brown died in 2009, and Jerome King, who was serving as dean of the denomination's St. Paul Institute, was officially anointed as his successor. He currently presides over the denomination.

Sanders, Oscar Haywood 1892–1972

A revered early leader in the **Pentecostal Assemblies of the World.** Sanders was born and educated in Lonoke, Arkansas near Little Rock and spent most of his boyhood in Pine Bluff, Arkansas. He came to faith in Christ at the age of fourteen. In 1913 Sanders moved to Indianapolis, Indiana and began working in a downtown furniture store. Sanders began attending Shiloh Baptist Church in Indianapolis and became involved in the choir and young people's ministry.

He was baptized in Jesus' name and received the experienced Pentecostal Holy Spirit in 1918 after attending a service at Garfield Haywood's integrated congregation where he was amazed to witness whites and blacks greeting each other with a "Holy Kiss." Sanders received a called to ministry a year later and assumed the short-lived pastorate of an all-white congregation in Frankfort, Indiana. When that church fell into dissension, Sanders returned to Indianapolis in 1922 and served under the major figure in the early PAW, Bishop **Garfield T. Haywood,** who took young Sanders under his wing and mentored him. Known as "sin-killing Sanders," the young preacher planted a congregation in Muncie, Indiana in 1922, then went on to assume the pastorate of Christ Temple Church, once held by Haywood.

After the failed attempt at merger with the Pentecostal Ministerial Alliance, Sanders, who had remained loyal to PAW was appointed to the committee that sought to bring reconciliation with the Pentecostal Churches of Jesus Christ. He was elected bishop with the PAW in 1948.

Among the positions he held within the PAW are charter member of the Apostolic Bible Student Association in the Indiana District of PAW (later the Indiana State Council of PAW), interim bishop of the Northwest District Council of the PAW, bishop of the State of Indiana of PAW, and founding bishop of the Home Board of Indiana.

One morning in April 1972, a gunman entered the building intending to kill Sanders. The gun was fired, and the bullet traveled through the pulpit, grazed Bishop's hand, followed through his suit-coat sleeve and out through the back of his chair. That chair remained on the platform at Christ Temple as a testimony of divine intervention. A few months later, he died of natural causes at the age of eighty.

Further Reading:

"Christ Temple Church Past Leaders." *The Muncie Times* 7.20 (1997) 33.
Fairley, David L. *Moved by Such a Man*. Muncie, IN: s.n., 1980.

Satchell, Ruth Brown 1910–2011

The fifth presiding bishop of the **Mt. Sinai Holy Church of America** was born in New Windsor, Maryland. In 1954, the year she turned forty-four, Satchell graduated from nursing school and worked as a nurse at the Hospital of the University of Pennsylvania, Albert Einstein Medical Center, and Newcomb Medical Center in Vineland, New Jersey.

In 1960 she founded the Christian Tabernacle Church in West Minister, Maryland, where she pastored for ten years. In 1966 Satchell came to Bethel Pentecostal Church, Bridgeton, New Jersey, with her husband, who was pastor. After his death, she was installed as pastor. In 1974 she took the pastorate at Port Norris, New Jersey. She had also served as first vice president, second vice president, a member of the Board of Directors and had been a member of the Mount Sinai board of directors since 1977. In 1978 she was consecrated as a bishop and became presiding prelate of the church's Mid-Atlantic Diocese in 1992. After the death of Bishop **Amy Stevens**, Satchell, in 2000, Satchell was appointed president of the denomination. That same year she earned a doctor of divinity degree from International Christian University. Satchell served only one year until 2001, when she became bishop emeritus at age ninety, making her the shortest-serving president in the denomination.

Saunders, Monroe Randolph Sr. 1919–2008

Founding presiding bishop of the **United Church of Jesus Christ (Apostolic)**. The son of farmers was born in Florence, South Carolina and raised in the Methodist Church. He had a promising future having been high school valedictorian and having earned a scholarship to Virginia State College for Negroes, now Virginia State University, in Petersburg.

After the death of his eldest brother, however, he left college and moved to Baltimore to help his brother's children, and soon joined his sister-in-laws in attending a Pentecostal congregation, Church of God in Christ #6, led by **Randolph A. Carr**. There, he received the Pentecostal Spirit baptism, and became active in church life. His enthusiasm caught the attention of Carr, who became his mentor and provided opportunities for leadership. Young Saunders edited and published the first newspaper, directed the sanctuary choir; organized street services; visited sick members; held prayer meetings; taught Sunday School; directed dramas; taught Bible class, and preached.

During World War II, he attained the rank of sergeant in the Army and was assigned as a chaplain. After the war, he attended Howard University earning a bachelor's degree in sociology and later a Master of Divinity degree. He also earned a doctorate of ministry degree, also from Howard.

In 1948 when Carr accepted the Oneness Pentecostal doctrine and left COGIC, Saunders followed and was sent to pastor Rehoboth Church of God in Christ Jesus (Apostolic) in Washington DC. In 1957, Carr ordained Saunders as a bishop in the **Church of God in Christ Jesus (Apostolic)** and appointed him assistant presiding bishop.

While Saunders appeared to be the heir to succeed Carr, in 1965, a major fracture developed in the two men's relationship, when the elder bishop went against his own teaching and that to the denomination to marry a divorced woman. Saunders established a second congregation, the First United Church of Jesus Christ Apostolic in Baltimore, Maryland. First United Church of Jesus Christ (Apostolic) was incorporated in November 1965 in Washington DC and several congregations that had been with Carr joined Saunders's group. In 1966, he and those who joined him established United Church of Jesus Christ (Apostolic). He served as the first presiding bishop of the new organization.

Though in the early years of ministry Saunders shunned political involvement and admonished his followers to do the same, he later became involved in a number of community causes. He served a twelve-year term as a commissioner of the Baltimore City School system as well as a term on the Maryland State Commission on Aging and retirement Education.

In 2000 the church's name was changed to Transformation Church of Jesus Christ. In 2004 Saunders was consecrated chief apostle of the United Church of Jesus Christ, Apostolic. In that year, due to ill health, he stepped down from the leadership of his congregation as well as the denomination he founded. His son, Monroe R. Saunders Jr. took both positions.

Further Reading:

Saunders, Monroe R. *Sermons and Hymns from My Heart.* Enumclaw, WA: Pleasant Word, 2004.

Schooler, Alexander Robinson (A. R.) 1882–1950

One of the original five bishops of the reorganized **Pentecostal Assemblies of the World.** There is little information on the particulars of the life of the Cleveland, Ohio native. He was born in Lancaster, Kentucky and spent time in Indianapolis, Indiana. He pastored The Apostolic Faith Church in Chicago, Illinois, which was founded in 1915, and The Church of Christ in Cleveland, Ohio where he served as one of four early black field supervisors and one of the founding fathers of the Ohio District Council. Schooler worked with **Joseph Turpin** to establish the Eastern District Council of the PAW.

In 1919 Schooler was elected Vice General Chairperson of the PAW. In 1920, Schooler was appointed Executive Vice Chair, a post he held until 1922, when he was replaced by **Garfield T. Haywood**. That same year, he was appointed to serve on the editorial board of *The Christian Outlook*, the official periodical of the denomination.

In 1924 Schooler was elected as a presbyter and by 1925 after the majority of white ministers pulled out to form three separate regional organizations and the PAW moved from a system of elders to an episcopal system, Schooler was one of the bishops elected to the Executive Board, serving there until 1927, when he was replaced by **Samuel N. Hancock**. By 1929, however, his name no longer appeared on the roster of PAW ministers.

Schooler wrote a number of distinctly Apostolic songs including "The Name," and "God Died for Me." His 1920 hymn "The Author and the Finisher" proclaims his defense of baptism in Jesus' name." His "The Bible Manifestation" is openly critical of what he considered apostate denominationalism and defends Pentecostal practices such as speaking in tongues, anointing of the sick by the bishopric, foot washing, and communion. He also co-authored several hymns with prolific hymnist, **Thoro Harris**.

In 1940 Schooler was living in Los Angeles, California and listed his occupation as proprietor, but he also listed his employer as the Union Church of Christ in that city. At some point he moved to Victorville, California, his last known place of residence, and he died in San Bernardino.

Scotton, Ralph 1909–1952?

An early black leader in the **Church of God of Prophecy**. Scotton joined COGOP in 1930, only seven years after founder and General Overseer, **A. J. Tomlinson,** formed the interracial body. He was born High Point, North Carolina and moved to Cleveland, Tennessee in the late 1930s where he apparently spent the rest of his life. Scotton was a bricklayer by trade and used that skill to help build many of the church buildings for the congregations he helped establish. Tomlinson ordained him a bishop in 1940. Still he served as a local pastor, evangelist, and a denominational representative, traveling across the United States and the Caribbean preaching and adding members to the church. His mother, Pattie K. Scotton, served as pastor of several local churches and was often involved in the denomination's healing services at the Annual Assemblies.

In 1941 COGOP founder **A. J. Tomlinson** appointed Scotton as one of two General Field Secretaries for the Church of God of Prophecy. He served in that position until 1952, traveling more than 150,000 miles and preaching over 2,000 sermons, assisting the General Overseer in reaching black Americans. Yet, though his ministry focused primarily on African Americans in the South, Scotton was highly respected among both races within COGOP and served as the general representative for the church at numerous district and state conventions, where whites and blacks worshipped together. He preached annually at the General Assembly, and used that pulpit to promote racial harmony in the church.

Seymour, Jennie Evans Moore 1874–1936

An early **Azusa Street Revival** participant who married founder **William Seymour**, and succeeded him as pastor of the local Azusa Street Mission congregation. Reportedly, she was among the first participants in the group to receive the Pentecostal Holy Spirit baptism and may have been the first woman to have had the experience. She was also among the first to take the news of the revival to the broader Los Angeles Christian community.

Moore was born in Austin, Texas. Nothing is recorded of her early education, family life, or religious background. In early 1906, she worked as a domestic for an influential, white Los Angeles family. She lived at 217 Bonnie Brae Street, near the home of Seymour's original Bible study and directly across the street from the cottage where **Julia Hutchins** and her Holiness congregation had a temporary home. Moore won to faith through this outreach and for a time was a member of Hutchins' congregation. Once Seymour moved his meeting to the Bonnie Brae home, Moore started attending.

After the group moved to Azusa Street, Moore took an increasingly active role in the mission and could be found leading singing, playing the piano, serving on the administrative board responsible for examining ministers for credentials, and eventually working as an evangelist throughout the city of Los Angeles. Moore became a powerful preacher in her own right, and between 1907 and 1908, when not at the Mission, was itinerating as an evangelist throughout the West and Midwest. Like others who went out from the mission, she regularly filed reports to the *Apostolic Faith* newspaper, such as an item n briefly describing a revival she held at William Durham's North Avenue Mission in Chicago:

In May 1908, little more than two years after the revival began, Seymour married Moore, setting off one of the major schisms that would challenge the mission's existence. Some within the mission questioned the expediency of the marriage, seeing the imminent return of Christ as leaving little room for such "worldly" pursuits. Other opposition was specifically lodged at Seymour's choice of a wife, since his close white friend and associate Clara Lum reportedly felt he might marry her. Soundly disappointed that he chose Moore, Lum left the Azusa Street Mission and moved to Portland to work with Florence Crawford.

After the marriage, the couple moved into a modest apartment above the mission, and Jennie played an ever-expanding leadership role. She regularly preached, filled in as pastor when William was away and occasionally traveled on his behalf. From time to time, she accompanied him when he traveled and was with him when he went to Oregon to confront Crawford and Lum about The Apostolic Faith mailing list.

Between 1910 and 1922, the waning years of the Azusa Street Mission, Jennie Seymour became more involved in decision-making, and soon became the only woman member of the Mission's official board of trustees. In 1911 her invitation of Durham to the mission proved disastrous for an already tenuous situation. Durham's open denunciation of the doctrine of entire sanctification resulted in a schism that saw a number of Seymour's congregation defect to his teaching.

By 1917 declining attendance and finances forced Jennie to return to the secular workforce to help augment the family's resources. Before Seymour's death, he placed the ministry's leadership in his wife's hands. When he died, she assumed the pastorate of the small remnant. In 1930 she and the congregation withstood a takeover attempt by R. C. Griffith. The resulting court battle, however, was costly and most remaining whites sided with Griffith and left.

Ultimately, the group succumbed to the financial strain. Jennie was forced to vacate the apartment she had shared with her husband when the building was condemned as a fire hazard, and moved the remaining congregation to her home to continue holding services until her health failed in 1933.

At one point in an attempt to save the mission, Seymour mortgaged her home. Yet, this measure did not stop the sale of the mortgages on the mission and her home to a Los Angeles bank. When she could no longer make payments, the bank foreclosed on the mission, and razed the building. Seymour died at the age of sixty-two, three years after she relinquished leadership of the church.

Further Reading:

Alexander, Estrelda. *The Women of Azusa Street.* Bowie, MD: Seymour, 2012.

Seymour, William Joseph 1871–1922

The leader of the 1906 **Azusa Street Revival** that was the seminal event that launched the of the contemporary American Pentecostal movement. The son of freed slaves, Seymour was born in Centerville, Louisiana. We know little of Seymour's childhood religious exposure, except that he was raised in the Baptist tradition, surrounded by a largely Catholic environment and probably had been baptized in the Roman Catholic Church. Growing up within the heady spiritual climate of Louisiana, Seymour repeatedly had dreams and visions that continued throughout his life. For a time at least, Seymour attended a freedman school where he learned to read and write. Seymour's family lived with devastation and poverty, and after his father's death during William's teen years, the family was thrown even further into poverty and William assumed his place, alongside his mother, as the male head of the family.

As a young man, Seymour headed north, stopping first in Memphis, Tennessee but by 1893, had moved to the Midwest stopping for times in Indiana, Ohio, Illinois and possibly Missouri and Tennessee, often working as a waiter in big city hotels. By age twenty-five, Seymour had settled in Indianapolis, Indiana. While there, he joined a Methodist Episcopal Church congregation where he had a conversion experience, but after becoming dissatisfied with the congregation's spiritual tenor and the racial climate beginning to develop in the Methodist church, he sought a deeper spiritual experience.

By 1900 Seymour was in Chicago, then moved to Cincinnati, Ohio where he encountered Martin Wells Knapp's Holiness teachings, attended his God Bible School and encountered the Church of God Reformation movement, the "Evening Light Saints," where he had the experience of sanctification and saw a level of racial tolerance unlike any other he had witnessed. The group ordained Seymour to the ministry, sending him out as an itinerant tent-making evangelist. He preached where he was invited, living off the work of his hands and free-will offerings. During this period, he came across their communal mutually supportive missionary homes that would later serve as a model for the Azusa Street mission.

While in Cincinnati, Seymour contracted, the potentially fatal disease, smallpox. During his recovery, he sensed a call to full-time ministry, answered affirmatively and was healed almost entirely, except the loss sight in his left eye so that he wore a glass eye the rest of this life.

Leaving that city in 1902, Seymour first moved to Houston looking for lost relatives. From there, he traveled and preached throughout Texas and Louisiana. During the summer of 1904, he reportedly traveled to Jackson, Mississippi to meet with Holiness leader **Charles Price Jones.** Later that year he was back in Houston attending **Lucy Farrow's** Holiness church, serving for a while as interim pastor while she traveled and worked for Charles Parham's family. Through this relationship, Seymour met Parham and sat under his teaching. Though Texas' segregation laws forced him to listen through the doorway as white students sat in the classroom, in the afternoons the two evangelized together in the black section of town, and by evenings, Seymour joined other black worshippers in Parham's multi-racial evangelistic services, though forced to sit in the section reserved for blacks.

In early spring 1906, Seymour left Houston travel to Los Angles, California to minister within the small Nazarene congregation pastored by **Julia Hutchins**, who subsequently reneged on her invitation after hearing Seymour's doctrine of the necessity of speaking in tongues with Holy Spirit baptism. This rejection put Seymour in the position of having to secure a new location for his ministry at the home of **Ruth and Richard Asbury** where the famous revival at the **Bonnie Brea Street Prayer Meeting** served as the prequel to the revival at the Azusa Street mission. In April 1906, when the earliest outbreak of tongue speaking first occurred and seven of those attending that meeting had the Pentecostal experience of Holy Spirit baptism, Seymour himself had not. Yet, three days later Seymour could testify to having had the experience, and as others began to have the experience, the group grew too large for the modest residence.

Seymour's ministry at Azusa Street was subject to several major challenges. Some in the congregation opposed his marriage to **Jennie Evans Moore**, an original member of the Bonnie Brae Street prayer meeting. Florence Crawford, an early leader in the mission, deserted the work to start her own Apostolic Faith Mission in Portland, Oregon. In 1911, William Durham, pastor of a leading Midwest Holiness congregation attempted to take over the Azusa Street congregation and introduced the Finished Work doctrine.

The high point of the **Azusa Street Revival** lasted approximately three years. As it begin to wane, Seymour prominence within the movement began to decline rapidly. Despite the major controversies, Seymour championed unity and racial reconciliation among fledgling Pentecostal bodies.

As important as Seymour's administrative and spiritual gifts were, an often-overlooked aspect of his leadership is his attempt at constructing a Pentecostal theological framework. Seymour gradually moved away from asserting that speaking in tongues was *the* initial evidence of Holy Spirit baptism or any insinuation that every believer who was filled with the Spirit of God had to show such evidence. Instead, he insisted, "a more sure sign . . . was love," and the [speaking in] Tongues alone was not an only true sign of baptism of the Holy Spirit. Further, for him, the experience of Holy Spirit baptism was not an essential element in conversion, but rather an added blessing or impartation of grace. Fully anticipating that such a stand might place him at odds with many other Pentecostals, he was not reluctant to write the issue because he was certain that many had settled for false hope in an outward physical sign without having an inward change in their spiritual condition. Seymour's concern seemingly was tied to the outworking of Holy Spirit baptism rather than any mechanical formulaic test of its reception.

For several years after the end of the revival, Seymour was in demand as a speaker among circle of supporters that was growing ever smaller. Seymour's greatest hope for a unified movement without regard to barriers based on race, gender, class never materialized. While the revival was in full swing, he took steps to ensure that this would be so, organizing a weekly meeting of pastors throughout the Los Angeles area to come together to pray, study scripture and share their struggles and triumphs. Using the mission as a meeting site, pastors regularly joined him for fellowship, succor, and an attempt to promote a unified spirit among the disparate Pentecostal congregations that were forming around Los Angeles.

In 1917 Seymour again called a meeting of Pentecostal leaders around Los Angeles to pray and fellowship, but the turnout was scandalously small considering his former prominence and the lack of any impropriety to discredit him. Throughout this period Seymour continued to travel to encourage existing congregations and plant new ones. In 1911 he visited Hansome, Virginia and left a congregation and appointed **Charles Lowe** as the pastor. By the end of his life, he often attended Pentecostal meetings as a member of the congregation, but without recognition by leaders, who often left him sitting in the congregation while others completely ignored him.

One place Seymour was always welcomed was with his friend **Charles Harrison Mason. The Church of God in Christ** leader found his Pentecostal experience in Seymour's meetings, considered him a father in the faith and frequently invited him to speak at Annual COGIC Convocations. John G. Lake, another colleague, remained in fellowship with Seymour and invited him to address a congregation of ten thousand believers in the Pacific Northwest who gave him a rousing reception and still revered him.

Despite his limited education, in 1915, Seymour took it upon himself to produce the first definitive work on polity for the fledgling movement, the Doctrine and Disciplines of the Azusa Street Mission that laid out his foundational beliefs and provided liturgies and orders of worship for several occasions. The doctrinal stances Seymour portrayed reflected his early Holiness affiliation, especially the Evening Light Saints, while his liturgical formulations clearly indicate an earlier tie to Methodism. The breadth of the structure of this document puts to bed the lie that Seymour was largely illiterate and portrays a man who valued education and had at least a rudimentary understanding of complex theological ideas. Within this document, he envisioned the establishment of educational institutions: primary and secondary schools, as well as colleges, universities, Bible schools and seminaries to train ministers.

By 1922 fifty-one-year-old Seymour was tired and discouraged. His congregation had dwindled to little more than a handful, his efforts to bring unity to the movement had apparently failed, and his personal influence had largely evaporated. By September of that year, he had succumbed, dying of what some have called a broken heart. After his death, his wife, **Jennie Evans Seymour,** took over leadership of the mission and the ministry.

Further Reading:

Alexander, Estrelda. *Black Fire: One Hundred Years of African American Pentecostalism.* Downers Grove, IL: InterVarsity, 2011.
Lewis, Scot. "William J. Seymour: Follower of the 'Evening Light.'" *Wesleyan Theological Journal* 39.2 (Fall 2004).
Nelson, Douglas J. *For Such a Time as This: The Story of Bishop William J. Seymour and the Azusa Street Revival, a Search for Pentecostal/Charismatic Roots.* PhD diss., University of Birmingham, 1981.
Tinney, James. "William J. Seymour: Father of Modern-Day Pentecostalism." In *Black Apostles: Afro-American Clergy Confront the Twentieth Century,* edited by Randall Burkett and Richard Newman. Boston: G.K. Hall, 1978.

Sharpton, Alfred Charles "Al" Jr. 1954–

The Prominent Civil Right activists, community organizer, politician and public media figure with ties to both the Pentecostal movement and the Baptist Church. Sharpton was born in Brooklyn, New York, and as a young man, he and his family attended famous Washington Temple **Church of God in Christ** in Brooklyn, New York where he sat under the ministry of politically active Bishop **Frederick D. Washington.**

Sharpton was baptized at age three, preached his first sermon there at the age of four, and by age seven, was touring with gospel singer Mahalia Jackson opening her musical performances with a sermon and becoming known as the "wonder boy preacher." He was ordained in COGIC at age ten by Bishop Washington, and soon became an evangelist whose charismatic style found him preaching at various Pentecostal congregations around Brooklyn. When Sharpton's father deserted his mother, leaving his formerly middle-class family in poverty, Sharpton used the love offerings he received from preaching to help support the family.

The young preacher eschewed the normal pastoral path designated for COGIC ministers, choosing rather to be involved in social activism. By 1969, at age fifteen, he had come under the tutelage of civil rights leader, Jesse Jackson, working for the New York City branch of Operation Breadbasket. At sixteen, Sharpton founded the National Youth

Movement Inc., which organized young people around the country to push for increased voter registration, cultural awareness, and job training programs

Sharpton first drew major national attention in 1987, when he defended fifteen-year-old Tawana Brawly, who alleged she had been abducted and assaulted by white policemen, though the grand jury ruled Brawley's accusations were unfounded. Twelve years later, Sharpton led a rally involving 1,200 people in a civil disobedience to protest the death Amadou Diallo, an unarmed, African immigrant, who was shot forty-one times and killed by four New York City police officers. In early 1991, Sharpton was stabbed by a white man while organizing a protest. At his attacker's trial, Sharpton forgave him, asking for lenience on his behalf.

Later that year, he created the National Action Network, a civil rights organization with over forty-five chapters and affiliates. In 1992 he ran for the Senate but lost in the primary election. Two years later, at age thirty-nine, Sharpton left the Pentecostal movement to affiliate with the Baptist Church because of disappointment in the level of Pentecostal engagement in social issues, and his conviction that aligning himself with the nation's largest Black Christian tradition would be a good tactical move for his political aspirations. Three years later, he ran for Mayor of New York City and in 2004, ran for the Democratic candidacy of the Presidency of the United States, losing both times.

After those defeats, Sharpton continued his social and political activism, but has turned his focus to public media. He began hosting a radio talk show, "Keepin' It Real," and is a frequent guest on national television venues such as Fox News, CNN, and MSNBC, which in 2011, named him host of their "PoliticsNation," a nightly talk show. He also continues to be highly visible as a spokesperson for much of the black community on social issues that arise within local communities and on the national front.

Further Reading:

Klein, Michael. *Man behind the Soundbites: The Real Story of the Rev. Al Sharpton.* New York: Carsillo International, 1991.

Sharpton, Al. *The Rejected Stone: Al Sharpton and the Path to American Leadership.* S.l.: Cash Money Content, 2013.

Sharpton, Al, and Anthony Walton. *Go and Tell Pharaoh: The Autobiography of the Reverend Al Sharpton.* New York: Doubleday, 1996.

Shelton, Omega Y. L. 1959–

Leader of one of the schismatic factions of **the Church of the Lord Jesus Christ of the Apostolic Faith**, who eventually took office of presiding bishop of the mother denomination. He was born Kenneth N. Thomas and legally became Kenneth Shelton when Bishop **S. McDowell Shelton** adopted him as the youngest of his children.

In 1976 Shelton was ordained an elder at age seventeen and given the spiritual name "Elder Omega Yediduth Limmud and is called "Bishop Omega." Shelton received his Bachelor of Arts degree in Political Science in 1982 from the American

College of Switzerland at Leysin. Two years later, he received his Master of Arts degree in Human Behavior and Political Science. In 1985 he earned an Alliance Français degree from École Schulz in Switzerland, and has a working knowledge of Spanish, Arabic, and Portuguese. In 1995, he returned to the American College of Switzerland, where he received an Honorary Doctor of Humane Letters for his outstanding accomplishments.

After the death of the elder Bishop Shelton in October 1991, Elder Omega became the spokesperson for his faction of the Church. Subsequently, after almost a decade of court battles, he won the right to become Bishop Omega, the third Bishop and General Overseer of the **Church of the Lord Jesus Christ of the Apostolic Faith.**

Like his predecessor, Shelton is revered by his followers and he continues the same lavish lifestyle. He is driven in a custom Rolls Royce, lives in a Philadelphia penthouse, sports expensive attire, and regularly takes evangelical "goodwill missions," trips around the globe, taking a group of aides with him. The Cherry Hill, New Jersey farm that was purchased by founder, **Sherrod Johnson**, during the Depression as a place for church members to grow food and a place of employment for families who could not find work elsewhere is the site of Omega's private dwelling, an Art Museum, and home of his Media home organization.

Shelton, Samuel McDowell 1929–1991

The second presiding Bishop and General Overseer of the Oneness Pentecostal denomination, the **Church of the Lord Jesus Christ of the Apostolic Faith.** The Philadelphia native was raised by his maternal grandparents. And, though little is known of his early life, he was probably born in Toledo, Ohio. He received his Bachelor of Arts in Sociology from Rutgers University, did graduate work at the University of Lisbon, Portugal, and was awarded an honorary Doctor of Divinity by Bethune-Cookman College, in Daytona Beach, Florida. He spoke six languages—English, German, Italian, French, Spanish, and Portuguese.

Prior to assuming leadership, Shelton had been prominent within the denomination and heavily involved in the initial development of its administrative structure for several years. He had served as former president of the National Young People's Department. At the time of Johnson's death, he was choir director. Nevertheless, that year, Shelton became Secretary General of the **Church of The Lord Jesus Christ of the Apostolic Faith.** His ordination as presiding bishop came more than a year after Johnson's death provoked lengthy court battles prompted from within the organization.

At the time of his assuming the position, he was thirty-three years old. For the next thirty years, Shelton led that denomination with the same rigid strictures put into place by Johnson. Yet, during his tenure, he also brought a greater degree of prominence to the organization, expanding the denomination's radio broadcast, "The Whole Truth," to several languages and broadcasting it in the United States, Canada, Europe, Asia, and Africa, with over sixty-two radio stations into the Caribbean, Europe, Africa, and India. On air, he carried on Johnson's tradition of contentious confrontation. Shelton was often heard to proclaim defiantly on his broadcast, "everybody can't be right." He also has been credited with bringing the church to a "debt-free" status, paying off enormous debt from investments made by the previous administration, and bringing a hint of respect to the denomination that was previously absent.

Within the Philadelphia area, outside of his local congregation, Shelton who followers referred to as "His Holy Apostolic Blessedness," was virtually unknown and fairly secretive. He rarely sought to publicize activities of the church, and granted few interviews. However, the world traveler is reported to have been granted audience with a myriad of global leaders, including heads of state such as King Hussein of Jordan, Emperor Haile Selassie of Ethiopia, Pope Paul VI at the Vatican in Rome, and Prime Minister Indira Gandhi of India.

A strong proponent of education and black self-help, he founded the Apostolic Institute in 1967, as well as the Apostolic Summer Youth Work program. In 1971 he built Apostolic Village, a thirty-two-unit independent living apartment complex for seniors, as a part of Apostolic square. Under Shelton's leadership, new churches were built in Newark, New Jersey, and Ellendale, Delaware. Other existing buildings and properties were purchased and renovated under his leadership.

Throughout his life, Shelton remained unmarried, and having no biological children, legally adopted individuals from within the denomination and groomed them for leadership. While the revered leader preached austerity to his followers, he chose a different lifestyle for himself. He lived in luxury, residing in opulent city penthouse apartments, driving luxury cars, wearing expensive clothes, eating the best food and drinking wine (which was a forbidden substance for regular members of the organization).

During the 1980s, Shelton's health began to fail and his travel schedule and personal appearances gradually declined. Shelton died in Philadelphia at age sixty-two in 1991, after a long battle with diabetes. After his death, a legal battle erupted among his adopted sons Elder Nehemiah Shelton and Bishop **Omega Shelton** over leadership succession and control over his assets.

Shields, Judge Pierce (J. P.) 1896-??

A former minister in the **Church of Our Lord Jesus Christ** who became the founding presiding bishop of Zion Assembly Churches in 1938 in the Jamaica Section of the Borough of Queens in New York City. That organization became the Zion Gospel Churches of the Apostolic Faith. Shields was born in Spring Hill, North Carolina. After serving in World War I, Shields migrated to New York City and located in Harlem by the early 1920s. By 1930 he was in the ministry and had relocated to the Jamaica area, and presumably, by then he was affiliated with the COOLJC. Not much is reported about his ministry except that he regularly advertised the congregation worship services in the African American periodical, *New York Age*, in the 1940s. In 1996 his son, Rev. Dr. Del P. Shields, a well-known entrepreneur in radio broadcasting left that arena to assume the pastorate of the Queens congregation.

Shiloh Apostolic Temple Church, Inc.

This Oneness Pentecostal denomination was founded by **Robert O. Doub Jr.** as a splinter group from the **Apostolic Church of Christ in God**. As a minister within the parent body, Doub established his first congregation in 1948 by preaching on the street corners of Philadelphia. He used that church as a home for conducting evangelistic campaigns and establishing other congregations throughout the community, first attempting to align the churches he had founded with the ACOG. After unsuccessfully seeking to be consecrated a bishop and not being able to work out an agreement, Doub, who was also dissatisfied with presiding bishop J. W. Aubrey's leadership, left the congregation.

His congregation became the mother church of local sponsored churches throughout the country, and Doub first attempted to align these congregations under his leadership with **Randolph A. Carr's** denomination, the **Church of God in Christ Jesus (Apostolic)**. When that merger did not materialize, he formed the Shiloh Apostolic Temple Church, Inc. in Philadelphia, Pennsylvania in 1953.

Doub's group quickly outgrew the body he left. By 1980, membership had grown to 4,500, and there were thirteen congregations in the United States, eight in Great Britain and two in Trinidad. By 1985 there were 7,500 member and 523 clergy serving 43 churches. Doub was killed in a car accident near Scranton, Pennsylvania in 1989.

Showell, Carolyn Denise 1952–

Prominent leader, educator, and conference speaker from the African-American Oneness Pentecostal tradition who has found wide acceptance within the broader Pentecostal/Charismatic realm. Showell was born in Baltimore, Maryland, into the second generation of a well-known Oneness Pentecostal dynasty. Her father, **Winfield Showell** (an early bishop in **Bible Way Church of Our Lord Jesus Christ**), her uncle, Joseph Marcelle (an early **Pentecostal Assemblies of the World** leader), and her brother, Cornelius Showell (former presiding bishop of International Bible Way Churches) have all made important contributions to the movement. Though she attends First Apostolic Faith Church in Baltimore—where her brother Bishop is the pastor and serves as a member of the Board of Presbyters—for most of her ministry, Showell has been ordained in the **Pentecostal Assemblies of the World**, where she served as president of "the Sacred College," the leadership development arm of the organization.

Showell is a certified licensed therapist and pastoral counselor, who holds bachelors of a arts degree from Goucher College in Towson, Maryland, a her Master of Divinity degree from Union Theological Seminary in New York, and a PhD in Counseling Psychology from the Carolina University of Theology. Further, she completed requirements for a second doctoral program in Jewish and Biblical studies at the Baltimore Hebrew University and the Advanced Studies Program in Psychology at Loyola University. She has served as the instructor of the Old Testament at Howard University (Washington DC) and Morgan State University.

Showell has founded and overseers organized Proposed Kingdom First Federal Credit Union and Kingdom Mortgage Company. She is founder and president of The Women's Institute of Lifelong Learning (The W.I.L.L.). She founded Transformed, Inc., a private Christian counseling practice and support service agency. In 1993, Dr. Showell served in several secular venues including as a consultant for AT&T in Racism and Cultural Diversity, a mental health specialist, a psychometrist for the Baltimore City Public School System, and a program and special projects developer for the Johns Hopkins School of Business and Administration.

In 1999 she was one of four finalists (out of 13,000) chosen for HUD's Community Builders Program. In 2001 and 2002, she served on the teaching staff of the Harvard University Summer Leadership Institute from which she received certification in Faith-based Economic Development and was selected as a member of the Steering Committee of the Black Alumni/ae Network of Harvard University Divinity School.

Showell, who is one of the most visible speakers on the African-American Pentecostal conference circuit, regularly speaks in settings as varied as women's and leadership conferences, national conclaves of denominational leaders, and ecumenical gatherings. She was consecrated as a Bishop in the Global United Fellowship under Bishop Neil C. Ellis, joining only a small group of women within any segment of the movement on whom that honor has been placed. Showell serves as one of four vice presiding bishops of the fellowship, overseeing the areas of Operational Programmatic Structuring, The Women's Department, Christian Education, and the Women's Protection Council.

Showell, Franklin Cornelius 1941–

Second presiding bishop of **International Bible Way Church of Jesus Christ, Inc.**, and pastor of First Apostolic Church in Baltimore, Maryland. Showell's great-uncle, Joseph Marcelle Turpin established the East Baltimore congregation in 1917 as one of the first Pentecostal congregations in the city. Showell's father, Bishop Winfield Amos Showell, one of the four founding Bishops of the Bible Way Churches Worldwide, took over in 1944, and in 1987, at his eightieth birthday celebration, named his son as senior pastor.

In the 1997 schismatic fracture over the failed succession agreement between bishops **Huie Rogers** and **Lawrence Campbell** after **Smallwood E. Williams'** death, Showell sided with Campbell and came to serve as his assistant presiding bishop. In 2002 Showell was consecrated to the Apostleship by the denomination's Executive Board. When Campbell retired in 2006, Showell was elected to preside over **Bible Way Church of Our Lord Jesus Christ**, moved the headquarters to his home congregation, and renamed the denomination International Bible Way Church of Jesus Christ, Inc.

As well as a leading Pentecostal pastor in Baltimore, Showell became a noted entrepreneur and business person involved in a successful mortuary business as well as real estate and business development and management for more than three decades. He also helped create more than 250 units of low-income and senior housing in impoverished Baltimore neighborhoods. More recently, as head of the church founded by his family, he helped set up an affiliated day care center.

Showell is an educator and a proponent of preserving black history. He has taught African American Religious Studies at Morgan State University, an historically black college, for a number of years and is founding executive director of the Commission on Negro History and Culture for the State of Maryland. His efforts helped bring AFRAM, Baltimore's highly acclaimed African American Heritage Festival into existence.

As presiding bishop, Showell continued the practice of ordaining women to the office of elder that Campbell introduced into the denomination and has personally ordained several women. Despite these overtures, his sister, Dr. **Carolyn Showell**, an educator and celebrated preacher who has a large following of black women and men inside and beyond the Pentecostal tradition and has been a long-time member of his congregation, was recently consecrated a bishop within the **Global United Fellowship** led by **Neil Ellis**.

Showell, Winfield Amos 1907–1988

A leader within the Oneness Pentecostal movement and one of the five founding bishops of the **Bible Way Churches of Our Lord Jesus Christ World Wide, Inc**. Showell was born in Frankford, Pennsylvania and raised on the Eastern Shore of Mayland. Before entering ministry, Winfield first completed two years of Morris College in Sumpter, South Carolina where he majored in Political Science with the ambition of becoming a lawyer. Then the accomplished saxophonist performed on Broadway and on the Boardwalk in Atlantic City, New Jersey for a short while.

Originally ordained in 1938 in the **Highway Christian Churches,** in 1940, he affiliated with the **Pentecostal Assemblies of the World** and attached himself to one of its congregations, First Apostolic Church, in Baltimore, Maryland, that was founded by his uncle, prominent PAW bishop **Joseph Marcelle Turpin**. Three years later in 1943, when Turpin died, Showell assumed the pastorate.

At some point Showell left PAW to join with **Robert Clarence Lawson's** denomination, **The Church of Our Lord Jesus Christ of the Apostolic Faith**. He remained with Lawson until 1957, when he responded to a call to join Smallwood Williams, along with McKinley Williams, Joseph Moore, and John S. Beane to form the Bible Way. He was appointed as diocesan bishop over an area that extended from Baltimore to the Philadelphia area and later as vice bishop of the denomination.

Showell served at the helm of First Apostolic Church for forty-three years and grew the congregation from a little more than two hundred members to well over one thousand, making it one of the most important African American Oneness Pentecostal congregations in the city. During his tenure, he started a radio broadcast in 1942 over which he was heard for more than forty years. He also built two high rise apartment complexes, and a 150-unit building for the elderly and disabled, and led the congregation in building two town-house projects for new homeowners, he set up a 22-acre youth camp.

Showell stayed with Williams' organization the rest of his life, and gained renown within Oneness circles for his preaching. Though the two men agreed on many areas of doctrine and polity, there was always a point of contention between them on the issue of ordination of women, with Showell taking the more liberal view.

In 1987 Showell turned the congregation over to his son, Cornelius, who later served a term as presiding bishop of International Bible Way Church of Jesus Christ, Inc., one of the two splinter groups that devolved from the parent body.

Sibley, Wallace Jerome 1938–

The highest ranking and most well-known African-American leader in the predominantly white, **Church of God (Cleveland, TN)** at the turn of the twenty-first century and the first to be elected to an international office or to serve on the Executive Council of that body.

The third-generation Church of God member was born and raised in St. Mary's, Georgia and became a Church of God minister in 1963. He is also one of the most educated blacks in the denomination, and attended Edward Waters College, where he received bachelor of science and master of education degrees from Florida A&M University, and a doctor of theology degree from Jacksonville Theological Seminary. As a pastor, he planted ten churches throughout Valdosta and Saint Mary's, Georgia and Jacksonville and Daytona Beach, Florida.

Among his many first for African Americans in the denomination, Sibley is the first to be elected Evangelism and Home Missions Assistant Director and Director, Executive Committee of the Church of God (Secretary General). He is also the first African American to be elected to the Executive Council of Eighteen and to the Executive Committee of the Church of God.

Sibley's national rise began on the regional level as Georgia state youth director for black congregations from 1965 until 1967. He then became youth and Christian education director for the Florida (Cocoa) region from 1971 until 1974, and Regional Evangelism Director for Southeast Black Churches from 1978 until 1982, and was Overseer of the Florida (Cocoa) jurisdiction from 1982 until 1986. He moved to the national level in 1986 serving for ten years on the General Board of Black Ministries Department, becoming chair in 1998 and serving in that position until 2000. While in that position, he also served as state overseer of the Southern New England jurisdiction from 1996 until 2000. As an overseer, he is credited with setting forth more than 150 churches and has preached at more than one hundred camp meetings and other events.

In 2004 Sibley was appointed director of Cross-Cultural Ministries and elected Assistant Director Evangelism and Home Missions, making him the first person of color to be elected to international office. Two years later, he was elected director of the office, a position he held until 2008, when he became the first black to be elected to the Executive Council as General Secretary. He was re-elected in 2012 as Third Assistant General Overseer. Due to tenure, he stepped down from the role in 2016.

His publications include *Evangelizing the Black Community,* published in 1984; *A Passion for Evangelism and Missions* and *Praying like Jesus,* both released in 2008; and his 2011 volume, *Prayer Changes People . . . People Change Things.*

Among his other honors, the Church of God's Pentecostal Theological Seminary inducted Sibley into their Hall of Prophets on July 12, 2012.

Skinner, Arthur Alfred (Arturo) 1924–1975

Founder and pastor of Deliverance Evangelistic Centers and a leading figure in the Deliverance wing of the Pentecostal movement. As a young man, his family lived in a heavily Jewish area of Brooklyn, New York and Skinner was able to easily learn Yiddish as a young age and to work as a translator for Jewish residents of his New York community who did not speak English. His father left the family to return to Barbados, and the fifteen-year-old dropped out of school to work to help maintain the household.

Though raised in a Christian home, the talented dancer began frequenting Harlem nightclubs and tap dancing on the street corners for coins. His talent soon landed him in Broadway musicals where he got involved in a lifestyle that including making and spending large sums of money, heavy drinking, and drug use.

After the death of his mother in 1952, twenty-eight-year-old Skinner considered suicide, but rather experienced a miraculous conversion. Afterward, he divested himself of the luxury items he had accumulated and entered the ministry. That same year, he was ordained an evangelist and soon began holding evangelistic services and tent meetings, and enrolled in the Bethel Bible Institute in Jamaica, Long Island, New York. After graduation, he continued preaching and within three years began a congregation in a local home, then moved to a storefront in Newark, New Jersey.

During the 1950s and 1960s Skinner was drawn to healing ministries being run by such people as healing evangelist William Brach. Soon Skinner became a black leader in this predominantly white movement. In 1957 he created the Deliverance Evangelistic Centers, Inc., Worldwide. In 1963 his ministry had grown to nearly 50 affiliated churches worldwide and Skinner was consecrated to the office of Apostle. By that time, his weekly "Supernatural Hour of Deliverance," radio broadcast reached over 20 million listeners and could be heard across the United States, Canada, Mexico, and the Caribbean. Skinner's "Deliverance Crusades," evangelistic and healing services were held around the world, drawing tens of thousands of people at a time. His *Deliverance Voice* magazine had a readership of 100,000.

Further Reading:

Lockwood, Lelia M. *When I Met the Master: The Story of Arturo Skinner.* S.l.: Park, 1976.
Blocker, James C. *Yours Because of Calvary.* S.l.: Xulon, 2012.

Slack, George Jr. 1893–1970

The second presiding bishop of the Church of God Congregational. Slack was born in Wilkinson, Mississippi. By 1930 he had relocated to East St. Louis, Illinois where he pastored for teaching that tithing was not a biblical principle. He joined the **Church of God in Christ Congregational,** a schismatic group that had broken from the parent body two years earlier, in objection to their episcopal polity. In 1945, when senior bishop, **Justus Bowe,** who had led the earlier break returned to COGIC, he had intended to bring the entire membership of the new body back with him. However, that proposal was rejected by the remaining leaders of the schismatic organization.

On Bowe's departure, George Slack became the senior bishop of the Church of God in Christ Congregational, serving in that position until his death in Illinois.

Smiley, Tavis 1964–

Prominent radio and television talk show host, political and social commentator, and philanthropist. The son of a single mother, Smiley was born in Gulfport, Mississippi, and grew up in Bunker Hill, Indiana. Later after his mother married his stepfather, the family moved to an all-white Indiana community, became involved in Pentecostalism, and attended New Bethel Tabernacle Church, a local congregation of the Oneness Pentecostal denomination, **Pentecostal Assemblies of the World,** where his mother became a Pentecostal minister. Smiley attributes his own later interest in mentoring young people, in part, to his attempt at emulating a Sunday School teacher within that congregation who mentored him.

During his time in college, he abandoned much of his Pentecostal teachings though he attended a storefront Pentecostal church for a while. On graduating, during the 1980s he worked as an aide to the first black Los Angeles mayor, Tom Bradley. Later, Smiley became the first African American to host his own syndicated talk show on National Public Radio.

At some point, after moving to Los Angeles, Smiley returned to the tradition, connecting with prominent pastor Noel Jones and his City of Refuge congregation. The relationship to this pastor and congregation became important enough to him that while working in Washington DC as host of a nightly Black Entertainment Television (BET) network talk show, Smiley retained his home in Los Angeles. He returned there every weekend to attend worship and seek spiritual counsel from Jones. When Smiley opened his new corporate Los Angeles headquarters, Jones was called on to bless it.

Smiley's philanthropic efforts have included numerous project, but chief among them has been his interest in the development of young black leaders. In its first sixteen years, the Tavis Smiley Foundation founded, which Smiley founded in 1999 as providing leadership training workshops and conferences for more than 6,000 young people. He has also given substantial support to institutions within the black community including The Smiley School of Communications and the Tavis Smiley Center for Professional Media Studies at the historically black, Texas Southern University in Houston.

Among his numerous honors, in 2009, Smiley was noted by *Time* magazine as being among "The World's 100 Most Influential People." In the same year, *Ebony* magazine named him among, the "Power 150: The Most Influential Blacks in America." A year earlier he received the WEB Du Bois Medal from Harvard University. He has also received six NAACP Image Awards for, "Best News, Talk or Information Series," in 1998, 1999, 2000, 2005, 2006, and 2007.

Further Reading:

Smiley, Tavis. *Keeping the Faith: Stories of Love, Courgae, Healing, and Hope from Black America.* New York: Doubleday, 2009.

Smiley, Tavis, and David Ritz. *What I Know for Sure: My Story of Growing Up in America.* New York: Doubleday, 2006.

Smith, Amanda Berry 1837–1915

African Methodist Episcopal lay preacher, Amanda Berry Smith, was among the most famous evangelist of the Holiness movement and addressed white camp meeting congregations at least as often as she did blacks.

The former slave was born in Long Green, Maryland, a small town in Baltimore County. After her father first purchased his freedom, he made it his mission to buy back his families. Though a slave, Smith had the advantage of learning to read and write. After her husband was killed in the American Civil War, she worked as a cook and a washerwoman to provide for herself and her daughter. In 1855 while Amanda was gravely ill, she dreamed that she was preaching at a camp meeting. She recovered miraculously from her illness and was converted not too long after that experience. When her second husband died in 1869, Smith began to preach and sing at holiness camp meetings. Becoming well-known for both of these talents.

In 1878 friends suggested she go to England to work with the churches there. While there, she made friends with Hannah Whitall Smith and Mary Broadman, opening an opportunity to attend the Keswick Conference for the Promotion of Higher Life, which furthered opened invitations to preach throughout the United Kingdom, and making her the first black woman to work as an international evangelist.

The next year, she was invited to India where she spent two years holding meetings in large cities such as Bombay and Calcutta, and numerous smaller towns and villages. Her ministry in India was curious not only because she was a woman minister within this highly male dominated culture, but as also as a black former slave within a highly stratified caste system. After returning to England, she traveled to Africa, where from 1881 through 1889, she ministered in churches and helped established temperance societies in Liberia and Sierra Leone.

Smith was never appointed by her AME Church, and her twelve years of missionary work was largely taken on by faith, with limited support from the Methodist Episcopal Church, supplemented by donations from friends and other supporters. While on the continent, Smith's work branched beyond preaching or leading temperance meetings. In addition, she was concerned with two causes: the status of women within the society and the need for education for Africa's children. She spent a great deal of her eight years on the continent attempting to ameliorate both. Her controversial work incurred criticism and strong opposition to her presence as a woman on the mission field and she suffered bouts of depression.

Smith remained in the AME Church throughout her life, though her relationships with individual congregations were often distant and the source of some of her harshest criticism. Nineteenth-century AME leaders criticized Smith for supporting Holiness teaching on sanctification, not contributing her gifts and talents to support the burgeoning AME women's effort in the Church, and focusing her attention on ministering to whites rather than to blacks.

After returning to the United States from her last missions trip, Smith concentrated her efforts of educating African-American children by founding the Amanda Smith Orphanage and Industrial Home for Abandoned and Destitute Colored Children in Harvey, Illinois in 1899. Despite relentless fundraising efforts, the school was never funded sufficiently. At the age of seventy-five, she left the school and moved to a home in Florida, where she passed away several years later.

Further Reading:

Smith, Amanda. *An Autobiography: The Story of the Lord's Dealings with Mrs. Amanda Smith, the Colored Evangelist: Containing an Account of Her Life Work of Faith, and Her Travels in America, England, Ireland, Scotland, India, and Africa as an Independent Missionary.* Chicago: Meyer & Brother, 1893.

Smith, Elias Dempsey ??–1920

The founder of the quasi-Pentecostal sect, **Triumph the Church and Kingdom of God**, had been an African Methodist Episcopal pastor in Issaquena County, Mississippi. Like others who were drawn to the Holiness movement, he sought what he felt was a deeper relationship with God than he had found possible in his Methodist setting.

As early as 1897, Smith reportedly had a vision from God prompting him to begin a new church. Five years later Smith traveled to New Orleans, Louisiana, where he organized his first congregation, Triumph the Righteous Church in 1902. In 1907 Smith joined forces with **Charles Harrison Mason**, founder of the **Churches of God in Christ** and for a short time, brought his congregation under Mason's organization. However, the relationship between the two was severed in 1912 when a schism occurred over Smith's teaching the doctrine of "Body Redemption," which Smith claimed was revealed to him by God. Further, while Mason was open to interracial cooperation, Smith distinguished the "church militant" of whites from, what he considered, the peace loving church of blacks. Finally, Smith rejected Mason's emphasis on speaking in tongues. After the break, he resumed leadership and reorganized Triumph the Holy Righteous Church.

Smith held the first National Congress was held in 1915. At this assembly, Smith was named, "Apostle, Priest and King," and the name of the church was changed to Triumph the Church and Kingdom of God in Christ. Smith chartered his body as denomination in 1918 in Washington DC. After World War I, he became enamored with Ethiopianism and Garvey's Back to Africa movement, and in 1919, he hosted the head of the Universal Negro Improvement Association at the denomination's international convention.

A year later, Smith and Prince J. D. Barbar sailed to Addis Ababa, Ethiopia which he referred to as Abyssinia. On his arrival, they were entertained by Empress Waizero Zandita and her nephew and co-ruler, Ras Tafari, and given a grand reception, including a lavish banquet. At a banquet that Smith threw for the rulers, he became ill and complained of stomach pains. The day after this elaborate ceremony, he died suddenly. After his death, leadership of the denomination shifted from one person to a board of seven bishops.

Smith, Francis Leonard 1915–1995

The sixth presiding bishop of the **Pentecostal Assemblies of the World** was born in Ironspot, Ohio, and raised by his grandparents, both of whom were Methodist ministers, who later adopted him and gave him their last name. In 1933, after serving the Methodist Church in several capacities, Smith attended a convention at the church pastored by his uncle, **Karl F. Smith**, received the Pentecostal Holy Spirit baptism, and was baptized in the Name of Jesus.

After a short stint as pastor in Springfield, Ohio, Smith became an instructor at PAW's **Aenon Bible College** in 1946. From 1951 to 1992, when he retired with the title pastor emeritus, he pastored the First Apostolic Church in Akron, Ohio. He was elevated to the Bishopric of the PAW in 1972 and appointed to the Southern Tri-State Council of Mississippi, Alabama and West Tennessee. That year, he began a two-year term as assistant presiding bishop of the organization under Ross Paddock, and became chair of the Board of Los Angeles extension of the college. In 1974 Smith became presiding bishop, serving two three-year terms before leaving that office in 1980. Following that, in 1989, he was appointed to the Third Episcopal Diocese in his home state of Ohio and served until the end of his life.

Smith, Helen 1929–1999

Oneness Pentecostal presiding founder of the **Cainhoy Miracle Revival Corporation**. Apostle Helen Smith was born in Beaufort, South Carolina, where she received her formal education in the public schools.

Helen was first converted to Christian faith in 1944. She contracted tuberculosis for three years from 1947 through 1949, was confined to the Pine Haven Sanatorium in Charleston, South Carolina. Each Christmas season of these three years she had visions, of a church but it had not entered her mind that these visions would have such an enormous impact on the work God had assigned to her hands.

After thirteen major operations in six years, she was healed but did not come to back to Christian faith until 1957, when she became a member of the Church of Our Lord Jesus Christ of the Apostolic Faith. Eleven years later, she sensed a call to preach.

In 1968 she began with a small group in the home of Mother Moriah Howard of Cainhoy, South Carolina. The revival spread quickly and soon the home was outgrown and the group relocated to a small shack in the same town. Since COOLJC did not acknowledge that God called women to preach, she was asked to stop the revival. When she refused, she and eleven others were excommunicated from the Church.

In 1969 Smith was ordained as the Apostle of the Cainhoy Miracle Revival Center, and used and evangelistic team to hold revivals in other cities. By the time of her death, Smith established fifteen churches.

Smith wrote four books: *You're Going to Be Somebody*; *In Case you Miss the Rapture*; *Can A Christian be Demon Possesses*; and *The Two Us and a Company of Angels*.

Further Reading:

Smith, Helen. *You're Going to Be Somebody*. Mobile, AL: Gazelle, 1999.

Smith, Horace E. 1950–

A physician, Oneness Pentecostal pastor, and former presiding bishop of the **Pentecostal Assemblies of the World**. Smith was baptized and received the gift of the Holy Ghost at seventeen. He earned his bachelor of science degree from Chicago State University, and his medical degree from the University of Illinois medical center, then completed a pediatric residency at the University of Illinois Hospital, before undertaking a clinical fellowship in pediatric hematology and oncology at Children's Medical Hospital of Northwestern University in Evanston, Illinois. Smith serves as director of the Comprehensive Sickle Cell/Thalassemia Program at Children's Memorial Hospital, and an assistant professor of pediatrics at Northwestern Feinberg School of Medicine.

Smith was born and raised in Chicago by parents who migrated from the South. His mother died when he was ten and his father was a Chicago police officer for decades. He was raised in the **Pentecostal Assemblies of the World**. In the 1970s Smith served as assistant pastor to prominent PAW bishop, **John S. Holly** who encouraged him to complete his medical studies. In 1980 following Holly's death, Smith became pastor of the Apostolic Faith Church in Chicago, Illinois and has led that congregation from 200 members to its present membership of 3,000. Simultaneously with his involvement in the medical field, Smith emerged as a leader within the **Pentecostal Assemblies of the World**. Appointed a District Elder of PAW's Illinois District Council in 1983; he served as chair from 1986 until 1991. In 1989 he was appointed to the board of Aenon Bible College.

Five years later he was consecrated a Suffragan Bishop and served as General Secretary of the denomination from 1996 until 1997. Smith was elevated to the office of full bishop in 1997. The next year, Smith was installed as Diocesan Bishop of the 14th Episcopal District that includes Kansas, Colorado and Western Missouri. In 2004 Bishop Smith was elected presiding bishop of the **Pentecostal Assemblies of the World**, Inc. He served until 2010, when Charles H. Ellis III of Detroit succeeded him.

Further Reading:

Poinsett, Alex. "The Ministry of the Rev. Horace E. Smith, M.D.: Healing Bodies and Souls." *Ebony Magazine* 46.6 (1999) 1.

Smith, Karl Franklin 1892–1972

The prominent educator, Bible scholar, pastor, and high-ranking leader in three Oneness Pentecostal denominations. Smith was born in Zanesville, Ohio to parents who were both African Methodist Episcopal Church ministers. He was the great grandson of Thomas Jefferson, third president of the United States and his black mistress, Salley Hennings. As a toddler, Smith survived a bout of scarlet fever, a disease, which at the time was often incurable.

Around 1912 Smith was converted to Christian faith in a revival service conducted by his mother. Shortly afterward, he accepted the call to ministry, and soon thereafter, enrolled at Payne Theological Seminary of Wilberforce University in Ohio. While there, Smith accepted a temporary pastorate of a small AME mission church in Columbus, Ohio. Six months later, he was introduced to Oneness Pentecostal doctrine by a former member of his congregation who had converted to the tradition. Tough he initially rejected, he secretly searched Scriptures to learn more it. In 1915 Smith had a change of heart. He was baptized in Jesus' name, sought and received the Pentecostal Spirit baptism and was ordained an elder in the **Pentecostal Assemblies of the World**.

Around 1916 Smith had permanently settled in Columbus, Ohio where he began attending PAW founder **Robert Clarence Lawson's** congregation, and soon became the assistant pastor to Lawson. For several years, he resided in Lawson's home, and in 1919, when Lawson left to evangelize in New York, Smith stepped into the pastorate. After Lawson founded his new body, the **Church of Our Lord Jesus Christ of the Apostolic Faith**, Smith soon followed him into his new work, and in 1920, Lawson appointed him as the first general secretary of the organization.

Five years later, however, the two men disagreed over the issue of divorce and remarriage, and the argument grew to the point that Smith broke with his former mentor and, within two years, had returned to the **Pentecostal Assemblies of the World** for the first time. Refusing to relinquish Lawson former's church back to him, Smith took the congregation with him into PAW. On returning to PAW, he was elected general secretary and was appointed to the founding committee of PAW's National Sunday School Association.

Following Haywood's death in 1931, Smith was among those ministers from PAW who joined with the Pentecostal Assemblies of Jesus Christ in attempt to form a larger interracial body, and became general secretary of foreign missions of that body. When that merger failed because of lingering attitudes that disparaged equal treatment of the races, Smith was among the majority of blacks who returned to PAW for the second time.

In 1940 he was elected to the bishopric. That same year, he and LaBaugh H. Stansbury, established Pentecostal Bible Training Center (which began **Aenon Bible College**).

Initially, with the first classes being held in his home church. By 1950, he had developed a four-year curriculum. But he found it harder to develop support for the institution among his PAW clergy colleagues who had yet to see the value in an educated clergy.

In the mid-1950s, Smith served for a short period as interim bishop of the Northwestern District Council, Inc. 14th Episcopal Diocese, which, at the time, included Minnesota, Colorado, Iowa, Kansas and Missouri. He had a far-reaching radio ministry, which he used to help bring the church he inherited from Lawson and led for a half century from a congregation of twenty to over fifteen hundred.

Further Reading:

Golder, Morris. *The Bishops of the Pentecostal Assemblies of the World.* Indianapolis, IN: s.n., 1980.

Smith, Lucinda Madden (Lucy) 1874–1952

Lucy Smith typifies many who came to the urban North during the Great Migration. She was born on a plantation in rural Woodstock, Georgia. Her impoverished family, which consisted of her mother and five siblings, lived in a one-room log cabin.

In 1896 Lucy married William Smith, and the couple moved to a nearby farm, where in 1898 the couple had their first of nine children. In 1908 the family moved from Woodstock to Athens, Georgia. By 1910, her husband William had abandoned the family and Lucy moved with her children first to Atlanta, then to Chicago where she worked as a seamstress. William at first remained in Athens, but later rejoined the family and stayed with them in Chicago until his death in 1938.

Smith, who had been Baptist since she was twelve years old, at first attended Olivet Baptist Church, but, like many other new immigrants, found the subdued worship of the large black congregation sterile and uninviting. By 1914 Smith found a temporary spiritual home at Stone Church, the predominantly white congregation founded in 1906 by Dowie's associate, William Piper. Here, Smith experienced the baptism of the Holy Spirit and her call to the "work of the Lord."

In 1916 she began holding prayer and faith healing services in her one-room apartment on the city's South Side with a small group of women. From that residence, Smith reached out to many in need, including the homeless and many who had newly arrived to Chicago from the South. She provided them with temporary shelter, food, and other assistance. From this initial outreach, Smith's ministry grew enough that she organized it into a congregation.

In 1925 her Sunday night worship services broadcast over local radio station WSBC, making Smith the first black religious leader to broadcast services. The broadcast was heard across the United States in the 1940s. In 1933 she added a Wednesday evening broadcast "The Glorious Church of the Air," that played gospel music and made appeals for the poor.

Smith was the first black woman to pastor a major congregation in Chicago. During thirty-six years of ministry, she claimed to have been used in the healing of more than 200,000 people, and maintained a "trophy room" in the basement of All Nation's Church to display the medical paraphernalia discarded by those healed through her ministry.

During the Depression, the largely uneducated and self-taught Smith formed alliances with prominent businessmen to garner their aid in carrying out a substantial outreach ministry throughout Chicago's South Side and become the first African-American pastor in Chicago to regularly distribute food and clothing without regard to race. Smith also formed alliances with other black churches in the Bronzeville section of Chicago despite the fact that several pastors in that area had significance opposition to women's ministry and leadership.

At the time of Smith's death, her congregation of nearly 5,000 members was one of the South Side's most influential congregations. Her funeral was one of the largest held in Chicago up to that time, as 60,000 people viewed her body and 50,000 lined the streets for the processional.

Further Reading:

Best, Wallace. *Passionately Human, No Less Divine: Religion and Culture in Black Chicago, 1915–1952*. Princeton, NJ: Princeton University Press, 2005.

Smith, Utah 1906–1965

An evangelist and gospel performer who recorded from the 1940s to 1960s and founded the Two Wing Temple **Church of God in Christ** in New Orleans, Louisiana. He was best known, however, for holding lively revival meetings, many of which were covered in the pages of the *Louisiana Weekly* newspaper. He was fairly famous in and around New Orleans, but toured from coast to coast with his singing, evangelistic ministry.

Smith was born in poverty in Cedar Grove, Louisiana, near Shreveport. He was deserted as a boy by his mother, and raised by a grandmother. He never got beyond the third grade, but took a job as a water boy in the cotton fields as a youth. He later worked in a chicken plant plucking and cleaning chickens. As a teenager, he had taken up harmonica then switched to a steel guitar, and finally an electric guitar, which he was using in his revival meetings by 1938.

By 1923 Smith felt called to become an evangelist in the **Church of God In Christ**. He was married in 1929 and set up a home in Shreveport, but had been on the road since 1925 where he would spend most of the next forty years.

Smith was one of the first black persons to have a radio broadcast in New Orleans on WJBW. He made three commercial recordings, that were issued on at least six different labels, three of which were versions of his theme song—"I Want Two Wings." In the

1950s, he toured with major gospel recording artists such as Mahalia Jackson, the Bells of Joy, and Joe May. By the time of his death, Smith, who suffered from diabetes and glaucoma, was blind and no longer able to play his guitar.

Further Reading:

Abbott, Lynn. *I Got Two Wings: Incidents and Anecdotes of the Two Winged Preacher and Electric Guitar Evangelist Elder Utah Smith*. Montgomery, AL: Case Quarter, 2008.

Smith, Willie Mae Ford 1904–1994

A prominent gospel singer and evangelist, first in the Baptist Church, and later, in the **Church of God Apostolic**. In the 1920s and 1930s, "Mother Smith," as she known, was among the first gospel singers to perform in Thomas A. Dorsey's blues-influenced gospel style.

Smith was born Willie Mae Ford, into a strict Baptist family in Rolling Fork, Mississippi. By age twelve, her father, a deacon and railroad brakeman had relocated the family first to Memphis, Tennessee, and later in 1918 to St. Louis, Missouri. Her early education was piecemeal and she quit school in the eighth-grade to help in her mother's restaurant while singing with family quartet, the Ford Sisters, until after her 1927 marriage, when she began the solo career that launched her into public view.

In 1926 Smith was ordained in the Baptist church, but prejudice against women in ministry in that denomination kept her from fully pursuing a preaching career. A high soprano, she considered pursuing classical music, but began touring to supplement her family's income. She, like her colleague, the legendary **Sallie Martin**, was among the first gospel performers to tour extensively to conduct musical revivals. In her travels, Smith crossed paths with Dorsey. In 1932 she helped him and Martin form the National Convention of Gospel Choirs and became the director of the convention's Soloist's Bureau until the late 1980s. She later formed a St. Louis chapter, and was the longtime head of the soloists' bureau. Smith left the Baptist Church in 1939, and joined the **Church of God Apostolic**.

Smith, who rarely recorded, made her first record in 1950 and later recorded for the Nashboro, Savoy, and Spirit Feel labels. Though by the early 1950s, she had turned to evangelistic work, in 1972, she began receiving national recognition after appearing at the Newport Jazz Festival. She appeared in the 1981 gospel documentary film *Say Amen, Somebody*, and received a National Heritage Award from the National Endowment for the Arts in 1988. Smith continued to perform regularly at the Lively Stone Apostolic Church in St. Louis until the early 1990s.

Further Reading:

Dargan, William Thomas, and Kathy White Bullock. "Willie Mae Ford Smith of St. Louis: A Shaping Influence upon Black Gospel Singing Style." *Black Music Research Journal* 9.2 (1989) 249–70.

Smith, Zollie Lennon Jr. 1949–

The first African American to serve on the executive leadership team of the Assemblies of God, which includes the general superintendent, assistant general superintendent, general secretary, general treasurer, and the executive director of Assemblies of God world missions. Smith is executive director of Assemblies of God US Missions, which oversees the national departments responsible for church planting, chaplaincy ministries, Teen Challenge, Chi Alpha Campus Ministries, intercultural ministries, Youth Alive, and the U.S. Mission America Placement Service. More than 1,000 missionaries, 500 chaplains, and 5,000 related field personnel minister under the direction of Assemblies of God U.S. Missions. He was elected to that position at the 52nd meeting of the General Council of the Assemblies of God in 2007.

Smith was ordained in the Assemblies of God in 1986, and served as Executive Presbyter representing the denomination's ethnic fellowships. He also served as president of the **National Black Fellowship**, an organization of African American Assemblies of God churches and ministers. He was the Assistant Superintendent of the New Jersey District Council of the Assemblies of God from 1998–2005, and served as Executive Secretary of the district from 2005–2007. Smith was the pastor of Eternal Life Christian Center of the Assemblies of God in Somerset, New Jersey for fifteen years. During his pastorate, church attendance exceeded three hundred, and the congregation completed an educational enrichment center valued over $2.5 million.

Smith grew up in the **Church of God in Christ** and received the Baptism of the Holy Spirit when he was fourteen. He was awarded the Bronze Star and the Purple Heart for his military service in the airborne infantry during the Vietnam War. He earned a bachelor's degree in criminology from Florida State University and holds the master's degree in business management from Regents University. In addition to his ministerial service, he was a police officer, detective, and U.S. Postal Service Inspector.

Sought Out Church of God in Christ

A Trinitarian Pentecostal denomination founded in 1947 in Brunswick, Georgia, by "Mother" **Mozella Cook**, a former Baptist who later affiliated with the **Church of God in Christ**. Two years after its founding, the denomination had four congregations and sixty members, and probably grew no larger than that figure. Despite these small numbers, however, it is significant because it represents one of the earliest denominations to splinter from the Church of God in Christ and the first organization formed out of COGIC specifically to give women the opportunity for full denominational leadership.

The full name of the group is The Sought Out Church of God in Christ and Spiritual House of Prayer, Inc. At least one congregation remains in Sylvania, Georgia that is pastored by Mattie Green.

Soul Saving Station for Every Nation

Soul Saving Station for Every Nation, Christ Crusaders of America began in 1940 through a revival in a mission church in Harlem, New York under Seattle, Washington evangelist Billy Roberts, who had been converted to Christian faith from a life of drugs and street crime. Following the meeting in which several people were converted and received Pentecostal Spirit baptism, Roberts launched a radio ministry, tent meetings, and prison ministries which led to the founding of the first congregation of the Soul Saving Station in Buffalo, New York with nine members. Roberts led the denomination until his death in 1958. Roberts was instrumental in launching other congregations throughout the Northeast using the same techniques he had employed in Buffalo.

At Roberts's death, Jesse Winley assumed leadership of the organization, serving as the second presiding bishop until his death. Winley was instrumental in leading the church into a member of the **Pentecostal and Charismatic Churches of North America**. Founded an orphanage in Haiti. At Winley's death, Alvin L. Tate assumed the office. He was followed by Richard S. Watkins, then Jesse Winley's grandson, Robert I. Winley.

In 1973 the organization, which is an association of autonomous churches who share the same beliefs, began negotiations to enter a loose affiliation with the white Pentecostal Holiness Church. Today, the organization has more than twenty congregations and a reported membership of approximately 5,000 in major cities along the East Coast and in the Midwest. Today, it is led by Arvell Garrett Sr.

Further Reading:

Roberts, Billy. *Out of Crime, Into Christ.* New York: Billy Roberts, s.d.
Winley, Jesse. *Jesse.* New Kensington, PA: Whitaker, 1976.

Spellman, Robert Clarence 1942–

The pastor, educator, author, and historian within the **Church of Our Lord Jesus Christ of the Apostolic Faith** and president of the denomination's **Church of Christ Bible Institute**. His father, Bishop Harry Spellman was National Sunday School Superintendent for the denomination; his mother had been raised by **Robert C. Lawson** and his wife, and young Spellman was named after the COOLJC founder.

In 2007 Spellman was consecrated as a bishop in the Church Of Our Lord Jesus Christ. Currently, Spellman is pastor of Macedonia Church of Our Lord Jesus Christ in Newark, New Jersey, and a senior professor at Essex County College, where he teaches humanities and formerly served as Associate Dean of Instruction, Dean Community Programs, and Vice President for Academic Affairs/Chief Academic Officer. Since 1975 he has served as President of the **Bible Institute** established in 1926 by the late Bishop **R. C. Lawson** and has also taught at New York Theological Seminary and the **W. L. Bonner College** in Columbia, South Carolina.

Spellman earned his bachelor of arts degree from Virginia State University, a master of arts degree from Rutgers University in New Jersey and a Doctor of Philosophy, PhD, from New York University in Fine Arts Education and the Administration of Higher Education.

As the COOLJC historian and editor of the *Contender for the Faith* magazine, the official international COOLJC publication, and expert on black Oneness Pentecostalism, Spellman regularly contributes articles and presentations on black and Oneness Pentecostalism. In 1983 he published his definitive biography of the COOLJC founder entitled, *The Life, Legend and Legacy of Bishop R. C. Lawson,* and wrote the Pentecostal Apostolic Section of the *Encyclopedia of African American Religious History*. Spellman He has made several presentations to predominantly white Pentecostal bodies such as the United Pentecostal Church International and the Society for Pentecostal Studies, as well as for the Schomburg Center for Research in Black Culture in Harlem.

Spencer, Herbert Joseph 1901–1974

The second presiding bishop of the **Church of Our Lord Jesus Christ of the Apostolic Faith** was born in Marytown, West Virginia. He was raised in the Baptist Church and converted to Christian faith as a boy of nine at Rockville Baptist Church in Gary, West Virginia. By age seventeen, he had transitioned into the Pentecostal movement and had a Pentecostal Holy Spirit baptism experience and a call to ministry. Prior to joining COOLJC, Spencer had been a presbyter within the **Pentecostal Assemblies of the World**.

As a young preacher, Spencer became friends with another young minister, **Smallwood E. Williams,** who was at that time a member of COOLJC and would later go on to become founder of **Bible Way Church of the Lord Jesus Christ World Wide, Inc.** Williams introduced him to Oneness doctrine, Spencer was rebaptized in Jesus' name and joined the denomination, and the two men would remain friends for life and cooperate on a number of ventures.

Spencer began his ministry in COOLJC as a traveling evangelist with Lawson. He also pastored several small churches including a congregation in Cleveland, Ohio. In 1925 a schism developed between Lawson and his assistant pastor, **Karl F. Smith,** who returned Lawson's Columbus, Ohio congregation to PAW. Lawson established a new congregation, Rehoboth Church of Christ, and placed Spencer at its head. In 1928 Lawson appointed him as one of the original bishops of COOLJC. Reportedly, however, after 1940 disagreement between Lawson and Spencer, the younger man vacated the property and chartered a new church under the name, "Rehoboth Temple Church of Christ," while remained in fellowship with Lawson.

After Lawson's death, the denomination established three-man board of apostles and elected Spencer, Maurice Hutner, and **William Lee Bonner** elected to fill those positions. Spencer was unanimously elected as presiding bishop and held that post from 1961 until 1973. He died a year later, and Bonner assumed the position.

Spirit: Journal Incident to African American Pentecostalism

The only semi-annual periodical dedicated to scholarly research related to African American Pentecostalism. The publication was founded and edited by **James S. Tinney**, a political scientist who was an assistant professor of journalism at Howard University and was affiliated with the Church of God in Christ.

It was published between 1977 and 1979 in Washington DC and there were only seven volumes of the journal published before the effort was disbanded. Yet even so, some of the major figures related to the study of African-American religion contributed articles including Tinney himself, and **James A. Forbes Jr.**, a **United Holy Church** minister who taught preaching at Union Theological Seminary in New York, but would go on to become senior minister of the prestigious Riverside Church in Harlem. There were also articles from **Herbert Daughtry**, presiding Bishop of the **House of the Lord and Church on the Rock, Pearl-Williams Jones,** a musicologist who was the daughter of **Smallwood E. Williams** of **Bible Way Church of Our Lord Jesus Christ World Wide** and educator and civil rights spokesperson, **Bennie Goodwin**. Further, along with dealing with such mundane issues as black Pentecostal history and worship, the journal addressed controversial topics such as women in role of women in ministry and leadership within the tradition. Moreover, it was cutting edge in that it dealt with issues that many Pentecostal leaders of that era shunned, including the topic of homosexuality with the Pentecostal community. The next to the last issue, volume 3.1, featured an annotated bibliography on Black Pentecostalism that had been compiled by Tinney.

Spooner, Kenneth E. M. (K. E. M.) 1884–1937

One of the earliest Pentecostal Holiness Church missionaries to Africa. Spooner, who was originally from in Barbados, British West Indies was born into an Anglican family. While in New York City in 1906, he felt called to go as a missionary to Africa when two women on two separate occasions approached him to tell him that God had called him to that continent. Spooner visited the **Azusa Street Revival** in 1909 after a series of miracles helped the Spooners clear their debts and pay for the trip, and became one of the Pentecostal Holiness Church's most effective missionaries in Africa.

The couple arrived in Africa in 1915. In 1922 Spooner began working with another missionary, Mr. Rhodes, and native workers to organize the South Africa Conference of the Pentecostal Holiness Church. He was elected Assistant Superintendent and served from that time until his death. While on the continent, Spooner worked among the Tswana people of Botswana, building a complex of sixty churches and schools out of a mission located near the town of Rustenburg, which was a platinum-mining and farming community, from 1913 until his death. At his death, John W. Brooks, a white missionary from Falcon, North Carolina, took his post. His wife, Geraldine, a native of Central America, however, remained in Africa until her death in 1990s.

Further Reading:

Spooner, Kenneth E. M. et al. *Sketches of the Life of K.E.M. Spooner*. Franklin Springs, GA: Pentecostal Holiness Publishing, 1940.

Stallings, George Augustus 1948–

The charismatic and controversial priest who pioneered neo-Pentecostal worship within the African-American Roman Catholic community before leaving the traditional church to form his own body, **African American Catholic Congregation**. His early training for the priesthood began at Asheville Catholic High School and even there he displayed a defiant attitude toward traditional rules, defying a bishop's order to shave off his mustache, insisting that it was part of his black identity.

A native of New Bern, North Carolina, Stallings attended St. Pius X Seminary in Kentucky, where he received a Bachelor of Arts degree in philosophy in 1970. Sent by his bishop to the Pontifical North American College in Rome, he earned three degrees from the Pontifical University of Saint Thomas Aquinas between 1970 and 1975: the Bachelor of Sacred Theology (STB), a master's degree in pastoral theology, and a Licentiate of Sacred Theology (STL).

After being ordained a priest in 1974, Stallings's first assignment was as associate pastor at Our Lady of Queen of Peace Church, an inner city Washington DC congregation that had a predominantly African American constituency. In 1976 at the age twenty-eight and just two years after ordination, he was named pastor of St. Teresa of Avila parish in one of the poorest sections of inner city, Washington, a position he held for fourteen years. During Stallings's pastorate, the parish became known for integrating African-American culture and gospel music in the traditional Mass. It also became known for its enthusiastic worship featuring a crucifix with a black Christ, a full-immersion baptismal font and a gospel choir within what became a three-hour mass. Its highly charismatic ritual drew former Catholics back to the church and enticed Protestants to explore Catholic worship, increasing St. Teresa's membership tenfold—from 200 to 2,000 parishioners.

Though in 1988 he was named to a new position as a diocesan evangelist, Stallings's spirituality drew concern from the Washington diocese, especially in his defiant attitude toward James Cardinal Hickey. In July 1989 Stallings established "Imani Temple," as an independent congregation. His first mass drew an estimated 2,300 people. A year later, Stallings founded a new denomination, the African-American Catholic Congregation. He was consecrated bishop of that body by Richard Bridges of the Independent Old Catholic Church—another breakaway denomination. By renouncing the authority of the Archbishop of Washington, Stallings was deemed to have broken canonical law regarding causing schism in the Roman Catholic Church. In response, the Archbishop of Washington, Cardinal James Hickey, concluded that Stallings had excommunicated himself from the Church in 1990. That same year, Stallings was consecrated as an independent Catholic bishop and adopted the title of "Archbishop."

In 2001 the fifty-three-year-old Stallings married twenty-four-year-old Sayomi Kamimoto in a mass wedding performed by the Unification Church's Rev. Sun Myung Moon. In 2006 the excommunicated former Catholic Archbishop Emmanuel Milingo performed a conditional consecration for Stallings and three other married independent Catholic bishops at the Imani Temple church in Washington.

By that same time, Stallings had become a highly visible fixture in the Washington community. His run for city council, though unsuccessful, included a highly publicized campaign. He is active in the Middle East Peace Initiative, promoting conflict resolution between Israeli Jews and Palestinian Muslims; serves on the Executive Board of the American Clergy Leadership Conference, an inter-religious and interracial coalition; and is president and CEO of SKS Press, a publishing company in Suitland, Maryland.

Further Reading:

Cramer, Jerome, and Richard Ostling. "Religion: Catholicism's Black Maverick." *Time Magazine,* May 14, 1990.

D'Apolito, Rosemary Ann. *An Analysis of African American Catholic Congregation: As a Social Movement.* PhD diss., University of Chicago, 1996.

Utietiang, Bekeh Ukelina. "Issues in the History and Development of the African American Catholic Church: A Study of Archbishop George Augustus Stallings, Jr." Unpublished manuscript.

Stevens, Amy Johnson Bell 1912–2000

As president and senior bishop of the **Mt. Sinai Holy Church of America**, Inc. from 1983 to 2000, Stevens was the fourth woman to successively hold that position. Elected to the post at age seventy-one she served until her death; like the women who preceded her, she had previously served in a number of increasingly responsible roles within the denomination.

In 1920 she was converted while still a young girl at the Union Grove Methodist Church in Hurlock, Maryland, where her family worshipped. In 1932, she received the Pentecostal baptism of the Holy Spirit at Mount Olive Holy Church where **Mt. Sinai Holy Church** founder Bishop **Ida Robinson** was the pastor.

Stevens worked closely with Mt. Sinai founder **Ida Robinson** both in the church and personally. In the church she served in several capacities including usher and Sunday school teacher. Outside the church, she worked as Robinson's personal nurse until her death in 1946. In return, Robinson mentored her, recognized her evangelistic ability and sent her on an extensive evangelistic tour in 1940 that began in Blackstone, Virginia. In 1941, Stevens returned to Hurlock, Maryland, and founded a Mount Sinai Holy Church congregation. Over the next several years, she ministered to communities from Boston, Massachusetts to Tallahassee, Florida.

Stevens was married three times. She married James Fuller Bell, presumably a relative of the founder, in 1932; he died in 1940. Twenty-five years later, in 1965, she married Minister Samuel Ray, who worked closely with her in ministry until his death. She became stepmother to his nine children. Then in 1973, she married Bishop Charles Stevens, who also preceded her in death.

In addition to the congregation she founded, Stevens held three pastorates within Mt. Sinai. In 1950 she was appointed pastor of Mount Nebo Holy Church in Mount Holly, New Jersey. In 1965 she was appointed pastor of Bethel Pentecostal Church in Wilmington, Delaware, where she remained for twenty-five years. After the death of Bishop Sylvester Webb in 1991, Bishop Stevens became the pastor of Mount Olive Holy Temple in Philadelphia, the mother church of the denomination, where she died nine years later.

In the interim, in 1962, while serving as the Secretary to the Board of Directors, Stevens became presiding elder of the Pennsylvania-New Jersey Diocese of Mount Sinai Holy Church of America, Inc. In 1970 **Mary E. Jackson**, who was then the senior bishop, consecrated her a bishop, and after the death of Bishop Annie B. Chamberlin in 1977, Stevens became the vice president of Mount Sinai, working with the presider until her death in 1983. Within that year, Stevens assumed the post as president. Under her administration, the denomination experienced structural growth. The Mount Sinai Training Institute was established, the ministry of Mount Sinai Farm was expanded, and new churches were added. Stevens' work saw her traveling and ministering to Mount Sinai's churches in Guyana and Cuba and supporting Mount Sinai's missionary endeavors in those countries as well as in India.

In 1984 Stevens along with Mt. Sinai Bishop, James F. Brown Jr., **Bishop James O. Patterson,** Bishop Joseph T Bowen of **United Holy Church of America,** and Bishop **J. Delano Ellis** of the **Pentecostal Church of Christ,** founded the **International Fellowship of Black Pentecostal Churche**s in Memphis, Tennessee.

Stevens's honors and awards include an Honorary Doctorate of Theology degree from Christian Bible Institute and Seminary. When she died at age eighty-eight in Winter Haven, Florida, she was the last president to have been with the founder.

Stokes, Cleveland H. 1887–1966

Co-founder and first General Secretary of the **Glorious Church of God in Christ** who left that organization to co-found the **Original Glorious Church of God in Christ.** Stokes was born in Cannellton, West Virginia, and previously had been a minister in **Triumph the Church and Kingdom of God**. In 1921 he moved to Eversville, West Virginia, where he worked as a coal miner and pastored a small Trinitarian house congregation, which he had named **Glorious Church of God in Christ**. That year, when the Triumph the Church congregations under the oversight of **Lulu Phillips** broke to form a new body, Stokes left with her. The group then adopted the name Stokes had coined, and subsequently adopted the Oneness Pentecostal understanding. Stokes, along with the group members, submitted himself for rebaptism. By the time of the separation, Stokes had been consecrated a bishop. After the new body formed, he was appointed to chair the West Virginia state board.

On Phillips's death in 1939, General Secretary **Sidney Coy Bass was elevated to p**residing bishop. When Bass married a divorced woman against church polity a decade and half later, Stokes joined **W. O. Howard** in resigning from the organization. They formed the **Original Glorious Church of God in Christ**. It is unclear what role Stokes served in the later body. He was possibly a bishop, but he preceded Howard in death so never served in the lead post.

T

Tate, Mary Magdalena Bell Street Lewis 1871–1930

Founder and presider of the **Church of the Living God the Pillar and Ground of the Truth**, the parent body of more than six schismatic groups that would form within the Pentecostal movement during the twentieth century. Tate was born in Vanleer, Tennessee. She spent most of her early life in the rural South with little opportunity to obtain a formal education and married her first husband, David Lewis, at age nineteen. The couple had two sons, **Walter Curtis Lewis** and **Felix Early Lewis**, both of whom would join her in ministry at early ages. By the time she married Robert Tate in 1914, she had been married twice before, and, before her death would be married five times.

"Mother Tate" or "Saint Mary Magdalena," as she became known by followers, began her ministry as a Holiness street preacher and home evangelist in 1903—two years after Parham's initial formulation of tongues as initial evidence and three years before the **Azusa Street Revival** outpouring—carrying out "missionary journeys" throughout the Ohio Valley and the South. Reportedly unaware of the Pentecostal revival springing from these other two leaders, her followers characterize her meetings as "the first great Pentecostal revival," insisting that, she came to the revelation of initial evidence on her own. That year Tate established her first congregation, The Latter Day Saints of the Foundation of Holiness and Sanctification. From there, she travelled throughout the South preaching and organizing her followers into prayer bands.

In 1908, Tate's miraculous healing from a near fatal illness was accompanied by a spontaneous episode of speaking in tongues, prompting her to add the doctrine of initial evidence to her message of sanctification. That year, she organized holiness bands formed under her leadership into the first congregations of the denomination, taking the title of bishop. In doing so, Tate became the first woman to hold that rank in a nationally recognized Protestant Christian denomination.

Tate insisted that the **Church of the Living God Pillar and Ground of the Truth** was the God-given revelation of the only name for the present day Church, and understood herself as exclusively called to "reestablish" and restore the New Testament church to a purity other Pentecostals missed, thereby ushering in the last days of true holiness. Her severe piety demanded tithing and forbid eating pork, swearing or taking oaths, and using alcohol products, including medicines containing alcohol.

In 1923 Tate opened the **New and Living Way Publishing House** in Nashville, Tennessee. Through it, she published doctrinal resources for the denomination. For though not formally educated, her mother had insisted that as a young girl she learn to read and write, and she used her skills to develop much of the church's early literature. Tate was also a songwriter; her hymns were published post humorously in a collection, when her daughter-in-law, **Mary Frankie Lewis Keith,** formally compiled them into a hymnal. These sectarian selections however were not widely sung or known outside of Tate's organization and the bodies that evolved from it.

Her followers saw a special significance of Tate's ministry, even among the already special significance Pentecostals generally ascribed to themselves, believing that her endeavor was "the beginning of true holiness in the last days. These followers, who informally addressed their leader as "Mother Tate" and publically ascribed more formal titles such as "Reviver" and "Chief Overseer," "Senior Bishop" and "Apostle Elder, were convinced of her, and their unique role in reviving the New Testament church. Though she suffered from chronic diabetes, Tate promoted divine healing and regularly prayed for the sick who reportedly, recounted "miraculous" healings through her intervention. She urged her followers to forego doctors and conventional medicine. Yet, both she and her older son succumbed prematurely to conditions that might have benefited from medical care. Tate died in 1930 at age fifty-nine from complications of diabetes and gangrene.

After her death, the denomination she led for twenty-one years separated into three sixteen-state dominions encompassing the then forty-eight United States. Each of these, along with smaller groups that came into being because of the early schisms, pays direct allegiance to Tate. Each retains some part of the original title, crediting Tate as founder and maintaining the distinctive elements she established.

Further Reading:

Alexander, Estrelda. *Limited Liberty: The Legacy of Four Pentecostal Women Pioneers.* Cleveland, OH: Pilgrim, 2008.

Lewis, Meharry H. *Mary Lena Lewis Tate: Vision! : A Biography of the Founder and History of The Church of the Living God, the Pillar and Ground of the Truth, Inc.* Nashville, TN: New and Living Way, 2005.

Taylor, Richard 1946–

The founder and presiding bishop of the **United Full Gospel Church, USA** and current president of the **Federated Pentecostal Church, International**. He was born in Seattle, Washington. He was converted to Christian faith in 1955 when he was nine years old, and acknowledged his call to the ministry at the early age of sixteen years old. His pastoral ministry began in 1971, when he founded Evangel Temple Full Gospel Church in Tacoma, Washington. That congregation grew and moved several times before settling in its present location in Bellevue, Washington.

As a young man, he attended God's Pentecostal Temple and was a part of the **Free Church of God in Christ** where he was mentored by Bishop **Ernest F. Morris**, founder and presiding bishop of the **Full Gospel Pentecostal Missionary Association** where he served as national youth president for several years. He was also affiliated with Bishop **Ulysses S. King** of the **Christ Holy Sanctified Church of America** and he served in several positions of the **Federated Pentecostal Church, International**.

Taylor holds bachelors and masters degrees in theology, as well as an earned Doctorate degree in Education. He served as a professional educator at the secondary and post-secondary levels since 1969, and was principal of a private elementary school for twenty-three years.

Terry, Neely

The woman who was instrumental is getting **William Joseph Seymour** to Los Angeles and facilitating his ministry in that city prior to the **Azusa Street Revival**.

Terry was a Los Angeles resident who belonged to the small Holiness church pastored by **Julia Hutchins**. In 1905 soon after the congregation was organized, Terry left Los Angeles to visit family in Houston, Texas. While there, she reportedly worked as a cook for the Charles Fox Parham family. There Terry met another Parham employee, **Lucy Farrow**, pastor of another small Holiness church, and through that association, met Seymour, who was standing in as interim pastor of Farrow.

Reportedly, while in Houston, she had already had the experience of speaking in tongues. On returning to Los Angeles, Terry convinced Hutchins to invite Seymour to serve as associate pastor. Though he preached only one sermon in that church before being locked out, it was this invitation that brought Seymour to that city. After Seymour was locked out of the church, Terry convinced her cousins, **Ruth and Richard Asberry** to allow him to use their home to conduct his initial Bible studies. It was there, at 214 Bonnie Brae Street, that the **Bonnie Brae Prayer Meeting** unfolded as the precursor to the **Azusa Street Revival**.

Once the revival moved into full swing, Terry presumably was a member of the congregation, following her pastor who had changed her mind regarding Seymour's ministry. It is unknown, however, what role, if any, Terry actually played in the revival from that point.

Tharpe, Rosetta 1915–1973

Gospel singer, songwriter, guitarist and recording artist who was among the first gospel singers to perform in secular venues and take gospel music into the mainstream. Born in Cotton Plant, Arkansas, by age four, "Little Rosetta Nubin," was playing guitar for her mother, Katie Bell Nubin, a **Church of God in Christ** traveling evangelist, singer, and mandolin player who encouraged her musical talents from a very young age. By age six, Rosetta was regularly performing in a traveling evangelical troupe.

In the mid-1920s, the duo settled in Chicago, Illinois, but traveled throughout the country to perform at church conventions, and young Rosetta developed considerable fame as a musical prodigy. In 1934 at the age of nineteen, Rosetta married Thomas

Thorpe, a COGIC minister who had accompanied the pair on their tours. While the marriage lasted only a short time, she decided to incorporate a version of her husband's surname into her stage name. She would be known as Sister Rosetta Tharpe for the rest of her career, though she would two more time. With her third marriage in 1951, she married her manager, Russell Morrison, in an elaborate ceremony at Griffith Stadium in Washington DC, attended by a paying audience of 25,000 and featured a gospel performance by Tharpe and a massive fireworks display.

In 1938 Tharpe moved to New York City, signed with Decca Records and recorded the first gospel songs on that label. The recordings became instant hits, and Tharpe became one of the first commercially successful gospel singers in the United States. Later that year, she performed at Carnegie Hall in John Hammond's legendary concert, "From Spirituals to Swing." Her gospel performances for secular audiences with blues and jazz musicians were highly unusual and were made more so by the fact that she was a woman performing guitar music. Later she performed regularly with Cab Calloway at Harlem's famous Cotton Club and with Lucky Millinder's orchestra, blues pianist Sammy Price.

All the while, Tharpe performed to racially mixed crowds. Her racial and stylist appeal allowed her to become one of only two African American gospel artists to be asked to record "V-Discs" (the "V" stood for "victory") for American troops overseas during World War II. Yet when she travelled in the deep South she was subjected to the same racial indignities of other blacks of her era.

In the mid-1940s, in the face of intense criticism from Christians who viewed her jazz collaborations as the devil's music, Tharpe returned to solely recording Christian music for a while. By 1953 however, she again deviated from gospel to record a blues album that turned out to be a commercial failure and drew widespread condemnation from Christian listeners. Tharpe spent the remaining two decades primarily performing gospel music on tour throughout Europe and the United States, including an acclaimed 1960 performance with James Cleveland at Harlem's Apollo Theatre and a 1967 performance at the Newport Jazz Festival.

While on a European blues tour with Muddy Waters in 1970, Tharpe was forced to return to the United States after suddenly becoming ill. Shortly after her return, she suffered a stroke and, due to complications from diabetes, had to have a leg amputated. Yet she continued to perform regularly until 1973, when she suffered a second stroke and died at the age of fifty-eight in Philadelphia, Pennsylvania.

In 1998 twenty-five years after death, the United States Postal Service issued a postage stamp in her honor. In 2003 the album *Shout, Sister Shout: A Tribute to Sister Rosetta Tharpe* was released, with versions of Tharpe's songs performed by female artists including Maria Muldaur, Odetta, and Marcia Ball. In 2013 the PBS series *American Masters* featured an episode on Tharpe, and she was inducted into the Arkansas Entertainers Hall of Fame.

Further Reading:

Wald, Gayle. *Shout, Sister, Shout!: The Untold Story of Rock-and-Roll Trailblazer Sister Rosetta Tharpe.* Boston: Beacon, 2007.

Thomas, Elsworth S. 1866–1936

The earliest known African-American ordained by the Assemblies of God, the largest classical Pentecostal denominations in the World. His name first appeared in the Assemblies of God ministers' directory in October 1915, as a "colored" pastor in Binghamton, New York.

Thomas was born in New York City about nine months after his father returned home from the Civil War. He was part of a flourishing, but small, community of free blacks that existed in Binghamton in the nineteenth century. After his father died in the early 1890s, Ellsworth lived with his mother and cared for her in a modest house in a predominantly white neighborhood. Though he did not attend school, he could read and write.

Thomas was a laundryman by trade, but by 1900, he had become a traveling evangelist. On the application, Thomas stated that he was originally ordained on December 7, 1913, by R. E. Erdman, pastor of a large congregation in Buffalo, New York. Correspondence in his ministerial file from reveals that he also pastored a congregation in Beaver Meadows, New York. Two years later, he sought and received AG credential. In 1917, the AG asked existing ministers to re-submit applications for credentials, apparently because earlier records had been lost. Robert Brown, influential pastor of Glad Tidings Tabernacle in New York City, endorsed Thomas' application at that time. Thomas, who served until his death, was the first, and possibly the only, AG minister to have carried the designation "(colored)" following his name on his credentials He was seventy years old and passed away in Binghamton after a serious illness.

Further Reading:

Kenyon, Howard. "Black Ministers in the Assemblies of God: Ellsworth S. Thomas First Black Minister Credentialed in 1915." *Assemblies of God Heritage* 7 (1987) 10–13, 20.

Thompson, Leroy 1946–

Televangelist and leader in the African American prosperity gospel community, probably most known in Charismatic circles for coining the phrase "money cometh to me, now!" The Louisiana native was converted to Christian faith in 1972. He attended Christian Bible College of Louisiana where he earned bachelor, master, and doctorate of theology degrees, and a doctorate of divinity. Thompson taught at his alma mater for several years.

In 1975 he entered pastoral ministry at Mt. Zion Baptist Church a small, 104-year-old traditional congregation in Darrow, Louisiana. In the 1980s he encountered the teachings of Kenneth Copeland and **Fred Price**. Price mentored him from 1980 to 1983, moving to California to study with him. He experienced Pentecostal Spirit baptism in 1983. Priced introduced him to his mentor, Kenneth Hagin, the father of the Word of Faith Movement and Thompson worked closely with Hagin throughout the 1990s. Thompson's message is focused on material and economic prosperity.

In 1984 Thompson changed the name of his congregation to Ever Increasing Word Ministries Church to reflect his new focus. Since then, the congregation has grown to become a megachurch.

Thompson is also chief overseer of Leroy Thompson Ministerial Association (LTMA), an interdenominational alliance of ministries and ministers. His Ever Increasing Word Ministries, the outreach ministry of Word of Life Christian Center has more than five thousand members who regularly support his ministry. In 1993 he established the Ever Increasing Word Training Center to train ministers within the Word of Faith teaching through a two-year, non-accredited course of study. He travels globally holding Money Cometh to You Conferences. He has authored numerous books including the best seller, *Money Cometh to the Body of Christ*.

Till, Emmett Louis 1941–1955

The fourteen-year-old, fifth generation **Church of God in Christ** teenager whose murder in Mississippi after reportedly flirting with a white woman is noted as a pivotal event motivating the African-American Civil Rights Movement. The Chicago, Illinois native was visiting relatives in Money, Mississippi, when the woman's husband and half-brother raided Till's great-uncle's (a COGIC preacher) house and kidnapped, brutally beat, and killed him.

Till's maternal grandmother was a member of the Church of God in Christ in Mississippi, where his mother Mamie had been raised. His great-great grandmother had been a personal friend of COGIC founder, **Charles Harrison Mason**, who had stayed at her house. She had become one of the first converts to his new Holiness organization.

Till's mother, who had raised him as a single parent within the church, insisted his body be returned to Chicago for a public funeral and that the casket remain open. The service, held at his mother's home church—the Roberts Temple Church of God in Christ, pastored by Rev. Isaiah Roberts on Chicago's South Side—exposed to the world her son's mutilated body over four days, as an estimated 250,000 people viewed his casket. Several thousand attended his funeral with several thousand more listening outside on a public address system. Further, black-oriented magazines and newspapers published images of his mutilated body, rallying popular black support and white sympathy across the US. Bishop **Louis H. Ford** of the St. Paul Church of God in Christ, noted for his involvement in the Civil Rights movement, gave the eulogy.

Tinney, James S. 1942–1988

A leading authority on the history of African-American Pentecostalism whose scholarly work was instrumental in promoting the legacy of **William Joseph Seymour** as the major leader of the early Pentecostal revival. Tinney was an outspoken gay rights activist who promoted a more inclusive posture within the African-American Pentecostal movement.

Born in Kansas City, Missouri, he was interested in the Christian faith at an early age and preached a three-week-long revival service at age fourteen. He was ordained in the **Church of God in Christ** at eighteen and while in his twenties pastored churches in Arkansas and Missouri and was an assistant editor of the *Kansas City Call*.

Though he married in 1962 at the age of twenty and fathered two daughters, seven years later, the marriage ended in divorce when Tinney publicly identified himself as a gay man. For the next ten years, Tinney lived quietly with two successive lovers who were also active Pentecostals, but was cut off from his family, his children, and the Pentecostal church. Yet, his scholarly interest in, and his personal commitment, to Pentecostal spirituality continued.

In 1973 Tinney moved to Washington DC and completed his graduate education in journalism at Howard University. During this period, he was the editor of *The Washington Afro-American* newspaper and a speechwriter for Congressman John Conyers, an African American, Democratic representative from Michigan, and for Samuel C. Jackson, undersecretary of the Department of Housing and Urban Development in the Nixon Administration.

In 1976 Tinney became an assistant professor of journalism at Howard University in Washington DC. While there, he established the first scholarly journal on Black Pentecostalism, *Spirit: A Journal of Issues Incident in Black Pentecostalism*, and was instrumental in establishing Howard's William J. Seymour Pentecostal Fellowship, an annual Black Religion Writers Workshop, and the Society for Blacks in Religious Communications.

In 1979 Tinney addressed the initial Third World Lesbian and Gay Conference. In 1980 he founded the Pentecostal Coalition for Human Rights in an attempt to help those Pentecostals who identified themselves as gay reconcile their Pentecostalism with their homosexuality.

In 1982 Bishop Samuel Kelsey excommunicated Tinney from the Church of God in Christ after he organized a three-day revival for gays and lesbians. Later that year, he founded Faith Temple, a nondenominational church in Washington with a largely black gay and lesbian congregation.

Tinney died at age forty-six from complications related to AIDS.

Tobin, Robert Franklin 1894–1947

The early Oneness Pentecostal leader who served as General Secretary of the **Pentecostal Assemblies of the World** and succeeded PAW founder, **Garfield T. Haywood**, as pastor of Christ Temple Apostolic Church in Indianapolis, Indiana. Tobin was born in Elizabethtown, Kentucky as the first of five children of an Irish father and former slave. His father died while Robert was a young man, leaving his mother to raise her children by herself. A year later, Tobin moved with his grandmother to Indianapolis. He did not finish high school, but worked as a janitor to help support his family. Between 1913 and 1918, he pitched baseball for the Negro National League. Afterward, he served in World War I in the all black 809th Pioneer Infantry unit.

During his absence, his wife began attending Haywood's church where she was baptized in Jesus' name, and received the Pentecostal Holy Spirit baptism. After his return home, Tobin joined his wife at Haywood's congregation and was converted to Oneness Pentecostal faith. He was called into the ministry at age twenty-four and was tutored by Haywood. In 1925 he became pastor of the Apostolic Faith Church in Grand Rapids, Michigan, and held this position for five and half years. After Haywood's death in 1931, the deacon board of Christ Temple requested that Tobin return as their pastor.

Tobin served as General Secretary of the **Pentecostal Assemblies of the World** from 1935 to 1947 when he died after a short illness.

Further Reading:

Garrett, Gary, and Morris E. Golder. *A Man For His Times: The Life and Times of Robert Franklin Tobin.* s.l.: Apostolic Christian, 2001.

Tomlinson, Ambrose Jessup (A. J.) 1865–1943

An early white advocate for racial equity within Pentecostalism, initially as the first general overseer of the predominantly white Church of God (Cleveland, TN), and then as the founder and presider of the more racially integrated Church of God of Prophecy. Tomlinson's grandparents, Robert and Lydia Tomlinson, were abolitionists who joined an "anti-slavery meeting of the Society of Friends." The Tomlinson family was also active in the Underground Railroad, and boycotted products produced by slave labor.

Due in part to his Quaker foundations, Tomlinson's attitude on race differed markedly from many of his colleagues. While he served as General Overseer of the Church of God he attempted, with some success, to introduce racially progressive measures into denominational polity and to integrate African Americans more fully into the church. He had much more success in organizing the new body to reflect a greater measure of integration from its founding.

He repeatedly spoke to the General Assemblies in both organizations of the desirability of full relationships between Christians regardless of race. Further, he openly lamented the limitation placed on interracial relationships south of the Mason-Dixon Line. His efforts, generally, met resistance from other leaders, or were ignored. In his 1913 work, *The Last Great Conflict*, he was among the earliest white Pentecostal leaders to acknowledge **William Seymour**'s influence on the Pentecostal movement.

On a number of occasions, Tomlinson made appointments of blacks to significant positions within the parent church. The first missionaries within the denomination, **Edmund and Rebecca Barr**, came into the Church of God in 1909 under the ministry of Tomlinson, who issued an Evangelist License to each in 1909 and ordained Edmund as a bishop in 1912, appointing him as state overseer of Black churches in Florida in 1915. In 1916, Tomlinson ordained **Crawford Bright** and appointed him to serve on the Questions and Answers Committee of the General Assembly, and, in 1919, as overseer of the churches in Pennsylvania, though at the time there was only one white church in the state. In that same year, Tomlinson invited him to preach in the denomination's General Assembly, an honor rarely extended to blacks, and appointed him as overseer of New Jersey in 1920.

In the earliest 1920s, Tomlinson appointed a small number of black ministers to leadership positions beyond the limited fellowship of the African-American churches. Thomas Richardson, for example, was appointed to the Education Committee and was one of three blacks who served on the Council of Seventy, along with W. V. Eneas and William Franks.

During the 1922 exodus of black Church of God ministers, Tomlinson attempted to quiet dissention by appointing black ministers to the Committee on Better Government. When a black delegation requested that he appoint a black person again to oversee their work, Tomlinson agreed, creating an autonomous structure for the black churches, The **Church of God (Colored Work)**, and appointing **Thomas Richardson** as overseer. Richardson served only one year at that post, however. In 1923, Richardson left with the former overseer to move to the newly formed Church of God of Prophecy where Tomlinson appointed him as the only African-American state overseer and to his newly formed Council, as well as the Bible Government Committee. Yet, when Tomlinson refused to appoint him as overseer of Florida, and offered him Bermuda instead, Richard left the COGOP.

Within his new denomination, however, Tomlinson worked to gain members of color and to be sure that they had visible positions throughout the denomination. He envisioned the Church God of Prophecy being the "The Great Specked Bird," spoken of in Jeremiah 12:9, and interpreted this passage to mean that church must be racially inclusive. In keeping with this vision, Tomlinson forged relationship with black Pentecostal leaders from other denominations. Perhaps, the most well-known of them was **Charles Harrison Mason** of the **Church of God in Christ**.

Further Reading:

Kinder, Christopher. "'The Great Speckled Bird': Prominent Black Ministers and Interracial Fraternity in the Church of God of Prophecy, 1923–1964." Paper presented to the Southern Studies Conference, Montgomery, AL: Auburn University, February 6–7, 2015.
Robins, R. G. *A. J. Tomlinson: Plainfolk Modernist.* New York: Oxford University Press, 2004.
Tomlinson, A. J. *Diary of A.J. Tomlinson.* New York: Church of God Headquarters, 1949.

Triumph the Church and Kingdom of God in Christ

The quasi-Pentecostal denomination, variably called The Triumph Church, was established in 1902 based on what its founder, **Elias Dempsey Smith,** called a divine revelation in which an eagle, a lion, and a brown-skinned young woman, dressed as a bride appeared to him. According to Smith, God revealed to him that the eagle meant that his church would be the highest religious group in existence. The lion indicated his message would be stronger than any other and without "carnal ordinances." The bride represented the church and the entire world, whom the bridegroom married and for whom the bridegroom holds the ability to birth all of her needs.

Though the revelation was given in 1897 with instruction to start a new church, it would be five years before the first congregation, Triumph the Righteous Church, was formed as a Methodist congregation in Baton Rouge, Louisiana. Still by that time, Smith reportedly kept the content of the vision secret for two more years, until 1904.

In 1907, before he had completely solidified his organization, Smith joined forces with Holiness movement leader, **Charles Harrison Mason**, founder of the **Church of God in Christ**. This union lasted until 1912. Smith objected to Mason's open cooperation with white Christians whom he considered the "church militant" as well as his Pentecostal emphasis on speaking in tongues. Mason, on the other hand, objected to Smith conception of "Body Redemption" in which he contended that was revealed to him by God.

Smith labeled this new understanding the "Everlasting Gospel," which he was instructed to share with the world to "prepare and call mankind, both soul and body, into everlasting existence on earth together." Triumph Church teaches a seven-step plan of salvation: conversion, justification, sanctification, baptism of the Holy Ghost with fire, redemption of the body, perfection and eternal life. Moreover, according to the message revealed to Smith, all of these are necessary for a person to be completely saved.

The first National Congress of Triumph Church was held in July 1915. At this assembly Smith was named "Apostle, Priest and King" and the name of the church was changed to Triumph the Church and Kingdom of God in Christ. The first International Congress was held in 1919, where over 1500 delegates registered. The meeting lasted for fifty days.

After World War I, Smith became involved in Marcus Garvey's "Back to Africa" movement and Ethopianism, and hosted the head of the Universal Negro Improvement Association at the 1919 convention. In 1920, he traveled to Ethiopia, which he referred to as Abyssinia. On his arrival, his host gave Smith a king's reception, including a lavish banquet with which he reciprocated with a banquet of his own. The day after these elaborate ceremonies, he died suddenly.

Prior to his trip to Africa, Smith relocated the denomination's headquarters to Birmingham, Alabama. After his death, leadership of the denomination shifted from one person to a board of seven bishops. In 1936 the church had only two congregations and thirty-six members. By 1972 it had grown to 475 congregations and 54,000 members in the United States, Africa, and the Philippines. Today it has congregations is thirty-six states and in Liberia, West Africa.

Trotter, Larry Darnell 1954?–

One of the founding bishops of the **Full Gospel Baptist Church Fellowship International.** During his eleven-year tenure with the FGBCFI, Trotter served as special assistant to founding presiding bishop **Paul S. Morton**, regional bishop of the Midwest jurisdiction, and third presiding bishop. He is also senior pastor of Chicago's Sweet Holy Spirit Church a congregation that grew from twenty-two members in 1981 to well over 10,000 presently, former presiding bishop of **United Covenant Churches of Christ International,** and a former board member of the **Joint College of African American Pentecostal Bishops**.

Born and raised in Chicago, Trotter came to Christian faith at age twelve. In 1976 he was licensed and ordained by both the Baptist Church and the Church of God in Christ. In his early ministry, he served as youth pastor in three Chicago area churches: Greater New Mount Eagle Baptist Church, New Faith Baptist Church, and House of Inspiration.

In 2000, Trotter led a delegation of more than fifty black Pentecostal church leaders, representing twenty-seven churches and more than 170 members of the JCAAPB from around the nation on a pilgrimage to Rome to build closer ecumenical relations with the Roman Catholic Church. The group visited the Vatican and gained an audience with the Roman Catholic pontiff, Pope John Paul, attended a three-day seminar at the Pontifical North American College, an elite seminary for Catholics, and participated in a Roman Catholic mass.

Trotter assumed the leadership of **Pentecostal Churches of Christ** in 2004 after the founder, **J. Delano Ellis**, stepped down because of ill health. After his installation, Trotter led the organization until 2009, moving its headquarters to Evergreen Park, Illinois and changing the name to United **Covenant Churches of Christ International**. That move drew the ire of Ellis who again took over interim leadership of the group, restoring its original name. In 2012 Trotter launched and became presiding prelate of New Century Fellowship of Churches and Ministries International.

Trotter is founder and CEO of the Utopia Music Group, Encouragement Plus Ministries, LaKheem Publishing, and Encouragement Plus Books. He is also a playwright and an author, and holds a seat on the Mayor's Advisory Council, the Judicial Board of the First Municipality Court of Illinois. He has also served for ten years as religious editor for *Gospel Today Magazine*, and five years as the chairperson of Clergy Speaks Interdenominational, a broad coalition of ministers engaged in social justice and community activism.

True Grace Memorial House of Prayer for All People Church on the Rock of the Apostolic Faith

An organization founded in 1961 as a challenge to the perceived authoritarian leadership of Bishop **Walter "Sweet Daddy" McCollough** who had been elected as leader of the **United House of Prayer for All People,** following the death of founder **Charles Emmanuel ("Sweet Daddy" Grace)**. Several elders challenged McCollough's right of succession and accused him of mishandling church funds. When the presider won the court-ordered election that allowed him to resume his post, a split became inevitable. That year, a Philadelphia congregation, under the leadership of Thomas Odell Johnson, a former Washington DC pastor whom McCollough had expelled for disloyalty, separately incorporated.

By 1962, however, several dismissed elders joined the dissident group. Originally, the body was organized congregationally with member churches working collaboratively instead of under an episcopal system. Eventually, the group elected a presiding bishop but continued their decentralized structure.

Johnson was dismissed from his pastorate in 1967 and died in 1970. William G. Easton took over leadership at his dismissal. In the 1970s there were eight congregations in Philadelphia, Pennsylvania where the headquarters for the group remains; Baltimore, Maryland; New York City; Savannah, Georgia; Hollywood, Florida; and North Carolina.

True Vine Pentecostal Churches of Jesus Christ (Apostolic Faith)

A Oneness Pentecostal denomination established in 1961 by Robert L. Hairston, who had previously co-founded and served as vice presiding bishop of the Trinitarian body, True Vine Pentecostal Holiness Church in 1949. After twenty-five year of affiliation with several Trinitarian denominations within the Pentecostal movement, Hairston aligned himself with Oneness Pentecostalism. His growing dissatisfaction with the former group centered largely on several polity issues with his organization and his understanding that baptism in Jesus name as the biblically correct formulation.

Since Hairston rejected some other tenets of the Apostolic movement including necessity of Jesus name baptism for salvation, and with it regenerational baptism, he might have been content to remain a minority voice in a denomination that had tolerated his deviation in doctrine. Yet, Hairston's departure was also prodded by his own personal situation, since his divorce and subsequent remarriage while his former wife was alive was problematic for several of his Oneness colleagues. Since remarriage while the former spouse was living was unacceptable to many of them, Hairston formed a new body.

Hairston used his Martinsville, Virginia congregation as the headquarters for the new organization. By 1976 when Bishop Thomas C. Williams brought several congregations under his leadership into the organization, several independent congregations had joined and a number of new congregations had been founded. Williams assumed the position of senior bishop and Hairston remained as presiding bishop. In 1980, the denomination, which encourages the leadership of women, reported only ten congregations and missions and approximatley nine hundred members.

Further Reading:

Richardson, James C., Jr. *With Water and Spirit: A History of Black Apostolic Denominations in the U.S.* Martinsville, VA: s.n., s.d.

True Vine Pentecostal Holiness Church

A Holiness-Pentecostal body co-founded in 1946 by **Robert L. Hairston** and **William Monroe Johnson,** in Winston-Salem, North Carolina. Johnson was consecrated as presiding bishop and Hairston as vice presiding bishop. In the 1960s, discord arose between the two leaders over a number of issues. First Hairston softened his stance on allowing women within the denomination to preach. Secondly, he became divorced from his wife, which was against church teaching. In 1961, after Hairston accepted the Oneness Pentecostal doctrine and the practice of baptism in Jesus' name, he was removed as vice bishop and he left to form a **True Vine Pentecostal Churches of Jesus Christ (Apostolic Faith)** as a Oneness body.

At Johnson's death in 1975, there were True Vine churches located throughout North Carolina, South Carolina, and Virginia. Johnson's son, Sylvester, became presiding bishop at this father's death. In 1997 the younger Johnson reorganization the denomination as True Vine Churches of Deliverance International (TVCOD).

Turner, William Clair, Jr. 1948–

The only African-American Pentecostal scholar to be appointed to a full professorship at Duke University School of Divinity in Durham, North Carolina where he teaches preaching. Turner was raised within a **United Holy Church of America** congregation in Richmond, Virginia. As a student, Turner played football at Duke and was the first to integrate Duke's football team as a walk-on player. During a period of fierce discrimination, Turner was relegated to the practice team and suffered racial indignities from teammates, coaches, and college administrators. Turner excelled in academics, however; in addition to earning a bachelor of science degree in electrical engineering in 1971, he went on to earn a master of divinity degree in 1974 and a doctorate in religion in 1984, also from Duke.

Turner has spent his entire academic career at Duke, since joining the faculty in 1982. He has served the university as assistant provost and dean of black affairs, acting director of the African and African-American Studies Department and director of black church affairs. He has taught theology for many years at Duke Divinity School and is now a professor of the practice of homiletics. His teaching and research focuses on pneumatology and the tradition of spirituality and preaching within the black church. Over the years, Turner has helped recruit an increasingly diverse student body.

Turner was ordained in the **United Holy Church of America**, and although he maintains his ordination in that body, he has served as the pastor of Mt. Level Baptist Church in Durham since 1990. Besides being widely sought out on the lecture circuit, Turner has authored several manuscripts, including *Preaching That Makes the Word Plain: Doing Theology in the Crucible of Life*; *The United Holy Church of America: A Study in Black Holiness-Pentecostalism, Discipleship for African American Christians: A Journey through the Church Covenant.*

Turpin, Joseph Marcel 1887–1943

One of the earliest bishops of the **Pentecostal Assemblies of the World** was born in Denton, on the Eastern Shore of Maryland. Turpin came to Christian faith as a young man and received the Pentecostal baptism of the Holy Spirit among those who taught the second definite work of grace or eradication theory. He later accepted the finished work of Calvary, was ordained within a Trinitarian organization, and accepted the Oneness Pentecostal doctrine of baptism in Jesus' name and the Oneness of God.

He affiliated his congregation with PAW around 1919. In 1920, he was listed as one of the denomination's general elders, and quickly rose with the PAW ranks, being appointed or elected to several key positions in consecutive years. First, he was appointed district elder, then presbyter and later he was consecrated a bishop, and appointed to preside over the Eastern Dioceses for approximately ten years. In 1923, when PAW reorganized under an eight-member board, Turpin was one of them. In 1925, when PAW dropped the district structure in favor of an episcopal structure Turpin was one of the five elected bishops

After the death of **Garfield T. Haywood** in 1931, Turpin favored the merger with the predominantly white, Pentecostal Ministerial Alliance into the Pentecostal Assemblies of Jesus Christ. After that took place, he became a presbyter in the new organizartion. When that merger failed only a few years later, however, Turpin stayed with the new group until the mid-1930s, then became an independent bishop, before returning to PAW.

Before his departure from PAW, Turpin had worked with **Alexander R. Schooler** to found the Eastern District Council. On his return, he was elected to PAW eldership, and served until his death in 1943 in Baltimore, Maryland, where he founded the First Apostolic Church.

U

Ulmer, Kenneth C. 1948–

The Neo-Pentecostal pastor, educator, and entrepreneur is presiding bishop of Macedonia International Bible Fellowship and senior pastor of Faithful Central Bible Church in Inglewood, California. In 1994 he was consecrated bishop of Christian Education of the **Full Gospel Baptist Church Fellowship,** where he also served on the Bishops Council.

Within the educational realm, Ulmer is a founding board member and former president of The King's College and Seminary, in Van Nuys, California. He also served on the Board of Directors of The Gospel Music Workshop of America, the Board of Trustees of Biola University, and the Board of Trustees of Southern California School of Ministry.

Before assuming that position of president of The King's College and Seminary, he served as both adjunct professor and summer dean. He also served as an instructor in Pastoral Ministry and Homiletics at Grace Theological Seminary, an instructor of African-American Preaching at Fuller Theological Seminary, an Adjunct Professor at Biola and Pepperdine Universities, and Doctor of Ministry mentor at United Theological Seminary.

Ulmer received his BA in Broadcasting & Music from the University of Illinois. After accepting his call to the ministry, he was ordained at Mount Moriah Missionary Baptist Church in Los Angeles, and shortly after founded Macedonia Bible Church in San Pedro, California. He has studied at Pepperdine University, Hebrew Union College, the University of Judaism, and Oxford University in England before receiving a PhD from Grace Graduate School of Theology in Long Beach, California and his Doctor of Ministry from United Theological Seminary

Ulmer also began the Macedonia International Bible Fellowship, with churches representing the countries of Zimbabwe, Namibia, Angola, and Republic of the Congo, South Africa, and the United States.

In 2000 Ulmer's more than 13,000-member congregation, where he has served since 1982, starting with 350 people, purchased the 17,500-seat Los Angeles Forum in Inglewood, California, a community with a 46 percent black and Hispanic constituency. Development plans for the property—a sports arena that once housed the games of the Los Angeles Lakers and Kings—includes a shopping mall, parking garage, restaurants, theaters and housing for the surrounding land with proceeds used to create an endowment fund for the church.

Ulmer has authored of six books including, *A New Thing: A Reflection on the Full Gospel Baptist Movement*, the most complete work on that movement to date.

United Church of Jesus Christ (Apostolic)

In 1965 four bishops—**Monroe R. Saunders Sr.** of Baltimore, Maryland; **Sydney A. Dunn** of Birmingham, England; John S. Watson of Kingston, Jamaica; Raymond Murray of Boston, Massachusetts—dissented with **Randolph A. Carr**, presiding bishop of **the Church of God in Christ (Apostolic),** over his decision to break church polity and marry a divorcee. Together, they established the United Church of Jesus Christ (Apostolic) and served as its first Board of Bishops. Saunders, who served as assistant presiding bishop under Carr, was elected as presiding bishop. Immediately, several of the congregations who also disagreed with Carr's actions joined the new denomination.

The denomination was incorporated in Washington DC where Saunders was pastoring at the time it was formed. He turned that congregation over to his assistant pastor, Charlie B. Burroughs and established a new congregation in Baltimore for Carr's former members, making that location the headquarters of the organization. The Baltimore site also houses an Institute for Biblical Studies, the Center for More Abundant Life and the Creative Learning Center, a preparatory school. The denomination also owns a shopping center in Baltimore.

The Oneness Pentecostal denomination has approximately seventy-five congregations, ten thousand churches across the United States and another fifty thousand in Canada, England, Jamaica, the Leeward Islands of the West Indies, and Liberia, West Africa.

Saunders, Sr. served the United Church of Jesus Christ (Apostolic) as presiding bishop from 1965 until 2004, when he retired. During the 38th International Convocation, the denomination affirmed Saunders as chief apostle in perpetuity and installed his oldest son, Bishop Monroe R. Saunders, Jr., as presiding prelate.

United Churches of God in Christ

In 1979 then **Church of God in Christ** presiding bishop, **James O. Patterson, Sr.,** dissolved the Northwestern Georgia Jurisdiction and directed its pastors to unite with one of the other Georgia jurisdictions. In response, "Superintendent" **Marshall Carter** organized and incorporated the **Church of God in Christ Incorporated** of Georgia as an Independent Fellowship that would "report to" and remain under the direct authority of the Church of God in Christ, headquartered in Memphis, Tennessee. He had hoped that Patterson would recognize the group as its own jurisdiction. By year's end, however, when Patterson failed to acquiesce, pastors from other states wanted to join with Carter in breaking with the parent denomination, dissolving the Church of God in Christ Incorporated of Georgia and forming the United Churches of God in Christ, Inc. Soon, congregation from other Georgia jurisdictions and other states had joined the body.

In 1980 Carter was elevated to the bishopric and formally installed as the first chief apostle and presiding bishop of the new denomination, serving in that position until his death in 2003. Aill Mannie of Albany, Georgia, then became the second chief apostle and presiding bishop. Later that year, the General Assembly of the new organization decided that the office of the presiding bishop would become an elected office, broken up into four-year terms and set the first quadrennial election for 2004. In that election, Bishop Spencer Lackey Sr. of Decatur, Georgia was elected to the position. At his death in 2009, the General Assembly allowed Bishop Aaron B. Lackey, Sr. to hold the office of chief apostle and presiding bishop for a thirteen-month interim period. In 2010, it elected him as the fourth chief apostle and presiding bishop.

Headquartered in Fairburn, Georgia, the vast majority of the denomination's US churches are in Georgia, and there are congregations in Wisconsin, North Carolina, and Indiana. There are also congregation in Canada, the Bahamas, Haiti, the Dominican Republic South Africa, the Philippines, Burkina Faso, Ghana, and Nigeria.

The polity and doctrine of the denomination closely paralleled that of the parent body. Further the nomenclature of the younger organization, which frequently fails to incorporate the distinction "United" within the name of individual local congregations often makes it difficult to distinguish their affiliation.

United Cornerstone Churches of Christ International

The Oneness denomination headquartered in Thomasville, North Carolina, formed in 2005, when several congregations affiliated with the **United Way of the Cross Church of Christ** left that body. Among the leaders of the group was Bishop **James H. Carter**, pastor of Cornerstone Church of Christ in Thomasville who had served the UWCCC as chairperson of the board of bishops, presiding prelate, and chief executive officer of the Board of Apostles, was consecrated as first presiding prelate of the UWCCC. Bishop Willie Davis, pastor of the Refuge Fundamental Church who also had been a member the UWCCC for twenty-one years, joined Carter as vice-presider.

In its first year, the denomination set the foundation of the United Cornerstone School of Divinity. Within nine years, that school has grown to become United Cornerstone University.

By 2006, UCCCI had chartered over forty-seven churches in North Carolina, South Carolina, Pennsylvania, Maryland, Washington DC, Virginia, West Indies and Africa. Currently, there are over sixty congregations affiliated with the group, including eleven churches in West Africa, and seventeen churches, two orphanages, and two schools in Haiti.

United Covenant Churches of Christ

A Neo-Pentecostal organization that integrates Pentecostal doctrine and practice with evangelical theology and sacramental ecclesiology. A notable feature of this integration is the adoption of the concept of apostolic succession through the laying-on of a bishop's hands during ordination.

The organization traces its founding to 1992, in Cleveland, Ohio as outgrowth of the work of Bishop **J. Delano Ellis, II**. That year, Ellis, pastor of the Pentecostal Church of Christ formed the Pentecostal Convocation as a gathering of independent churches. In 1993, its first bishops were consecrated, overseers were appointed, and Ellis assumed the position of presiding bishop and president.

Nine years later, in 2004, Ellis, who was struggling with health issues, stepped down from leadership. At the time, there were three hundred congregations in the United States, India and Africa. In his place, Ellis nominated **Larry D. Trotter**, pastor of the 5,000-member Sweet Holy Spirit Full Gospel Baptist Church in Chicago, Illinois. Trotter led the organization until 2009 and while at the helm, moved the headquarters to Evergreen Park, Illinois and changed the name to **United Covenant Churches of Christ International**. These moves drew the ire of Ellis and other pastors who were originally associated with the UPCC, who considered Trotter actions unconstitutional. Since Ellis had regained his health, he resumed leadership of the original body, while Trotter and his followers formed the United Covenant Churches of Christ as a separate group.

Later that year, Trotter resigned from the new organization he had started. In his place, and the organization installed Eric Garnes, pastor of Tabernacle of Praise Cathedral Brooklyn, New York, as presiding bishop and moved the headquarters to his home city. UCCC currently has more than 20,000 members globally.

United Fellowship Convention of the Original Apostolic Faith Mission

An organization of six Trinitarian Pentecostal bodies all of which are based in Virginia and claim an affiliation to each other because of their direct tie to the personal evangelistic endeavors of early Pentecostal pioneer, **William Joseph Seymour**. In 1907, Seymour made a stop in Virginia, meeting with **Charles Lowe** and leaving several congregations in place that either developed as independent bodies or conglomerated with existing groups to form small denominations. With few minor exceptions, though a number of schisms and realignments occurred over the next eighty years, the groups retained similar doctrine, but developed their individual polities. Also with few exceptions, the organizations remained fairly small and relatively unknown—even among other Pentecostal groups.

In 1987, Bishop **Oree Keyes** of the **Apostolic Faith Churches of God,** headquartered in Hansome, Virginia, extended an invitation to the leaders of five other bodies to collaborate on how they might present a common witness to their **Azusa Street Revival** heritage. The group which met in Norfolk, Virginia, had representation from his body as well as from the **Apostolic Faith Church of God in Christ** in Hereford, North Carolina; the **Apostolic Faith Church of God Live On!** in Suffolk, Virginia, under the leadership of Bishop Richard Cross; **The Church of Christ Holiness Unto the Lord, Inc.,** in Savannah, Georgia, under the leadership of Bishop Moses Lewis; **The Saints at Runneymede Holiness Church** headquartered in Elberon, Virginia; and **Sweet Haven Holiness Church** in Carrollton, Virginia. The group initially formed a Historical Society of Apostolic Faith and chose C. Larry Hill as chair.

Each of the groups also had a direct link to Lowe, who had been converted to Pentecostal faith at the **Azusa Street Revival** and went on to become founder of the Apostolic Faith Churches of God. That organization became the parent of many of the other denominations within the fellowship, which meets annually for a convention in the headquarters at Hansome.

United Full Gospel Church, USA

An organization established by **Richard Taylor**, pastor of Evangel Temple Full Gospel Church in Bellevue, Washington in 1974 as an informal association to sustain the ministers, missionaries and other ministries that were being supported by congregations that he had established over several years of ministry. The organization was incorporated in 1984 in Washington State as United Crusade Fellowship, Missions Conference International and operated under that loose umbrella for twelve years.

In 1996 the organization changed its name and reorganized with a more formal structure. Within the United States, there are several congregations in Washington State, as well as in Cleveland, Ohio, St. Paul, Minnesota. UFGC has a heavy missions emphasis with churches in Guinea Bissau, Sierra Leone, Zimbabwe, Russia, Ukraine and the Philippines. It is organized under three dioceses—Northern, Southern, and Western—and is a member of the larger umbrella organization, **Federated Pentecostal Church International, Inc.**

United Holy Church of America

The **United Holy Church of America** is one of the five original black Holiness-Pentecostal bodies along with the **Fire Baptized Holiness Church**, the Church of the Living God (Christian Workers for Fellowship), the **Church of Christ Holiness USA** and the **Church of the Living God Pillar and Ground of the Truth**. The denomination is among the most prominent black Holiness bodies swept into the new tide of Pentecostalism, contending with the Church of God (Cleveland, TN) as the oldest Pentecostal body in the nation while singularly reserving its distinction as the oldest African-American Pentecostal body.

There was no single founder of the UHC, but rather a number of men and women came together to forge a series of alliances that eventually led to its formation. The initial impetus was a succession of late nineteenth-century revival meetings conducted throughout North Carolina. The first of these was conducted by Isaac Cheshier in 1886 in Method, a small town near the capital of Raleigh, which served as the catalyst for formation of a fellowship that would become the nucleus of black Holiness revivalism in that area. The congregation that grew out of the Method revival became the first congregation formed under the aegis of this fellowship, but Cheshier did not take over leadership of the group. Instead, on the heels of his successful meeting, he joined several others including L. M. Mason, G. A. Mials, H. C. Snipes, **William L. Fulford**, and **Henry. L. Fisher** in forming a fellowship of people from several independent black Holiness congregations throughout the state who would simply refer to themselves as the Holy People. By year's end, they regularly were meeting for worship, and were becoming known as the Holy Churches in North Carolina.

In 1892, another significant revival took place when Elijah Lowney of Cleveland, Ohio preached to large crowds in a Baptist church in Wilmington, North Carolina. Several new Holiness congregations were formed in the wake of these meetings. More importantly, however, during these meetings, Henry Fisher, one of the earliest leaders of the **United Holy Church**, came to embrace the message and experience of sanctification.

Sometime later, **William Fulford**, a former African Methodist Episcopal pastor who had later affiliated with the **Fire Baptized Holiness Church** and who had been involved in the 1886 meeting, established a large congregation in Wilmington, which grew quickly to more than fifteen hundred members and would become one of the major early **United Holy Church** congregations.

For the next year, the loosely affiliated Holiness congregations continued to meet independently. It would not be until 1894 that the first convocation of the fellowship was held in Durham, North Carolina. By that time several congregation in the neighboring state Virginia had joined the group, which now went by the name the Holy Churches of North Carolina and Virginia.

There was no attempt to establish a formal organization until 1900 when Charles and Craig, who had established one of the oldest congregations in the denomination, called a meeting of the loosely affiliated black Holiness leaders throughout the region to organize an independent association of Holiness congregations. That year, C. J. Wilcox, Joseph Silver, and John Scott convened the Union Holiness Convention in which Fisher was ordained. In that same meeting, the Convention chose L. M. Mason, who informally served as president of the loose affiliation from 1894, as first president and P. M. Marable as vice president. One year later, the two groups merged, becoming the Holiness Church of North Carolina. At the next annual meeting, Fulford was chosen as president and W. C. Carlton as vice president. This pair served for fifteen years, from 1901 to 1916. During this period, the **United Holy Church** embraced the tenets of Pentecostalism, so that after existing for two decades as a Holiness group, this body was swept into the Pentecostal movement.

Throughout Fulford's tenure, Fisher had been a prominent, behind-the-scenes, leader. He served as editor-in-chief of the Holiness Union, the organizations newspaper, and as chairperson of the Foreign Missions Board, and Sunday School superintendent. By 1910 he had headed a team responsible for developing a manual. In it, the name was changed to the **United Holy Church of America**. Two years later, and four years before he was elected president, the organization was incorporated under that name. It was 1916, Fisher was chosen as president, and the group came to be known as the **United Holy Church of America**.

As one of the most significant leaders to emerge throughout UHCA history, Fisher introduced a level of organizational structure that had previously been missing from the denomination. During his entire tenure, Vice President **General Johnson (G. J.) Branch** who was a moderately wealthy real estate owner with exceptional business skills also served as president of the Northern District, and helped set the UHC on strong administrative footing.

In 1918 the Board of Missions was established and sending Isaac and Annie Williams to Liberia as the denomination's first missionaries. For much of the early 1900s the UHC missionary work was concentrated in that country and several other missionaries joined Williams, establishing stations throughout the country. Other works were begun in the Caribbean with churches were established in Bermuda, Barbados and Jamaica.

For the first forty-five years, UHC congregations were concentrated in the Southern part of the country, primarily in North Carolina, South Carolina, and Virginia, and the early headquarters for the church was Durham, North Carolina. From this work, the Southern District came into being and remains the largest and strongest district in the body. The Northern District was formed in 1920; the Northwestern District followed in 1924. By that year the **United Holy Church** had spread to the West Coast and churches had been established in California and. It has also reached to the Caribbean and churches had been established in Bermuda and Barbados. The Barbados congregations, however, later affiliated with another Pentecostal body. It would not be until twenty-five years later that the **United Holy Church** had a presence on that Island, when Bishop Henry Gentles founded the Mt. Olive United Holy Church and brought several existing independent congregations into the denomination. The current constituency of the denomination consists of 516 churches, seventeen districts, and eight territories.

Just before the outbreak of World War I, the UHC purchased land in Dunn, North Carolina in a triangle connecting, Raleigh, Fayetteville and Goldsboro to build an educational facility, but abandoned the project during the War. Nearly twenty years later, in 1936, land was purchased in Greensboro, North Carolina and plans for a Bible training school were developed. When bank funding for the project could not be secured the funds were raised internally. The building was completed in and the first classes of the Bible Training School were held in 1944.

When Fisher died in 1947, Branch assumed the leadership of the denomination, serving only two years until his death in 1949. He was followed by Henry H. Harrison, 1949–1963, Walter Strohbar, 1963–1980, and under his leadership, the Virginia and North Carolina Districts were organized. Nearly ten years into his tenure, a major fission broke out that threatened to split it permanently. In an attempt to diffuse some of that influence, UHCA leaders suggested subdividing the existing Southern district into smaller jurisdictions by state. In reaction to that proposal, in 1972, **James A. Forbes, Sr.** and the lead officers of the District took the unauthorized action of dissolving the UHCA and drawing up a new charter as the Southern District of the **United Holy Church**. Relationships between the leadership of the two groups deteriorated until 1977, when most Southern district ministers with one hundred congregations (all but seven) formed what became the **Original United Holy Church International**.

After twenty years in which a lengthy trial unfolded and the new body approaching the International Pentecostal Holiness Church about possible affiliation the schism was resolved. During that time, other smaller bodies that had split from the parent group joined the Forbes faction or formed other organizations. In 2000, the two major factions joined with these smaller factions to reunite. By that time, most of the leaders who had been involved in the original schism were out of leadership, and many of the local congregations and individual pastors within these bodies had continued to fellowship with each other.

Joseph Bowen came into the position of General President during the middle of the schismatic period and served from 1980 to 1992. By that year, the denomination had put new polity in place limiting the term of the General President to four years, and voted not to return Bowen to the position. Instead, Walter Talley, who had served as first president of the Virginia District, was elected as the first General President elected to serve under the new rule, but died in 1996, several months before his term would have expired. Odell McCullom was elected to complete his term, re-elected to a new term in 1996 and, again, re-elected in 2000 and 2004. At McCollum's death in 2005, Elijah Williams filled out his term, and then was re-elected twice.

Further Reading:

Gregory, Chester W. *The History of the United Holy Church of America, Inc., 1886–1986.* Baltimore, MD: Gateway, 1986.
Fisher, Henry L. *The History of the United Holy Church of America, Inc.* S.L.: s.n., s.l.
Turner, William C. *The United Holy Church of America: A Study in Black Holiness-Pentecostalism.* Piscataway, NJ: Gorgias, 2006.

United House of Prayer for All People

The quasi-Holiness denomination founded in 1919 and incorporated in 1927 by Marcelino Manuel da Graca, also known as **Charles Manuel "Sweet Daddy" Grace in** Washington, D.C. The organization was founded as The United House of Prayer for All People of the Church on the Rock of the Apostolic Faith, a denomination within the **Holiness Movement**. By the 1950s, the denomination had become a religious empire of at least 500,000 members in 300 congregations in nearly 70 cities, primarily, along the East Coast. Contemporary estimates, however, indicate that there has been a sizeable decline in the body so that current estimates are that there are approximately 145 congregations in 29 cities primarily in the Southern and Eastern parts of the United States.

While some respected sources categorize the group as a Pentecostal Holiness denomination, its designation as a quasi-Holiness derives, in part, from the fact within a short time after its establishment, Grace had introduced elements into the structure and polity of the organization that placed it within the genre of a personality cult rather than within the authentic classical Pentecostal tradition. Grace, for example, made claims regarding his own deity, saying that church members should look to him as God's emissary, not to God directly, for salvation. Later, he reportedly, claimed for himself the authority to grant and withhold salvation, allegedly asserting at one point, "[n]ever mind about God. . .[s]alvation is by Grace only. Grace has given God a vacation. If you sin against God, Grace can save you, but if you sin against Grace, God can't save you." Though worship within the congregations incorporates elements of classical Holiness-Pentecostalism such as shouting (spiritual dancing) and speaking in tongues, lyrics of songs within the denomination's worship were often altered to lift up the name of "Daddy" rather than God or Jesus, incorporating such lines as "life Daddy higher" for classical refrain, "life Jesus higher." Further, his authoritarian one-man rule provided that many offerings went directly to Grace, who held the singular authority to excommunicate members and even leaders who did not fall in line with his authority.

Over its nearly ninety-year history, the organization has been headed by a succession of senior bishops who each have practiced his authoritarian style of leadership to some degree. At Grace's death in 1960, **Walter McCollough** took office and served for more than thirty years, until 1991, after winning a court fight and two elections. McCollough launched a nationwide building program, erecting low-income and affordable housing for parishioners, as well as others in the community. He also built a number of new churches, day care centers and senior citizens homes, and renovated older edifies.

After McCollough's death, **Samuel Christee Madison** was elected and continued his predecessor's building program. Under his administration, over 123 Houses of Prayer received major renovation or were constructed, and numerous apartments, senior citizens' dwellings, parsonages, houses, and commercial properties were erected.

After winning ninety-one percent approval by the General Assembly, the current presider, **C.M. Bailey** a native of Newport News, Virginia, and former pastor apostle of the United House of Prayer for All People in Augusta, Georgia (the mother church for the state of Georgia) came into leadership.

While not crediting to them the level of deity that Grace held for himself, adherents hold successive leaders as intermediaries with God. Each successive has continued the one-man leadership style initiated by Grace and bears the moniker "Daddy," and continued the founder's extravagant lifestyle. Presiding bishops receive such royal treatment as riding on a throne surrounded by a uniformed entourage in the marching parades, being driven around in custom made limos, giving them ownership or access to several luxury homes and other benefits.

The organization is known for feeding those in communities that surround its churches, affordable soul food restaurants, annual colorful "Christian Saints" marching parades with shout bands, mass baptisms, sometimes performed on public streets using fire hoses in which hundreds of white appareled congregants are baptized. The McCollough Theological Seminary founded in Richmond, Virginia in 1967 offers an unaccredited training program for its ministers.

There have been two major schisms within the ranks of the organization. In 1927, **Alonzo Daughtry** became disillusioned with Grace's claims to divinity, and after attempting to temper the adulation some followers heaped on him left to establish the House of the Lord and Church on the Mount Pentecostal Church in Brooklyn, New York. In 1962, several elders challenged Walter McCollough's right of succession to Grace and accused him of mishandling church funds. When the presider won the court ordered election a Philadelphia congregation, under the leadership of Thomas Odell Johnson, this group separately incorporated as the True Grace Memorial House of Prayer.

Further Reading:

Brune, Danielle Elizabeth. *Sweet Daddy Grace: The Life and Times of a Modern Day Prophet.* PhD Dissertation, University of Texas at Austin, 2002.

Dallam, Marie. *Daddy Grace: A Celebrity Preacher and His House of Prayer.* New York: New York University Press, 2007.

Whiting, Albert N. *The United House of Prayer for All People: A Case Study of a Charismatic Sect.* PhD Dissertation, American University, 1952.

U

United Pentecostal Church International, Race Relations in

The largest Oneness body in the United States—the predominantly white United Pentecostal Church—began as a splinter group from the interracial **Pentecostal Assemblies of the World** and currently exhibits a racial position that mirrors its Trinitarian siblings. Formation of the UPCI resulted from an amalgamation of the whites who left PAW in 1924 (rather than remain under black leadership) to form the Apostolic Churches of Jesus Christ with another predominantly white denomination which would come to be known as the Apostolic Church of Jesus Christ.

In 1931 the group's leaders proposed a merger with the PAW that would allow the two bodies to again form a multi-racial denomination. With that possibility rejected, the white groups came together to form the Pentecostal Assemblies of Jesus Christ. Despite its beginnings, the new organization took steps to ensure that racial disparity within its ranks would be minimized. Early on, its leaders determined that the governing Presbyter Board would consist of twelve members—six white and six black. Four of the first five General Assemblies had to be held in the North because black members could not secure adequate accommodations in the South. Yet this caused a hardship for Southern white pastors who could not afford the cost associated with traveling north.

In 1936 the General Assembly made the policy that Presbyter Board representation should reflect the denomination's racial composition, which at that time was 80 percent white and 20 percent black. Yet, apparently, such overtures were not sufficient for many of the blacks who remained in the organization. At the 1937 General Assembly, several blacks resigned and returned to the PAW. Presumably, this included all of the blacks on the Presbyter Board since after their departure, for the first time, this board was made up entirely of whites. Between 1928 and 1945, several more blacks left the organization to return to PAW. In 1945 the Pentecostal Assemblies of Jesus Christ and the Pentecostal Churches, Inc. merged and formed the United Pentecostal Church. Though a small number of blacks have historically been affiliated with the UPC since its founding, initially African American ministers were not listed in the regular section of the ministerial directory with the white ministers. Instead, they were listed in the back of the directory in a section labeled "the colored branch."

Throughout much of the Civil Rights era, the United Pentecostal Church maintained the same relatively silent posture as its Trinitarian siblings. Still, the denomination has generally characterized itself as interracial. When the **Pentecostal Fellowship of North America** was formed in 1948 as an Anglo-American organization, the UPCI declined to join on two points: while it rejected the Trinitarian doctrinal stance of the group, it also refused to relinquish its own interracial policy.

In recent years, the UPCI has become more ethnically diverse. Today, evangelistic efforts targeting blacks are centered on a national Black Evangelism Conference that annually addresses the special interest of the African-American community and trains UPCI ministers and laity involved in reaching that community. Several thousand persons attend the events that elect a director of Black Ministries who is supported by a Black Evangelism Board under the direction of the Home Missions Division. While the denomination does keep racial statistics, the majority of UPCI's black constituency is

Caribbean with most of these coming from Jamaica. The largest black congregation in North American, Faith Sanctuary in Toronto, Ontario, has over one thousand members. Granville McKenzie, the pastor of that largely Jamaican congregation is the highest-ranking black in the denomination, serving as the Executive Superintendent of Canada. His church is one of the more successful congregations in the UPCI and includes Faith Academy that goes to grade six; Faith Institute, a Bible college; and a 150-unit nonprofit senior residence located on site.

Interestingly, while there are a number of majority black or integrated UPCI congregations throughout the United States, African Americans have been reluctant to attach themselves to the denomination, and black Oneness denominations have been reluctant to associate with white Oneness colleagues, choosing rather to focus ecumenical efforts on black Trinitarian Pentecostal affiliations. Caribbean blacks have been less so, presumably, because they do not attach the same racial history to its beginnings and unfolding. Within the US, the largest black UPC congregations are located in large metropolitan areas along the east coast. Further, there are a number of multi-racial congregations scattered throughout the country, and a number of African-American pastors, presbyters and district superintendents currently hold leadership positions in the UPCI today.

United Pentecostal Council of the Assemblies of God

In 1917 African-American missionaries Alexander and Margaret Howard approached denominational leaders within the New England region of the Assemblies of God for support as missionaries in Liberia, West Africa. However, they were refused support primarily because of race. Two years later, the Howards, along with a committee including members from three African-American Pentecostal churches in Cambridge, Massachusetts, formed the New England District Council of the Assemblies of God, specifically to financially and spiritually support missionaries working out of their district.

Howard joined this community of New England churches that became The UPCAOG in 1920. That year, members of the group provided the Howards with $1,200, allowing them to begin ministry in Africa. Since the AG already had a New England District, the group renamed their body the United Pentecostal Council of the Assemblies of God.

George Phillips, a member of the founding of UPCAG and a professor at the Zion Bible Institute in Providence, Rhode Island, emerged as the first UPCAG president. When he died in 1948, another founding member, Conrad Dottin, was chosen as president, serving until his death in 1953. Allan C. Miller assumed the post that year, serving in that position until 1964 when the Presbytery Board consecrated him national bishop. In 1962, When Miller declined to be re-nominated, **Roderick Caesar**, pastor of Bethel Gospel Tabernacle in Queens, New York was elevated to national president.

The Trinitarian denomination holds belief similar to its predominantly white parent body. In 2014, after four years of negotiations, prompted by an overture from UPCAG, the two denominations entered an agreement through retained their own governance and credentialing process but partner as a cooperative network, allowing any UPCAG congregation fellowship into local AG districts, as well as all national AG programs and missions.

The UPCAG has thirty congregations in the United States, fifteen in Barbados, and twenty-two congregations. The headquarters of the organization is in Cambridge, Massachusetts.

Further Reading:

Greene, Herman L. *UPCAG: The First 90 Years; Volume 1: 1919 to 1945.* Monsey, NJ: Geda, 2005.
Harrup, Scott. "A Larger Family." *Pentecostal Evangel,* Jan. 16, 2011.

United Progressive Pentecostal Church Fellowship

The denomination founded in 2008 by Bishop **O. C. Allen III**, as an organization that is "unapologetically Pentecostal and unashamedly welcoming to all" is a body that insists, contrary to the vast majority of Pentecostal leaders and congregations, that homosexuality is a biblically acceptable lifestyle. Allen, senior pastor of the 3500-plus member **Vision Church International** in Atlanta, Georgia, that is lauded in liberal Christian circles and the secular press as one the fastest growing churches in the United States, serves as presiding bishop. The rapid success of Allen's **Vision Church International** led other gay or affirming churches and pastors to seek him out as spiritual covering for their ministries.

The organization does not consider itself a denomination, but rather a fellowship with membership open to local members, congregations are fully autonomous and meet yearly for its annual convocation, which to date has been held in Atlanta. The first of these events, held in 2009, drew delegates from more than ninety affirming congregations.

The organization's statement of belief revolves around five principles or "pillars" Three of these resound with classical Evangelical tenets—exaltation of the name of Jesus, understanding of Christ as head of the church, and seeing God's plan of salvation as coming through Christ. The other two—God's call for Justice and Peace for all humanity and God's "inclusive love exemplified in and offer through Christ"—relate to the protestation that accepting persons within the gay community into the full life of the church is a biblical mandate. This is a claim that the vast majority of Pentecostal Christians would reject. Further, while incorporating classically Pentecostal language such as Christ-like lifestyle, healing and restoration for the entire Body of Christ, member churches are expected to incorporate principles that are antithetical to historical Pentecostal principles. These include the expectation that member congregation become "welcoming, inclusive, "Whosoever" churches" and "teach the principles of inclusion," They further incorporate the affirmation that "spiritual unity is . . . expressed among all Christians by . . . acceptance of . . . one another regardless of . . . sexual orientation." Moreover, UPPC insists that one hallmark of Pentecostalism is not only the demonstration of the Holy Spirit, but the "eradication of . . . orientational . . . barriers."

Further Reading:

Wilson, Derick. *Progressive Pentecostalism.* S.l., Lulu Com, 2013.

United Way of the Cross Churches of Christ of the Apostolic Faith

A Oneness Pentecostal denomination founded in 1974 by Joseph H. Adams of Axton, Virginia, formerly of the **Way of the Cross Church of Christ** who had concerns regarding the administration of his former body; Harrison Twyman, pastor of **Bibleway World Wide** congregation in North Carolina; and James Pritchard, formerly of the **Apostolic Church of Christ in God**.

In 1998 Bishop **James H. Carter** was elevated as an archbishop and appointed chairperson of the Board of Bishops. In 2003 after Adams's death, Carter became presiding bishop and chief executive officer of the Board of Apostles. After serving in that office for only two years, however, Carter left the UWCCC to found the **United Cornerstone Churches of Christ International.**

UWCCC is headquarters is in Danville, Virginia. The denomination grew primarily from the addition of congregations that had left other Oneness Pentecostal bodies. There are approximately fifty churches in North Carolina, South Carolina, Virginia, Maryland, New Jersey, Ohio and the West Indies with approximately one thousand members, thirty ministers, and four bishops.

Universal Christian Spiritual Faith and Church for All Nations

Founded in 1952 as a merger of three quasi-Pentecostal religious bodies—the National David Spiritual Temple of Christ Church Union, Inc. which had been founded in 1932 by David William Short in Kansas City, Missouri, St. Paul's Spiritual Church Convocation formed in 1937 in Washington DC, King David's Spiritual Temple of Truth Association. Short, a former Baptist minister, became archbishop of the new body.

This is one of the rare African-American Pentecostal bodies in the United States that teaches a two-crisis salvation experience of regeneration and baptism in the Holy Spirit and that holds that sanctification is an on-going process in distinct contract to the predominately Wesleyan understanding of a three stage salvation experience of regeneration, sanctification and Holy Spirit baptism. The group differs from classical Pentecostals in that denies the assertion that only those who have spoken in tongues have received the Holy Spirit. Yet, UPPC insists that full Holy Spirit baptism is accompanied by speaking in tongues as well as the demonstration of other gifts.

The denominational educational institution is St. David's Spiritual Seminary in Des Moines, Iowa. The headquarters is in Los Angeles, California. The monthly publication is the *Christian Spiritual Voice* and the current membership unknown. However, in the mid-1960s there were reportedly sixty churches and approximately 41,000 members.

Utterbach, Clinton 1931–2005

Utterbach, Sarah 1937–

Clinton was a conductor, composer, and arranger and director of the ground breaking Utterbach Gospel Ensemble that was prominent on the black gospel choir circuit in the 1960s and 1970s. His parents, who were Pentecostal gospel musicians, attended Refuge **Church of Our Lord Jesus Christ** in Harlem, pastored by **Robert Clarence Lawson**.

Prior to becoming a pastor, Clinton Utterbach was intimately involved with music. In his teen years, he was a church choir director. In 1961 he founded the Ensemble, which gained widespread acclaim and established a number of "firsts" for the gospel genre of music, including performances on college campuses, on national television, and at Carnegie Hall in New York City.

Sometime around 1979, the couple embraced the Word of Faith (prosperity gospel) message. In that year, Clinton left his successful career in gospel music and Sarah left her corporate career to attend Rhema Training Center, a Word of Faith institution in Tulsa, Oklahoma. While there, Clinton was introduced to praise music, which was distinctly different from the traditional hymns, spirituals, and gospel music of his early church experience.

In 1996 the Utterbachs purchased a 53-acre campground in the Pocono Mountains of Pennsylvania. They named it Redeeming Love Christian Village, a family-oriented location, housing residential cabins and a conference center containing a chapel, banquet hall, and meeting rooms.

In 1980 Clinton and Sarah founded Redeeming Love Christian Center as a nondenominational, multi-racial congregation in their home in Hackensack, New Jersey. Within a few months, they relocated to a larger facility, and finally settled in a 3,000-seat auditorium in Nanuet, New York. They launched a school and a media ministry, and in 2002, expanded to include a second church, the Redeeming Love Christian Center at the Village.

Clinton was so intent on introducing praise music instead of gospel to the congregation that he did not form a church choir. Instead, four years after establishing the congregation, twenty-two singers were selected for the Praisers. The group ministered for the first time in 1985 and recorded several albums with Utterbach.

In part the ministry growth was due to radio outreach through the live, call-in program "Listen to Jesus," which at one point had expanded to thirty stations—three of which were in the Caribbean. Sarah also edited a quarterly devotional magazine, *Horizons Unlimited*.

Though the Utterbach's ministry centered in part on divine healing, Clinton suffered a number of physical conditions including an aneurism, near stroke, kidney failure and transplant. After his death, Sarah continued the ministry as senior pastor emeritus. In 2006 she installed Edward Pfundstein and Gregory Carr, both of whom had served under the couple for more than twenty years as her co-pastors.

V

Vision Church of Atlanta

The local church was founded by Bishop **O. C. Allen, III**—an openly homosexual, self-proclaimed "progressive" Pentecostal pastor—and twelve followers in 2005 as a multiracial, Pentecostal congregation, that is the founding congregation of the United Progressive Pentecostal Church Fellowship a welcoming and affirmation denomination. The first worship service drew twenty new members, and within three months, the congregation had grown to fifty. By the end of eighteen months, membership had reached 675. Currently there are approximately 3,000 members, majority of whom are self-identified homosexual, lesbian bi-sexual, or transgender individuals or families.

The congregation runs a number of major ministries including the Vision Cathedral, Vision Empowerment Center, the Vision Institute for Life Enrichment, Vision Seminary and a Family Life Center. The Bread of Life Ministry (an outreach arm of the church) feeds over 12,000 individuals annually in downtown Atlanta.

The church's theology of gender and sexuality runs counter to the vast majority of classical Pentecostal denominations or congregations as well as most Charismatic and Neo-Pentecostal groups. Further, though the majority of Pentecostal leaders openly oppose the homosexual lifestyle as not in line with biblical moral precepts, the church and its leader have found tacit support from more liberal factions within the broader Christian community.

In the fall of 2010, the Atlanta congregation purchased a 2.9 million dollar property in the Grant Park area of the city to house the new Vision Church "Cathedral" and a variety of outreach ministries. Allen's partner, Rashad Burgess, serves as first gentleman of the congregation, as parallel to the role of first lady generally reserved for pastor's wives.

W

Waddles, Charleszetta Campbell 1912–2001

Pastor and community organizer and activist who founded the Perpetual Mission for Saving Souls of All Nations in Detroit, Michigan after overcoming an tumultuous early life. Her father died when she was twelve, after suffering financial ruin. She left school in eighth grade to work as a house cleaner to help support her family. While working in a rag factory the following year, she became pregnant by her boyfriend, who ended up leaving her. In 1933, at age twenty-one, she married a thirty-seven-year-old truck driver, and had six children together before divorcing him twelve years later. She then lived in a common-law marriage and produced three more children. By 1937, as a twice married, single mother of ten young children, she was receiving public assistance and reading voraciously to educate herself. She moved to Detroit from St. Louis where she met her third husband, Payton Waddles, an employee of Ford Motor Company while selling barbeque at a church fundraiser, and later married him.

At some point in the late 1940s, Waddles had a vision in which, "the Lord told [her] to feed the hungry and clothe the naked." Armed with this dream, Waddles began holding prayer meetings at her house for small groups of local women, exhorting them to involve themselves in practical, charitable actions rather than religious rhetoric. She taught that no one was too poor to help someone the less fortunate.

In 1956, nineteen years after moving to Detroit, Waddles was ordained in the First Pentecostal Church. A year later, sixty year old "Mother Waddles," as she came to be known, convinced an inner-city property owner to let her use a vacant storefront at no cost and founded the Perpetual Mission for Saving Souls of All Nations. At its height, it housed a mission that sheltered the homeless each evening, and offered between 90,000 and 100,000 meals annually for thirty-five cents per person. The ministry drew on more than two hundred volunteers providing emergency financial assistance, job training, a graphic arts program, and other programs to unwed mothers, prostitutes, abused children, the handicapped, the elderly, and the poor without using government funding. Over time, her mission became the most frequent source for referral services in the city.

Waddle worked twelve-hour days as the head of the ministry, until she was eighty-two years old. Her work drew accolades from the secular press, city officials, and even Richard Nixon, then president of the United States. It also garnered her dozens of awards from local, state and national organizations including the Sojourner Truth Award, and the National Urban League, and the Lane Bryant Citizens Award. For many years, the governor of Michigan and the mayor of Detroit sponsored an annual Mother Waddles Week, focusing local attention on the importance of community service.

Waddles died at the age of eighty-eight.

Further Reading:

Hine, Darlene Clark, ed. "Charleszetta Waddles." In *Black Women in America: An Historical Encyclopedia.* New York: Carlson, 1993.

Wagner, Norman L. 1942–2010

Former presiding bishop of the **Pentecostal Assemblies of the World,** sought after as a preacher and teacher in Pentecostal apostolic circles, and longtime pastor of Mount Calvary Pentecostal Church of Youngstown, Ohio, the city where he was raised. He graduated from Youngstown State University, where he later served as a lecturer, before earning bachelor's and master's degrees in theology from Aenon Bible College in Columbus and Indiana Bible College in Indianapolis.

In 1969 he began traveling extensively as a national evangelist, gaining a reputation as a powerful preacher and gifted musician. In 1971 he was installed as pastor of the Mount Calvary congregation, where he served for thirty-nine years. His mother had been a charter member of that congregation where he grew up and served as youth leader before becoming assistant pastor under James Tyson. Under his pastorate, the church established Calvary Christian Academy; a nation-wide weekly television program, "The Power of Pentecost," which aired on the Praise the Lord (PTL) and Armed Forces networks; Saints Saving and Trust Credit Union; and Calvary Towers Senior Citizen Complex. When Calvary Christian Academy closed in 2001, Wagner directed the opening of a charter school, Legacy Academy for Leaders and Arts and served as board chair. He also founded Pentecost in Perspective International, an annual leadership conference. Along with his civic work, and preaching Wagner was known across this country and the world for the several books he authored. The respected singer, songwriter and arranger was also nominated with his choir for two Stellar Gospel Music Awards.

Within PAW Wagner served president of the National Young People's Union from 1973 to 1976, as bishop 13th Episcopal district that incorporated the state of Texas and the European Council of Nations of PAW, a network of forty churches throughout that continent. He was elected Assistant General Secretary and remained in that office until being elected presiding bishop of the denomination in 1998, becoming one of the youngest presiding prelates in PAW history. He served in that position until 2004.

In recognition for his work, in 1976, *The [Youngstown] Vindicator* named him one of the ten most progressive pastors in the city. In 1982 President Ronald Reagan recognized him as among one hundred "Outstanding Black Clergymen in America."

Walker, Joseph Warren III

The second International presiding bishop of the **Full Gospel Baptist Church Fellowship International,** succeeding founder, **Paul S. Morton Sr.,** at the head of the Neo-Pentecostal organization. In 1992 twenty-four-year-old Walker assumed the pastorate of Mt. Zion Baptist Church, a congregation of 175 members in Nashville, Tennessee. In 2006, his launched the first church plant of Zion Baptist, Zion Church in Jackson, Tennessee. By 2013, the ministry had grown to over 28,000 with seven weekly services in three physical locations and included www.mtzionanywhere.org, its fourth church location. It hosts five weekly television broadcasts and two daily radio ministries.

In 2009, after losing his first wife Diane to cancer, Walker married Dr. Stephaine Hale. In 2010 the couple founded the Dr. Joseph & Stephaine Walker Foundation, an education, mentorship, and outreach organization. Within four years, the foundation awarded over $500,000 in scholarships through the Dr. Diane Greer Walker Memorial Scholarship Fund.

Born and raised in Shreveport, Louisiana, Walker received a Bachelor of Arts degree from Southern University in Baton Rouge, Louisiana, a Master of Divinity degree from Vanderbilt University and a Doctor of Ministry degree from Princeton Theological Seminary. He has authored eight books, been the recipient of numerous awards and honors, sits on several boards including the American Red Cross, and holds a seat on the Tennessee Human Rights Commission.

Walker's community involvement includes launching the New Level Community Development Corporation (NLCDC) in 2001, to provide housing and other services to low-and moderate-income families, and economic development to the community surrounding his church. He also launched ChurchFit, a comprehensive health and wellness program designed to promote healthy lifestyles within the faith community. The program strives to preserve good health, revive fitness goals and promote/improve overall health and wellness among program participants.

In 2010 the *Nashville Post Magazine* recognized his efforts by naming him one of the city's most influential leaders. In 2013, theroot.com named Walker one of the twenty Top Black Preachers in the country, and most recently, EBONY recognized him on its "Power 100" list as one of the nation's most influential Afro-American leaders. He also has been a guest on CNN and on CBS Morning News and was featured in the film "Black, White and Blues," directed by award-winning Mario Van Peebles.

Throughout this time, Walker's role in the Full Gospel Baptist Church Fellowship, International Full Gospel Baptist Church Fellowship International was expanding. He was first was appointed to the Executive Council, and then bishop of senior pastors. Prior to heading FGBCFI, Walker found himself embroiled in controversy when five women in his Nashville congregation accused him of sexual misconduct. Though he refuted the charges as an attempt to extort money from him and the church, following these allegations, some were surprised at his selection to head the sprawling FGBCFI.

His election prompted Bishop **Neil Ellis**, who as second presiding bishop, expected to take on the senior post, to leave the FGBCFI and establish a new organization, **The Global United Fellowship.**

Washington, Ernestine Beatrice Thomas 1914–1983

Touted as the "Song Bird of The East" by the **Church of God in Christ** music community and referred to as Madame Ernestine Washington by many, the onetime official COGIC soloist was originally from Little Rock, Arkansas. Her mother was a popular sanctified church singer in the community, and Ernestine started singing at age four. While in high school, she did domestic work while she sang in the church.

Washington traveled across the country to churches, then worked with her husband, **F. D. Washington**, to establish two congregations, the first in Montclair, New Jersey, and finally the renowned Washington Temple COGIC in Brooklyn, New York.

Earlier COGIC gospel singer, **Arizona Dranes**, heavily influenced Washington. However, while at the height of her career, she gave several hundred concerts a year and recorded with secular artists in a style that incorporated jazz elements. Unlike Dranes, she refused to cross into secular music, or sing in venues such as nightclubs. Most of the mezzo-soprano's recordings were made during the 1940s when she worked with such groups as secular jazz trumpeter William Geary "Bunk" Johnson and his band, the Dixie Hummingbirds, and with the Southern Sons. She also performed in live appearances on church bills with such luminary friends as Mahalia Jackson, Roberta Martin, and the Selah Jubilee Singers.

After coming to Brooklyn in 1951, she continued to record but at a slower pace, and she traveled less, choosing to remain near home to work with her husband to build the congregation. Washington's 1940s recordings were re-released in the 1990s on the Documents Records label.

Further Reading:

Boyer, Horace Clarence. "Gospel in New York." In *The Golden Age of Gospel*. Urbana, IL: University of Illinois Press, 2000.

Washington, Frederick Douglas (F. D.) 1914–1988

Prominent **Church of God in Christ**, bishop, pastor, evangelist, and radio personality who built one of the most widely known COGIC congregations of the mid-twentieth century. Born in Dermott, Arkansas, he was named after the civil rights leader Frederick Douglass. Washington, the son of a COGIC pastor, began preaching as adolescent and was ordained as a minister during his teen years.

He first served as a pastor of a COGIC congregation in Montclair, New Jersey, before moving to Brooklyn, New York, to hold tent revival services. From these meetings, he established a congregation that grew to become Washington Temple Church of God in Christ. Washington went on to purchase the old Loew's Theatre and to launch a radio broadcast that featured his preaching and the singing of his wife, **Ernestine Washington**, who was tagged "The Songbird of the East." Working as a team, the two drew large numbers of people and eventually Washington Temple COGIC, with about 3,000 members, became one of the largest congregations of any denomination located in Brooklyn during that period.

Washington served as assistant jurisdictional bishop of New York under **O. M. Kelly** before finally succeeding him in 1983. He also served on the General Board of the Church Of God In Christ as second assistant to **Bishop J.O. Patterson, Sr,** and as the first president of the Church of God in Christ Publishing House.

Washington was influential in the lives of many who would go to become successful in COGIC as well as in the broader community. One of the most well-known personalities to come out of his congregation is **Al Sharpton**, whom he licensed and ordained as a minister at the age of nine. Ultimately, he introduced Sharpton to Reverend William Augustus Jones Jr., who converted Sharpton to his current Baptist faith. Besides Sharpton, Washington mentored several others who would go on to become prominent leaders with COGIC and the broader Pentecostal realm including Timothy Wright, world famous gospel artist.

He died of heart failure in Brooklyn at the age of seventy-five.

Washington, Johnnie Lee 1929–1986

Faith healer, traveling Evangelist and founding bishop of the Tabernacle of Prayer for All People, a megachurch congregation within the Deliverance segment of the Pentecostal movement. Washington was born in a small, mostly black town of Mound Bayou, Mississippi, where he first became a minister in the Christian Church (Disciples of Christ) before affiliating with the **Church of God in Christ**. The gifted singer first moved to New Orleans, then New York City where he travelled and sang with a gospel group, called "The Gospel Wonders," and rejoined the Disciples of Christ.

In 1968 he established his first congregation in the Red Hook section of Brooklyn, Tabernacle of Prayer For all People, the Center of Hope" with approximately fifteen people. In 1972 Washington opened the Manhattan Bible Institute with approximately fifty students. Two years later, he launched a tent ministry in Brooklyn. In 1977, the congregation moved into their newly renovated building in Jamaica, New York, an historic 1920s Jewish Synagogue with a seating capacity of more than 3,500.

Washington's preaching and singing regularly drew a packed house of worshippers. His organization grew to include several congregations throughout the United States

As the years progressed, Apostle Johnnie Washington expanded his ministry through radio programs around the country. In the early 1980s, Washington used the newly available technology of cable TV to launch a national television broadcast.

The faith healer suffered from several medical problems including a bout with cancer. Yet he resolutely preached against use of traditional medical care and refused to seek care for himself. Washington apparently suffered several strokes and a heart attack and died after a short illness at the age of fifty-six. By the time of his death, there were thirty-six congregations within Tabernacle Fellowship primarily along the East Coast.

Way of the Cross Church of Christ

Bishop **Henry Chauncey Brooks** had come to Washington DC to plant an independent congregation in 1927. Six years later, in 1933, that congregation was granted charter credentials from Bishop **Robert Clarence Lawson** and became an affiliate of Lawson's **Church of our Lord Jesus Christ of the Apostolic Faith**, one the largest **African-American** Oneness Pentecostal bodies in United States.

In 1933 Lawson approached Brooks about relinquishing his still fledging congregation to **Smallwood E. Williams** on the assumption that one strong congregation would better serve the denomination than two smaller churches. Instead, Brooks broke away to lead an independent work. Brooks initially had no desire to start an organization and was content to remain independent. However, as other ministers and churches sought to work with him, he officially started the **Way of the Cross Churches of Christ**. Within a short period, a second congregation in Henderson, North Carolina became the first of several to join WOTCCC. Brooks continued to pastor the mother church for forty years while building the denomination's membership to over 3,000 before his death in 1967, only ten years after founding the organization.

Under his leadership, the organization grew to about twenty-five churches throughout the Eastern United States. After Brooks' death, Joseph Weathers, who had served as a chief assistant to Brooks, appeared most likely to succeed him. Instead, Brooks' brother, Bishop John Luke Brooks served as presiding bishop and pastor of the mother congregation. During his administration, seven churches were added in Ghana, West Africa, and a national foreign missions effort was begun.

When he did not receive the appointment as presiding bishop, Weathers broke away with approximately one hundred members of the Washington congregation to form the Holy Temple Church of Christ as an independent congregation. In 1974 another disgruntled leader, Joseph H. Adams of Axton, Virginia, pull out of the organization over concerned with Brooks' administration to form **United Way of the Cross Churches of Christ of the Apostolic Faith**.

Brooks stepped down from the pastorate of the mother congregation in 1978, turning it over to the founder's son, Alphonzo Brooks. However, he continued to preside over the denomination until his death in 1981, when Harry Clay Eggleston became the third presiding bishop. He served in that position until his death in 1985.

On assuming the position of presiding bishop in that year, **LeRoy Cannady** introduced organizational structure into the denomination with formation of the Executive Board of Bishops, the General Board of Bishops, the Pastoral Council, the Ministers and Elders Council, the National Sunday School Department, the diaconate, the Pastor's Wives Council, and other ministries at the national and international level.

A year later, the denomination added thirteen churches and missions in Ghana and Liberia. Today the Way of the Cross Church of Christ International consists of nearly one hundred churches including congregation in twelve states, seventy-two congregations in India, and a congregation in Ghana, West Africa.

Wenyika, Reggies

The educator and church leader is the first African-American president of Southwestern Christian University, a Pentecostal Holiness Church institution in Oklahoma City, Oklahoma. Born and raised in Zimbabwe, Wenyika earned a Certificate, Diploma, and Bachelor of Religious Arts degree at the University of Zimbabwe.

He and his wife arrived in the United States in 2000 where he pursued a master's degree and doctorate in Education from Oral Roberts University and a master's degree from Southwestern Christian University. Prior to leaving Zimbabwe, Wenyika worked in the biomedical field. He also served on the pastoral staff of Hear the Word Church (Celebration Church) in Harare for four years, first as youth pastor and later as an associate on the pastoral team. He also served as an adjunct lecturer at the Bible College and assisted with leadership development.

Wenyika first became employed in education in 1993, as a public school substitute teacher, then worked as a graduate assistant at ORU while he completed graduate work. He began at Southwestern as Provost and Vice-President for Academic Affairs in 2008, after previously serving for nearly two years as Assistant Director of the Veritas Worldview Institute at Oklahoma Wesleyan University

In 2014 Wenyika was elected the 12th president of Southwestern Christian University, a liberal arts university institution with more than 800 students. At the same time, he serves as a vice president for Faith Community Churches International, a fellowship of Pentecostal churches in over forty-seven countries.

Wheelock, Donald Ray 1947–

A scholar, educator and preacher in the **Church of God in Christ**. Wheelock was born in Houston, Texas. He preached his first sermon at seventeen years of age and from that point was convinced he should dedicate his education to pursue his call to ministry. Wheelock changed his undergraduate major at Southern University in Baton Rouge from Speech and Theater, in which he had excelled in high school, to Speech Pathology and Audiology. Following that, he earned a Master of Divinity degree at Colgate-Rochester Divinity School in Rochester, New York.

Returning to Louisiana in 1971, he was ordained. Then in the summer 1972, he served as interim pastor of Holy Temple COGIC in Norwalk, Connecticut. That year, he began pursuing his PhD at Candler School of Theology at Emory University in Atlanta, GA where, in 1983, he was awarded the PhD in Philosophical Theology, completing a dissertation entitled "Spirit Baptism in American Pentecostal Thought."

While serving as pastor of the Fairburn Church of God in Christ, he accepted a position as academic dean and ultimately president of **Saints College and Academy** in Lexington, Kentucky succeeding **Arenia Mallory**. Wheelock led the institution in acquiring both state and regional accreditation while serving in several COGIC jurisdictional leadership posts. In 1985 Wheelock was sent to pastor the historical Mount Moriah Church of God in Christ in Mendenhall, Mississippi. In 1991, while continuing to serve at Saints, he became adjunct professor of Religion at Tougaloo College in Tougaloo, Mississippi. He remained pastor of the Mendenhall congregation as well as Saints College and Academy until his retirement from the pastorate in 1993.

White, Archibald Henry (A. H.) 1929–1981

Founder and first presiding bishop of the **House of God, Church of the Living God Pillar and Ground of the Truth.** White was converted and received the Pentecostal experience of Holy Spirit baptism in 1910 while **Mary Magdalena Lewis Tate**, the chief overseer of the **Church of the Living God Pillar and Ground of the Truth** was conducting a revival in Waycross, Georgia.

White was called to the ministry in 1911, an in 1914 Tate sent him to pastor a Lumber City, Georgia congregation, then to Greenville, Alabama where he built a congregation while presiding over the States of Mississippi and Alabama. In 1915 he was appointed to a Douglas, Georgia congregation and that same year was consecrated as one of the first four state bishops of Tate's original denomination.

For several years, White set up churches under the auspices of the **House of God Church of the Living God, Pillar and Ground of the Truth,** as an affiliate of Tate's group before relocating to Philadelphia, Pennsylvania to establish a storefront congregation that quickly grew from twenty members to several hundred. In 1929 White pulled the congregations he had started out of Tate's body to establish a separate organization under the name he had been using. He remained the senior bishop until his demise when bishop James H. Smith was unanimously elected as the next senior bishop and president general.

White, John C. (J. C.) 1939–

The second presiding bishop of the **Institutional Church of God in Christ, International,** a schism group from the **Church of God in Christ,** is a native of Brooklyn, New York. In his early ministry, he served as a deacon at the Institutional Church of God in Christ in his home city and director of the Grammy-nominated Institutional Church of God in Christ Radio Choir. His composition "Stretch Out" launched the Institutional Radio Choir on the road to popularity.

In 1979 white who was serving as an elder and assistant pastor was called to lead Turner's Faith Temple Church of God in Christ, International in Bridgeport, Connecticut. Within a short time, he was elevated to the office of bishop over the States of Connecticut and Virginia He was later called to serve as chairperson of the Board of Bishops and as vice presiding bishop. In 2000 he was appointed presiding prelate of the **Churches of God in Christ International**.

White holds an honorary doctorate of Sacred Music from the Pillar of Fire College in York, England, a doctorate of Divinity from the Eastern American University in Indianapolis, Indiana, and a doctorate of Theology from the North Carolina College of Theology.

White's local congregation, Cathedral of Praise, houses an elementary school; a senior citizen high-rise complex; a full-time day care center; a training center for ex-offenders; a halfway house; and a house for unwed teenage mothers. Bishop White has also established the International Bible Institute that awards graduating students certificates in biblical studies.

White, Joseph

Founder of the **Church of the Living God, International** in Columbus, Ohio, as one of several organizations that evolved from the ministry of **Mary Magdalena Tate**'s denomination, **Church of the Living God Pillar and Ground of the Truth.** In 1966, White's mother, Beulah M. White, assumed leadership of the congregation where she had served as assistant pastor. During her pastorate, her son, Joseph was appointed assistant pastor. A year after her death, in 1968, Joseph was appointed the pastor.

Over the next ten years, the younger White saw substantial growth in his ministry within that congregation, which was part of the **Keith Dominion** of Tate's devolving structure. In 1979 White began an expansion program throughout Ohio and neighboring states. A number of churches were started and he was appointed state bishop over what eventually came to be known as the Great Lakes Diocese. Soon he was traveling abroad, bringing congregations in Germany into the organization and starting congregations in Holland, the United Kingdom, Japan, South Korea, Suriname, South America, and Africa.

In 1994 White organized several of the congregations he had founded or nurtured into The Church of the Living God International, Inc. At that time he installed a Board of Bishops, reserving the position of presiding bishop for himself and continues to hold that position.

White Ministers in COGIC

From 1907 until 1914, the **Church of God in Christ** was in a unique position as the only body within the new movement registered with the federal government to grant recognized ministerial credentials. Because of this, COGIC founder, **Charles Harrison Mason** provided the critical service of signing credentials for both black and white Pentecostal ministers asked to surrender their credentials to mainline congregations and denominations. With COGIC credentials in hand, they were not only able to function as pastors and evangelists, but to take advantage of discounted clergy railroad fairs and register as conscientious objectors during World War I.

In the seven years following COGIC's break from **Charles Price Jones** and rebirth as a Pentecostal denomination, Mason credentialed nearly three hundred and fifty white ministers. In 1910 the first white group joined under Elder **Leonard P. Adams.** In 1911 a second group joined under E. B. Bell and Goss. By 1914, however, this arrangement proved to be untenable for the majority of them. The breach began to form some time earlier, when several white leaders approached Mason to suggest that he no longer issue individual credentials, but sign a number of blank certificates and allow them to distribute them and handle all affairs of white ministers. By the later date, the breach culminated in the Hot Springs, Arkansas meeting that signaled the end of formal ties with Mason and the beginning of a new fellowship in which he was, apparently, not invited to participate as a leader.

Though not formally invited, Mason attended that first meeting, preached to the assembled delegates and gave his blessing to the new organization. Once the split became formal, leaders of the Assemblies of God reportedly entered into a "sisterly" agreement with Mason to divide the work of evangelizing along racial lines with the AG reaching out to whites and COGIC doing the same for blacks. Though never corroborated, the "sisterhood myth" as this arrangement was known, persisted until the late twentieth century, coloring the race politics and evangelism strategies of the two bodies. Yet, Mason worked hard to maintain racial unity with other Pentecostal ministers within the young movement. He maintained close alliances with sympathetic white leaders such as **A. J. Tomlinson** of the Church of God (Cleveland, TN) and J. H. King of the Pentecostal Holiness Church.

With the exodus to form the Assemblies of God, a number of white ministers remained with Mason. Whites continued to participate in COGIC worship services and several COGIC congregations continued to have white members. Nevertheless, as white denominations sprang up, participation in the churches declined steadily. For example, **E. R. Driver's** interracial Los Angeles congregation saw a dramatic decline in white members once Aimee Simple McPherson established Angelus Temple.

Even as the number of white ministers in COGIC continued to decline, among those who remained loyal to COGIC and Mason was the "Kentucky Cyclone Evangelist" **James Logan Delk**, who met Mason in 1904 in Conway, Arkansas. Delk was one of few early white Pentecostals to renounce racism publically and became Mason's close confidante–an association often proved costly for him within the white community. Because of it, for example, he was beaten twice by members of the Ku Klux Klan. Yet Delk, a strong leader in his own right, ran revivals throughout the country and hosted a radio broadcast. He maintained relationships with local and national political leaders and ran political office several times, including for governor of Missouri in 1932. During World War II, he used his political connections to secure steel to complete construction of Mason Temple in Memphis. Delk stayed with the organization until death in 1963, two years after Mason.

William B. Holt, a blond-haired German COGIC pastor, who served as the National Field Secretary before becoming COCIC's first General Secretary from 1910 to 1920, was another trusted confident who regularly accompanied Mason as his aide and secretary, and served as superintendent of COGIC Spanish missions in California. The relationship between the two appeared even closer than that maintained by Mason and Delk, for later, presiding bishop, Louis Ford, noted that pair were like blood brothers. Their close friendship drew suspicion from the FBI who monitored them during World War I, believing that Mason might incite blacks to align with Germany. When Mason was arrested by federal agents and thrown into a Lexington, Mississippi, jail for violating the Sedition Act, Holt raised two thousand dollars for his bail. After his release, Mason continued to fellowship with whites, while, all the time, condemning segregation.

Leonard P. Adams, a lawyer and the pastor of Grace and Truth Church, a Holiness congregation near Mason's church in Memphis, had been part of the Cumberland Presbyterian Church. After experiencing the Pentecostal Spirit-baptism in 1908, Adams joined the Church of God (Cleveland, TN). However, in 1910, following a disagreement with General Overseer **A. J. Tomlinson**, Adams left the denomination and his congregation affiliated with COGIC. He was one of the first white ministers to unite with Mason in Memphis and led several other white congregation into the denomination. Though Adams was present at the 1914 AG organizing meeting he did not join the new organization deciding, instead, to continue to work with Mason.

August Feick, had worked with famed evangelist Maria Woodward-Etter in the first quarter of the twentieth century and later served as pastor of the Woodworth-Etter Tabernacle in Indianapolis, Indiana. Reportedly, after Mason asked him to organize the white COGIC churches, he withdrew from the Assemblies of God to work with the black leader.

Around 1916 the White Branch of the Church of God in Christ was known as the Western Department since many of the congregations were located in the Midwest or West. But from 1914 to 1924, there were over three hundred white COGIC congregations throughout the South and Southwest. Though the denomination established a minority conference for white congregations and ministers from across the country, which remained in existence until the mid-1930s, by 1924, pressure for racial separation had increased, and by 1933, COGIC had dismissed Holt and the denomination's interracial period effectively ended.

COGIC has remained explicit regarding its commitment to racial unity, even spelling out a policy of racial tolerance in its polity manual. By the end of the twentieth century, however, white congregations in the Church of God in Christ had all but disappeared, though some individual white members continued to frequent COGIC worship services. Further, some more prominent COGIC congregations, particularly mega-churches such as West Angeles COGIC in Los Angeles, continued to attract a fairly larger number of white to their congregations.

Further Reading:

Clemons, Ithiel. *Bishop C.H. Mason and the Roots of the Church of God in Christ*. Bakersfield, CA: Pneuma Life, 1996.

Newman, Joe. *Race and the Assemblies of God: The Journey from Azusa Street to the "Miracle of Memphis."* Youngstown, NY: Cambria, 2007.

Williams, Dempsey Lawrence (D. Lawrence) 1905–1971

The early **Church of God in Christ** leader was born in Washington, North Carolina where his family became members of the local COGIC congregation. At the age of twelve, he received the Pentecostal experience of Holy Spirit baptism. After graduating from high school, Williams moved to Newport News, Virginia, where he became a master barber and was ordained to the ministry, and finally settled in the nearby Norfolk. In that early period, he travelled as an evangelist and served several churches as pastor before being assigned to the Mother church in that city by COGIC founder, **Charles Harrison Mason**, in 1935.

Ten years later, Mason appointed Williams Overseer for the State of Maryland after **Randolph Carr**, another early COGIC leader, accepted Oneness Pentecostal doctrine and left COGIC to launch the **Church of God in Christ Jesus (Apostolic).** Williams served in that position from 1945 through 1959.

Throughout the 1950s, Williams served as COGIC representative and the first African American Secretary of the Presidium of the World Pentecostal Conference, the organization's executive board, which met in Atlanta, Georgia. His attendance at these sessions insured that he would experience the indignities of the Jim Crow South regarding accommodations, transportation and other amenities. He served two years as president of the Hampton Ministerial Conference and four years as president of the Fellowship of Pentecostal Ministers.

When Mason died in 1961, dissention between senior bishop, **Ozro T. Jones Sr.** and the special commission caused a great deal of anxiety and turmoil. During that time, Williams was elected as chairperson of the Board of Bishops of the Church Of God In Christ, Inc. and member of the General Board that was responsible for making decisions regarding the administrative functioning of the denomination. In the schism between Chairperson, **A. B. McEwen,** and Jones, Williams stood against the majority of board members in support of Jones.

As pastor of Mason Memorial Church of God in Christ, Williams led his congregation in building two housing complexes for the poor and the elderly, Williams Village housing development in Virginia Beach, Virginia and COGIC Memorial Home for the Elderly, Inc. known as COGIC high-rise apartments. He also spearheaded the opening of a child day care center and a well-baby clinic. Williams was eventually appointed bishop of the Second Ecclesiastical Jurisdiction of Virginia, where he served until his death in Norfolk.

Williams, Frank W. ??–d. 1932

We know little of Williams's early life, except that he was from the South, probably from Mississippi and reportedly received the Pentecostal baptism while the meeting was still at **Bonnie Brae Street Prayer Meeting**. He was a long-time friend of **William Joseph Seymour**. As missionaries began to go out from the **Azusa Street Revival**, Williams was among the early wave to carry the Pentecostal message to the South, and was one of the first to give **Charles Harrison Mason** an eyewitness account of the revival.

Yet, his initial attempts to start a congregation in Mississippi failed. His efforts in Mobile, Alabama, however, were more successful. He founded his organization there when, under his preaching, an entire Primitive Baptist Church congregation was converted to Pentecostalism, giving Williams their building as the first meetinghouse for the Apostolic Faith Mission Alabama. Initially, the church was organized in July 10, 1906, as an outreach of Seymour's Los Angeles work. He also planted an African-American Pentecostal congregation in Chicago and the first such congregation in New York City.

In 1915 however, Williams became one of the first to adopt Oneness theology, and broke with Seymour and renamed his church the **Apostolic Faith Mission Church of God**. Williams was influential in leading several future leaders, first into the Pentecostal Movement, then into the Oneness movement. Among them was **W. T. Phillips**, a former Methodist Holiness minister who founded the **Apostolic Overcoming Holiness Church**, whom Williams ordained in 1913.

Williams, Harold Ivory, Sr. 1921–2014

The second presiding bishop of the **Mount Calvary Holy Churches of America** was born in Denton, Maryland, but spent his early life in Baltimore. In 1958, Williams co-founded the Mount Calvary Holy Temple in Baltimore, Maryland with his mother, Rev. Ethel Williams, and his late companion, Dr. Amanda Williams, while he pastored a sister congregation in Washington DC as well as the Winston Salem North Carolina congregation he inherited from MCHCA founder, **Brumfield Johnson**. At the same time, Williams worked as a piano tuner in the Baltimore area. Shortly before he died in 1972, Johnson designated Williams as his successor. Under Williams' leadership, the organization grew to include churches in over fifteen states as well as Europe, Africa, Asia, and the Caribbean.

Williams, an accomplished pianist and songwriter, married prominent gospel singer and pastor, **Shirley Caesar**, in 1983, and from that time, the two served as co-pastors of Raleigh's Mount Calvary Word of Faith Church for over thirty years. From time to time, the couple also worked together as a music team recording. Williams led their local congregation until 2000 when he turned leadership over to his wife, but continued to lead the national church until his retirement in 2008. Following retirement, Williams served as patriarch of the national church.

In the 1990s Williams was one of the first Pentecostals invited to address the historic, Hampton Ministers Conference. His musical acumen was handed down to his late son and namesake, Harold Ivory Williams Jr. The younger Williams was a well-known jazz keyboardist who worked with Miles Davis, Michal Urbaniak, and James Cleveland.

Williams, Joseph David, Sr. 1892-1966

Founding bishop of the Oneness Pentecostal body, the **Progressive Church of the Lord Jesus Christ**. Williams was pastor of Pilgrim Church of Christ, a congregation he established in Cleveland, Ohio under the **Church of Our Lord Jesus Christ of the Apostolic Faith, Inc.** While visiting family in the South, Williams was instrumental in the miraculous divine healing of his wife's niece, who had been diagnosed as terminal cancer, and subsequently was converted to the Pentecostal faith and experienced Pentecostal Holy Spirit baptism.

In 1944 Williams resigned his Cleveland pastorate and moved to Columbia, South Carolina to start a single congregation with his niece and her family as charter members. From there, he traveled and sent workers first throughout the city of Columbia, then to other South Carolina cities, and finally throughout the South to establish congregations. Williams traveled to each of the newly founded Progressive Churches to help lay a strong foundation and help ensure their success.

One night in 1955, while preaching in Lugoff, South Carolina, someone slashed his car tires and fired shots through the window of the church. On another occasion, as he preached in Mullins, South Carolina, a man entered the church with a shotgun, threatening to kill him. As members of the congregation prayed, the man suddenly turned around and walked out of the church. Later that evening, the man was killed with his own gun in a fight. On a separate occasion, while traveling to pray for a member, Williams' car was hit head-on by a drunken driver. His only major injury was a broken leg that was placed in a cast for several weeks. During his recuperation, though he was unable to stand, he preached sitting down until his leg healed and the cast was removed.

Williams led the denomination for twenty-two years. In late 1965 his health began to deteriorate and he set up a plan for succession for the denomination. He died early the next year.

Williams, Marion 1927-1994

Prominent American gospel singer who influenced both secular and religious music, but refused to leave the Church to crossover from the gospel-recording realm. Williams was born in Miami, Florida, to a religiously devout mother and musically inclined father. She was only three years old when she started singing with her mother, a church soloist and left school at nine to help support the family, worked as a domestic and factory worker, though she eventually graduated from Pacific Union College in 1987.

Williams began singing in front of audiences while young and though she learned African-American blues and jazz, alongside Caribbean calypso, she stayed with gospel in spite of pressure to switch to popular blues tunes or the opera. In 1946 she joined the famous Ward Singers and stayed with them until 1958. That year, she and other members of the Ward Singers left to form the Stars of Faith. That group was unable, however, to reproduce the success the Ward Singers had enjoyed, as Williams retreated from the spotlight to give other members of the group more opportunity to star. The group's career recovered, however, in 1961, when it appeared in *Black Nativity,* an off-Broadway production, and toured across North America and Europe.

In 1965 Williams began a solo career, touring college campuses across the country in Africa and the West Indies. Her best-known hit, "Standing Here Wondering Which Way to Go," is from this period.

Throughout much of her adult life, Williams was a member and church mother at the BM Oakley Memorial **Church of God in Christ** in Philadelphia under the pastorate of the late Mother Irene A. Oakley. She recorded ten albums and her music has appeared in the movies *Fried Green Tomatoes* and *Mississippi Masala*. She was also featured in Bill Moyers' PBS documentary *Amazing Grace*. In 1993 Williams received the Kennedy Center Honor and the $374,000 MacArthur Foundation Fellowship, becoming the first singer to win the so-called "genius" award.

Williams, Riley F. 1897–1952

A pioneer COGIC leader who served as the first National Chairperson of the **Church of God in Christ** Board of Bishops and was among the first five bishops selected by COGIC founder **Charles Harrison Mason** to serve as overseers of the COGIC National headquarters, Mason Temple in Memphis.

Born in St. Francisville, Louisiana, near Baton Rouge, his father died before his birth and he was raised by his uncle, a Baptist deacon. Williams was converted and called to the ministry in the Baptist Church at the age twelve years. He attended Selma University in Selma, Alabama, Baptist College in Birmingham, Alabama, and Cleveland Bible College in Cleveland, Ohio before graduating with a bachelor degree in theology. He did graduate work in business law and philosophy at Western Reserve University in Cleveland, took correspondence courses in philosophy, and received the Doctor of Divinity Degree from Greater Payne University of Birmingham, Alabama.

In 1914 Williams received the Pentecostal experience of baptism of the Holy Spirit and became a member of a Holiness Church in New Orleans. He moved to Memphis, Tennessee in 1918, where he joined the Church of God in Christ. Williams' ministry began in New Orleans, Louisiana, where he preached in churches and on street corners, and helped a number of other missions in Louisiana and on the coast of Mississippi. His first pastorate was at Donaldsonville, Louisiana; the second at Burton, Louisiana.

In 1919 Mason ordained him and, a year later, appointed him Overseer of Georgia, where he served for twenty-three years. During this period, the Georgia jurisdiction grew from seven original missions to thirty-three churches.

He established churches in Memphis, Tennessee and Jackson, Mississippi, while he continued preaching on the streets while playing the guitar, or in a cornfield, praying for people on the road, or starting missions and turning them over to others to pastor; Mason had appointed Williams to represent the Church of God in Christ at the Great Unity Council at Valdosta, Georgia. Following his speech at the council, one hundred and sixty churches, including twenty-two in Florida, were united with the COGIC. In 1931 Williams was appointed overseer of Ohio and Alabama.

Mason consecrated him bishop in 1933 and appointed him as national chairperson of the Church of God in Christ, president of the Home and Foreign Mission Board, and vice president of the Education Board. In 1940 several years after the National Temple in Memphis, Tennessee had been destroyed by fire, Mason appointed Williams chairperson of the commission to oversee rebuilding of the structure. It was completed in 1945.

Further Reading:

Clark, Otis G., ed. *Life History of Bishop R. F. Williams, National Chairman of the Churches of God in Christ Dictated by Riley F. Williams.* Oakland, CA: O. G. Clark, 1950.

Williams, Roy Constantine 1929–2010

Founder and first presiding bishop of the Oneness Pentecostal denomination, the **Church of Jesus Christ (Apostolic) Inc.** He was born in Camaguey, Cuba. The family migrated to Jamaica, West Indies when he was three years old. Williams was christened within the Catholic Church in Cuba, yet an early age, he made a personal commitment to faith and was baptized. His father died when he was twelve years old. In 1946, he experienced Pentecostal Holy Spirit baptism. At the age of twenty, he was ordained to the ministry and began traveling throughout Jamaica preaching.

After marrying, he began traveling between the United States and Jamaica, finally settling in Paterson, NJ, where he established a single storefront congregation, the Church of Jesus Christ Apostolic (Inc.), in 1962. Under his leadership, the single congregation grew into a denomination and expanded to Canada, England, Africa, India and many parishes in Jamaica, and throughout the United States. In 1993 Williams was consecrated an apostle over the body.

Apostle Williams attended Kingston Technical, and St. Simon College, both in Jamaica. He also holds a Certificate from the American Association of Christian Counselors, Center for Biblical Counseling in Forest, Virginia, a Master of Biblical Studies from the Institute of American Bible in the same city, and a Doctor of Philosophy from Kingdom Bible College in Fort Worth, TX.

Williams, Smallwood Edmonds 1907–1991

The Oneness Pentecostal leader, social activist and founding presiding bishop of **Bible Way Church Worldwide**, was considered by some the most prominent Apostolic leader in the Civil Rights Movement during his error. He was born in Lynchburg, Virginia to a young mother widowed several days before her son's birth. She soon moved the family to Columbus, Ohio where as a young man, Williams became involved in **Robert Clarence Lawson's** denomination, the **Church of Our Lord Jesus Christ of the Apostolic Church**. The onetime sidewalk preacher began preaching at the age of fourteen and was licensed to the ministry by the age of sixteen.

In 1927 Lawson sent twenty-year-old Williams to Washington DC to plant a congregation. His street preaching skills allowed him to begin his congregation in services held in large tents. He subsequently moved to a storefront edifice. In 1941 the congregation began featuring Williams' sermons on Sunday evening broadcasts in which he frequently announced catchy subjects. These programs brought the church to the attention with many in the Washington area who would come out to see how the sermons would be developed. Many remained as members so that by 1947, the congregation was able to build a 3,000-seat edifice, allowing his local Bible Way church to become one of the first black Pentecostal megachurches.

By 1957 Williams had risen to the rank of General Secretary of COOLJC. In that year, however, he and four other bishops—John S. Beane, McKinley Williams, **Winfield A. Showell**, and Joseph Moore—pulled away from Lawson's organization with about seventy churches to form the Bible Way Church, citing Lawson's autocratic leadership style. One of the most egregious concerns was Lawson's decision to no longer consecrate anyone other than himself as bishops and designate then existing bishops to the rank of "State Overseer." On the other hand, Lawson objected to what he saw as Williams' progressive, moderate stances on doctrinal issues.

Like Lawson, Williams became one of few Oneness leaders to engage consistently the issue of social injustice and politics. His social activism began as early as 1952, when Williams launched a sit-in to protest segregation in the Washington public schools. At one time, he served as president of the Washington DC chapter of the Southern Christian Leadership Conference and on the Board of Directors of the National Association for the Advancement of Colored People (NAACP). Astute at using the political system to the advantage of his congregation and other as well as other blacks in Washington, Bible Way built the $3.3 million federally financed Golden Rule housing complex for low- and middle-income members of his congregation and the surrounding community, and opened a grocery store in a neighborhood shunned by the larger chains. Further, Williams was able to thwart demolition of a portion of the community surrounding his church for the construction Interstate Highway I-95, a major north/west thoroughfare, forcing travelers along the East Coast to travel around rather than through the Nation's Capital,

Williams presided over Bible Way for thirty-four years. By the time of his death following heart surgery at age eighty-three, the denomination had more than 100,000 members in 330 congregations in the United States, Britain, Africa, and Latin America.

Further Reading:

Williams, Smallwood Edmond. *This Is My Story: A Significant Life Struggle: Autobiography of Smallwood Edmond Williams*. Washington DC: Willoughby, 1981.

Wilson, Grady Demond 1946–

An American actor, minister, and author, who was born in Valdosta, Georgia and grew up in the Harlem section of New York City. Though he was acting on Broadway by age four, after a ruptured appendix threatened to take his life, Wilson vowed to God that he would serve him in some kind of ministry later in life.

In 1968 after returning from the Vietnam War, Wilson began working in live theatre in Broadway and off-Broadway productions before moving to Hollywood where he performed in small roles in several successful television series including blockbusters series such as *Mission: Impossible* and *All in the Family* and films including, *The Dealing* in 1970, and *The Organization* in 1971. He is best known for working with comedian Redd Fox as his long-suffering offspring in the 1970s situation comedy, *Sanford and Son*. His work with Foxx in a prime-time situation comedy featuring an African American family was a first, opening doors for many that came after them.

In the late 1980s at age forty and at the height of his acting career, Wilson, who had acquired a $1,000-a-week cocaine habit, left that program. He walked away from a promising career and the Hollywood high life that included a $40,000-a-week salary, a 27-room Bel-Air mansion, and a Rolls-Royce to become an evangelist, at first preaching in small churches. He soon was preaching to megachurch congregations and on broadcast on religious television stations.

In 1984 he became an ordained interdenominational evangelist, fulfilling his childhood vow. Later, in 1995, he founded Restoration House, a center near Lynchburg, Virginia that provides rehabilitation to former prison inmates. Wilson has written several Christian books refuting the New Age Movement and what he considers is its hidden dangers to society. *New Age Millennium* was released in 1998. In 1999 Demond wrote a screenplay about the life and times of an ex-slave, entitled, *The Legend of Ned Turner* and in 2010 he returned to the screen to star in an inspirational film, "Faith Ties."

Further Reading:

Moses, Gavin. "Sanford's Son, Demond Wilson, Leaves His Demons Behind to Become a Full-Time Evangelist." *People* 23.15 (1985).

Wilson, Quander L., Sr. 1918–2003

The Oneness Pentecostal founder and first presiding bishop of the **Greater Emmanuel Apostolic Churches** was born in Berywn, Pennsylvania, and raised in Philadelphia. He preached his first sermon in 1937, was licensed to ministry in 1940 and ordained the next year. He attended Bible Truths Center and the Philadelphia School of the Bible both in Philadelphia. He also attended Crozier Bible Institute and Chester Theological Seminary, both in Chester, Pennsylvania, and the Florida State Christian College in Fort Lauderdale, Florida where he received his Ph.D. in 1971.

From 1953 until 1956, Wilson had been a pastor and then a General Secretary in the **Glorious Church of God in Christ.** Wilson's first pastorate was in Philadelphia, after which he relocated to Oberlin, Ohio to establish a congregation there before landing in Portsmouth, Ohio. In 1960 those three congregations became the nucleus of Greater Emmanuel Apostolic Faith Churches. That organization incorporated in 1961, later took the name Greater Emmanuel International Fellowship, Inc.

In 1986 Wilson established Greater Life Evangelistic Temple, which currently serves as denominational headquarters. A year later, he consecrated prominent televangelist, **Thomas Dexter (T.D.) Jakes**, with whom he has had a long collegial relationship to the bishopric of the denomination. At the senior Wilson's death, his elder son, Quander L. Wilson Jr. assumed leadership.

Winbush, Roy Lawrence Hailey 1931–

A progressive pastor and educator as well as jurisdictional and auxiliary leader in the **Church of God in Christ.** Winbush was born in Crowley, Louisiana. He graduated from Southern University in Baton Rouge, attended Union Theological Seminary in New York, received his Master of Divinity Degree from the New Orleans Baptist Theological Seminary, and his Doctorate of Ministry Degree from C. H. Mason Theological Seminary of the Interdenominational Theological Center in Atlanta, Georgia. He also holds two honorary doctorate degrees. He was consecrated a bishop in 1983 and served the First Jurisdiction of Louisiana.

Winbush has served as a Member of the General Board, organized and chaired the United National Auxiliaries Convention, now known as the Auxiliaries in Ministry (AIM) Convention, chaired the Saints Center Board, organized the COGIC Bookstore and produced the COGIC Hymnal. He also served as president of the National Publishing Board for twenty-five years. Throughout this period, Winbush has pastored Gethsemane Church of God in Christ in Lafayette, Louisiana, where he remains until now.

In 1979 Winbush acted on his educational interest, which range from preschool through higher education to work with his wife, Dr. Mae C. Winbush, to establish the Gethsemane Christian Academy in Lafayette, which now educates kindergarten through eighth grade students, and a development center for newborn through four years of age. The couple also co-founded the Roy-Mae Winbush School in Haiti. At the college level, he has served on the Board of Trustees at the C. H. Mason Theological Seminary of the Interdenominational Theological Center (ITC) in Atlanta, where he was former chair and as director of Curriculum for the **Charles Harrison Mason System of Bible Colleges**. His own institution, the Winbush Bible Institute, trains Christian workers at the local congregation level.

From 1996 through 2002, Winbush represented COGIC as chair of the Congress of National Black Churches (CNBC), the interdenominational umbrella association for the eight major black denominations (African Methodist Episcopal; African Methodist Episcopal Zion; Christian Methodist Episcopal; Church of God in Christ; National Baptist Convention of America, Inc.; the National Baptist Convention, USA, Inc., National Missionary Baptist Convention of America; and Progressive National Baptist Convention, Inc.). It represents more than 65,000 churches and over 20 million individuals.

Winbush is the presiding prelate of the First Jurisdiction of Louisiana for COGIC. He also currently serves as pastor of the Gethsemane Church of God in Christ in Lafayette, Louisiana.

Yarborough, Nellie Constance 1925–2015

One of the first two women consecrated to the office of bishop in the **Mount Calvary Holy Churches of America**. Born in Cedar Grove, North Carolina, Yarborough began praying at age twelve that she was called to the ministry. She joined the MCHCA at age fifteen and remained active within the church the rest of her life. At seventeen she persuaded her father to let her travel with **Brumfield Johnson**, founder of Mount Calvary Holy Church. Although Johnson felt she was destined for leadership within the MCHCA organization, he initially did not consecrate her bishop because she was not a man. With Johnson, Yarborough helped open churches in Durham, North Carolina, and Buffalo. She also went with evangelical groups to foreign countries and through the South, journeys that presented challenges to African Americans.

She became Johnson's administrative assistant and their travels led them to Boston, where they helped establish the church's headquarters. They also opened Bishop Yarborough's future church on Otisfield Street, just off Blue Hill Avenue. She was appointed assistant pastor of Johnson's congregation, Mount Calvary Holy Church in 1962. She became senior pastor ten years later, when Johnson died and left the role to her. She served that congregation until a few months before her death.

In 1994 Bishop Yarborough became the second woman to be ordained as a bishop in the Mount Calvary Holy Church of America. When she died, she was the only woman holding the title. She devoted much of her time to her proudest accomplishment, establishing and becoming principal of the Dr. Brumfield Johnson Christian Academy in Dorchester.

Earlier in her life, she went to a Bible school in Chicago and was ordained as a minister. Bishop Yarborough studied religion and philosophy at Eastern Nazarene College in Quincy and graduated with a bachelor's degree. She also received a master's in business administration from Cambridge College, and until the end of her life, at age eighty-seven, continued to take graduate courses in pursuit of a doctorate.

Y

Young, David Johnson (D. J.) 1861–1926

The early **Church of God in Christ** leader who sided with **Charles Harrison Mason** in his break from **Charles Price Jones**. He later founded the first publishing operation of Mason's group, the D. J. Publishing House. Young, a former public school teacher and AME presiding elder, was born in South Carolina and educated at Morehouse College in Atlanta and Benedict College in Columbia, South Carolina. At one time after accepting the doctrine of sanctification, Young was affiliated with Burning Bush Association, the Holiness group headed by Martin Wells Knapp, completing their Bible school in Chicago.

Around the turn of the nineteenth century, after moving to Memphis, Young became a close companion of Mason and belonged to the association of Holiness churches formed by Mason and Jones. He began traveling throughout the South as an evangelist, preaching on street corners and in rented halls in several large cities. Eventually, he established the first black Holiness church in Pine Bluff, Arkansas.

In 1906 Mason, Young, and **J. A. Jeter** travelled as a committee appointed by Jones's to investigate reports of **William Joseph Seymour**'s Los Angeles revival. Their job was to determine the validity of the phenomenon being experienced there. Mason and Young accepted the teaching and both received the experience of Pentecostal Holy Spirit baptism during the revival.

Once back East, Young sided with Mason in his assessment that the revival was an authentic work of God and that the spiritual manifestations were authentic. Subsequently, he was among those who left Jones' group when Mason was ex-communicated in 1907 and joined Mason in establishing a new Pentecostal association.

During the formative years of Mason's splinter group, which retained the name, Church of God in Christ, Young initially continued to minister in Pine Bluff while establishing a second congregation in Beaumont, Texas where membership quickly grew from 50 to 250. In 1912 Mason appointed him as overseer of Texas and as the first COGIC representative to Dallas, Texas. His efforts there, however, proved unsuccessful and drew widespread opposition from the community as well as other churches. In some instances, that opposition flared into violence, vandalism and sabotage against church members and property, leading Mason to replace him with **E. M. Page**. By 1914 Young had returned to the evangelistic circuit.

The multi-talented Young was also an inventor who, in 1910, invented the "Young Musical Attachment for Automobiles." This tool patented in Canada and the United States allowed him to produce played music from his very own automobile.

By 1916 he was settled in Kansas to establish the first COGIC congregation in that state. That year, he was also elected as editor of COGIC Sunday School literature and as overseer of Kansas, a position in which he served until his death. Later, Arkansas and Oklahoma were added to his oversight. In 1918 an arson destroyed the church building. While the edifice was being rebuilt, Young first held services under a tree, then in members' homes. The trained educator began publishing the *Whole Truth* magazine from his home in Argentia, Arkansas near Little Rock. He founded the **D. J. Young Publishing House** in Kansas City, Kansas. Over the next twenty years, Young worked through the company to continue to publish the Sunday school literature for fifty years. Over his lifetime, Young founded more than twenty-five churches, most of them in the state of Kansas. At his death, his wife, Priscilla took over operations of the publishing house. She worked with the young family to continue publishing COGIC materials for thirty years.

By the time of his death, he had established more then twenty-five churches within the state of Kansas.

Further Reading:

Brown, Ladrian, ed. *Great was the Company of those that Published: The D. J. Young Papers.* Kansas City, KS: D.J. Young Heritage Foundation, 2010.

Young, Elzie William 1913–1989

The third presiding bishop of the **Pentecostal Churches of the Apostolic Faith**, was born in Lexington, Kentucky, had a conversion experience, and was baptized in the Oneness Pentecostal formula at age eight. He received his Pentecostal Holy Spirit baptism in 1932, at the age of nineteen. Young attended St. Mary's College near Lebanon Kentucky, but left to work as a jockey for a short time. When he became too heavy to ride professionally, his chosen occupation proved untenable.

Young acknowledged his call to the ministry and evangelized across the country for a number of years before founding Greater Bethlehem Temple Apostolic Church in Cincinnati, Ohio in 1950, a congregation within the **Pentecostal Assemblies of the World**. Not long after, **Samuel Hancock** left the PAW to found the Pentecostal Churches of the Apostolic Faith in 1957, Young Joined him. Within that denomination, he was soon promoted to the office of District Elder of Ohio; the next year he was consecrated to the bishopric. In 1962 Young became the assistant presiding bishop and was elected to the position of presiding bishop in 1964, after Willie Lee was disfellowshipped for promulgating a heretical doctrine concerning the deity of Jesus.

Young was the only presider to serve a life term in as presiding bishop of the PCAF, remaining in office for twenty-five years until his death at the age of seventy-six. At the time he stepped into the position of presider, there was $5.00 in the treasury and by the end of his tenure; the organization was worth over $1,000,000.00

Z

Zion Gospel Churches of the Apostolic Faith

A Oneness Pentecostal body founded in 1938 as Zion Assembly Church in the Jamaica area of Queens, New York by Bishop **Judge Pierce Shields.** Shields pastored Refuge Church of Christ, a congregation of the **Church Of Our Lord Jesus Christ of the Apostolic Faith** that was organized in 1927 in the Jamaica section of the borough of Queens in New York City. When Shields broke away from the parent body that congregation became the headquarters of the new body.

Sometime later, the organization was renamed Zion Gospel Church, Inc. and Shields assumed the position of general bishop. There are congregations in New York, Ohio, and Virginia.

In 1996 his son, Rev. Dr. Del P. Shields, a well-known entrepreneur and radio broadcaster, assumed the pastorate of the congregation. Building on his business and media expertise, the younger Shields continued his role as a spokesman for the African-American community and has moved the congregation to be actively involved with other congregations in taking on a variety of social issues.

Index of Denominations

Affirming Pentecostal Church International, 4
African American Catholic Congregation, 5, 6, 391
African Methodist Episcopal Church, 7, 8, 29, 37, 61, 144, 174, 193, 193, 216, 217, 249, 250, 278, 344, 349, 360, 379, 383
African Methodist Episcopal Zion Church, 8, 73, 164, 169, 254
African Universal Church and Commercial League, 9, 10, 255
African Universal Church, Inc., 11, 256, 303
All Nations Pentecostal Church, 12
Alpha and Omega Pentecostal Church of God of America, 14–15, 331
Apostle Church of Christ in God, 16, 83, 347
Apostolic Assemblies of Christ, Inc., 17, 48–49
Apostolic Church of Christ, 17
Apostolic Church of Christ in God, 1, 27, 141, 298, 344, 371
Apostolic Faith Church of Christ (Pentecostal), 18
Apostolic Faith Church of God and True Holiness, 18, 19, 20, 264
Apostolic Faith Church of God Giving Grace, Inc., 18
Apostolic Faith Church of God Live On, 18, 19, 249, 411
Apostolic Faith Churches of God, 18, 19, 249, 411
Apostolic Faith Churches of God in Christ, 20
Apostolic Faith Fellowship International, 21, 234–36, 325
Apostolic Overcoming Holy Church, 23, 27, 331, 355
Assemblies of God, 1, 2, 23–26, 55, 88, 156, 159, 182, 199–201, 245, 246, 265, 270, 276, 280, 295, 298 305, 349–50, 385, 396, 414, 429, 430
Associated Churches of Christ (Holiness), 26–27

Beth-El Churches of Christ, Inc., 41, 154
Bible Way Church of Our Lord Jesus Christ, Inc., 41
Bible Way Churches of Our Lord Jesus Christ World Wide, Inc., 43, 373
Bible Way Church Worldwide, 438

Cainhoy Miracle Revival Corporation, 68, 381–82
Christ Holy Sanctified Church, 74–75, 158–59, 251, 252, 253, 288, 396
Christ's Sanctified Holy Church, 74, 75, 251, 252
Christian Church (Disciples of Christ), 426
Christian Methodist Episcopal Church, 74–75, 441, see also Colored Methodist Episcopal Church
Church in the Lord Jesus Christ of the Apostolic Faith, 77, 217
Church of Christ Holiness unto the Lord, 78, 120, 303, 411
Church of Christ (Holiness) USA, 27, 31, 78–80, 110, 185, 242–43, 271, 284, 334
Church of Christ Written in Heaven, 45, 81, 161
Church of God (Apostolic), 16, 17, 18, 27, 83–84, 260, 293
Church of God and Saints of Christ, 81–82, 127–28, 334–35
Church of God and True Holiness, 14, 180, 181, 266
Church of God Holiness Unto the Lord, 249
Church of God in Christ, 1–2, 5, 13, 16, 21, 24, 29, 31, 34, 36, 37, 38, 40, 43, 48, 50–51, 52, 56, 57, 62, 64, 70, 72, 79, 88–95, 96, 97, 101, 103, 109, 110, 114–15, 116, 117, 118, 119, 122, 124
    White Ministers in, 1, 138, 161, 212–13, 433–35
    Women in, 34, 52, 114, 119–20, 122, 126, 132, 146, 156, 225–28, 274, 279, 339, 351–52, 354–55, 398–99, 427
Church of God in Christ, Congregational, 89, 94
Church of God in Christ International, 91, 95, 96, 221, 229, 344, 357
Church of God in Christ International (Arkansas), 95

Index of Denominations

Church of God in Christ Jesus (Apostolic), 95, 141, 363, 373, 433
Church of God in Christ United, 96, 160
Church of God (Anderson, IN), 273; see also Evening Light Saints
Church of God (Apostolic), 16, 17, 18, 27, 83, 260, 293
Church of God (Cleveland, TN), 82, 110, 130. 133, 174, 225, 259, 274, 283, 284, 300, 349, 378, 403, 414, 433, 434; see also Church of God (Colored Work)
Church of God by Faith, Inc., 56, 84–85
Church of God of Prophecy, 82, 86, 134, 257, 347, 364, 401
Church of God (Sanctified Church), 99, 305
Church of God Which He Purchased With His Own Blood, 99, 104, 167
Church of Jesus Christ (Apostolic) Inc., 437
Church of Our Lord Jesus Christ of the Apostolic Faith, 41, 45, 46–47, 55, 58, 59, 83, 100, 109, 111, 112, 146, 153, 192, 207, 233, 236, 237, 243, 259–61, 278, 324, 341, 372, 381, 383, 388, 389, 419, 427, 435, 438, 445
Church of the Living God (Christian Workers for Fellowship), 77, 102–4, 105, 107, 108, 167, 412
Church of the Living God, International, 430
Church of the Living God Pillar and Ground of the Truth, 44, 81, 104–7, 108, 213, 214, 232, 236, 247, 264, 279, 394, 412, 429, 430
Church of the Living God Pillar and Ground of the Truth (General Assembly, 107, 108
Church of the Living God Pillar and Ground of the Truth (Lewis Dominion), 107, 363
Church of the Living God Pillar and Ground of the Truth of Muskogee Oklahoma, 107, 108
Church of the Lord Jesus Christ of the Apostolic Faith, 77, 78, 109, 154, 184, 217, 231, 236, 370–72
Churches of God and True Holiness, 14, 82–83, 109–10, 180–81
Churches of God, Holiness, 62, 80, 110
Churches of God in Christ, International, 110–11, 432
Colored Methodist Episcopal Church, 74, 75, 79, 201 see also Christian Methodist Episcopal Church

Emmanuel Pentecostal Church of Our Lord, Apostolic Faith, 152, 262
Emmanuel Tabernacle Baptist Church of the Apostolic Faith, 152, 190

Ethiopian Overcoming Holy Church of God, 22, 332 see Apostolic Overcoming Holy Church
Evangelical Churches of Christ (Holiness), 153
Evangelistic Churches of Christ, 97, 153, 235–36
Evening Light Saints, 366, 368

Faith Tabernacle Council of Churches International, 155, 309
Federated Pentecostal Church, International, Inc., 155
Fellowship of Affirming Ministries, 159, 167
Fellowship of Christian Believers, 159, 308
Fire Baptized Holiness Church of God of the Americas, 160–65, 175, 178–79, 223, 269, 328, 329, 412, 413
First Born Church of the Living God, 44, 81, 105, 148, 162–63, 263
First Church of Our Lord Jesus Christ, 46, 110, 163, 230
Free Church of God in Christ, 89, 172–74, 288, 289, 395
Free Church of God in Christ in Jesus Name, Inc., 174
Free Unity Church of God in Christ, 89, 174, 265
Freewill Baptist Church, 52, 165
Full Gospel Baptist Church Fellowship International, 176, 239, 279, 290, 404, 424
Full Gospel Pentecostal Missionary Association, 174, 288, 289, 395

Glorious Church of God in Christ, 38, 182–85, 189, 195, 216, 305, 331, 393, 440
Gospel Spreading Church of God, 185–86
Greater Emmanuel International Fellowship, Inc., 189

Higher Ground Always Abounding Assemblies, 189, 207
Highway Christian Church of Christ, 197, 207, 288, 343
House of God International, 23, 343
House of God, the Church of the Living God, Pillar and Ground of the Truth, Inc., 213
House of God which is the Church of the Living God Pillar and Ground of the Truth without Controversy, Inc. (Keith Dominion), 104, 106, 147, 214, 247, 258, 363, 430
House of the Lord and Church on the Mount Pentecostal Church, 120, 131–34, 215–16, 308, 390

Index of Denominations

Institutional Church of God in Christ, International, 430
Intercollegiate Pentecostal Conference International (IPCI), 133
International Bible Way Church of Jesus Christ, Inc., 42, 220–21, 374–75
International Church of the Foursquare Gospel, 121, 182, 187–88, 194, 222–23, 282, 307, 351

King's Apostle's Holiness Church, 166, 192–93, *see also*, King's Apostle Holy Church World Ministries
King's Apostle Holy Church World Ministries, 254
Kodesh Church of Immanuel, 249–50, 254–55

Latter House of the Lord for All People and the Church of the Mountain, Apostolic Faith, 258
Living Witness of the Apostolic Faith, Inc., 265, 335

Methodist Episcopal Church, 138, 150, 166, 331, 9, 344, 360, 366, 379
Missionary African Universal Church, 11, 256, 303
Mount Calvary Holy Churches of America, 67, 158, 221, 233, 292, 299, 309–10, 332, 434, 442
Mount Hebron Apostolic Temple of Our Lord Jesus Christ, 84, 393
Mount Sinai Holy Church of America, 15–16, 39, 122, 193, 221, 227, 230, 257, 293–95, 317, 321, 354, 359, 362, 389, 392–93

Nation of Islam, 7, 231, 348
National Church of God, Inc., 298
National Fellowship Churches of God, Inc., 298–99
National Tabernacles of Deliverance, 292, 298
New Born Lighthouse Church of the Apostolic Faith, Inc., The, 14, 301
New Church of Christ Holiness unto the Lord of the Apostolic Faith, 78, 119, 302
New Day Church International, 90, 189, 303

Oral Roberts University, 43, 44, 137, 209, 244, 281, 315, 319, 320, 340, 430,
Original Church of God or Sanctified Church, 98, 305
Original Glorious Church of God in Christ of the Apostolic Faith, 39, 119, 183, 195, 216, 305, 308, 393

Original United Holy Church, 170–71, 306–7, 414

Peace Mission Movement, 156, 162, 318
Pentecostal Assemblies of the World, 2, 3, 21, 50, 53, 54, 55, 56, 70, 96, 98, 99, 144, 154, 183, 186, 187, 19, 193, 200, 205, 207, 209, 211, 213, 238, 261, 264, 266, 267, 280, 289, 290, 310, 314, 324, 327, 336, 346, 363, 365, 365, 377, 380, 383, 384, 385, 391, 402, 405, 417, 425, 446
Pentecostal Churches of Christ, 151, 239, 302, 326, 404
Pentecostal Churches of the Apostolic Faith, 48–49, 195–96, 262, 324, 327, 336, 444
Pilgrim Assemblies International, 60, 239, 279, 332
Progressive Church of Our Lord Jesus Christ, Inc., 101, 341
Progressive National Baptist Convention, Inc., 443
Pure Holiness Church of God, 342

Quakers, 97, 150; *see also* Society of Friends

Reformed Churches of God in Christ International, 344, 356
Reformed Zion Union Apostolic Church, 344–46
Refuge Temple Assembly of Yahweh, 101, 346
Roman Catholic Church, 4–7, 60, 152, 240, 326, 366, 391, 404

Saints at Runneymede Holiness Church, The, 409
Scott's Revival Center, 249
St. Mark's Holy Gospel Church of America Inc., 122, 294, 359
Shiloh Apostolic Temple Church, Inc., 16, 296, 373
Society of Friends, 403
Sought Out Church of God in Christ, 90, 120, 387
Soul Saving Station for Every Nation, 329, 388

Tabernacle of God Holiness Church, 249
Triumph the Church and Kingdom of God, 38, 89, 182, 331, 380, 393, 402–3
True Grace Memorial House of Prayer for All People Church on the Rock of the Apostolic Faith, 404
True Vine Pentecostal Churches of Jesus Christ (Apostolic Faith), 239, 405, 406
True Vine Pentecostal Holiness Church, 239, 405, 406

Index of Denominations

Unification Church, 7, 391
Union Zion Apostolic Church, 217, 345
United Church of Jesus Christ (Apostolic), 96, 181, 362–63, 409
United Churches of God in Christ, 72, 409–10
United Cornerstone Churches of Christ International, 410, 418
United Covenant Churches of Christ International, 410
United Fellowship Convention of the Original Apostolic Faith Mission, 19, 20, 21, 78, 259, 266, 411
United Full Gospel Church, USA, 158, 395, 412
United Holy Church of America, 14 52, 138, 164–65, 170–71, 176–75, 221, 231, 258, 292, 306, 317, 352, 393, 406, 412–14
United House of Prayer for All People, 35, 131, 186, 215, 267, 274, 405

United Pentecostal Church International, 101, 199, 220, 389, 415
United Pentecostal Council of the Assemblies of God, 26, 66, 146, 418
United Progressive Pentecostal Church Fellowship, 13, 419, 423
United Way of the Cross Churches of Christ of the Apostolic Faith, 1, 420, 430
Universal Christian Spiritual Faith and Church for All Nations, 420
United Way of the Cross Churches of Christ of the Apostolic Faith, 1, 71, 412, 420, 430

Vision Church of Atlanta, 13, 419, 423

Way of the Cross Church of Christ, 58, 69, 71, 221, 420, 429, 430

Zion Gospel Churches of the Apostolic Faith, 372, 445

Index of Names

Abrams, Allyson Nelson, 7
Adams, Joseph H, 1
Adams, Leonard P., 1, 431-32
Allen, Oliver Clyde (O.C.) III, 13
Amos, Barbara M., 15-16, 283, 321
Audrey, J. W., 16-17, 27, 84
Ayers, George Washington, 23, 27-28, 355

Bailey, Annie Lee Pennington, 34, 36, 93, 118, 225, 277
Bailey, Clarence M. (C. M.), 35, 416
Bailey, John Seth, 34, 36, 113, 248, 276, 310
Baker, George; see Father Divine
Baldwin, James Arthur, 26-27, 213, 328
Barr, Edmund S., 37-38, 401,
Barr, Rebecca, 37-38, 401,
Bass, Sidney Coy Sr., 393,
Bell, Joseph, 16, 39-40, 294
Bell, William Yancey, 75
Bennett, Harold V., 40-41
Bethune, Mary McLeod, 118, 284,
Blake, Charles Edward Sr., 13, 43-44, 92, 127, 131, 240, 282, 311, 316, 348
Blake, Junious Augustus Jr., 43, 127, 280
Blakely, Jesse Clarence, 44, 81, 105, 162-63
Bonner, Ethel Mae Smith, 45-46
Bonner, William Lee, 45, 46-47, 101-2, 192, 346, 389
Boone, George Marshall (G. M.), 17, 48-49
Boone, Wellington, 49-50
Bowdan, Frank Reuben Joseph, 3, 50, 324, 325
Bowe, Justus, 50-51, 89-90, 92, 94, 221, 245, 378
Bowen, Frank, 221
Brandhagen, Gladys, 53, 328
Bragg, Bernard Nathaniel, 41, 51
Bram-Bibby, Emily, 52
Brazier, Arthur 53-55, 325
Brisbin, Lawrence E., 56, 324
Broadie, Benjamin H (B. H.), 57
Bronson, Audrey Flora, 57-58,
Brooks, Henry Chauncey, 58-59, 69, 101
Brown, Rosie J. Wallace, 59
Brown, Roy Edmund, 60, 151, 239, 279, 332
Brown, William, 60, 360

Bryant, John Richard, 7-8, 61-62
Burruss, King Hezekiah, 62, 80, 110
Burruss, Titus Paul Sr., 62-63, 110
Bush, George W., 351
Butler, Keith, 63
Bynum, Juanita, 64-65, 360

Caesar, Roderick R., Sr., 66-67, 418
Caesar, Shirley Ann, 15, 67-68, 436
Campbell, Lawrence G., 42, 43, 68, 220-21, 356, 374, 375
Cannady, Leroy H. Sr., 69-70, 428
Carr, Randolph Adolphus, 70-71, 95 -96, 141, 265, 362-63, 373, 409-10, 433
Carter, James H., 71, 410, 420
Carter, James Earl (Jimmy), 67, 337
Carter, Marshall, 72, 409
Carver, George Washington, 284
Cashwell, Gaston Barnabas, 2, 29, 31, 32, 161
Cherry, John A. Sr., 8-9, 73
Christian, William, 102, 105, 107, 108
Clark, James I. Jr., 102, 111
Clark, James I. Sr., 102, 112
Clark, Mattie Juliet Moss, 93, 112-13, 318
Clark, Otis G., 113-14
Clemmons, Frank, 55, 114-15
Clemmons, Ithiel, 91, 115-16, 117, 282, 321
Clemmons, Joseph, 116-17
Cleveland, Elmer Elijah (E. E.), 139
Cleveland, James, 59, 338, 437
Clinton, Hillary, 134
Clinton, William Jefferson (Bill), 90, 125, 133, 134, 172, 225, 311, 337
Coffey, Lillian Brooks, 34, 117-18, 126, 154, 224, 225, 248., 351, 352
Collier, Lucy Smith, 12, 119
Colty, Benjamin Franklin, 78, 119-20, 302
Conry, Inez, 120, 132, 216
Cook, Glenn, 204, 323
Cook, Mozella, 90, 120, 387
Cotton, Emma, 121-22, 222, 251, 288
Cotton, Henry, 121-22, 222, 251, 288
Counts, Beulah, 122
Courts, James A., 122-23, 313, 359
Cox, John Thomas, 123

Index of Names

Cox, Thomas J., 20, 83, 123, 243, 260, 266, 299
Crawford, Florence, 30, 322, 338, 365, 367
Crouch, Andraé Edward, 94, 124
Crouch, Emma Frances, 125 225 314 350
Crouch, Samuel Martin Sr., 43, 114 122, 126–27 194, 276
Crowdy, William Saunders, 81–82, 127–28, 334–35
Curry, John Henry, 85–86, 129

Daughtry, Alonzo, 120, 131–32, 215, 416
Daughtry, Herbert, 120, 133–34, 215, 308, 390
Daughtry, Leah, 133
Deadricks, D. M. and Dorothy, 98, 134
DeLee, Victoria Way, 134–35
Delk, James Logan, 136, 352, 431, 432
Dickerson, Ernestine Cleveland Reems, 137
Diggs, Jefferson Davis (J. D.), 138
Dollar, Creflo Augustus Jr., 140, 149
Dorsey, Thomas, 143, 269–70, 286, 386
Doub, Robert O. Jr., 16, 141, 298, 373
Douglas, Floyd Ignatius (F.I.), 142, 204
Douglass, Frederick, 155
Dranes, Arizona Juanita, 93, 143–43, 425
Driver, Edward Robert Sr., 126, 143–44, 271, 313, 431
DuBois, Joshua, 144–45
Dunn, Sydney A., 95, 409
DuPree, Sherrie Sherrod, 145–46

Easter, Rufus, 18–19, 20
Eason, Willie Claude, 147, 358
Eason, Troman, 358
Easter, Rufus, 18, 20,
Eckhardt, John, 147
Echols, Joseph Henry, 148, 163
Eikerenkoetter, Frederick J. II, 149–50
Eisenhower, Dwight David, 186, 285
Eisenhower, Mamie, 186, 285
Elaw, Zilpha, 150
Ellis, Jesse Delano II, 151–52, 393, 404, 410–11
Ellis, Neil, 177, 276, 374, 375, 427
Evans, Robert Jr., 51, 153–54, 207
Ewart, Frank J., 50, 204, 323
Exume, Dorothy Mae Webster, 154

Farrakhan, Louis, 7, 231
Farrow, Lucy, 30, 157–58, 221, 369, 398
Father Divine, 156–58, 162, 212, 318
Feick, August, 159, 434
Feltus, James Jr., 96, 160–61
Ferguson, Stanley, 98
Finney, Charles, 97
Fisher, Henry Lee, 52–53, 138, 164–65, 175, 293, 412–13, 424

Fisher, Violet, 166–67, 193
Fizer, William Jordan, 99, 103–4, 167
Flunder, Yvette Adrienne, 159, 167–68, 360
Foote, Julia, 169,
Forbes, James Alexander Jr., 169–70
Forbes, James Alexander Sr., 170–71, 306, 329, 414
Ford, Louis Henry, 91, 125, 171–72, 173, 434
Ford, Willie L., 86, 172
Franklin, Robert Michael, Jr., 91, 173
Frazee, J. J., 204, 322, 323
Fulford, William, 165, 174–75, 412–13
Fuller, William Edward, 161–62, 165, 178–79, 230, 328

Garlington, John Wesley Jr., 83, 180
Garlington, John Wesley Sr., 82, 180–81
Garlington, Joseph, 181–82
Garr, Alfred Garrison (A.G.) and Lillian, 31, 32
Garvey, Marcus, 10, 75, 257–58
Gandhi, Indira, 372
Gibson, Bruce K., 24, 182
Goodwin, Bennie Eugene II, 183, 390,
Goodwin, Randolph, 110, 184
Golder, Morris Ellis, 184–85
Goss, Howard, 2, 156, 204, 323
Grace, Charles Manual "Sweet Daddy," 186–87, 215, 267–68, 274, 284, 404, 415–16
Graham, Billy, 199, 229, 280, 351
Gray, Arthur J., II 187–88, 223
Grayson, David W. Sr., 90, 189, 303
Gregory, Martin Rawleigh, 152, 190, 260
Grimes, Samuel Joshua, 190–91, 196, 205, 211, 312, 324, 327, 344
Grimes, Sobrina Kathleen McDowell Washington, 191–92, 211
Groover, Gentle L., 47, 102, 192
Gurrey, Carrie V., 166, 192–93, 254

Hagee, John, 63
Hagin, Kenneth, Sr. 63, 339, 398
Hagin, Kenneth, Jr., 340
Hamiter, Isaiah Warren (I.W.) Jr., 195, 216, 306
Hancock, Samuel Nathan, 49, 152, 195–96, 262, 265, 324, 325, 327, 336, 364, 446
Haney, Oliver J., 196–97
Harewood, Gladstone Theophilus, 197
Harris, James Frank, 197
Harris, Robert Lee, 197
Harris, Thoro, 197, 198, 222, 364
Harrison, Robert Emmanuel, 199–200
Hart, Robert Eber, 201, 271
Hawkins, Edwin, 93, 202
Hawkins, Walter Lee, 93, 113, 168, 202–3

Index of Names

Hayford, Jack, 182, 282
Hayward, Garfield T, 50, 55, 101, 184, 191, 194, 203–5, 210, 259, 261, 262, 264, 287, 322, 323–24, 335, 339, 344, 361, 363, 400
Hickson, Peter Callahan, 206,
Hill, Edward Victor, Sr. (E. V.), 330
Hill, Edward Victor II, 208, 330
Hilliard, Ira Van (I.V.), 27, 209
Holly, John Silas, 209–10, 335, 382
Holman, William C., 80, 110, 153
Holt, William B., 144, 159, 210–11, 434
Hopkins, Ellen Moore, 191, 193, 211–12
Horn, Jessie, 53, 328
Horn, Rosa Artemis, 36–37, 53, 212 -213, 284, 327–28
Horne, Lena, 284
Howard, W. O., 183, 195, 216, 306, 393
Howell, James Richard, 216–17, 344–246
Hunter Lenist J., 77, 219
Hutchins, Julia 23, 30–31, 47, 158, 220–21, 367, 369, 398

Ironsides, Harry A., 32
Irwin, B. H., 160, 164–65, 178–79

Jackson, Jesse, 133, 135, 180, 369,
Jackson, Mahalia, 143, 358, 369, 386, 427, 442
Jackson, Michael, 124
Jackson, Mary, 227, 294, 393
Jakes, Thomas Dexter (T. D.), 64, 189, 207, 227–29, 282, 319, 442
Jefferson, Illie Louis, 91, 229
Jeffries, Elmira, 227, 230, 294
Jennings, Gino N., 110, 163–64, 230–31
Jeter, John A. (J. A.), 79, 88, 231–32, 241, 271, 334, 445
Jewell, Mattie Lou Tate McLeod, 108, 232–33, 279
Johnson, Brumfield, 158, 233, 292, 332, 436, 444
Johnson, Celeste Ashe, 233–34
Johnson, Charles Edward, 21, 234, 325
Johnson, Lymus Leewood, 101, 153, 235–36
Johnson, Rufus Abraham Reid (R. A. R.), 213, 236
Johnson, Sherrod Charlotte (S. C.), 77, 100, 109, 164, 184, 217, 235, 236–38, 371
Johnson , W. J. ("Blind" Willie), 238
Johnson, William Monroe, 239, 406
Jonas, Mack E., 241
Jones, Charles Price, 2, 26, 31, 50, 62, 79, 87, 99, 102, 139, 143, 165, 185, 201, 231, 242–43, 270, 305, 313, 333, 334, 350, 367, 433, 445
Jones, Curtis P., 243

Jones, Jim, 164, 319
Jones, Ozro Thurston, Jr., 92, 244, 245, 311
Jones, Ozro Thurston, Sr. 89, 90, 95, 110–11, 130, 160, 244–45, 276, 313, 314, 435
Jones, Pearl-Williams, 390
Jones, Quincy, 124
Jones, Spencer, 25, 245–46, 297

Kee, John P., 94
Keith, Mary Frankie Giles Lewis (M. F. L.), 106, 214–15, 247–48, 395
Kelly, Leontyne, 167
Kelly, Otha Miema (O.M.), 115, 116, 248–49, 276, 318, 351, 428
Kennedy, John, 59, 118
Keyes, Oree Sr., 20, 249, 411
Killingsworth, Frank Russell, 249–50, 254
Kinchlow, Harvey Benjamin (Ben), 250–51
King Hussein of Jordan, 372
King, J. H., 272
King, Judge, 251, 252, 253, 288
King, Martin Luther, Jr., 14, 54, 69, 71, 116, 135, 173, 180, 183, 244, 270, 282, 316
King, Sarah Ann, 251, 252
King, Saunders Samuel, 252
King, Ulysses Stephen, Sr., 74, 158, 251, 252, 253, 396
Knapp, Martin Wells, 366, 445
Koffey, Laura Adorkor, 9–12, 255–56, 303–4

La Fleur, David, 85–86, 257
Lambert, Eva Gertrude Bell, 122, 257, 359
Larkin, Clarence, 32
Lawrence, Mary D., 258
Lawson, Robert Clarence, 41–42, 45 46, 55, 58–59, 83, 100–102, 109, 112, 123, 146, 153, 190, 204, 235–36, 237, 243, 259–61, 264, 272, 278, 323, 324, 341, 246, 375, 383, 384, 388, 389, 421, 429, 440,
Layne, Austin Augustus, 261–62, 265
Lee, Willie, 17, 152, 262, 327, 446
Lewis, Felix Early, 106, 107, 247, 262, 263, 264, 279, 301, 394
Lewis, Helen Middleton Matchett, 108, 263, 301
Lewis, Walter Curtis, 247, 262, 264, 394
Lightford, Susan Gertrude, 50, 55, 263, 266
Linsey, Nathaniel, 76
Looper, Sumpter Eziel (S. E.), 265
Louis, Joe, 284
Lovett, Leonard, 266, 360
Lowe, Charles Wesley, 18, 19–20, 123, 411, 266, 299, 411

Madonna, 124

Index of Names

Madison, Samuel Christee (S. C.), 35, 267–68, 416,
Mallory, Arenia, 92, 118, 123, 268–69, 359–60
Mandella, Nelson, 135
Mandela, Wnnie, 135
Martin, Roberta, 119, 427
Martin, Sallie, 70, 386
Mason, Charles Harrison, 1, 2, 13, 24, 29, 31, 32, 34, 36, 40, 50–51, 62, 70, 77, 79–80, 87–88, 89, 90, 91, 92, 93, 94, 95, 96, 99, 102, 105, 110, 115, 116, 117, 123, 126, 130, 136, 139, 142, 143–44, 159, 160, 165, 192, 201, 210, 211, 214, 223–24, 225, 231–32, 241, 242–43, 244, 245, 248, 251, 260, 268, 270–72, 273, 276, 289, 305, 310, 313, 314, 316, 317, 333, 338, 344, 350, 352–53, 359, 368, 380, 399, 402, 403, 433–34, 435, 436, 438–39, 445
Mason, Elsie Louise Washington, 270, 272–73
Massey, James Earl, 273
McClurkin, Donnie, 94
McCollough, Walter M. ("Sweet Daddy"), 35, 267, 268, 274, 404, 405, 415, 416,
McCullough, Jacqueline E. (Jackie), 275–76, 279
McEwen, A. B. Sr., 90, 154, 245, 248, 276, 317, 435
McGlothen, Mattie Mae Carter, 93, 277
McGoings, Robert J. Jr., 278
McKinley, Wilbert Sterling 151, 239, 275, 278–79
McKinney, George Dallas, 279
McLeod, Bruce Lee, 106, 108, 232, 247, 279, 280, 287, 301
McPherson, Aimee Simple, 121, 187, 18, 199, 288, 351, 433
Meares, John Levin, 281–82
Meredith, Don, 283
Michaux, Lightfoot Solomon, 62, 284–85
Mix, Sarah Ann Freeman, 285–86
Moales, Kenneth H., Sr., 286–87
Moon, Sun Yun, 7
Moore, Benjamin Thomas, 287
Moore, Faye, 109, 287–88
Moore, Joanna Patterson, 242, 352
Morgan, G. Campbell, 32
Morris, Elias Camp, 79, 242
Morris, Ernest Fredrick (E. F.), 158, 173, 174, 288, 289, 395
Morris, James Thomas, 207, 288, 34
Morris, John Henry, 173, 289
Morton, Clarence Leslie (C. L.), Sr., 289–90
Morton, Paul Sylvester, 151, 176–77, 239, 279, 290–91, 404, 426

Neal, Elijah Nathan (Eli N.), 16, 83–84, 123, 299–300, 347
Neeley Isaac S, 24, 300
Neeley, Martha A. (Mattie), 24, 300
Nelson, Douglas Johnson, 300–301
Nixon, Richard, 424
Nyombolo, Eli B'usabe, 11, 303–4

O'Quinn Doretha Ann, 307
Opperman, D.C.O., 204, 323
Osborne, Grace C., 155, 160, 308, 309
Osborne, Louis W. Sr., 155, 308, 309
Outlaw, Wanda Cecilia, 7
Owens, Alfred A, Jr., 292, 309–10
Owens, Chandler David, Sr., 91, 310–11, 314, 318, 350

Paddock, Ross Perry 50, 312–13, 324, 381
Page, Emmett Morey (E. M.), 80, 92, 122, 313, 314
Parks, Rosa, 201
Parham, Charles Fox, 31, 83, 111, 157–58, 369, 396, 398
Patterson, Gilbert Earl (G. E.), 13, 43, 92 189, 303, 311, 314–16, 321
Patterson, James Oglethorpe, Jr., 13, 151, 316–17
Patterson, James Oglethorpe, Sr. 13, 34, 36, 52, 66, 72, 90, 92, 113, 139, 171 189, 221, 245, 248, 249, 276, 315, 316–18, 370, 409, 428
Pearson, Carlton D., 28, 240, 319 -321
Pendleton, William, 322
Phillips, Lulu, 39, 182, 305, 331, 393
Phillips, Magdalene Mabe, 14–15, 331
Phillips, William Thomas, 22, 331–32, 355, 436
Pitts, Gertrude Louise Norris, 292, 332
Pleas, Charles, 333
Pleasant, William S. (W. S.), 79, 66, 271, 334
Plummer, William Henry, 81, 334–35
Poole, Charles Edward, 262, 265, 335–36
Poole, Mattie Belle Robinson, 265, 335–36
Pope John Paul 240, 404
Pope Paul VI, 372
Portier, Harcourt Garfield (H. G.), 87, 337
Powell, Adam Clayton, Jr., 260, 264, 269
Powell, Adam Clayton, Sr., 264
Powell, Sarah Jordan, 93, 94, 337–38
Prentiss, Henry S., 191, 203, 264, 322, 338–39
Presley, Elvis, 124
Price, Frederick K. C., 149, 319, 339–40, 398

Rawlings, Simon Peter (S.P.), 213, 343
Reeder, Hilda, 344
Reems, Ernestine Cleveland, 90, 137
Richardson, James C. Sr, 16, 27, 84, 346–47

Index of Names

Richardson, Thomas, 85, 97, 257, 347, 402
Rivers, Eugene F. III, 348–49
Rivers, Willie Mae, 93, 125, 226, 349–50
Roberson, Paul, 284
Roberts, William Matthew, 89, 248, 313, 350–51
Robertson, Cornelia Jones, 199, 351–52
Robertson, Marion Gordon (Pat), 49, 250
Robinson, Bill, 284
Robinson, Elizabeth Isabelle Smith Woods (Lizzie), 34, 93, 117, 136 225, 272, 277, 352–53
Robinson, Ida Bell, 15, 39, 122, 193, 227, 230, 257, 293 -294, 354, 359, 392
Roby, Jasper C., 23, 27, 355
Rogers, Huie, 42, 43, 69, 220, 355, 374
Rogers, Kendrick J., 344, 356–57
Roosevelt, Eleanor, 118, 186, 285

Sanders, Oscar Haywood, 361
Satchell, Ruth Brown, 289, 362
Saunders, Monroe Randolph, 70, 95, 181, 220, 237, 278, 362–63, 409
Schooler, Alexander Robinson, 198, 209, 323, 363
Scotton, Ralph, 98, 134
Selassie, Haile, 262, 374
Seymour, Jennie Evans Moore, 48, 218, 365–66, 367
Seymour, William Joseph, xi, 18, 19, 21, 23, 29, 31, 32, 47, 74, 88, 97, 155, 156, 192, 220, 251, 252, 259, 266, 271, 300, 331, 338, 350, 366–69, 396, 399, 401, 411, 436, 445
Shamana, Beverly, 167
Sharpton, Alfred Charles "Al" Jr., 369–70, 428
Shelton, Nehemiah, 110, 372
Shelton, Omega Y. L., 370–71, 372
Shelton, Samuel McDowell, 109, 110, 184, 238, 371–72
Showell, Carolyn Denise, 373–74, 375
Showell, Franklin Cornelius, 42, 69, 221, 373, 374–75, 376
Showell, Winfield Amos, 41, 69, 112, 373, 374, 375–76, 441
Sibley, Wallace Jerome, 376–77
Skinner, Arthur Alfred (Arturo), 377
Slack, George Jr., 51, 90, 94, 378
Smallwood, Richard, 113
Smiley, Tavis, 378–79
Smith, Amanda Berry, 270, 379–80
Smith, Elias Dempsey, 38, 89, 380–81, 402
Smith, Francis Leonard, 57, 324, 381
Smith, Helen, 381–82
Smith, Horace E., 324–25, 382

Smith, Karl Franklin, 2, 100, 260, 325, 381, 383–84, 389
Smith, Lucinda Madden (Lucy), 384–85
Smith, Utah, 93, 385–86
Smith, Willie Mae Ford, 386
Smith, Zollie Lennon Jr., 26, 297, 387
Spellman, Robert Clarence, 388–89
Spencer, Herbert Joseph, 46, 101, 260, 346, 389
Spooner, Kenneth E. M. (K. E. M.), 390
Stallings, George Augustus, 5–7, 391–293
Stevens, Amy Johnson Bell, 183, 221, 294, 317, 362, 392–93
Stokes, Cleveland H., 182, 305, 393
Swancy, Howard, 4

Tate, Mary Magdalena Lewis, 104, 108, 214, 232, 247, 262–63, 279, 301, 394–95, 431, 432
Taylor, Richard, 158, 412
Terry, Neely, 23, 396
Tharpe, Rosetta, 143, 358, 396–97
Thomas, Elsworth S., 398
Thompson, Leroy, 398–99
Till, Emmett Louis, 171, 399
Tinney, James S, 389- 390, 399 -400
Tobin, Robert Franklin, 184, 400
Tomlinson, Ambrose Jessup (A. J.), 2, 37–38, 56, 85, 96–98, 257 271, 347–48, 364, 401–2, 433, 434
Torrey, Rueben Archer (R. A.), 32
Townsley, Nathaniel, Jr., 359
Townsley, Nathaniel, Sr., 359
Trask, Thomas, 284
Trotter, Larry Darnell, 151–52, 176, 291, 302, 326, 404, 411
Truman, Harry S., 138
Turner, William Clair, Jr., 406
Turpin, Joseph Marcel, 207, 289, 324, 363, 374, 375, 407

Ulmer, Kenneth C. 176, 291, 408–9
Underwood, Bernard E., 116, 282–83, 330
Utterbach, Clinton, 421–22
Utterbach, Sarah, 421–22

Waddles, Charlezetta, 424–25
Wagner, Norman L., 324, 425
Walker, Hezekiah, 113
Walker, Joseph Warren III, 426
Ward, Clara, 143
Washington, Ernestine Beatrice Thomas, 427, 428
Washington, Frederick, 427–28
Washington, Johnnie Lee, 428–29
Wenyika, Reggies, 430

Index of Names

Wheelock, Donald Ray, 360, 431
White, Archibald Henry (A. H.), 105, 213–14, 431
White, John C. (J. C.) 111, 432
White, Joseph, 104, 432
Wilder, L. Douglas, 1
Williams, Carl E, 94, 111
Williams, Dempsey Lawrence (D. Lawrence), 117, 435
Williams, Deniece, 94
Williams, Diana, 7
Williams, Frank W., 21, 48, 331, 436
Williams, Harold Ivory, Sr., 292, 310, 436–37
Williams, Joseph David, 437
Williams, Lillie Perry, 18–19, 20
Williams, Marion, 437–38
Williams, Raymond, 76
Williams, Riley F., 89, 438
Williams, Roy Constantine, 100, 439
Williams, Smallwood Edmund, 41, 43, 59, 68, 100, 112, 210, 237, 243, 260, 356, 374, 475, 389 429, 440–41
Williams, William David Charles (WDC), 90, 94, 111
Wilson, Grady Demond, 441
Wilson, Quander L., Sr., 189, 228, 442
Winbush, Roy Lawrence Hailey, 442–43
Wonder, Stevie, 124

Yarborough, Nellie Constance, 444
Young, David Johnson (D. J.), 50, 79, 139, 231, 271, 313, 333, 334, 445, 446
Young, Elzie William, 327, 446

Index of Terms

abolition, 155, 216, 345; *see also* anti-slavery activism
Aenon Bible College, 2, 50, 185, 211, 235, 260, 287, 308, 325, 381, 383, 383, 423
Aenon School of Theology & Bible College, 3, 325
African-American Catholic Charismatics, 4, 5–7, 391–293
African People's Christian Organization, 133
All Saints Bible College, 13, 71, 91
anti-war activism, 144
anti-segregation protest, 54, 69, 157, 210, 434, 440
anti-slavery activism, 169, 401
Angelus Temple, 121, 222, 288, 433,
Apostolic World Christian Fellowship, 17
Arkansas Baptist College, 77, 231, 242, 270
Association of Biblical Higher Education, 45, 93, 102
Azusa Interdenominational Fellowship of Christian Churches, 28, 320,
Azusa Street Revival, xi, 2, 18, 19, 20, 47, 50, 79, 80, 88, 97, 121, 122, 155–56, 192, 199, 203, 218, 231, 241, 249, 259, 266, 271, 299, 300–301, 322, 331, 334, 338, 350, 351, 365, 366–69, 390, 394, 396

Back to Africa Movement, 381, 403
Bay Ridge Christian College, 39
Bethune-Cookman College, 58, 268, 371
Billy Graham Evangelistic Association, 25, 199, 200
Bonnie Brae Street Prayer Meeting, 29, 47, 121, 367, 434
Black Entertainment Television (BET), 317, 380
Black Hebrew Pentecostals, 79–80, 126–28, 176, 213, 346
Black Pentecostal Fellowship of North America, 66
Black United Front, 133, 308
Blind Boys of Alabama, the, 358

C. H. Mason System of Bible Colleges, 13, 72, 91, 92, 317, 360, 443

C. H. Mason Theological Seminary, 44, 72, 92, 154, 266, 280, 360, 440, 441
Charismatic Movement, xii, 28, 75
Church of God (Colored Work), 56, 85–87, 97, 129–31, 172, 206, 257, 298, 337, 402
Church of God in Christ Publishing House, 91, 273, 276, 317, 333, 428
City College, 40, 115, 234
Civil Rights Movement, 19, 23, 69, 83, 98, 110, 133, 198, 321, 329, 332, 351, 399, 440
Columbia University, 40, 111, 261
Congress of National Black Churches (CNBC), 91, 317, 443

deliverance churches, 428
divine healing, 5, 21, 29, 79, 84, 205, 283, 289, 291, 317, 395, 422, 437
D. J. Young Publishing House, 141, 446
Dove Awards, 67, 94, 124

Eastern Baptist Theological Seminary, 16, 166, 167, 348
emancipation, 77, 285
Evening Light Saints, 366, 368

Faith Home and Industrial School of Geridge, 50, 92, 314
Federal Bureau of Investigation (FBI), 107, 144, 146, 210, 271, 285, 434
Fordham University, 40
Full Gospel Pentecostal Association for Women on the Move, 178

Garveyism, 9; *see also* Universal Negro Improvement Association
glossolalia, xii, 9, 75, 76, 80, 218, 245; *see also* speaking in tongues
Gospel Music Hall of Fame, 67, 113, 124, 146, 286
Gospel Music Workshop of America, 338, 408
Grammy Awards, 15, 44, 67, 94, 113, 124, 202, 229, 316, 432
Great Depression, 12, 48, 143, 157–58, 196, 233, 237, 284, 318

Index of Terms

Hampton Institute, 52
Hampton University, 16, *see also* Hampton Institute
  Ministers' Conference, 117, 145, 435, 436
Hebrew Pentecostals, 346
Harvard University, 14, 134, 173, 234, 348, 349, 374, 379
HIV/AIDS, 14, 44, 58, 170, 312
homosexuality, 4, 7, 13-14, 161, 169-70, 200, 201, 240, 284, 310, 320, 390 400-401 419, 421
Howard University, 5, 37, 40, 42, 58, 75, 116, 151, 154, 169, 220, 284, 301, 309, 310, 362, 374, 390, 400

initial evidence (of Holy Spirit baptism), 4, 62, 74, 80, 87, 96, 104, 155, 177, 218, 243, 254, 368, 394
Industrial Home for Abandoned and Destitute Colored Children, 380
Interdenominational Theological Center, 40, 43, 44, 58, 115, 154, 173, 183, 198, 266, 317, 442, 443
International Women's Department of the Church of God in Christ, 34, 93, 223-25, 269, 272, 277, 349, 350, 351, 352, 359
Interdenominational World Wide Women Ministers Alliance, 166

Jim Crow era, 2, 96, 125, 165, 272, 313
Joint College of African American Pentecostal Bishops, 14, 60, 151, 229-40, 278, 310, 310, 404

Kennedy Center Honors, 438
Ku Klux Klan, 39, 96, 136, 204, 222, 433

Lee College, 87
Lighthouse Institute for Foursquare Evangelism (L.I.F.E.) Bible College, 188, 194, 222
lynching, 134, 157, 165, 318

Memphis Miracle, 117, 284, 317, 323, 332; *see also* Pentecostal and Charismatic Churches of North America
missions work, 25, 30-31, 118, 126, 154, 158, 205, 211-12, 215, 223, 225, 272, 311, 333, 344, 353, 379-80, 413, 429
Morehouse College, 14, 40, 117, 151, 173, 266, 445
Morgan State University, 14, 62, 278, 374, 375
music, 59, 67, 93, 94, 112-13, 121, 124, 142-43, 145, 146, 147, 193, 197, 202, 269, 270, 286, 318, 337-38, 350, 359, 385, 391, 396-97, 421-22, 437-38

Gospel, 59, 67, 113, 119, 124, 142-43, 145, 146, 147, 202, 269, 270, 286, 337-38, 350, 359, 385, 391, 396-97, 421

National Apostolic Fellowship Association, Inc., 298
National Association for the Advancement of Colored People (NAACP), 67, 71, 112, 137, 141, 172, 183, 355, 379, 440
National Association of the Churches of God (Anderson, Indiana, 296
National Baptist Convention, 79, 90, 173, 242, 289
National Baptist Convention of America, Inc., 443
National Baptist Convention, USA, Inc., 89, 290, 443
National Black Fellowship of the Assembly of God, 25, 26, 202, 248, 299, 389
National Black Justice Coalition, 13
National Committee of Black Churchmen, 62
National Council of Churches, 146, 266
  Faith and Order Commission of, 266
National Memorial to the Progress of the Colored Race in America, 186, 285
National Missionary Baptist Convention of America, 443
National Urban League, 137, 172, 425
Negro Women's League, 118
Neo-Pentecostalism, xii, 6, 7-9, 61, 73, 75-77, 166, 176, 239, 240, 379, 290-91, 298, 320, 331, 391, 408, 410, 423, 426
Network of Politically Active Christians (NPAC), 49
New and Living Way Publishing Company, 108, 263, 301, 394
New Apostolic Movement, 147
New York Theological Seminary, 58, 168, 388
Norfolk State University, 16

Oral Roberts University, 43, 44, 137, 209, 244, 266 281-82, 315, 319-20, 340, 430

Page Normal Industrial and Bible Institute, 124, 126, 315
pacifism, 75, 77, 129, 144, 163, 173, 258, 271, 289, 326
Pentecostal and Charismatic Churches of North America (PCCNA), 16, 115, 283, 321-22, 390
Pentecostal Fellowship of North America (PFNA), 16, 98, 116, 321, 330, 417
political involvement and leadership, 6, 42, 96, 115, 133, 135-36, 144, 172, 198, 260, 266, 270, 274, 348-49, 363, 369-70, 434, 440

Index of Terms

Prosperity Gospel, 398, 421; *see also* Word of Faith Movement

Quakers, 83, 110, 150, 403, *see also* Society of Friends
Quasi-Holiness Groups, xii, 35, 156, 162, 186, 215, 318, 415
Quasi-Pentecostalism, xii, 9, 10, 11, 255, 303, 346, 380, 402, 418

racism, 16, 98, 116, 200, 321, 330, 340, 367, 417, 433
Rhema Bible Training Center, 63, 340, 421
Roberta Martin Singers, 119

Sabbath keeping, 82, 103, 105, 106, 174, 213, 236, 346
Sacred Steel Guitar Tradition, 147, 215, 358–59, 385,
Saints Industrial and Literary School, 92, 122, 268, 313, 359
Samuel DeWitt Proctor School of Theology, 16
Sarah Lawrence College, 40
Second Vatican Council, 4, 5
segregation, 23–25, 48, 54, 131, 134, 165, 282, 313, 349, 367
slavery, 77, 97, 103, 150, 155, 164, 169
Society of Friends, 403
Soul Stirrers, the, 358, 393
Southern Christian Leadership Committee (SCLC), 76, 183, 440
speaking in tongues, xii, 9, 26, 30, 47, 48, 50, 74, 75, 78, 80, 84, 88, 96, 98, 99, 102, 104, 105, 106, 143, 155, 176, 177, 184, 218, 232, 241, 242, 24, 254, 271, 284, 291, 305, 313, 332, 333, 334, 350, 364, 367, 368, 380, 394, 396, 403, 415, 402
Spirit Baptism, xii, 2, 5, 9, 12, 18, 29, 30, 32, 34, 38, 46, 48, 50, 53, 55, 56, 59, 74, 75, 78, 79, 80, 87, 98, 102, 104, 105, 128, 131, 142, 152, 155, 156, 158, 173, 177, 178, 179, 184, 190, 191, 192, 194, 195, 197, 203, 218, 219, 228, 230, 232, 235, 237, 239, 241, 242, 243, 245, 248, 252, 254, 259, 261, 262, 263, 264, 268, 271, 277, 284, 288, 289, 312, 315, 322, 332, 334, 335, 336, 338, 343, 344, 349, 350, 362, 365, 367, 368, 381, 383, 38, 389, 398, 401, 420, 431, 434, 435, 437, 439, 445, 446
Stellar Gospel Music Awards, 67, 316, 425

Teen Challenge, 25, 124, 387
Trinity Broadcasting Network (TBN), 64, 286, 315

Union Theological Seminary 45, 111, 115, 169, 170, 373, 390, 442
Universal Negro Improvement Association, 10, 144, 254, 256, 381, 405

Vatican, The, 4, 5, 133, 240, 372, 404

White House, the, 68, 118, 145–45, 198, 337
Wilberforce University, 304, 383
W. L. Bonner Bible College, 45, 233
women, 5, 6, 7, 12, 15, 17, 21, 23, 27, 30, 41, 42, 43, 44, 46, 51, 69, 75, 78, 81, 83, 99, 100, 101, 104, 105, 107, 109, 121, 122, 137, 153, 162, 164, 166–67, 178, 190, 191, 205, 207, 214, 215, 221, 227, 228, 237, 243, 259, 292, 293–94, 302, 303, 305, 324, 325, 326, 333, 341, 351, 352, 354, 375, 376, 380, 381–82, 385, 386, 387, 390, 405, 406, 426
  In Church of God in Christ 34, 52, 114, 119–20, 122, 126, 132, 146, 156, 225–28, 274, 279, 339, 351–52, 354–55, 398–99, 427,
Word of Faith Movement, 63, 140, 176, 209, 319, 339–40 399–400, 421, 436
World Council of Churches, 317
  Black Church Summit of, 317
World Fellowship of Black Pentecostal Churches, 91, 95, 221, 317
World Methodist Council on Evangelism, 62
World Pentecostal Conference, 435

Yeshiva University, 40

www.ingramcontent.com/pod-product-compliance
Lightning Source LLC
Chambersburg PA
CBHW060416300426
44111CB00018B/2873